D1284032

SQL Queries 2012 Joes 2 Pros® Volume 2

The SQL Query Techniques Tutorial for SQL Server 2012

(SQL Exam Prep Series 70-461 Volume 2 of 5)

By

Rick A. Morelan

MCDBA, MCTS, MCITP, MCAD, MOE, MCSE, MCSE+I

Pinal Dave

Founder of SQLAuthority.com

EAN: 978-1-939666-01-7

Rick A. Morelan
INFO@JOES2PROS.COM

Table of Contents

About the Authors

We write each book in this series to help anyone seeking knowledge about SQL Server – whether an intermediate looking to fill gaps in their knowledge, an expert looking for new features in the 2012 version of SQL Server, or even a developer picking up SQL Server as their second or third programming language. At the heart of the mission as an educator remains the dedication to helping people with the power of SQL Server. The goal of education is action.

Rick Morelan

In 1994, you could find Rick Morelan braving the frigid waters of the Bering Sea as an Alaskan commercial fisherman. His computer skills were non-existent at the time, so you might figure such beginnings seemed unlikely to lead him down the path to SQL Server expertise at Microsoft. However, every computer expert in the world today woke up at some point in their life knowing nothing about computers.

Making the change from fisherman seemed scary and took daily schooling at Catapult Software Training Institute. Rick got his lucky break in August of 1995, working his first database job at Microsoft. Since that time, Rick has worked more than 10 years at Microsoft and has attained over 30 Microsoft technical certifications in applications, networking, databases and .NET development.

His books are used the world over by individuals and educators to help people with little experience learn these technical topics and gain the ability to earn a Microsoft certification or have the confidence to do well in a job interview with their new found knowledge.

Rick's speaking engagements have included SQL Saturdays and SQL Server Intelligence Conferences. In addition to these speaking engagements Rick gives back to the community by personally teaching students at both Bellevue College and MoreTechnology in Redmond, WA.

Pinal Dave

Pinal Dave is a technology enthusiast and avid blogger. Prior to joining Microsoft, his outstanding community service helped to earn several awards, including the Microsoft Most Valuable Professional in SQL Server Technology (3 continuous years) and the Community Impact Award as an Individual Contributor for 2010.

Playing an active role in the IT industry for over eight years, his career has taken him across the world working in both India and the US, primarily with SQL Server Technology, from version 6.5 to its latest form. His early work experience includes being a Technology Evangelist with Microsoft and a Sr. Consultant with

SolidQ, and he continues to work on performance tuning and optimization projects for high transactional systems.

Pinal's higher education degrees include a Master of Science from the University of Southern California, and a Bachelor of Engineering from Gujarat University. In addition to his degrees, Pinal holds multiple Microsoft certificates and helps to spread his knowledge as a regular speaker for many international events like TechEd, SQL PASS, MSDN, TechNet and countless user groups.

At the time of this writing, Pinal has co-authored three SQL Server books:

- o SQL Server Programming
- o SQL Wait Stats
- o SQL Server Interview Questions and Answers

Pinal's passion for the community drives him to share his training and knowledge and frequently writes on his blog http://blog.SQLAuthority.com covering various subjects related to SQL Server technology and Business Intelligence. As a very active member of the social media community it is easy to connect with him using one of these services:

- o Twitter: http://twitter.com/pinaldave
- o Facebook: http://facebook.com/SQLAuth

When he is not in front of a computer, he is usually travelling to explore hidden treasures in nature with his lovely daughter, Shaivi, and very supportive wife, Nupur.

Acknowledgements from Rick Morelan

As a book with a supporting web site, illustrations, media content and software scripts, it takes more than the usual author, illustrator and editor to put everything together into a great learning experience. Since my publisher has the more traditional contributor list available, I'd like to recognize the core team members:

Editor: Lori Stow
Technical Editor: Richard Stockhoff
Technical Review: Tony Smithlin
User Acceptance Testing: Sandra Howard

Thank you to all the teachers at Catapult Software Training Institute in the mid-1990s. What a great start to open my eyes. It landed me my first job at Microsoft by August of that year. A giant second wind came from Koenig-Solutions, which gives twice the training and attention for half the price of most other schools. Mr. Rohit Aggarwal is the visionary founder of this company based in New Delhi,

India. Rohit's business model sits students down one-on-one with experts. Each expert dedicates weeks to help each new IT student succeed. The numerous twelve-hour flights I took to India to attend those classes were pivotal to my success. Whenever a new generation of software was released, I got years ahead of the learning curve by spending one or two months at Koenig.

Dr. James D. McCaffrey at Volt Technical Resources in Bellevue, Wash., taught me how to improve my own learning by teaching others. You'll frequently see me in his classroom because he makes learning fun. McCaffrey's unique style boosts the self-confidence of his students, and his tutelage has been essential to my own professional development. His philosophy inspires the *Joes 2 Pros* curriculum.

Introduction

Does the following story sound familiar to you? The first SQL book I bought left me confused and demoralized at Chapter 1. Enrolling in my first class totally overwhelmed me and left me nearly hopeless, with only a partial tuition refund. Progress was expensive and slow. Countless times I was tempted to give up.

After years of trial and error, I finally got into my groove. While grinding away at my own work with SQL, those key "ah-ha" moments and insights eventually came. What took me over five years of intense study is now a high tide that lifts my students to the same level in just a few months.

Each lesson and chapter builds sequentially. The labs have been created and delivered by me over several years of teaching SQL. If a lab offered one of my classrooms an exciting "ah-ha" experience with students leaning forward on every word and demo, it's a keeper. However, when a lab caused more of a trance or tilted squint, it was discarded or revised with a better approach. The labs in this book are the end result, and each one consistently elicits "ah-ha" moments in my classes.

This book follows what students told me worked for them and launched their careers. This curriculum has helped many people achieve their career goals. If you would like to gain the confidence that comes with really knowing how to get things done, this book is your ticket. This book offers the following ways to help:

Most learning for the money: What if you could get more from this book than the average $1,800 class? Perhaps there is even more material here – proven teaching tools presented by someone whose goal is for you to succeed and achieve a high level of SQL knowledge and proficiency. More importantly, we can learn SQL with demos and practice. When you finish this book, you will be reading and writing in SQL with ease. This book can easily give you more than a typical 18-hour class costing $1,800.

Truly getting it: Is there a better way to learn SQL than from a giant book of concepts with only a few examples? You bet there is, and you're reading it. Just wait until you finish the Points to Ponder section of each chapter. It exists in written and video format to bring life and action to concepts. The Points-to-Ponder section represents a wrap-up of each chapter, which is like getting 10 pages of lengthy reading into one. This is a concise way to finalize the new points you have just used.

Downloadable files bring text to life: Answer keys, quiz games and setup scripts will prepare your SQL Server for the practices that will hone your skills. The files can be found at www.Joes2Pros.com.

Bug Catcher game reviews: After you have run the right code several times, you are ready to write code and help others do the same by spotting errors in code samples. Each chapter's interactive Bug Catcher section highlights common mistakes people make and improves your code literacy. In the classroom setting, this segment is a fun chapter wrap-up game with a wireless buzzer system. Try this game at home for yourself.

This book is an essential tool. When used correctly, we can determine how far and fast we can go. It has been polished and tuned for your use and benefit. In fact, this is the book I really wish was in my possession years ago when I was learning about SQL. What took me years of struggle to learn can now be yours in only months in the form of efficient, enjoyable and rewarding study.

Skills Needed for this Book

SQL stands for Structured Query Language. Since SQL uses English words like select, set and where, SQL statements can be created using basic English. Beyond that you only need to be able to turn on your computer, click a mouse, type a little and navigate to files and folders.

You should be able to install SQL Server on your computer. Your options are to search the internet for a free download or buy a licensed copy. The official download site gets updated to a new location constantly. To get the most current installation steps go to www.Joes2Pros.com.

The preferred option is to get the Microsoft SQL Server 2012 Developer edition for under $50. The Joes2Pros site has a link to make this purchase. Microsoft offers a real bargain for students learning how to use SQL Server. For only $50 you can install and use the fully-enabled Developer edition as long as you agree to use it only for your own learning and to create your own code. This is an outstanding deal considering that businesses generally spend $10,000 to obtain and implement SQL Server Enterprise. More on these options and installation instructions can be found on the Joes2Pros.com site.

About this Book

By far the most common usage of SQL is to handle data. When you change or look at data, you are running queries. If you want to be a go-to person on queries and look forward to all such challenges, then this book strives for the same goal.

For those of you who have read my 2008 series for the 70-433 exam you will find a lot of the same material from the 2008 series in this series. This is because much of the 70-461 exam covers the same material as the 70-433. I have added material that is new to the exam and removed material that is no longer relevant. If you have already read this series or have already passed the 70-433 exam you may choose to read my book which covers only the changes from 70-433 to 70-461. This book has a publication date of December 2012.

Most of the exercises in this book are designed around proper database practices in the workplace. The workplace also offers common challenges and process changes over time. For example, it is good practice to use numeric data for IDs. If you have ever seen a Canadian postal code (zip code), you see the need for character data in relational information. You will occasionally see an off-the-beaten-path strategy demonstrated so you know how to approach a topic in a job interview or workplace assignment.

To put it simply, there is a recipe for success and you can choose your own ingredients. Just learn the lesson, do the lab, view the Points to Ponder and play the review game at the end of each chapter.

How to Use this Book

There is a video on the Joes2Pros website that can be watched while online, or downloaded and watched offline that demonstrates how to install SQL Server on a computer. If SQL Server 2012 is already installed on a computer, then open your favorite web browser and type www.Joes2Pros.com to be taken directly to the website for this book series *and follow the download instructions.*

Taking the practice quizzes is another great use of this book. Some multiple choice questions may only have one answer, while others will require multiple answers. There is a standard that most tests have adopted that is good for you to know as you study and prepare.

Here is an example of a question with a single answer:

1.)   What is the result of the equation: 2 + 3?

O a.   2
O b.   3
O c.   5

The correct answer to question #1 is (c). Notice that each choice has a round bubble symbol to the left of the letter selection. This symbol means that there will only be a single answer for this question.

Sometimes a question will have more than one correct answer, and for these multiple-answer types of questions, a square box symbol is shown to the left of the letter selection. An example of this is shown in question #2.

2.)   Which numbers in the following list are greater than 2?

☐ a. 0
☐ b. 2
☐ c. 3
☐ d. 4

The correct answers to question #2 are (c) and (d). Notice that each choice has a square box symbol to the left of the letter selection. This symbol means that there will be more than one answer for this question.

I'm often asked about the Points to Ponder feature, which is popular with both beginners and experienced developers. Some have asked why I don't simply call it a Summary Page. While it's true that the Points to Ponder page generally captures key points from each section, I frequently include options or technical insights not contained in the section. Often these are points which my students have found helpful and will likely enhance your understanding of SQL Server.

These books are also available as video books. To see the latest in this learning format visit the www.Joes2Pros.com website and click on Videos. Many of our students find that using the text and video together often help in their learning.

How to Use the Downloadable Labs

To help get you started, the first three chapters are in video format for free downloading. Videos show labs, demonstrate concepts, and review Points to Ponder along with tips from the appendix. Ranging from 3-15 minutes in length, they use special effects to highlight key points. You can go at your own pace and pause or replay within these lessons as needed. To make knowing where to start even easier, the videos are numbered. You don't even need to refer to the book to know what order they should be viewed in. There is even a "Setup" video that shows you how to download and use all other files.

Clear content and high-resolution multimedia videos coupled with code samples will make learning easy and fun. To give you all this and save printing costs, all supporting files are available with a free download from www.Joes2Pros.com. The breakdown of the offerings from these supporting files is listed as follows:

Answer keys: The downloadable files also include an answer key. All exercise lab coding answers are available for peeking if you get really stuck.

Resource files: If you are asked to import a file into SQL, you will need that resource file. Located in the resources sub-folder from the download site are your practice lab resource files. These files hold the few non-SQL script files needed for certain labs.

Lab setup files: SQL Server is a database engine and we need to practice on a database. The Joes 2 Pros Practice Company database is a fictitious travel booking company that has been shortened to the database name of JProCo. The scripts to set up the JProCo database can be found here.

Chapter review files: Ready to take your new skills out for a test drive? We have the ever popular Bug Catcher game located here.

DVD or Videos as a Companion

Training videos: These books are also available for sale as video books. In these videos I guide you through the lessons of each section of the book. Every lab of every chapter of this book series has multimedia steps recorded into videos. The content of the five book series fits into 10 DVDs. When comparing prices, you will find the costs are much less than the existing ad-hoc options on the market today.

If you have done some shopping around you will have noticed there are video training sets that cost over $300. You might also have seen single certification books for $60 each. Do the math and you see one book from other leading publishers will set you back nearly $400.

What this Book is Not

This book will start you off on the cornerstones of the language behind SQL. It will cover the most commonly used keywords. In short, this book won't attempt to 'boil the ocean' by teaching you every single keyword and command in SQL. However, you will become advanced enough at using the ones covered in this series to qualify for working in positions requiring SQL Server knowledge. In your continued study of SQL Server through more advanced books, you will acquire more of these keywords and continually add to your fluency of programming with SQL on your way to becoming a SQL expert.

This is not a memorization book. Rather, this is a skills book to make part of preparing for the 70-461 certification test a familiarization process. This book prepares you to apply what you have learned to answer SQL questions in the job setting. The highest hopes are that your progress and level of SQL knowledge will soon have business managers seeking your expertise to provide the reporting and information vital to their decision making. It's a good feeling to achieve and to help others at the same time. Many students commented that the training method used in *Joes 2 Pros* was what finally helped them achieve their goal of certification.

When you go through the *Joes 2 Pros* series and really know this material, you deserve a fair shot at SQL certification. Use only authentic testing engines to measure your skill. Show you know it for real. At the time of this writing, MeasureUp® at http://www.measureup.com provides a good test preparation simulator. The company's test pass guarantee makes it a very appealing option.

Chapter 1.   Data, Information and Tables

Most of my students laugh when they hear me say the prerequisite for learning in my classes is the ability to click a mouse and breathe oxygen. A beginning class should be welcoming for beginners.

The first book in this series, *SQL Queries 2012 Joes 2 Pros Volume 1*, addresses this very reasonable request. In this book (*Volume 2*), the first chapter will begin with a quick refresher on data, information and tables previously covered in the first book. This is a great help to the beginner students, who have decided to read this book first, and is a quick refresher for those who have already completed the first book. Anyone already familiar with SQL can treat Chapter 1 as a warm up and get ready for some fun. *HINT: there are tips-n-tricks included in this chapter that many experienced SQL Server Developers are not aware of.*

Each chapter in this book will include instructions for when a setup script will need to be run to create the database objects necessary to follow along with the examples or labs. These setup scripts allow the freedom to practice any code without fear of damaging the database beyond repair.

So, if any data, tables, or even an entire database is intentionally or mistakenly changed, deleted, or dropped, the corresponding setup script can be run to quickly restore all databases, objects and data necessary to accomplish the exercises in this book.

Many sections within each chapter and all labs will require executing a specific setup script for the exercise to be successfully completed as described. This process is good practice for beginners and intermediates alike, as these are frequently performed tasks when working with SQL Server.

READER NOTE: *Please run the SQLQueries2012Vol2Chapter1.0Setup.sql script in order to follow along with the examples in the first section of Chapter 1. All scripts mentioned in this chapter are available at www.Joes2Pros.com. Also on this site are many free videos to watch. Also, on our site there is a selection of free videos to watch to help you get started. Our entire video instruction library is available via online subscription and DVD.*

Single Table Queries

When we want information from a database, we write a query, such as SELECT *data* FROM *TableName*. In English we might say, "Show me the information!"

Let's write a simple query. We will use the dbBasics database context and request all records and fields from the ShoppingList table as part of the result set. The keyword SELECT requests information to be displayed and the asterisk (*) sign is a shortcut for all the field names. The keyword FROM chooses a specific table.

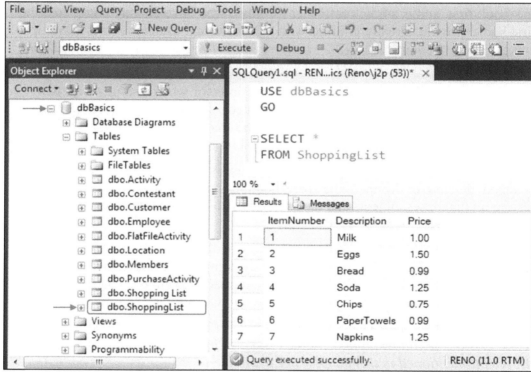

Figure 1.1 This shows a query for all records and all fields from the ShoppingList table.

We are able to run this query to retrieve the information by either clicking on the '**! Execute**' button in the toolbar above the query window, or by pressing the F5 button on our keyboard (Some keyboard configurations require pressing the fn (function) + F5 keys simultaneously).

Basic Query Syntax

A group of students in one of my weekend classes helped to write a neatly summarized guide listing the meaning of words in a basic SQL query. To honor their request for adding it to this book, here is the code sample:

```
USE dbBasics          --choose DATABASE Context
GO                    --complete USE statement

SELECT *              --choose Field(s) to display
FROM ShoppingList     --choose Table(s) containing fields
```

Now is a good time to point out that words can be placed in a query window that have nothing to do with the SQL code itself. We can write non-SQL words and notes like "I wrote this query today" above the SELECT statement. In order to do this, we must tell SQL Server to ignore this text since it's not intended to be code. In fact, it should be non-executing code known as comments. To make comments, we need to begin the line with two hyphen signs, one after the other with no spaces between them. Change the database context back to JProCo with the drop-down window in the toolbar and then use this example of code:

```
SELECT * FROM Location
```

The code above runs fine in JProCo. SQL Server ignores the first line because of the double hyphens. It's there only for the benefit of the human eye reading it. This is a useful way to make notes that later provide us, or our team with key hints or details explaining what the code is attempting to accomplish.

Table names can optionally have square brackets around them, and will not change the result set. Changing back to the dbBasics context, we can run the following two queries. Although one query uses square brackets and the other does not use brackets, they will both operate identically by returning a result set.

```
SELECT * FROM [ShoppingList]
SELECT * FROM ShoppingList
```

When coding, we rarely use square brackets because it requires extra typing. The only time it is helpful is when we can't tell when a table name starts or stops. For this demo, the dbBasics database has two identical tables named 'ShoppingList' and 'Shopping List'. The latter contains a space in its name, which is generally a bad naming practice for any database object.

For situations like this, we must use a delimiter, such as square brackets. Without these delimiters, SQL Server will think the table is named 'Shopping' and there is a command named 'List', which it does not recognize and will result in an error message (Figure 1.2).

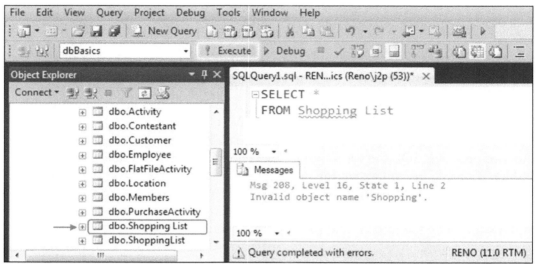

Figure 1.2 This shows a table with a space in the name will not run without using square bracket delimiters.

Of course, as shown in the two earlier queries, we can put square brackets around any table. In fact, code generated automatically by SQL Server always creates these delimiters for every object in the database. The only time we must use the square bracket delimiters is when table names are separated by a space, have the same name as a SQL Server keyword (bad idea), or otherwise named in a way that is not obvious or easily interpreted by SQL Server.

We can easily correct this error message by placing square bracket delimiters around the 'Shopping List' table name. Once this is complete, the query will successfully run without an error (Figure 1.3) and we will get the same seven records in our result set, as the first query using the ShoppingList table (Not the [Shopping List] table).

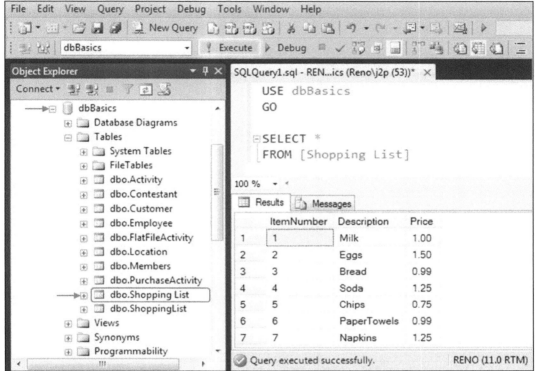

Figure 1.3 Delimiting a table whose name includes a space will allow the query to run.

Using delimiters for table names helps us in another way, too. As previously mentioned, it is a bad idea to name a table after known SQL Server keywords. For example, a table named 'From' would look like this:

```
SELECT * FROM From
```

The vocabulary of SQL Server has grown over the years, with new keywords continually added to the existing list. Take an example where a company database, named 'Grant', keeps track of charity grants. The company upgrades to a newer version of SQL Server where Grant is now a keyword used to administer database permissions. The following code would create problems:

```
SELECT * FROM Grant
```

In this case, SQL Server interprets the word 'Grant' as a keyword. We can tell this is happening because the word 'Grant' appears in the color blue (just like the keywords SELECT and FROM). We can solve all conflicts between a table name and keyword(s) by using square bracket delimiters. By placing these delimiters around the Grant table name, SQL Server will know that this is not a keyword.

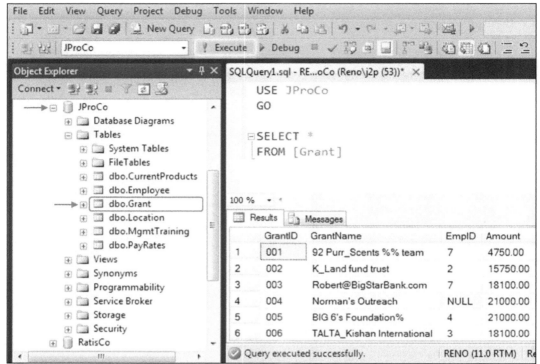

Figure 1.4 Delimiters instruct SQL Server that Grant is a table, not the keyword GRANT.

Square brackets work on all database objects, so we could place square brackets around the Employee table, if we wanted to. This means field names can use delimiters. For example, the Location table in the JProCo database has a field named 'state'. STATE is a keyword first introduced with SQL Server 2008. There is more on selecting fields later in this chapter.

Over time, we will find that in reality, delimiters are only necessary on rare occasions, as most database objects created use proper naming practices.

Exact Criteria

There is a big difference between selecting everything and being selective. When questioning the business importance of database systems, we need only to look at what a highly profitable search engine company does every day. The world has billions of websites and when we want a search narrowed down to just a few sites of interest, the database a search engine company uses will make the necessary calculations based on our unique search query and make the selections best suited for our needs. This information, presented as a plethora of links, entices us to click on them and visit a specific website, which drives revenue created by the search engine company's advertising business.

Trying to obtain information by looking at all records in a table is about as useful as trying to look at all web sites on the internet to find what we want. Instead, the preferred way is to add criteria to a query. With criteria, we can deliver the exact information needed. All queries must have the SELECT and FROM keywords together to be valid. We also have other choices available, such as the WHERE clause, which is the most common optional keyword.

When we query the entire ShoppingList table, we have two items costing $1.25. It is easy to spot two records out of seven with our own eyes. However, finding two records from a million with our own eyes is like looking for a needle in a haystack. So, let's tunnel through that haystack with the WHERE clause. We want to limit our result set based on the Price field being exactly $1.25. This is accomplished by adding this specific criteria immediately after the WHERE clause (Figure 1.5).

```
SELECT *
From ShoppingList
WHERE Price = 1.25
```

	ItemNumber	Description	Price
1	4	Soda	1.25
2	7	Napkins	1.25

2 rows

Figure 1.5 The WHERE clause limits the number of records in your result set.

The perfect tool for filtering data is the WHERE clause. There are still seven records contained in the ShoppingList table, even though the number of records in the result set of our query is now two.

Any type of data can be filtered by the WHERE clause. If we wanted to see all people in the Employee table of the JProCo database, with a first name of David, we can use the WHERE clause with this criteria. It is important to know that we must enclose any characters or words in a set of single quotation marks.

The next query example uses a WHERE clause to filter on the FirstName field looking for all values that are equal to David. We have data represented by twelve records stored in the Employee table. The WHERE clause will show only those records that exactly match the criteria we give it and expects a logical statement to evaluate each record. This logical statement (FirstName = 'David') is commonly known as a *predicate*. By predicating on the FirstName field, our goal is to filter the results to provide us with only the information that we want to see.

```
SELECT *
FROM Employee
WHERE FirstName = 'David'
```

Let's try running the next few examples by ourselves, checking the results after completing each query. Use the JProCo database context for these examples.

Of the twelve employees, there are ten not named David. The reverse of this query will show all records that do not have David as a FirstName:

```
SELECT *
FROM Employee
WHERE FirstName != 'David'
```

When we place an exclamation point before the equals sign, it means 'Not Equals'. This will filter all exact matches out of the result set. In the previous versions to SQL Server 2008, the '< >' operator was used as 'Not Equals,' as shown in the next code sample.

```
SELECT *
FROM Employee
WHERE FirstName <> 'David'
```

The risk in using the '< >' operator is that it looks exactly like an HTML or XML tag. When SQL Server needs to talk with other languages, it's better to use '! =' operator for 'Not Equals' as shown in this code sample:

```
SELECT *
FROM Employee
WHERE FirstName != 'David'
```

Using the '=' operator provides an exact match. What if we wanted to look for all the values of Lisa or David in the FirstName field? One option is to use this code:

```
SELECT *
FROM Employee
WHERE FirstName = 'Lisa'
OR FirstName = 'David'
```

This works fine, except for the logical rule that only allows for one exact match after the '=' operator. Some people like using the equals sign and simply write an additional line for each criterion that they are looking for.

To enumerate a set of exact matches in a query with a single criterion requires the use of the IN operator. This code shows another way to find the same result set:

```
SELECT *
FROM Employee
WHERE FirstName IN ('Lisa', 'David')
```

What if the goal is to find everyone in the company except for Lisa and David? By putting the word NOT in front of the IN operator we give the opposite result.

Since there are twelve employees and three named Lisa or David, there will be nine employees not named Lisa or David. This code is an example of how to use the NOT IN operator when specifying a list:

```
SELECT *
FROM Employee
WHERE FirstName NOT IN ('Lisa', 'David')
```

Pattern Criteria

What do the names Brian and Bo have in common? They both start with the letter 'B'. Yes, there are other similarities, but let's go with the most obvious. Using the '=' operator with the letter 'B' would not find either name. The query would look for the name 'B,' which is only one letter long and produces an empty result set. A query that searches for a partial match needs an approximate logical operator combined with something called a *wildcard* character to return a result set.

The operator that allows for an approximate predicate is LIKE. The LIKE operator allows us to perform special relative searches to filter the result set.

To find everyone with a FirstName beginning with the letter 'B', we will need to predicate on the letter 'B' followed by a wildcard character, which allows for any number of characters to follow it. For example, **WHERE FirstName LIKE 'B%'** is the proper format for finding all FirstName fields with a value (name) beginning with the letter 'B' (Figure 1.6).

```
SELECT *
FROM Employee
WHERE FirstName LIKE 'B%'
```

	EmpID	LastName	FirstName	HireDate	LocationID	ManagerID
1	2	Brown	Barry	2002-08-12…	1	11
2	12	O'Neil	Barbara	1995-05-26…	4	4

2 rows

Figure 1.6 Using the approximate operator LIKE allows for a wildcard in the predicate.

READER NOTE: *SQL Server does not care if the FirstName value (name) is Barry or barry, as it is case insensitive by default (unless this setting has been intentionally changed). This means that SQL Server merely looks at the letters themselves, not which case they are, to determine if there is a match in the predicate. EXAMPLE: Predicating on a FirstName using these spellings, 'Barry', 'BARRY', 'barry', 'baRRy', 'barrY' will all return the same results.*

The % wildcard character represents any number of characters of any length. Let's find all first names that end in the letter 'A'. By using the percentage '%' sign with the letter 'A', we achieve this goal using the code following sample:

```
SELECT *
FROM Employee
WHERE FirstName LIKE '%A'
```

Lisa and Barbara both end in the letter 'A'. In this example, a capital letter 'A' found all FirstName records ending in 'A', even if the letter was in lower case.

Lisa has three characters before the ending letter 'A' while Barbara has six. The '%' wildcard can mean one character, three, nine or even zero characters. If the FirstName value is the letter 'A', then it would also appear in this result set.

The next goal is to find records with FirstName values where the letter 'A' is the second letter. We want exactly one character of any type followed by an 'A', then any number of letters afterwards. The wildcard sign representing exactly one character is the underscore '_' sign.

Writing a query searching for one character before the letter 'A', and any amount of characters afterward will find David, James and several others (Figure 1.7). The '%' sign wildcard can represent many characters while the '_' sign wildcard always represents exactly one character.

```
SELECT *
FROM Employee
WHERE FirstName LIKE '_A%'
```

	EmpID	LastName	FirstName	HireDate	LocationID	ManagerID	Status
1	2	Brown	Barry	2002-08-12…	1	11	NULL
2	4	Kennson	David	1996-03-16…	1	11	Has Tenure
3	7	Lonning	David	2000-01-01…	1	11	On Leave
4	9	Newton	James	2003-09-30…	2	3	NULL
5	11	Smith	Sally	1989-04-01…	1	NULL	NULL
6	12	O'Neil	Barbara	1995-05-26…	4	4	Has Tenure

7 rows

Figure 1.7 The underscore wildcard will find exactly one character.

Alphabetical Range Criteria

To find all FirstName values beginning with the letters 'A' or 'B' we can use two predicates in our WHERE clause by separating them with OR.

```
SELECT *
FROM Employee
WHERE LastName LIKE 'A%'
OR LastName LIKE 'B%'
```

	EmpID	LastName	FirstName	HireDate	LocationID	ManagerID	Status
1	1	Adams	Alex	2001-01-01…	1	11	NULL
2	2	Brown	Barry	2002-08-12…	1	11	NULL
3	5	Bender	Eric	2007-05-17…	1	11	NULL

3 rows

Figure 1.8 Using the OR operator to find FirstName values starting with letters A or B.

Finding names beginning with an 'A' or 'B' is easy and this works fine until we want a larger range of letters as in the following example for 'A' thru 'K':

```
SELECT *
FROM Employee
WHERE FirstName LIKE 'A%'
OR FirstName LIKE 'B%'
OR FirstName LIKE 'C%'
OR FirstName LIKE 'D%'
OR FirstName LIKE 'E%'
OR FirstName LIKE 'F%'
OR FirstName LIKE 'G%'
OR FirstName LIKE 'H%'
OR FirstName LIKE 'I%'
OR FirstName LIKE 'J%'
OR FirstName LIKE 'K%'
```

The previous query does find FirstName values beginning with the letters 'A' through 'K'. However, when a query requires a large range of letters, the LIKE operator has an even better option. Since the first letter of the FirstName field can be 'A', 'B', 'C', 'D', 'E', 'F', 'G', 'H', 'I', 'J' or 'K', simply list all these choices inside a set of square brackets followed by the '%' wildcard, as in the following example:

```
SELECT *
FROM Employee
WHERE FirstName LIKE '[ABCDEFGHIJK]%'
```

A more elegant example of this technique recognizes that all these letters are in a continuous range, so we really only need to list the first and last letter of the range inside the square brackets, followed by the '%' wildcard allowing for any number of characters after the first letter in the range (Figure 1.9).

```
SELECT *
FROM Employee
WHERE LastName LIKE '[A-K]%'
```

	EmpID	LastName	FirstName	HireDate	LocationID
1	1	Adams	Alex	2001-01-01 00:00:00.000	1
2	2	Brown	Barry	2002-08-12 00:00:00.000	1
3	4	Kennson	David	1996-03-16 00:00:00.000	1
4	5	Bender	Eric	2007-05-17 00:00:00.000	1
5	6	Kendall	Lisa	2001-11-15 00:00:00.000	4

5 rows

Figure 1.9 This uses square brackets with LIKE to find LastName values in the range from A-K.

READER NOTE: *A predicate that uses a range will not work with the '=' operator (equals sign). It will neither raise an error, nor produce a result set. An = sign is an exact operator and is looking for records where the FirstName is exactly [A-K]%.*

```
SELECT *
FROM Employee
WHERE FirstName = '[A-K]%'
```

We have now discovered that a range of characters can be found using LIKE accompanied with the appropriate characters inside square brackets. The '%' wildcard is used when working with a string pattern and must be enclosed in single quotes. Simply place the starting letter followed by a hyphen and then the ending letter of the range inside a set of brackets followed by the '%' wildcard inside of single quotes.

Notice that Alex is in this result set. This is because 'A' is considered to be in the [a-k] range. The same logic applies to Lisa. There is a similar trick we can use when working with a range of numbers.

Numerical Range Criteria

Now we'll examine a similar trick with number ranges. Looking at the Grant table, we notice there are values for the Amount field as low as $4,750 and as high as $41,000 (Figure 1.10).

```
SELECT *
FROM [Grant]
```

	GrantID	GrantName	EmpID	Amount
1	001	92 Purr_Scents %% team	7	4750.00
2	002	K_Land fund trust	2	15750.00
3	003	Robert@BigStarBank.com	7	18100.00
4	004	Norman's Outreach	NULL	21000.00
5	005	BIG 6's Foundation%	4	21000.00
6	006	TALTA_Kishan International	3	18100.00

10 rows

Figure 1.10 All fields and all records from the Grant table.

There are many values for grants over $20,000 in the Amount field. In the following query we use a 'greater than' operator to find values over 20000:

```
SELECT *
FROM [GRANT]
WHERE Amount > 20000
```

There are also multiple grants under $20,000 in the Amount field. The following query uses a 'less than' operator to find the values under 20000:

```
SELECT *
FROM [GRANT]
WHERE Amount < 20000
```

We need to be careful when looking for amounts over $21,000 (Figure 1.11), because we have some Amount values that are exactly $21,000. Using a greater than '>' operator will not include this amount, but a greater than or equal to '>=' operator will include the amount matching $21,000.

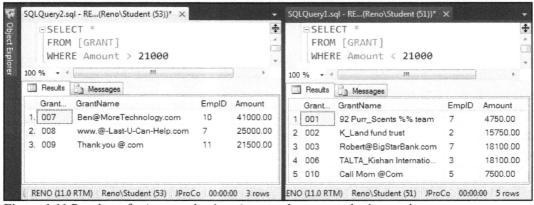

Figure 1.11 Result set for 'greater than' vs. 'greater than or equal to' operations.

When someone asks us to pick a number between one and ten, what are valid answers? Zero would be out of range. How about an edge case answer of one? Is one between one and ten? Yes! When we use the word, between, in everyday life the numbers on the edge are inclusive. The same is true with the BETWEEN operator in SQL Server.

After the WHERE clause, we can place a BETWEEN operator with the AND operator to specify two numbers that define a range. When looking for values between 21000 and 30000 in the Amount field, we get four records in our result set as seen in Figure 1.12.

```
SELECT *
FROM [Grant]
Where Amount BETWEEN 21000 AND 30000
```

	GrantID	GrantName	EmpID	Amount
1	004	Norman's Outreach	NULL	21000.00
2	005	BIG 6's Foundation%	4	21000.00
3	008	www.@-Last-U-Can-Help.com	7	25000.00
4	009	Thank you @.com	11	21500.00

4 rows

Figure 1.12 Using BETWEEN with AND to find a range of values.

Notice that two of the results are exactly 21000. Using a BETWEEN operator offers results that are inclusive of the numbers in the predicate.

Querying Special Characters

We learned about two special characters earlier called wildcards. When using the percentage sign '%' or the underscore '_' we can perform relative searches. There is a GrantName field with a value of '92 Purr_Scents %%% team' which has two percentage signs as part of the name. There are also other values in the GrantName field containing the percentage sign.

How do we search for a percentage sign? Do we simply place a wildcard '%' on either side of it? No. SQL Server will interpret this as a request to search for three wildcards and return all records as seen in the following query:

```
SELECT *
FROM [GRANT]
WHERE GrantName LIKE '%%%'
```

The Code above is looking for a GrantName with any number of characters before and after any number of characters. Since every GrantName has characters either before or after other characters, every record will be returned in the result set.

So, we need a method of identifying a literal percentage sign as being different from a wildcard '%' sign. Help is on the way again with the square bracket! In this case, we place the literal percentage sign inside the square brackets and then surround the square brackets with the '%' wildcards on either side.

By using this method, we can write a query that will show the two records having a percentage sign within the GrantName field (Figure 1.13). In this example, the square brackets tell SQL Server to interpret the '%' sign inside of them as a literal percentage sign and not a wildcard character.

```
SELECT *
FROM [Grant]
WHERE GrantName LIKE '%[%]%'
```

	GrantID	GrantName	EmpID	Amount
1	001	92 Purr_Scents %% team	7	4750.00
2	005	BIG 6's Foundation%	4	21000.00

2 rows

Figure 1.13 Finding a literal '%' sign in a relative search predicate.

There is a GrantName with a value of 'K_Land fund trust' containing an actual underscore in the name. There are other grants with underscores as well. How do we search for an underscore sign? Do we simply place the '%' wildcard on each side? No. SQL Server will interpret this as a request to search for all records with one or more characters in the GrantName field, as seen in the following query:

```
SELECT *
FROM [GRANT]
WHERE GrantName LIKE '%_%'
```

The code above is searching for any number of characters including zero characters before or after a single character. Since every GrantName has at least one character all the records will be returned.

So, we have two special characters ('%' and '_') in the predicate without a single literal underscore sign. Once again, square brackets come to the rescue! We need to place the literal underscore inside a set of square brackets, and then surround the brackets by a '%' wildcard on either side.

By running the query shown here, we can see the three records in the Grant table that have an underscore somewhere in the GrantName field. This example instructs SQL Server that the underscore sign inside the square brackets is a literal underscore and not a '_' wildcard character (Figure 1.14).

```
SELECT *
FROM [Grant]
WHERE GrantName LIKE '%[_]%'
```

	GrantID	GrantName	EmpID	Amount
1	001	92 Purr_Scents %% team	7	4750.00
2	002	K_Land fund trust	2	15750.00
3	006	TALTA_Kishan International	3	18100.00
				3 rows

Figure 1.14 Finding a literal '_' sign using a relative search predicate.

Finding Names with an Apostrophe

What if finding values having an apostrophe (single quote sign), such as 'Norman's Outreach', in the GrantName field is our goal? Everything inside single quotes after the LIKE operator evaluates every record and returns a result set.

Remember that SQL Server requires words or characters be enclosed within a ***pair*** of single quotes. In this example, the first single quote marks the beginning of a string and the next single quote marks the end of a string. Everything between these single quotes is part of the search string. Everything before the first single quote and after the second single quote is not part of the search string, so a pair of single quotes acts as delimiters for the string pattern we are searching for.

This presents a new challenge. The following query will produce a syntax error.

```
--Bad query syntax results in an error.
SELECT *
FROM [GRANT]
WHERE GrantName LIKE '%'%'
```

The problem lies in the fact that SQL Server follows the rule that any predicate based on a string is complete after finding the second single quote. In other words, SQL Server interprets any character after the second single quote as an error in the code it is trying to execute. Thus, our intentions with this code are either lost or misunderstood in the translation from human to computer.

To have SQL Server interpret a predicate searching for a literal single quote, we need to precede it with another single quote, as shown in Figure 1.15.

```
SELECT *
FROM [Grant]
WHERE GrantName LIKE '%''%'
```

	GrantID	GrantName	EmpID	Amount
1	004	Norman's Outreach	NULL	21000.00
2	005	BIG 6's Foundation%	4	21000.00

2 rows

Figure 1.15 Two single quotes enclosed by '%' filters a result set for an apostrophe.

We now have two records with a single quote in the result set. To view all names without a single quote (apostrophe) we simply change the LIKE operator to a NOT LIKE operator in the WHERE clause.

Exclusion Criteria

So far, all of our pattern matching queries have searched for an item based on either what it is like or not like. For example, finding all the names starting with the letter 'O', would use LIKE 'O%' for the predicate. Finding all names that do not start with the letter 'O', would use NOT LIKE 'O%' for the predicate to return the proper result set.

What if we wanted to find every name with a first letter beginning with an 'O', and the second letter cannot be an 'S'? In other words, the search results would not contain any names like Osborn or Osmond, although it would contain the name Olsen. To accomplish this, we would want to use code like the sample shown here:

```
--First letter is 'O' and the second letter is not 'S'.
SELECT *
FROM Employee
WHERE LastName LIKE 'O[^S]%'
```

The carrot sign '^' instructs SQL Server to ignore values that match this pattern. We can use this feature with a range of values as well.

The next code sample will eliminate any name where the second letter is in the range from 'A' thru 'Z'. OK, that covers all the letters in the alphabet. What could possibly remain in the result set after ignoring the entire alphabet as the second character in the LastName field? Let's run the code shown here and find out what records are shown for this query.

```
--First letter is 'O' and second letter is not 'A-Z'
SELECT *
FROM Employee
WHERE LastName LIKE 'O[^A-Z]%'
```

Aha! We can find names with special characters immediately after the first letter in the LastName field. So, any names like O'Neil, O'Dowd, or O'Hanlon are perfectly acceptable results in this query, as the second character is not a letter from 'A' thru 'Z'. That is pretty cool!

Field Selection Lists

Since we rarely need to see all the records in a table we often use the WHERE clause to limit the result set to just what we are interested in seeing. We simply do not want more records to sift through than necessary and just want to see what matters. Similarly, it is also possible to see too many fields in a set of results. When this happens, we need a way to limit the number of columns returned in our result set.

So far all of our queries have used the asterisk * sign right after the SELECT clause. This is both handy and common for an initial look at the information in a table, or when building more complicated queries. The asterisk sign frees us from needing to know the names of the fields. One drawback to this method is returning all fields in the query. Oftentimes we only want a few specific fields in our result set.

SQL Server allows tables with up to 1024 fields. Trying to view this many fields in one query would require a great deal of horizontal scrolling. If we wanted to see only some of these fields, we can pick them individually. Simply itemize the field list in the SELECT clause. Of course, to accomplish this task we need to know the names of the available fields.

The Employee table of the JProCo database has seven fields (Figure 1.16). A few more fields and we would need to scroll right or left to view all the information.

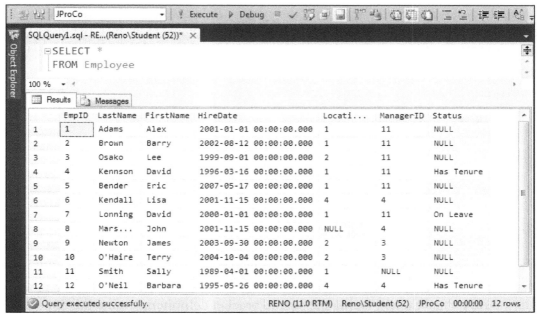

Figure 1.16 Using the SELECT * (asterisk) displays all fields in the table.

By listing the FirstName and LastName fields separated by a comma, we will only get two fields in our result set (Figure 1.17).

```
SELECT FirstName, LastName
FROM Employee
```

	FirstName	LastName
1	Alex	Adams
2	Barry	Brown
3	Lee	Osako
4	David	Kennson
5	Eric	Bender
6	Lisa	Kendall
		12 rows

Figure 1.17 Choosing specific fields in the SELECT list to show FirstName and LastName only.

We now know that we can choose to display only the fields we wish to view by specifically listing them in the SELECT clause, separated by commas, one after the other. We can list one, many or all the fields available from any table listed in the FROM clause. Of course, it's easier to type '*' than to know and type out all those names separated by commas.

We can optionally use a two-part name of the field by listing the table identifier and then the field identifier separated by a '.' (Sign for a period). This requires extra typing, which we will learn how to avoid in Chapter 4.

Using two-part names for fields uses the syntax, *TableName.FieldName*. This means that Employee.FirstName and Employee.LastName (Figure 1.18) gives us the same results as specifying the FirstName and LastName fields (Figure 1.17).

```
SELECT Employee.FirstName, Employee.LastName
FROM Employee
```

	FirstName	LastName
1	Alex	Adams
2	Barry	Brown
3	Lee	Osako
4	David	Kennson
5	Eric	Bender
6	Lisa	Kendall

12 rows

Figure 1.18 Field SELECT list using a two-part naming convention… *TableName.FieldName.*

Field names can clash with an existing keyword. For example, the Location table has a field named State. Placing the square bracket delimiters around the State field tells SQL Server we're referring to an object and not the keyword command. The following example demonstrates a query for the Street, City and State fields.

```
SELECT Street, City, [State]
FROM Location
```

Anatomy of a SQL Query

Remember that query keyword order must be followed in your SQL code. Here is the full breakdown of the anatomy of a basic query.

```
USE JProCo                      ⟹  Choose the Database context
GO                              ⟹  Finishes the USE statement


SELECT FirstName, LastName      ⟹  Choose the Field(s)
FROM Employee                   ⟹  Choose the Table(s)
WHERE FirstName = 'Lisa'        ⟹  Filter the Result Set
```

Comparison Operators Used in Criteria

The following table lists the T-SQL comparison operators. Comparison operators evaluate expressions in order to display the precise data required in a result set.

Table 1.1 Comparison operators used in T-SQL queries.

Operator	Description
=	Equality for one value
<>	Non-equality (deprecated)
!=	Non-equality
<	Less than
<=	Less than or equal to
!<	Not less than
>	Greater than
>=	Greater than or equal to
!>	Not greater than
BETWEEN	Between two specified values
IN	Equality for enumeration of values
NOT IN	Non-equality for enumeration of values
LIKE	Equality for matching a string pattern

Lab 1.1: Basic Queries

Lab Prep: Each lab has one or more Skill Checks. Start with Skill Check 1 and proceed until reaching the Points to Ponder section.

Before beginning this lab, verify that SQL Server 2012 is properly installed and operating. Before running the lab setup script for resetting the database (SQLQueries2012Vol2Chapter1.1Setup.sql), please make sure to close all query windows within SSMS. An open query window pointing to a database context can lock that database preventing it from updating when the script is executing. A simple way to assure all query windows are closed, is to exit out of SSMS, then open a new instance of SSMS, and lastly run the setup script.

Since this is the first lab, please watch the first few videos relating to this book by visiting the www.Joes2Pros.com website.

Skill Check 1: Write a query to show all records from the CurrentProducts table of the JProCo database with a RetailPrice less than $200.00. When done, the result set should resemble Figure 1.19.

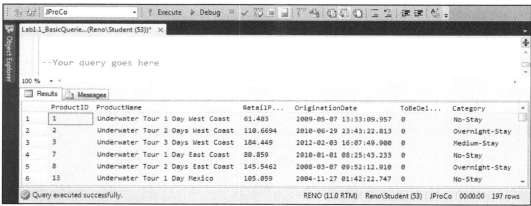

Figure 1.19 Skill Check 1 should produce 197 records.

Skill Check 2: Find all the records from the CurrentProducts table that have the word Canada in the ProductName. Show all fields from the CurrentProducts table. When done, the results should resemble Figure 1.20.

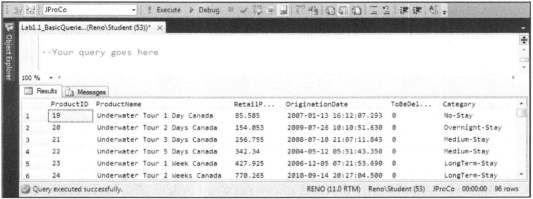

Figure 1.20 Skill Check 2 produces 96 records.

Skill Check 3: Grant is a table in the JProCo database. Show all the Grant records with Amount values between 21000 and 30000. Show only the GrantName and Amount fields. When done, the results should resemble Figure 1.21.

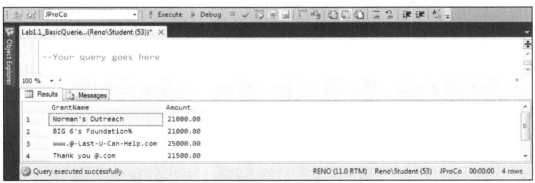

Figure 1.21 Skill Check 3 produces four records.

Answer Code: The T-SQL code for this lab is located in the downloadable files as a file named Lab1.1_BasicQueries.sql.

Points to Ponder - Single Table Queries

1. A query written in the SQL language is a request for information created from data stored in a table within a database.

2. Microsoft SQL Server uses the Transact Structured Query Language (T-SQL) standard for writing database queries.

3. Database context refers to which database the current query will find the required data from.

4. The FROM clause tells SQL which table or tables contain searchable data.

5. When writing a SQL query, if a letter is missing, a punctuation mark forgotten, or a spelling error made, SQL Server returns an error message.

6. Always maintain the following query keyword order: SELECT, FROM, and WHERE.

7. A SELECT clause with an '*' (asterisk) will choose all available fields.

8. To see only a subset of fields in a query, make sure to itemize each field name, separated by commas, after the SELECT clause.

9. The WHERE clause filters records in the result set to only include the information needed by the user.

10. The WHERE clause is optional in a SELECT statement. When omitting the WHERE clause, all records in a table are returned in the result set.

11. Changing the WHERE clause affects the records shown in the result set.

12. The WHERE keyword is always followed by a logical expression called a predicate.

13. Using the equal '=' sign finds exact matches to the criteria.

14. Wildcard characters such as '%' and '_' can be used in a WHERE clause.

15. The '%' (percent sign) is the most common wildcard. This sign represents any number of characters. For example, **WHERE FirstName LIKE '%N'** would find a name that ends in 'N' regardless of how long the name is. Examples may include Ann, MaryAnn and Dean among others.

16. The '%' sign can even represent zero characters. For example, **'%A%'** would find Alex and Lisa.

17. The SQL Server operator, LIKE can be used to return a range of names, such as those beginning with a letter ranging from 'A' thru 'M'. For example, **WHERE FirstName LIKE '[a-m]%'**

18. To exclude a value from a pattern match search, use the '^' (carrot sign) placed in square brackets followed by the value or values to be omitted. For example, **LIKE '[^O]%'** gets all names not starting with the letter 'O'.

19. To have SQL Server interpret '%' as a literal percent sign and not as a wildcard, place the literal percent sign inside square brackets and surround the square brackets on either side with the wildcard '%'. For example, **LastName LIKE '%[%]%'**. This technique can be used to search for names that include these special signs like the password R%per!est and all other names with a percent sign in them.

Relational Data in Tables

When was the last time we received a vague answer to a question? For most of us, it happens every day. Let's say we asked someone where they worked. We are anticipating a response that may include a city name or address, except the answer we actually get is, "I work at headquarters". While this answer is accurate, it does not contain the detail we wanted to know.

After detecting a slight New England accent from James Newton, we decide to look him up in the Employee table and discover that he works at LocationID 2. In what City or State is this mysterious LocationID 2 located? A quick query of the Location table shows us the following data (Figure 1.22).

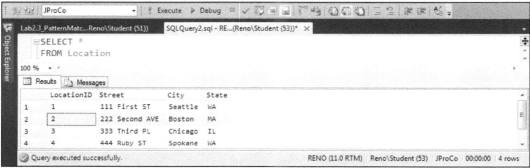

Figure 1.22 All records and fields from the Location table of JProCo.

Now, each time we see an employee listed for LocationID 2 we know the Street, City and State information for where they work. Why not store City, State and Street information in the Employee table? In fact, why not place all of the data in a single giant table so we only have to go to one place for our information? That is a common interview question about database design, so let's review a few database design best practices to add to our interviewing arsenal.

One reason is a lot of space in memory is saved by not replicating all three data items for each employee in a table. Another reason for having location fields only in the Location table is that it saves us time as well. For example, what would happen if the office at LocationID 2 physically moved from Boston to a new building in nearby Cambridge? If all the data were in a giant table, then we would have to update every Street, City and State for each employee individually. This very tedious task leaves a great deal of room for errors and inconsistency in entering data. Placing the LocationID field only in the Location table means all employees with LocationID 2 map to an update we can make just once.

So, how do we find an employee's address if the information is spread between two tables? Each table has a LocationID field inside it. We can then use a two-part identifier, to distinguish them as the Employee.LocationID field corresponds to the Location.LocationID field.

Refer to Figure 1.23 for a look at Alex Adams and Barry Brown. These employees both work at LocationID 1. If we were new to the company and only had access to the Employee table, we would not have enough detailed information to send a parcel to Alex Adams. What if we put two tables next to one another on our screen? By physically drawing a line from the Employee.LocationID field to the Location.LocationID field we can get more location details for each employee. LocationID 1 is located at 111 First ST in Seattle, WA (Figure 1.23).

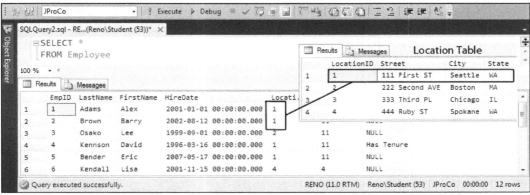

Figure 1.23 The Employee and Location tables are correlated on the LocationID field.

What about a global company with locations in all 50 states and over 100 different countries? We will have many records in our Location table and probably will not be able to look at both tables very efficiently on one screen.

How can we effectively see information in two different tables at the same time? Our ultimate goal is to show the Employee and Location information in one result set (Figure 1.24). Since we have not learned the code on how to do this yet, it is not shown in this figure. The results shown are the goal of the upcoming example.

	EmpID	LastName	FirstName	HireDate	LocationID	ManagerID	Status	LocationID	Street	City	State
1	1	Adams	Alex	2001-01-01 00:00:00.000	1	11	NULL	1	111 First ST	Seattle	WA
2	2	Brown	Barry	2002-08-12 00:00:00.000	1	11	NULL	1	111 First ST	Seattle	WA
3	3	Osako	Lee	1999-09-01 00:00:00.000	2	11	NULL	2	222 Second AVE	Boston	MA
4	4	Kennson	David	1996-03-16 00:00:00.000	1	11	Has Tenure	1	111 First ST	Seattle	WA
5	5	Bender	Eric	2007-05-17 00:00:00.000	1	11	NULL	1	111 First ST	Seattle	WA
6	6	Kendall	Lisa	2001-11-15 00:00:00.000	4	4	NULL	4	444 Ruby ST	Spok...	WA

Query executed successfully.   RENO (11.0 RTM)   Reno\j2p (53)   JProCo   00:00:00   11 rows

Figure 1.24 Two related tables showing as one result set.

INNER JOIN

So far, we have learned that each query can have only one result set and will only allow a single FROM clause. How can we place two tables in one FROM clause? We can include many tables in one FROM clause by using a JOIN operator. In special instances it is possible to join a table to itself (This is known as a Self-Join and is covered in Chapter 11). The most common join type is the INNER JOIN.

READER NOTE: *Prior to SQL Server 2008, the limit was 256 tables. The only limitation now is the amount of available resources.*

An INNER JOIN clause allows us to join multiple tables in a single query, although it requires a specific condition in order for it to work correctly. We must ensure that the INNER JOIN statement has two tables with at least one common or overlapping field. We already know the Employee and Location tables share a common field (LocationID). The relationship is between Employee.LocationID and Location.LocationID, so we instruct SQL Server that the INNER JOIN is on this field and voila! We have combined two tables into one result set.

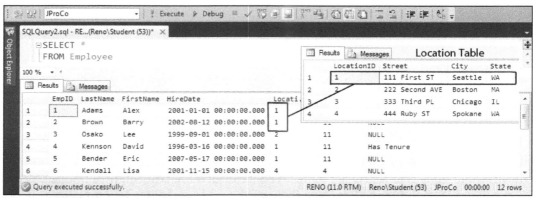

Figure 1.25 The LocationID field is a common field between the Employee and Location tables.

Every time a value is found in Employee.LocationID, the INNER JOIN searches for the matching record in the Location.LocationID field. If a match is found, data from both tables are displayed as a single record. Both tables will show all their fields if we type SELECT * at the beginning of our query.

In looking at the Grant table we can see 'Ben@MoreTechnology.com' is the GrantName with the largest value (41000.00) in the Amount field (Figure 1.26).

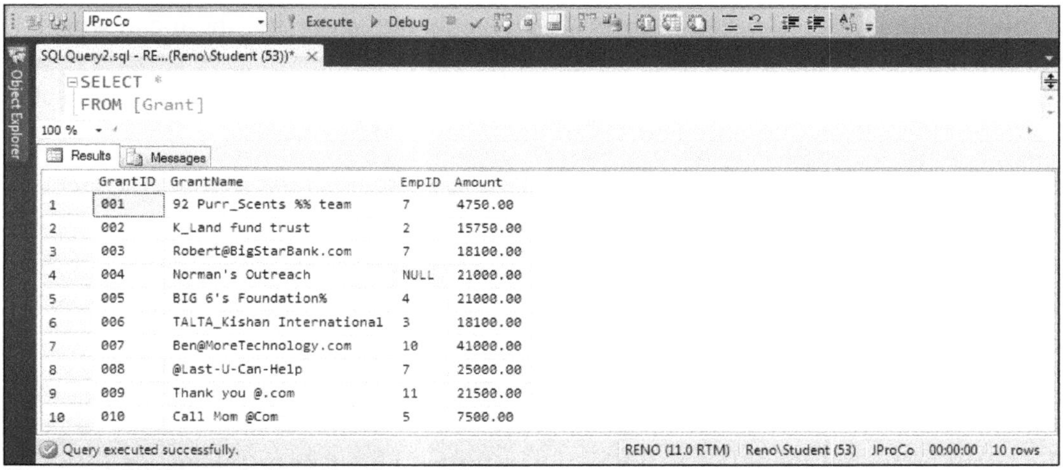

Figure 1.26 All records from the Grant table.

The employee who made that procurement has an EmpID of 10. What if we wanted to find more information about this employee? Is this employee a man or woman? When was this employee hired?

We are unable to get answers to detailed questions about this employee, without looking beyond the Grant table.

For visual purposes, let's put these two tables next to one another. We can see that the EmpID field correlates data between these two tables. Grant.EmpID equates to Employee.EmpID. If we look at EmpID 10 on both tables, we can see Terry O'Haire is the employee who found the $41,000 grant Amount (Figure 1.27).

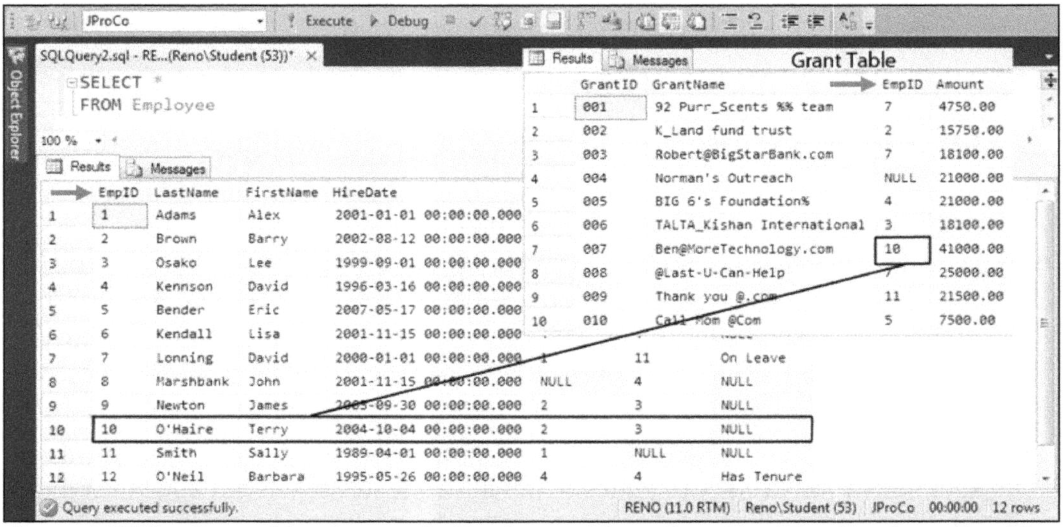

Figure 1.27 The Grant table relates to the Employee table on Grant.EmpID to Employee.EmpID.

Again, placing these two small tables side by side and analyzing them can work, but it's time-consuming and not very efficient, especially if we have two very large tables. Instead, we can use SQL Server to put both tables into one result set. Putting information into one report is of great value to businesses.

READER NOTE: *The tables in Figure 1.27 share the common field of EmpID. Knowing this is a key step.*

To put all these records into one result set, we will need both tables in the FROM clause and a join which requires a field that corresponds to both tables. The ON clause after the INNER JOIN is how we show this relationship.

Looking closely at Figure 1.27 and Figure 1.28 we can see something unusual that might cause us to be cautious when using an INNER JOIN. There are ten grants in the Grant table, but the INNER JOIN only returned nine records. Thus, an INNER JOIN can produce what seems to be a loss of data. We will explore how to know when this will happen and when it is necessary to use a different type of join.

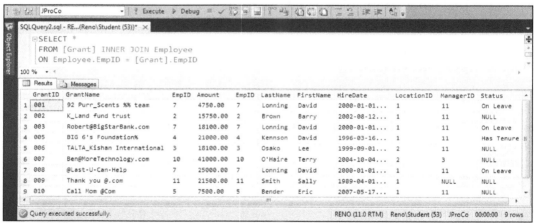

Figure 1.28 Grant and Employee tables in an INNER JOIN show 9 of the 10 grants matching on EmpID.

The GrantName, 'Norman's Outreach' was an online registration, so there is no employee listed as receiving credit for obtaining this grant. The right-hand side of Figure 1.27 shows this record has a NULL value for the EmpID field. We briefly talked about NULL values in this chapter. NULL values will ***never*** match records in another table. Since there is no match found, the record containing the 'Norman's Outreach' GrantName is not included in the result set.

The core behavior of an INNER JOIN is to include only those records where there is an exact match found in both tables. Unmatched records will not appear in the result set.

EQUI JOIN

This is an older, rarely used technique, for joining two tables together. While widely used in years past, with the advent of the INNER JOIN operator, the EQUI JOIN is no longer considered a best practice in modern coding. However, it is possible to encounter this syntax in the workplace, especially when reviewing code that has been in use for a number of years, so it is important to have an understanding of what it does.

The result set produced by the following code sample is the same as that of an INNER JOIN operator on the same two tables.

```
SELECT *
FROM Employee, Location
WHERE Employee.LocationID = Location.LocationID
```

Of course, it is also possible to use table aliases and two-part names with this type of query, as seen in the next code sample.

```
SELECT *
FROM Employee AS em, Location AS lo
WHERE em.LocationID = lo.LocationID
```

	EmpID	LastName	FirstName	HireDate	LocationID	ManagerID	State	LocationID	Street	City	State
1	1	Adams	Alex	2001-01-01...	1	11	NULL	1	111 First ST	Seattle	WA
2	2	Brown	Barry	2002-08-12...	1	11	NULL	1	111 First ST	Seattle	WA
3	3	Osako	Lee	1999-09-01...	2	11	NULL	2	222 Second AVE	Boston	MA
4	4	Kennson	David	1996-03-16...	1	11	Has Tenure	1	111 First ST	Seattle	WA
5	5	Bender	Eric	2007-05-17...	1	11	NULL	1	111 First ST	Seattle	WA
6	6	Kendall	Lisa	2001-11-15...	4	4	NULL	4	444 Ruby ST	Spokane	WA

Query executed successfully.   RENO (11.0 RTM)   Reno\j2p (53)   JProCo   00:00:00   11 rows

Figure 1.29 The older style EQUI JOIN yields the same results as the INNER JOIN operator.

OUTER JOIN Types

Being able to understand how an INNER JOIN works makes it much easier to learn how the different OUTER JOIN types work. They both display records found by a match between two tables. Both types of joins require us to specify the matching field(s) in an ON clause. The primary difference is that each of the different OUTER JOIN types will find records that an INNER JOIN omits from its result set.

LEFT OUTER JOIN

Before we begin writing an OUTER JOIN query, we need to state the goal for what records we want to see in the query result set. There is a record in the Employee table for an employee who works remotely and has a NULL value for the LocationID. Also, there is a location under construction in Chicago that has not had any employees assigned to it yet, so it is not in the Employee table at all.

Are we looking for an employee report or a location report? In an employee report, it is all right if Chicago does not show in the results. We simply need a list of all employees from the Employee table. Thus, the OUTER JOIN must favor the Employee table to ensure all employee records are shown (Figure 1.30).

SQLQuery1.sql - RE...oCo (Reno\j2p (53))* ×

```
SELECT *
FROM Employee LEFT OUTER JOIN Location
ON Employee.LocationID = Location.LocationID
```

	EmpID	LastName	FirstName	HireDate	LocationID	ManagerID	Status	LocationID	Street	City	State
1	1	Adams	Alex	2001-01-01...	1	11	NULL	1	111 First ST	Seattle	WA
2	2	Brown	Barry	2002-08-12...	1	11	NULL	1	111 First ST	Seattle	WA
3	3	Osako	Lee	1999-09-01...	2	11	NULL	2	222 Second AVE	Boston	MA
4	4	Kennson	David	1996-03-16...	1	11	Has Tenure	1	111 First ST	Seattle	WA
5	5	Bender	Eric	2007-05-17...	1	11	NULL	1	111 First ST	Seattle	WA
6	6	Kendall	Lisa	2001-11-15...	4	4	NULL	4	444 Ruby ST	Spokane	WA
7	7	Lonning	David	2000-01-01...	1	11	On Leave	1	111 First ST	Seattle	WA
8	8	Marshb...	John	2001-11-15...	NULL	4	NULL	NULL	NULL	NULL	NULL
9	9	Newton	James	2003-09-30...	2	3	NULL	2	222 Second AVE	Boston	MA
10	10	O'Haire	Terry	2004-10-04...	2	3	NULL	2	222 Second AVE	Boston	MA
11	11	Smith	Sally	1989-04-01...	1	NULL	NULL	1	111 First ST	Seattle	WA
12	12	O'Neil	Barbara	1995-05-26...	4	4	Has Tenure	4	444 Ruby ST	Spokane	WA

Query executed successfully.   RENO (11.0 RTM)   Reno\j2p (53)   JProCo   00:00:00   12 rows

Figure 1.30 A LEFT OUTER JOIN favors the Employee table listed to the *left* of the join.

The query shown in Figure 1.30 is written in a way to help illustrate that the Employee table is to the left of the Location table. Since we want all employees to be included in our results, we need to use a *LEFT OUTER JOIN*. Notice, that John Marshbank, JProCo's remote worker, appears in this result set. When filtering data, a LEFT OUTER JOIN will first return all records from the table on the left and then tries to find matches with the table on the right.

In this example, all records from the Employee table are shown and then matches for the LocationID field in the Location table are populated and displayed. By looking closer at the results shown in Figure 1.30, we see fields from the left table (Employee) sorted by EmpID, and all the fields from the right table (Location) are displayed by aligning values of the matching LocationID fields.

RIGHT OUTER JOIN

A notification from OSHA states they are going to inspect all JProCo buildings, and we need to provide location details for our buildings. They also want to know which employees work in these buildings. Since John Marshbank works remotely, they have no interest in him. They want to inspect each building even if it is under construction and no employees work there.

To show all records from the table on the right, we need a *RIGHT OUTER JOIN* (Figure 1.31). Since the RIGHT OUTER JOIN favors the Location table in this query, all locations are shown in the result set. Because LocationID 3 (Chicago) does not appear in the Employee table, these fields receive NULL values.

Figure 1.31 The RIGHT OUTER JOIN shows all locations, even if nobody works there.

Notice the EmpID values are no longer in order and it is the LocationID values from 1 to 4 that determine how the results are sorted. This is because the right table (Location) is the dominant table finding records matching on LocationID. All the records are shown from the right table (Location), including Chicago.

FULL OUTER JOIN

When we want to see all employees with information obtained from both the Employee table and the Location table, including employees without a location, a LEFT OUTER JOIN works great. Using these same tables, if we want to see all locations, even those without employees, a RIGHT OUTER JOIN will give us the results we need for our location report.

If we wanted to see all employees and all locations regardless of whether each employee matches to a location and regardless of whether each location matches to an employee, we would use a *FULL OUTER JOIN* (Figure 1.32).

Figure 1.32 The FULL OUTER JOIN shows all records from both tables.

The Employee table has 12 records and the Location table has 4 records. A query using a FULL OUTER JOIN with these tables will return 13 records, showing all records from both tables at least one time each.

A FULL OUTER JOIN will show all matched *and* all unmatched records from both tables. So, this type of join can contain results with NULL values in the field(s) listed in the ON clause.

Here is another example of a FULL OUTER JOIN query returning all records from both tables. We need to find all employees with no grants and all grants with no employees by joining the Employee and Grant tables, as seen in Figure 1.33.

As expected, a query with a FULL OUTER JOIN finds all records whether they are matched or unmatched. Until now, none of our queries using a join have included a WHERE clause, so our results always included all possible records.

When filtering any type of a query using a WHERE clause, only the records that satisfy the criteria in the predicate will be included in the result set. By adding the statement, WHERE LocationID = 1 to the code shown in Figure 1.33, all records in the tables not matching this criteria would be removed from the result set. This reduces the original result set of 15 records to 10 records for the Seattle location. Without the WHERE clause, our result set includes all matched and unmatched records. Unmatched records between tables will show as NULLs.

```
SELECT *
FROM [Grant] FULL OUTER JOIN Employee
ON [Grant].EmpID = Employee.EmpID
```

	GrantID	GrantName	EmpID	Amount	EmpID	LastName	FirstName	HireDate	LocationID	ManagerID	Status
1	001	92 Purr_Scents %%...	7	4750.00	7	Lonning	David	2000-01-0...	1	11	On Leave
2	002	K_Land fund trust	2	15750.00	2	Brown	Barry	2002-08-1...	1	11	NULL
3	003	Robert@BigStarBa...	7	18100.00	7	Lonning	David	2000-01-0...	1	11	On Leave
4	004	Norman's Outreach	NULL	21000.00	NULL	NULL	NULL	NULL	NULL	NULL	NULL
5	005	BIG 6's Foundation%	4	21000.00	4	Kennson	David	1996-03-1...	1	11	Has Tenure
6	006	TALTA_Kishan Inter...	3	18100.00	3	Osako	Lee	1999-09-0...	2	11	NULL
7	007	Ben@MoreTechnol...	10	41000.00	10	O'Haire	Terry	2004-10-0...	2	3	NULL
8	008	@Last-U-Can-Help	7	25000.00	7	Lonning	David	2000-01-0...	1	11	On Leave
9	009	Thank you @.com	11	21500.00	11	Smith	Sally	1989-04-0...	1	NULL	NULL
10	010	Call Mom @Com	5	7500.00	5	Bender	Eric	2007-05-1...	1	11	NULL

Query executed successfully.   (local) (11.0 RTM)   Reno\Student (51)   JProCo   00:00:00   15 rows

Figure 1.33 The FULL OUTER JOIN between the Grant and Employee tables shows all records.

Table Aliasing

When people ask me, "How did you do that?" oftentimes they are asking about ordinary work that got done quickly. This is great for deadlines. Table aliasing is a big saver of keystrokes. As we know, tables are listed in the FROM clause. We had to retype the table names again in the ON clause as seen in the following code:

```
SELECT *
FROM Location INNER JOIN Employee
ON Location.LocationID = Employee.LocationID
```

Setting Aliases

Our next goal is to get the FROM clause to refer to the Employee table as 'emp' and the Location table as 'loc'. It's like giving a nickname to a friend. They respond and use it, but their birth certificate still has the original name. In other words, the tables will not change names literally, but our query can use a shorter name. Simply alias the table name as another name in the FROM clause and we can then reuse the shorter name. Here is a SQL example:

```
SELECT *
FROM Location AS loc
INNER JOIN Employee AS emp
ON loc.LocationID = emp.LocationID
```

In this example, the payoff is only slightly obvious. As we write more and more complex queries, we will find that some queries will use a table name in dozens of places. It's far quicker to type *Loc* many times versus *Location*.

Using Aliases

At this point, we are probably not big fans of two-part field names in a query. In fact, the simple name seems to do the same thing with far fewer keystrokes. In comparing the following two queries, we see identical results.

```
--Simple Field Names
SELECT FirstName, LastName, State
FROM Location
INNER JOIN Employee
ON Location.LocationID = Employee.LocationID
```

```
--Two-part Field Names
SELECT Employee.FirstName, Employee.LastName, Location.State
FROM Location
INNER JOIN Employee
ON Location.LocationID = Employee.LocationID
```

The truth is we have lucked out on all our past queries. The simple field name query from above is looking for FirstName from either table. Since there is a FirstName field in the Employee table only, FirstName must really mean Employee.FirstName, so SQL Server implicitly does this behind the scenes for us. The same is true with the State field. When SQL Server looks for the State field in the Employee table and realizes it isn't present, it does us the courtesy of pulling it in from the Location table.

Warning: *Please do not do any of the following steps regarding renaming fields. They are only for demonstration and assume a knowledge level that hasn't been discussed yet. For now, enjoy the concept and feel free to come back and experiment with altering field names after finishing this book.*

Why has everything worked so far by using the simple name? Let's use an example. The Employee table has a Status field (Figure 1.34).

```
SELECT *
FROM Employee
WHERE Status IS NOT NULL
```

	EmpID	LastName	FirstName	HireDate	LocationID	ManagerID	Status
1	4	Kennson	David	1996-03-16…	1	11	Has Tenure
2	7	Lonning	David	2000-01-01…	1	11	On Leave
3	12	O'Neil	Barbara	1995-05-26…	4	4	Has Tenure

3 rows

Figure 1.34 The Employee table has a Status field.

What if the Status field in the Employee table is renamed as the State field? We could end up with two table designs like the ones shown in Figure 1.35.

Figure 1.35 The Employee table's Status field renamed to State. This move could lead to confusion as the Location table already has a State field with an entirely different meaning.

This brings up a question. If a SELECT field list includes State, will SQL Server choose the Employee.State field or the Location.State field? The sheer risk of picking the wrong field means SQL Server will give an error message requesting more information. If we use a 'SELECT *' we will get both fields with no error.

When itemizing fields, we must specify exactly which ones we want. Suppose we want to include the State field in our report. If we use the simple name for a field when two fields with the same name exist, our list will be ambiguous and SQL Server displays an error message (Figure 1.36).

```
SELECT FirstName, LastName, City, State
FROM Location AS loc
INNER JOIN Employee AS emp
ON loc.LocationID = emp.LocationID
```

Messages
Msg 209, Level 16, State 1, Line 1
Ambiguous column name 'State'.
0 rows

Figure 1.36 SQL Server can't tell which State field has been requested to be shown.

Notice the error message coupled with an explanation that SQL Server does not make guesses for what field we want to see. The only time it allows simple field names in a multiple table query is when there is only one field with that name in either table. A good tip to remember is that a 'SELECT *' statement does not give ambiguous column name errors since it will display all fields.

```
SELECT *
FROM Employee
INNER JOIN Location
ON Employee.LocationID = Location.LocationID
```

	EmpID	LastName	FirstName	HireDate	LocationID	ManagerID	State	LocationID	Street	City	State	
1	1	Adams	Alex	2001-01-01...	1	11	NULL	1	111 First ST	Seattle	WA	
2	2	Brown	Barry	2002-08-12...	1	11	NULL	1	111 First ST	Seattle	WA	
3	3	Osako	Lee	1999-09-01...	2	11	NULL	2	222 Second AVE	Boston	MA	
4	4	Kennson	David	1996-03-16...	1	11	Has Tenure	1	111 First ST	Seattle	WA	
5	5	Bender	Eric	2007-05-17...	1	11	NULL	1	111 First ST	Seattle	WA	
6	6	Kendall	Lisa	2001-11-15...	4	4	NULL	4	444 Ruby ST	Spokane	WA	

Query executed successfully. RENO (11.0 RTM) | Reno\j2p (53) | JProCo | 00:00:00 | 11 rows

Figure 1.37 SELECT * displays the State fields from both the Location and Employee tables.

We wanted the City and State fields displayed from the Location table. This error can be fixed by using a two-part field name. Let's modify the field selection list to specify the Location.City and the Location.State fields with table aliases.

We used the Loc alias for the Location table in this query. Doing so allows us to use a shorter name each time we reference that table. This allows the State field to work in our query. We did not need to prefix the City field to get this query to work. Is it possible to guarantee that tomorrow someone will not add a City field to the Employee table in our database denoting where the employee resides? This action would break many queries that use a simple or single-part table name.

We want to ensure that our queries will work today and into the future. A good way to do this is to use two-part names for all fields listed in our SELECT statement. This seems like extra typing, which can be significantly reduced by the use of aliases for the table names.

```
SELECT FirstName, LastName, loc.City, loc.State
FROM Employee
INNER JOIN Location AS loc
ON Employee.LocationID = loc.LocationID
```

	FirstName	LastName	City	State
1	Alex	Adams	Seattle	WA
2	Barry	Brown	Seattle	WA
3	Lee	Osako	Boston	MA
4	David	Kennson	Seattle	WA
5	Eric	Bender	Seattle	WA
6	Lisa	Kendall	Spokane	WA

11 rows

Figure 1.38 Using the loc alias for the Location table to use the two-part names loc.City and loc.[State].

In Figure 1.39 we have changed every listed field to use the two-part name. The aliasing we did in our FROM clause allowed us to use the shorter names. Aliasing is a time-saving way to allow you to create robust and durable code more easily.

```
SELECT emp.FirstName, emp.LastName,
loc.City, loc.State
FROM Employee AS emp
INNER JOIN Location AS loc
ON emp.LocationID = Loc.LocationID
```

	FirstName	LastName	City	State
1	Alex	Adams	Seattle	WA
2	Barry	Brown	Seattle	WA
3	Lee	Osako	Boston	MA
4	David	Kennson	Seattle	WA
5	Eric	Bender	Seattle	WA
6	Lisa	Kendall	Spokane	WA

11 rows

Figure 1.39 All four fields in the SELECT list are aliased with two-part names.

Lab 1.2: Joining Tables and Aliases

Lab Prep: Each lab has one or more Skill Checks. Start with Skill Check 1 and proceed until reaching the Points to Ponder section.

Before beginning this lab, verify that SQL Server 2012 is properly installed and operating. Before running the lab setup script for resetting the database (SQLQueries2012Vol2Chapter1.2Setup.sql), please make sure to close all query windows within SSMS. An open query window pointing to a database context can lock that database preventing it from updating when the script is executing. A simple way to assure all query windows are closed, is to exit out of SSMS, then open a new instance of SSMS, and lastly run the setup script.

Skill Check 1: In a single query, show the employees and cities where they work. Join the Employee and Location tables of the JProCo database on the field they share in common (LocationID). The field selection list should only include FirstName, LastName, City and State. When done, the results should have 11 records and resemble Figure 1.40.

	FirstName	LastName	City	State
1	Alex	Adams	Seattle	WA
2	Barry	Brown	Seattle	WA
3	Lee	Osako	Boston	MA
4	David	Kennson	Seattle	WA
5	Eric	Bender	Seattle	WA
6	Lisa	Kendall	Spokane	WA

11 rows

Figure 1.40 Skill Check 1 shows all employees and where they work.

Skill Check 2: Set the database context to JProCo. Write a query that shows a list of records (grants) from the Grant table, plus the first and last names for the employees who acquired them. If an employee has not found a grant, display a NULL where their names would have been.

Accomplish this Skill Check by joining the Employee and Grant tables together. Include the FirstName, LastName, GrantName and Amount fields in the selection list. When done, the results should have 10 records and resemble Figure 1.41.

	FirstName	LastName	GrantName	Amount
1	David	Lonning	92 Purr_Scents %% team	4750.00
2	Barry	Brown	K_Land fund trust	15750.00
3	David	Lonning	Robert@BigStarBank.com	18100.00
4	NULL	NULL	Norman's Outreach	21000.00
5	David	Kennson	BIG 6's Foundation%	21000.00
6	Lee	Osako	TALTA_Kishan International	18100.00
				10 rows

Figure 1.41 Skill Check 2 shows all records from Grant table and matching Employee table.

Answer Code: The T-SQL code for this lab is located in the downloadable files as a file named Lab1.2_JoiningTables.sql.

Points to Ponder - Table Joins and Aliases

1. A single query can consist of tables joined together on a related field.

2. An INNER JOIN only returns a result set with exact matches on a field in two or more tables.

3. An INNER JOIN is the default join type. When omitting the INNER keyword from the join clause, SQL Server defaults to an INNER JOIN.

4. Using the word INNER is optional. INNER JOIN means the same thing as JOIN in a query.

5. Outer join types can return more records in the result set than just an equal record match list from the INNER JOIN.

6. There are three types of outer joins: LEFT OUTER JOIN, RIGHT OUTER JOIN and FULL OUTER JOIN.

7. In a LEFT OUTER JOIN, the left table might have records that appear even if SQL Server finds no matching records in the right table.

8. In a RIGHT OUTER JOIN, the right table might have records that appear even if SQL Server finds no matching records in the left table.

9. In a FULL OUTER JOIN, all matched and unmatched records from both tables are included in the result set.

10. Using the word OUTER is optional. LEFT OUTER JOIN means the same thing as LEFT JOIN in a query.

11. Regardless of the joining type used, the records produced can be filtered with criteria in the WHERE clause. The joining operation takes place first and then these records are filtered with the WHERE clause.

12. Databases, tables and columns have names called Identifiers. There is an Employee table in the JProCo database. This table is an object and the Identifier of the object is Employee.

13. Aliasing a table with SQL usually means a shorter name than the original Identifier is used.

14. Aliases must be declared immediately after the name of the table in the FROM clause.

15. Once aliased, every reference to the table or the fields in the table must use this alias throughout the query.

16. The process of qualifying fields with two-part names ensures that a query will be unambiguous.

17. Using a shorter alias name, instead of the complete table name, reduces some of the extra work with qualifying fields.

18. Although using the keyword AS when specifying an alias is optional it is considered best practice and makes reading the code easier.

Bulk Copy Program (BCP)

There are many ways to get data into a SQL Server database. We have discussed scripts extensively in Volume 1 and seen many ways to run these scripts. Most of the time, the source of our data will be plain, raw data. Raw data often comes to us as a block of values separated by commas with no SQL code whatsoever. In our SQL career, we will no doubt receive inputs in the form of spreadsheets, text files, Microsoft Access databases or another company's database.

There are utilities that understand data, and SQL Server can manage the inserting of data for us by using these different utilities and services. Some programs like *SQL Server Integration Services* (SSIS) can take just about any source of data and move it into or out of SQL Server. In this chapter, we explore how to use the *Bulk Copy Program* (BCP) utility, which is designed to expedite the flow of data between SQL Server and text files. This simple utility does one of the most common types of bulk copying.

Importing Data

If we have data in a text file and need to move it into a SQL table, then we are ready to import that file into SQL Server using the BCP utility. A quick visual comparison of data in the input file and destination table will really help. We must confirm that the text data supplied can populate each field by matching the design of the destination table.

Let's start off by looking at the destination where we intend to import this new data into. Usually this will be an existing table. In this example, let's look at the Movie table of the dbMovie database to examine the records (Figure 1.42).

```
SELECT * FROM Movie
```

	m_ID	m_Title	m_Runtime	m_Rating	m_Teaser	m_Release
1	1	A-List Explorers	96	PG-13	Description Coming Soon	2000
2	2	Bonker Bonzo	75	G	Description Coming Soon	2000
3	3	Chumps to Champs	75	PG-13	Description Coming Soon	2000
4	4	Dare or Die	110	R	Description Coming Soon	2000
5	5	EeeeGhads	88	G	Description Coming Soon	2000
						6 rows

Figure 1.42 The destination of the data will be the Movie table of the dbMovie database.

We currently have six fields, which can also be stated as "We need six values for each record in this table". There are also five records in our Movie table and two records in the file called Ch1MovieFeed.txt (Figure 1.43). Our goal is to import movies 6 and 7 into the Movie table using the BCP utility.

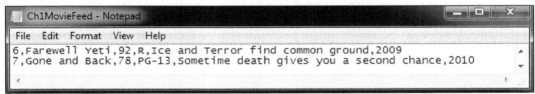

Figure 1.43 A text file with data is used to copy two records into the Movie table.

Locate the file Ch1MovieFeed.txt inside the Resources folder of the C:\Joes2Pro folder location. Copy this file directly into the C:\Joes2Pros folder.

The first record of the text file is m_id 6. Note the value 6 is terminated with a comma to separate it from the second field value of 'Farewell Yeti', which is separated by a comma from the third field, which shows a runtime of 92 minutes. The pattern repeats until the final field in each record is reached. At that point, a return (a carriage return or the equivilant of pressing the 'Enter' key) signals the end of the record. Keep in mind that *commas separate fields*, and after each line the *carriage return separates records*.

OK, we've confirmed the data in the source file and now are confident the data conforms to the destination format of our Movie table. The BCP utility should be able to run without a problem. We need to provide a few logistical items to BCP:

- o The filepath of the source file.
- o Which table we want the data copied into (Destination).
- o The type of field terminators designated (commas, tabs, hash mark).

Close any query window that is open to the Movie database and minimize the Management Studio window to the taskbar, then press the keyboard combination

'▓⊞ + R' (Windows key plus R key). This will open a dialog box. In the '***Run***' dialog box type the word '**cmd**' and then press 'OK' (Figure 1.44).

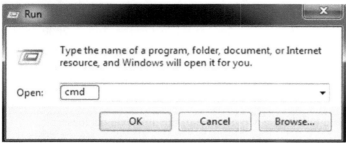

Figure 1.44 Starting the Command Prompt.

With the Command Prompt open (Figure 1.45), we can go to the root of the C:\ drive with a '**cd**' command and then press 'Enter'. Set the folder context to C:\Joes2pros with the command '**cd Joes2Pros**' then press 'Enter'. While in the folder, a good practice is to make sure the Ch1MovieFeed.txt is actually located in the directory. We can verify this by simply typing the command '**dir**', which will show us all the folders and files in the Joes2Pros folder. Once this is confirmed, we can proceed to invoke the file using the BCP utility.

We want to tell BCP to expect character data '**-c**' with fields terminated by commas '**-t,**'. The Windows Operating System has already authenticated our password, and SQL Server trusts Windows authentication. Since we are logged on as a user with permissions, we don't need to re-type our password. Use the Trusted connection switch by typing an upper case '**-T**'. Lastly, we have multiple records in the text file. Each record is separated by a new line '**\n**' or a carriage return '**r\n**' (carriage return\newline) in our text file. Place all these command switches together in the command line shown in Figure 1.45.

Caution: *SQL Express Users… to successfully complete this exercise, the '-S' switch will require the SQL Server instance name (found in Object Explorer) followed by a backslash '\' sign and then the word '**SQLExpress**'. Please look to the end of this section for Figure 1.51 and Figure 1.52 and the accompanying paragraphs as an example.*

Figure 1.45 The path is C:\Joes2Pros, run BCP to add two new records into the Movie table.

Query the Movie table and notice the two new records for a total of seven. This verifies that the m_id 6 and m_id 7 records were successfully added via BCP.

```
SELECT * FROM Movie
```

	m_ID	m_Title	m_Runtime	m_Rating	m_Teaser	m_Release
2	2	Bonker Bonzo	75	G	Description Coming Soon	2000
3	3	Chumps to Champs	75	PG-13	Description Coming Soon	2000
4	4	Dare or Die	110	R	Description Coming Soon	2000
5	5	EeeeGhads	88	G	Description Coming Soon	2000
6	6	Farewell Yeti	75	R	Ice and Terror find a…	2009
7	7	Gone and Back	75	R	Sometimes death gives…	2010

7 rows

Figure 1.46 The result set after running BCP shows there are now seven movie records.

Exporting Data

We are now being asked to share this information with a parent company. That company needs all seven records from our Movie table. Since they do not have permissions to our SQL Server, they have requested that we send them the data in a text file terminated (delimited) by hash # marks.

Essentially, we will be reversing the import process we just completed using the BCP utility. So, we will be moving data from our table in SQL Server and then saving it as a text file in the file system. In the Command Prompt window we will use BCP to specify the Movie table is going out to the Ch1PartnerFeed.txt using character data terminated by hash marks (Figure 1.47).

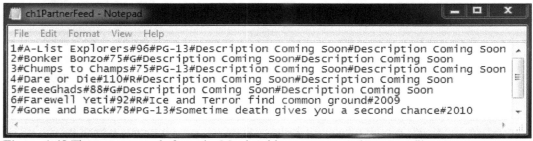

Figure 1.47 The BCP process is saving all seven files as a text file.

Next, we will open the file C:\Joes2Pros\Ch1PartnerFeed.txt and examine its contents. We can do this by locating the file with Windows Explorer and then double-clicking on the file name. We can use the command line and type the command '**notepad C:\Joes2Pros\Ch1PartnerFeed.txt**'. We can easily see that our file uses hash marks as delimiters and has seven records in total (Figure 1.48).

Figure 1.48 The seven records from the Movie table were exported to a text file.

There are many options to tell BCP how to perform a task. Different file types and security settings are among the choices. To view the list of all command line switches for the BCP utility we can type this command '**BCP /?**' and then press the 'Enter' button on our keyboard. The results are shown in Figure 1.49.

```
C:\Windows\system32\cmd.exe

C:\>BCP /?
usage: BCP {dbtable | query} {in | out | queryout | format} datafile
  [-m maxerrors]              [-f formatfile]           [-e errfile]
  [-F firstrow]               [-L lastrow]              [-b batchsize]
  [-n native type]            [-c character type]       [-w wide character type]
  [-N keep non-text native]   [-V file format version]  [-q quoted identifier]
  [-C code page specifier]    [-t field terminator]     [-r row terminator]
  [-i inputfile]              [-o outfile]              [-a packetsize]
  [-S server name]            [-U username]             [-P password]
  [-T trusted connection]     [-v version]              [-R regional enable]
  [-k keep null values]       [-E keep identity values]
  [-h "load hints"]           [-x generate xml format file]
  [-d database name]          [-K application intent]

C:\>_
```

Figure 1.49 All the options of the BCP can be seen with the BCP help command 'BCP /?'.

In order for BCP to communicate with SQL Server, it needs the right password or credential. This means we must either supply it with a trusted connection or a password.

If we want to see what the text file would look like if we accidently missed specifying a terminator in the previous example (Figure 1.47), we can type in the following command at the flashing cursor.

```
BCP dbMovie.dbo.Movie OUT Ch1TabFeed.txt –c -T -r\n
```

If a field terminator is not specified, a tab-delimited text file is created by default. A best practice is to specify a delimiter, otherwise BCP will choose the default tab delimiter. We can see what this looks like in Figure 1.50. With tab delimited files, it can be difficult to see where fields of varying lengths end, since columns don't line up uniformly and sometimes the gap for a tab is the same as a single space. In this case, a comma-delimited text file would be easier to visually scan and verify.

```
Ch1TabFeed - Notepad

File   Edit   Format   View   Help

1       A-List Explorers        96      PG-13   Description Coming Soon Desc
2       Bonker Bonzo    75      G               Description Coming Soon Description
3       Chumps to Champs        75      PG-13   Description Coming Soon Desc
4       Dare or Die     110     R               Description Coming Soon Description
5       EeeeGhads       88      G               Description Coming Soon Description
6       Farewell Yeti   92      R               Ice and Terror find common ground
7       Gone and Back   78      PG-13   Sometime death gives you a second ch
```

Figure 1.50 A tab-delimited text file is the default for BCP without specifying a terminator type.

SQL Server Express Users: To complete this exercise with SQL Server Express edition, we will need to know the exact name of our SQL Server instance. To do this, verify our server name at the top of the Object Explorer. For example, in Figure 1.51 we see the name of the instance is Reno. The full path name for this instance is 'SQL Server 11.0.2100 - Reno\Student'.

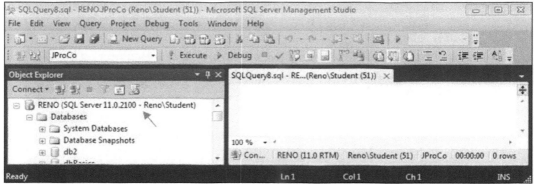

Figure 1.51 SQL Express on the Reno server will have the instance name of Reno\SQLExpress.

Users of SQL Server Express must explicitly name their server. So, to run our CreateDBMovie.sql script with SQLCMD, use the correct Server switch '**-S**' and then type the name of our SQL Server instance (found in Object Explorer) followed by a backslash '\' sign and then the word '**SQLExpress**'. An example of what this looks like appears in Figure 1.52.

```
C:\Joes2Pros>SQLCMD -S Reno\sqlexpress -E -iCreateDBMovie.sql
Changed database context to 'master'.
Changed database context to 'dbMovie'.

(0 rows affected)

C:\Joes2Pros>
```

Figure 1.52 SQL Server Express users must explicitly identify the server name in SQLCMD.

Lab 1.3: Using BCP

Lab Prep: Each lab has one or more Skill Checks. Start with Skill Check 1 and proceed until reaching the Points to Ponder section.

Before beginning this lab, verify that SQL Server 2012 is properly installed and operating. Before running the lab setup script for resetting the database (SQLQueries2012Vol2Chapter1.3Setup.sql), please make sure to close all query windows within SSMS. An open query window pointing to a database context can lock that database preventing it from updating when the script is executing. A simple way to assure all query windows are closed, is to exit out of SSMS, then open a new instance of SSMS, and lastly run the setup script.

Skill Check 1: Copy the Ch1SalesInvoiceFeed.txt' file to the C:\Joes2Pros folder. Run BCP utility with the correct switches to place these 1877 records into the JProCo.dbo.SalesInvoice table as seen in Figure 1.53.

```
Starting copy...
1000 rows sent to SQL Server. Total sent: 1000

1877 rows copied.
Network packet size (bytes): 4096
Clock Time (ms.) Total      : 121      Average : (15512.40 rows per sec.)

C:\Joes2Pros>
```

Figure 1.53 BCP has copied 1877 rows into the SalesInvoice table.

Skill Check 2: The Customer table of JProCo has five test records inside. The Ch1CustomerFeed.txt in the C:\Joes2Pros\Resources folder has 775 verified records.

```
SELECT * FROM Customer
```

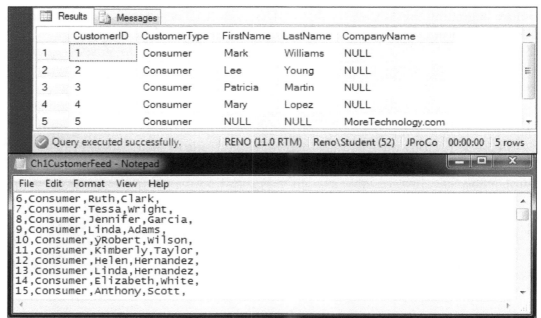

Figure 1.54 Ch1CustomerFeed.txt is a comma-delimited text file ready to import into the Customer table.

We need to delete the five test records from the Customer table and then import the 775 comma-delimited rows of data from the Ch1CustomerFeed.txt file. When done, the Command Prompt window will resemble the BCP utility results shown here in Figure 1.55.

Figure 1.55 BCP shows 775 records have been inserted.

Answer Code: The T-SQL code for this lab is located in the downloadable files as a file named Lab1.3_BCP.sql.

Points to Ponder - Using BCP

1.   BCP stands for Bulk Copy Program.

2.   BCP lets you to perform data imports and exports using a command-line utility.

3.   In BCP, the '**–t**' switch is used to specify how your fields are terminated. For example: To use commas between each field, use '**–t,**' and to use ampersands between each field, use '**–t&**' for the switch.

4.   Upper and lower case switches have different meanings in BCP and all Command Prompt utilities.

5.   To see the list of BCP usage commands, type BCP from the command line. **Start > Run > CMD > BCP**

Creating Tables

To build a new table you need the CREATE TABLE statement. CREATE is a DDL statement (If you need a review, then see *SQL Queries 2012 Joes 2 Pros Volume 1* "Data Definition Language" and Chapter 12 "SQL Language Statement Types").

Do not run this code yet – later you will run it as part of Lab 1.4.

```
USE JProCo
GO

CREATE TABLE SalesInvoiceDetail (
InvoiceDetailID INT PRIMARY KEY,
InvoiceID INT NOT NULL,
ProductID INT NOT NULL,
Quantity INT NOT NULL,
UnitDiscount SMALLMONEY)
GO
```

This T-SQL code creates the SalesInvoiceDetail table. The field names and data types are in the parentheses. The InvoiceDetailID is the primary key for the table, which means we can't have two records with the same InvoiceDetailID. Fields with primary keys do not allow NULLs even if you don't specify NOT NULL when creating the field. The second field definition states that the InvoiceID cannot contain NULL values. The ProductID field will accept integer (INT) data and cannot be NULL. If the UnitDiscount is not known, we can leave that NULL until a later time. We can create records and still enter some of the values at a later date when they are known (This topic will be further explored in Chapter 3).

The following is a preview of the steps you will take in Lab 1.4 to create, populate and query a table. The screenshots are a visual recap of the steps you would take to create a new table and populate it with records.

Step 1. CREATE TABLE

SQL Server builds the table structure with the CREATE TABLE statement. Query the table with a SELECT clause as shown in Figure 1.56. Since this table is brand new, it has no records. The unpopulated table is seen in Figure 1.56 with five fields.

```
SELECT *
FROM SalesInvoiceDetail
```

InvoiceDetailID	InvoiceID	ProductID	Quantity	UnitDiscount
				0 rows

Figure 1.56 This query shows the SalesInvoiceDetail table, which is not yet populated with data.

Inserting Data

Tables are created for the purpose of holding data. Every table begins its life as an unpopulated table. The only way to populate a table is by inserting data. T-SQL coding that starts with the INSERT keyword are DML statements. INSERT statements add new records to tables.

Currently the SalesInvoiceDetail table is unpopulated, meaning it has no records. How much data you need to add depends on how many fields the table has.

Step 2. INSERT INTO Table VALUES (insert the first record).

To populate the first record, we need to supply five values. In an INSERT statement you separate each field value with a comma. To add the first record, use the following code:

```
INSERT INTO SalesInvoiceDetail VALUES (1, 1, 76, 2, 0)
```

Step 3. INSERT INTO Table VALUES (insert the next two records).

If you want to insert two records at the same time, you always have the option to run multiple INSERT INTO statements together. We can insert InvoiceDetailID 2 and InvoiceDetailID 3 at the same time as shown in Figure 1.57.

```
INSERT INTO SalesInvoiceDetail VALUES (2, 1, 77, 3, 0)
INSERT INTO SalesInvoiceDetail VALUES (3, 1, 78, 6, 0)
```

Messages
(1 row(s) affected)
(1 row(s) affected)
0 rows

Figure 1.57 Two INSERT INTO statements each inserted one record.

There was no need to run these INSERT INTO statements in separate batches with GO statements. DML statements like INSERT INTO use Transaction Control Language (TCL) instead of batches. Each insert statement in Figure 1.57 inserted one record, resulting in two additional records in the SalesInvoiceDetail table (Figure 1.57). Note *that this example shows the SQL 2005 INSERT syntax where an insert statement can only insert one record. Since the 2008 version we can insert many records at once with one insert statement. All remaining INSERT statements in this book will use the SQL Server 2008 row constructor syntax.*

Step 4. SELECT * FROM SalesInvoiceDetail (query the table).

Run a simple SELECT * FROM query to show all records from the SalesInvoiceDetail table and confirm how many records you have (Figure 1.58).

```
SELECT *
FROM SalesInvoiceDetail
```

	InvoiceDetailID	InvoiceID	ProductID	Quantity	UnitDiscount
1	1	1	76	2	0.00
2	2	1	77	3	0.00
3	3	1	78	6	0.00

3 rows

Figure 1.58 The SalesInvoiceDetail table now contains three records.

Lab 1.4: Creating and Populating Tables

Lab Prep: Each lab has one or more Skill Checks. Start with Skill Check 1 and proceed until reaching the Points to Ponder section.

Before beginning this lab, verify that SQL Server 2012 is properly installed and operating. Before running the lab setup script for resetting the database (SQLQueries2012Vol2Chapter1.4Setup.sql), please make sure to close all query windows within SSMS. An open query window pointing to a database context can lock that database preventing it from updating when the script is executing. A simple way to assure all query windows are closed, is to exit out of SSMS, then open a new instance of SSMS, and lastly run the setup script.

Skill Check 1: Create the dbo.StateList table in the JProCo database with the table design shown in Figure 1.59. *Hint: This table has no primary key.*

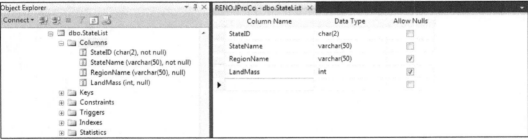

Figure 1.59 The design view of the StateList table.

Next use the BCP utility to import Ch1StateListFeed.txt into the StateList table. Verify the results by running a simple query for all fields and records of the StateList table. When done, the results should resemble Figure 1.60.

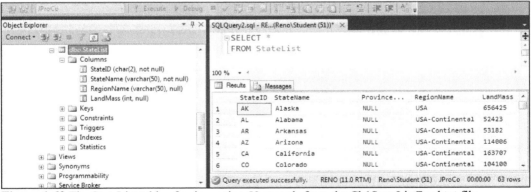

Figure 1.60 The StateList table after importing 53 records from the Ch1StateListFeed.txt file.

Skill Check 2: Drop, re-create and then populate the SalesInvoiceDetail table in the JProCo database. Use the table design shown in Figure 1.61.

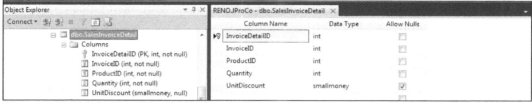

Figure 1.61 The design view of SalesInvoiceDetail.

Populate the table with the Ch1SalesInvoiceDetailFeed.txt using the BCP utility. During the import into the database, the results will look like Figure 1.62.

```
C:\joes2pros>BCP JProCo.dbo.SalesInvoiceDetail IN Ch1SalesInvoiceDetailFeed.txt
-c  -r \n  -T

Starting copy...
1000 rows sent to SQL Server. Total sent: 1000
1000 rows sent to SQL Server. Total sent: 2000
1000 rows sent to SQL Server. Total sent: 3000
1000 rows sent to SQL Server. Total sent: 4000
1000 rows sent to SQL Server. Total sent: 5000
1000 rows sent to SQL Server. Total sent: 6000

6960 rows copied.
Network packet size (bytes): 4096
Clock Time (ms.) Total     : 341      Average : (20410.56 rows per sec.)

C:\joes2pros>
```

Figure 1.62 BCP copied 6960 records into the SalesInvoiceDetail table.

A quick check of the table after importing the data should verify the results shown in Figure 1.63.

```sql
SELECT *
FROM SalesInvoiceDetail
```

	InvoiceDetailID	InvoiceID	ProductID	Quantity	UnitDiscount
1	1	1	76	2	0.00
2	2	1	77	3	0.00
3	3	1	78	6	0.00
4	4	1	71	5	0.00
5	5	1	72	4	0.00
6	6	2	73	2	0.00

6960 rows

Figure 1.63 A simple query of SalesInvoiceDetail shows the table is now populated.

Answer Code: The T-SQL code for this lab is located in the downloadable files as a file named Lab1.4_CreatingAndPopulatingTables.sql

Points to Ponder - Creating and Populating Tables

1. The CREATE TABLE statement is the T-SQL way of adding a table object to a database.

2. A CREATE TABLE statement is a DDL (Data Definition Language) statement.

3. CREATE is used to make new objects in SQL Server including tables, or even whole databases. The CREATE keyword is part of a DDL statement.

4. DROP removes objects in SQL Server (tables, databases). The DROP keyword is the beginning of a .

5. At the time a table is created, the required fields and data types must also be specified.

6. Column names must be unique within a specific table, although the same column name can be used in a different table.

7. When a field is defined as NOT NULL, this means a field value can never be empty. Each time a new row is added, a value must be entered.

Chapter Glossary

Alias: An abbreviated name for database objects which save keystrokes while writing queries.

ALTER: A DDL command that changes the design or properties of database objects.

BCP: Bulk Copy Program is a command-line utility for importing or exporting data from a delimited text file.

BETWEEN Operator: An operator used in SQL that selects a range of data between two values.

Clause: A type of keyword used for a query. SELECT is both a clause and a keyword.

CREATE: A DDL statement that creates database objects.

Database Context: Refers to which database the current query is run against.

DDL Statement: A statement that can CREATE, DROP, or ALTER a database or database objects.

DDL: Data Definition Language.

DELETE: Removes records from a table, without changing the structure of the table, or removing the table itself from the database.

Delimiter: A character which separates one object or entity from another.

DML: Data Manipulation Language.

DROP: A DDL statement that removes a database or database object.

Export: A process to take data from a table and save it with another type of data storage.

Filter: A clause that limits the records in the query results.

FROM: A keyword which chooses the table to query for information.

Import: A process to bring data into a SQL Server table.

IN: An operator used to enumerate a set of exact matches in a query.

INNER JOIN: Combines records from two or more tables where matching values are found.

INSERT: A DML keyword used to add new records to tables.

Join Clause: The clause used to join tables in SQL.

Keyword: A word built into the SQL language.

LEFT OUTER JOIN: Combines records from two or more tables and shows all records from the left table and matching records from the right table.

LIKE: An operator that allows a relative search to filter a result set for a specified pattern in a column.

Operator: Words or signs used by SQL to make calculations or evaluations. Some commonly used operators are AND, OR, <, > and =.

OUTER JOIN: Combines records from two or more tables and shows matching and unmatched values.

Populate: The process of adding data to a table.

Predicate: A logical statement evaluating to true, false, or unknown for each record.

PRIMARY KEY: An attribute of a field that prevents records with duplicate values in this specific field.

Relational Database: A database containing more than one table.

RIGHT OUTER JOIN: Combines records from two or more tables and shows all records from the right table and matching records from the left table.

Row Constructors: Allow multiple records in one INSERT INTO statement.

Script: SQL code saved as a file with a '.sql' file extension.

SELECT: A SQL command used to choose which fields to return in a result set.

System Table: A table created by SQL Server to track design and settings used by SQL Server.

Tab-Delimited File: A text file where each field is separated by a tab character.

Terminator: This type of marker designates the ending of a column or a row.

Unpopulated Table: A table with no records.

UPDATE: A statement that changes, or *manipulates* existing data without adding any new records.

WHERE (clause): The most common optional keyword used to filter result sets.

Wildcard: Special characters that are used in conjunction with the LIKE keyword to match patterns for a result set.

Review Quiz - Chapter One

1.) Which record will not return with the following WHERE clause?

```
WHERE LastName LIKE 'T%'
```

O a. Thomas
O b. Atwater
O c. Tompter
O d. TeeTee

2.) Look at the following T-SQL statement:

```
SELECT *
FROM Employee LEFT OUTER JOIN Location
ON Location.LocationID = Employee.LocationID
```

What will be displayed in the result set?

O a. All records where both tables match.
O b. All records in Employee including matches from Location.
O c. All records from Location including matches from Employee.

3.) What is the correct way to alias the sales table?

O a. FROM Sales AS sl

O b. FROM sl AS Sales sl

O c. SELECT Sales AS sl

4.) You have a table named Employee. You write the following query:

```
SELECT *
FROM Employee em
```

You plan to join the Location table and fear there may be some employees with no location. You want to make sure that the query returns a list of all employee records. What join clause would you add to the query above?

O a. `LEFT JOIN Location lo ON em.LocationID = lo.LocationID`

O b. `RIGHT JOIN Location lo ON em.LocationID = lo.LocationID`

O c. `INNER JOIN Location lo ON em.LocationID = lo.LocationID`

O d. `FULL JOIN Location lo ON em.LocationID = lo.LocationID`

5.)   BCP is a command-line utility that does what?

O a. It runs SQL scripts.
O b. It installs SQL Server.
O c. It imports data from any type of file.
O d. It imports data from a text file.

6.)   If you do not specify a way to delimit your fields what does BCP do?

O a. You get an error message.
O b. It picks the most recently used delimiting option.
O c. You don't get any delimited file.
O d. You get a comma delimited file.
O e. You get a tab delimited file.

7.)   You want to find all first names that start with the letters A-M in your Customer table. Which T-SQL code would you use?

O a. ```
SELECT * FROM Customer
   WHERE FirstName <= 'm%'
```

O b.  ```
SELECT * FROM Customer
   WHERE FirstName  = 'a-m%'
```

O c. ```
SELECT * FROM Customer
   WHERE FirstName LIKE 'a-m%'
```

O d.  ```
SELECT * FROM Customer
   WHERE FirstName  = '[a-m]%'
```

O e. ```
SELECT * FROM Customer
   WHERE FirstName LIKE '[a-m]%'
```

**8.)**    You want to find all scores for contestants who scored in the range of 20-30 points. Which T-SQL code would you use?

O a.  ```
SELECT * FROM contestant
   WHERE score BETWEEN 20 OR 30
```

O b. ```
SELECT * FROM contestant
   WHERE score BETWEEN 20 AND 30
```

O c.  ```
SELECT * FROM contestant
   WHERE score IS BETWEEN 20 AND 30
```

O d. ```
SELECT * FROM contestant
   WHERE score MIDDLE RANGE (20,30)
```
```

9.) You want to find all first names that have the letter A as the second letter and do not end with the letter Y. Which T-SQL code would you use?

O a. `SELECT * FROM Employee`
`WHERE FirstName LIKE '_A% ' AND FirstName NOT LIKE 'Y%'`

O b. `SELECT * FROM Employee`
`WHERE FirstName LIKE '_A% ' AND FirstName NOT LIKE '%Y'`

O c. `SELECT * FROM Employee`
`WHERE FirstName LIKE 'A_% ' AND FirstName NOT LIKE 'Y%'`

10.) You work for a commercial CA (certificate authority) which helps identify trusted third party URLs. You have a table named ApprovedWebSites. Some are ftp:// sites and some are http:// sites. You want to find all approved .org sites listed in the URLName field of the ApprovedWebSites table. All URL names will have the :// with at least one character before them. All sites will have at least one character after the :// and at least one character before the .org at the end. What code will give you all .org records?

O a. `SELECT * FROM ApprovedWebSites`
`WHERE URLName LIKE '%://_[.org]'`

O b. `SELECT * FROM ApprovedWebSites`
`WHERE URLName LIKE '_%[.org]'`

O c. `SELECT * FROM ApprovedWebSites`
`WHERE URLName LIKE '_%://_%.org'`

O d. `SELECT * FROM ApprovedWebSites`
`WHERE URLName = '%://%.org'`

11.) You have a table named Performance. The Duration field shows the total time, in milliseconds, it took for a query to run. You have a field called CPU, which shows the processing time in milliseconds. You have a field called EventClassID, which is an integer that maps to the dbo.EventClass table. The company worries there may be queries running slowly in the CPU, or quickly in the CPU but spending too much time for the total duration. You want to find all records from EventClassID 7 that are taking more than 1 second of CPU time or more than 2 seconds of total duration. Which predicate do you use?

O a. `WHERE EventClassID = 7 AND (CPU > 1 OR Duration > 2)`

O b. `WHERE EventClassID = 7 AND (CPU > 1000 OR Duration > 2000)`

O c. `WHERE EventClassID = 7 AND (CPU > 1000 AND Duration > 2000)`

Answer Key

1.) Because '%' represents zero or more characters and the first character in the pattern to be matched is 'T' the only names that will be returned will start with 'T'. Since 3 of the names do start with 'T' (a) Thomas, (c) Tompter and (d) TeeTee are all wrong. Since Atwater is the only one that does not start with 'T', (b) is the correct answer.

2.) An INNER JOIN will return 'All records where both tables match', so (a) is incorrect. RIGHT OUTER JOIN-ing to Location, would return 'All records from Location including matches from Employee, making (c) wrong too. Because Employee is on the left and Location is on the right of the LEFT OUTER JOIN operator (b) is correct and will return 'All records in Employee including matches from Location'.

3.) 'FROM sl AS Sales sl' will alias the 'sl' tables as 'Sales' then display a syntax error because of the second 'sl', making (b) wrong. 'SELECT Sales AS sl' will alias the 'Sales' field as 'sl', so (c) is also wrong. 'FROM Sales AS sl' will alias the 'Sales' table as 'sl', so (a) is correct.

4.) RIGHT JOIN Location lo ON em.LocationID = lo.LocationID will return all location records including any matches from the employee table, so (b) is wrong. INNER JOIN Location lo ON em.LocationID = lo.LocationID will only return the employee records that have a matching location, so (c) is wrong too. FULL JOIN Location lo ON em.LocationID = lo.LocationID will return the superset of both tables, making (d) incorrect. LEFT JOIN Location lo ON em.LocationID = lo.LocationID will return all employee records including any matches from the location table, making (a) the correct answer.

5.) SQL Server runs SQL scripts, so (a) is incorrect. Installation discs are used for installing SQL Server, so (b) is wrong too. Programs like SQL Server Integration Services (SSIS) can import data from most types of files, so (c) is also wrong. The correct answer is (d) because BCP (Bulk Copy Program) imports data from text files.

6.) Since, by default, you get a tab delimited file when you do not specify a way to delimit your fields using the –t switch, then (a), (b), (c) and (d) are all wrong. BCP will create a tab delimited file if the –t switch is not used, making (e) the correct answer.

7.) Wildcards (%, _) only work with the LIKE keyword, making (a), (b) and (d) all incorrect. 'LIKE 'a-m%'' would only match strings where the first three characters are 'a-m', so (c) is also wrong. The correct answer is (e) because the predicate uses the LIKE keyword and ends in %, meaning zero or more characters following the first character, which has its range defined correctly with [a-m].

8.) BETWEEN uses the AND operator, so (a) is incorrect because it used the OR operator. The IS operator is not used with the BETWEEN operator, so (c) is also incorrect. There is no such operator as MIDDLE RANGE, so (d) is wrong too. The BETWEEN operator requires the AND operator but doesn't need the IS operator, so (b) is correct.

9.) When pattern matching, the use of NOT LIKE 'Y%' only ensures that the first character in the string is not 'Y', it does not check to see what the string ends in, so (a) and (c) are both wrong. The use of LIKE '_A%' will match strings with any character in the first position followed by 'A' followed by zero or more characters. The use of NOT LIKE '%Y' ensures that the last character in the string is not 'Y', so (b) is correct.

10.) The wildcard '%' can match zero characters, so (a) and (d) are both wrong because they would match a string starting with '://'. The pattern we need to match must include '://' and (b) doesn't include this, so it is wrong too. The two wildcards '_' and '%' used side by side ensure that a pattern contains at least one character immediately followed by zero or more characters, therefore (c) is the correct answer.

11.) 1 second is 1000 milliseconds. Since the data is stored in milliseconds, (a) is wrong. Since we are looking for a long CPU time or a long total Duration, we don't need both to be high, making (c) wrong. Since either the CPU time or the total Duration can be high, (b) is the correct answer.

Bug Catcher Game

To play the Bug Catcher game, run the SQLQueries2012Vol2BugCatcher01.pps file from the BugCatcher folder of the companion files. These files are available from the www.Joes2Pros.com website.

[THIS PAGE INTENTIONALLY LEFT BLANK.]

Chapter 2.   Query Options

Often times when shopping at the store I will select an items based on its price. After making my selection and heading home the price tag is no longer needed. We can search for everyone with an April birthdate without showing the actual birthdate in the final report. What we look for and what we show are sometime two different things.

You may not need to sort your family names alphabetically but the phone books of yesteryear need this feature. Even if you have the right data you might want to put some effort into making sure it is formatted the way you want it. Perhaps the results need to be sorted alphabetically by name or in order by revenue amounts, so the highest or lowest data will stand out at the top of your list.

In this chapter, we will encounter similar issues trying to get table data to answer the questions we ask, as well as arranging data in the order we'd like to view the information. You will work with multi-table joins every day of your career working with SQL Server and data. As well, the sorting techniques introduced in this chapter are key skills you will need in Chapters 4 through 7.

READER NOTE: *Please run the SQLQueries2012Vol2Chapter2.0Setup.sql script in order to follow along with the examples in the first section of Chapter 2. All scripts mentioned in this chapter are available at www.Joes2Pros.com.*

Sorting Data

Now that you've mastered building basic queries with T-SQL, you are eager to power forward in your understanding SQL Server. Beware – at first glance the sorting topics in this section may simply seem like optional finishing touches. Up until now, the result sets we've built have been small enough to visualize all records in one glance and to answer questions without needing to rearrange the order of the data. However, data sorting is one capability that differentiates SQL Joes from SQL Pros. Two things you will encounter in a data-intense job setting are fast motivators to learn sorting: 1) very large record sets (thousands, millions, even billions of records!), and 2) managers and decision makers who are very specific and require precise appearance of information in your reports. In short, the ability to properly sort data can keep you out of hot water!

Just like table joins and filtering, when you sort data it affects only the view of the information in your result set. Sorting does not physically change the way the underlying table stores the data. Sorting is a key step in turning your data into report information.

We can sort any field in ascending or descending order. Ascending (keyword ASC) will order characters alphabetically A to Z; numbers from lowest to highest; and dates from oldest to newest. Descending (keyword DESC) does just the opposite and gives you the newest dates, highest numbers, and a reverse alphabetical sort Z to A. SQL Server's default sort order is ascending, so your result will appear in ascending order if you don't specify.

Sorting Single Table Queries

Let's begin by simply selecting all the records in the Employee table of the JProCo database without specifying a sort order (Figure 2.1).

```
SELECT *
FROM Employee
```

	EmpID	LastName	FirstName	HireDate	LocationID	ManagerID	Status
1	1	Adams	Alex	2001-01-01…	1	11	NULL
2	2	Brown	Barry	2002-08-12…	1	11	NULL
3	3	Osako	Lee	1999-09-01…	2	11	NULL
4	4	Kennson	David	1996-03-16…	1	11	Has Tenure
5	5	Bender	Eric	2007-05-17…	1	11	NULL
6	6	Kendall	Lisa	2001-11-15…	4	4	NULL

12 rows

Figure 2.1 SQL Server naturally sorts by an indexed field, such as EmpID.

Note SQL Server naturally sorts this table on the EmpID field (Figure 2.1). If there is no ID field or indexed field, table data will generally display in the order the records were inserted. Now change your SELECT statement to include just LastName and FirstName (Figure 2.2). Notice that SQL Server still orders the records by this table's natural sort (EmpID).

```
SELECT LastName, FirstName
FROM Employee
```

	LastName	FirstName
1	Adams	Alex
2	Brown	Barry
3	Osako	Lee
4	Kennson	David
5	Bender	Eric
6	Kendall	Lisa

12 rows

Figure 2.2 SQL Server still orders by EmpID, even if the result set does not show EmpID.

To sort on the LastName field (ascending), add an ORDER BY clause after the FROM clause in your previous query (Figure 2.3).

When specifying sort order SQL Server will not recognize the full words "ascending" or "descending". Therefore, you must use the keywords ASC and DESC.

```
SELECT LastName, FirstName
FROM Employee
ORDER BY LastName ASC
```

	LastName	FirstName
1	Adams	Alex
2	Bender	Eric
3	Brown	Barry
4	Kendall	Lisa
5	Kennson	David
6	Lonning	David

12 rows

Figure 2.3 The Employee data now sorted by LastName (ascending) Compare to Figure 2.2.

Sorting Multiple Table Queries

When you join two or more tables in a query, we can then sort on any field of any table in the query (Figure 2.4).

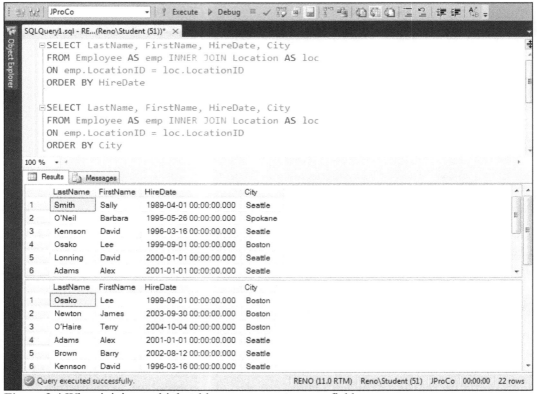

Figure 2.4 When joining multiple tables, we can sort on any field.

Sorting Data with NULLs

Oftentimes the fields you sort will contain NULL values. NULLs always sort before any data. So in an ascending query, the NULLs always show first. In a descending query, the NULLs always show last. Open a new query window to the JProCo database, type the following code, and observe the different way each query handles NULL values (Figure 2.5).

```
--Status in DESC order, NULLs appear last
SELECT *
FROM Employee
ORDER BY Status DESC

--Status defaults to ASC order and NULLs appear first
SELECT *
FROM Employee
ORDER BY Status
```

	EmpID	LastName	FirstName	HireDate	LocationID	ManagerID	Status
1	7	Lonning	David	2000-01-01 00:00:00.000	1	11	On Leave
2	4	Kennson	David	1996-03-16 00:00:00.000	1	11	Has Tenure
3	12	O'Neil	Barbara	1995-05-26 00:00:00.000	4	4	Has Tenure
4	5	Bender	Eric	2007-05-17 00:00:00.000	1	11	NULL
5	6	Kendall	Lisa	2001-11-15 00:00:00.000	4	4	NULL
6	1	Adams	Alex	2001-01-01 00:00:00.000	1	11	NULL

	EmpID	LastName	FirstName	HireDate	LocationID	ManagerID	Status
1	1	Adams	Alex	2001-01-01 00:00:00.000	1	11	NULL
2	2	Brown	Barry	2002-08-12 00:00:00.000	1	11	NULL
3	3	Osako	Lee	1999-09-01 00:00:00.000	2	11	NULL
4	8	Marshb...	John	2001-11-15 00:00:00.000	NULL	4	NULL
5	9	Newton	James	2003-09-30 00:00:00.000	2	3	NULL
6	10	O'Haire	Terry	2004-10-04 00:00:00.000	2	3	NULL

Query executed successfully.　　RENO (11.0 RTM)　Reno\Student (51)　JProCo　00:00:00　24 rows

Figure 2.5 The effects of descending vs. ascending sort order on a field with NULL values.

Running both queries at once gives you the two result sets you see in Figure 2.5. The first query is descending and puts the NULLs last, and the second query shows the NULLs first.

Sorting Hidden Results

In your SQL Server career, you will frequently encounter reports where you must sort by a field not displayed in your final report. For example, you might be asked to show an employee list sorted by highest to lowest pay. However, because of confidentiality reasons, you can't show any actual pay numbers in the report.

You can sort your results on any field in your query, including field(s) not contained in the SELECT list. This example sorts by the YearlySalary field but doesn't show YearlySalary in the result set:

We have four employees who receive a yearly salary. Of those employees, Sally Smith is the highest paid employee and Lisa Kendall is the lowest. In Figure 2.6 we see these employees in order while not revealing any of the salary fields in our report.

```
SELECT FirstName, LastName, HireDate
FROM Employee AS emp
INNER JOIN PayRates AS pr
ON emp.EmpID = pr.EmpID
WHERE YearlySalary IS NOT NULL
ORDER BY YearlySalary DESC
```

	FirstName	LastName	HireDate
1	Sally	Smith	1989-04-01 00:00:00.000
2	Barry	Brown	2002-08-12 00:00:00.000
3	Alex	Adams	2001-01-01 00:00:00.000
4	Lisa	Kendall	2001-11-15 00:00:00.000

4 rows

Figure 2.6 We can sort by YearlySalary without displaying the field in our result set.

Sorting Levels

The ORDER BY clause allows you to sort using multiple fields. In Figure 2.7 the sort is done first on City, so all three Boston employees appear first in the result set. Within the Boston group of records Newton comes before O'Haire and Osako is the last Boston Employee. The next group is Seattle, which has six records in its group. Adams is first and Smith is last.

```
SELECT FirstName, LastName, City, State
FROM Employee AS emp
INNER JOIN Location AS loc
ON emp.LocationID = loc.LocationID
ORDER BY City, LastName
```

	FirstName	LastName	City	State
1	James	Newton	Boston	MA
2	Terry	O'Haire	Boston	MA
3	Lee	Osako	Boston	MA
4	Alex	Adams	Seattle	WA
5	Eric	Bender	Seattle	WA
6	Barry	Brown	Seattle	WA
7	David	Kennson	Seattle	WA
8	David	Lonning	Seattle	WA
9	Sally	Smith	Seattle	WA

11 rows

Figure 2.7 We can sort on multiple fields.

SQL Server will display those "tie" records in their natural order. If you apply two fields in a sort, then your second field acts as a "tie breaker".

In the Grant table, two grants each show an amount of $21,000 (Figure 2.28 to Figure 2.29). This illustrates the difference a secondary sort field (GrantName) makes when sorting the Grant table by Amount.

```
SELECT *
FROM [Grant]
ORDER BY Amount DESC, GrantName
```

	GrantID	GrantName	EmpID	Amount
1	007	Ben@MoreTechnology.com	10	41000.00
2	008	www.@-Last-U-Can-Help.com	7	25000.00
3	009	Thank you @.com	11	21500.00
4	005	BIG 6's Foundation%	4	21000.00
5	004	Norman's Outreach	NULL	21000.00
6	003	Robert@BigStarBank.com	7	18100.00

10 rows

Figure 2.8 The secondary sort on this table is by GrantName.

Lab 2.1: Sorting Data

Lab Prep: Each lab has one or more Skill Checks. Start with Skill Check 1 and proceed until reaching the Points to Ponder section.

Before beginning this lab, verify that SQL Server 2012 is properly installed and operating. Before running the lab setup script for resetting the database (SQLQueries2012Vol2Chapter2.1Setup.sql), please make sure to close all query windows within SSMS. An open query window pointing to a database context can lock that database preventing it from updating when the script is executing. A simple way to assure all query windows are closed, is to exit out of SSMS, then open a new instance of SSMS, and lastly run the setup script.

Skill Check 1: Show all records from the Grant table sorted alphabetically by GrantName. Your result should look like Figure 2.9.

	GrantID	GrantName	EmpID	Amount
1	001	92 Purr_Scents %% team	7	4750.00
2	007	Ben@MoreTechnology.com	10	41000.00
3	005	BIG 6's Foundation%	4	21000.00
4	010	Call Mom @Com	5	7500.00
5	002	K_Land fund trust	2	15750.00
6	004	Norman's Outreach	NULL	21000.00

10 rows

Figure 2.9 The result of Skill Check 1 shows 10 records sorted by GrantName.

Skill Check 2: Show all fields from the Employee table. The most recent HireDate should appear first (Figure 2.10).

	EmpID	LastName	FirstName	HireDate	LocationID	ManagerID	Status
1	5	Bender	Eric	2007-05-17…	1	11	NULL
2	10	O'Haire	Terry	2004-10-04…	2	3	NULL
3	9	Newton	James	2003-09-30…	2	3	NULL
4	2	Brown	Barry	2002-08-12…	1	11	NULL
5	6	Kendall	Lisa	2001-11-15…	4	4	NULL
6	8	Marshbank	John	2001-11-15…	NULL	4	NULL

12 rows

Figure 2.10 Skill Check 2 shows the most recently hired person listed first.

Skill Check 3: Query the CurrentProducts table for just the ProductName and Category fields. Sort the table by the most expensive RetailPrice on top and the least on the bottom. When you're done, your result should resemble the figure you see here (Figure 2.11 shows the first 6 of 480 rows):

	ProductName	Category
1	Lakes Tour 2 Weeks West Coast	LongTerm-Stay
2	Lakes Tour 2 Weeks East Coast	LongTerm-Stay
3	Rain Forest Tour 2 Weeks East Coast	LongTerm-Stay
4	River Rapids Tour 2 Weeks East Coast	LongTerm-Stay
5	Wine Tasting Tour 2 Weeks West Coast	LongTerm-Stay
6	Ocean Cruise Tour 2 Weeks West Coast	LongTerm-Stay

480 rows

Figure 2.11 Shows the most expensive products first without showing RetailPrice in the SELECT list.

Skill Check 4: Now sort all the fields of the Grant table from highest to lowest amount. If any Grants have a tying amount, then list the ties alphabetically by GrantName (Figure 2.12). Amount ($21,000), Big 6 is listed before Norman's because the secondary sort is alphabetical by GrantName.

	GrantID	GrantName	EmpID	Amount
1	007	Ben@MoreTechnology.com	10	41000.00
2	008	www.@-Last-U-Can-Help.com	7	25000.00
3	009	Thank you @.com	11	21500.00
4	005	BIG 6's Foundation%	4	21000.00
5	004	Norman's Outreach	NULL	21000.00
6	003	Robert@BigStarBank.com	7	18100.00
				10 rows

Figure 2.12 Skill Check 4 shows the highest amounts listed first. Where two grants have the same value the first GrantName value shows up first in an A to Z sort.

Skill Check 5: Join the Employee and Location tables together in an OUTER JOIN that shows all the employee records even if they have no location. Show the fields FirstName, LastName and City. Sort your result so that NULL City names appear first and the remaining values appear in ascending order (Figure 2.13).

	FirstName	LastName	City
1	John	Marshbank	NULL
2	James	Newton	Boston
3	Terry	O'Haire	Boston
4	Lee	Osako	Boston
5	David	Kennson	Seattle
6	Eric	Bender	Seattle
			12 rows

Figure 2.13 Skill Check 5 shows Employee names and City listed in order by City with NULLs appearing first.

Answer Code: The T-SQL code for this lab is located in the downloadable files as a file named Lab2.1_SortingData.sql

Points to Ponder - Sorting Data

1. The ORDER BY clause enables you to sort your query results.

2. You can append the DESC (descending) and ASC (ascending) keywords to your ORDER BY clause.

3. If you do not specify DESC or ASC, then the default is to sort ascending.

4. SQL Server will not recognize the full words "descending" or "ascending" – you must specify the keywords as DESC or ASC.

5. You can sort by more than one field. This is useful when the primary sort field has many identical values.

6. If NULL values appear in your sort, they are first in ASC queries and last in DESC queries.

7. SQL Server's natural sort order is first by indexed fields (the primary key field or an ID field). If no such fields are present, then SQL Server displays records in the order they were created.

8. In a simple query you choose the field(s) you wish to sort on.

9. The ORDER BY clause generally appears last.

10. You can sort on any field in your query even if you leave that field out of the SELECT list.

Exploring Related Tables

A relational database contains many related tables. The Employee and Location tables of JProCo relate on the LocationID field (Figure 2.14).

```
SELECT  *  FROM Employee
SELECT  *  FROM Location
```

	EmpID	LastName	FirstName	HireDate	Location...	ManagerID	Status
1	1	Adams	Alex	2001-01-01 00:00:00.000	1	11	NULL
2	2	Brown	Barry	2002-08-12 00:00:00.000	1	11	NULL
3	3	Osako	Lee	1999-09-01 00:00:00.000	2	11	NULL
4	4	Kennson	David	1996-03-16 00:00:00.000	1	11	Has Tenure
5	5	Bender	Eric	2007-05-17 00:00:00.000	1	11	NULL
6	6	Kendall	Lisa	2001-11-15 00:00:00.000	4	4	NULL

	LocationID	Street	City	State
1	1	111 First ST	Seattle	WA
2	2	222 Second AVE	Boston	MA
3	3	333 Third PL	Chic...	IL
4	4	444 Ruby ST	Spok...	WA

Query executed successfully.   RENO (11.0 RTM)   Reno\Student (51)   JProCo   00:00:00   12 rows

Figure 2.14 These two tables relate on the LocationID field.

This gives us the ability to take these same tables and put them into the same query using a join. We also have the ability to join many tables in one query.

We can see that Alex Adams works in Location 1, which is in Seattle. Barry Brown also works in Location 1. Lee Osako works in Location 2, which is on 2nd Avenue in Boston.

This second table referencing Location is known as a lookup table. It contains more detailed information about the LocationID as referenced from the Employee table.

Let's next look at the Grant table, where we can see Ben@MoreTechnology.com was the largest grant at $41,000 (Figure 2.15).

```
SELECT *
FROM [Grant]
```

	GrantID	GrantName	EmpID	Amount
1	001	92 Purr_Scents %% team	7	4750.00
2	002	K_Land fund trust	2	15750.00
3	003	Robert@BigStarBank.com	7	18100.00
4	004	Norman's Outreach	NULL	21000.00
5	005	BIG 6's Foundation%	4	21000.00
6	006	TALTA_Kishan International	3	18100.00
7	007	Ben@MoreTechnology.com	10	41000.00
8	008	www.@-Last-U-Can-Help.com	7	25000.00

Query executed successfully.   (local) (11.0 RTM)   Reno\Student (51)   JProCo   00:00:00   10 rows

Figure 2.15 All records from the Grant table.

The employee who procured the grant from Ben@MoreTechnology.com was EmpID 10. What if we wanted to find more information about this employee? Is this employee a man or woman? When was this employee hired? In which of JProCo's four locations does this employee work?

To answer detailed questions about this employee, we need to look beyond the Grant table. Expand JProCo in the Object Explorer and look at the other tables to find data relating to the Grant table fields (GrantID, GrantName, EmpID, Amount).

Employee is the only other table in the JProCo database to share a common field with the Grant table. The field [Grant].EmpID matches with Employee.EmpID. In Chapter 1, we learned that two tables may be joined if they share a common field. In this case, EmpID links Grant and Employee.

READER NOTE: *Having the same field name (EmpID) helped us quickly find the link and related table in this case. But even if the field names weren't exactly the same, this field could still link the two tables because the data and data type within EmpID is the same in both tables. In your database career, you frequently will find overlapping fields (containing the same data with the same data type) between tables, but the fields will have different names. For example, if the field in Grant had been called [Grant].EmployeeID, it still would be a match with Employee.EmpID. [Grant].EmployeeNumber would also still be a match with Employee.EmpID. As long as the data and data type in both fields match, you will be able to join the tables. We will explore this topic further in Chapter 9.*

Let's resume our quest for more insight to the individual who procured JProCo's largest grant. We've identified Employee as the other table that relates to Grant. Looking at EmpID 10 on both tables, we see Terry O'Haire is the employee who found the $41,000 grant (Figure 2.16).

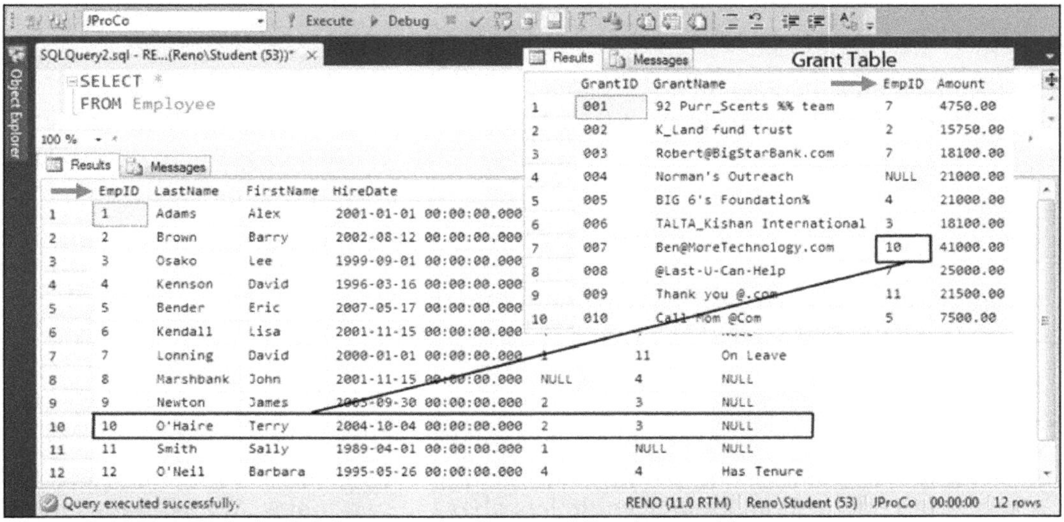

Figure 2.16 EmpID is the link between the Grant and Employee tables.

In the next section we will see these two tables joined by a query. What else can the Employee table tell us about Terry O'Haire? Earlier we wondered when this employee had been hired, whether this is a man or woman, and in which location the employee works.

Besides EmpID, LastName and FirstName, the Employee table contains these fields: HireDate, LocationID, ManagerID and Status. Our HireDate question is answered (10/4/2004). However, we can't tell from this table whether Terry is male or female. And while the Employee table tells us Terry works in Location 2, it doesn't explicitly tell us the city.

To find the name of the city where Terry O'Haire works, we must repeat the process of checking other tables in the database to find a link to location data. As was the case with the Grant and Employee tables, we luck out and quickly find the field LocationID is the logical link to the Location table. By looking up Location 2 in the Location table, we now know that Terry O'Haire works in Boston.

Our curiosity about the employee who secured JProCo's largest grant took us on a quick tour of JProCo and told us more about Terry O'Haire. But more importantly, in the process we logically linked three tables (Grant, Employee and Location) in order to answer our questions.

Joining Two Tables

We know the Grant and Employee tables overlap on the EmpID field Said another way, these tables are related on EmpID. We will now write an actual join of the Grant and Employee tables, which we logically joined when we wanted more information about the person who secured the largest grant (Figure 2.16).

The FROM clause decides in which table or tables the query will take place. Joining two tables happens in the FROM clause so begin by Placing both tables in the FROM clause:

```
SELECT *
FROM [Grant] Employee
```

Listing tables in the FROM clause will not join them in a SQL query. We will need to separate the two tables with an INNER JOIN:

```
SELECT *
FROM [Grant]
INNER JOIN Employee
```

To keep our code neat and manageable lets alias the two tables. We will alias the Grant table AS gr and the Employee table AS em.

```
SELECT *
FROM [Grant] AS gr
INNER JOIN Employee AS em
```

For these tables to be joined SQL has to know where to join them. This happens in the ON clause. To define the field that joins them we need to specify a field they have in common that is pertinent to our query. In this case they both have the EmpID field in common so we will use that:

```
SELECT *
FROM [Grant] AS gr
INNER JOIN Employee AS em
ON gr.EmpID = em.EmpID
```

Now run the code. In each row, we see all fields from the Grant table and all fields for the employee who procured the grant.

```
SELECT *
FROM [Grant] AS gr
INNER JOIN Employee AS em
ON gr.EmpID = em.EmpID
```

	GrantID	GrantName	EmpID	Amount	EmpID	LastName	FirstName	HireDate	
1	001	92 Purr_Scents %% team	7	4750.00	7	Lonning	David	2000-01-01 0	
2	002	K_Land fund trust	2	15750.00	2	Brown	Barry	2002-08-12 0	
3	003	Robert@BigStarBank.com	7	18100.00	7	Lonning	David	2000-01-01 0	
4	005	BIG 6's Foundation%	4	21000.00	4	Kennson	David	1996-03-16 0	
5	006	TALTA_Kishan International	3	18100.00	3	Osako	Lee	1999-09-01 0	
6	007	Ben@MoreTechnology.com	10	41000.00	10	O'Haire	Terry	2004-10-04 0	

Query executed successfully.   RENO (11.0 RTM) | Reno\Student (51) | JProCo | 00:00:00 | 9 rows

Figure 2.17 An INNER JOIN on EmpID joins the Grant and Employee tables.

For information on the other types of joins, review the Chapter 1 coverage of Outer Joins, Left Outer Joins, Right Outer Joins, Full Outer Joins, and unmatched Queries. Chapter 1 also contains a section on Table Aliasing.

Joining Three Tables

So far we have seen examples querying a single table or two tables. In business and reporting settings however, it's more common to see three or more tables joined together (SQL Server can join many tables in a single query).

Once you are proficient at joining two tables together, adding one more table to your query is not difficult. As we did with basic joins, we always begin building our query with a "SELECT *" statement. Only after all needed tables are joined and we see them working properly do we narrow down our field selection list.

In the section "Exploring Related Tables," we logically joined three tables. Let's now do an actual join of those tables and see Grant, Employee and Location data combined within a single result set.

We've already joined the Grant and Employee tables. Aside from the EmpID field appearing twice, the result looks like a single table. Any of the fields you see in Figure 2.18 may be used to join additional tables to this result.

Since LocationID appears in the combined Grant-Employee result, we know the Location table may be joined using the overlapping field (LocationID).

```
SELECT gr.GrantName, gr.EmpID, gr.Amount,
em.EmpID, em.LastName, em.FirstName, em.LocationID,
loc.LocationID, loc.Street
FROM [Grant] AS gr
INNER JOIN Employee AS em ON gr.EmpID = em.EmpID
INNER JOIN Location AS loc ON em.LocationID = loc.LocationID
```

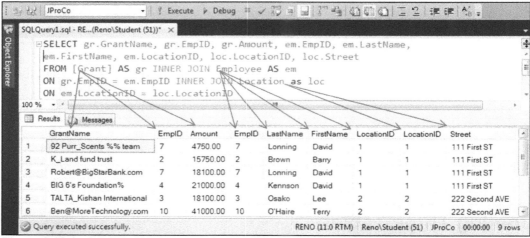

Figure 2.18 An INNER JOIN on LocationID adds the Location table to the Grant-Employee query.

Now specify just the three fields we want to see in our report. Waiting to narrow your field selection list until all needed tables have been joined in the FROM clause is a best practice for SQL Pros (Figure 2.19).

```
SELECT GrantName, Amount, City
FROM [Grant] AS gr
INNER JOIN Employee AS em ON gr.EmpID = em.EmpID
INNER JOIN Location AS loc ON em.LocationID = loc.LocationID
```

	GrantName	Amount	City
1	92 Purr_Scents %% team	4750.00	Seattle
2	K_Land fund trust	15750.00	Seattle
3	Robert@BigStarBank.com	18100.00	Seattle
4	BIG 6's Foundation%	21000.00	Seattle
5	TALTA_Kishan International	18100.00	Boston
6	Ben@MoreTechnology.com	41000.00	Boston

9 rows

Figure 2.19 Make specifying your field SELECT list your last step when working with joins.

The first thing SQL Server evaluates in a query is the FROM clause, so it makes sense to first completely build that. When you try specifying the fields too early, you run the risk of getting column ambiguity errors which waste time and are frustrating. Build all your joins and see them successfully run with "SELECT *" before narrowing down the fields you want to display in your result.

We now see the GrantName, Amount and City fields in our report (Figure 2.19). Open a new query window and look at all fields from just the Grant and Location tables (SELECT * FROM [Grant], SELECT * FROM Location). Notice these two tables do not have a common field. We cannot directly join these two tables. We were able to connect them indirectly because each table relates to the Employee table.

Could we add a fourth table here? Absolutely, given our curiosity about Terry O'Haire, we could have gone an additional step to logically link to the PayRates table using EmpID. But for the moment we will focus on three table queries, since those pave the way to our next major topic: Many-To-Many Relationships.

Lab 2.2: Three Table Query

Lab Prep: Each lab has one or more Skill Checks. Start with Skill Check 1 and proceed until reaching the Points to Ponder section.

Before beginning this lab, verify that SQL Server 2012 is properly installed and operating. Before running the lab setup script for resetting the database (SQLQueries2012Vol2Chapter2.2Setup.sql), please make sure to close all query windows within SSMS. An open query window pointing to a database context can lock that database preventing it from updating when the script is executing. A simple way to assure all query windows are closed, is to exit out of SSMS, then open a new instance of SSMS, and lastly run the setup script.

Skill Check 1: Show all the city names and rates of pay for each employee in those cities. You will need to join the Location, Employee and PayRates tables. Show the City field from the Location table. Include FirstName and LastName from the Employee table and all fields from the PayRates table. When you're done, your result should resemble Figure 2.20.

```
SELECT lo.City, em.FirstName, em.LastName, pr.*
--Remaining Code Here
```

	city	firstname	lastname	EmpID	YearlySalary	MonthlySalary	HourlyRate	Selector	Estimate
1	Seattle	Alex	Adams	1	76000.00	NULL	NULL	1	1
2	Seattle	Barry	Brown	2	79000.00	NULL	NULL	1	1
3	Boston	Lee	Osako	3	NULL	NULL	45.00	3	2080
4	Seattle	David	Kennson	4	NULL	6500.00	NULL	2	12
5	Seattle	Eric	Bender	5	NULL	5800.00	NULL	2	12
6	Spokane	Lisa	Kendall	6	52000.00	NULL	NULL	1	1

Query executed successfully.   RENO (11.0 RTM)   Reno\Student (53)   JProCo   00:00:00   11 rows

Figure 2.20 A query joining the Location, Employee and PayRates tables together.

Answer Code: The T-SQL code for this lab is located in the downloadable files as a file named Lab2.2_ThreeTableQuery.sql

Points to Ponder - Three Table Query

1. In SQL Server we can join many tables in a single query. Prior to SQL Server 2008, you could include up to a maximum of 256 tables in a single query. The number of tables we can join is now limited only by available resources.

2. The steps for joining three (or more) tables are the same as joining two tables. First – join all tables and confirm they are working properly using a "SELECT *" statement. Narrow down the SELECT list to include the specific fields you need only after all tables have been joined.

3. While table aliasing saves keystrokes on two table joins, it greatly helps readability when joining three or more tables.

Many-to-Many Relationships

How many kids do you have? The question implies we can have many. We also know we can have just one or even zero children. Asking a child "How many parents do you have?" again would give you different results. The relationship between parents and children goes beyond a single join on one ID field.

"Joan" is the soccer mom of the "Jay" family. Her two active children are named "Joey" and "Janet". Joan picks up her children from school each day. She is also authorized to get them from school early if they become sick or injured. Since Joan is a parent and she could have more than one child, we need to be able to handle her authorization to be the guardian for many children.

Figure 2.21 Parents can have many children and children can have many parents.

The reason you don't list a ParentID in the child table is because most children have more than one ParentID. Which parent would you pick?

Let's say Joey gets sick and the school nurse calls home. Joan is out of town so Joey's father Ed shows up to get him. The problem is there is only one ParentID listed in the child table and it refers to Joan. The Parent and Child tables in this example don't have an efficient way to join directly.

Figure 2.22 Joey has Ed as his Father.

We need a new process to map this complex relationship. Sometimes tables exist for the sole purpose of allowing indirect relationships between tables. Common terms for these type of tables are Mapping tables, Bridge tables, or Junction tables.

Using the example above, a school might handle the Jay family and many other families with the design you see here (Figure 2.23).

dbo.Parent		dbo.ParentChild		dbo.Child	
P_ID	**P_Name**	**P_ID**	**C_ID**	**C_ID**	**C_Name**
1001	Joan	1001	2001	2001	Janet
1002	Sue	1001	2002	2002	Joey
1003	Sara	1002	2003	2003	Kayla
1004	Ed	1003	2004	2004	Robby
1005	Jeff	1003	2005	2005	Andy
		1004	2001		
		1004	2002		
		1005	2003		

Figure 2.23 The ParentChild table handles the many-to-many relationship between parents and children.

The Bridge table tells us that P_ID of 1001 has two children of Janet and Joey.

dbo.Parent		dbo.ParentChild		dbo.Child	
P_ID	**P_Name**	**P_ID**	**C_ID**	**C_ID**	**C_Name**
1001	Joan	1001	2001	2001	Janet
1002	Sue	1001	2002	2002	Joey
1003	Sara	1002	2003	2003	Kayla
1004	Ed	1003	2004	2004	Robby
1005	Jeff	1003	2005	2005	Andy
		1004	2001		
		1004	2002		
		1005	2003		

Figure 2.24 Looking at the ParentID of 1001, the table dbo.ParentChild tells us Joan's children are Janet and Joey.

It also tells us that Joey has two parents of Joan and Ed. One parent can have many children and one child can have many parents (Figure 2.25).

dbo.Parent		dbo.ParentChild		dbo.Child	
P_ID	**P_Name**	**P_ID**	**C_ID**	**C_ID**	**C_Name**
1001	Joan	1001	2001	2001	Janet
1002	Sue	1001	2002	2002	Joey
1003	Sara	1002	2003	2003	Kayla
1004	Ed	1003	2004	2004	Robby
1005	Jeff	1003	2005	2005	Andy
		1004	2001		
		1004	2002		
		1005	2003		

Figure 2.25 We can see that Joey has the parents Joan and Ed.

Invoicing Systems

These JProCo tables use a many-to-many relationship to show which products were ordered on which invoices, the same way a school relates parents to children. A Product can appear on many invoices and an invoice can have many products. The relationship between Products and Invoices is known as a many-to-many relationship (Figure 2.26).

dbo.Product		dbo.InvoiceDetail		dbo.Invoice	
P_ID	P_Name	P_ID	Inv_ID	Inv_ID	Inv_Date
1	Toy Car	1	5631	5631	1/1/2009
2	Furchee	2	5631	5632	3/5/2009
3	Timbot	2	5632	5633	7/15/2009
4	Go-Duck	5	5632	5634	9/22/2009
5	Pet Mock	1	5633		
		4	5633		
		4	5634		
		1	5634		

Figure 2.26 A many-to-many relationship exists between Products and Invoices.

Look at Figure 2.26 above. If you were to ask yourself "What Products are on Invoice 5631?" or "Go-Duck was ordered on how many invoices?" you could resolve this query. Figure 2.27 shows us how to resolve both mappings.

dbo.Product		dbo.InvoiceDetail		dbo.Invoice	
P_ID	**P_Name**	**P_ID**	**Inv_ID**	**Inv_ID**	**Inv_Date**
1	Toy Car	1	5631	5631	1/1/2009
2	Furchee	2	5631	5632	3/5/2009
3	Timbot	2	5632	5633	7/15/2009
4	Go-Duck	5	5632	5634	9/22/2009
5	Pet Mock	1	5633		
		4	5633		
		4	5634		
		1	5634		

Figure 2.27 We can see Go-Duck was ordered twice. We also see that Invoice 5631 has a Toy Car and a Furchee.

Now we'll take a look at many-to-many relationships between JProCo's sales invoices and products (Figure 2.28).

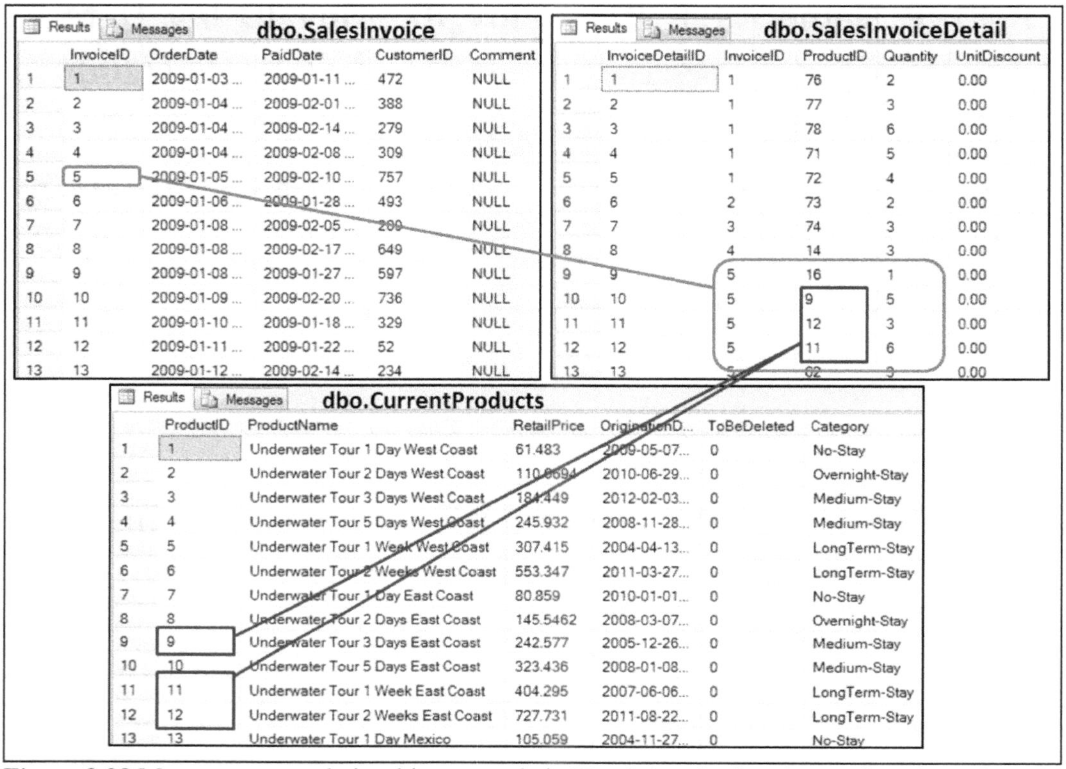

dbo.SalesInvoice

	InvoiceID	OrderDate	PaidDate	CustomerID	Comment
1	1	2009-01-03 ...	2009-01-11 ...	472	NULL
2	2	2009-01-04 ...	2009-02-01 ...	388	NULL
3	3	2009-01-04 ...	2009-02-14 ...	279	NULL
4	4	2009-01-04 ...	2009-02-08 ...	309	NULL
5	5	2009-01-05 ...	2009-02-10 ...	757	NULL
6	6	2009-01-06 ...	2009-01-28 ...	493	NULL
7	7	2009-01-08 ...	2009-02-05 ...	200	NULL
8	8	2009-01-08 ...	2009-02-17 ...	649	NULL
9	9	2009-01-08 ...	2009-01-27 ...	597	NULL
10	10	2009-01-09 ...	2009-02-20 ...	736	NULL
11	11	2009-01-10 ...	2009-01-18 ...	329	NULL
12	12	2009-01-11 ...	2009-01-22 ...	52	NULL
13	13	2009-01-12 ...	2009-02-14 ...	234	NULL

dbo.SalesInvoiceDetail

	InvoiceDetailID	InvoiceID	ProductID	Quantity	UnitDiscount
1	1	1	76	2	0.00
2	2	1	77	3	0.00
3	3	1	78	6	0.00
4	4	1	71	5	0.00
5	5	1	72	4	0.00
6	6	2	73	2	0.00
7	7	3	74	3	0.00
8	8	4	14	3	0.00
9	9	5	16	1	0.00
10	10	5	9	5	0.00
11	11	5	12	3	0.00
12	12	5	11	6	0.00
13	13	5	62	3	0.00

dbo.CurrentProducts

	ProductID	ProductName	RetailPrice	OriginationD...	ToBeDeleted	Category
1	1	Underwater Tour 1 Day West Coast	61.483	2009-05-07...	0	No-Stay
2	2	Underwater Tour 2 Days West Coast	110.0694	2010-06-29...	0	Overnight-Stay
3	3	Underwater Tour 3 Days West Coast	184.449	2012-02-03...	0	Medium-Stay
4	4	Underwater Tour 5 Days West Coast	245.932	2008-11-28...	0	Medium-Stay
5	5	Underwater Tour 1 Week West Coast	307.415	2004-04-13...	0	LongTerm-Stay
6	6	Underwater Tour 2 Weeks West Coast	553.347	2011-03-27...	0	LongTerm-Stay
7	7	Underwater Tour 1 Day East Coast	80.859	2010-01-01...	0	No-Stay
8	8	Underwater Tour 2 Days East Coast	145.5462	2008-03-07...	0	Overnight-Stay
9	9	Underwater Tour 3 Days East Coast	242.577	2005-12-26...	0	Medium-Stay
10	10	Underwater Tour 5 Days East Coast	323.436	2008-01-08...	0	Medium-Stay
11	11	Underwater Tour 1 Week East Coast	404.295	2007-06-06...	0	LongTerm-Stay
12	12	Underwater Tour 2 Weeks East Coast	727.731	2011-08-22...	0	LongTerm-Stay
13	13	Underwater Tour 1 Day Mexico	105.059	2004-11-27...	0	No-Stay

Figure 2.28 Many-to-many relationships example in JProCo's sales invoices and products data.

Here is an example of JProCo's sales invoices mapping to a bridge table (SalesInvoiceDetail) in order to map over to the CurrentProducts table. The CurrentProducts table gives us all the detail of the current products that have been ordered.

Let's take a look at SalesInvoice 5 (Figure 2.28). It looks like many products were ordered on that one invoice (Products 9, 11, 12, and 16). To see what those products are, we would look over to the CurrentProducts table. We see Product 9 is an Underwater Tour 3 Days East Coast. Product 11 is an Underwater Tour 1 Week East Coast, and so forth.

So a SalesInvoice can have many products, and products can be ordered on multiple sales invoices.

Lab 2.3: Many-to-Many Relationships

Lab Prep: Each lab has one or more Skill Checks. Start with Skill Check 1 and proceed until reaching the Points to Ponder section.

Before beginning this lab, verify that SQL Server 2012 is properly installed and operating. Before running the lab setup script for resetting the database (SQLQueries2012Vol2Chapter2.3Setup.sql), please make sure to close all query windows within SSMS. An open query window pointing to a database context can lock that database preventing it from updating when the script is executing. A simple way to assure all query windows are closed, is to exit out of SSMS, then open a new instance of SSMS, and lastly run the setup script.

Skill Check 1: In JProCo write a query that shows all the invoices ordered by customer 490. Show all fields from just 2 tables (SalesInvoice and SalesInvoiceDetail). When you're done your result should resemble Figure 2.29.

	InvoiceDetailID	InvoiceID	ProductID	Quantity	UnitDiscount	InvoiceID	OrderDate	PaidDate	CustomerID	Comment
1	5057	1285	64	4	0.00	1285	2011-11-04 ...	2011-12-23 ...	490	NULL
2	5568	1459	70	2	0.00	1459	2012-03-16 ...	2012-04-27 ...	490	NULL
3	6700	1804	49	1	0.00	1804	2012-12-25 ...	2013-01-24 ...	490	NULL

Query executed successfully. RENO (11.0 RTM) Reno\Student (53) JProCo 00:00:00 3 rows

Figure 2.29 Skill Check 1 shows the Customer who ordered each invoice.

Skill Check 2: Write a query that combines SalesInvoice, SalesInvoiceDetail and CurrentProducts. Show the following fields:

- o SalesInvoice.CustomerID
- o SalesInvoice.InvoiceID
- o SalesInvoice.OrderDate
- o SalesInvoiceDetail.Quantity
- o CurrentProducts.ProductName
- o CurrentProducts.RetailPrice

When you are done your result should resemble Figure 2.30.

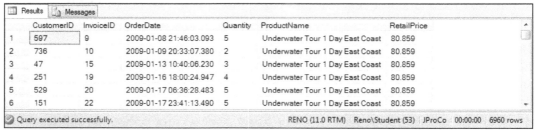

Figure 2.30 Skill Check 2 shows all the product details for each InvoiceID.

Answer Code: The T-SQL code for this lab is located in the downloadable files as a file named Lab2.3_Many-to-Many_Relationships.sql

Points to Ponder - Many-to-Many

1. Databases often contain tables which exist for the sole purpose of allowing indirect relationships between tables.

2. These tables are known as mapping tables, bridge tables, or junction tables.

Chapter Glossary

Ascending (ASC keyword): A SQL keyword used to order the results of a query from lowest to highest. SQL Server does not recognize the full word so the ASC keyword must be used.

Bridge Tables: A common term used to identify tables that exist for the sole purpose of allowing indirect relationships between tables. See also Junction tables and Mapping tables.

Descending (DESC keyword): A SQL keyword that does the opposite of ASC in that, it returns data highest to lowest. SQL Server does not recognize the full word so the DESC keyword must be used.

Junction Table: A common term used to identify tables that exist for the sole purpose of allowing indirect relationships between tables. See also Bridge tables and Mapping tables.

Lookup Table: The second table in a join that references the field in common with the first table.

Mapping Tables: A common term used to identify tables that exist for the sole purpose of allowing indirect relationships between tables. See also Bridge tables and Junction tables.

ORDER BY: This clause allows you to sort result data and can also be used to sort using multiple fields.

Related Tables: Tables within a database that has a related field. SQL has the ability to join many tables in one query. In SQL Server 2008, the maximum number of tables we can join is limited only by available resources.

Sorting: A key step in turning data into report information. It does not physically change the way the underlying table stores the data.

Review Quiz - Chapter Two

1.)   You have a table named CurrentProducts and need to display just the ProductName and Category. You want the highest RetailPrice listed first and the lowest price listed last. Which query should you use?

O a.   **SELECT** ProductName, Category
      FROM CurrentProducts
      ORDER BY ProductName, Category **DESC**

O b.   **SELECT** *
      FROM CurrentProducts
      ORDER BY ProductName, Category **DESC**

O c.   **SELECT** ProductName, Category
      FROM CurrentProducts
      ORDER BY RetailPrice **ASC**

O d.   **SELECT** ProductName, Category
      FROM CurrentProducts
      ORDER BY RetailPrice **DESC**

2.)   You have a table named Employee and need to display just the FirstName, LastName, and HireDate. You want the most recent hire date listed first. Which query will achieve this goal?

O a.   **SELECT** FirstName, LastName, HireDate
      FROM Employee
      ORDER BY FirstName **DESC**

O b.   **SELECT** FirstName, LastName, HireDate
      FROM Employee
      ORDER BY LastName **DESC**

O c.   **SELECT** FirstName, LastName, HireDate
      FROM Employee
      ORDER BY HireDate **DESC**

O d.   **SELECT** FirstName, LastName, HireDate
      FROM Employee
      ORDER BY FirstName **ASC**

O e.   **SELECT** FirstName, LastName, HireDate
      FROM Employee
      ORDER BY LastName **ASC**

3.)   You need a report of all invoice numbers that have an InvoiceID of over 500. Each invoice should be listed each time it was a customer that placed an order. The report should show the first name and last name of the customer who placed the order. This report will be sorted alphabetically by ProductName and lists all the dates each product was ordered. Which query should you use?

O a.
```
SELECT cu.FirstName, cu.LastName, si.InvoiceID,
si.OrderDate
FROM Customer cu
INNER JOIN SalesInvoice si
ON cu.CustomerID =  si.CustomerID
WHERE InvoiceID < 500
ORDER BY ProductName
```

O b.
```
SELECT cu.FirstName, cu.LastName, si.InvoiceID,
si.OrderDate
FROM Customer cu
INNER JOIN SalesInvoice si
ON cu.CustomerID =  si.CustomerID
WHERE InvoiceID > 500
ORDER BY ProductName
```

O c.
```
SELECT cu.FirstName, cu.LastName, si.InvoiceID,
si.OrderDate
FROM Customer cu
INNER JOIN SalesInvoice si
ON cu.CustomerID =  si.CustomerID
WHERE InvoiceID < 500
ORDER BY ProductName DESC
```

O d.
```
SELECT cu.FirstName, cu.LastName, si.InvoiceID,
si.OrderDate
FROM Customer cu
INNER JOIN SalesInvoice si
ON cu.CustomerID =  si.CustomerID
WHERE InvoiceID > 500
ORDER BY ProductName DESC
```

4.) Your manager wants to see all employees in alphabetical order for each state. She has asked you to sort by State, LastName and FirstName columns. Without creating any additional tables how can you view this report?

O a. Specify State, LastName and FirstName in the ORDER command.

O b. Create a file format that has an export operation.

O c. Specify State, LastName and FirstName in the ORDER BY clause.

O d. Copy the data into a new table that has a clustered index set on State, LastName and FirstName.

5.) You have two tables named dbo.SalesInvoice and dbo.SalesInvoiceDetail. CustomerID is located in the SalesInvoice table and InvoiceID is located in both tables. You have been told to show the discount amounts from the SalesInvoiceDetail table that correspond to the sales of a specific CustomerID of 490. Which Transact SQL statement should you use?

O a.
```
SELECT CustomerID, DiscountAmt
FROM dbo.SalesInvoiceDetail sd
INNER JOIN dbo.SalesInvoice si
ON sd.InvoiceID= si.InvoiceID
WHERE si.CustomerID= 490
```

O b.
```
SELECT CustomerID, DiscountAmt
FROM dbo.SalesInvoiceDetail sd
WHERE si.CustomerID= 490
```

O c.
```
SELECT CustomerID, DiscountAmt
FROM dbo.SalesInvoiceDetail sd
WHERE EXISTS (dbo.SalesInvoice si
ON sd.InvoiceID= si.InvoiceID
WHERE si.CustomerID= 490)
```

6.) You have tables named Sales.InvoiceDetails and Sales.Invoice. You need to update the discount amounts for the sales of a particular salesperson. You need to set Discount to .25 for all entries in Sales.InvoiceDetails that correspond to SalesPersonID 290. Which T-SQL statement should you use?

O a.
```
UPDATE d
SET Discount = .25
FROM Sales.InvoiceDetails d
INNER JOIN Sales.Invoice h
ON h.SalesOrderID = d.SalesOrderID
WHERE h.SalesPersonID = 290;
```

O b.
```
UPDATE Sales.InvoiceDetails
SET Discount = .25
FROM Sales.Invoice h
WHERE h.SalesPersonID = 290;
```

Answer Key

1.) The code in (a) is sorting the result set by ProductName and Category instead of the RetailPrice as requested, so it is incorrect. SELECT * would return every field rather than limiting the field list to just the ProductName and Category as requested, so (b) is incorrect too. To order a result set from highest to lowest you would use the DESC keyword not the ASC keyword, so (c) is also incorrect. The code in (d) limits the field list to only ProductName and Category and sorts the result set by RetailPrice from highest to lowest using the DESC keyword, making (d) the correct answer.

2.) Because the code in (a) and (d) are sorting the result set in ORDER BY FirstName instead of HireDate, they are wrong. Sorting the results in ORDER BY LastName, as in (b) and (e), make them both wrong too. To list the result set in 'ORDER BY HireDate' from the most recent to the furthest in the past, use the DESC keyword because newer dates are greater in value than older dates which makes (c) the correct answer.

3.) Since using 'WHERE InvoiceID < 500' will return all records that have an InvoiceID of 499 or lower, (a) and (c) are both incorrect. Because the code in (d) is sorting the results in ORDER BY ProductName DESC they will be displayed in reverse alphabetical order, making it wrong too. The right answer is (b) because it is filtering the records WHERE InvoiceID > 500 and is sorting the results in ORDER BY ProductName (by default ORDER BY uses ASC).

4.) 'ORDER' is not a command but part of the 'ORDER BY' clause, so (a) is wrong. 'Creating a file format that has an export operation' has nothing to do with sorting a result set, so (b) is wrong too. Because your manager specifically requested not creating any additional tables, (d) is also incorrect. To meet the requirements 'Specify State, LastName and FirstName in the ORDER BY clause' which makes (c) the correct answer.

5.) The code in (b) does not look at the SalesInvoice Table which contains the CustomerID field so it will return an error. The use of EXISTS with a subquery (see Chapter 13) in the WHERE clause will either return every row in the SalesInvoiceDetail table or none of them, regardless of the CustomerID, so (c) is also incorrect. Because 'dbo. SalesInvoiceDetail sd INNER JOIN dbo.SalesInvoice si ON sd.InvoiceID = si.InvoiceID' will return only records that have a match from both tables and 'WHERE si.CustomerID = 490' will filter the results to only display records having a CustomerID of 490, (a) is the correct answer.

6.) We can use an Aggregate as a field without either using GROUP BY or OVER, making (b) incorrect. There is no sense in multiplying the answer by 2, making (c) wrong. You need to join Sales.Invoice to get the entire company total and you need to use OVER with nothing in the parentheses, making (a) correct.

Bug Catcher Game

To play the Bug Catcher game, run the SQLQueries2012Vol2BugCatcher02.pps file from the BugCatcher folder of the companion files. These files are available from the www.Joes2Pros.com website.

[THIS PAGE INTENTIONALLY LEFT BLANK.]

Chapter 3. NULL, Expression and Identity Fields

Can we truly say we know what is going to happen next? The names or values of most future data points can only be known after they occur. If you've ever seen an organizational chart for a rapidly growing company, then you are familiar with the placeholder value "TBH" meaning the employee is yet "to be hired". To the hiring manager and team carrying a heavy workload, that "TBH" represents a person with some known attributes (the job requirements include SQL certification, a valid driver's license, and working in the Seattle office) and some unknown attributes (name, address, hire date). However, the CFO treats "TBH" entries as zeros, because no salary is paid out until the employee is actually hired.

On the other hand, there are a few scenarios where you actually can predict the next value. If you're now 33, the numeric value of your age following your next birthday is certain to be 34. If your last invoice number was #10752, the next invoices created will be #10753 and #10754.

This chapter deals with NULL values – the database equivalent of the uncertain future data point signified by "TBH". This chapter also handles identity fields, which SQL Server uses to logically choose and populate data for you, like invoice numbers.

READER NOTE: *Please run the SQLQueries2012Vol2Chapter3.0Setup.sql script in order to follow along with the examples in the first section of Chapter 3. All scripts mentioned in this chapter are available at www.Joes2Pros.com.*

Working With NULLs

What does "NULL" really mean? Most dictionary entries associate the term "NULL" with zero, much like the math world does. In the database world, NULL is a keyword and signifies that no value exists.

If you asked ten data worker colleagues about NULL, most would say it means a field is empty or has a value of zero. While that's not a bad interpretation – just like the CFO's view of "TBH" – we need more precision when dealing with a powerful RDMS like SQL Server. Similar to the overworked team looking forward to its new hire, SQL Server views the NULL as representing a future entity – not as empty or a zero. It views NULL as a placeholder which could represent any name or value. If HR generated a list of employees split out by gender, the TBH record(s) couldn't be included in either category because it's unknown whether the new hire(s) will be male or female.

Consider another real world example using NULL. Movie audiences watch trailers for upcoming features while they wait for the main attraction to start. We know who stars in the movie and what it will be titled. At the end, a big black banner with white letters reads "This film has not yet been rated". Suppose our database includes an ongoing list of all known films, including future releases. Films must be rated before they can be shown, but until then, our Movie table will have to store some interim data. The field or column containing rating will have to be set to NULL until the rating is known.

Nullable Fields in Database Tables

For most students at this point, the concept of NULL values is somewhat familiar. But for those newer to SQL Server or relational databases, I usually digress at this point to talk more about NULLs and why they're useful tools in table design.

When you see a nullable field, it means that most records will have data in the field but by design the table is flexible enough to allow exceptions to the rule. Throughout your SQL Server career you will design tables knowing that some records might have fields containing no data, at least temporarily. Most movies do have a rating, but our "not yet rated" trailer example is a situation where it's wise to allow a NULL value to be stored in the Rating field.

Another case where your table should accept a NULL value is if you planned to hire Madonna – your Employee table must allow her record to have a NULL LastName. This can be done by putting NULL next to the LastName field as seen in the following code:

```
CREATE TABLE dbo.Employee (
EmpID INT PRIMARY KEY,
LastName VARCHAR(30) NULL,
FirstName VARCHAR(20) NOT NULL,
HireDate DATETIME NULL,
LocationID CHAR(3) NULL,
ManagerID INT NULL,
[Status] CHAR(12) NULL)
GO
```

The Employee table is typical of most tables you will see in your database work. The designer thought carefully about the expected data for the Employee table. It is not uncommon for only one or two vital fields to be non nullable.

A good way to think about whether to allow NULLs in your table is to consider the "required" fields you encounter when filling out an online registration form or making an online purchase. Online transactions cannot complete without key credit card data points (card type, card #, expiration date, cardholder name and cardholder address). The database view of that shopping cart form would indicate "NOT NULL" for all the "required" fields. The database table(s) must reject any record that does not contain all the "required" fields. Similarly, the shopping cart's optional fields like secondary street address or phone number usually allow NULL values.

In today's world of online commerce and services, we know how important registrations and transactions can be for an organization's success. More registrations and customers increase the business's bottom line. While there are a few key data points without which we can't accept a registration (email address, zip code) or a purchase (valid credit card data, valid cardholder data), you would never want your web form to discourage transactions by being unduly rigid or restrictive.

Remember this example when designing tables and you're unsure whether a field should be nullable. "NOT NULL" fields are like those unforgiving "required" fields where you truly want your table to reject a record if those fields don't contain proper values. "NULL" fields offer more flexibility and are like the optional fields on a web form.

Inserting NULLs

The following code shows the syntax for adding NULL records to your table. As you'll see in the Working With NULLs video (Lab3.1_WorkingWithNulls.wmv), Phil is a new JProCo hire whose record must be entered today in the Employee table, even though we don't presently have data for all seven Employee fields.

```
--Insert Phil's partial record into Employee
INSERT INTO Employee VALUES
(13, NULL, 'Phil', NULL, 1, 4, 'Pending Hire')
```

Notice we code NULL for a field that has no values. A common student mistake is to attempt the incorrect code 'NULL' – the quotes tell SQL Server to store the literal character value. If you incorrectly attempted to code 'NULL' here as LastName, it would run. However, SQL Server would store Phil's name as "Phil Null" instead of what you intended.

Querying NULLs

Along the same lines as our bad practice example above of incorrectly providing 'NULL' as a field value, we need to be clear on proper syntax when querying for NULLs.

Recall we said SQL Server interprets the presence of NULL as an uncertain future entity. So we can't query for the string literal 'NULL' or search for a value equal to NULL.

```
--Incorrect query syntax for NULLs
SELECT * FROM Employee
WHERE Status = NULL

SELECT * FROM Employee
WHERE Status LIKE 'NULL'

--Correct query syntax for NULLs
SELECT * FROM Employee
WHERE Status IS NULL

SELECT * FROM Employee
WHERE Status IS NOT NULL
```

Think for a moment about our new Employee record with a LastName value of NULL. If you asked SQL Server to show you a list of all records where LastName is not Smith, would you expect to see Phil's record in the result? (Recall Phil's last name shows as NULL. Hint: remember our TBH example.)

The answer is no, SQL Server won't include a NULL in the result (Figure 3.1). Just like "TBH", NULL could potentially be any name – including Smith.

```
SELECT *
FROM Employee
WHERE LastName != 'Smith'
```

	EmpID	LastName	FirstName	HireDate	LocationID	ManagerID	Status
1	1	Adams	Alex	2001-01-01 …	1	11	NULL
2	2	Brown	Barry	2002-08-12 …	1	11	NULL
3	3	Osako	Lee	1999-09-01 …	2	11	NULL
4	4	Kennson	David	1996-03-16 …	1	11	Has Tenure
5	5	Bender	Eric	2007-05-17 …	1	11	NULL
6	6	Kendall	Lisa	2001-11-15 …	4	4	NULL
7	7	Lonning	David	2000-01-01 …	1	11	On Leave
8	8	Marshbank	John	2001-11-15 …	NULL	4	NULL
9	9	Newton	James	2003-09-30 …	2	3	NULL
10	10	O'Haire	Terry	2004-10-04 …	2	3	NULL
11	11	Smith	Sally	1989-04-01 …	1	NULL	NULL
12	12	O'Neil	Barbara	1995-05-26 …	4	4	Has Tenure

Query executed successfully.   RENO (11.0 RTM)   Reno\Student (51)   JProCo   00:00:00   12 rows

Figure 3.1 Notice that SQL Server does not return the NULL LastName record to this result set.

Updating NULLs

We can set a NULL field to a real value or replace a real value with a NULL.

Throughout our discussion of NULLs, we've talked about values in JProCo's Employee table which temporarily may be NULL. We inserted two NULL values in our new record for Phil, who was just hired for the Seattle office. His record needed to be inserted quickly into the company database, even though his exact HireDate or LastName weren't readily available.

We now have Phil's last name and hire date and are ready to properly update his Employee record.

```
UPDATE Employee
SET LastName = 'Wilconkinski'
WHERE EmpID = 13
```

```
UPDATE Employee
SET HireDate = '6/11/2009'
WHERE EmpID = 13
```

Recall the Status field in the Employee record. That field is generally empty for most employees unless they have an unusual status note, such as "Has Tenure" or "On Leave". Now that Phil's hire process is complete, we want to remove the "Pending Hire" note and give him the same NULL status shared by most of his fellow JProCo employees.

```
UPDATE Employee
SET Status = NULL
WHERE EmpID = 13
```

Finally, run this code to replace the NULL values in the Status field with "Active". The CEO Sally Smith noticed the NULL values for all the active employees and wants the field updated with a better descriptor (Figure 3.2).

```
UPDATE Employee
SET Status = 'Active'
WHERE Status IS NULL
```

Let's take a look at the Employee table.

```
SELECT * FROM Employee
```

	EmpID	LastName	FirstName	HireDate	LocationID	ManagerID	Status
1	1	Adams	Alex	2001-01-01...	1	11	Active
2	2	Brown	Barry	2002-08-12...	1	11	Active
3	3	Osako	Lee	1999-09-01...	2	11	Active
4	4	Kennson	David	1996-03-16...	1	11	Has Tenure
5	5	Bender	Eric	2007-05-17...	1	11	Active
6	6	Kendall	Lisa	2001-11-15...	4	4	Active
7	7	Lonning	David	2000-01-01...	1	11	On Leave
8	8	Marshbank	John	2001-11-15...	NULL	4	Active
9	9	Newton	James	2003-09-30...	2	3	Active
10	10	O'Haire	Terry	2004-10-04...	2	3	Active
11	11	Smith	Sally	1989-04-01...	1	NULL	Active
12	12	O'Neil	Barbara	1995-05-26...	4	4	Has Tenure
13	13	Wilconkin...	Phil	2009-06-11...	1	4	Active

Query executed successfully.   RENO (11.0 RTM)   Reno\Student (51)   JProCo   00:00:00   13 rows

Figure 3.2 The Employee table should now appear as seen here.

Lab 3.1: Working With NULLs

Lab Prep: Each lab has one or more Skill Checks. Start with Skill Check 1 and proceed until reaching the Points to Ponder section.

Before beginning this lab, verify that SQL Server 2012 is properly installed and operating. Before running the lab setup script for resetting the database (SQLQueries2012Vol2Chapter3.1Setup.sql), please make sure to close all query windows within SSMS. An open query window pointing to a database context can lock that database preventing it from updating when the script is executing. A simple way to assure all query windows are closed, is to exit out of SSMS, then open a new instance of SSMS, and lastly run the setup script.

Skill Check 1: The Employee table in JProCo has a field called ManagerID. Write a query to show all Employees who don't have a ManagerID. When you're done, your result should resemble Figure 3.3.

	EmpID	LastName	FirstName	HireDate	LocationID	ManagerID	Status
1	11	Smith	Sally	1989-04-01…	1	NULL	Active

1 rows

Figure 3.3 Skill Check 1 shows all JProCo Employees who have no ManagerID.

Skill Check 2: Find the two records in the Customer table where the company name is not NULL, as shown in Figure 3.4.

	CustomerID	CustomerType	FirstName	LastName	CompanyName
1	5	Consumer	NULL	NULL	MoreTechnology.com
2	117	Business	NULL	NULL	Puma Consulting

2 rows

Figure 3.4 Find the 2 records in the Customer table where the field CompanyName is not NULL.

Skill Check 3: Using your result set from Skill Check 2, write a statement to update the CustomerType field of the Customer table to "Business" for each record where the company name is not NULL. When you are done, you should have two records with the value "Business" in the CustomerType field (Figure 3.5).

	CustomerID	CustomerType	FirstName	LastName	CompanyName
1	5	Business	NULL	NULL	MoreTechnology.com
2	117	Business	NULL	NULL	Puma Consulting

2 rows

Figure 3.5 Skill Check 3 changes the CustomerType to "Business" if CompanyName is not NULL.

Skill Check 4: You have 10 grants in your Grant table. One grant was procured by EmpID 5 and the other nine grants were not. Show all grants found by employees other than EmpID 5, as well as all grants for which EmpID is NULL. When you're done, your result should resemble Figure 3.6.

	GrantID	GrantName	EmpID	Amount
1	001	92 Purr_Scents %% team	7	4750.00
2	002	K_Land fund trust	2	15750.00
3	003	Robert@BigStarBank.com	7	18100.00
4	004	Norman's Outreach	NULL	21000.00
5	005	BIG 6's Foundation%	4	21000.00
6	006	TALTA_Kishan International	3	18100.00

9 rows

Figure 3.6 Skill Check 4 shows the nine grants not found by EmpID 5.

Answer Code: The T-SQL code for this lab is located in the downloadable files as a file named Lab3.1_WorkingWithNulls.sql

Points to Ponder - Working With NULLs

1.   When filtering for NULLs in queries, use the IS NULL or IS NOT NULL operators. Since NULL denotes the absence of a value, the Equals (=) or Not Equals (!=) operators do not recognize NULLs.

2.   If you were to ask two women how old they are you would likely hear them decline to answer the question. Both women would give you a NULL. Since they gave you the same answer does that mean they have the same age? No! There is nothing that can be equal to a NULL. Not even a NULL can be equal to a NULL!!

3.   Note the syntax used to assign a NULL value to a field (SET Status = NULL). Here the equal sign is not acting as a comparison operator, so it does not conflict with Point #1.

4.   We can set a NULL field to a real value or replace a real value with a NULL.

5.   When you create a table we can specify each field as NULL or NOT NULL. If you don't specify then Microsoft SQL Server defaults NULLs to ON (nullable) for those fields.

6.   The "ANSI NULL default" standard specifies that if you don't explicitly specify nullability for a field then it should be NOT NULL. Microsoft SQL Server does the opposite of this and sets the "ANSI NULL default" to OFF (non-nullable).

Expression Fields

Expression fields in SQL Server are also known as dynamic fields, derived fields, and calculated fields.

Up until now, all our code and queries have involved actual data stored in tables. We might have sorted that data or filtered our results, but the information displayed in our reports is the same data just as you would see it physically stored in the tables. As you may have guessed from the term "calculated field," one capability of Expression Fields is to perform data calculations. Other capabilities include.

- o Combining column data, or concatenation in geek speak
- o Dynamically renaming fields
- o Altering the formatting of data in your result set

You are familiar with SQL Server's ability to dynamically join tables, sort data in our result set, and alias table names – all while never altering the actual physical table data. Expression Fields similarly have dramatic and useful effects on reports. But the underlying data and tables are never altered. For example, we can make 10.6779 appear rounded and as a currency value ($10.68), but the actual data point physically stored in the table remains untouched (10.6779).

If you haven't already done so, this is a good point to pause and view the Expression Fields video (Lab3.2_ExpressionFields.wmv).

Calculated Fields

SQL Server can perform any imaginable calculation on numeric data.

Let's begin with a few examples using JProCo's CurrentProducts table, which contains all product offerings and prices.

Example 1: JProCo's current price list (ProductName, RetailPrice) appears along with two dynamic fields calculating after-tax prices for California and Ohio (Figure 3.7).

```
SELECT ProductName, RetailPrice,
--6.25% sales tax
(RetailPrice * 1.0625) AS California,
--7% sales tax
(RetailPrice * 1.07) AS Ohio
FROM CurrentProducts
```

	ProductName	RetailPrice	California	Ohio
1	Underwater Tour 1 Day West Coast	61.483	65.32568750	65.786810
2	Underwater Tour 2 Days West Coast	110.6694	117.58623750	118.416258
3	Underwater Tour 3 Days West Coast	184.449	195.97706250	197.360430
4	Underwater Tour 5 Days West Coast	245.932	261.30275000	263.147240
5	Underwater Tour 1 Week West Coast	307.415	326.62843750	328.934050
6	Underwater Tour 2 Weeks West Coast	553.347	587.93118750	592.081290

480 rows

Figure 3.7 Two dynamic fields calculate after-tax prices for California and Ohio.

Example 2: JProCo's current price list has been filtered to show just the 160 LongTerm-Stay products. Lodging and utility rates are expected to increase next year, so the sales and marketing teams must prepare recommendations to increase LongTerm-Stay prices. Alongside ProductName and current RetailPrice, your report includes the effect of a 5% and 8% increase (Figure 3.8).

```
SELECT ProductName, RetailPrice AS CurrentPrice,
(RetailPrice * 1.05) AS [5% Price Increase],
(RetailPrice * 1.08) AS [8% Price Increase]
FROM CurrentProducts
WHERE Category = 'LongTerm-Stay'
```

	ProductName	CurrentPrice	5% Price Increase	8% Price Increase	
1	Underwater Tour 1 Week West Coast	307.415	322.785750	332.008200	
2	Underwater Tour 2 Weeks West Coast	553.347	581.014350	597.614760	
3	Underwater Tour 1 Week East Coast	404.295	424.509750	436.638600	
4	Underwater Tour 2 Weeks East Coast	727.731	764.117550	785.949480	
5	Underwater Tour 1 Week Mexico	525.295	551.559750	567.318600	
6	Underwater Tour 2 Weeks Mexico	945.531	992.807550	1021.173480	

Query executed successfully.   RENO (11.0 RTM)   Reno\Student (51)   JProCo   00:00:00   160 rows

Figure 3.8 The impact of potential price increases for JProCo's LongTerm-Stay products.

Example 3: JProCo's largest customers receive discounts. To get a rough idea of how discounting works, let's take a look at the top 10 discounted invoices found in the SalesInvoiceDetail table. For each invoice, multiply the discount rate by RetailPrice to see how much the customer saved. Subtract the customer savings expression field from RetailPrice to see what the customer actually paid (Figure 3.9).

```
SELECT TOP (10) sd.UnitDiscount, sd.InvoiceID,
cp.RetailPrice AS [Retail Price],
(sd.UnitDiscount * cp.RetailPrice) AS [Customer Saved],
(cp.RetailPrice - (sd.UnitDiscount * cp.RetailPrice)) AS
[Customer Paid]
FROM SalesInvoiceDetail AS sd
INNER JOIN CurrentProducts AS cp
ON sd.ProductID = cp.ProductID
ORDER BY sd.UnitDiscount DESC
```

	UnitDiscount	InvoiceID	Retail Price	Customer Saved	Customer Paid	
1	0.40	15	580.59	232.236	348.354	
2	0.40	249	145.5462	58.2185	87.3277	
3	0.40	471	189.1062	75.6425	113.4637	
4	0.40	473	556.74	222.696	334.044	
5	0.40	655	446.94	178.776	268.164	
6	0.40	857	122.441	48.9764	73.4646	

Query executed successfully.   RENO (11.0 RTM)   Reno\Student (51)   JProCo   00:00:00   10 rows

Figure 3.9 Two calculated fields show the impact of discounting for JProCo's best customers.

Notice in each case where we added an expression field, we gave the column a descriptive name. We also enclosed the new name inside square bracket delimiters to include spaces in the column headers for readability. SQL Server does not require you to provide a name and gives a default column header ("No Column Name") to any expression field you don't name.

Another best practice is to include parentheses around calculations within your queries. SQL Server doesn't require them, but they improve your code's readability.

The TOP 10 command shown in this example will be explained in Chapter 6.

Field Functions

We can format our dynamic fields using the CAST or CONVERT functions.

Cast and convert are used nearly interchangeably. CAST is the newer method preferred by ISO (International Organization for Standardization). However, CONVERT allows you to take advantage of Microsoft's style functionality.

The example here (Figure 3.10) refers back to JProCo's current price lookup list and the dynamic fields we added to show after-tax prices for our two busiest states (CA, OH) (Figure 3.7). We'll use the CAST function to limit each of the post-tax totals to just two digits after the decimal, so sales reps can easily quote prices to customers without needing to mentally round the figure.

```
SELECT ProductName, RetailPrice,
--6.25% sales tax
CAST(RetailPrice * 1.0625 AS DECIMAL(6,2)) AS California,
-- 7% sales tax
CAST(RetailPrice * 1.07 AS DECIMAL(6,2)) AS Ohio
FROM CurrentProducts
ORDER BY RetailPrice DESC
```

	ProductName	RetailPrice	California	Ohio
1	Lakes Tour 2 Weeks West Coast	1161.099	1233.67	1242.38
2	Lakes Tour 2 Weeks East Coast	1147.986	1219.74	1228.35
3	Rain Forest Tour 2 Weeks East Coast	1144.773	1216.32	1224.91
4	River Rapids Tour 2 Weeks East Coast	1116.108	1185.86	1194.24
5	Wine Tasting Tour 2 Weeks West Coast	1101.969	1170.84	1179.11
6	Ocean Cruise Tour 2 Weeks West Coast	1101.969	1170.84	1179.11

480 rows

Figure 3.10 The CAST function used to limit after-tax prices to just 2 decimal places.

The CAST function displays an expression using the data type you specify.

```
CAST(RetailPrice * 1.0625 AS DECIMAL(6,2)) AS California
```

The data type here is decimal, and we have specified the output length should be (6, 2). This indicates a precision (total digits, a.k.a. "significant digits") of 6, and a scale (number of places after the decimal) of 2. JProCo's current prices are a maximum of 4 places before the decimal, and we want to round them to the penny (2 decimal places).

If we wanted to allow 3 digits to follow the decimal in this price list, we would instead specify a precision of 7 and a scale of 3.

The ROUND( ) function is used to round data in a numeric field to the number of decimals you specify.

```
ROUND(RetailPrice, 2) AS RoundedPrice
```

The example here (Figure 3.11) shows the CAST and ROUND functions used to accomplish the same task: limit RetailPrice to just 2 digits following the decimal.

```
SELECT ProductName, RetailPrice,
CAST (RetailPrice AS DECIMAL (6,2)) AS Price_Cast,
ROUND (RetailPrice, 2) AS PriceRounded2Places
FROM CurrentProducts
```

	ProductName	RetailPrice	Price_Cast	PriceRounded2Places
1	Underwater Tour 1 Day West…	61.483	61.48	61.48
2	Underwater Tour 2 Days West…	110.6694	110.67	110.67
3	Underwater Tour 3 Days West…	184.449	184.45	184.45
4	Underwater Tour 5 Days West…	245.932	245.93	245.93
5	Underwater Tour 1 Week West…	307.415	307.42	307.42
6	Underwater Tour 2 Weeks West…	553.347	553.35	553.35

480 rows

Figure 3.11 In this example, both CAST and ROUND are used to round prices to the penny.

The CONVERT function can be used to modify date formatting in your reports. The following example (Figure 3.12) shows the HireDate field (DATETIME data type) converted to character data (NVARCHAR data type) and output using several of Microsoft's date formats.

If you look closely at the code, you'll notice the result is sorted by the original HireDate field. Since the other fields contain character data, they can't actually be sorted by the date.

```
SELECT FirstName +' '+LastName AS [Employee Name], HireDate,
CONVERT (NVARCHAR, HireDate, 1) AS [MM/DD/YY],
CONVERT (NVARCHAR, HireDate, 101) AS [MM/DD/YYYY],
CONVERT (NVARCHAR, HireDate, 103) AS [DD/MM/YYYY],
CONVERT (NVARCHAR, HireDate, 106) AS [European Letter],
CONVERT (NVARCHAR, HireDate, 107) AS [Business Letter],
CONVERT (NVARCHAR, HireDate, 110) AS [MM-DD-YYYY]
FROM Employee
ORDER BY HireDate DESC
```

	Employee Name	HireDate	MM/DD/YY	MM/DD/YYYY	DD/MM/YYYY	European Letter	Business Letter	MM-DD-YYYY
1	Phil Wilconkinski	2009-06-11...	06/11/09	06/11/2009	11/06/2009	11 Jun 2009	Jun 11, 2009	06-11-2009
2	Eric Bender	2007-05-17...	05/17/07	05/17/2007	17/05/2007	17 May 2007	May 17, 2007	05-17-2007
3	Terry O'Haire	2004-10-04...	10/04/04	10/04/2004	04/10/2004	04 Oct 2004	Oct 04, 2004	10-04-2004
4	James Newton	2003-09-30...	09/30/03	09/30/2003	30/09/2003	30 Sep 2003	Sep 30, 2003	09-30-2003
5	Barry Brown	2002-08-12...	08/12/02	08/12/2002	12/08/2002	12 Aug 2002	Aug 12, 2002	08-12-2002
6	Lisa Kendall	2001-11-15...	11/15/01	11/15/2001	15/11/2001	15 Nov 2001	Nov 15, 2001	11-15-2001

Query executed successfully.   RENO (11.0 RTM) Reno\Student (51) JProCo 00:00:00 13 rows

Figure 3.12 Example of CONVERT used with date formatting.

Aliasing Expression Fields

Back in Volume 1 we saw the geek speak term "concatenate" which means to link together in a series. Here is an example concatenating two fields (Figure 3.13).

```
SELECT EmpID, FirstName, LastName,
(FirstName + LastName) AS FullName
FROM Employee
```

	EmpID	FirstName	LastName	FullName
1	1	Alex	Adams	AlexAdams
2	2	Barry	Brown	BarryBrown
3	3	Lee	Osako	LeeOsako
4	4	David	Kennson	DavidKennson
5	5	Eric	Bender	EricBender
6	6	Lisa	Kendall	LisaKendall

13 rows

Figure 3.13 Concatenating two fields into one new field (FirstName + LastName).

Now for readability, let's add a space in the new column to separate the last name from first name (Figure 3.14).

```
SELECT EmpID, FirstName, LastName,
(FirstName + ' ' + LastName) AS FullName
FROM Employee
```

	EmpID	FirstName	LastName	FullName
1	1	Alex	Adams	Alex Adams
2	2	Barry	Brown	Barry Brown
3	3	Lee	Osako	Lee Osako
4	4	David	Kennson	David Kennson
5	5	Eric	Bender	Eric Bender
6	6	Lisa	Kendall	Lisa Kendall

13 rows

Figure 3.14 Adding a space between FirstName and LastName aids in the legibility.

Sorting Expression Fields

Note the order of Employee records in our prior example. Since we didn't specify a sort order, the table uses its natural sort on the EmpID field.

What will happen if we try to sort by the dynamic field FullName? This new column appears in our result set but is not a part of the underlying table data.

The answer is shown in Figure 3.15. Yes indeed… the power of SQL Server to dynamically create and sort on new expression fields on the fly is impressive.

```
SELECT EmpID, FirstName, LastName,
(FirstName + ' ' + LastName) AS FullName
FROM Employee
ORDER BY FullName
```

	EmpID	FirstName	LastName	FullName
1	1	Alex	Adams	Alex Adams
2	12	Barbara	O'Neil	Barbara O'Neil
3	2	Barry	Brown	Barry Brown
4	4	David	Kennson	David Kennson
5	7	David	Lonning	David Lonning
6	5	Eric	Bender	Eric Bender

13 rows

Figure 3.15 Dynamically sorting the result set on the FullName expression field.

Lab 3.2: Expression Fields

Lab Prep: Each lab has one or more Skill Checks. Start with Skill Check 1 and proceed until reaching the Points to Ponder section.

Before beginning this lab, verify that SQL Server 2012 is properly installed and operating. Before running the lab setup script for resetting the database (SQLQueries2012Vol2Chapter3.2Setup.sql), please make sure to close all query windows within SSMS. An open query window pointing to a database context can lock that database preventing it from updating when the script is executing. A simple way to assure all query windows are closed, is to exit out of SSMS, then open a new instance of SSMS, and lastly run the setup script.

Skill Check 1: Using the CurrentProducts table of JProCo, make another field to express the price in Canadian currency called CDN$ that is 1.1 times the stated RetailPrice in JProCo's CurrentProducts table. Then create two additional fields named Aussie$ (1.4 times the RetailPrice) and Euro (which is .82 times the RetailPrice). When you're done your result should resemble Figure 3.16.

```
SELECT ProductName, RetailPrice,
--Remaining Code Here
```

	ProductName	RetailPrice	Cnd$	Aussie$	Euro
1	Underwater Tour 1 Day West Coast	61.483	67.63	86.08	50.42
2	Underwater Tour 2 Days West Coast	110.6694	121.74	154.94	90.75
3	Underwater Tour 3 Days West Coast	184.449	202.89	258.23	151.25
4	Underwater Tour 5 Days West Coast	245.932	270.53	344.30	201.66
5	Underwater Tour 1 Week West Coast	307.415	338.16	430.38	252.08
6	Underwater Tour 2 Weeks West Coast	553.347	608.68	774.69	453.74
					480 rows

Figure 3.16 Three new currency columns calculated from RetailPrice (US dollars).

Skill Check 2: In JProCo find the 773 records in your Customer table where the CustomerType is Consumer. Show the CustomerID, CustomerType field and the FullName expression field. Your results should be sorted by the FullName field (Z-A). When you're done your result should resemble Figure 3.17.

	CustomerID	CustomerType	FullName
1	266	Consumer	William Wright
2	328	Consumer	William Wright
3	594	Consumer	William Wilson
4	374	Consumer	William Turner
5	357	Consumer	William Thomas
6	555	Consumer	William Parker
			773 rows

Figure 3.17 Add the expression field FullName.

Skill Check 3: Join the SalesInvoiceDetail table to the CurrentProducts table. Show the ProductID, ProductName and RetailPrice from the CurrentProducts table. Show Quantity from the SalesInvoiceDetail table. Create an expression field called SubTotal which multiplies RetailPrice by Quantity. Your result should look like Figure 3.18.

	ProductID	ProductName	RetailPrice	Quantity	SubTotal
1	7	Underwater Tour 1 Day East…	80.859	5	404.295
2	7	Underwater Tour 1 Day East…	80.859	2	161.718
3	7	Underwater Tour 1 Day East…	80.859	3	242.577
4	7	Underwater Tour 1 Day East…	80.859	4	323.436
5	7	Underwater Tour 1 Day East…	80.859	5	404.295
6	7	Underwater Tour 1 Day East…	80.859	5	404.295
					6960 rows

Figure 3.18 Skill Check 3 adds dynamic field SubTotal.

Skill Check 4: Modify your query from Skill Check 3. Using the Round function, show Retail Price and the SubTotal expression field rounded to the nearest penny. When you're done, your result will resemble Figure 3.19.

```
SELECT cp.ProductID, cp.ProductName,
--Remaining Code Here
```

	ProductID	ProductName	RetailPrice	Quantity	SubTotal
1	7	Underwater Tour 1 Day East…	80.86	5	404.30
2	7	Underwater Tour 1 Day East…	80.86	2	161.72
3	7	Underwater Tour 1 Day East…	80.86	3	242.58
4	7	Underwater Tour 1 Day East…	80.86	4	323.44
5	7	Underwater Tour 1 Day East…	80.86	5	404.30
6	7	Underwater Tour 1 Day East…	80.86	5	404.30
					6960 rows

Figure 3.19 Use the ROUND function to display Skill Check 3 results rounded to the nearest penny.

Answer Code: The T-SQL code for this lab is located in the downloadable files as a file named Lab3.2_ExpressionFields.sql.

Points to Ponder - Expression Fields

1. We can create expression fields in our query and base them upon other fields (like having a foreign currency price based upon the US price).

2. An expression field is sometimes called a calculated field, a dynamic field, or a derived field.

3. We can have many dynamic fields in one query.

4. In SQL Server parentheses are optional around calculated fields in your expression field queries. A best practice is to include these to make your code more readable.

5. Expression fields can have names. Put the expression name after the AS keyword (just like you would rename a column or alias a table).

6. You can sort by expression fields only if you have named them.

7. You can format your dynamic fields using the CAST() or CONVERT() function.

8. Use CAST() instead of CONVERT() if you want to use the newer ISO (International Organization for Standardization) compliant method.

9. Use CONVERT() instead of CAST() if you want to take advantage of style functionality from Microsoft.

10. Precision is the total number of digits in a number.

11. Scale is the number of digits to the right of the decimal point in a number.

12. In the following code "6" is the precision and "2" is the scale.>> decimal(6,2)

13. The number 561.28 has a precision of 5 and a scale of 2.

14. The ROUND(*expression, length after decimal*) function is used to round a numeric field to the number of decimals specified.

15. The ROUND() Function will keep the number of decimal places you started with while rounding up the numbers. For example:

    o ROUND(`3.80, 0`) = `4.00`
    o ROUND(`3.8, 0`) = `4.0`

Identity Fields

An identity field uniquely differentiates (or "identifies") each record in a table. In the case of an identity field, that distinct value is an identifying number (e.g., InvoiceID, ProductID). The noteworthy feature of identity fields is that the identity property enforces data integrity by automatically generating the ID value each time you add a new record to the table.

Discovering Identity Fields

To know whether a table contains an identity field, view the table's properties. To check the CurrentProducts table, open the Object Explorer, right-click on the CurrentProducts table, and select Design. Then click on ProductID to view its properties (Figure 3.20). In the lower section of the Column Properties tab, we see the Identity Specification is set to 'Yes'. ProductID begins with a value of 1 (Identity Seed) and adds 1 to the value of ProductID for each new record that is added (Identity Increment).

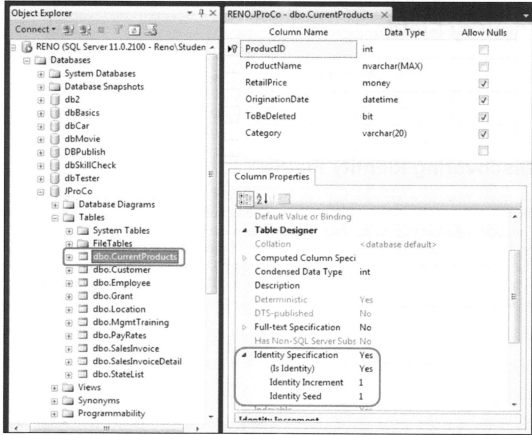

Figure 3.20 ProductID is the identity field for the CurrentProducts table.

Creating Identity Fields

We want to create a table name TestTable that uses an identity field. This code creates a table TestTable with an identity field called TestID:

```
--An identity field TestID (seed 100, increment 50)
USE JProCo
GO

CREATE TABLE TestTable (
TestID INT IDENTITY(100,50),
FName VARCHAR(20),
Middle CHAR(1),
LName VARCHAR(30))
GO
```

Since most identity fields have a seed of 1 and an increment of 1, this example uses different values to better illustrate their behavior. In TestTable, the seed of 100 means the first record's ID will be 100. The increment of 50 means each subsequent ID increases by 50.

```
INSERT TestTable (FName, Middle, LName) VALUES
('Sarah', 'F', 'Smith'),
('John', 'Q', 'Public'),
('Mary', 'B', 'Goode')

SELECT * FROM TestTable
```

	TestID	FName	Middle	LName
1	100	Sarah	F	Smith
2	150	John	Q	Public
3	200	Mary	B	Goode

3 rows

Figure 3.21 The TestTable has an identity field with seed of 100, increment of 50.

If you haven't seen a real world invoice table, you may wonder why you wouldn't always use a seed of 1. Businesses prefer lengthier invoice numbers and a static number of digits for invoice IDs. Instead of beginning with 1, their first invoices would be more like 101000, 101001, etc. New bank customers also tend to request a higher seed (e.g., 300 or 1000) for their check register, rather than beginning with Check#1.

The identity property enforces non-nullability. View the Column Properties tab for TestTable (Figure 3.22) and notice that SQL Server created our TestID field as non-nullable, even though we didn't specify "NOT NULL".

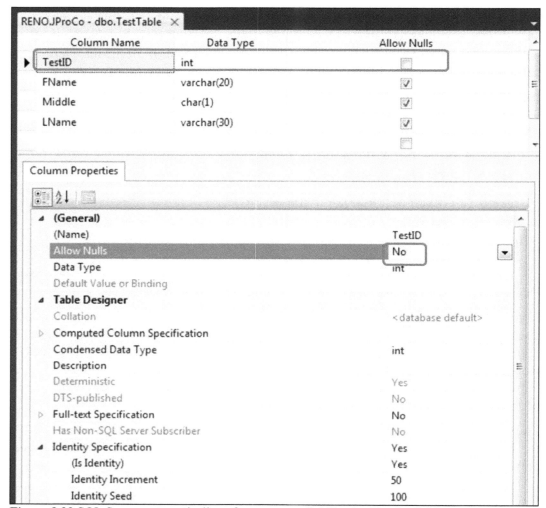

Figure 3.22 SQL Server automatically enforces non-nullability for identity fields.

Using the following code lets Drop the test table from the JProCo database:

```
DROP TABLE TestTable
GO
```

Using Identity Fields in Database Tables

As we did earlier with NULLs, we'll quickly digress here to explore why you might use – and when not to use – the identity property. Old hands with Microsoft Access or relational databases are already familiar with these ideas.

For students new to the database world, it helps to begin thinking about ID fields in the context of larger organizations with lots of activity. A customer service department has a constant flow of activity and many representatives entering data in the system simultaneously. The same is true for large billing departments. These are examples where an identity field helps to ensure the entities you care about get tracked properly. A CustomerID that is automatically generated with each new record makes sure each new customer gets a unique number – even if you have many reps all entering data at the same time.

The CustomerID field is one we wouldn't want accidentally duplicated, altered, or deleted. Similarly, the billing department would not want to have mistaken entries in the InvoiceID field. A missing InvoiceID could indicate a serious error (e.g., a customer wouldn't get billed and JProCo wouldn't get paid for that order) or even fraud. A duplicate InvoiceID might result in a customer's payment being applied to the wrong customer.

Identity fields help prevent these unwanted scenarios. For large tables, like JProCo's CurrentProducts, having ProductID as an identity field ensures each ProductID value will be unique and sequential. It also saves JProCo's product managers from having to track down which ProductID to use each time they quickly need to add new products.

One hint about the identity property is to count the number of times we've used the words "large" and "active" in this section. For large tables where new records get added daily, the identity property saves time and helps enforce data integrity. But with smaller tables where records don't often change, using the identity property to create your ID field is unnecessary and its automatic incrementing can make extra work for you. Tables where records are frequently deleted also make poor candidates for the identity property. In our next example, we will see that an identity field's ability to auto-increment and keep track of the next expected value can require extra maintenance tasks when fields are deleted.

Overriding Identity Fields

There are exception cases when you will need to alter a value in the identity field. When training a new database user, you might temporarily allocate them a few empty invoice records to practice on. Later the practice records will be deleted, but you'll want to make sure your next invoice number appears in proper sequence.

Now imagine a more complex scenario, where several records in a large table (CurrentProducts) accidentally get deleted. Customers have purchased those products, and the ProductID appears on their invoices. In this case, we must add back the missing product records AND have these records retain the original ProductID sequence.

Let's step through a similar example using the CurrentProducts table and a new Yoga product offering. Open a new query window to quickly scan the 6 fields and see the table's 480 records. Pretend we don't already know that ProductID is an identity field, so we can read the error message SQL Server generates when you attempt to enter an ID into the identity field (Figure 3.23).

```
INSERT INTO CurrentProducts VALUES
(481,'Yoga Mtn Getaway 5 Days',875,'9/1/2009',0,
'Medium-Stay')
```

Messages
Msg 8101, Level 16, State 1, Line 1
An explicit value for the identity column in table 'CurrentProducts' can only
be specified when a column list is used and IDENTITY_INSERT is ON.
0 rows

Figure 3.23 SQL Server generates an error when you attempt to insert an ID into an identity field.

Remove the 481 value (ProductID) from the code, and then insert the record with the following statement (Figure 3.24).

```
INSERT INTO CurrentProducts VALUES
('Yoga Mtn Getaway 5 Days',875,'9/1/2009',0,'Medium-Stay')
```

Messages
(1 row(s) affected)
0 rows

Figure 3.24 Removing the ProductID value permits us to successfully insert the new record.

Run your query again (SELECT * FROM CurrentProducts) and notice the new record was inserted with SQL Server auto-assigning the next correct ProductID of 481. Repeat the step after inserting the next two Yoga products.

```
INSERT INTO CurrentProducts VALUES
('Yoga Mtn Getaway 1 week',995.00,'6/11/2009',0,
'LongTerm-Stay'),
('Yoga Mtn Getaway 2 week',1695.00,GETDATE(),0,
'LongTerm-Stay')
```

Messages
(2 row(s) affected)
0 rows

Figure 3.25 The two new yoga product records are successfully inserted.

Products 481, 482 and 483 have been added.

```
SELECT * FROM CurrentProducts
```

	ProductID	ProductName	RetailPrice	OriginationDate	ToBeDeleted	Category
478	478	Wine Tasting Tour 5 Days Scandina...	162.256	2008-07-17 06:36:31.183	0	Medium-Stay
479	479	Wine Tasting Tour 1 Week Scandina...	202.82	2007-08-30 21:27:24.520	0	LongTerm-Stay
480	480	Wine Tasting Tour 2 Weeks Scandin...	365.076	2005-02-23 19:33:03.767	0	LongTerm-Stay
481	481	Yoga Mtn Getaway 5 Days	875.00	2009-09-01 00:00:00.000	0	Medium-Stay
482	482	Yoga Mtn Getaway 1 week	995.00	2009-06-11 00:00:00.000	0	LongTerm-Stay
483	483	Yoga Mtn Getaway 2 week	1695.00	2012-09-20 22:35:34.730	0	LongTerm-Stay

Query executed successfully. RENO (11.0 RTM) Reno\Student (51) JProCo 00:00:00 483 rows

Figure 3.26 SQL Server auto-assigns the ProductID values for the yoga products.

Now let's "accidentally" delete all the yoga products, in order to simulate the accidental deletion scenario.

```
DELETE FROM CurrentProducts
WHERE ProductName LIKE '%yoga%'
```

	ProductID	ProductName	RetailPrice	OriginationDate	ToBeDeleted	Category
475	475	Wine Tasting Tour 1 Day Scandinavia	40.564	2007-09-08 07:00:27.480	0	No-Stay
476	476	Wine Tasting Tour 2 Days Scandina...	73.0152	2010-08-01 11:26:21.703	0	Overnight-Stay
477	477	Wine Tasting Tour 3 Days Scandina...	121.692	2007-02-05 02:32:57.397	0	Medium-Stay
478	478	Wine Tasting Tour 5 Days Scandina...	162.256	2008-07-17 06:36:31.183	0	Medium-Stay
479	479	Wine Tasting Tour 1 Week Scandina...	202.82	2007-08-30 21:27:24.520	0	LongTerm-Stay
480	480	Wine Tasting Tour 2 Weeks Scandin...	365.076	2005-02-23 19:33:03.767	0	LongTerm-Stay

Query executed successfully. RENO (11.0 RTM) Reno\Student (51) JProCo 00:00:00 480 rows

Figure 3.27 The yoga products are deleted, the table now contains just the original 480 records.

Next, attempt to reinsert those 3 yoga products we just "accidentally" deleted. Note the identity property of ProductID keeps track of all records you insert and delete. It knows the records you just deleted were 481, 482, and 483 and it knows the next sequential ProductID values should be 484, 485, and 486 (Figure 3.28).

```
INSERT INTO CurrentProducts VALUES
('Yoga Mtn Getaway 5 Days',875.00,'9/1/2009',0,
'Medium-Stay'),
('Yoga Mtn Getaway 1 Week',995.00,'6/11/2009',0,
'LongTerm-Stay'),
('Yoga Mtn Getaway 2 Weeks',1695.00,GETDATE(),0,
'LongTerm-Stay')

SELECT * FROM CurrentProducts
```

Figure 3.28 The yoga products are re-inserted, but the ProductID values are incorrect.

Alright, we've now arrived at the heart of our lesson. The "accidentally" deleted records have been re-inserted causing SQL Server to jump ahead to the next unused ProductID values.

We don't want this gap between ProductID values, and we want the yoga products to retain their original ProductID values (481, 482, 483). To accomplish this goal, we must temporarily halt the automatic counter and insert our records. While the automatic identity counter is halted, we can manually assign the correct ProductID values. Delete the yoga records again by re-running this DELETE statement:

```
DELETE FROM CurrentProducts
WHERE ProductName LIKE '%yoga%'
```

Our next step is to temporarily set the IDENTITY_INSERT property to ON. We successfully ran the first command by setting the IDENTITY_INSERT property to ON for the CurrentProducts table. We next will attempt to run the INSERT statement for the three yoga records.

```
SET IDENTITY_INSERT CurrentProducts ON
INSERT INTO CurrentProducts VALUES
(481,'Yoga Mtn Getaway 5 Days',875.00,'9/1/2009',0,
'Medium-Stay'),
(482,'Yoga Mtn Getaway 1 Week',995.00,'9/1/2009',0,
'Medium-Stay'),
(483,'Yoga Mtn Getaway 5 Weeks',1695.00,'9/1/2009',0,
'Medium-Stay')
```

Messages
```
Msg 8101, Level 16, State 1, Line 2
An explicit value for the identity column in table 'CurrentProducts' can only
be specified when a column list is used and IDENTITY_INSERT is ON.

                                                               0 rows
```

Figure 3.29 A column list is needed when manually inserting records with an identity field.

The error message prompts us to include a column list whenever we manually insert records to a table with an identity field. In other words, when manually inserting records, we have to pass the values by name and not position. It is required to only add data in specified columns. In other words find the names of all the fields in the table and list them in parenthesis after the INSERT INTO keywords but before the VALUES keyword as seen in this code:

```
INSERT INTO CurrentProducts (ProductID, ProductName,
RetailPrice, OriginationDate, ToBeDeleted, Category)
VALUES (...
```

When inserting with IDENTITY_INSERT set to on you must specify the column names where the data will be inserted. Here's a trick to get the CurrentProducts column list to appear in our code window (Figure 3.30). In the Object Explorer, navigate to the table you need and expand the table until you see the "Columns" folder. Click and drag the folder into your code window. The field list appears in the same order it appears in the table. Try this yourself by opening a new query window and seeing how nicely this works. It saves many keystrokes and may impress a few colleagues in your SQL Server journey.

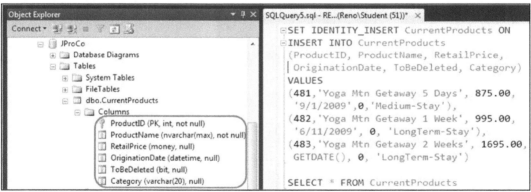

Figure 3.30 Click and drag a table's "Columns" folder to reproduce the column list in your code.

After you've added the column list, enclose the list in parentheses and move the keyword VALUES to follow the column list. Now reattempt to insert the 3 yoga records. After SQL Server gives you confirmation ("3 row(s) affected"), run a SELECT statement and confirm the yoga records show in the table, as expected (Figure 3.31). Lastly, set IDENTITY_INSERT to OFF (Figure 3.32).

```
SET IDENTITY_INSERT CurrentProducts ON
INSERT INTO CurrentProducts (
ProductID, ProductName, RetailPrice, OriginationDate,
ToBeDeleted, Category) VALUES
```

```
(481,'Yoga Mtn Getaway 5 Days',875.00,'9/1/2009',0,
'Medium-Stay'),
(482,'Yoga Mtn Getaway 1 Week',995.00,'6/11/2009',0,
'LongTerm-Stay'),
(483,'Yoga Mtn Getaway 2 Weeks',1695.00,GETDATE(),0,
'LongTerm-Stay')
```

```
SELECT * FROM CurrentProducts
```

	ProductID	ProductName	RetailPrice	OriginationDate	ToBeDeleted	Category
478	478	Wine Tasting Tour 5 Days Scandina...	162.256	2008-07-17 06:36:31.183	0	Medium-Stay
479	479	Wine Tasting Tour 1 Week Scandina...	202.82	2007-08-30 21:27:24.520	0	LongTerm-Stay
480	480	Wine Tasting Tour 2 Weeks Scandin...	365.076	2005-02-23 19:33:03.767	0	LongTerm-Stay
481	481	Yoga Mtn Getaway 5 Days	875.00	2009-09-01 00:00:00.000	0	Medium-Stay
482	482	Yoga Mtn Getaway 1 Week	995.00	2009-06-11 00:00:00.000	0	LongTerm-Stay
483	483	Yoga Mtn Getaway 2 Weeks	1695.00	2012-09-20 23:16:48.157	0	LongTerm-Stay

Query executed successfully.   RENO (11.0 RTM)   Reno\Student (51)   JProCo   00:00:00   483 rows

Figure 3.31 After you run the INSERT INTO, confirm the 3 yoga records appear in the table.

SQL Server will allow you to utilize IDENTITY_INSERT with just one table at a time in your database. After you've completed the needed work, it's very important to reset the IDENTITY_INSERT back to OFF. A best practice recommendation is to write the OFF statement as a reminder at the same time you write the ON statement.

```
SET IDENTITY_INSERT CurrentProducts OFF
```

Messages
Command(s) completed successfully.
0 rows

Figure 3.32 Once done be sure to set the IDENTITY_INSERT to OFF.

Recall we used GETDATE() as the OriginationDate value for the yoga product 483. GETDATE() is a function that returns the date and time in your time zone.

CURRENT_TIMESTAMP is a property whose value is the time in your time zone and produces a result identical to the GETDATE() function.

GETDATE() was invented by Microsoft, and CURRENT_TIMESTAMP is the ANSI (American National Standards Institute) equivalent for displaying the current date and time (Figure 3.33).

```
SELECT GETDATE() AS GetDateFunction,
CURRENT_TIMESTAMP AS CurrentTimestampProperty
```

	GetDateFunction	CurrentTimestampProperty
1	2012-09-21 00:04:16.180	2012-09-21 00:04:16.180

1 rows

Figure 3.33 The function GETDATE( ) and the property CURRENT_TIMESTAMP.

Lab 3.3: Identity Fields

Lab Prep: Each lab has one or more Skill Checks. Start with Skill Check 1 and proceed until reaching the Points to Ponder section.

Before beginning this lab, verify that SQL Server 2012 is properly installed and operating. Before running the lab setup script for resetting the database (SQLQueries2012Vol2Chapter3.3Setup.sql), please make sure to close all query windows within SSMS. An open query window pointing to a database context can lock that database preventing it from updating when the script is executing. A simple way to assure all query windows are closed, is to exit out of SSMS, then open a new instance of SSMS, and lastly run the setup script.

Skill Check 1: The MgmtTraining table in JProCo has ClassID as an identity field. Previously, this table had many records deleted from it. We want to insert a value of 'Empowering Others' in the ClassName field with a ClassID of 4.

If we run a simple INSERT statement, the identity counter is already past the number 4. We must set the table's property for inserting values to allow manually inserting all fields for this record. The ApprovedDate field should be set using the CURRENT_TIMESTAMP property.

When done, the results should resemble those shown in Figure 3.34.

```
--Skill Check 1 Code Here
SELECT * FROM MgmtTraining
```

	ClassID	ClassName	ClassDurationHours	ApprovedDate
1	1	Embracing Diversity	12	2007-01-01 00:00:00.000
2	2	Interviewing	6	2007-01-15 00:00:00.000
3	3	Difficult Negotiations	30	2008-02-12 00:00:00.000
4	4	Empowering Others	18	2012-09-21 00:06:39.763

Query executed successfully.   RENO (11.0 RTM)   Reno\Student (53)   JProCo   00:00:00   4 rows

Figure 3.34 Manually inserting ClassID 4 "Empowering Others" into the MgmtTraining table.

Answer Code: The T-SQL code for this lab is located in the downloadable files as a file named Lab3.3_IdentityFields.sql.

Points to Ponder - Identity Inserts

1. When explicitly entering a DATETIME value, enclose the date value inside a set of single quotes. For example, enter the date for March 1st, 2009 as '3/1/2009'.

2. To include the current system time into a DATETIME field Microsoft SQL Server provides the GETDATE() function.

3. The ANSI equivalent of GETDATE() is CURRENT_TIMESTAMP.

4. Identity fields are used to auto-increment values in a table.

5. When inserting data into a table containing an identity field, explicitly omit the value for the identity field from the VALUES clause of the INSERT statement. In other words, omit the explicit values from the INSERT statement for the auto-incremented field, when inserting data into a table with an identity field.

6. If you need to enter a specific value of your choosing into an identity field, you must set IDENTITY_INSERT to ON for that table.

7. Only one database table per session can have the IDENTITY_INSERT property set to ON.

8. When IDENTITY_INSERT is ON, your INSERT statement must pass the values by name and not by position.

9. It is considered a best practice to return the IDENTITY_INSERT setting to OFF immediately after completing all record inserts that required IDENTITY_INSERT to be set to ON.

10. If you alias an expression field with the same name as the original field then any ORDER BY clause will refer to the aliased field.

Chapter Glossary

ANSI: American National Standards Institute

Calculated Fields: Expression fields in SQL that are used to perform data calculations, concatenating data, dynamically renaming fields, and altering the formatting of data in a result set. See also expression fields, derived fields and dynamic fields.

CAST(): A function used to format expression fields. This is the newer ISO (International Organization for Standardization) compliant method.

Concatenate: To link together in a series, such as joining FirstName and LastName fields together to show the full name in one field.

CONVERT(): A function used to modify data formatting in reports.

CURRENT_TIMESTAMP: A property representing the current time of the time zone the machine is located in. CURRENT_TIMESTAMP is the ANSI equivalent of the Microsoft function: GETDATE().

Derived Fields: Expression fields in SQL that are used to perform data calculations, concatenating data, dynamically renaming fields and altering the formatting of data in a result set. See also expression fields, dynamic fields and calculated fields.

Descriptive Names: Names designated for columns in an expression field.

Dynamic Fields: Expression fields in SQL that are used to perform data calculations, concatenating data, dynamically renaming fields and altering the formatting of data in a result set. See also expression fields, derived fields and calculated fields.

Expression Fields: Expression fields in SQL that are used to perform data calculations, concatenating data, dynamically renaming fields and altering the formatting of data in a result set. See also dynamic fields, derived fields and calculated fields.

GETDATE(): A property whose value is the time in your time zone. This is the Microsoft version. CURRENT_TIMESTAMP is the ANSI version.

Identity Fields: A field that enforces data integrity by automatically generating unique identity values to each record in a table.

Identity Increment: Located within the Column Properties, this indicates the value for each new record. For example, a new record in the CurrentProducts table with 486 records would have the next ProductID of 487. If the increment were set to a value of five (5), the next ProductID would be 491.

IDENTITY_INSERT: A SQL Server setting that can be turned off to allow for entry of a specific value in an identity field.

Identity Seed: The starting value used by an Identify field to number records.

Identity Specification: Located within the Column Properties, this indicates whether the identity is set to Yes or No.

Nullable field: A nullable field is one that allows the field to contain data or to be empty waiting for future data. NULL is acting as a placeholder for future data.

Output length: Used by CAST() to indicate the length of the possible results displayed.

Precision: Used by CAST() to indicate the total number of significant digits to potentially display.

ROUND(): A SQL Server function used to round data in a numeric field to the number of decimals specified.

Row constructors: A method used to insert values via SQL code that has been available since SQL Server 2008.

Scale: The number of places after the decimal in a CAST() as decimal function.

UPDATE: A statement that changes – or *manipulates* – existing data without adding any new records.

VALUES: A SQL Server keyword used with an INSERT statement.

Review Quiz - Chapter Three

1.) You need to find all records in your Employee table that have a NULL value for the LocationID field. Which criterion should you use in your query?

O a. `WHERE LocationID = 'NULL'`

O b. `WHERE LocationID IS 'NULL'`

O c. `WHERE LocationID = NULL`

O d. `WHERE LocationID IS NULL`

2.) You need to take the number 3.85 and round it to the nearest whole number while still keeping the decimal place. In other words, 3.85 should round to 4.00. Which code will achieve this result?

O a. `SELECT ROUND(3.85, 0)`

O b. `SELECT ROUND(3.85, 2)`

O c. `SELECT ROUND(3.85, 1.00)`

O d. `SELECT UPPER(3.85, 2, 0)`

3.) You have a table named Products defined with the following code:

```
CREATE TABLE Products(
ProductID INT IDENTITY (1,1),
Product Rating INT NOT NULL,
ProductName VARCHAR(50),
CreationDate DATETIME NOT NULL)
```

You must insert a new Product record with a rating of 75 called "Go Duck" with today's Creation date and time. Which statement should you use?

O a. `INSERT INTO Products VALUES`
`(75,'Go Duck', DEFAULT)`

O b. `INSERT INTO Products VALUES`
`(NULL,75,'Go Duck', DEFAULT)`

O c. `INSERT INTO Products VALUES`
`(75,'Go Duck', CURRENT_TIMESTAMP)`

O d. `INSERT INTO Products VALUES`
`(NULL,75,'Go Duck', CURRENT_TIMESTAMP)`

4.) You need to write a query that returns the City field from the Location table and a FullName expression field. FullName is a concatenation of FirstName and LastName with a space in the middle. Sort the result set by the FullName field from 'A' to 'Z'. Only show employees who were hired after January 1st, 2000. What T-SQL statement will achieve this result?

O a.
```
SELECT FirstName+ ' ' + LastName AS FullName,
HireDate, City
FROM Employee e
INNER JOIN Location l
ON e.LocationID = l.LocationID
WHERE HireDate > '1/1/2000'
ORDER BY FullName ASC
```

O b.
```
SELECT FirstName + ' ' + LastName AS FullName,
HireDate, City
FROM Employee e
INNER JOIN Location l
ON E.LocationID = L.LocationID
WHERE HireDate > '1/1/2000'
```

O c.
```
SELECT FirstName + ' ' + LastName AS FullName,
HireDate, City
FROM Employee e
INNER JOIN Location l
ON E.LocationID = L.LocationID
WHERE HireDate > '1/1/2000'
ORDER BY FullName DESC
```

5.) You need to insert an explicit value into an identity field for the SalesInvoice table. You want to execute the INSERT statement successfully, which two steps must be implemented at the same time? (Choose two)

☐ a. Turn the IDENTITY_INSERT to ON for the SalesInvoice table

☐ b. Turn the IDENTITY_INSERT to OFF for the SalesInvoice table

☐ c. Insert your values by position

☐ d. Insert your values by name

6.)   You have a database named JProCo with a table named Products. The record for ProductID 481 has been deleted from this table. You need to re-insert the same record into the Products table with ProductID value 481. ProductID is an identity field. Which T-SQL code should you use?

O a. `INSERT INTO Products (`
`ProductID, ProductName, OriginationDate, Category)`
`VALUES (481,'Yoga 5 Days', CURRENT_TIMESTAMP, 'Medium')`

O b. `SET IDENTITY_INSERT Products ON`
`INSERT INTO Products (`
`ProductID, ProductName, OriginationDate, Category)`
`VALUES (481,'Yoga 5 Days', CURRENT_TIMESTAMP, 'Medium')`
`SET IDENTITY_INSERT Products OFF`

O c. `ALTER TABLE Products`
`ALTER COLUMN InvoiceID INT`
`INSERT INTO Products (`
`ProductID, ProductName, OriginationDate, Category)`
`VALUES (481,'Yoga 5 Days', CURRENT_TIMESTAMP, 'Medium')`

O d. `ALTER DATABASE JProCo SET MULTI-USER`
`INSERT INTO Products (`
`ProductID, ProductName, OriginationDate, Category)`
`VALUES (481,'Yoga 5 Days', CURRENT_TIMESTAMP, 'Medium')`

7.)   You have the following rows and fields in your dbo.Customer table.

CustomerID	Status
1	Active
2	NULL
3	Frozen

Which predicate will find the 2 records that do not have a NULL status?

O a. `WHERE status NOT IN (NULL)`

O b. `WHERE status != NULL`

O c. `WHERE status IS NOT NULL`

O d. `WHERE status IS NOT (NULL)`

8.)   You need to round the value 2.94 to the nearest whole number. Which code segment should you use?

O a. `SELECT ROUND(2.94, 0)`

O b. `SELECT ROUND(2.94, 1)`

O c. `SELECT ROUND(2.94, 2)`

9.) You want to see all the full names of your sales people Hired after '2009/01/01' listed in alphabetical order. The result set must be sorted by the concatenated field. What T-SQL code will do this?

O a.
```
SELECT FName + ' ' + LName AS FullName
FROM Person.SalesPerson
WHERE Hired > '2009/01/01'
ORDER BY LName ASC, FName ASC
```

O b.
```
SELECT FName + ' ' + LName AS FullName
FROM Person.SalesPerson
WHERE Hired > '2009/01/01'
ORDER BY FullName ASC
```

Answer Key

1.) When comparing values, NULL will match a string of that value, so (a) and (b) are both incorrect answers. When determining if a value is NULL, use the IS operator instead of the = operator, making (c) an incorrect answer also. 'WHERE LocationID IS NULL' is the only code that uses the IS operator and NULL without quotes together, so (d) is the correct answer.

2.) ROUND (3.85, 2) will return a value rounded to the 2nd decimal place (3.85), so (b) is incorrect. 'ROUND (3.85, 1.00) will return a value rounded to the 1st decimal place (3.9), so (c) is also incorrect. The UPPER function is used to change string values to all upper case, making (d) an incorrect answer too. To round to the nearest whole number, use 0 as the precision parameter of the ROUND function, as in 'ROUND (3.85, 0), which makes (a) the correct answer.

3.) The CreationDate field does not have a DEFAULT value defined, so (a) is incorrect. Because ProductID is an IDENTITY field which does not allow NULL values, (b) and (d) are also incorrect. The correct code will list only the three values for ProductRating, ProductName and CreationDate and because CURRENT_TIMESTAMP will return the current date and time (c) is the correct answer.

4.) Because the code in (b) does not sort the results and (c) sorts the results by FullName from Z to A with the DESC keyword, both of them are incorrect answers. Because the code in (a) is the only one that sorts the result set by FullName from A to Z using the ASC keyword it is the correct answer.

5.) If you need to enter a specific value of your choosing into an IDENTITY field, you must set INDENTITY_INSERT to ON for that table, so (b) is incorrect. When IDENTITY_INSERT is ON, the INSERT statement must pass the values by name and not position, so (c) is also incorrect. Because you are required to set INDENTITY_INSERT to ON and you must pass the values by name and not position, so (a) and (d) are the correct answers.

6.) Because the code in (a) does not set IDENTITY_INSERT ON for the Products table, it is incorrect. Since the ALTER TABLE statement in (c) and the ALTER DATABASE statement in (d) will both return errors they are not correct either. Because you are required to set INDENTITY_INSERT to ON, pass the values by name and not position, then set IDENTITY_INSERT to OFF immediately afterwards, (b) is the correct answer.

7.) Because the = and IN operators require an exact match, both (a) and (b) do not work. Since NOT does not use parentheses, (d) is not correct either. NULL must be used with IS, making (c) the correct answer.

8.) ROUND (2.94, 1) will return a value rounded to the first decimal place (2.90), so (b) is incorrect. ROUND (2.94, 2) will return a value rounded to the second decimal place (2.94), so (c) is also incorrect. To round to the nearest whole number use zero (0) as the precision parameter of the ROUND function, as in ROUND (3.00, 0), which makes (a) correct.

9.) The code in (a) does not sort on the concatenated field. The ORDER BY on FullName in (b) makes this the correct answer.

Bug Catcher Game

To play the Bug Catcher game, run the SQLQueries2012Vol2BugCatcher03.pps file from the BugCatcher folder of the companion files. These files are available from the www.Joes2Pros.com website.

[THIS PAGE INTENTIONALLY LEFT BLANK.]

Chapter 4.　Aggregating Data

If the term "aggregating data" sends you running for the dictionary, relax – it's just fancy geek speak that means "totaling data". Even if your only exposure to the database world is what you know so far from your Joes2Pros books, you are aware that databases can contain tens of millions of records and track a huge number of transactions and details. So knowing how to accurately total, subtotal and "slice and dice" data is actually serious business. Decision makers and managers rely on database professionals and SQL Server analysts to be the definitive experts who originate, store and retrieve their valuable data.

SQL Server's data aggregating functions do the magic of turning mountains of transaction detail into meaningful information. Viewing raw detail in tables can be interesting, but that detail becomes actionable information to decision makers only when it reports things like: 1) January's sales amounts, 2) the percent of sales in California versus all regions, 3) the performance of Product A versus Product B, or 4) yearly sales broken down to show which regional team made more sales. This chapter gets you acquainted with these powerful functions.

READER NOTE: *Please run the SQLQueries2012Vol2Chapter4.0Setup.sql script in order to follow along with the examples in the first section of Chapter 4. All scripts mentioned in this chapter are available at www.Joes2Pros.com.*

Using GROUP BY

The GROUP BY statement does just what the name implies – it groups the results of your query by one or more columns, so that you may apply an aggregate function. Here are the most common aggregate functions you will encounter in your SQL Server journey:

- o **COUNT**(expression) - number of matching records (per group)
- o **SUM**(expression) - sum of given values (per group)
- o **MIN**(expression) - minimum of given values (per group)
- o **MAX**(expression) - maximum of given values (per group)
- o **AVG**(expression) - average of given values (per group)

You want to become an expert at using GROUP BY. Since there's no other way in SQL Server to aggregate numerical data (like prices, grant amounts, or salary data), the GROUP BY statement will be a permanent fixture in your SQL Server work.

GROUP BY with SUM()

Let's begin by looking at JProCo's current Grants. Seven employees successfully solicited 10 grants, with one person (EmpID 7) procuring three. One grant was unsolicited, so the EmpID is NULL because no employee is associated with it.

```
SELECT EmpID, GrantName, Amount
FROM [Grant]
ORDER BY EmpID
```

	EmpID	GrantName	Amount
1	NULL	Norman's Outreach	21000.00
2	2	K_Land fund trust	15750.00
3	3	TALTA_Kishan International	18100.00
4	4	BIG 6's Foundation%	21000.00
5	5	Call Mom @Com	7500.00
6	7	92 Purr_Scents %% team	4750.00
7	7	Robert@BigStarBank.com	18100.00
8	7	www.@-Last-U-Can-Help.com	25000.00
9	10	Ben@MoreTechnology.com	41000.00
10	11	Thank you @.com	21500.00

10 rows

Figure 4.1 The Grant table is showing the EmpID associated with each grant.

If we wanted to show the total grant amount each employee obtained, we first need to GROUP BY EmpID in order to apply the aggregate function SUM.

```
SELECT EmpID, SUM(Amount)
FROM [Grant]
GROUP BY EmpID
```

	EmpID	(No column name)
1	NULL	21000.00
2	2	15750.00
3	3	18100.00
4	4	21000.00
5	5	7500.00
6	7	47850.00

8 rows

Figure 4.2 Grouping on the EmpID field lets us SUM total grant amount values found by employees.

GROUP BY with COUNT()

Let's stay with the Grant table and instead, show the number of grants each employee has obtained so far (Figure 4.3).

```
SELECT EmpID, COUNT(Amount)
FROM [Grant]
GROUP BY EmpID
```

	EmpID	(No column name)
1	NULL	1
2	2	1
3	3	1
4	4	1
5	5	1
6	7	3

8 rows

Figure 4.3 The COUNT function shows the number of grants each employee procured.

On a side note, we could have counted using any field in the Grant table besides EmpID (GrantID, GrantName, or Amount) and gotten the same result. This is because the COUNT(expression) function counts the number of records where the expression is NOT NULL. (In Figure 4.3 we specified Amount as the field to count on.) Database analysts often use identity fields (e.g., GrantID) for counting. Here we've chosen Amount for practice, since we can use all our aggregate functions (COUNT, SUM, MIN, MAX, and AVG) on this field.

GROUP BY with MAX()

Next we'll use the MAX function to show the highest grant for each employee (Figure 4.4).

```
SELECT EmpID, MAX(Amount)
FROM [Grant]
GROUP BY EmpID
```

	EmpID	(No column name)
1	NULL	21000.00
2	2	15750.00
3	3	18100.00
4	4	21000.00
5	5	7500.00
6	7	25000.00

8 rows

Figure 4.4 The MAX function shows the largest grant each employee obtained.

Recall most employees obtained a single grant. For them, the highest grant amount is the same as the amount of their grant. But for the employee (EmpID 7) who secured three grants, the MAX function tells us his highest grant was $25,000.

Suppose we want to add one more field to our query, in order to see the name of each employee's highest grant alongside the grant amount (Figure 4.5).

```
SELECT EmpID, GrantName, MAX(Amount)
FROM [Grant]
GROUP BY EmpID
```

Messages
Msg 8120, Level 16, State 1, Line 1
Column 'Grant.GrantName' is invalid in the select list because it is not
contained in either an aggregate function or the GROUP BY clause.

0 rows

Figure 4.5 All non-aggregated fields in the SELECT list must appear in the GROUP BY statement.

The error message shown in Figure 4.5 illustrates an important rule for GROUP BY statements. The GROUP BY statement must include every non-aggregated field from your SELECT statement.

Figure 4.6 shows how the modified code ran with all non-aggregated fields from the SELECT statement appearing in the GROUP BY. It runs successfully, but look closely at the data. Adding the grant name detail disaggregated our result, which is not what we intended (Figure 4.6).

Results | Messages

	EmpID	(No column name)	GrantName
1	7	4750.00	92 Purr_Scents %% team ←
2	10	41000.00	Ben@MoreTechnology.com
3	4	21000.00	BIG 6's Foundation%
4	5	7500.00	Call Mom @Com
5	2	15750.00	K_Land fund trust
6	NULL	21000.00	Norman's Outreach
7	7	18100.00	Robert@BigStarBank.com ←
8	3	18100.00	TALTA_Kishan International
9	11	21500.00	Thank you @.com
10	7	25000.00	www.@-Last-U-Can-Help.com ←

Query executed successfully. | RENO (11.0 RTM) | Reno\Student (51) | JProCo | 00:00:00 | 10 rows

Figure 4.6 The code runs, but our data is now disaggregated.

When working with aggregate functions, keep an eye on your result. By trying to show too much detail, we can inadvertently undo the good effect the aggregate function has in your report. In Chapter 5, we will learn ways to include both aggregation and detail in our reports.

Drop the following code into a new query window to view the highest price in each of JProCo's product categories:

```
SELECT Category, COUNT(ProductID), MAX(RetailPrice)
FROM CurrentProducts
GROUP BY Category
```

The following code includes optional finishing touches, which improve the appearance of your report. The column headers have descriptive names and prices are rounded to the penny.

```
SELECT Category,
COUNT(ProductID) AS [ProductID Count],
ROUND(MAX(RetailPrice), 2) AS [High Price]
FROM CurrentProducts
GROUP BY Category
```

	Category	ProductID Count	High Price
1	LongTerm-Stay	162	1695.00
2	Medium-Stay	161	875.00
3	No-Stay	80	129.01
4	Overnight-Stay	80	232.22

4 rows

Figure 4.7 Improving our MAX price report with column names and rounding.

Counting Records vs. Counting Values

Earlier we saw the behavior of the Count function with an expression field (see section "GROUP BY With Count"). In the Figure 4.3 example, the function counted the number of records where the value in the field specified (Grant.Amount) was NOT NULL. COUNT(*) is another use of COUNT and counts all records, including NULLs:

- COUNT(*FieldName*) counts all records found where a field is NOT NULL
- Count(*) counts all records found in any fields (even if they are NULL)

To demonstrate the different behaviors of these two aggregate functions, we need sample data which includes several NULL values. Let's start with JProCo's locations and employees. We know there is an unoccupied location (Chicago), with a salesperson (John Marshbank) who travels and has no fixed office location.

```
--The base query before grouping or aggregation
SELECT *
FROM Employee AS emp
FULL OUTER JOIN Location as loc
ON emp.LocationID = loc.LocationID
```

In Figure 4.8 the FULL OUTER JOIN is the tool that shows all unmatched records. All the NULL Location values for John Marshbank say "there is no relationship between John Marshbank and a location". Chicago's NULL values on the Employee side of the result tell a similar story, "Chicago has no relationship with any JProCo employee".

	EmpID	LastName	FirstName	HireDate	LocationID	ManagerID	Status	LocationID	Street	City	State
1	1	Adams	Alex	2001-01-01 ...	1	11	Active	1	111 First ST	Seattle	WA
2	2	Brown	Barry	2002-08-12 ...	1	11	Active	1	111 First ST	Seattle	WA
3	3	Osako	Lee	1999-09-01 ...	2	11	Active	2	222 Second AVE	Boston	MA
4	4	Kennson	David	1996-03-16 ...	1	11	Has Tenure	1	111 First ST	Seattle	WA
5	5	Bender	Eric	2007-05-17 ...	1	11	Active	1	111 First ST	Seattle	WA
6	6	Kendall	Lisa	2001-11-15 ...	4	4	Active	4	444 Ruby ST	Spokane	WA
7	7	Lonning	David	2000-01-01 ...	1	11	On Leave	1	111 First ST	Seattle	WA
8	8	Marshbank	John	2001-11-15 ...	NULL	4	Active	NULL	NULL	NULL	NULL
9	9	Newton	James	2003-09-30 ...	2	3	Active	2	222 Second AVE	Boston	MA
10	10	O'Haire	Terry	2004-10-04 ...	2	3	Active	2	222 Second AVE	Boston	MA
11	11	Smith	Sally	1989-04-01 ...	1	NULL	Active	1	111 First ST	Seattle	WA
12	12	O'Neil	Barbara	1995-05-26 ...	4	4	Has Tenure	4	444 Ruby ST	Spokane	WA
13	13	Wilconkinski	Phil	2009-06-11 ...	1	4	Active	1	111 First ST	Seattle	WA
14	NULL	NULL	NULL	NULL	NULL	NULL	NULL	3	333 Third PL	Chicago	IL

Query executed successfully.   RENO (11.0 RTM) | Reno\Student (51) | JProCo | 00:00:00 | 14 rows

Figure 4.8 The unmatched query shows no relationship between John Marshbank and Location. No relationship between Chicago and Employee.

Now we add grouping and aggregated COUNT fields (Figure 4.9). We know COUNT(*) will look at each city grouping (Boston, Chicago, etc.) and count its records, including NULL values. COUNT(*) finds three records in the Boston group, one in the Chicago group, seven in the Seattle group and so on. A NULL City group is listed because John Marshbank has no location.

Consider the different result produced by COUNT(FirstName), which counts values. In this case, COUNT looks at each city grouping and counts the records where the value of FirstName isn't NULL. It finds three records in the Boston group, seven in Seattle, two in Spokane, etc. Since FirstName in the Chicago record is NULL, COUNT(FirstName) shows zero records for the Chicago group. For the NULL City group, it finds one record (John Marshbank).

```
SELECT City,
COUNT(*),
COUNT(FirstName)
FROM Employee AS emp
FULL OUTER JOIN Location AS loc
ON emp.LocationID = loc.LocationID
GROUP BY City
```

	City	(No column name)	(No column name)
1	NULL	1	1
2	Boston	3	3
3	Chicago	1	0
4	Seattle	7	7
5	Spokane	2	2

5 rows

Figure 4.9 Counting records (middle field) versus counting values (right field).

The following two queries show that COUNT(*) finds 10 records in the Grant table. COUNT(EmpID) finds nine records where the value of EmpID is not NULL. Recall JProCo currently has 10 grants, each averaging $19,370. Nine are associated with an EmpID because they were found by employees. However, one grant has a NULL EmpID because Norman's Outreach used JProCo's web form to submit an unsolicited grant (Figure 4.10).

```
SELECT COUNT(*) AS CountRecords,
AVG(Amount)
FROM [Grant]

SELECT COUNT(EmpID) AS CountValues,
AVG(Amount)
FROM [Grant]
```

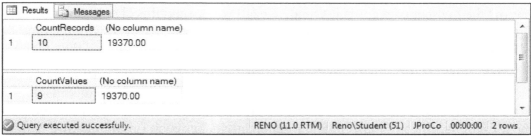

Figure 4.10 JProCo has 10 grants, each averaging $19,370.

Note that the AVG(Amount) is the same for both queries since it is the average over the entire table, even when the EmpID is NULL (Figure 4.10).

```
SELECT emp.EmpID,
COUNT(*) AS CountRecords,
COUNT(GrantName) AS CountValues
FROM Employee AS emp
FULL OUTER JOIN [Grant] AS gr
ON emp.EmpID =gr.EmpID
GROUP BY emp.EmpID
```

	EmpID	CountRecords	CountValues
1	1	1	0
2	2	1	1
3	3	1	1
4	4	1	1
5	5	1	1
6	6	1	0
7	7	3	3
8	8	1	0
9	9	1	0
10	10	1	1
11	11	1	1
12	12	1	0
13	13	1	0
14	NULL	1	1

14 rows

Figure 4.11 Another view of grants and employees counting records vs. counting fields.

A related view of grants and employees appears in Figure 4.11. When counting values, COUNT(GrantName) looks through each EmpID and counts records where GrantName isn't NULL. Add up the figures in the CountValues column to get the expected total of 10. All 10 grants have grant names – no grant is nameless. For each EmpID with a non-NULL GrantName, the COUNT function

171

returns the number of records it found. Recall we opened this chapter looking at the Grant table and observing that seven employees were involved with the nine solicited grants. One individual (EmpID 7) obtained three grants, and the other six each obtained one.

Now look at the CountRecords column, where COUNT(*) found 16 records in our unmatched query results (FULL OUTER JOIN). It counted one record for most EmpIDs, since our GROUP BY statement makes each EmpID its own group. For EmpID 7, COUNT(*) found three records. And since Norman's Outreach (the grant not associated with any employee) adds a NULL EmpID record to our results, COUNT(*) counts that as one record in the NULL EmpID group.

Multiple Level Grouping

We can have more than one field in our GROUP BY statement. In fact, an earlier example explained that the GROUP BY statement sometimes requires you to list additional fields.

The GROUP BY statement must include every non-aggregated field from your SELECT statement, or else SQL Server generates an error message. In other words, you must group on all non-aggregated fields which appear in your SELECT statement.

Suppose we wanted to create a quick tally of employees and how many grants each person obtained. With just 10 grants and 13 employees, this should be an easy query.

We'll need to use an outer join on the Employee table, since some employees haven't yet obtained grants. Alongside the number of grants, we'll list just first name for this informal tally sheet.

```
SELECT emp.FirstName,
COUNT(GrantID) AS GrantCount
FROM Employee AS emp
LEFT OUTER JOIN [Grant] AS gr
ON emp.EmpID =gr.EmpID
GROUP BY FirstName
```

	FirstName	GrantCount
1	Alex	0
2	Barbara	0
3	Barry	1
4	David	4
5	Eric	1
6	James	0

12 rows

Figure 4.12 Grouping by just FirstName lumps together David Kennson & David Lonning.

We run the query and spot an unexpected result (Figure 4.12). The four jumps out as an odd number – we know the most anyone obtained was three grants. Then we remember there are two employees named "David".

```
SELECT FirstName, LastName,
COUNT(GrantID) AS GrantCount
FROM Employee AS emp
LEFT OUTER JOIN [Grant] AS gr
ON emp.EmpID =gr.EmpID
GROUP BY FirstName, LastName
```

	FirstName	LastName	GrantCount
1	Alex	Adams	0
2	Eric	Bender	1
3	Barry	Brown	1
4	Lisa	Kendall	0
5	David	Kennson	1
6	David	Lonning	3
7	John	Marshbank	0
8	James	Newton	0
9	Terry	O'Haire	1
10	Barbara	O'Neil	0
11	Lee	Osako	1
12	Sally	Smith	1
13	Phil	Wilconkinski	0

13 rows

Figure 4.13 Grouping by FirstName and LastName shows all 13 employees and their grants

To fix the flaw in our query, we add the LastName to the SELECT statement and the GROUP BY statement. Each David now shows in the tally with his respective number of grants.

Note that our query is grouping on multiple levels: by FirstName and LastName.

Finally, let's join the Employee and Location tables in another unmatched query (FULL OUTER JOIN). Group on State to get the count of JProCo employees working in each state. The result shows the number of employees working in each state, as well as our sales employee with no fixed location (Figure 4.14).

```
SELECT State, COUNT(FirstName)
FROM Employee AS E
FULL OUTER JOIN Location AS L
ON E.LocationID = L.LocationID
GROUP BY State
```

	State	(No column name)
1	NULL	1
2	IL	0
3	MA	3
4	WA	9

4 rows

Figure 4.14 The COUNT of employees by State.

```
SELECT State, COUNT(FirstName)
FROM Employee AS E
FULL OUTER JOIN Location AS L
ON E.LocationID = L.LocationID
GROUP BY State
ORDER BY State DESC
```

	State	(No column name)
1	WA	9
2	MA	3
3	IL	0
4	NULL	1

4 rows

Figure 4.15 The Sorting rows using ORDER BY.

```
SELECT State, COUNT(FirstName)
FROM Employee AS E
FULL OUTER JOIN Location AS L
ON E.LocationID = L.LocationID
GROUP BY State
ORDER BY COUNT(FirstName) DESC
```

	State	(No column name)
1	WA	9
2	MA	3
3	NULL	1
4	IL	0
		4 rows

Figure 4.16 Employee counts are shown in descending order by state.

Add an ORDER BY clause to organize the list in reverse alphabetical order by state. Lastly, revise the ORDER BY clause to organize the list in descending order of employee count.

Take a moment to notice the different behavior of the ORDER BY clause when used with GROUP BY and aggregate functions. Similar to the restrictions on items allowed by the GROUP BY statement, here the ORDER BY clause can accept only the aggregate function(s) or fields appearing in the GROUP BY statement.

If an expression is used in the GROUP BY and you want that same expression to show in the SELECT list then it must be listed the same way in both clauses. If the expression has an alias in the SELECT clause, the alias can be used in the ORDER BY. An alias cannot be used in a GROUP BY.

The following error (Figure 4.17) was produced by attempting to ORDER BY a field not included in the GROUP BY statement and not an aggregate function. Recall we previously used ORDER BY to sort results by any field contained in a query, even when the field does not display in the result (i.e., is not listed in the SELECT statement) (See Chapter 2 topic "Sorting Hidden Results").

```
SELECT State, COUNT(FirstName)
FROM Employee E
FULL OUTER JOIN Location L
ON E.LocationID = L.LocationID
GROUP BY State
ORDER BY FirstName DESC
```

Messages
Msg 8127, Level 16, State 1, Line 6
Column "Employee.FirstName" is invalid in the ORDER BY clause because it is
not contained in either an aggregate function or the GROUP BY clause.
0 rows

Figure 4.17 ORDER BY behaves differently when used with GROUP BY and aggregate functions.

Lab 4.1: Using GROUP BY

Lab Prep: Each lab has one or more Skill Checks. Start with Skill Check 1 and proceed until reaching the Points to Ponder section.

Before beginning this lab, verify that SQL Server 2012 is properly installed and operating. Before running the lab setup script for resetting the database (SQLQueries2012Vol2Chapter4.1Setup.sql), please make sure to close all query windows within SSMS. An open query window pointing to a database context can lock that database preventing it from updating when the script is executing. A simple way to assure all query windows are closed, is to exit out of SSMS, then open a new instance of SSMS, and lastly run the setup script.

Skill Check 1: Query the Employee table of JProCo to see how many people work for each ManagerID. Select the ManagerID and Count the EmpID field. Alias the field as EmpIDCount. When you're done, your result should resemble the figure you see here (Figure 4.18).

	ManagerID	EmpIDCount
1	NULL	1
2	3	2
3	4	4
4	11	6

Query executed successfully. RENO (11.0 RTM) Reno\Student (53) JProCo 00:00:00 4 rows

Figure 4.18 Skill Check 1 displays the count of people associated with each ManagerID.

Skill Check 2: Perform a grouping query on the Customer table to get a count of how many consumers versus Business customers you have. Alias the field as CustomerCount. Group on the CustomerType field. When you're done your result should resemble the figure you see here (Figure 4.19).

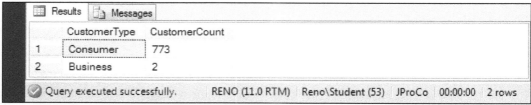

	CustomerType	CustomerCount
1	Consumer	773
2	Business	2

Query executed successfully. RENO (11.0 RTM) Reno\Student (53) JProCo 00:00:00 2 rows

Figure 4.19 Group on CustomerType to show numbers of Consumer vs. Business customers.

Skill Check 3: Get a list of all Customers and how many Invoice orders each one has placed. You will need to join the Customer and SalesInvoice tables. Alias the aggregated field as InvoiceIDCount. If a Customer has not ordered yet, then you should still see their name with a zero next to it. Hint: this will require an OUTER JOIN between Customer and SalesInvoice (Figure 4.20). Your results should have 775 records.

	CustomerID	FirstName	LastName	InvoiceIDCount
1	1	Mark	Williams	3
2	2	Lee	Young	1
3	3	Patricia	Martin	3
4	4	Mary	Lopez	2
5	5	NULL	NULL	0
6	6	Ruth	Clark	0

Query executed successfully.   RENO (11.0 RTM)   Reno\Student (53)   JProCo   00:00:00   775 rows

Figure 4.20 Skill Check 3 shows each customer and the COUNT of their invoices.

Skill Check 4: Make a slight modification to Skill Check 3 so that only Customers who have placed at least one order appear in the query (Hint: change the type of join). Notice CustomerID 5 does not appear in this result.

	CustomerID	FirstName	LastName	InvoiceIDCount
1	1	Mark	Williams	3
2	2	Lee	Young	1
3	3	Patricia	Martin	3
4	4	Mary	Lopez	2
5	7	Tessa	Wright	1
6	8	Jennifer	Garcia	2

Query executed successfully.   RENO (11.0 RTM)   Reno\Student (53)   JProCo   00:00:00   711 rows

Figure 4.21 Skill Check 4 shows only customers who placed at least one order.

Answer Code: The T-SQL code for this lab is located in the downloadable files as a file named Lab4.1_UsingGroupBy.sql.

Points to Ponder - GROUP BY

1. The GROUP BY clause summarizes data on a field or group of fields.

2. The GROUP BY clause must include all non-aggregated fields listed in the SELECT statement.

3. Using COUNT(*FieldName*) will count the number of records found where that field is NOT NULL.

4. Using COUNT(*) counts all records found in any fields, including NULLs.

5. An aggregated query can be sorted by placing an ORDER BY clause at the end of the query statement.

6. ORDER BY, if used, is always the last keyword in a query statement.

7. In a GROUP BY query, ORDER BY must choose from the fields in the SELECT list.

8. When using aggregated functions in a SELECT list, such as SUM(), or COUNT(), they must have supporting aggregated language. This chapter shows how to accomplish this with a GROUP BY clause.

Aggregation Criteria

At this point, take a moment to congratulate yourself. In this chapter you've covered a wealth of material and have quickly ramped up on data aggregation concepts. We are now comfortable seeing and writing aggregate functions (COUNT(), SUM(), MIN(), MAX(), and AVG()) in our queries.

The next two sections layer a few helpful techniques on top of the impressive foundation you've forged in your understanding of data grouping and aggregation.

This section is all about filtering criteria. Back when we first learned simple filtering techniques (WHERE, ORDER BY), we instantly gained more control over the content and ordering of our simple query results. The filtering techniques which follow are sharp tools which will enable us to produce more precise and customized information from our robust queries.

The HAVING Clause

The HAVING clause allows you to filter your aggregated results.

Let's begin with the Employee table. We want a list of locations with more than two employees.

```
--list of locations and their employee counts
SELECT LocationID, COUNT(*)
FROM Employee
GROUP BY LocationID
```

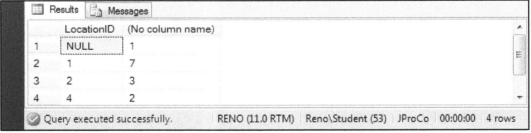

Figure 4.22 This shows a list of locations and their employee counts

```
--list of locations and their employee counts
SELECT LocationID, COUNT(*)
FROM Employee
WHERE COUNT(*) > 2    --WHERE clause won't work
GROUP BY LocationID   --with aggregated fields
```

Try running the code sample above and notice the error SQL Server shows. Our basic syntax and idea are on the right track, but it's the HAVING clause we need in order to filter aggregated results. Locations 1 and 2 (Seattle, Boston) both have more than two employees (Figure 4.23).

```
SELECT LocationID, COUNT(*)
FROM Employee
GROUP BY LocationID
HAVING COUNT(*) > 2
```

	LocationID	(No column name)
1	1	7
2	2	3

2 rows

Figure 4.23 The HAVING clause allows you to filter your aggregated results.

The majority of JProCo's employees are based in Seattle, WA. First run a query showing the employee count for all states which have a JProCo location (even if that location does not yet contain employees). Filter your final result to answer the question, "How many total employees are located in Washington State?"

Let's start by assembling a basic query before adding GROUP BY and COUNT. We should Use an OUTER JOIN since some locations may not have employees and some employees may not have a location:

```
--Step 1
SELECT State, emp.FirstName
FROM Location AS loc
FULL OUTER JOIN Employee AS emp
ON loc.LocationID = emp.LocationID
```

Next lets GROUP BY Loc.State and instead of listing the FirstName values let's COUNT the emp.FirstName values:

```
--Step 2
SELECT loc.State, COUNT(emp.FirstName)
FROM Location AS loc
FULL OUTER JOIN Employee AS emp
ON loc.LocationID = emp.LocationID
GROUP BY loc.State
```

Lastly, we need to filter down to just WA State. Let's use a WHERE clause and set loc.State equal to WA:

```
--Step 3
SELECT loc.State, COUNT(emp.FirstName)
FROM Location AS loc
FULL OUTER JOIN Employee AS emp
ON loc.LocationID = emp.LocationID
WHERE loc.State = 'WA'
GROUP BY loc.State
```

Run the WA state example in SQL Server and see the second query answered our question – one of the records told us there are nine employees in WA. In our prior work, we would have declared victory and stopped there. But we went one step further in narrowing down our result to show only the precise information we wanted (Figure 4.24).

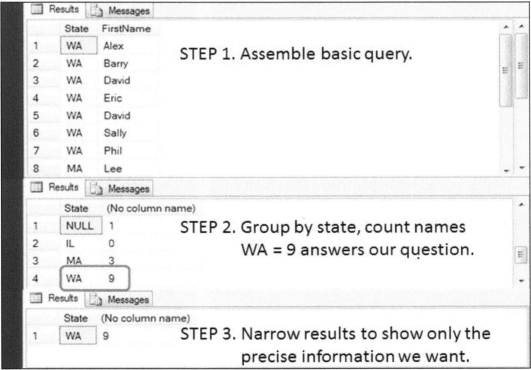

Figure 4.24 Our final result shows only the precise information we want.

Using what we've learned, let's create a list that shows just those states having more than two JProCo employees (Figure 4.25).

```
SELECT loc.[State], COUNT(emp.FirstName)
FROM Location AS Loc
FULL OUTER JOIN Employee AS emp
ON Loc.LocationID = emp.LocationID
GROUP BY loc.State
HAVING COUNT(emp.FirstName) > 2
```

	State	(No column name)
1	MA	3
2	WA	9

2 rows

Figure 4.25 Filtering with the HAVING clause shows just the information you specify.

Here we could have achieved the same result with the same FULL OUTER JOIN we used earlier. (Take a moment to ponder why that is true. Be curious and try the query both ways in SQL Server.) . Notice that the HAVING clause must refer to the aggregated field and can't refer to the field alias of empCount.

Next, we'll put our new filtering abilities to work on an example involving employees and the grants amounts they have obtained.

```
--Assemble basic query without group, aggregate function
SELECT FirstName, LastName, Amount
FROM Employee AS emp
INNER JOIN [Grant] AS gra
ON emp.EmpID = gra.EmpID
```

You will notice our basic query lists all the grant amounts and employees who found them. If an employee found more than one grant, the employee will be listed multiple times. David Lonning appears three times, once for each of his grants (Figure 4.26).

```
SELECT FirstName, LastName, Amount
FROM Employee AS emp
INNER JOIN [Grant] AS gra
ON emp.EmpID = gra.EmpID
```

	FirstName	LastName	Amount
1	David	Lonning	4750.00
2	Barry	Brown	15750.00
3	David	Lonning	18100.00
4	David	Kennson	21000.00
5	Lee	Osako	18100.00
6	Terry	O'Haire	41000.00
7	David	Lonning	25000.00
			9 rows

Figure 4.26 David Lonning appears three times because he found three grants.

Let's aggregate the results by summing multiple grants and double grouping on FirstName and LastName. We want to see each employee once in this list alongside the total of each employee's grants (Figure 4.27).

```
SELECT emp.FirstName, emp.LastName, SUM(Amount)
FROM Employee AS emp
INNER JOIN [Grant] AS gra
ON emp.EmpID = gra.EmpID
GROUP BY FirstName, LastName
```

	FirstName	LastName	(No column name)
1	Eric	Bender	7500.00
2	Barry	Brown	15750.00
3	David	Kennson	21000.00
4	David	Lonning	47850.00
5	Terry	O'Haire	41000.00
6	Lee	Osako	18100.00
7	Sally	Smith	21500.00
			7 rows

Figure 4.27 David Lonning appears just once along with the sum of his three grants.

Now narrow down the list to employees having total grants that exceed $40,000 (Figure 4.28).

```
SELECT FirstName, LastName, SUM(Amount)
FROM Employee AS emp
INNER JOIN [Grant] AS gra
ON emp.EmpID = gra.EmpID
GROUP BY FirstName, LastName
HAVING SUM(Amount) > 40000
```

	FirstName	LastName	(No column name)
1	David	Lonning	47850.00
2	Terry	O'Haire	41000.00

2 rows

Figure 4.28 The list now includes only those employees having more than $40,000 in grants.

WHERE clause in Aggregated Queries

Think back to the previous grant example. It's important to be clear on David Lonning's grant profile versus that of Terry O'Haire. Terry obtained one $41,000 grant, whereas David obtained three grants (ranging from $4750 to $25,000) which sum to $47,850. Using HAVING with the aggregate function includes single records in the group (FirstName, LastName) with an Amount >40000 OR a group (FirstName, LastName) of records whose Sum >40000.

We can use a WHERE clause in an aggregated query, you just can't use it on an aggregated field. In earlier examples we intentionally caused an error to underscore the latter point (we attempted WHERE COUNT(*) >2 to filter locations with more than 2 employees). But we easily could have included a WHERE clause to filter location in one of the aggregated query examples.

```
SELECT LocationID, COUNT(*)
FROM Employee
WHERE LocationID != 3
GROUP BY LocationID
HAVING COUNT(*) > 2
```

Contrast the following query using a WHERE clause with the result shown back in Figure 4.28.

```
SELECT FirstName, LastName, SUM(Amount)
FROM Employee AS emp
INNER JOIN [Grant] AS gra
ON emp.EmpID = gra.EmpID
WHERE Amount > 40000
GROUP BY FirstName, LastName
```

	FirstName	LastName	(No column name)
1	Terry	O'Haire	41000.00

| | | | 1 rows |

Figure 4.29 The WHERE clause allows only single records with Amount > $40,000.

If the intent was to limit results to just single grants exceeding $40,000, then this is the right query to use. A common mistake would be to attempt this WHERE clause hoping to achieve the same result as shown in Figure 4.28.

Using DISTINCT

DISTINCT and GROUP BY are very powerful querying tools. Most times you use them separately, but there are occasions where you will use them together. Let's look at all the records in JProCo's Customer table.

```
SELECT * FROM Customer
```

	CustomerID	CustomerType	FirstName	LastName	CompanyName
1	1	Consumer	Mark	Williams	NULL
2	2	Consumer	Lee	Young	NULL
3	3	Consumer	Patricia	Martin	NULL
4	4	Consumer	Mary	Lopez	NULL
5	5	Business	NULL	NULL	MoreTechnology.com
6	6	Consumer	Ruth	Clark	NULL

| | | | | | 775 rows |

Figure 4.30 JProCo has 775 customers showing in the Customer table.

This section is about achieving more specific result outputs, so let's narrow down to just those customers who purchased from JProCo in 2006. Join the SalesInvoice table to the Customer table and then filter the list on purchases with an OrderDate in calendar year 2006.

READER NOTE: *By going from midnight on January 1st 2009 to the final second leading up to midnight January 1st 2010 we get all the records for 2009. Figure 4.31 gets exactly one year's worth of data.*

```
SELECT *
FROM Customer AS cu
INNER JOIN SalesInvoice AS sv
ON cu.CustomerID = sv.CustomerID
WHERE OrderDate >= '1/1/2009' AND OrderDate < '1/1/2010'
```

	CustomerID	CustomerType	FirstName	LastName	CompanyName	InvoiceID	OrderDate	PaidDate	CustomerID	Comment
1	8	Consumer	Jennifer	Garcia	NULL	161	2009-05-14 ...	2009-06-07...	8	NULL
2	9	Consumer	Linda	Adams	NULL	425	2009-12-24 ...	2010-02-08...	9	NULL
3	12	Consumer	Helen	Hernandez	NULL	316	2009-09-21 ...	2009-10-14...	12	NULL
4	12	Consumer	Helen	Hernandez	NULL	318	2009-09-22 ...	2009-11-08...	12	NULL
5	12	Consumer	Helen	Hernandez	NULL	69	2009-03-01 ...	2009-03-25...	12	NULL
6	15	Consumer	Anthony	Scott	NULL	350	2009-10-18 ...	2009-11-25...	15	NULL

Query executed successfully. RENO (11.0 RTM) Reno\Student (51) JProCo 00:00:00 438 rows

Figure 4.31 JProCo has 438 customer purchases showing for 2009.

Our initial SELECT statements showed 775 Customer records and 1877 SalesInvoice records. Now the result set has narrowed to 438 customer purchase records for 2009, so this is progress.

Run this query in SQL Server and look at the table data. If you look at your own results and scroll you will notice customers like Helen Hernandez, Daniel Nelson and William Green have multiple records indicating they purchased multiple times. If we wanted to send a special mailer to 2009 customers, this list wouldn't work because of the repeat instances of the same customer. Sending five mailers to one customer not only is wasteful but makes JProCo seem like an organization that has trouble managing its data.

Figure 4.32 demonstrates SELECT DISTINCT achieving our goal. There is just one instance of each 2009 customer in the list.

```
SELECT DISTINCT cu.*
FROM Customer AS cu
INNER JOIN SalesInvoice AS sv
ON cu.CustomerID = sv.CustomerID
WHERE OrderDate BETWEEN '1/1/2009' AND '1/1/2010'
```

	CustomerID	CustomerType	FirstName	LastName	CompanyName
1	8	Consumer	Jennifer	Garcia	NULL
2	9	Consumer	Linda	Adams	NULL
3	12	Consumer	Helen	Hernandez	NULL
4	15	Consumer	Anthony	Scott	NULL
5	22	Consumer	George	Hall	NULL
6	26	Consumer	Sandra	Williams	NULL

333 rows

Figure 4.32 SELECT DISTINCT includes a single record for each 2009 customer.

DISTINCT can also be used with the COUNT function.

We'll continue to work with the product and sales invoice data, and we'll also want to bring in data from the SalesInvoiceDetail table.

Instead of querying the tables directly, we will write queries pulling from vSales, which is a view.

Views are like virtual tables and offer many advantages over directly querying tables, particularly in multi-user settings. While we won't study views in this book, you will frequently use views in your work with SQL Server. Views are covered in depth in the subsequent Joes2Pros book, which focuses on design and implementation.

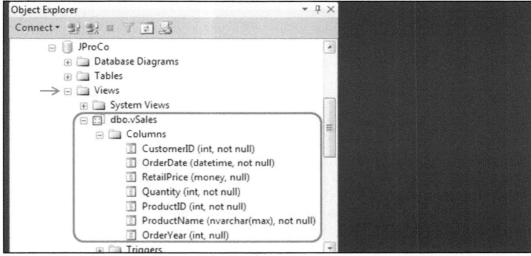

Figure 4.33 vSales appears in your Object Explorer.

In the **Views** folder of JProCo, we can see **vSales** and the columns which it contains (Figure 4.33). To peek at the code to build this view, right-click **dbo.vSales** > **Script View As** > **Create To** > **New Query Editor Window**

```
SELECT * FROM vSales
```

	CustomerID	OrderDate	RetailPrice	Quantity	ProductID	ProductName	OrderYear
1	597	2009-01-08 ...	80.859	5	7	Underwater Tour 1 Day East Coast	2009
2	736	2009-01-09 ...	80.859	2	7	Underwater Tour 1 Day East Coast	2009
3	47	2009-01-13 ...	80.859	3	7	Underwater Tour 1 Day East Coast	2009
4	251	2009-01-16 ...	80.859	4	7	Underwater Tour 1 Day East Coast	2009
5	529	2009-01-17 ...	80.859	5	7	Underwater Tour 1 Day East Coast	2009
6	151	2009-01-17 ...	80.859	5	7	Underwater Tour 1 Day East Coast	2009

Query executed successfully.   RENO (11.0 RTM)   Reno\Student (51)   JProCo   00:00:00   6960 rows

Figure 4.34 All the columns available in the virtual table (view) vSales.

As seen above (Figure 4.34), vSales contains key fields (CustomerID, OrderDate, RetailPrice, Quantity, ProductID, ProductName) for every product order sold by JProCo.

Add a counting field (CustomerID) to get a list of each ProductID that has been sold and the number of times it's been purchased (Figure 4.35).

```
SELECT ProductID, COUNT(CustomerID)
FROM vSales
GROUP BY ProductID
```

	ProductID	(No column name)
1	23	1
2	69	60
3	29	106
4	75	144
5	9	126
6	15	192

60 rows

Figure 4.35 JProCo's sales activity data grouped by product (ProductID) and showing the number of times each product has ever been purchased.

Product#23 has been purchased just once. Product#69 has been purchased 60 times (Figure 4.35). The logical next question is to want to know how many different customers actually made the purchases. Product#69 appears to be popular, but was it bought by 60 different people? Or did just three or four customers buy in bulk?

To answer these questions, we must add COUNT DISTINCT to our query. Our result shows us that Product#69 was purchased by 59 distinct customers, so only one customer made a repeat purchase of this product. Product#72 showed 142 sales in our original query, and we now see those sales were made by 132 distinct customers.

```
SELECT ProductID,
COUNT(DISTINCT CustomerID)
FROM vSales
GROUP BY ProductID
```

Results | Messages

	ProductID	(No column name)
50	68	117
51	69	59
52	70	180
53	71	151
54	72	132
55	73	135

Query executed successfully. | RENO (11.0 RTM) | Reno\Student (51) | JProCo | 00:00:00 | 60 rows

Figure 4.36 COUNT with DISTINCT shows the number of distinct customers who purchased.

Lab 4.2: Filtering Aggregated Results

Lab Prep: Each lab has one or more Skill Checks. Start with Skill Check 1 and proceed until reaching the Points to Ponder section.

Before beginning this lab, verify that SQL Server 2012 is properly installed and operating. Before running the lab setup script for resetting the database (SQLQueries2012Vol2Chapter4.2Setup.sql), please make sure to close all query windows within SSMS. An open query window pointing to a database context can lock that database preventing it from updating when the script is executing. A simple way to assure all query windows are closed, is to exit out of SSMS, then open a new instance of SSMS, and lastly run the setup script.

Skill Check 1: Using the SalesInvoice table, write a query which groups on CustomerID and counts the number of orders (also called invoices) each customer has made. Return only the records where the CustomerID has ordered more than 7 times. Show the aggregated field as OrderCount.

When done, the results should resemble Figure 4.37.

	CustomerID	OrderCount
1	252	9
2	155	9
3	388	8

3 rows

Figure 4.37 Skill Check 1 results show CustomerIDs with more than 7 orders.

Skill Check 2: Query the SalesInvoiceDetail table and show just the ProductID and InvoiceID fields. Change the query to group on ProductID and count the InvoiceID field. Return only the records where the ProductID has been ordered more than 200 times. When done the result should resemble Figure 4.38.

There is no need to join to the CurrentProducts table since we will be grouping on ProductID which is already in the SalesInvoiceDetail table.

	ProductID	InvoiceCount
1	52	236
2	49	312
3	50	222
4	70	204
5	53	309
6	51	254

6 rows

Figure 4.38 Skill Check 2 looks for products ordered more than 200 times.

Answer Code: The T-SQL code for this lab is located in the downloadable files as a file named Lab4.2_FilteringAggregatedResults.sql.

Points to Ponder - Filtering Aggregated Results

1. The HAVING clause always appears after the GROUP BY clause.

2. HAVING sets conditions on the aggregated values of the GROUP BY clause similar to the way WHERE interacts with SELECT.

3. The HAVING predicate can filter against aggregate functions. It can also filter against non-aggregated fields.

4. WHERE can only filter a single value for each individual row.

5. WHERE Sales > 100000 would find any single sales transaction totaling more than 100 grand.

6. If Tom made four separate $30,000 sales, then WHERE sales > 100000 would not show Tom in your result set.

7. HAVING SUM(Sales) > 100000 would find the grouped totals over 100 grand.

8. The DISTINCT clause is useful to show all items in your query once, regardless of how many times they are listed.

9. Use DISTINCT to eliminate duplicates or multiple listings of the same entity value when they are not relevant to your report.

10. We can combine DISTINCT and HAVING to find aggregates that don't count repeating records multiple times.

11. ORDER BY items must appear in the SELECT list if SELECT DISTINCT is specified.

Aggregation in Stored Procedures

There are parts to anything that you build. A car is made up of batteries, lights, chasses and many other items. A stored procedure is always made up from one or many statements. Aggregated queries are one of many things that can be used in stored procedures.

Creating the Aggregated query

Let's build a robust query using employee and location data. We want all four JProCo locations included, even though the Chicago office is not yet occupied (which is a hint you need an outer join).

```
SELECT loc.LocationID, COUNT(*)
FROM Location AS loc
LEFT OUTER JOIN Employee as emp
ON loc.LocationID = emp.LocationID
GROUP BY loc.LocationID
```

Let's check our result set. We want to perfect the query before we create the stored procedure which will store and reuse this code.

```
SELECT Loc.LocationID, COUNT(*)AS EmployeeCt
FROM Location AS loc
LEFT OUTER JOIN Employee AS emp
ON Loc.LocationID = emp.LocationID
GROUP BY Loc.LocationID
```

Figure 4.39 Initial build of aggregate query incorrectly shows one employee in Location 3.

Our employee counting logic isn't quite right, since we know Location 3 (Chicago) should be showing zero employees. By changing COUNT(*) to COUNT(EmpID) we are now counting the records that have values for the EmpID field. Also to make this easier to read we are putting the highest EmployeeCount sorted on the top with an ORDER BY clause.

```
SELECT Loc.LocationID,
COUNT(EmpID) AS EmployeeCount
FROM Location AS loc
LEFT OUTER JOIN Employee AS emp
ON Loc.LocationID = emp.LocationID
GROUP BY Loc.LocationID
ORDER BY COUNT(EmpID) DESC
```

	LocationID	EmployeeCount
1	1	7
2	2	3
3	4	2
4	3	0

4 rows

Figure 4.40 Testing and perfecting the query logic before creating a stored procedure.

Creating the Stored Procedure

Now we are ready to create the stored procedure, also called a sproc.

Step 1. Add keywords BEGIN and END above and below the query, then indent the query code.

```
BEGIN
  SELECT Loc.LocationID, COUNT(EmpID) AS EmployeeCt
  FROM Location AS loc
  LEFT OUTER JOIN Employee AS emp
  ON Loc.LocationID = emp.LocationID
  GROUP BY Loc.LocationID
  ORDER BY COUNT(EmpID) DESC
END
```

Step 2. Add the CREATE PROC command, sproc title and the AS keyword.

```
CREATE PROC GetLocationCount AS
BEGIN
  SELECT Loc.LocationID, COUNT(EmpID) AS EmployeeCt
  FROM Location AS loc
  LEFT OUTER JOIN Employee AS emp
  ON Loc.LocationID = emp.LocationID
  GROUP BY Loc.LocationID
  ORDER BY COUNT(EmpID) DESC
END
GO
```

READER NOTE: *we can use either "CREATE PROC" or spell out the full command "CREATE PROCEDURE" – SQL Server recognizes both terms.*

Step 3. Now run the code and be sure you see that the command completed successfully, as indicated in the Messages tab (Figure 4.41).

```
CREATE PROC GetLocationCount AS
BEGIN
  SELECT Loc.LocationID, COUNT(EmpID) AS EmployeeCount
  FROM Location AS loc
  LEFT OUTER JOIN Employee AS emp
  ON Loc.LocationID = emp.LocationID
  GROUP BY Loc.LocationID
  ORDER BY COUNT(EmpID) DESC
END
GO
```

Messages
Command(s) completed successfully.
0 rows

Figure 4.41 Step 3 – run code, confirm the command completes successfully.

Step 4. Check the Object Explorer and see the new object.

READER NOTE*: you will likely need to right-click and refresh the Databases folder to see the newly created object. SQL Server conserves resources by not automatically refreshing the Object Explorer list every time you make a change.*

Object Explorer > Databases > JProCo > Programmability > Stored Procedures

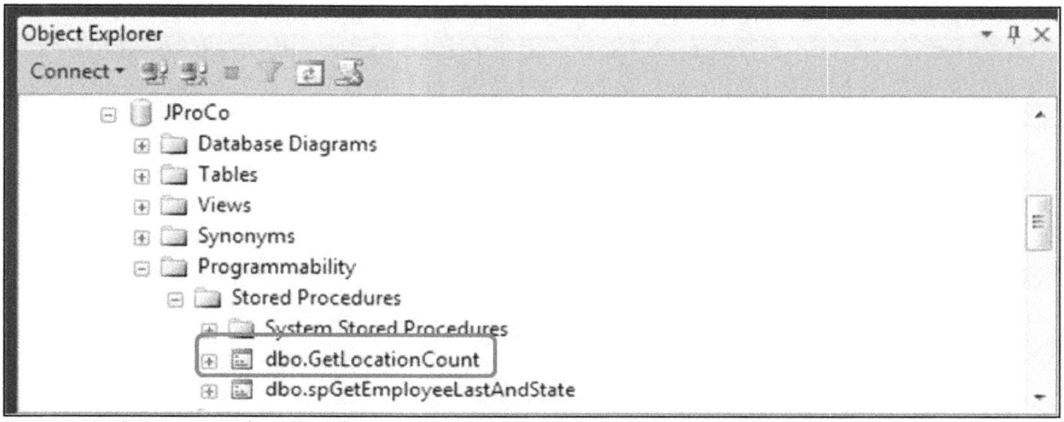

Figure 4.42 Step 4 – visualize the newly created object in the Object Explorer window.

Step 5. In a new query window, run the command EXEC GetLocationCount.

```
USE JProCo
GO

EXEC GetLocationCount
```

	LocationID	EmployeeCount
1	1	7
2	2	3
3	4	2
4	3	0

4 rows

Figure 4.43 Step 5 – running the command EXEC GetLocationCount.

Lab 4.3: Aggregation in Stored Procedures

Lab Prep: Each lab has one or more Skill Checks. Start with Skill Check 1 and proceed until reaching the Points to Ponder section.

Before beginning this lab, verify that SQL Server 2012 is properly installed and operating. Before running the lab setup script for resetting the database (SQLQueries2012Vol2Chapter4.3Setup.sql), please make sure to close all query windows within SSMS. An open query window pointing to a database context can lock that database preventing it from updating when the script is executing. A simple way to assure all query windows are closed, is to exit out of SSMS, then open a new instance of SSMS, and lastly run the setup script.

Skill Check 1: Using what you've learned, create a stored procedure called GetCategoriesByProductCount. This will join the CurrentProducts and the SalesInvoiceDetail tables and show the total number of orders for each Category.

When done, execute the stored procedure and view the results. The results should resemble those shown in Figure 4.44.

EXEC GetCategoriesByProductCount

	Category	ProductCount
1	LongTerm-Stay	2370
2	Medium-Stay	2186
3	No-Stay	1103
4	Overnight-Stay	1301

4 rows

Figure 4.44 Skill Check 1 creates the stored procedure GetCategoriesByProductCount.

Answer Code: The T-SQL code for this lab is located in the downloadable files as a file named Lab4.3_AggregationInStoredProcedures.sql.

Points to Ponder - Aggregation in Stored Procedures

1. A stored procedure can use any type of query including one that uses grouping and aggregation functions.

2. It is considered good practice to surround the body of your stored procedure with a BEGIN…END block.

3. To view newly created objects (stored procedures, tables, databases, schemas, views, etc.) in the Object Explorer, you must first refresh the Object Explorer.

Chapter Glossary

Aggregating Data: The totaling of data.

AVG(expression): The average of the given values (per group).

COUNT(*): A version of the COUNT expression that counts all records, including NULLs.

COUNT(expression): When followed by a field name this expression counts the number of records found where that field isn't NULL.

CREATE PROC: Also "Create Procedure", used to save code that will be reused.

DISTINCT: Using this clause in a query shows each item only once, eliminating duplicates and multiple listings.

GROUP BY: This statement in a query groups the results by one or more columns. The GROUP BY statement must include every non-aggregated field from your SELECT statement.

HAVING: A clause in SQL that sets conditions on aggregated values of the GROUP BY function. It can also filter against both aggregated and non-aggregated data.

MAX(expression): Maximum of given values (per group).

MIN(expression): Minimum of given values (per group).

Non-aggregated Data: Data in a result that are not totaled.

ORDER BY: A clause used in a query to organize the results displayed. If used, this is always the last keyword in a query statement. If used with a GROUP BY, the ORDER BY must choose from the fields in the SELECT list.

SELECT: A SQL command used to choose which stored data to retrieve and view as information.

Stored Procedures: A set of defined, precompiled SQL statements stored on a SQL Server; also called a sproc. A sproc can use grouping and aggregation functions.

Views: Covered more thoroughly in SQL Programming, Book 4 in the Joes2Pros series, for this chapter we will consider them to be a virtual table or version of a table.

Review Quiz - Chapter Four

1.) Which of the following is NOT true about the ORDER BY keyword?

O a. ORDER BY can go above or below the WHERE clause.

O b. ORDER BY can sort descending with the use of the DESC keyword.

O c. We can order by one or more fields in one ORDER BY clause.

O d. ORDER BY is optional.

2.) How does ORDER BY work with NULL?

O a. ORDER BY ignores NULLs in a random manner.

O b. ORDER BY puts all NULLs first in ascending order.

O c. ORDER BY puts all NULLs first in descending order.

3.) What is the appropriate placement of ORDER BY and GROUP BY in a query?

O a. ORDER BY always goes before GROUP BY.

O b. ORDER BY always goes after GROUP BY.

O c. Use them in any placement you want.

4.) Which statement(s) about WHERE and HAVING is/are true?

O a. WHERE and HAVING can both be used as criteria.

O b. WHERE and HAVING if present must be listed before the ORDER BY clause.

O c. HAVING clauses can reference any one of the items that appear in the SELECT list.

O d. WHERE can be used as criteria in aggregate operations.

O e. HAVING can be used as criteria in aggregate operations.

5.) You are writing a query that returns a list of products which have grossed more than $2,000,000 during the year 2007. Which clause allows you to filter on aggregated totals?

O a. ON

O b. WHERE

O c. HAVING

O d. GROUP BY

6.) Your JProCo database has two tables named Customer and SalesInvoice. Not all customers have placed an order yet. You would like to see a list of customers who have placed at least one order and the total number of SalesInvoice values listed next to the CompanyName. Which query should you use?

○ a.
```
SELECT CompanyName,
SUM(ord.SalesInvoicerID) AS OrderCount
FROM Customers cust
INNER JOIN SalesInvoice ord
ON cust.CustomerID = ord.CustomerID
GROUP BY CompanyName
```

○ b.
```
SELECT COUNT(Ord.SalesInvoicerID) AS OrderCount
FROM Customers Cust
INNER JOIN SalesInvoice Rod
ON Cust.CustomerID = Ord.CustomerID
```

○ c.
```
SELECT CompanyName,
SUM(Ord.SalesInvoicerID) AS OrderCount
FROM Customers Cust
INNER JOIN SalesInvoice Rod
ON Cust.CustomerID = Ord.CustomerID
GROUP BY OrderCount
```

○ d.
```
SELECT CompanyName,
COUNT(Ord.SalesInvoicerID) AS OrderCount
FROM Customers Cust
INNER JOIN SalesInvoice Rod
ON Cust.CustomerID = Ord.CustomerID
GROUP BY CompanyName
```

7.) You have a virtual table named vSales and need to list all ProductID values that have been sold to fewer than 100 different CustomerIDs. You need to write a query to help complete this report. Which query should you use?

○ a.
```
SELECT ProductID,
COUNT(DISTINCT CustomerID) AS CustomerCount
FROM vSales
GROUP BY ProductID
HAVING COUNT(CustomerID) < 100
```

○ b.
```
SELECT DISTINCT  ProductID,
COUNT(DISTINCT CustomerID) AS CustomerCount
FROM vSales
GROUP BY ProductID
HAVING COUNT(DISTINCT CustomerID) < 100
```

8.) Your database has two tables named Customers and Orders. Not all customers have placed an order yet. You would like to see a list of customers and the total number of orders listed next to the CustomerID. Which query should you use?

O a. **SELECT** COUNT(ord.OrderID) **AS** OrderCount
       FROM Customers Cust
       INNER JOIN Orders Rod
       ON Cust.CustomerID = Ord.CustomerID

O b. **SELECT** Cust.CustomerID, SUM(ord.OrderID) **AS** OrderCount
       FROM Customers Cust
       INNER JOIN Orders Rod
       ON Cust.CustomerID = Ord.CustomerID
       GROUP BY Cust.CustomerID

O c. **SELECT** Cust.CustomerID, COUNT(Ord.OrderID) **AS** OrderCount
       FROM Customers Cust
       INNER JOIN Orders Rod
       ON Cust.CustomerID = Ord.CustomerID
       GROUP BY Cust.CustomerID

9.) You have a table named Orders. You need to produce a report listing customers that have placed more than 7 orders. Which query should you use?

O a. **SELECT** CustomerID, COUNT(OrderID) **AS** CustomerCount
       FROM dbo.orders
       GROUP BY CustomerID
       HAVING COUNT(OrderID) > **7**

O b. **SELECT** CustomerID, COUNT(OrderID) **AS** CustomerCount
       FROM dbo.orders
       GROUP BY CustomerID
       HAVING SUM(OrderID) > **7**

O c. **SELECT** CustomerID, COUNT(OrderID) **AS** CustomerCount
       FROM dbo.orders
       GROUP BY CustomerID
       WHERE COUNT(OrderID) > **7**

10.) You work for a company that sells major appliances. You are creating a report to list sales reps and their total sales for the current month. The report must include only those reps who meet their sales quota of $9,000 per Sales Agent. The date parameters are stored in variables named @FromDate and @ToDate. You need to meet these requirements. Which SQL query should you use?

O a.
```
SELECT AgentName, SUM(o.SubTotal) AS SumOrderTotal
FROM SalesRep s
INNER JOIN SalesInvoice o
ON s.SalesRepID = o.SalesRepID
WHERE o.OrderDate BETWEEN @FromDate AND @ToDate
GROUP BY AgentName AND s.SubTotal >= 9000
```

O b.
```
SELECT AgentName, SUM(o.SubTotal) AS SumOrderTotal
FROM SalesRep s
INNER JOIN SalesInvoice o
ON s.SalesRepID = o.SalesRepID
WHERE o.OrderDate BETWEEN @FromDate
AND @ToDate AND o.SubTotal >= 9000
GROUP BY AgentName
HAVING SUM(o.SubTotal) >= 9000
```

O c.
```
SELECT AgentName, SUM(o.SubTotal) AS SumOrderTotal
FROM SalesRep s
INNER JOIN SalesInvoice o
ON s.SalesRepID = o.SalesRepID
WHERE o.OrderDate BETWEEN @FromDate AND @ToDate
GROUP BY AgentName
HAVING SUM(o.SubTotal) >= 9000
```

11.) You want to find products that grossed over 10,000 for the year 2010. The following query gives you all the totals of all products.

```
SELECT ProductID, SUM(UnitPrice * Quantity) AS YrTotl
FROM Orders WHERE [Year] = 2010
GROUP BY ProductID
```

Some of your product gross totals are over 10,000 and some are under. The criteria for the products grossing over 10,000 are as follows:

```
SUM(UnitPrice * Quantity) > 10000
```

Which clause filters this aggregated query?

O a. ON

O b. WHERE

O c. HAVING

12.) You have a table named InvoiceDetails. You need to find products that have been sold to less than 25 customers. Which T-SQL statement should you use?

O a. ```
SELECT ProductID,
COUNT(DISTINCT CustomerID) AS CustomerCount
FROM InvoiceDetails
GROUP BY ProductID
HAVING COUNT(DISTINCT CustomerID) < 25;
```

O b. ```
SELECT ProductID, COUNT(*) AS CustomerCount
FROM InvoiceDetails
GROUP BY ProductID, CustomerID
HAVING COUNT(*) < 25;
```

O c. ```
SELECT ProductID, CustomerID,
COUNT(DISTINCT CustomerID) AS CustomerCount
FROM InvoiceDetails
GROUP BY ProductID, CustomerID
HAVING COUNT(DISTINCT CustomerID) < 25;
```

**13.)** You have two tables named Customers and Invoices. For each customer found in both the Customers and Invoices tables, you need to query for the customer's name and the number of Invoices ordered by that customer. Which query should you use?

O a. ```
SELECT c.CustomerName, COUNT(o.OrderId) AS [OrderCount]
FROM Customers c
INNER JOIN Invoices o
ON c.CustomerId = o.CustomerId
GROUP BY c.CustomerName
```

O b. ```
SELECT c.CustomerName, COUNT(o.OrderID) AS [OrderCount]
FROM Customers c
INNER JOIN Invoices o
ON c.CustomerID = o.CustomerID
GROUP BY c.CustomerName
HAVING COUNT(o.OrderID) > 1
```

# Answer Key

**1.)** Because sorting the results with the ORDER BY clause is optional, the results can be ordered by more than one field by separating the fields with a comma and it is possible to sort a field in descending order with the DESC keyword, making (b), (c) and (d) all wrong. The right answer is (a) because the ORDER BY clause is required to be after or below the WHERE clause.
```

2.)   The default behavior of the ORDER BY clause is to consider NULL values less than all other values and list them first in ascending order or last in descending order, so (a) and (c) are both incorrect. Because the default behavior of the ORDER BY clause is to list NULLs first in ascending order or last in descending order (b) is the correct answer.

3.)   ORDER BY always goes after GROUP BY, so (a) is wrong for saying it goes before and (c) is incorrect for saying use them in any placement. Because ORDER BY always goes after GROUP BY (b) is the correct answer.

4.)   Because HAVING is used as criteria in aggregate operations, not WHERE, which is used as criteria in filtering records, (d) is incorrect. Since WHERE is used as criteria for filtering records and HAVING is used as criteria for aggregate operations, (a) is a correct answer. Since it is required that the ORDER BY clause must come after the WHERE and HAVING clauses, (b) is also correct. Because HAVING is used as criteria in aggregate operations and it can reference any of the field list items, (c) and (e) are both correct answers too.

5.)   Because ON is a condition of the JOIN operation, (a) is incorrect. Because WHERE predicates or filters on a single value for each record, (b) is incorrect too. GROUP BY collects records for use in an aggregate function, so (d) is also incorrect. Filtering on aggregated values requires using the HAVING clause, making (c) the correct answer.

6.)   Since 'Sum (Ord.OrderID)' will add up the value of all the OrderIDs instead of counting them, (a) is incorrect. Because the code in (b) does not GROUP the records by CompanyName the result will be one record counting all of the sales, so it is wrong too. The GROUP BY clause must include every non-aggregated field, so the code in (c) is incorrect because it does not include CompanyName. The correct code will GROUP BY CompanyName and Count the OrderIDs, making (d) the correct answer.

7.)   'HAVING COUNT (CustomerID)' will display the wrong number of CustomerIDs because it includes the duplicates, so (a) will be the wrong answer. 'HAVING COUNT (DISTINCT CustomerID)' will remove the duplicate CustomerIDs counted for each product, so (b) is the correct answer.

8.) Since the code in (a) does not return CustomerID and there is no GROUP BY clause it will return a count of every matched record so it is wrong. Because the second field is being aggregated as a SUM instead of a COUNT, (b) is also wrong. Since the code in (c) is the only one that uses GROUP BY Cust.CustomerID to COUNT the number of OrderIDs, it is the correct answer.

9.) 'HAVING SUM(OrderID) > 7' incorrectly filters the records on a sum of all the OrderIDs for each CustomerID when it should be counting them, so (b) is wrong. The proper way to filter a GROUP BY operation is to use HAVING, not WHERE, so the code in (c) is incorrect. The requirement is to display customers with 7 or more orders, therefore filtering the 'GROUP BY CustomerID' clause with 'HAVING COUNT (OrderID) > 7' makes (a) the correct answer.

10.) The code in (a) is incorrect as it returns a syntax error because of the AND keyword in the GROUP BY clause. The 'AND o.SubTotal >= 9000' in the WHERE clause of (b) makes it incorrect because it will only use records that have 9000 or more in the o.SubTotal field rather than 9000 or more for the sum of those fields. Since the WHERE clause in (c) is properly filtering the records that will be summed according to the OrderDate field and 'GROUP BY Agent Name HAVING SUM (o.SubTotal) >= 9000' will filter the results for those Agents that have met the sales quota of $9000.00, it is the correct answer.

11.) The code in (a) is incorrect since ON is used for joins (not filter criteria). The WHERE in (b) is incorrect because it will only filter row data (not aggregated data) . Since the HAVING clause in (c) can filter aggregated data, it is the correct answer.

12.) Having CustomerID included in the GROUP BY clause means each ProductID group will have its records grouped by CustomerID, therefore counting the records in ProductID/CustomerID groups, making both (b) and (c) wrong answers. 'COUNT (DISTINCT CustomerID)' is removing the duplicates from the count of records after GROUP(ing) BY only ProductID, making (a) the correct answer.

13.) The 'HAVING COUNT(o.OrderID) > 1' clause filters the result set, only showing customers that have ordered twice or more, and the goal is to show all customer order counts, so (b) is wrong. The right answer is (a) because the INNER JOIN will show all Customers who have placed orders.

Bug Catcher Game

To play the Bug Catcher game, run the SQLQueries2012Vol2BugCatcher04.pps file from the BugCatcher folder of the companion files. These files are available from the www.Joes2Pros.com website.

[THIS PAGE INTENTIONALLY LEFT BLANK.]

Chapter 5.   Aggregation Strategies

As your database grows, you will have many related tables of various sizes. Oftentimes new data (e.g., transaction detail, new price lists) comes to you from a data partner or external feed and could contain errors you need to find before allowing the new data into your database. Even if your system has rigorous processes in place to check feeds before new records are allowed in, troubleshooting anomalies and exceptions in your data is an integral part of your mission as a SQL Pro.

Errors in small tables are more obvious, while subtle errors in tables with millions of records can be difficult to find. In this lesson we learn techniques useful in analyzing and scrubbing data. Pay close attention because these are also common database interview questions!

The ability to investigate and confirm whether data complies with your organization's business rules is an important skill for every database professional. Aggregation techniques are useful tools for diving into your data. Another theme in this chapter is the importance of being very familiar with the detailed data contained in your tables and databases.

READER NOTE: *Please run the SQLQueries2012Vol2Chapter5.0Setup.sql script in order to follow along with the examples in the first section of Chapter 5. All scripts mentioned in this chapter are available at <u>www.Joes2Pros.com</u>.*

Duplicate Data

Duplicates in your data can sometimes be a bad thing. Finding identical duplicate entries in the daily feed of sales transactions would be a red flag situation warranting further investigation. In other cases, duplicates can be positive. A customer returning to make another purchase is a good thing – finding the same customer entities across multiple invoices means your customers appreciate your products and want to buy them. It all depends on the data. Whether duplicates are expected (the good kind) or unexpected (the bad kind), it's important to comprehend and be able to explain what they signify in your data.

Sorting to Find Duplicates

Let's begin with a table we know well, JProCo's Employee table. We know two employees have the same first name of David. A quick way to detect duplicates is to compare a SELECT query on the target field(s) against a SELECT DISTINCT query. Add an ORDER BY clause to make any duplicates display contiguously.

SELECT DISTINCT will only display each unique name one time. The Employee table has 13 records but since David is in two records the DISTINCT keyword will only display David once so this query will only return 12 of the 13 records:

```
SELECT DISTINCT FirstName
FROM Employee
```

By adding an ORDER BY clause on the FirstName field we will group together any duplicates (Figure 5.1).

```
SELECT FirstName
FROM Employee
ORDER BY FirstName
```

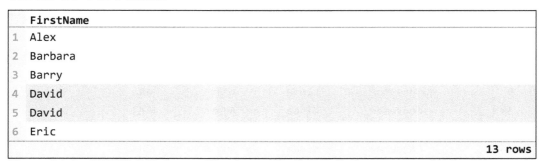

	FirstName
1	Alex
2	Barbara
3	Barry
4	David
5	David
6	Eric

13 rows

Figure 5.1 An ORDER BY clause will make any duplicates display next to each other.

This approach works just as well on a larger table or record set where you suspect duplicates. In larger tables, you won't be able to effectively eyeball duplicates

(Figure 5.1). However, if you get a lower row count when changing your query to SELECT DISTINCT, then duplicates exist in your data.

Let's try this approach on JProCo's Customer table to get a sense of how much duplication (if any) may be present among customers' last names. There are 775 total records in the customer table which we found by running the following query:

```
SELECT * FROM Customer
```

By running this following query using a SELECT DISTINCT LastName we find there are 52 unique LastName values in the 775 Customer table records:

```
SELECT DISTINCT LastName
FROM Customer
```

There are obviously some duplicates so by using ORDER BY LastName we can see all the unique LastName values listed together.

```
SELECT LastName
FROM Customer
ORDER BY LastName
```

In Figure 5.2 a similar query shows customers who share the same popular first and last names. You might have to scroll to see all the examples. The different CustomerIDs confirm these are all separate individuals (e.g., two named Jason Adams, four named Linda Adams and two named Betty Allen).

```
SELECT *
FROM Customer
ORDER BY LastName, FirstName
```

	CustomerID	CustomerType	FirstName	LastName	CompanyName
6	178	Consumer	George	Adams	NULL
7	49	Consumer	Jason	Adams	NULL
8	747	Consumer	Jason	Adams	NULL
9	110	Consumer	John	Adams	NULL
10	112	Consumer	Laura	Adams	NULL
11	9	Consumer	Linda	Adams	NULL
12	38	Consumer	Linda	Adams	NULL
13	223	Consumer	Linda	Adams	NULL
14	344	Consumer	Linda	Adams	NULL
15	746	Consumer	Pedro	Adams	NULL

775 rows

Figure 5.2 An ORDER BY clause displays duplicate names in JProCo's customer population.

Figure 5.2 also hints at a problem with duplicate entries in large record sets. While we've confirmed these duplicates in the Customer table are all the "good" kind, it would be a real chore to scroll through all 775 rows and manually count how many sets of JProCo customers share the same name.

In order to efficiently answer the question, "How many JProCo customers share the same name?" we must use some additional techniques.

Grouping to Find Duplicates

Adding grouping and a counting field to our display of FirstName and LastName combinations shows how many times each customer name appears (Figure 5.3).

```
SELECT FirstName, LastName, COUNT(*)
FROM Customer
GROUP BY LastName, FirstName
ORDER BY LastName
```

	FirstName	LastName	(No column name)
5	George	Adams	1
6	Jason	Adams	2
7	John	Adams	1
8	Laura	Adams	1
9	Linda	Adams	4
10	Pedro	Adams	1

653 rows

Figure 5.3 Grouping and aggregating better displays the duplicate names in the Customer table.

This view is better because GROUP BY shows just one record for each combination of names it finds. Now let's filter using the HAVING clause to exclude any name combination that appears only once.

```
SELECT FirstName, LastName, COUNT(*)
FROM Customer
GROUP BY LastName, FirstName
HAVING COUNT(*) > 1
ORDER BY LastName
```

	FirstName	LastName	(No column name)
1	NULL	NULL	2
2	Jason	Adams	2
3	Linda	Adams	4
4	Betty	Allen	2
5	John	Allen	2
6	Pedro	Allen	2
			103 rows

Figure 5.4 The criteria in the HAVING clause filters on just the 103 repeat name combinations.

Let's look back to the Employee table for a moment. Observe the impact of this grouping and filtering technique to display the duplicate first names shared by JProCo employees (Figure 5.5).

```
SELECT FirstName, COUNT(*)
FROM Employee
GROUP BY FirstName
HAVING COUNT(*) > 1
```

	FirstName	(No column name)
1	David	2
		1 rows

Figure 5.5 A summary view of the duplicate employee names. Compare to Figure 5.1.

Now return to our Customer table query to add one final level of specificity to our code. Instead of ordering by last name, we will order by count so we can see which name(s) appears most often on the JProCo customer list. There is a three-way tie for the most popular name: Linda Adams, Donald Turner and Susan Wright (Figure 5.6).

```
SELECT FirstName, LastName, COUNT(*)
FROM Customer
GROUP BY LastName, FirstName
HAVING COUNT(*) > 1
ORDER BY COUNT(*) DESC
```

	FirstName	LastName	(No column name)
1	Donald	Turner	4
2	Linda	Adams	4
3	Susan	Wright	4
4	Tessa	Allen	3
5	Tessa	Anderson	3
6	Donald	Taylor	3

103 rows

Figure 5.6 There is a 3-way tie for most popular name among JProCo customers.

Lab 5.1: Finding Duplicates

Lab Prep: Each lab has one or more Skill Checks. Start with Skill Check 1 and proceed until reaching the Points to Ponder section.

Before beginning this lab, verify that SQL Server 2012 is properly installed and operating. Before running the lab setup script for resetting the database (SQLQueries2012Vol2Chapter5.1Setup.sql), please make sure to close all query windows within SSMS. An open query window pointing to a database context can lock that database preventing it from updating when the script is executing. A simple way to assure all query windows are closed, is to exit out of SSMS, then open a new instance of SSMS, and lastly run the setup script.

Skill Check 1: Go to the JProCo database and count all employees having multiple grants listed in the Grant table. Your result should resemble Figure 5.7.

	FirstName	LastName	(No column name)
1	David	Lonning	3

1 rows

Figure 5.7 Skill Check 1 looks for employees with multiple entries in the Grant table.

Skill Check 2: Query the StateList table to find any duplicate records. List all duplicated StateID values you find. Title your aggregated field IDCount. When you're done, your result should resemble Figure 5.8.

	StateID	StateName	IDCount
1	NH	New Hampshire	2

1 rows

Figure 5.8 Find records with a duplicate StateID in the table JProCo.dbo.StateList.

Answer Code: The T-SQL code for this lab is located in the downloadable files as a file named Lab5.1_FindingDuplicates.sql.

Points to Ponder - Finding Duplicates

1. A differing record count using a SELECT query vs. SELECT DISTINCT can be a rapid way to know if duplication exists.

2. Sorting your data can help spot duplicates, but aggregating techniques (GROUP BY, COUNT) are more efficient for summarizing and explaining duplicate data. Aggregating techniques also allow you to isolate and view just the duplicate data, whereas sorting does not.

3. The GROUP BY clause shows only one result for each combination it finds. For example, if you GROUP BY FirstName, then "Tom" will appear as a row only once in your result no matter how many Tom records exist.

4. The GROUP BY clause allows you to use aggregating functions like COUNT(), SUM(), AVG(), and so forth.

5. To find records with repeating or duplicative values, use GROUP BY with a HAVING clause that looks for a count greater than 1.
   HAVING COUNT(*) > 1.

6. De-duping is short for "de-duplicating". You won't find either term in the dictionary, but de-dupe is a geek speak term used in data intensive environments where you will find SQL Server databases. De-duping usually includes removal of the duplicates, as well as locating them. But techniques and tools you use to locate duplicates also fall in the category of de-duping. Related terms you may hear are "merge-purge" (for mailing lists) and "data cleansing". De-duplication is one component of both of these processes.

Combining Individual Rows with Aggregates

From these last two chapters ("Aggregating Data" and "Aggregation Strategies") hopefully you're seeing aggregation as useful and important. Aggregation is your friend and is a necessary part of your transformation from "SQL Joe" to "SQL Pro".

But glance back to how we began investigating whether our employee and customer data contained duplicates. We started by looking at the individual record detail.

Every big, impressive item you will ever construct in SQL Server begins with your understanding of the data contained in your tables and databases.

This section demonstrates the OVER() clause, which allows you to combine aggregated and non-aggregated data. In the same row containing detail from each individual table record, we can view aggregated data right alongside it.

The OVER() clause debuted as a new feature in SQL Server 2005. Prior to that version, SQL Pros had to write more code and use a messy workaround to achieve what OVER() accomplishes cleanly. It is a great way to combine totals or subtotals next to individual records.

Aggregation Functions

Until now we've never seen aggregation without a GROUP BY with some of your fields using an aggregated function.

With GROUP BY you are limited to including only aggregated data in your result set. We only see totals and not the individual table records when we use functions like SUM() or COUNT(). Those aggregate functions require supporting language so they know how to run.

For every query we began with a "SELECT *" statement, we had to modify it once we introduced an aggregate function. To support the aggregate function, we had to add GROUP BY and drop the "SELECT *", since every non-aggregated field in the SELECT statement must be listed in the GROUP BY clause.

Using the OVER Clause

Let's launch into an example beginning with JProCo's Grant table.

The two simple queries (Figure 5.9) show all the Grant table records and the sum of the grant amounts.

```
SELECT SUM(Amount) AS SumOfGrants
FROM [Grant]

SELECT *
FROM [Grant]
```

	SumOfGrants
1	193700.00

	GrantID	GrantName	EmpID	Amount
1	001	92 Purr_Scents %% team	7	4750.00
2	002	K_Land fund trust	2	15750.00
3	003	Robert@BigStarBank.com	7	18100.00
4	004	Norman's Outreach	NULL	21000.00
5	005	BIG 6's Foundation%	4	21000.00
6	006	TALTA_Kishan Internatio...	3	18100.00
7	007	Ben@MoreTechnology.c...	10	41000.00
8	008	www.@-Last-U-Can-Hel...	7	25000.00
9	009	Thank you @.com	11	21500.00
10	010	Call Mom @Com	5	7500.00

Query executed successfully.   RENO (11.0 RTM)   Reno\Student (51)   JProCo   00:00:00   11 rows

Figure 5.9 The Grant table contains 10 grants totaling $193,700.

If we want to show the total amount next to every record of the table – or just one record of the table – SQL Server gives us the same error. It does not find the language needed to support the aggregate function (Figure 5.10).

```
SELECT *, SUM(Amount)
FROM [Grant]

SELECT *, SUM(Amount)
FROM [Grant]
WHERE GrantID = '001'
```

Messages
```
Msg 8120, Level 16, State 1, Line 1
Column 'Grant.GrantID' is invalid in the select list because it is not
contained in either an aggregate function or the GROUP BY clause.
```
0 rows

Figure 5.10 SQL gives an error because it finds no language to support the function SUM().

Adding the OVER() clause allows us to see the total amount next to each grant record (Figure 5.11).

```
SELECT *, SUM(Amount) OVER()
FROM [Grant]

SELECT *, SUM(Amount) OVER()
FROM [Grant]
WHERE GrantID = '001'
```

	GrantID	GrantName	EmpID	Amount	(No column name)
1	001	92 Purr_Scents %% team	7	4750.00	193700.00
2	002	K_Land fund trust	2	15750.00	193700.00
3	003	Robert@BigStarBank.com	7	18100.00	193700.00
4	004	Norman's Outreach	NULL	21000.00	193700.00
5	005	BIG 6's Foundation%	4	21000.00	193700.00
6	006	TALTA_Kishan International	3	18100.00	193700.00
7	007	Ben@MoreTechnology.com	10	41000.00	193700.00
8	008	www.@-Last-U-Can-Help.com	7	25000.00	193700.00
9	009	Thank you @.com	11	21500.00	193700.00
10	010	Call Mom @Com	5	7500.00	193700.00

	GrantID	GrantName	EmpID	Amount	(No column name)
1	001	92 Purr_Scents %% team	7	4750.00	4750.00

Query executed successfully. RENO (11.0 RTM) Reno\Student (51) JProCo 00:00:00 11 rows

Figure 5.11 OVER() applies the aggregation SUM(Amount) across all rows of a query.

Later we will see examples showing OVER() used with an argument. Here we have left the parentheses blank, which causes OVER() to apply the aggregation across all rows of each query. In the top query, we see SUM(Amount) for all 10 rows in the query. The bottom query also shows SUM(Amount) applied across all rows of the query, which in this case is just one row. The same would be true if your query contained two rows (Figure 5.12).

```
SELECT *, SUM(Amount) OVER()
FROM [Grant]
WHERE GrantID IN (001, 006)
```

	GrantID	GrantName	EmpID	Amount	(No column name)
1	001	92 Purr_Scents %% team	7	4750.00	22850.00
2	006	TALTA_Kishan International	3	18100.00	22850.00
					2 rows

Figure 5.12 OVER() applies an aggregate function across all rows of a query.

By listing the total amount of all grants (aliased as CompanyTotal in Figure 5.13) next to each individual grant, we automatically get a nice reference for how each individual grant compares to the total of all JProCo grants.

The sum of all 10 grants is $193,700. Recall the largest single grant (007) is $41,000. Doing the quick math in our head, we recognize $41,000 is around 1/5 of ~$200,000 and guesstimate that Grant 007 is just over 20% of the total.

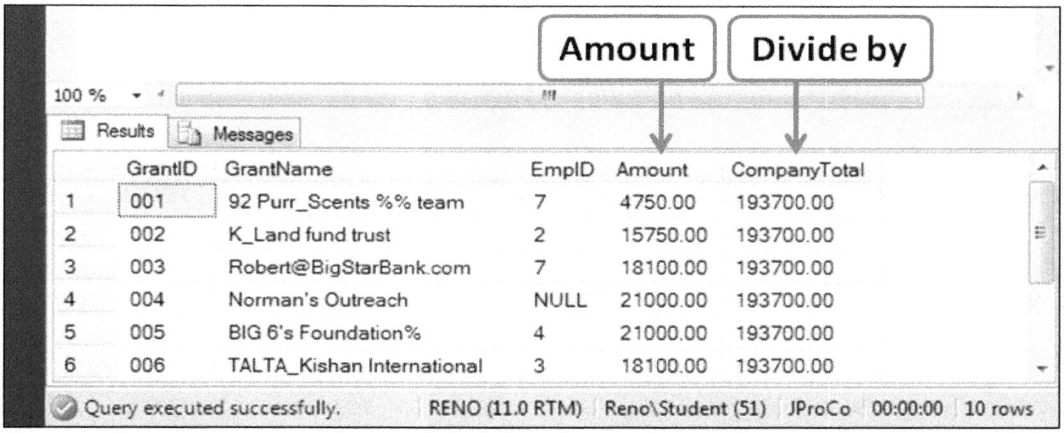

Figure 5.13 We want a new column dividing each grant amount by the total of all grants.

Thanks to the OVER clause, there's no need to guess. We can get the precise percentage. To accomplish this, we will add an expression that does the same math we did in our head. We want the new column to divide each grant amount by $193,700 (the total of all the grants).

```
SELECT *, SUM(Amount) OVER() AS CompanyTotal
FROM [Grant]
```

The new column is added and confirms our prediction that Grant 007 represents just over 21% of all grants (Figure 5.14).

```
SELECT *, SUM(Amount) OVER() AS CompanyTotal,
Amount / SUM(Amount) OVER()
FROM [Grant]
```

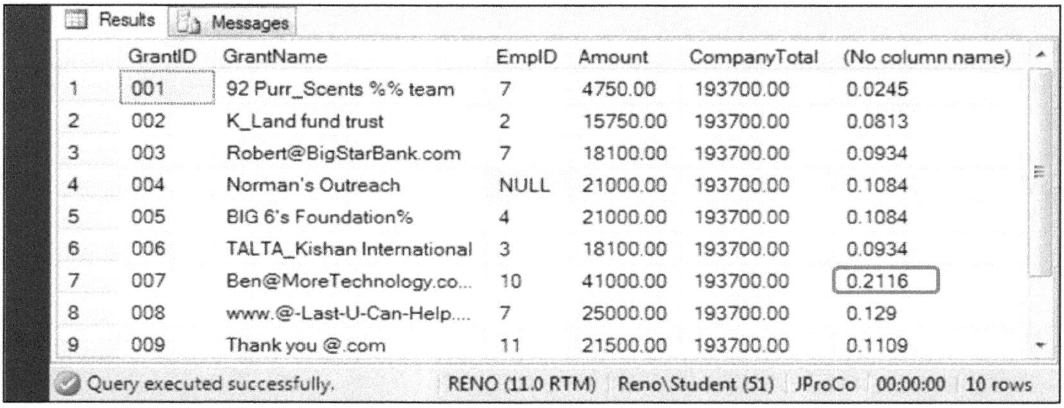

Figure 5.14 Grant 007 represents just over 21% of all grants.

Notice that the figures in our new column appear as ratios. Percentages are 100 times the size of a ratio. Example: the ratio 0.2116 represents a percentage of 21.16% (Figure 5.15).

```
SELECT *,
SUM(Amount) OVER() AS CompanyTotal,
Amount / SUM(Amount) OVER() * 100
FROM [Grant]
```

	GrantID	GrantName	EmpID	Amount	CompanyTotal	(No column…
1	001	92 Purr_Scents %% team	7	4750.00	193700.00	2.45
2	002	K_Land fund trust	2	15750.00	193700.00	8.13
3	003	Robert@BigStarBank.com	7	18100.00	193700.00	9.34
4	004	Norman's Outreach	NULL	21000.00	193700.00	10.84
5	005	BIG 6's Foundation%	4	21000.00	193700.00	10.84
6	006	TALTA_Kishan Internati…	3	18100.00	193700.00	9.34

10 rows

Figure 5.15 Multiplying a ratio by 100 will show the percentage.

To finish, give the column a descriptive title, PctOfTotal (Figure 5.16).

```
SELECT *,
SUM(Amount) OVER() AS CompanyTotal,
Amount / SUM(Amount) OVER() * 100 AS PctOfTotal
FROM [Grant]
```

	GrantID	GrantName	EmpID	Amount	CompanyTotal	PctOfTotal
1	001	92 Purr_Scents %% team	7	4750.00	193700.00	2.45
2	002	K_Land fund trust	2	15750.00	193700.00	8.13
3	003	Robert@BigStarBank.com	7	18100.00	193700.00	9.34
4	004	Norman's Outreach	NULL	21000.00	193700.00	10.84
5	005	BIG 6's Foundation%	4	21000.00	193700.00	10.84
6	006	TALTA_Kishan Internatio…	3	18100.00	193700.00	9.34

10 rows

Figure 5.16 Alias the new column with a descriptive field name of PctOfTotal.

Now let's try an example using the aggregate function COUNT() with the OVER() clause. We'll start with a simple query on the Employee table (Figure 5.17).

```
SELECT FirstName, LastName, LocationID
FROM Employee
```

	FirstName	LastName	LocationID
1	Alex	Adams	1
2	Barry	Brown	1
3	Lee	Osako	2
4	David	Kennson	1
5	Eric	Bender	1
6	Lisa	Kendall	4

13 rows

Figure 5.17 There are 13 total employees in the Employee table.

Since there are 13 total employees, we want to see a 13 alongside each individual record in the table. Attempting this without OVER() gives an error (Figure 5.18).

```
SELECT FirstName, LastName, LocationID, COUNT(*)
FROM Employee
```

Messages
Msg 8120, Level 16, State 1, Line 1
Column 'Employee.FirstName' is invalid in the select list because it is not contained in either an aggregate function or the GROUP BY clause.

0 rows

Figure 5.18 An aggregate function must have GROUP BY or an OVER() clause.

```
SELECT FirstName, LastName, LocationID,
COUNT(*) OVER() AS TotalEmployees
FROM Employee
```

	FirstName	LastName	LocationID	TotalEmployees
1	Alex	Adams	1	13
2	Barry	Brown	1	13
3	Lee	Osako	2	13
4	David	Kennson	1	13
5	Eric	Bender	1	13
6	Lisa	Kendall	4	13

13 rows

Figure 5.19 The addition of the OVER() clause displays the total count 13 next to each record.

Now let's look at Alex Adams. He works in Location 1.

How many of JProCo's employees are in Location 1 (Seattle)? How many of the total employees work in Boston? Alongside the existing table records, we want to add a column showing the count of employees at each location.

But what code do we write for this new column?

Recall that blank parentheses cause OVER() to apply the aggregation across all rows of a query. Our instruction to show employee count at each location means we don't just want a total of all locations in our query – we already have that data displayed in the TotalEmployees column.

We must include an argument inside the parentheses.

PARTITION BY divides the result set into partitions. In this case we've added a partition by LocationID. Similar to the behavior of GROUP BY, the command to PARTITION BY LocationID takes the LocationID for each employee and counts the number of records in that group which shares the same LocationID. Thus, each of the Seattle employees shows a 7 for LocationCount. The Boston employees have a LocationCount of 3, and the Spokane records have LocationCount of 2. John Marshbank shows LocationCount of 1, since he's the only one with a NULL LocationID (Figure 5.20).

```
SELECT FirstName, LastName, LocationID,
COUNT(*) OVER() AS TotalEmployees,
COUNT(*) OVER(PARTITION BY LocationID) AS LocationCount
FROM Employee
```

	FirstName	LastName	LocationID	TotalEmployees	LocationCount
1	John	Marshbank	NULL	13	1
2	Sally	Smith	1	13	7
3	Alex	Adams	1	13	7
4	Barry	Brown	1	13	7
5	David	Kennson	1	13	7
6	Eric	Bender	1	13	7
7	David	Lonning	1	12	6
8	Lee	Osako	2	12	3
9	James	Newton	2	12	3
10	Terry	O'Haire	2	12	3
11	Barbara	O'Neil	4	12	2
12	Lisa	Kendall	4	12	2

13 rows

Figure 5.20 PARTITION BY divides the result set into partitions.

Be curious and try out a few variations on your own to get familiar with the behavior of PARTITION BY (Figure 5.21). Note that the PARTITION BY and ORDER BY aren't limited to fields listed in the SELECT statement. They can use any field made available by the FROM clause. Try partitioning on duplicate values (such as Status, LocationID, or FirstName) versus partitioning on EmpID which does not repeat for any employee.

```
SELECT FirstName, LastName, LocationID,
COUNT(*) OVER() AS TotalEmployees,
COUNT(*) OVER(PARTITION BY Status) AS StatusCount
FROM Employee
```

	FirstName	LastName	LocationID	TotalEmployees	StatusCount
1	Alex	Adams	1	13	10
2	Barry	Brown	1	13	10
3	Lee	Osako	2	13	10
4	John	Marshbank	NULL	13	10
5	James	Newton	2	13	10
6	Terry	O'Haire	2	13	10
7	Sally	Smith	1	13	10
8	Eric	Bender	1	13	10
9	Lisa	Kendall	4	13	10
10	Phil	Wilconkinski	1	13	10
11	Barbara	O'Neil	4	13	2
12	David	Kennson	1	13	2
13	David	Lonning	1	13	1

13 rows

Figure 5.21 Be curious and test drive the behavior of PARTITION BY with various fields.

Now let's look back to Figure 5.20, where we added the total count of employees at all locations, as well as a LocationCount showing the location occupancy for each employee record.

Like the Grant table example, we want to use those columns to show an occupancy percentage alongside each employee record. The calculation method is the same as with the grants (Figure 5.13). We want to divide each smaller amount (LocationCount) by the total amount (13 TotalEmployees).

Since Seattle has 7 of the total 13 employees, we can guesstimate that just over ½ or more than 50% of JProCo employees work in Seattle (LocationID 1). Let's run the query (Figure 5.22) and check the results.

```
SELECT FirstName, LastName, LocationID,
COUNT(*) OVER() AS TotalEmployees,
COUNT(*) OVER(PARTITION BY LocationID) AS LocationCount,
COUNT(*) OVER(PARTITION BY LocationID) / COUNT(*) OVER()
FROM Employee
```

Figure 5.22 Our first calculation attempt shows only integers (whole numbers) instead of ratios.

Our result set shows no ratios and all 0s. This is because our calculation involved only integers. An open query window pointing to a database context can lock that database preventing it from updating when the script is executing. Rather than writing additional code using CAST, we'll use a trick that works with many programming languages. Multiply the numerator by 1.0 to make each figure display as a decimal instead of an integer (Figure 5.23).

```
SELECT FirstName, LastName, LocationID,
COUNT(*) OVER() AS TotalEmployees,
COUNT(*) OVER(PARTITION BY LocationID) AS LocationCount,
COUNT(*) OVER(PARTITION BY LocationID) * 1.0 /
COUNT(*) OVER()
FROM Employee
```

	FirstName	LastName	LocationID	TotalEmployees	LocationCount	(No column…
1	John	Marshbank	NULL	13	1	0.076923076923
2	Sally	Smith	1	13	7	0.538461538461
3	Alex	Adams	1	13	7	0.538461538461
4	Barry	Brown	1	13	7	0.538461538461
5	David	Kennson	1	13	7	0.538461538461
6	Eric	Bender	1	13	7	0.538461538461
						13 rows

Figure 5.23 Multiply the numerator by 1.0, so results appear as decimals instead of integers.

This result is a big improvement – each result is now in decimal form. The Seattle occupancy rate is about 53.85%.

Now multiply instead by 100 so the values show as percentages, like we did with the Grant example (Figure 5.15). In this instance be sure to multiply by 100.0, so the values show as decimals and not integers (Figure 5.24).

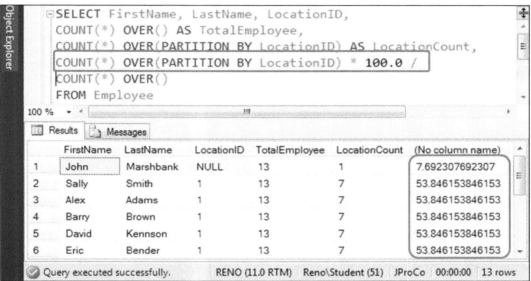

Figure 5.24 Multiply the numerator by 100.0, so results appear as percentages.

Finally, polish your report by adding the descriptive title Pct in place of the blank column header. Sort your report in descending order of occupancy (Pct) and LastName (Figure 5.25).

```
SELECT FirstName, LastName, LocationID,
COUNT(*) OVER() AS TotalEmployees,
COUNT(*) OVER(PARTITION BY LocationID) AS LocationCount,
COUNT(*) OVER(PARTITION BY LocationID) * 100.0 /
COUNT(*) OVER() AS Pct
FROM Employee
ORDER BY Pct DESC, LastName
```

	FirstName	LastName	LocationID	TotalEmployee	LocationCount	Pct
1	Alex	Adams	1	13	7	53.846153846153
2	Eric	Bender	1	13	7	53.846153846153
3	Barry	Brown	1	13	7	53.846153846153
4	David	Kennson	1	13	7	53.846153846153
5	David	Lonning	1	13	7	53.846153846153
6	Sally	Smith	1	13	7	53.846153846153

Query executed successfully.   RENO (11.0 RTM)   Reno\Student (51)   JProCo   00:00:00   13 rows

Figure 5.25 Polish your final report with sorting and titling any blank column headers.

Lab 5.2: The OVER Clause

Lab Prep: Each lab has one or more Skill Checks. Start with Skill Check 1 and proceed until reaching the Points to Ponder section.

Before beginning this lab, verify that SQL Server 2012 is properly installed and operating. Before running the lab setup script for resetting the database (SQLQueries2012Vol2Chapter5.2Setup.sql), please make sure to close all query windows within SSMS. An open query window pointing to a database context can lock that database preventing it from updating when the script is executing. A simple way to assure all query windows are closed, is to exit out of SSMS, then open a new instance of SSMS, and lastly run the setup script.

Skill Check 1: Use the JProCo database and query the CurrentProducts table for the fields ProductName, RetailPrice and Category. Create an expression field that combines AVG() with an OVER() clause and call it AvgPrice. When you are done, your result should resemble the figure you see here (Figure 5.26).

	ProductName	RetailPrice	Category	AvgPrice	
1	Underwater Tour 1 Day West Coast	61.483	No-Stay	316.671	
2	Underwater Tour 2 Days West Coast	110.6694	Overnight-Stay	316.671	
3	Underwater Tour 3 Days West Coast	184.449	Medium-Stay	316.671	
4	Underwater Tour 5 Days West Coast	245.932	Medium-Stay	316.671	
5	Underwater Tour 1 Week West Coast	307.415	LongTerm-Stay	316.671	
6	Underwater Tour 2 Weeks West Co...	553.347	LongTerm-Stay	316.671	

Query executed successfully.   RENO (11.0 RTM)   Reno\Student (51)   JProCo   00:00:00   483 rows

Figure 5.26 Skill Check 1 creates a new expression field combining AVG() with an OVER clause.

Skill Check 2: Take the query from Skill Check 1 and add another expression field called AvgCatPrice that shows the average price for the Category for any given product. When you are done, your result will resemble Figure 5.27.

	ProductName	RetailPrice	Category	AvgPrice	AvgCatPrice	
1	Underwater Tour 1 Week West Coast	307.415	LongTerm-Stay	316.671	559.0931	
2	Underwater Tour 2 Weeks West Coast	553.347	LongTerm-Stay	316.671	559.0931	
3	Underwater Tour 1 Week East Coast	404.295	LongTerm-Stay	316.671	559.0931	
4	Underwater Tour 2 Weeks East Coast	727.731	LongTerm-Stay	316.671	559.0931	
5	Underwater Tour 1 Week Mexico	525.295	LongTerm-Stay	316.671	559.0931	
6	Underwater Tour 2 Weeks Mexico	945.531	LongTerm-Stay	316.671	559.0931	

Query executed successfully.   RENO (11.0 RTM)   Reno\Student (51)   JProCo   00:00:00   483 rows

Figure 5.27 Skill Check 2 adds a new expression field showing AvgCatPrice.

Skill Check 3: Use the JProCo database and query the CurrentProducts table. Show each distinct category and calculate the percentage (with decimals) of products for each Category. Since we have more LongTerm-Stay products, that category will represent the highest percentage of the total (Figure 5.28).

	Category	PctCategory
1	LongTerm-Stay	33.540372670807
2	Medium-Stay	33.333333333333
3	No-Stay	16.563146997929
4	Overnight-Stay	16.563146997929

Query executed successfully. RENO (11.0 RTM) Reno\Student (51) JProCo 00:00:00 4 rows

Figure 5.28 Skill Check 3 calculates the percentage of products in each product Category.

Skill Check 4: Join the Location, Employee and Grant tables and display FirstName, LastName, GrantName, City and Amount. Add an expression field called CityTotal that compares each grant to the total amount in the same City (See the expected result in Figure 5.29).

	FirstName	LastName	GrantName	City	Amount	CityTotal
1	Lee	Osako	TALTA_Kishan International	Boston	18100.00	59100.00
2	Terry	O'Haire	Ben@MoreTechnology.com	Boston	41000.00	59100.00
3	Barry	Brown	K_Land fund trust	Seattle	15750.00	113600.00
4	David	Kennson	BIG 6's Foundation%	Seattle	21000.00	113600.00
5	Eric	Bender	Call Mom @Com	Seattle	7500.00	113600.00
6	David	Lonning	92 Purr_Scents %% team	Seattle	4750.00	113600.00

Query executed successfully. RENO (11.0 RTM) Reno\Student (51) JProCo 00:00:00 9 rows

Figure 5.29 Compare each individual grant to the total grant amounts in the same city (CityTotal).

Answer Code: The T-SQL code for this lab is located in the downloadable files as a file named Lab5.2_TheOVER_Clause.sql.

Points to Ponder - The OVER() Clause

1. With the OVER()clause we can integrate both actual base fields and aggregates in the same row.

2. OVER() allows aggregation without requiring you to use a GROUP BY clause.

3. Leaving the parentheses in OVER() with nothing between them (empty) causes it to apply the aggregation across all rows of the query.

4. The OVER() clause can aggregate rows across groups of another field using the PARTITON BY keyword. For example, a grocery chain can find how sales of bananas compare to total produce sales instead of the entire food total sales.

5. Note that PARTITION BY and ORDER BY aren't limited to fields listed in the SELECT statement. They can use any field made available by the FROM clause.

6. To get your integer number scaling to decimals you can multiply the OVER() results by a decimal like 1.0. If you multiply by 1 then you'll get the nearest integer (whole number).

Chapter Glossary

De-duping: Short for "de-duplicating". This involves removal and location of duplicate records in a database.

Duplicate Data: Identical duplicate records.

OVER(): This clause allows you to combine aggregated and non-aggregated data.

PARTITION BY: This keyword divides result sets into partitions.

Review Quiz - Chapter Five

1.) You think there may be duplicate ContractorID values in the Contractor table. Which query should you use to find these duplicates?

O a. **SELECT** ContractorID
    FROM dbo.Contractor
    GROUP BY ContractorID
    HAVING (*) > **1**

O b. **SELECT** ContractorID
    FROM dbo.Contractor
    GROUP BY ContractorID
    HAVING (*) >= **1**

O c. **SELECT** ContractorID
    FROM dbo.Contractor
    GROUP BY ContractorID
    HAVING COUNT(*) > **1**

O d. **SELECT** ContractorID
    FROM dbo.Contractor
    GROUP BY ContractorID
    HAVING COUNT(*) >= **1**

2.) You want to display each grant in your Grant table and have an expression field that shows the total amount of all grants. Which query should you use?

O a. **SELECT** *,
    COUNT(Amount) **OVER**() **AS** CompanyTotal
    FROM [Grant]

O b. **SELECT** *,
    SUM(Amount) **OVER**() **AS** CompanyTotal
    FROM [Grant]

O c. **SELECT** *,
    COUNT(Amount) **AS** CompanyTotal
    FROM [Grant]
    GROUP BY *

O d. **SELECT** *,
    SUM(Amount) **AS** CompanyTotal
    FROM [Grant]
    GROUP BY *

3.)   You want to show all fields of the Employee table. You want an additional field called StartDate that shows the first HireDate for all Employees. Which query should you use?

O a.
```
SELECT *,
MIN(HireDate) AS StartDate
FROM Employee
```

O b.
```
SELECT *,
MAX(HireDate) AS StartDate
FROM Employee
```

O c.
```
SELECT *,
MIN(HireDate) OVER() AS StartDate
FROM Employee
```

O d.
```
SELECT *,
MAX(HireDate) OVER() AS StartDate
FROM Employee
```

4.)   You have a table named CurrentProducts. The table contains a column named Category. You need to make a T-SQL statement that calculates the percentage (with decimals) of products in each product Category. Which query should you use?

O a.
```
SELECT DISTINCT Category,
COUNT(*) OVER(PARTITION BY Category) * 100 /
COUNT(*) OVER() AS pctCategory
FROM CurrentProducts
```

O b.
```
SELECT DISTINCT Category,
COUNT(*) OVER(PARTITION BY Category) * 100.0 /
COUNT(*) OVER() AS PctCategory
FROM CurrentProducts
```

O c.
```
SELECT DISTINCT Category,
COUNT(*) OVER() * 100.0 /
COUNT(*) OVER(PARTITION BY Category) AS PctCategory
FROM CurrentProducts
```

5.) You have a table named CurrentProducts. The table contains a column named Category. You need to make a T-SQL statement that calculates a decimal ratio of products in each product Category. Which query should you use?

O a.
```
SELECT Category,
COUNT(*) OVER(PARTITION BY Category) AS CategoryRatio
FROM CurrentProducts
GROUP BY Category
```

O b.
```
SELECT Category,
COUNT(*) OVER() * 1.0 /
COUNT(*) OVER(PARTITION BY Category) AS CategoryRatio
FROM CurrentProducts
GROUP BY Category
```

O c.
```
SELECT DISTINCT Category,
COUNT(*) OVER(PARTITION BY Category) * 1.0 /
COUNT(*) OVER() AS CategoryRatio
FROM CurrentProducts
```

O d.
```
SELECT DISTINCT Category,
COUNT(*) OVER() * 1.0 /
COUNT(*) OVER(PARTITION BY Category) AS CategoryRatio
FROM CurrentProducts
```

6.) You need to return sales data from the Sales table, ordered by customer name and date of order. You want to keep the customer names together and, for each customer, the most recent order must be listed first. Which query should you use?

O a.
```
SELECT CustomerName, OrderDate
FROM Sales
ORDER BY CustomerName, OrderDate;
```

O b.
```
SELECT CustomerName, OrderDate
FROM Sales
ORDER BY OrderDate DESC, CustomerName;
```

O c.
```
SELECT CustomerName, OrderDate
FROM Sales
ORDER BY CustomerName DESC;
```

O d.
```
SELECT CustomerName, OrderDate
FROM Sales
ORDER BY CustomerName, OrderDate DESC;
```

7.) You want to list all records of your CurrentProducts table and put the Average retail price as an expression field named CompanyAverage next to each row. Which T-SQL statement should you use?

O a. `SELECT *,`
`AVG(RetailPrice) OVER() AS CompanyAverage`
`FROM CurrentProducts`

O b. `SELECT *,`
`AVG(RetailPrice) AS CompanyAverage`
`FROM CurrentProducts`

O c. `SELECT *, (RetailPrice * 2) AS CompanyAverage`
`FROM CurrentProducts`

8.) You want to list all records of your CurrentProducts table and put the Average retail price as an expression field named CompanyAverage for each SupplierID next to each row. Which T-SQL statement should you use?

O a. `SELECT *,`
`AVG(RetailPrice) OVER() AS CompanySupplierAverage`
`FROM CurrentProducts`

O b. `SELECT *,`
`AVG(SupplierID) OVER() AS CompanySupplierAverage`
`FROM CurrentProducts`

O c. `SELECT *,`
`AVG(RetailPrice) OVER(PARTITION BY SupplierID) AS`
`CompanySupplierAverage`
`FROM CurrentProducts`

O d. `SELECT *,`
`AVG(SupplierID) OVER(PARTITION BY RetailPrice) AS`
`CompanySupplierAverage`
`FROM CurrentProducts`

Answer Key

1.)   Incorrect syntax near '*' will be returned from (a) and (b), making them wrong answers. 'HAVING Count (*) >= 1', as in (d), will incorrectly include those ContractorIDs with only 1 occurrence. Use 'GROUP BY ContractorID HAVING Count (*) > 1' to find duplicate ContractorIDs as in (c), which is the correct answer.

2.)   COUNT (Amount) will not total the amounts but count how many grants there are, so (a) and (c) are both incorrect. Because 'GROUP BY' requires that each field is specified rather than using the * wildcard, (d) will not work either. The only way to include every field of every record along with an aggregated field in the results is to use the OVER clause as supporting language for the SUM, making (b) the correct answer.

3.)   Because there is no supporting language for the aggregated field, both (a) and (b) will not be correct. Because MAX(HireDate) will return the greatest or most recent HireDate, (d) is also incorrect. The correct code is (c) which uses the MIN aggregate function and the OVER () clause as supporting language.

4.)   Because multiplying an aggregate by 100 (an integer) will result in the nearest integer, (a) will not work. Since calculating a category's percentage of the total products is done by dividing the quantity in the category by the quantity of all the products then multiplying by 100.0, (c) will be incorrect, because it is dividing the total (COUNT(*) OVER ()) by the category (COUNT(*) OVER(PARTITION BY Category)) instead. Because the category's quantity is being multiplied by 100.0 (a decimal) before being divided by the quantity of all the products, it will result in a decimal, making (b) the correct answer.

5.)   To calculate a ratio, the code must divide two numbers but the code in (a) is only counting one field, making it incorrect. Since calculating a category's ratio of the total products is done by dividing the quantity in the category (COUNT (*) OVER (PARTITION BY Category)) by the quantity of all the products (COUNT (*) OVER ()) then multiplying by 1.0, (b) and (d) will both be incorrect because they are dividing the quantity of all the products by the quantity in the category instead. Because the category's quantity is being multiplied by 1.0 (a decimal) before being divided by the quantity of all the products, it will result in a decimal rather than an integer, making (c) the correct answer.

6.)   If we don't specify DESC, then OrderDate will be sorted in ascending order. Since we want the most recent order listed first, (a) is incorrect. Because we want to keep the customer names together, the CustomerName field must be the first field listed in the ORDER BY clause, so (b) is also wrong. There is no OrderDate field in the ORDER BY clause (c), making that answer incorrect too. The CustomerName will be sorted in alphabetical order, by default, and OrderDate DESC will result in the most recent dates on top, making (d) the correct answer.

7.)   You are not looking for a number double each RetailPrice, so (c) incorrect. You can not use AVG() unless you use OVER or GROUP BY, so (b) is incorrect. You want the average over the retail price, making (a) correct.

8.)   Since you need a partitioned total, your OVER clause must not be empty, making (a) and (b) incorrect. We want to Partition by SupplierID, making (c) correct.

Bug Catcher Game

To play the Bug Catcher game, run the SQLQueries2012Vol2BugCatcher05.pps file from the BugCatcher folder of the companion files. These files are available from the www.Joes2Pros.com website.

[THIS PAGE INTENTIONALLY LEFT BLANK.]

Chapter 6.   TOP(*n*) Record Queries

One of my fondest childhood memories is of my year old Samoyed puppy, Strider, receiving a second place ribbon during the graduation ceremony for his obedience class. I was there with Strider when they awarded him the bright red ribbon for earning a total score of 94 points. This was a proud moment, as there were thirty other dogs also vying for one of the top three spots on the podium.

A friend, with a Samoyed of his own, referred this very good obedience school to my family. His Samoyed, Sebastian, being a year older than Strider had taken the same class during the previous year. I asked how Sebastian did in the contest last year and discovered that Sebastian had won fourth place. I proudly said, "Wow, my dog did better!" I later found out that this wasn't exactly true, as Sebastian had scored 96 points in his obedience class, which was two points more than Strider. It seems Sebastian was in a class with very stiff competition.

This is how I learned that a specific score like 94 or 96 points isn't always a true measure for the top 3 places in every competition. The cutoff value is dependent on how each score compares with other scores measured at the same time.

It is possible to find the top *n* number of records without using a WHERE clause, by implementing the TOP clause. This chapter will demonstrate many of the best tips and tricks for mastering queries using the TOP(*n*) clause.

READER NOTE: *Please run the SQLQueries2012Vol2Chapter6.0Setup.sql script in order to follow along with the examples in the first section of Chapter 6. All scripts mentioned in this chapter are available at www.Joes2Pros.com.*

TOP(*n*) Queries

Our manager has instructed us to find the three most expensive products currently sold by JProCo. What type of query can we write to get this result set?

A quick way to get the answer is to query the CurrentProducts table, sorting on the RetailPrice field in descending order placing the most expensive value first. We can then look for the first three records at the top of the list.

```
SELECT *
FROM CurrentProducts
ORDER BY RetailPrice DESC
```

	ProductID	ProductName	RetailPrice	OriginationDate	ToBeDeleted	Category
1	483	Yoga Mtn Getaway 2 Weeks	1695.00	2012-10-20 19:17:38.773	1	LongTerm-Stay
2	336	Lakes Tour 2 Weeks West ...	1161.099	2011-09-29 18:15:51.907	1	LongTerm-Stay
3	342	Lakes Tour 2 Weeks East C...	1147.986	2008-08-31 13:21:02.883	1	LongTerm-Stay
4	372	Rain Forest Tour 2 Weeks ...	1144.773	2007-04-21 16:51:51.403	1	LongTerm-Stay
5	402	River Rapids Tour 2 Weeks ...	1116.108	2009-10-23 09:28:35.167	1	LongTerm-Stay
6	456	Wine Tasting Tour 2 Weeks...	1101.969	2011-09-09 11:30:06.323	1	LongTerm-Stay

Query executed successfully.   RENO (11.0 RTM)   Reno\j2p (51)   JProCo   00:00:00   483 rows

Figure 6.1 Sorting the CurrentProducts table in descending order of RetailPrice places the most expensive product at the top of the result set (each product below it is successively cheaper).

Now that we know the value of the third highest RetailPrice (1147.986), we can use this value to filter the list to show only the three most expensive products. Run the following sample code and observe the results in Figure 6.2.

```
SELECT *
FROM CurrentProducts
WHERE RetailPrice >= 1147.986
ORDER BY RetailPrice DESC
```

	ProductID	ProductName	RetailPrice	OriginationDate	ToBeDeleted	Category
1	483	Yoga Mtn Getaway 2 Weeks	1695.00	2012-10-20 19:17:38.773	1	LongTerm-Stay
2	336	Lakes Tour 2 Weeks West Coast	1161.099	2011-09-29 18:15:51.907	1	LongTerm-Stay
3	342	Lakes Tour 2 Weeks East Coast	1147.986	2008-08-31 13:21:02.883	1	LongTerm-Stay

Query executed successfully.   RENO (11.0 RTM)   Reno\j2p (51)   JProCo   00:00:00   3 rows

Figure 6.2 Hard-coded values in this query provide the right answer today, but are not flexible.

The result set in Figure 6.2 clearly shows the records reflecting JProCo's three most expensive products, so we have answered the question. Will this last query answer the question correctly sometime in the future?

What would happen if JProCo stopped selling these products, or added products that are even more expensive than one of these three? Our code is not robust enough to anticipate changes, because in reality, this query will always show any product with a RetailPrice value that is greater than or equal to $1147.986. If the JProCo management team decided to restructure its pricing so all products cost less than $1000, this query would return zero records.

In the world of programmers, using actual values as criteria in a predicate has a term known as *hard coding*, and generally is not a good practice. The preferred method is to write flexible, robust code that anticipates changes and by design will always deliver the expected result. Let's insert a more expensive record into the CurrentProducts table to help visualize the problems created by *hard coding* values in the predicate.

```
INSERT INTO CurrentProducts VALUES
('Summer Trip Cabo',4500,GETDATE(),0,'SuperLong')
```

Messages
(1 row(s) affected)

0 rows

Figure 6.3 Inserting an expensive record into the CurrentProducts table is successful.

We can now run the same query that moments ago, provided the three most expensive products in the CurrentProducts table. Will it work again?

```
SELECT *
FROM CurrentProducts
WHERE RetailPrice >= 1147.986
ORDER BY RetailPrice DESC
```

Results | Messages

	ProductID	ProductName	RetailPrice	OriginationDate	ToBeDeleted	Category
1	485	Summer Trip Cabo	4500.00	2012-10-20 19:40:55.777	0	Super Long
2	483	Yoga Mtn Getaway 2 Weeks	1695.00	2012-10-20 19:17:38.773	1	LongTerm-Stay
3	336	Lakes Tour 2 Weeks West Coast	1161.099	2011-09-29 18:15:51.907	1	LongTerm-Stay
4	342	Lakes Tour 2 Weeks East Coast	1147.986	2008-08-31 13:21:02.883	1	LongTerm-Stay

Query executed successfully. | RENO (11.0 RTM) Reno\j2p (51) JProCo 00:00:00 4 rows

Figure 6.4 This result set shows the flaw of using hard-coded values as criteria in the predicate.

The result set in Figure 6.4 is now returning four records. What happened? After adding the 'Summer Trip Cabo' product for $4500 to the CurrentProducts table, it became JProCo's most expensive product. The criteria for the query finds every RetailPrice value greater than or equal to $1147.986, so in addition to the three products found the first time we ran the query, this newest record is now part of the result set.

Since this *hard-coded* query is unable to reliably answer the question "What are the three most expensive products that JProCo currently sells?", we must find a better solution that is flexible enough to adapt to changes in the table.

Fortunately, there is another clause recognized by SQL Server that we can place in a SELECT statement to ensure we will always get the correct results, no matter how many changes are made to the CurrentProducts table. The TOP(*n*) clause is the solution we are looking for. Run this code and view the results in Figure 6.5.

```
SELECT TOP(3) *
FROM CurrentProducts
ORDER BY RetailPrice DESC
```

	ProductID	ProductName	RetailPrice	OriginationDate	ToBeDeleted	Category
1	484	Summer Trip Cabo	4500.00	2013-01-03 15:59:42.890	0	SuperLong
2	483	Yoga Mtn Getaway 2 Weeks	1695.00	2013-01-03 15:59:05.960	1	LongTerm-Stay
3	336	Lakes Tour 2 Weeks West Coast	1161.099	2011-09-29 18:15:51.907	1	LongTerm-Stay

Query executed successfully. (local) (11.0 RTM) Reno\Student (55) JProCo 00:00:00 3 rows

Figure 6.5 The TOP(*n*) clause reliably returns the desired results, even with changes to the table.

Even if we add another more expensive product, our query will always return the top 3 most expensive products in the table. We can test this by adding yet another new expensive product to the CurrentProducts table.

```
INSERT INTO CurrentProducts VALUES
('Summer Trip Aussie', 7500, GETDATE(), 0, 'Super Long')
```

```
Messages
(1 row(s) affected)
0 rows
```

Figure 6.6 Inserting an expensive record into the CurrentProducts table is successful.

Run the query again to test if this newest record appears in the result set.

```
SELECT TOP(3) *
FROM CurrentProducts
ORDER BY RetailPrice DESC
```

	ProductID	ProductName	RetailPrice	OriginationDate	ToBeDeleted	Category
1	485	Summer Trip Aussie	7500.00	2013-01-03 16:00:43.147	0	Super Long
2	484	Summer Trip Cabo	4500.00	2013-01-03 15:59:42.890	0	SuperLong
3	483	Yoga Mtn Getaway 2 Weeks	1695.00	2013-01-03 15:59:05.960	1	LongTerm-Stay

Query executed successfully. (local) (11.0 RTM) Reno\Student (55) JProCo 00:00:00 3 rows

Figure 6.7 The TOP(3) result set provides the correct results even after new products are added.

We can see by the results in Figure 6.7 that the TOP(3) query has delivered the result set exactly as requested. The best way to know when to use a TOP(*n*) clause in a query is to take a moment to understand more clearly how it works.

Let's follow along with the basic steps SQL Server took to create the result set for our most recent query.

1) The FROM clause is the foundation of every SQL query, as this is the source that defines the scope of available objects, such as tables, where the data is located. In this case, it makes the CurrentProducts table available to the rest of the clauses, keywords, statements or functions in the query.

2) The ORDER BY clause sorts the records in descending order of the RetailPrice field. This sorting process will place the highest RetailPrice values at the top of the record list and the lowest values at the bottom.

3) The SELECT * statement requests all fields in the CurrentProducts table be shown in the result set.

4) The TOP(3) clause acts as a row-limiter which will only deliver the first three rows returned by the query as the result set. Therefore, even though the query finds 483 records, the TOP(3) clause limits the result set to only the first (top) three records.

What if finding the three least expensive products currently available from JProCo were the requirement? Is there a BOTTOM (*n*) clause also? No, SQL Server only makes the TOP(*n*) clause available as the tool to limit rows returned by a query. So can we still find the three least expensive products as easily as we located the three most expensive products? We sure can!

Take a moment to examine the four basic steps SQL Server took with our query to find the three most expensive products available in the CurrentProducts table. In step 2, the ORDER BY clause is sorting the records in descending order, which places the most expensive values at the top and the least expensive at the bottom.

What if we sorted the records in ascending order? What effect would that have on the same query? Changing the ORDER BY clause to sort the RetailPrice values in ascending order will place the least expensive products at the top of the list and the most expensive at the bottom (reversing the previous order of the list).

Step 4 states that the TOP(3) clause acts as a row-limiter to the records returned by the query, so if the least expensive values are now at the top of the record list found by our query, we can anticipate a result set with only the three least expensive items. In fact, this is exactly what happens as shown in Figure 6.8.

```
SELECT TOP (3) *
FROM CurrentProducts
ORDER BY RetailPrice ASC
```

	ProductID	ProductName	RetailPrice	OriginationDate	ToBeDeleted	Category
1	313	Cherry Festival Tour 1 Day Mexico	31.909	2007-04-11 07:44:34.653	0	No-Stay
2	145	Mountain Lodge 1 Day Scandinavia	32.574	2012-01-04 05:55:45.417	0	No-Stay
3	73	Ocean Cruise Tour 1 Day Mexico	32.601	2010-01-01 06:01:01.907	0	No-Stay

Query executed successfully. RENO (11.0 RTM) Reno\j2p (51) JProCo 00:00:00 3 rows

Figure 6.8 Sorting RetailPrice in ascending order yields the three least expensive products.

READER NOTE: *Before reading the next section, 'Using TOP(n) with tied Values', either run the SQLQueries2012Vol2Chapter6.1Setup.sql reset script, or delete the two newest records added to the CurrentProducts table. Either action will restore the table to its original condition.*

Using TOP(*n*) with Tied Values

Our two TOP(3) queries were able to find either the three most expensive, or three least expensive products in the CurrentProducts table. While we are sure that these two queries worked correctly, what happens if two or more of the products had the same value for a RetailPrice?

```
SELECT *
FROM CurrentProducts
ORDER BY RetailPrice DESC
```

	ProductID	ProductName	RetailPrice	OriginationDate	ToBeDeleted	Category
1	483	Yoga Mtn Getaway 2 Weeks	1695.00	2012-10-20 19:17:38.773	1	LongTerm-Stay
2	336	Lakes Tour 2 Weeks West ...	1161.099	2011-09-29 18:15:51.907	1	LongTerm-Stay
3	342	Lakes Tour 2 Weeks East C...	1147.986	2008-08-31 13:21:02.883	1	LongTerm-Stay
4	372	Rain Forest Tour 2 Weeks ...	1144.773	2007-04-21 16:51:51.403	1	LongTerm-Stay
5	402	River Rapids Tour 2 Weeks ...	1116.108	2009-10-23 09:28:35.167	1	LongTerm-Stay
6 →	456	Wine Tasting Tour 2 Weeks...	1101.969	2011-09-09 11:30:06.323	1	LongTerm-Stay
7 →	66	Ocean Cruise Tour 2 Week...	1101.969	2009-05-04 07:48:04.043	1	LongTerm-Stay
8	30	Underwater Tour 2 Weeks ...	1045.062	2011-12-24 14:10:22.090	1	LongTerm-Stay
9	210	Horseback Tour 2 Weeks S...	1023.426	2007-04-01 08:32:59.657	1	LongTerm-Stay

Query executed successfully. RENO (11.0 RTM) Reno\j2p (51) JProCo 00:00:00 483 rows

Figure 6.9 ProductID 456 and 66 tied for 6th place with a value of $1101.969.

Suppose we wanted to get the six most expensive items. We can see Figure 6.9 shows a tie for 6th place with ProductID 456 and 66 having the same value of $1101.969. Since there is a two-way tie for sixth place, will a TOP(6) query return six records or seven?

```
SELECT TOP (6) *
FROM CurrentProducts
ORDER BY RetailPrice DESC
```

	ProductID	ProductName	RetailPrice	Origination...	ToBeDeleted	Category
1	483	Yoga Mtn Getaway 2 Weeks	1695.00	2012-09-25...	1	LongTerm-Stay
2	336	Lakes Tour 2 Weeks West Coast	1161.099	2011-09-29...	1	LongTerm-Stay
3	342	Lakes Tour 2 Weeks East Coast	1147.986	2008-08-31...	1	LongTerm-Stay
4	372	Rain Forest Tour 2 Weeks East ...	1144.773	2007-04-21...	1	LongTerm-Stay
5	402	River Rapids Tour 2 Weeks Eas...	1116.108	2009-10-23...	1	LongTerm-Stay
6	66	Ocean Cruise Tour 2 Weeks We...	1101.969	2009-05-04...	1	LongTerm-Stay

Query executed successfully. RENO (11.0 RTM) Reno\Student (51) JProCo 00:00:00 6 rows

Figure 6.10 A TOP(6) query returns only six records, even if tied values exist.

The result set in Figure 6.10 clearly shows the TOP(6) query returned only six records, even though there should be seven records in the result set. The same would be true if there had been 10, 1000, or millions of records with a RetailPrice value of \$1101.969, a TOP(6) query will strictly limit the result set to six records.

Once again, SQL Server has a solution for us. One of the TOP(*n*) optional clauses, WITH TIES, is available to solve this issue. Simply make the change to the query shown in the following code sample to display all seven records.

```
SELECT TOP (6) WITH TIES *
FROM CurrentProducts
ORDER BY RetailPrice DESC
```

	ProductID	ProductName	RetailPrice	Origination...	ToBeDeleted	Category
1	483	Yoga Mtn Getaway 2 Weeks	1695.00	2012-09-2...	1	LongTerm-Stay
2	336	Lakes Tour 2 Weeks West Coast	1161.099	2011-09-2...	1	LongTerm-Stay
3	342	Lakes Tour 2 Weeks East Coast	1147.986	2008-08-3...	1	LongTerm-Stay
4	372	Rain Forest Tour 2 Weeks East C...	1144.773	2007-04-2...	1	LongTerm-Stay
5	402	River Rapids Tour 2 Weeks East ...	1116.108	2009-10-2...	1	LongTerm-Stay
6	456	Wine Tasting Tour 2 Weeks West ...	1101.969	2011-09-0...	1	LongTerm-Stay
7	66	Ocean Cruise Tour 2 Weeks West...	1101.969	2009-05-0...	1	LongTerm-Stay

Query executed successfully. RENO (11.0 RTM) Reno\Student (51) JProCo 00:00:00 7 rows

Figure 6.11 Altering the query to read, TOP(6) WITH TIES, returns all seven records.

Using TOP(*n*) and DELETE

An easy way to learn how to use the TOP(*n*) clause with a DELETE statement is to use the CurrentProducts table of the JProCo database. This table has a field called ToBeDeleted that has a value of zero (0), or one (1).

    o   A value of zero (0) indicates the record is a current JProCo offering.

    o   A value of one (1) indicates the record is a product no longer offered by JProCo and scheduled for removal from the table.

Before attempting to remove any records from the CurrentProducts table, it is a good idea to build any DELETE statement as a SELECT statement first to make sure only the records intended for deletion are part of the result set prior to running the DELETE statement.

```
SELECT *
FROM CurrentProducts
WHERE ToBeDeleted = 1
```

	ProductID	ProductName	RetailPrice	OriginationDate	ToBeDeleted	Category
1	6	Underwater Tour 2 Weeks ...	553.347	2011-03-27 20:40:38.760	1	LongTerm-Stay
2	12	Underwater Tour 2 Weeks ...	727.731	2011-08-22 19:59:47.407	1	LongTerm-Stay
3	18	Underwater Tour 2 Weeks ...	945.531	2004-12-20 14:17:02.213	1	LongTerm-Stay
4	24	Underwater Tour 2 Weeks ...	770.265	2010-09-14 20:27:04.500	1	LongTerm-Stay
5	30	Underwater Tour 2 Weeks ...	1045.062	2011-12-24 14:10:22.090	1	LongTerm-Stay
6	36	History Tour 2 Weeks West ...	671.598	2005-09-08 09:10:33.740	1	LongTerm-Stay
7	42	History Tour 2 Weeks East ...	964.431	2010-05-17 23:20:28.873	1	LongTerm-Stay
8	48	History Tour 2 Weeks Mexico	640.278	2010-10-13 01:38:31.447	1	LongTerm-Stay
9	54	History Tour 2 Weeks Cana...	1019.583	2004-10-08 21:31:21.890	1	LongTerm-Stay
10	60	History Tour 2 Weeks Scan...	1005.615	2004-12-02 20:46:04.163	1	LongTerm-Stay
11	66	Ocean Cruise Tour 2 Week...	1101.969	2009-05-04 07:48:04.043	1	LongTerm-Stay
12	72	Ocean Cruise Tour 2 Week...	556.74	2008-08-30 21:28:44.060	1	LongTerm-Stay
13	78	Ocean Cruise Tour 2 Week...	293.409	2004-12-18 10:48:19.740	1	LongTerm-Stay
14	84	Ocean Cruise Tour 2 Week...	562.896	2010-08-09 13:56:57.833	1	LongTerm-Stay
15	90	Ocean Cruise Tour 2 Week...	964.575	2008-03-29 19:25:18.263	1	LongTerm-Stay

Query executed successfully.   RENO (11.0 RTM) Reno\j2p (51) JProCo 00:00:00 81 rows

Figure 6.12 There are 81 records with ToBeDeleted = 1 in the CurrentProducts table.

The results shown in Figure 6.12 confirm that there are 81 records ready for deletion, as indicated with a number 1 in the ToBeDeleted field. While it is a simple task for SQL Server to delete these 81 records at the same time, what if there were 81,000 records ready for deletion?

Deleting several thousand, let alone millions of records from a table during a single pass requires SQL Server to lock the table for an excessive amount of time, which denies access to all other users and applications until the deletion process is complete. We can use a TOP(n) clause to avoid these extended locks while deleting records, as it limits the number of records deleted at a single time.

By adding a TOP(10) clause to our previous query we will know exactly which records are about to be removed from the table as seen in Figure 6.13.

```
SELECT TOP(10) *
FROM CurrentProducts
WHERE ToBeDeleted = 1
```

	ProductID	ProductName	RetailPrice	OriginationD...	ToBeDeleted	Category
1	6	Underwater Tour 2 Weeks Wes...	553.347	2011-03-27...	1	LongTerm-Stay
2	12	Underwater Tour 2 Weeks East...	727.731	2011-08-22...	1	LongTerm-Stay
3	18	Underwater Tour 2 Weeks Mex...	945.531	2004-12-20...	1	LongTerm-Stay
4	24	Underwater Tour 2 Weeks Can...	770.265	2010-09-14...	1	LongTerm-Stay
5	30	Underwater Tour 2 Weeks Sca...	1045.062	2011-12-24...	1	LongTerm-Stay
6	36	History Tour 2 Weeks West Coast	671.598	2005-09-08...	1	LongTerm-Stay
7	42	History Tour 2 Weeks East Coast	964.431	2010-05-17...	1	LongTerm-Stay
8	48	History Tour 2 Weeks Mexico	640.278	2010-10-13...	1	LongTerm-Stay
9	54	History Tour 2 Weeks Canada	1019.583	2004-10-08...	1	LongTerm-Stay
10	60	History Tour 2 Weeks Scandina...	1005.615	2004-12-02...	1	LongTerm-Stay

Query executed successfully.   RENO (11.0 RTM)   Reno\Student (51)   JProCo   00:00:00   10 rows

Figure 6.13 A TOP(10) clause allows the first ten rows to be examined prior to deletion.

READER NOTE: *Recall the syntax for DELETE queries. The DML statement, DELETE, removes entire records, so there are no fields to specify in the query.*

Now that we have verified the first ten records are ready for deletion, we can change the SELECT TOP(10) * query to a DELETE TOP(10) query by using the code sample shown here.

```
DELETE TOP(10)
FROM CurrentProducts
WHERE ToBeDeleted = 1
```

Messages
(10 row(s) affected)
0 rows

Figure 6.14 The first 10 records ToBeDeleted = 1 have been successfully deleted.

CAUTION: *Although omitting a set of parentheses around the parameter value in a TOP clause will typically work with a SELECT statement, neglecting to place the parameter in a set of parentheses with a DELETE statement will cause SQL Server to issue an incorrect syntax error message. Thus, it is always a best practice to place parameter values inside a set of parentheses, i.e. TOP(5).*

Using a bit of simple math, we can determine that $(81 - 10) = 71$. We can verify that there are 71 records with a ToBeDeleted value of one (1) remaining in the CurrentProducts table, with this code sample.

```
SELECT *
FROM CurrentProducts
WHERE ToBeDeleted = 1
```

	ProductID	ProductName	RetailPrice	Origination...	ToBeDeleted	Category	
1	66	Ocean Cruise Tour 2 Weeks ...	1101.969	2009-05-04...	1	LongTerm-Stay	
2	72	Ocean Cruise Tour 2 Weeks ...	556.74	2008-08-30...	1	LongTerm-Stay	
3	78	Ocean Cruise Tour 2 Weeks ...	293.409	2004-12-18...	1	LongTerm-Stay	
4	84	Ocean Cruise Tour 2 Weeks ...	562.896	2010-08-09...	1	LongTerm-Stay	
5	90	Ocean Cruise Tour 2 Weeks ...	964.575	2008-03-29...	1	LongTerm-Stay	
6	96	Fruit Tasting Tour 2 Weeks ...	773.397	2004-04-19...	1	LongTerm-Stay	

Query executed successfully. RENO (11.0 RTM) Reno\Student (51) JProCo 00:00:00 71 rows

Figure 6.15 There are 71 records with a ToBeDeleted = 1 remaining in the CurrentProducts table.

The results in Figure 6.15 confirm there are 71 records remaining in the CurrentProducts table with a ToBeDeleted value of 1. If we take a moment to review the results shown in Figure 6.12, we will see that the first, second and third records in Figure 6.15 were originally the 11th, 12th and 13th records. In other words, after deleting the first ten records from the original result set, the current results begin with the original eleventh record.

Complete the requirement to remove these records from the JProCo database by running a DELETE statement on the remaining records marked for deletion.

```
DELETE
FROM CurrentProducts
WHERE ToBeDeleted = 1
```

Messages
(71 row(s) affected)
0 rows

Figure 6.16 Removing the remaining 71 records in the CurrentProducts table marked for deletion.

Our last step is to verify that there are no longer any records remaining in the CurrentProducts table with the number 1 in the ToBeDeleted field (Figure 6.17).

```
SELECT *
FROM CurrentProducts
WHERE ToBeDeleted = 1
```

Figure 6.17 There are no records left in the CurrentProducts table with ToBeDeleted = 1.

As a reminder, using the FROM clause is optional with a DELETE statement. Many SQL Developers and DBAs prefer to use it as they are typically writing the query as a SELECT statement first. After verifying the records in the result set for deletion, it is simple to change the SELECT keyword to the DELETE keyword.

An example of deleting all records in a table without using the FROM clause is shown in this code sample.

```
DELETE CurrentProducts
```

Lab 6.1: TOP(*n*) Queries

Lab Prep: Each lab has one or more Skill Checks. Start with Skill Check 1 and proceed until reaching the Points to Ponder section.

Before beginning this lab, verify that SQL Server 2012 is properly installed and operating. Before running the lab setup script for resetting the database (SQLQueries2012Vol2Chapter6.1Setup.sql), please make sure to close all query windows within SSMS. An open query window pointing to a database context can lock that database preventing it from updating when the script is executing. A simple way to assure all query windows are closed, is to exit out of SSMS, then open a new instance of SSMS, and lastly run the setup script.

READER NOTE: *Some of the Skill Checks in Lab 6.1 will not work properly unless there are 81 records with 'ToBeDeleted = 1' in the CurrentProducts table.*

Before starting the first Skill Check, run the following query filtering on this criterion to verify 81 records are present.

```
SELECT *
FROM CurrentProducts
WHERE ToBeDeleted = 1
```

Skill Check 1: In the JProCo database, display only the two EmpID records with the oldest HireDate in the Employee table.

When done, the result set should resemble the one shown in Figure 6.18.

	EmpID	LastName	FirstName	HireDate	LocationID	ManagerID	Status
1	11	Smith	Sally	1989-04-01 00:00:00.000	1	NULL	Active
2	12	O'Neil	Barbara	1995-05-26 00:00:00.000	4	4	Has Tenure

Query executed successfully.   RENO (11.0 RTM)   Reno\Student (51)   JProCo   00:00:00   2 rows

Figure 6.18 Skill Check 1 finds the two employees with the oldest HireDate.

Skill Check 2: In the JProCo database, display the six largest grants found in the Grant table. Make sure any tied values will also appear in the result set.

When done, the result set should resemble the one shown in Figure 6.19.

	GrantID	GrantName	EmpID	Amount
1	007	Ben@MoreTechnology.com	10	41000.00
2	008	www.@-Last-U-Can-Help.com	7	25000.00
3	009	Thank you @.com	11	21500.00
4	004	Norman's Outreach	NULL	21000.00
5	005	BIG 6's Foundation%	4	21000.00
6	006	TALTA_Kishan International	3	18100.00
7	003	Robert@BigStarBank.com	7	18100.00

Query executed successfully.   RENO (11.0 RTM)   Reno\Student (51)   JProCo   00:00:00   7 rows

Figure 6.19 Skill Check 2 finds the top six grant values, including any ties for fourth and sixth place.

Skill Check 3: In the JProCo database, display the ten most expensive single day trips found in the CurrentProducts table. Since an overnight stay is not required, a day trip has a value of No-Stay in the Category field.

When done, the results should resemble those shown in Figure 6.20.

	ProductID	ProductName	RetailPrice	OriginationD...	ToBeDeleted	Category
1	331	Lakes Tour 1 Day West Coast	129.011	2006-08-08...	0	No-Stay
2	337	Lakes Tour 1 Day East Coast	127.554	2009-10-23...	0	No-Stay
3	367	Rain Forest Tour 1 Day East Coast	127.197	2007-03-01...	0	No-Stay
4	397	River Rapids Tour 1 Day East Coast	124.012	2012-03-12...	0	No-Stay
5	61	Ocean Cruise Tour 1 Day West Coast	122.441	2007-04-13...	0	No-Stay
6	451	Wine Tasting Tour 1 Day West Coast	120.198	2004-03-31...	0	No-Stay
7	25	Underwater Tour 1 Day Scandinavia	116.118	2010-11-03...	0	No-Stay
8	205	Horseback Tour 1 Day Scandinavia	113.714	2012-03-28...	0	No-Stay
9	355	Lakes Tour 1 Day Scandinavia	113.354	2010-10-16...	0	No-Stay
10	49	History Tour 1 Day Canada	113.287	2010-01-04...	0	No-Stay

Query executed successfully.   RENO (11.0 RTM)   Reno\Student (51)   JProCo   00:00:00   10 rows

Figure 6.20 Skill Check 3 displays the top ten most expensive day trips.

Skill Check 4: Our sister company is now handling all trips lasting two weeks and thus need to be deleted from our CurrentProducts table. There are 81 records in the CurrentProducts table marked ToBeDeleted with a value of one (1).

Run a query to delete the first 10 records in the CurrentProducts table. Once this is complete, verify there are only 71 ToBeDeleted records with a value of one (1) remaining in the CurrentProducts table.

When done, the results should resemble those shown in Figure 6.21.

```
SELECT * FROM CurrentProducts
WHERE ToBeDeleted = 1
```

	ProductID	ProductName	RetailPrice	Origination...	ToBeDeleted	Category
1	66	Ocean Cruise Tour 2 Weeks ...	1101.969	2009-05-04...	1	LongTerm-Stay
2	72	Ocean Cruise Tour 2 Weeks ...	556.74	2008-08-30...	1	LongTerm-Stay
3	78	Ocean Cruise Tour 2 Weeks ...	293.409	2004-12-18...	1	LongTerm-Stay
4	84	Ocean Cruise Tour 2 Weeks ...	562.896	2010-08-09...	1	LongTerm-Stay
5	90	Ocean Cruise Tour 2 Weeks ...	964.575	2008-03-29...	1	LongTerm-Stay
6	96	Fruit Tasting Tour 2 Weeks ...	773.397	2004-04-19...	1	LongTerm-Stay

Query executed successfully.   RENO (11.0 RTM)   Reno\Student (51)   JProCo   00:00:00   71 rows

Figure 6.21 Confirm 71 ToBeDeleted records remain in the CurrentProducts table.

Answer Code: The T-SQL code for this lab is located in the downloadable files as a file named Lab6.1_Top_n_Queries.sql.

Points to Ponder - TOP(*n*) Queries

1. The TOP(*n*) clause is a row-limiter that specifies how many records found by the query will be in the result set.

2. It is good practice to use an ORDER BY clause with any statement containing a TOP(*n*) clause.

3. The result set produced by a TOP(*n*) clause relies on the sorting order of the records in the query. For example, when sorting the Sales field in descending order, the largest sales will appear at the top of the record set. Conversely, sorting the Sales field in ascending order will place the smallest sales at the top of the result set.

4. TOP(*n*) ignores tie values. It simply slices off the TOP(*n*) number of records requested. Should two people tie for 5th place in a TOP(5) query, only one of the tied records will be listed in the result set.

5. When a TOP(*n*) query needs to include tied values in the result set, it must have a WITH TIES clause following it.

6. TOP(*n*) is strictly a row-limiter and does not evaluate or read the actual data values. It simply relies upon the sort order and slices off the specified number of records from the upper part of the result set.

7. When adding the WITH TIES clause, any values tied on the last record will be included in the result set. For example, the statement "TOP(10) WITH TIES Price" will select the first 10 rows from the top of the record set. Then it will look at the next record(s) and evaluate whether the 11th row value for Price is the same as the 10th row. If the 11th value is the same, then row 11 appears in the result set. The statement will continue checking and including the next rows (rows 12, 13, 14, etc.) until it finds a different value. If rows 10-15 all contain the same value for Price, then the "TOP(10) WITH TIES Price" query will return rows 1-15.

8. The TOP(*n*) clause limits records affected by the SELECT statement.

TOP(*n*) Query Tricks

The TOP(n) clause is a handy tool. In this section, we will see some creative uses for answering questions, including one or two of my favorite interview questions. Interviews for IT and database jobs can actually be enjoyable when approaching these challenging coding questions as though they are a puzzle.

TOP(*n*) Queries with Variables

Our fun begins by looking at how to use variables with the TOP(*n*) clause. Students with little exposure to variables should not worry, as we will do a quick review of using variables to make sure everyone is familiar with these concepts.

Recall we opened this chapter with an example showing *hard-coded* values as a bad practice. One alternative to using hard-coded values in a query is to use variables in their place, as they are much more flexible and efficient. In short, variables allow for easily altering values in a query without having to change the code each time.

READER NOTE: *In SQL, a single '@' (ampersand) sign precedes the name of any local variable (e.g., @MinPrice, @MaxGrantAmount).*

Using variables to pass input values (also called parameters) to a query or stored procedure is an even better way to make sure queries are robust, flexible and avoid using hard-coded values. Depending on which version of SQL Server is running the code, there are two different ways to implement a variable. The next two coding samples will show the syntax and basic usage of variables in a query.

This first code sample demonstrates the only available way to declare and set a variable with versions of SQL Server prior to 2008, although it is acceptable in current versions as well.

```
DECLARE @MinPrice INT
SET @MinPrice = 800

SELECT *
FROM CurrentProducts
WHERE RetailPrice > @MinPrice
```

This second code sample demonstrates the newest way to declare and set a variable that became available with SQL Server 2008 and is acceptable in every version since then, including SQL Server 2012. *Notice how in a single statement, the variable has been declared and assigned a value.*

```
DECLARE @MinPrice INT = 800

SELECT *
FROM CurrentProducts
WHERE RetailPrice > @MinPrice
ORDER BY RetailPrice DESC
```

	ProductID	ProductName	RetailPrice	OriginationDate	ToBeDeleted	Category
1	483	Yoga Mtn Getaway 2 Weeks	1695.00	2012-10-23 22:19:49.757	1	LongTerm-Stay
2	336	Lakes Tour 2 Weeks West C...	1161.099	2009-01-02 18:15:51.907	1	LongTerm-Stay
3	342	Lakes Tour 2 Weeks East C...	1147.986	2005-12-05 13:21:02.883	1	LongTerm-Stay
4	372	Rain Forest Tour 2 Weeks E...	1144.773	2004-07-25 16:51:51.403	1	LongTerm-Stay
5	402	River Rapids Tour 2 Weeks ...	1116.108	2007-01-27 09:28:35.167	1	LongTerm-Stay
6	456	Wine Tasting Tour 2 Weeks ...	1101.969	2008-12-13 11:30:06.323	1	LongTerm-Stay

Query executed successfully.　　RENO (11.0 RTM)　Reno\j2p (51)　JProCo　00:00:00　31 rows

Figure 6.22 The result set returned by a query using a variable in the filtering criteria.

We can also declare two variables, set them at different values and use them as range filtering criteria in our query. Run the code sample here and compare the results to those shown in Figure 6.23.

```
DECLARE @MinPrice INT = 900
DECLARE @MaxPrice INT = 1000

SELECT *
FROM CurrentProducts
WHERE RetailPrice BETWEEN @MinPrice AND @MaxPrice
ORDER BY RetailPrice DESC
```

	ProductID	ProductName	RetailPrice	OriginationDate	ToBeDeleted	Category
1	482	Yoga Mtn Getaway 1 Week	995.00	2012-10-23 22:19:49.753	0	LongTerm-Stay
2	120	Fruit Tasting Tour 2 Weeks ...	984.438	2007-02-11 15:00:38.513	1	LongTerm-Stay
3	414	River Rapids Tour 2 Weeks ...	978.858	2001-11-10 18:21:42.790	1	LongTerm-Stay
4	312	Cherry Festival Tour 2 Week...	976.968	2006-03-15 21:45:41.527	1	LongTerm-Stay
5	90	Ocean Cruise Tour 2 Week...	964.575	2005-07-03 19:25:18.263	1	LongTerm-Stay
6	42	History Tour 2 Weeks East ...	964.431	2007-08-21 23:20:28.873	1	LongTerm-Stay

Query executed successfully.　　RENO (11.0 RTM)　Reno\j2p (53)　JProCo　00:00:00　9 rows

Figure 6.23 Two variables are used to set the minimum and maximum price range.

We are now ready to write a TOP(*n*) query that we can modify to use a variable as a parameter. Since we will be looking for the most expensive products, make sure to sort the records in descending order based on the RetailPrice value.

```
SELECT TOP(4) *
FROM CurrentProducts
ORDER BY RetailPrice DESC
```

	ProductID	ProductName	RetailPrice	OriginationDate	ToBeDeleted	Category
1	483	Yoga Mtn Getaway 2 Weeks	1695.00	2012-10-23 22:19:49.757	1	LongTerm-Stay
2	336	Lakes Tour 2 Weeks West Coast	1161.099	2009-01-02 18:15:51.907	1	LongTerm-Stay
3	342	Lakes Tour 2 Weeks East Coast	1147.986	2005-12-05 13:21:02.883	1	LongTerm-Stay
4	372	Rain Forest Tour 2 Weeks East...	1144.773	2004-07-25 16:51:51.403	1	LongTerm-Stay

Query executed successfully. RENO (11.0 RTM) Reno\j2p (53) JProCo 00:00:00 4 rows

Figure 6.24 TOP(4) records with the most expensive RetailPrice values appearing first.

It is a simple process to change the TOP(*n*) clause to accept a variable as a parameter. All we need to do is create a variable named @TopNum and set its value to the number 4. Once the @TopNum variable has been declared and assigned a value, we can place the variable name inside the parentheses of the TOP clause. Run the code sample shown here and verify the results are the same as those shown in the previous query with the hard-coded value of 4 (Figure 6.24).

```
DECLARE @TopNum INT = 4

SELECT TOP(@TopNum) *
FROM CurrentProducts
ORDER BY RetailPrice DESC
```

	ProductID	ProductName	RetailPrice	OriginationDate	ToBeDeleted	Category
1	483	Yoga Mtn Getaway 2 Weeks	1695.00	2012-10-23 22:19:49.757	1	LongTerm-Stay
2	336	Lakes Tour 2 Weeks West Coast	1161.099	2009-01-02 18:15:51.907	1	LongTerm-Stay
3	342	Lakes Tour 2 Weeks East Coast	1147.986	2005-12-05 13:21:02.883	1	LongTerm-Stay
4	372	Rain Forest Tour 2 Weeks East...	1144.773	2004-07-25 16:51:51.403	1	LongTerm-Stay

Query executed successfully. RENO (11.0 RTM) Reno\j2p (53) JProCo 00:00:00 4 rows

Figure 6.25 TOP(@TopNum) records with the most expensive RetailPrice values appearing first.

READER NOTE: *When using a variable as the parameter in the TOP clause, enclosing it inside a set of parentheses is required to avoid receiving a SQL Server incorrect syntax error message. This should reinforce the habit of always using parentheses with the TOP(n) clause, as it will always perform correctly.*

It is quite understandable if variables are still an abstract concept. Hang in there, nearly all SQL Server Pros began learning these important programming concepts in much the same way.

Whichever value we choose to pass to the @TopNum variable, it will run and change the result accordingly. At this point, the benefits of using a variable in a query might not be readily apparent, since it is just as easy for us to change the hard-coded parameter value, as it is to change the variable parameter value as long as we are working inside SSMS. The advantages will become much more obvious when we begin using stored procedures, functions and applications with variables.

Here's another example. Most readers have probably used a web application in their daily routine. Many of these web applications interact with a SQL Server, or other RDMS database behind the scenes.

When making an online payment, look at the date range choices the web form allows. Some systems won't accept a payment on the same day, forcing us to choose a date at least one day out in the future before accepting the payment. Other systems won't allow payments scheduled further in advance than 30 days.

Both of these cases are examples of a user inputting a date value and the system sending that input value (parameterized variable) to a stored procedure, then proceeding to the next step in the transaction. It is highly unlikely the system takes the date value parameter and evaluates it against a hard-coded list of acceptable payment dates. Rather, it takes the date value parameter and passes it as a variable to the stored procedure, which plugs the date into the query logic and produces a result, which either returns Yes or No to the payment date requested.

Much like red cars, variables are everywhere once we begin noticing them!

Customizing TOP(*n*) Queries

What if a hiring manager asked us an interview question, similar to this one:
"What are two ways to find the 5th highest record of the CurrentProducts table?"

The easiest answer is to write a simple query like the one shown here and point to the fifth record in the result set.

```
SELECT *
FROM CurrentProducts
ORDER BY RetailPrice DESC
```

Of course, now that we know how to use the TOP(*n*) clause, we would certainly consider showing this skill off by writing a query similar to this one and pointing to the last item on the list (Figure 6.26).

```
SELECT TOP (5) *
FROM CurrentProducts
ORDER BY RetailPrice DESC
```

	ProductID	ProductName	RetailPrice	OriginationDate	ToBeDeleted	Category
1	483	Yoga Mtn Getaway 2 Weeks	1695.00	2012-10-23 22:19:49.757	1	LongTerm-Stay
2	336	Lakes Tour 2 Weeks West ...	1161.099	2009-01-02 18:15:51.907	1	LongTerm-Stay
3	342	Lakes Tour 2 Weeks East C...	1147.986	2005-12-05 13:21:02.883	1	LongTerm-Stay
4	372	Rain Forest Tour 2 Weeks ...	1144.773	2004-07-25 16:51:51.403	1	LongTerm-Stay
5	402	River Rapids Tour 2 Weeks...	1116.108	2007-01-27 09:28:35.167	1	LongTerm-Stay

Query executed successfully.   RENO (11.0 RTM) Reno\j2p (53) JProCo 00:00:00 5 rows

Figure 6.26 The fifth most expensive item in the CurrentProducts table is ProductID 402.

What if the hiring manager had actually asked this question with a slight twist: *"What query will show only the 5th highest record in the CurrentProducts table?"*

Hmmm… that is quite different. It is very important to listen to every question asked to determine what the actual meaning or intent of the question is, regardless of whether the question is asked during an interview, by the manager, team lead, or the customer themselves.

Our first two queries displayed more than just the fifth record in their respective result sets. They also relied on a human capable of manually pointing out the fifth record in the result set. Neither of these solutions will answer this question.

So how do we remove those other four records and leave only the fifth record in the result set? Solving this puzzle starts with answering the question we just asked ourselves.

In other words, we need to write two queries; the first will find the five highest priced products and another query that shows only the four most expensive products. The results of these two queries are in Figure 6.27.

```
SELECT TOP(5) *
FROM CurrentProducts
ORDER BY RetailPrice DESC
```

```
SELECT TOP(4) *
FROM CurrentProducts
ORDER BY RetailPrice DESC
```

Figure 6.27 ProductID 402 is the only record in the TOP(5) not contained in the TOP(4).

Both of the result sets in Figure 6.27 have four records in common. There is only one record in the TOP(5) query that is not contained in the TOP(4) query. It looks like we could solve this problem if there were a way to subtract, or exclude, the records in the TOP(4) query from the result set of the TOP(5) query.

Another perspective on the problem is that ProductID 402 from the TOP(5) query is the one record not in the result set of the TOP(4) query. OK, looking at it from this perspective, we can actually write a query that matches our description.

```
SELECT TOP(1) *
FROM CurrentProducts
WHERE ProductID NOT IN (483,336,342,372)
ORDER BY RetailPrice DESC
```

Figure 6.28 The River Rapids Tour is the only record in the TOP(5) not contained in the TOP(4).

Very good! We have found a way to display only the fifth most expensive record (ProductID 402) in the result set, by looking for the single record, or TOP(1), with a ProductID that is NOT IN the four ProductID values from our previous TOP(4) query results.

While this is a correct answer, we know very well that hard-coded values limit flexibility for this query. If tomorrow, products get added, deleted, or re-priced, then it is quite possible an incorrect result will show for the fifth highest record.

We need a creative way to achieve the same result from this query without using hard-coded ProductID values for our criteria. Let's look closer at how the TOP(4) query determined which four hard-coded ProductID values to use, by rewriting it to only show the ProductID field in the results (Figure 6.29).

```
SELECT TOP(4) ProductID
FROM CurrentProducts
ORDER BY RetailPrice DESC
```

	ProductID
1	483
2	336
3	342
4	372

4 rows

Figure 6.29 The TOP(4) ProductID query results are the hard-coded values in the first query.

The results shown in Figure 6.29 have the same ProductID values as those used for our hard-coded criteria. Is it possible to substitute this entire query for the hard-coded values? Yes, it really is that easy.

Placing (nesting) code inside another query goes by the term *subquery*. Notice that the indented code in the *subquery* makes it easier to read by separating it from the outer query. Run the code sample shown here and observe that we get the desired results in Figure 6.30.

```
SELECT TOP(1) *
FROM CurrentProducts
WHERE ProductID NOT IN (
   SELECT TOP(4) ProductID
   FROM CurrentProducts
   ORDER BY RetailPrice DESC)
ORDER BY RetailPrice DESC
```

	ProductID	ProductName	RetailPrice	OriginationDate	ToBeDeleted	Category
1	402	River Rapids Tour 2 Weeks Ea...	1116.108	2007-01-27 09:28:35.167	1	LongTerm-Stay

Query executed successfully.   RENO (11.0 RTM)   Reno\j2p (51)   JProCo   00:00:00   1 rows

Figure 6.30 Replacing hard-coded criteria values with a subquery shows the same results.

Success! This is a much better way of answering this interview question about displaying only the fifth highest record. Our latest solution uses some creative thinking to deliver the required results *and* avoids the poor practice of hard coding values in the filtering criteria.

This latest solution uses most of what we have learned so far about the TOP(n) clause, except for using a variable as a parameter. At first, using a variable as a parameter in this query might not seem appropriate. After all, an application will most likely ask a user to input directly the value for the record they want to find.

If the application asks the user for which of the highest records they want to see and were to pass a variable with a value of 5 to our previous query, we would get the sixth highest record in the result set, which is incorrect, as seen in Figure 6.31.

```
DECLARE @TopNum INT = 5

SELECT TOP(1) *
FROM CurrentProducts
WHERE ProductID NOT IN (
   SELECT TOP(@TopNum) ProductID
   FROM CurrentProducts
   ORDER BY RetailPrice DESC)
ORDER BY RetailPrice DESC
```

	ProductID	ProductName	RetailPrice	OriginationDate	ToBeDeleted	Category
1	456	Wine Tasting Tour 2 Weeks W...	1101.969	2008-12-13 11:30:06.323	1	LongTerm-Stay

Query executed successfully. RENO (11.0 RTM) Reno\j2p (51) JProCo 00:00:00 1 rows

Figure 6.31 Passing the user entered value directly as a parameter will give the wrong result.

This is a great example of why testing is an important part of code development. Had this query been released into production prior to testing, it would certainly have prompted a complaint from the user(s) and required significantly more time to track down the problem, as it would be necessary to eliminate any potential mistakes in both the front-end application and the back-end database code.

Fortunately, SQL Server allows expressions as the parameter in the TOP(*n*) clause. Since we know that the parameter value passed in from the users application causes our query to return a record one higher than what the user wants to see, we need to use a mathematical expression to subtract one from the parameters value.

In other words, we know the parameter value in the subquery that gives us the correct record is 4 and the parameter value that is passed from the application is 5, so if our expression is (5 - 1), SQL Server will interpret this as being equal to 4. Let's modify the query to replace the variable in the TOP(@TopNum) clause with our expression TOP(@TopNum - 1). Run the code sample shown here and check the results against those shown in Figure 6.32 and notice that the query now provides the correct record (ProductID 402) in the result set.

```
DECLARE @TopNum INT = 5

SELECT TOP(1) *
FROM CurrentProducts
WHERE ProductID NOT IN (
  SELECT TOP(@TopNum - 1) ProductID
  FROM CurrentProducts
  ORDER BY RetailPrice DESC)
ORDER BY RetailPrice DESC
```

	ProductID	ProductName	RetailPrice	OriginationDate	ToBeDeleted	Category
1	402	River Rapids Tour 2 Weeks Ea...	1116.108	2007-01-27 09:28:35.167	1	LongTerm-Stay

Query executed successfully. RENO (11.0 RTM) Reno\j2p (51) JProCo 00:00:00 1 rows

Figure 6.32 Using the expression (@TopNum - 1) for the parameter will give the correct result.

The power of using variables with the TOP(*n*) clause is now much more obvious. We can test our code a little further by using a value of 10 for the @TopNum variable and make sure it returns the record for ProductID 360 (Figure 6.33).

```
DECLARE @TopNum INT = 10

SELECT TOP(1) *
FROM CurrentProducts
WHERE ProductID NOT IN (
  SELECT TOP(@TopNum - 1) ProductID
  FROM CurrentProducts
  ORDER BY RetailPrice DESC)
ORDER BY RetailPrice DESC
```

	ProductID	ProductName	RetailPrice	OriginationDate	ToBeDeleted	Category
1	360	Lakes Tour 2 Weeks Scandina...	1020.186	2002-02-09 01:20:30.970	1	LongTerm-Stay

Query executed successfully. RENO (11.0 RTM) Reno\j2p (51) JProCo 00:00:00 1 rows

Figure 6.33 Testing the query with a different variable value will confirm that it works correctly.

Fantastic! We now have a TOP(*n*) trick up our sleeves that is sure to impress any experienced SQL Developer or hiring manager. This is definitely a skill to keep.

READER NOTE: *This latest query example briefly touched on using a subquery to achieve the desired results. Chapter 12 will delve much deeper into different techniques using subqueries. In Chapter 7, we will use ranking functions to discover additional ways of answering interview questions like this.*

Our next example uses the Employee table to apply what we have learned using the DATETIME data type with our new found knowledge of the TOP(*n*) clause.

Display all records from the Employee table sorted by the HireDate value for each employee from the oldest date to the most recent. The three employees with the most seniority will now appear at the top of the record set (Figure 6.34).

```
SELECT *
FROM Employee
ORDER BY HireDate ASC
```

	EmpID	LastName	FirstName	HireDate	LocationID	ManagerID	Status
1	11	Smith	Sally	1989-04-01 00:00:00.000	1	NULL	Active
2	12	O'Neil	Barbara	1995-05-26 00:00:00.000	4	4	Has Tenure
3	4	Kennson	David	1996-03-16 00:00:00.000	1	11	Has Tenure
4	3	Osako	Lee	1999-09-01 00:00:00.000	2	11	Active
5	7	Lonning	David	2000-01-01 00:00:00.000	1	11	On Leave
6	1	Adams	Alex	2001-01-01 00:00:00.000	1	11	Active

Query executed successfully.   RENO (11.0 RTM)   Reno\Student (51)   JProCo   00:00:00   13 rows

Figure 6.34 The employees appearing at the top of the record set have the most seniority.

Of course, adding a TOP(3) clause will display only the three employee records with the most seniority (Figure 6.35).

```
SELECT TOP(3) *
FROM Employee
ORDER BY HireDate ASC
```

	EmpID	LastName	FirstName	HireDate	LocationID	ManagerID	Status
1	11	Smith	Sally	1989-04-01 00:00:00.000	1	NULL	Active
2	12	O'Neil	Barbara	1995-05-26 00:00:00.000	4	4	Has Tenure
3	4	Kennson	David	1996-03-16 00:00:00.000	1	11	Has Tenure

Query executed successfully.   RENO (11.0 RTM)   Reno\Student (51)   JProCo   00:00:00   3 rows

Figure 6.35 Results show the three JProCo employees with the most seniority.

By changing the sort order of this query from ascending to descending order, we will display the three employee records that were most recently hired to work at JProCo (Figure 6.36).

```
SELECT TOP(3) *
FROM Employee
ORDER BY HireDate DESC
```

	EmpID	LastName	FirstName	HireDate	LocationID	ManagerID	Status
1	13	Wilconkinski	Phil	2009-06-11 00:00:00.000	1	4	Active
2	5	Bender	Eric	2007-05-17 00:00:00.000	1	11	Active
3	10	O'Haire	Terry	2004-10-04 00:00:00.000	2	3	Active

Query executed successfully. | RENO (11.0 RTM) | Reno\Student (51) | JProCo | 00:00:00 | 3 rows

Figure 6.36 Results show the three newest employees at JProCo.

In this chapter, we have learned to consider where records appear physically in a result set. We then discovered how using this knowledge helps to answer difficult questions. Similarly, it is helpful to know what effects a WHERE, ORDER BY and TOP clause have on the result set. Here is a quick review of these clauses:

The WHERE clause is processed immediately after the FROM clause, which is the first clause SQL Server processes in a query. The WHERE clause filters, or limits, the records available to the rest of the query, by applying criteria to individual records, and excluding those that do not meet the criteria. This filtering takes place before any aggregation or sorting takes place. We saw examples in Chapter 4 that taught us to use caution when combining a WHERE clause with a GROUP BY clause, as the former works on individual records and the latter works on groups (sets) of records. This mismatch in behavior can cause unintended results. *It is recommended to use the HAVING clause with the GROUP BY clause for filtering, as it too works on sets of records.*

The ORDER BY clause sorts all records made available to it in either an ascending or descending order as instructed by the query. If a sort order is not explicitly stated then SQL Server will default to an ascending sort order. The ORDER BY clause is usually the last statement to appear in a query and can work with or without aggregation. When used with aggregation, ORDER BY can accept the aggregated field(s) or any other field(s) contained after the SELECT or GROUP BY clauses.

The TOP(*n*) clause acts as a row limiter, by returning only the number of records requested by the value of its parameter to the result set. Since the TOP(*n*) clause will only operate on records at the top of a list, it is highly recommended, and in many cases a requirement, to implement an ORDER BY clause whenever the TOP(*n*) clause is used in a DML statement, as this is the only way to predetermine which records are at the top of the list.

Our last exercise in this section will compare the effect these three clauses have on the records marked for deletion in the CurrentProducts table.

Recall from Skill Check 4 in Lab 6.1 that the sister company for JProCo is taking over all trips lasting two weeks, thus a mass deletion of these records from the CurrentProducts table is evident by the value 1 in the ToBeDeleted column.

We can easily see how many records are marked for deletion by querying the CurrentProducts table and using the WHERE clause to eliminate all records that do not have a ToBeDeleted value equal to 1, as seen in Figure 6.37.

```
SELECT *
FROM CurrentProducts
WHERE ToBeDeleted = 1
```

	ProductID	ProductName	RetailPrice	OriginationDate	ToBeDeleted	Category
1	6	Underwater Tour 2 Weeks ...	553.347	2008-06-30 20:40:38.760	1	LongTerm-Stay
2	12	Underwater Tour 2 Weeks ...	727.731	2008-11-25 19:59:47.407	1	LongTerm-Stay
3	18	Underwater Tour 2 Weeks ...	945.531	2002-03-26 14:17:02.213	1	LongTerm-Stay
4	24	Underwater Tour 2 Weeks ...	770.265	2007-12-19 20:27:04.500	1	LongTerm-Stay
5	30	Underwater Tour 2 Weeks ...	1045.062	2009-03-29 14:10:22.090	1	LongTerm-Stay
6	36	History Tour 2 Weeks West ...	671.598	2002-12-13 09:10:33.740	1	LongTerm-Stay

Query executed successfully. RENO (11.0 RTM) Reno\j2p (51) JProCo 00:00:00 81 rows

Figure 6.37 The 81 records in the CurrentProducts table marked for deletion.

READER NOTE: If you ran Skill Check 4 of Lab 6.1 then you will only have 71 records in this table. If you want to see all records then run the In fact, querying the SQLQueries2012Vol2Chapter6.2Setup.sql script.

CurrentProducts table with its records sorted in descending order of RetailPrice will show that all but two (ProductID 482 and 481) of the first fifty records are slated for deletion (Figure 6.38).

```
SELECT *
FROM CurrentProducts
ORDER BY RetailPrice DESC
```

	ProductID	ProductName	RetailPrice	OriginationDate	ToBeDeleted	Category
23	168	Spa & Pleasure Getaway 2 ...	887.328	2003-04-23 13:11:56.973	1	LongTerm-Stay
24	198	Horseback Tour 2 Weeks M...	884.979	2007-12-06 20:05:46.043	1	LongTerm-Stay
25	180	Spa & Pleasure Getaway 2 ...	879.894	2006-12-29 15:40:43.627	1	LongTerm-Stay
26	481	Yoga Mtn Getaway 5 Days	875.00	2012-10-23 22:19:49.753	0 ←	Medium-Stay
27	390	Rain Forest Tour 2 Weeks ...	844.308	2001-11-11 14:21:21.500	1	LongTerm-Stay
28	174	Spa & Pleasure Getaway 2 ...	840.393	2003-02-20 03:23:21.510	1	LongTerm-Stay
29	384	Rain Forest Tour 2 Weeks ...	836.838	2005-10-29 22:57:08.080	1	LongTerm-Stay
30	264	Winter Tour 2 Weeks Canada	816.255	2002-10-27 03:27:34.523	1	LongTerm-Stay

Query executed successfully. RENO (11.0 RTM) Reno\j2p (51) JProCo 00:00:00 483 rows

Figure 6.38 Scroll through the results to find the highest prices not marked for deletion.

Once deleting these records from the CurrentProducts table, the two highest priced products remaining will be the aforementioned ProductID 482 with a RetailPrice value of $995 and ProductID 481 with a RetailPrice value of $875, as shown in the second set of results (bottom) of Figure 6.40.

```
DELETE
FROM CurrentProducts
WHERE ToBeDeleted = 1
```

Messages
(81 row(s) affected)
0 rows

Figure 6.39 Confirmation message after deleting 81 records from the CurrentProducts table.

The next two queries demonstrate the syntax and behavior of the ORDER BY clause for sorting the same table in ascending and descending order. Notice in the first query the ORDER BY defaulted to ascending sort order with the cheapest items at the top. The second query descending (DESC) order was specified in the second query so the most expensive items are at the top of the result set (Figure 6.40).

```
SELECT *
FROM CurrentProducts
ORDER BY RetailPrice
```

```
SELECT *
FROM CurrentProducts
ORDER BY RetailPrice DESC
```

	ProductID	ProductName	RetailPrice	OriginationDate	ToBeDeleted	Category
1	313	Cherry Festival Tour 1 Day Mexico	31.909	2007-04-11 07:44:34.653	0	No-Stay
2	145	Mountain Lodge 1 Day Scandinavia	32.574	2012-01-04 05:55:45.417	0	No-Stay
3	73	Ocean Cruise Tour 1 Day Mexico	32.601	2010-01-01 06:01:01.907	0	No-Stay
4	265	Winter Tour 1 Day Scandinavia	34.506	2011-03-06 16:07:52.060	0	No-Stay
5	319	Cherry Festival Tour 1 Day Canada	34.944	2009-07-02 04:27:57.853	0	No-Stay
6	421	Snow Ski Tour 1 Day West Coast	35.308	2009-11-18 16:07:46.500	0	No-Stay

	ProductID	ProductName	RetailPrice	OriginationDate	ToBeDeleted	Category
1	482	Yoga Mtn Getaway 1 Week	995.00	2013-01-03 16:03:19.573	0	LongTerm-Stay
2	481	Yoga Mtn Getaway 5 Days	875.00	2013-01-03 16:03:19.573	0	Medium-Stay
3	335	Lakes Tour 1 Week West Coast	645.055	2011-01-31 11:16:43.800	0	LongTerm-Stay
4	341	Lakes Tour 1 Week East Coast	637.77	2012-02-19 15:52:06.277	0	LongTerm-Stay
5	371	Rain Forest Tour 1 Week East Coast	635.985	2008-02-06 04:21:43.127	0	LongTerm-Stay
6	401	River Rapids Tour 1 Week East Coast	620.06	2011-10-11 11:49:26.597	0	LongTerm-Stay

Query executed successfully.　　　　(local) (11.0 RTM)　Reno\Student (56)　JProCo　00:00:00　804 rows

Figure 6.40 ORDER BY sorts to show cheapest (query #1) and most expensive items (query #2).

Our final two examples will add a TOP(10) clause limiting the result set to displaying only the first ten records made available after the WHERE clause filtering process and the ORDER BY clause performing its sorting process.

Display the TOP(10) most expensive products in the CurrentProducts table.

```
SELECT TOP (10) *
FROM CurrentProducts
WHERE ToBeDeleted = 0
ORDER BY RetailPrice DESC
```

	ProductID	ProductName	RetailPrice	OriginationDate	ToBeDeleted	Category
1	482	Yoga Mtn Getaway 1 Week	995.00	2012-10-23 22:19:49.753	0	LongTerm-Stay
2	481	Yoga Mtn Getaway 5 Days	875.00	2012-10-23 22:19:49.753	0	Medium-Stay
3	335	Lakes Tour 1 Week West C...	645.055	2008-05-06 11:16:43.800	0	LongTerm-Stay
4	341	Lakes Tour 1 Week East Co...	637.77	2009-05-25 15:52:06.277	0	LongTerm-Stay
5	371	Rain Forest Tour 1 Week E...	635.985	2005-05-12 04:21:43.127	0	LongTerm-Stay
6	401	River Rapids Tour 1 Week ...	620.06	2009-01-14 11:49:26.597	0	LongTerm-Stay
7	65	Ocean Cruise Tour 1 Week ...	612.205	2003-12-07 22:54:33.533	0	LongTerm-Stay
8	455	Wine Tasting Tour 1 Week ...	600.99	2003-04-28 15:31:54.427	0	LongTerm-Stay
9	29	Underwater Tour 1 Week S...	580.59	2004-03-08 01:03:05.267	0	LongTerm-Stay
10	209	Horseback Tour 1 Week Sc...	568.57	2002-11-28 14:16:04.533	0	LongTerm-Stay

Query executed successfully.   RENO (11.0 RTM) Reno\j2p (51) JProCo 00:00:00 10 rows

Figure 6.41 TOP slices the first 10 records from the top of the record set (most expensive items).

Display the TOP(10) least expensive products in the CurrentProducts table.

```
SELECT TOP (10) *
FROM CurrentProducts
WHERE ToBeDeleted = 0
ORDER BY RetailPrice ASC
```

	ProductID	ProductName	RetailPrice	OriginationDate	ToBeDeleted	Category
1	313	Cherry Festival Tour 1 Day Mexico	31.909	2004-07-15 07:44:34.653	0	No-Stay
2	145	Mountain Lodge 1 Day Scandinavia	32.574	2009-04-09 05:55:45.417	0	No-Stay
3	73	Ocean Cruise Tour 1 Day Mexico	32.601	2007-04-07 06:01:01.907	0	No-Stay
4	265	Winter Tour 1 Day Scandinavia	34.506	2008-06-09 16:07:52.060	0	No-Stay
5	319	Cherry Festival Tour 1 Day Canada	34.944	2006-10-06 04:27:57.853	0	No-Stay
6	421	Snow Ski Tour 1 Day West Coast	35.308	2006-02-22 16:07:46.590	0	No-Stay
7	415	River Rapids Tour 1 Day Scandina...	36.042	2001-12-20 20:30:48.670	0	No-Stay
8	475	Wine Tasting Tour 1 Day Scandina...	40.564	2004-12-12 07:00:27.480	0	No-Stay
9	403	River Rapids Tour 1 Day Mexico	41.837	2003-02-02 15:10:00.777	0	No-Stay
10	187	Horseback Tour 1 Day East Coast	41.979	2006-02-28 03:44:36.443	0	No-Stay

Query executed successfully.   RENO (11.0 RTM) Reno\j2p (51) JProCo 00:00:00 10 rows

Figure 6.42 TOP slices the first 10 records from the top of the record set (least expensive items).

Using TOP(*n*) and WHERE

The TOP(*n*) clause can also be used with a WHERE clause. Let's build a query using these two clauses and analyze the result at each step. It is important to understand the impact each of these clauses have on the result set.

Our first step is a familiar one. Write a simple query to find all fields and records of the CurrentProducts table.

```
SELECT *
FROM CurrentProducts
```

Figure 6.43 All fields and records of the CurrentProducts table (402).

The second step is to add a WHERE clause to this query that is predicated on finding all records with an OriginationDate greater than or equal to 1/1/2009. This will remove all products added prior to 2009.

```
SELECT *
FROM CurrentProducts
WHERE OriginationDate >='1/1/2009'
```

Figure 6.44 Adding a WHERE clause filter to show all products added since 1/1/2009 (194 rows).

For the third step, we will add an ORDER BY clause to sort these 194 records in ascending alphabetical order from A to Z based on the ProductName field.

```
SELECT *
FROM CurrentProducts
```

```
WHERE OriginationDate >='1/1/2009'
ORDER BY ProductName
```

	ProductID	ProductName	RetailPrice	OriginationDate	ToBeDeleted	Category
1	289	Acting Lessons Tour 1 Day Canada	78.95	2012-05-25 01:45:29.600	0	No-Stay
2	277	Acting Lessons Tour 1 Day East Coast	52.67	2011-04-16 20:55:56.943	0	No-Stay
3	293	Acting Lessons Tour 1 Week Canada	394.75	2010-06-30 10:58:17.560	0	LongTerm-Stay
4	281	Acting Lessons Tour 1 Week East Coast	263.35	2009-10-01 03:01:55.500	0	LongTerm-Stay
5	287	Acting Lessons Tour 1 Week Mexico	505.34	2012-01-07 15:07:35.297	0	LongTerm-Stay
6	275	Acting Lessons Tour 1 Week West Coast	556.83	2011-08-28 06:23:43.763	0	LongTerm-Stay
7	278	Acting Lessons Tour 2 Days East Coast	94.806	2011-11-15 06:40:15.900	0	Overnight-Stay

Query executed successfully.   (local) (11.0 RTM)   Reno\Student (56)   JProCo   00:00:00   194 rows

Figure 6.45 The filtered records sorted in alphabetical order (A-Z) on the ProductName field.

Our final step is to add a TOP(12) clause to limit the number of records returned by the filtered and sorted query to the twelve records at the top of the list.

```
SELECT TOP(12) *
FROM CurrentProducts
WHERE OriginationDate >='1/1/2009'
ORDER BY ProductName
```

	ProductID	ProductName	RetailPrice	OriginationDate	ToBeDeleted	Category
1	289	Acting Lessons Tour 1 Day ...	78.95	2012-05-25 01:45:29.600	0	No-Stay
2	277	Acting Lessons Tour 1 Day ...	52.67	2011-04-16 20:55:56.943	0	No-Stay
3	293	Acting Lessons Tour 1 Wee...	394.75	2010-06-30 10:58:17.560	0	LongTerm-Stay
4	281	Acting Lessons Tour 1 Wee...	263.35	2009-10-01 03:01:55.500	0	LongTerm-Stay
5	287	Acting Lessons Tour 1 Wee...	505.34	2012-01-07 15:07:35.297	0	LongTerm-Stay
6	275	Acting Lessons Tour 1 Wee...	556.83	2011-08-28 06:23:43.763	0	LongTerm-Stay

Query executed successfully.   RENO (11.0 RTM)   Reno\j2p (51)   JProCo   00:00:00   12 rows

Figure 6.46 The TOP(12) clause limits the number of records in the result set to 12.

After completing this exercise, we should have a good understanding of how the WHERE, ORDER BY and TOP(*n*) clauses affect the results in a query. Every query needs a FROM clause to identify the database object that will be available to the other clauses, statements, functions and keywords.

The four steps in this exercise should help reinforce the principle to always construct, deconstruct and test SQL Server queries beginning with the FROM clause. When everything works, customize the SELECT statement as the last step.

Lab 6.2: TOP(*n*) Tricks

Lab Prep: Each lab has one or more Skill Checks. Start with Skill Check 1 and proceed until reaching the Points to Ponder section.

Before beginning this lab, verify that SQL Server 2012 is properly installed and operating. Before running the lab setup script for resetting the database (SQLQueries2012Vol2Chapter6.2Setup.sql), please make sure to close all query windows within SSMS. An open query window pointing to a database context can lock that database preventing it from updating when the script is executing. A simple way to assure all query windows are closed, is to exit out of SSMS, then open a new instance of SSMS, and lastly run the setup script.

Skill Check 1: In the JProCo database, write a query to find and then display only the third most expensive record from the Grant table based on the Amount field. *Hint: Locate the most expensive single GrantID that is not in the TOP(2) results.*

When done the results should resemble those shown in Figure 6.47.

```
SELECT TOP(1) *
--Remaining Code Here
```

	GrantID	GrantName	EmpID	Amount
1	009	Thank you @.com	11	21500.00

Query executed successfully.   RENO (11.0 RTM)   Reno\Student (51)   JProCo   00:00:00   1 rows

Figure 6.47 Skill Check 1 finds and displays the third most expensive record in the Grant table.

Skill Check 2: In the JProCo database context, write a query to find the three newest employees from the Employee table with a LocationID of 1.

When done, the results should resemble those shown in Figure 6.48.

	EmpID	LastName	FirstName	HireDate	LocationID	ManagerID	Status
1	13	Wilconkinski	Phil	2009-06-11 00:00:00.000	1	4	Active
2	5	Bender	Eric	2007-05-17 00:00:00.000	1	11	Active
3	2	Brown	Barry	2002-08-12 00:00:00.000	1	11	Active

Query executed successfully.   RENO (11.0 RTM)   Reno\Student (51)   JProCo   00:00:00   3 rows

Figure 6.48 Skill Check 2 shows the three most recently hired employees from LocationID 1.

Answer Code: The T-SQL code for this lab is located in the downloadable files as a file named Lab6.2_Top_n_Tricks.sql.

Points to Ponder - TOP(*n*) Tricks

1. The WHERE clause first filters out rows not wanted in the result set. The TOP(*n*) clause then displays the specified number of rows in a result set based on the remaining records.

2. A query looking for the TOP(1) row with filtering criteria looking for the TOP(4) rows not listed in the results will return the fifth highest record.

3. Using NOT IN with filtering criteria allows enumeration over a list of values that will not be included in a result set.

4. Using a query as a part of another query's criteria is a type of subquery.

TOP(*n*) PERCENT Queries

I make the trip to the Puyallup Fair in Washington State nearly every year and on many occasions have had the opportunity to enjoy an act called the Gentleman Jugglers. The jugglers like to tell a joke about halfway through their act about how they placed in the top two of all jugglers in a worldwide competition. The audience loudly applauds for their success on such a grand scale.

As the fanfare begins to quiet, they sheepishly say, "Well there were only two teams in the contest…" and the audience laughs aloud as they recognize that placing 2nd in a contest of only two teams is not as impressive as the original claim seemed.

In an equivalent example, someone from Rhode Island could boast that their state is one of the largest 50 states in the USA. There is a better way to look for an upper tier of records that takes into account the size of the competition pool, by looking for the top percentage of performers in the competition.

TOP(10) PERCENT

To find the best performers in any field we often will look for the top 10%. Take a moment to look at the following query. It has returned a list of all the states and provinces in order by LandMass largest to smallest.

```
SELECT *
FROM StateList
ORDER BY Landmass DESC
```

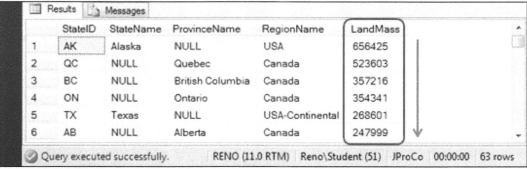

Figure 6.49 This Shows the StateList table in order by LandMass.

What if we need to find the TOP 10% LandMass values? How many of the 63 records make up 10% of the total? If 10% of zero to 10 records is 1, and 11 to 20 records is two, then 63 total records should return seven. The TOP (7) records should be the TOP 10% State or Province by LandMass.

```
SELECT TOP (7) *
FROM StateList
ORDER BY Landmass DESC
```

	StateID	StateName	ProvinceName	RegionName	LandMass
1	AK	Alaska	NULL	USA	656425
2	QC	NULL	Quebec	Canada	523603
3	BC	NULL	British Columbia	Canada	357216
4	ON	NULL	Ontario	Canada	354341
5	TX	Texas	NULL	USA-Continental	268601
6	AB	NULL	Alberta	Canada	247999
7	SK	NULL	Saskatchewan	Canada	228445

Query executed successfully.   RENO (11.0 RTM) Reno\Student (51) JProCo 00:00:00 7 rows

Figure 6.50 This shows the TOP (7) of the 63 States and Provinces by LandMass.

Going through all the calculations of finding 10%, and worrying about what to do with a remainder can become cumbersome. SQL has an option that allows us to run the TOP() PERCENT.

```
SELECT TOP (10) PERCENT *
FROM StateList
ORDER BY Landmass DESC
```

	StateID	StateName	ProvinceName	RegionName	LandMass
1	AK	Alaska	NULL	USA	656425
2	QC	NULL	Quebec	Canada	523603
3	BC	NULL	British Columbia	Canada	357216
4	ON	NULL	Ontario	Canada	354341
5	TX	Texas	NULL	USA-Continental	268601
6	AB	NULL	Alberta	Canada	247999
7	SK	NULL	Saskatchewan	Canada	228445

Query executed successfully.   RENO (11.0 RTM) Reno\Student (51) JProCo 00:00:00 7 rows

Figure 6.51 This shows the TOP 10% of the 63 States and Provinces by LandMass.

When we queried for the TOP(10) PERCENT, SQL rounded to the next whole number and returned seven records.

TOP(0-100) PERCENT

TOP(10) PERCENT is a common choice however any valid percentage will work in this function. Take a look at the following examples.

```
SELECT TOP (50) PERCENT *
FROM StateList
ORDER BY Landmass DESC
```

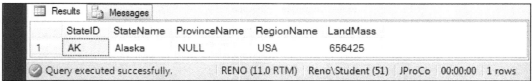

Figure 6.52 This shows the TOP(50) PERCENT of the StateList table by LandMass.

Using TOP(50) PERCENT returned 32 records which are the TOP half of all the records by LandMass (Figure 6.52). This example broadened the search. What if we need to narrow it down? Take a look at this example querying for the TOP(1) PERCENT.

```
SELECT TOP (1) PERCENT *
FROM StateList
ORDER BY Landmass DESC
```

	StateID	StateName	ProvinceName	RegionName	LandMass
1	AK	Alaska	NULL	USA	656425

Query executed successfully.   RENO (11.0 RTM)   Reno\Student (51)   JProCo   00:00:00   1 rows

Figure 6.53 This shows the TOP(1) PERCENT of the StateList table by LandMass.

Any valid percentage works in the TOP(n) PERCENT function including TOP(0) which returns no records and TOP(100) to return every record.

Lab 6.3: TOP(*n*) PERCENT Queries

Lab Prep: Each lab has one or more Skill Checks. Start with Skill Check 1 and proceed until reaching the Points to Ponder section.

Before beginning this lab, verify that SQL Server 2012 is properly installed and operating. Before running the lab setup script for resetting the database (SQLQueries2012Vol2Chapter6.3Setup.sql), please make sure to close all query windows within SSMS. An open query window pointing to a database context can lock that database preventing it from updating when the script is executing. A simple way to assure all query windows are closed, is to exit out of SSMS, then open a new instance of SSMS, and lastly run the setup script.

Skill Check 1: From the Employee table of the JProCo database, show the top 50% most senior employees by HireDate.

	EmpID	LastName	FirstName	HireDate	LocationID	ManagerID	Status
1	11	Smith	Sally	1989-04-01 00:00:00.000	1	NULL	Active
2	12	O'Neil	Barbara	1995-05-26 00:00:00.000	4	4	Has Tenure
3	4	Kennson	David	1996-03-16 00:00:00.000	1	11	Has Tenure
4	3	Osako	Lee	1999-09-01 00:00:00.000	2	11	Active
5	7	Lonning	David	2000-01-01 00:00:00.000	1	11	On Leave
6	1	Adams	Alex	2001-01-01 00:00:00.000	1	11	Active
7	8	Marshb...	John	2001-11-15 00:00:00.000	NULL	4	Active

Query executed successfully.   RENO (11.0 RTM)   Reno\Student (51)   JProCo   00:00:00   7 rows

Figure 6.54 Skill Check 1 shows the top 50% of most senior employees.

Skill Check 2: From the CurrentProducts table of the JProCo database, show the top 2% most expensive products from the CurrentProducts table.

	ProductID	ProductName	RetailPrice	Origination...	ToBeDeleted	Category
1	483	Yoga Mtn Getaway 2 Weeks	1695.00	2012-09-25...	1	LongTerm-S
2	336	Lakes Tour 2 Weeks West ...	1161.099	2011-09-29...	1	LongTerm-S
3	342	Lakes Tour 2 Weeks East ...	1147.986	2008-08-31...	1	LongTerm-S
4	372	Rain Forest Tour 2 Weeks ...	1144.773	2007-04-21...	1	LongTerm-S
5	402	River Rapids Tour 2 Week...	1116.108	2009-10-23...	1	LongTerm-S
6	456	Wine Tasting Tour 2 Week...	1101.969	2011-09-09...	1	LongTerm-S

Query executed successfully.   RENO (11.0 RTM)   Reno\Student (51)   JProCo   00:00:00   10 rows

Figure 6.55 Skill Check 2 shows the top 2% most expensive products.

Answer Code: The T-SQL code for this lab is located in the downloadable files as a file named Lab6.3_Top_Percent_Queries.sql.

Points to Ponder - Top Percent Queries

1. PERCENT is an optional clause that can be used with the TOP(n) clause.

2. A parameter value used with the PERCENT clause is a FLOAT data type.

3. A parameter passed into a PERCENT clause with a decimal value (12.5) will be rounded upwards to the nearest integer value (whole number).

4. PERCENT values must be between 0 and 100.

5. Any number from 0-100 is a valid parameter for the PERCENT clause used in conjunction with TOP(n). For example, the top 49.9 % of RetailPrice values in the CurrentProducts table can be shown with the following syntax:

    ```
    SELECT TOP(49.9) PERCENT *
    FROM CurrentProducts
    ORDER BY RetailPrice DESC
    ```

Chapter Glossary

Hard-Coding: This is a coding style using actual values as criteria for logic in a query. Because the actual value does not adapt to changes occurring in a database object or query, the code is hard and not flexible.

PERCENT: An optional clause used in conjunction with the TOP(n) clause. A parameter passed into a PERCENT clause is a FLOAT data type and when passed in as a decimal value it will be round upwards to the nearest integer value.

TOP(n): A clause used in conjunction with DML statements limiting the n number of records specified to display in the result set. To achieve consistent results and avoid potential error messages, always have an ORDER BY clause with the TOP(n) clause. The TOP(n) clause does not evaluate data, as it simply limits the number of records returned by the query to the amount specified by its parameter value.

Variable: A variable is a database object capable of holding a single value for a specific data type. A common use is to store a value used by a stored procedure or function, or as a counter for a loop to control how many times the loop iterates.

WITH TIES: A clause used in conjunction with the TOP(n) clause that specifies the query result set will include any additional rows that match values in the ORDER BY column or columns in the last row returned.

This might cause more rows returned than the value specified by the TOP(n) parameter. For example, if the parameter is set to 5, but the next row is tied with the values of the ORDER BY column(s) in row 5, the result set will contain 6 rows.

TOP(n)...WITH TIES can be specified in SELECT statements only, and must include an ORDER BY clause. Since the returned order of tying records is arbitrary, the ORDER BY clause does not affect this rule.

Review Quiz - Chapter Six

1.) In a TOP(5) query what happens to ties for 5th place by default?

   O a. Each record tied for fifth place will show up.

   O b. None of the records tied for fifth place will show up.

   O c. All of the records tied for fifth place will show up when specifying the WITH TIES clause.

2.) In a TOP(8) query you have a WHERE clause that finds a criteria match for 10 records. How many records will show up in your result set?

   O a. 2

   O b. 8

   O c. 10

   O d. 18

3.) We can limit the number of affected records in a SELECT statement using the TOP keyword. What statement works with the TOP keyword?

   O a. DML

   O b. DDL

   O c. TCL

4.) You have 1 million rows to delete from the TempProducts table. If the field called PlsDelete is marked with the number 1, then you need to write a T-SQL batch that will delete exactly 5000 rows at a time. Which code batch should you use?

   O a.
```
DELETE TOP(5000) dbo.TempProducts
WHERE PlsDelete = 1
```

   O b.
```
DELETE TOP(5000) dbo.TempProducts
WHERE PlsDelete != 1
```

   O c.
```
DELETE BOTTOM (5000) dbo.TempProducts
WHERE PlsDelete = 1
```

   O d.
```
DELETE BOTTOM (5000) dbo.TempProducts
WHERE PlsDelete != 1
```

5.) Each month you rate your salespeople for the three highest sales amounts. Those salespeople making this list receive bonuses. Last month Terry Anders got third place and a $1000 bonus. Chris Zowalski complained that his sales amount was the same as Anders, but he got no reward. You check the data in the SalesPerson table and see Zowalski listed as the fourth record in the table, because alphabetically his last name starts with Z, even though his sales totals were the same as Terry Anders.

After hearing from HR, you gave him the bonus and then instituted a policy that any tie for third place in the future will split the prize money. How do you write a query so that ties in the top three values for TotalSales will show up, in case this happens again?

O a. `SELECT TOP(3) *`
     `FROM SalesPerson`
     `ORDER BY TotalSales`

O b. `SELECT TOP(3) *`
     `FROM SalesPerson`
     `ORDER BY TotalSales DESC`

O c. `SELECT TOP(3) WITH TIES *`
     `FROM SalesPerson`
     `ORDER BY TotalSales`

O d. `SELECT TOP(3) WITH TIES *`
     `FROM SalesPerson`
     `ORDER BY TotalSales DESC`

O e. `SELECT TOP(3) WITH TIES *`
     `FROM SalesPerson`

Answer Key

1.) By default, a TOP(5) query will only return five results regardless of any tied values, so (a) is incorrect. Because one of the records tied for fifth place will appear in the result set, (b) is also incorrect. Since a TOP(5) result set can only include more than five records when specifying the WITH TIES clause, (c) is the correct answer.

2.) Because a TOP(8) query will return eight records, (a), (c) and (d) are all incorrect, which makes (b) the correct answer.

3.) TOP(*n*) is compatible with all DML statements in most situations, making (a) correct.

4.) Since 'PlsDelete != 1' would act on records not marked for deletion, (b) is incorrect. Because BOTTOM is not a recognized built-in clause, both (c) and (d) are incorrect. Because 'PlsDelete = 1' will act only on records marked for deletion and includes the TOP(5000) clause, (a) is correct.

5.) Since a TOP(3) query not including a WITH TIES clause will only return three records, (a) and (b) are both wrong. Since the queries in both (c) and (e) are not sorting the records from the highest TotalSales value to the lowest value, they are also wrong. To query for the three highest TotalSales including ties, the code must contain the WITH TIES clause and the ORDER BY clause must use the DESC keyword, making (d) the correct answer.

Bug Catcher Game

To play the Bug Catcher game, run the SQLQueries2012Vol2BugCatcher06.pps file from the BugCatcher folder of the companion files. These files are available from the www.Joes2Pros.com website.

[THIS PAGE INTENTIONALLY LEFT BLANK.]

Chapter 7.   Ranking Functions

Now that we have a lot of experience with the OVER() and ORDER BY clauses, we can leverage them during our study of how to use ranking functions. Each of the ranking functions used by SQL Server **must** use the OVER() clause that contains an ORDER BY clause identifying which field is the target of the ranking criteria and how the ranked data will be sorted (highest to lowest or vice versa).

There are four ranking functions used by SQL Server:

1) RANK()
2) DENSE_RANK()
3) ROW_NUMBER()
4) NTILE()

Ranking functions are just one type of analytical functions available in every version since its introduction with SQL Server 2005. The TOP(n) clause is a perfect segue to working with the different ranking functions, as neither will interpret nor make qualitative judgments about data.

While each of the ranking functions will always begin ranking the result set with the numeral one (1), the logic used by the individual function will determine which rows receive a specific rank and corresponding numeric value.

In this chapter, we will learn how the four ranking functions treat data with the same value (ties) and whether they rank results sequentially or allow gaps.

READER NOTE: *Please run the SQLQueries2012Vol2Chapter7.0Setup.sql script in order to follow along with the examples in the first section of Chapter 7. All scripts mentioned in this chapter are available at www.Joes2Pros.com.*

The RANK() Function

The RANK(), DENSE_RANK() and ROW_NUMBER() ranking functions used by SQL Server exhibit the same basic behavior. If we were to provide these three functions the exact same data, without any duplicate values (ties), then they will each return the same result set. The primary difference between these functions is how they treat ties within the data supplied to them in a query.

We can see an example of how ranking functions handle a tie by observing the results shown in Figure 7.1. Two of the players (Josh and Kevin) have the same value (9.6) in the Score column. Notice that until encountering a tie, the first four records have the same ranking. After each of the three ranking functions find a tie, they treat the numerical ranking of the remaining two records differently.

	Player	Score	RANK()	DENSE_RANK()	ROW_NUMBER()
1	Tom	9.9	1	1	1
2	Daryl	9.8	2	2	2
3	Bill	9.7	3	3	3
4	Josh	9.6	4	4	4
5	Kevin	9.6	4	4	5
6	Eric	9.2	6	5	6

6 rows

Figure 7.1 How the Rank(), DENSE_RANK() and ROW_NUMBER() functions treat tie values.

Before we begin to work with the RANK() function, let's write a query finding all the fields and records in the Grant table and sort the results based on the largest to smallest Amount (descending order) as shown in Figure 7.2.

```
SELECT *
FROM [Grant]
ORDER BY Amount DESC
```

	GrantID	GrantName	EmpID	Amount
1	007	Ben@MoreTechnology.com	10	41000.00
2	008	www.@-Last-U-Can-Help.com	7	25000.00
3	009	Thank you @.com	11	21500.00
4	004	Norman's Outreach	NULL	21000.00
5	005	BIG 6's Foundation%	4	21000.00
6	006	TALTA_Kishan International	3	18100.00

10 rows

Figure 7.2 The Grant table sorted from the largest to smallest Amount.

A good way to build a query that uses a ranking function is to see what errors are produced when accidently making one of the two most common mistakes for this type of query. This way we can recognize the error and quickly correct it.

The first example demonstrates what happens when the RANK() function is not immediately followed by the OVER() clause. Remember, every ranking function **must** implement the OVER() clause to obtain a result set. Figure 7.3 shows the error message for this query.

```
SELECT *,
RANK()
FROM [Grant]
ORDER BY Amount DESC
```

Messages
Msg 10753, Level 15, State 3, Line 2
The function 'RANK' must have an OVER clause.
0 rows

Figure 7.3 All ranking functions must implement an OVER() clause to obtain a result set.

The next example shows the RANK() function immediately followed by an OVER() clause for the entire table, yet it still produces an error. Why? We can look at the error message supplied by SQL Server (Figure 7.4) and find that the OVER() clause is missing the required ORDER BY clause.

This is important to know, because all ranking functions need a target field specified so it can determine which values to rank and the ranking order. It is the ORDER BY clause that supplies these two critical pieces of information to the OVER() clause for the ranking functions to work properly.

```
SELECT *,
RANK() OVER()
FROM [Grant]
ORDER BY Amount DESC
```

Messages
Msg 4112, Level 15, State 1, Line 2
The function 'RANK' must have an OVER clause with ORDER BY.
0 rows

Figure 7.4 Ranking functions expect to find the ORDER BY info inside the OVER() clause.

Let's put this new found information to work by writing a query with a RANK() function that will provide us with the results we are looking for. Remember to place an OVER() clause that contains an ORDER BY clause using the field we want to have ranked, along with the order to sort the ranked field (descending). Alias the column with the RANK() function as *GrantRank*, so we can easily identify it in our result set (Figure 7.5).

```
SELECT *,
RANK() OVER(ORDER BY Amount DESC) AS GrantRank
FROM [Grant]
```

Figure 7.5 The Grant table ranked over the Amount column, showing 2 pairs of tied amounts.

Observe that we no longer need to have an ORDER BY clause at the end of the query, since we have moved it inside the parentheses of the OVER() clause.

READER NOTE: *Many SQL Developers prefer to build their ranking function queries as shown in the second example with the ORDER BY clause at the end of the query and then cutting and pasting it inside the parentheses of the OVER() clause to take advantage of the 'Intellisense' feature in SSMS for the field name.*

Great! Our data is now displayed in ranked order on the GrantRank column. By examining what the RANK() function has produced, we can see the first three rows are ranked sequentially (1, 2, and 3) based on the unique values in the Amount field. When the RANK() function encountered the first tie between GrantID 004 and GrantID 005, it assigned each of them a fourth place rank. The next tie is between GrantID 006 and GrantID 003, so the RANK() function assigns each of these rows a sixth place rank. The remaining three rows in the table each have unique values for the Amount field and will have the sequentially ranked values of 8, 9 and 10.

RANK() Function Logic

Wait a minute… what happened to the fifth and seventh place rankings? These values have been intentionally skipped as part of the logic used by the RANK() function, which is what makes it different from the other ranking functions.

When the RANK() function encounters a tie value it will assign the same ranked value to every row that is tied. As soon as a non-tied value is found, a ranking value is assigned by adding 1 for each tied row from the previous ranked value. In our example, the first tie is assigned a ranked value of 4 and there are two records assigned this value, so 4 + 2 = 6. This means the next ranked value assigned will be the number 6, thereby skipping a fifth place ranked value for this result set. When looking at Figure 7.5, we see this is exactly what happened.

If there had been a three-way tie for fourth place, what would the next untied ranked value have been? Simply add the tied ranked value (4) to the number of rows in the tie (3) to find the ranked value for the next row that breaks the tie (4 + 3 = 7). By using this easy calculation, we can determine the next ranking value would have been seventh place had there been a three-way tie.

The DENSE_RANK() Function

At the beginning of this chapter, we discovered that the results of Figure 7.1 showed how the DENSE_RANK() function does not skip values (leave gaps) when it performs its ranking calculations. As we will soon see, this is the opposite of how the RANK() function evaluates ranking values.

Let's query the CurrentProducts table to view the ProductName and RetailPrice fields in descending order of the RetailPrice value (largest to smallest). When we run the code shown here the results should resemble those shown in Figure 7.6.

```
SELECT ProductName, RetailPrice
FROM CurrentProducts
ORDER BY RetailPrice DESC
```

	ProductName	RetailPrice
1	Yoga Mtn Getaway 2 Weeks	1695.00
2	Lakes Tour 2 Weeks West Coast	1161.099
3	Lakes Tour 2 Weeks East Coast	1147.986
4	Rain Forest Tour 2 Weeks East Coast	1144.773
5	River Rapids Tour 2 Weeks East Coast	1116.108
6	Wine Tasting Tour 2 Weeks West Coast	1101.969

483 rows

Figure 7.6 The CurrentProducts table result set in descending order of RetailPrice.

To better illustrate the differences between the ranking results produced by the RANK() and DENSE_RANK() functions, we can simply use the previous query format to build two new queries individually using these functions and compare their ranking results.

We will use RetailPrice as the targeted ranking field and ask for the highest priced ProductName to receive the ranked value of first place and each successively lower RetailPrice value to receive the next lower ranked value available (second place, third place, fourth place, etc…). In other words, our query will be ranking each value from the highest RetailPrice down to the lowest. That's another way of saying, "Place the ranking results for the RetailPrice field in descending order".

Run the following code sample and see the results resemble those in Figure 7.7.

```
SELECT ProductName, RetailPrice,
RANK() OVER(ORDER BY RetailPrice DESC) AS RankNo
FROM CurrentProducts
```

	ProductName	RetailPrice	RankNo
4	Rain Forest Tour 2 Weeks East Coast	1144.773	4
5	River Rapids Tour 2 Weeks East Coast	1116.108	5
6	Wine Tasting Tour 2 Weeks West Coast	1101.969	6
7	Ocean Cruise Tour 2 Weeks West Coast	1101.969	6
8	Underwater Tour 2 Weeks Scandinavia	1045.062	8
9	Horseback Tour 2 Weeks Scandinavia	1023.426	9

483 rows

Figure 7.7 The RANK() function breaks sequential order after the tie for 6th place (creates gaps).

Notice that in Figure 7.7 the RANK() function breaks the sequential ranking order when it encounters a tie between the two rows with a RetailPrice of 1101.969.

Now let's change the query to use the DENSE_RANK() function. We can see by the results shown in Figure 7.8 that when this same tie is encountered by the DENSE_RANK() function, it continues on by ranking the next non-tied distinct amount in sequential order (leaving no gaps in the ranking values).

```
SELECT ProductName, RetailPrice,
DENSE_RANK() OVER(ORDER BY RetailPrice DESC) AS DRankNo
FROM CurrentProducts
```

	ProductName	RetailPrice	DRankNo
4	Rain Forest Tour 2 Weeks East Coast	1144.773	4
5	River Rapids Tour 2 Weeks East Coast	1116.108	5
6	Wine Tasting Tour 2 Weeks West Coast	1101.969	6
7	Ocean Cruise Tour 2 Weeks West Coast	1101.969	6
8	Underwater Tour 2 Weeks Scandinavia	1045.062	7
9	Horseback Tour 2 Weeks Scandinavia	1023.426	8

483 rows

Figure 7.8 The DENSE_RANK() function distinctly ranks in sequential order – no skips or gaps!

DENSE_RANK() Function Logic

Hmmm… why is it important, or even necessary to display the rankings in a sequential order? There are times when the logic used in a business decision will demand the *n* number of highest or lowest distinct values. The only ranking function that can provide this type of solution is DENSE_RANK(), as it does not skip a ranking value as part of its logic, thus the ranking values will always be in sequential order (no gaps).

READER NOTE: *We will see more examples of why this is important in the next section ~ RANK() & DENSE_RANK() in the Real World.*

When the DENSE_RANK() function encounters a tie value it will assign the same ranked value to every row that is tied. As soon as a non-tied value is found, it is assigned a ranked value determined by adding 1 to the previous ranked value. In our example, the first tie is assigned a ranked value of 6, so 6 + 1 = 7. This means the next non-tied row will have a seventh place ranked value for this result set, which is exactly what happened (Figure 7.8).

By carefully observing the results in Figure 7.7 and comparing them to the results in Figure 7.8. When we do this on our screen and see all the records we will find that the RANK() function only produces seven unique values for the first eight places, while the DENSE_RANK() function produces eight unique values for the first eight places in the ranked results as shown here:

Table 7.1 Side-by-Side representation of RANK() and DENSE_RANK() results.

RANK()	RetailPrice	DENSE_RANK()
1	1695.00	1
2	1161.099	2
3	1147.986	3
4	1144.773	4
5	1116.108	5
6	1101.969	6
6	1101.969	6
8	1045.062	7
	1023.426	8

If there had been a three-way tie (or more) for sixth place, what would the next non-tied ranked value have been? Simply add the tied ranked value (6) to the number 1 to find the ranked value for the next row that breaks the tie (6 + 1 = 7). When performing this calculation, we can easily see that the DENSE_RANK() function will always assign ranking values in sequential order for each distinct value evaluated by the function, regardless of how many rows are involved in a tie.

RANK() & DENSE_RANK() in the Real World

In Chapter 6, we learned how to solve a difficult interview question about retrieving only the 5th highest record from all possible results by using some query tricks to manipulate records returned by using the TOP() command.

Now that we have learned the basics about how to use the RANK() and DENSE_RANK() functions, it looks like this could be an even simpler way to solve the interview question for finding only the 5th highest record.

Let's use our last query and filter the results by predicating on DRankNo = 5.

```
SELECT ProductName, RetailPrice,
DENSE_RANK() OVER(ORDER BY RetailPrice DESC) AS DRankNo
FROM CurrentProducts
WHERE DRankNo = 5
```

Messages
Msg 207, Level 16, State 1, Line 4
Invalid column name 'DRankNo'.
0 rows

Figure 7.9 DRankNo is not recognized in a WHERE clause, since it is an expression, not a field.

It seems we have confused the SQL Server Query Optimizer... an error message indicates the WHERE clause cannot recognize DRankNo as a valid column name (Figure 7.9). This is because the aliased expression, DRankNo, is not included in a temporary object.

READER NOTE: *In simple terms, SQL Server does not store the entire set of values that can be created by an expression in memory, so it is unable to use an expression as criteria in a WHERE clause. However, a temporary object, such as a derived table, will store these values in memory as long as the query is running. There will be more examples of this to practice in Chapters 8, 9, 10 and 11.*

To turn DRankNo into a column that can be used in a WHERE clause, it must first be materialized as a field in a temporary object called a derived table. This is accomplished by nesting the previous query (without the WHERE clause) inside a SELECT statement, which allows SQL Server to recognize DRankNo as a field. Follow along with these basic steps to build a query with a derived table:

Step 1: Write or locate the query to be turned into a derived table.

```
SELECT ProductName, RetailPrice,
DENSE_RANK() OVER(ORDER BY RetailPrice DESC) AS DRankNo
FROM CurrentProducts
```

Step 2: Write a basic SELECT query that has a set of empty parentheses (aliased as *RankedProducts*) after the FROM keyword.

```
SELECT * FROM () AS RankedProducts
```

Step 3: Place the query from Step 1 inside the empty parentheses starting on a new line below the FROM keyword. Visually separate this code block by indenting it from the main outer query.

```
SELECT * FROM (
  SELECT ProductName, RetailPrice,
  DENSE_RANK() OVER(ORDER BY RetailPrice DESC) AS DRankNo
  FROM CurrentProducts) AS RankedProducts
```

Step 4: Finally, place the WHERE clause (without indenting) on the last line marking the end of the main outer query.

```
SELECT * FROM (
  SELECT ProductName, RetailPrice,
  DENSE_RANK() OVER(ORDER BY RetailPrice DESC) AS DRankNo
  FROM CurrentProducts) AS RankedProducts
WHERE DRankNo = 5
```

READER NOTE: *In Figure 7.10, an example shows how easy it is to indent a section of code (code block). Simply highlight the code to be indented and either left-click on the Increase Indent button or press the Tab key on the keyboard.*

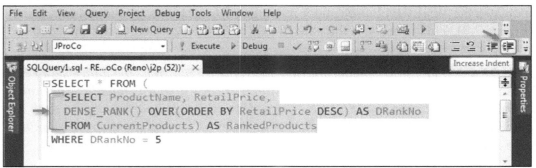

Figure 7.10 The **Increase Indent** button makes indenting easy. The tab key also indents.

Let's compare the results of running this derived table query, first without the WHERE clause criteria and then with the WHERE clause criteria. Run the first code sample to see what this query looks like without filtering the result set.

```
SELECT * FROM (
  SELECT ProductName, RetailPrice,
  DENSE_RANK() OVER(ORDER BY RetailPrice DESC) AS DRankNo
  FROM CurrentProducts) AS RankedProducts
```

	ProductName	RetailPrice	DRankNo
4	Rain Forest Tour 2 Weeks East Coast	1144.773	4
5	River Rapids Tour 2 Weeks East Coast	1116.108	5
6	Wine Tasting Tour 2 Weeks West Coast	1101.969	6
7	Ocean Cruise Tour 2 Weeks West Coast	1101.969	6
8	Underwater Tour 2 Weeks Scandinavia	1045.062	7
9	Horseback Tour 2 Weeks Scandinavia	1023.426	8

483 rows

Figure 7.11 RankedProducts behaves like an actual table with three fields, including DRankNo.

Notice the result set produced from the derived table query (Figure 7.11) is the same as our query of the CurrentProducts table shown in Figure 7.8. This is proof positive that both the standard query and the derived table query will return the same result set. The primary difference is that SQL Server stores all the data for the three fields (ProductName, RetailPrice and DRankNo) of the derived table named RankedProducts in temporary memory.

By design, temporary objects like derived tables allow any of these fields, and the data they contain, to be referenced (called) in the same way as any other table in the database, so long as the query is running.

We can now run this same code block with the addition of the filter for DRankNo value equal to five. Use the following code sample to run the query and observe that the results are the same as those shown in Figure 7.12.

```
SELECT * FROM (
  SELECT ProductName, RetailPrice,
  DENSE_RANK() OVER(ORDER BY RetailPrice DESC) AS DRankNo
  FROM CurrentProducts) AS RankedProducts
WHERE DRankNo = 5
```

	ProductName	RetailPrice	DRankNo
5	River Rapids Tour 2 Weeks East Coast	1116.108	5

1 rows

Figure 7.12 With RankedProducts materialized as a table, we can now find the 5th highest record.

Alright! We can now solve the difficult interview question in multiple ways with two different tools called TOP() and DENSE_RANK().

What if this same manager asked us another interview question, similar to this: *"What are the five highest amounts found in the Grant table?"*

It is very important to listen to every question asked to determine what the actual meaning or intent of the question is, regardless of whether the question is asked during an interview, by the manager, team lead, or the customer themselves.

For instance, in this second interview question, it is critical to take notice what the interviewer is not asking, *"What are the five highest grants in the Grant table?"*

The distinction here is the question's syntax. When searching for the five highest amounts, it is necessary to account for distinct values in this field, as it is possible that the five highest values (amounts) are occupying more than five records or ranks.

Alternatively, accounting for distinct values is not part of searching for the five highest grants. Because ties produce gaps in the ranked values, there is a possibility to have fewer than five distinct values in the result set for the Amount field.

Oftentimes we will encounter such precisely worded statements in design specifications, exams and very likely during interviews. When asked questions like this during the course of an interview, it is usually an attempt to test how closely we listen to and assimilate a specific request. Sometimes, using this tactic may trip us up and other times it is simply a test to see how we respond to the question. In other words, do we clarify the question before attempting to solve it, or do we immediately begin working on a solution.

Before we begin to answer this most recent question, it is a good idea to look at the data stored in the Grant table to see if there is anything that can help us solve the problem. Since we are being asked to find the highest amounts, let's go ahead and sort the table with the Amount field in descending order.

```
SELECT *
FROM [Grant]
ORDER BY Amount DESC
```

	GrantID	GrantName	EmpID	Amount
1	007	Ben@MoreTechnology.com	10	41000.00
2	008	www.@-Last-U-Can-Help.com	7	25000.00
3	009	Thank you @.com	11	21500.00
4	004	Norman's Outreach	NULL	21000.00
5	005	BIG 6's Foundation%	4	21000.00
6	006	TALTA_Kishan International	3	18100.00
7	003	Robert@BigStarBank.com	7	18100.00
8	002	K_Land fund trust	2	15750.00
9	010	Call Mom @Com	5	7500.00
10	001	92 Purr_Scents %% team	7	4750.00

10 rows

Figure 7.13 The Grant table with the Amount field sorted in descending order.

OK, we can see from the results in Figure 7.13 that there are ten records ranging from $41,000 (highest) to $4,750 (lowest). Fortunately, this table only has ten records and we can easily spot the two sets of ties in the Amount field ($21,000 and $18,100 respectively). Our next step is to add a ranking function to this query. Let's test the results found when using the RANK() function (alias this expression as *RankNo*). Run the following code sample and view the results shown in Figure 7.14.

```
SELECT *,
RANK() OVER(ORDER BY Amount DESC) AS RankNo
FROM [Grant]
```

	GrantID	GrantName	EmpID	Amount	RankNo
1	007	Ben@MoreTechnology.com	10	41000.00	1
2	008	www.@-Last-U-Can-Help.com	7	25000.00	2
3	009	Thank you @.com	11	21500.00	3
4	004	Norman's Outreach	NULL	21000.00	4
5	005	BIG 6's Foundation%	4	21000.00	4
6	006	TALTA_Kishan International	3	18100.00	6
7	003	Robert@BigStarBank.com	7	18100.00	6
8	002	K_Land fund trust	2	15750.00	8
9	010	Call Mom @Com	5	7500.00	9
10	001	92 Purr_Scents %% team	7	4750.00	10

10 rows

Figure 7.14 The Grant table query re-written to show results from the RANK() function.

We're on the right track; however: we must create a derived table in our query before we can filter the results. Make sure to follow the four basic steps to materialize the RankNo column inside the derived table named RankedGrants.

Step 1: Write or locate the query to be turned into a derived table.

Step 2: Write a basic SELECT query that has a set of empty parentheses (aliased as *RankedGrants*) after the FROM keyword.

Step 3: Place the query from Step 1 inside the empty parentheses starting on a new line below the FROM keyword. Indent this code block to visually separate it from the main outer query.

Step 4: Finally, place the WHERE clause (without indenting) on the last line marking the end of the main outer query.

We can now filter the entire query with the RankNo column searching for the five highest amounts (Figure 7.15).

```
SELECT * FROM (
  SELECT *,
  RANK() OVER(ORDER BY Amount DESC) AS RankNo
  FROM [Grant]) AS RankedGrants
WHERE RankNo <= 5
```

	GrantID	GrantName	EmpID	Amount	RankNo
1	007	Ben@MoreTechnology.com	10	41000.00	1
2	008	www.@-Last-U-Can-Help.com	7	25000.00	2
3	009	Thank you @.com	11	21500.00	3
4	004	Norman's Outreach	NULL	21000.00	4
5	005	BIG 6's Foundation%	4	21000.00	4

5 rows

Figure 7.15 Filtering results by the RANK() function returns five grants and only four amounts.

Are we done yet? To answer that question, we must determine if the result set shown in Figure 7.15 satisfies the specific requirements of the original question. So, do these results give us five distinct values representing the five highest amounts available in the Grant table? No. We only have four unique values in the Amount field, so we are missing the next highest amount from the table.

In other words, our work would be done, if it were not for the tie for 4th place. Since the logic design for the RANK() function intentionally creates a gap in ranked values when it encounters a tie, it should never be used when there is a necessity to obtain an *n* number of distinct values in a result set (no gaps).

The ranking function having a logic design to assign ranked values sequentially when it encounters a tie (no gaps), is the DENSE_RANK() function. It looks like we can now fulfill the requirements of this interview question. Let's test this theory out by modifying our previous query to replace the RANK() keyword with the DENSE_RANK() keyword and rename the alias to *DRankNo*.

Run the code sample shown and check the results against those in Figure 7.16.

```
SELECT * FROM (
  SELECT *,
  DENSE_RANK() OVER(ORDER BY Amount DESC) AS DRankNo
  FROM [Grant]) AS RankedGrants
WHERE DRankNo <= 5
```

	GrantID	GrantName	EmpID	Amount	DRankNo
1	007	Ben@MoreTechnology.com	10	41000.00	1
2	008	www.@-Last-U-Can-Help.com	7	25000.00	2
3	009	Thank you @.com	11	21500.00	3
4	004	Norman's Outreach	NULL	21000.00	4
5	005	BIG 6's Foundation%	4	21000.00	4
6	006	TALTA_Kishan International	3	18100.00	5
7	003	Robert@BigStarBank.com	7	18100.00	5

7 rows

Figure 7.16 Filtering results by the DENSE_RANK() function returns five distinct amounts.

Excellent! We now know that we can reliably use the DENSE_RANK() function whenever we need to find a specific number of highest (or lowest) distinct values, because it is designed to not leave any gaps in its ranked numbering sequence.

READER NOTE: *Some of my students say they are able to remember this because the ranking function that finds **d**istinct values is **D**ENSE_RANK() and both of these begin with the letter 'D'.*

Lab 7.1: RANK() & DENSE_RANK()

Lab Prep: Each lab has one or more Skill Checks. Start with Skill Check 1 and proceed until reaching the Points to Ponder section.

Before beginning this lab, verify that SQL Server 2012 is properly installed and operating. Before running the lab setup script for resetting the database (SQLQueries2012Vol2Chapter7.1Setup.sql), please make sure to close all query windows within SSMS. An open query window pointing to a database context can lock that database preventing it from updating when the script is executing. A simple way to assure all query windows are closed, is to exit out of SSMS, then open a new instance of SSMS, and lastly run the setup script.

Skill Check 1: In the JProCo database, use the correct ranking function to assign ranked values for each record in the Employee table based on the HireDate. The most recent HireDate should have a ranked value of 1 and each distinct date older than the first date should add 1 to the ranked value without any gaps.

The newest hires will appear at the top of the list and the oldest hire dates will be at the bottom of the list. The ranked field should be aliased as *GreenRank*.

When complete the results should resemble those shown in Figure 7.17.

	EmpID	LastName	FirstName	HireDate	LocationID	ManagerID	Status	GreenRank
1	13	Wilconkinski	Phil	2009-06-11...	1	4	Active	1
2	5	Bender	Eric	2007-05-17...	1	11	Active	2
3	10	O'Haire	Terry	2004-10-04...	2	3	Active	3
4	9	Newton	James	2003-09-30...	2	3	Active	4
5	2	Brown	Barry	2002-08-12...	1	11	Active	5
6	6	Kendall	Lisa	2001-11-15...	4	4	Active	6

Query executed successfully.   RENO (11.0 RTM)   Reno\Student (51)   JProCo   00:00:00   13 rows

Figure 7.17 Skill Check 1 uses DENSE_RANK( ) to rank employees by the most recent HireDate.

Skill Check 2: In the JProCo database, join the Employee and PayRates tables together to display the FirstName, LastName, YearlySalary and a ranking expression aliased as *yrRank*. Order the ranked values based on the highest to lowest YearlySalary values.

The result set should only contain the fields for the first two ranked values provided by the RANK() function. ***Hint:*** *It is possible to complete this exercise without implementing a derived table when using the TOP(n) clause.*

When done, the results of the query should resemble those shown in Figure 7.18.

	FirstName	LastName	YearlySalary	yrRank
1	Sally	Smith	115000.00	1
2	Barry	Brown	79000.00	2

2 rows

Figure 7.18 The Employee and PayRates tables joined to display the two highest paid employees.

Skill Check 3: In the JProCo database, write a query that will display all the fields and records of the Grant table, plus a field to display the results of a ranking function that is aliased as *AmountRank*.

The ranking function should assign the ranked values based on sorting the Amount field from the highest to the lowest value. When encountering a tie, assign the same ranked value to each of the tied rows, allowing for gaps in the ranked values to occur when finding the next non-tied row.

When done, the query results should resemble those shown in Figure 7.19.

	GrantID	GrantName	EmpID	Amount	AmountRank
1	007	Ben@MoreTechnology.com	10	41000.00	1
2	008	www.@-Last-U-Can-Help.com	7	25000.00	2
3	009	Thank you @.com	11	21500.00	3
4	004	Norman's Outreach	NULL	21000.00	4
5	005	BIG 6's Foundation%	4	21000.00	4
6	006	TALTA_Kishan International	3	18100.00	6
7	003	Robert@BigStarBank.com	7	18100.00	6
8	002	K_Land fund trust	2	15750.00	8
9	010	Call Mom @Com	5	7500.00	9
10	001	92 Purr_Scents %% team	7	4750.00	10

10 rows

Figure 7.19 Skill Check 3 ranks the Grant table showing ties and gaps.

Skill Check 4: In the JProCo database context, write a query that uses the DENSE_RANK() function to find only the 5th highest RetailPrice value in the CurrentProducts table. The expression field should be aliased as *PriceRank*. The field selection list should display only these fields in the following order: PriceRank, ProductID, ProductName, RetailPrice and Origination Date.

Hint: Use a derived table to materialize the expression field, so it can be used as criteria to find the fifth record.

When done the query results should resemble those shown in Figure 7.20.

	PriceRank	ProductID	ProductName	RetailPrice	OriginationDate
1	5	402	River Rapids Tour 2…	1116.108	2009-10-23…

1 rows

Figure 7.20 Using DENSE_RANK() with a derived table to filter for the 5th ranked record.

Answer Code: The T-SQL code for this lab is located in the downloadable files as a file named Lab7.1_Rank&DenseRank.sql.

Points to Ponder - RANK() & DENSE_RANK()

1. RANK() and DENSE_RANK() are ranking functions.

2. Ranking functions can analyze multiple rows like an aggregate function but are different because it will return many rows instead of a single number summarizing the results. For example; SUM() will produce a numeric total for 100 rows, whereas RANK() can produce 100 numbers, one for each row.

3. Until a set of tied values are encountered, RANK() and DENSE_RANK() will produce identical results.

4. By design, the RANK() function counts tied values and assigns ranking values in non-sequential order, which creates gaps in the ranking values.

5. When the RANK() function encounters a tie value it will assign the same ranked value to every row that is tied (three records tied for 6th place will all receive the ranked value of 6). As soon as a non-tied value is found, it is assigned a ranked value determined by adding 1 for each tied row from the previous ranked value (adding $6 + 3 = 9$, so the next ranking value will be 9th place).

6. By design, the DENSE_RANK() function counts ties and will always assign ranking values in sequential order, which eliminates gaps in ranking values.

7. When the DENSE_RANK() function encounters a tie value it will assign the same ranked value to every row that is tied (three records tied for 6th place will all receive the ranked value of 6). As soon as a non-tied value is found it is assigned a ranked value determined by adding 1 to the previous ranked value(thus, adding $6 + 1 = 7$, so the next ranking value will be 7th place).

8. When querying on an expression field, one approach is to make a derived table from the query in which the expression field appears. The expression will then appear as an actual column in the derived table, allowing access to the aliased column by the query. The derived table behaves like an actual table, as long as the current query is running.

9. There are three components to building a derived table:

   1) If any expression fields are present, they must be aliased, as they will become the new column names.

   2) Nest the query inside a SELECT statement:
   ```
   SELECT * FROM (SELECT * FROM TableName)
   ```

   3) The nested query (derived table) must be aliased:
   ```
   SELECT * FROM (SELECT * FROM TableName) AS Derived
   ```

10. Derived tables aren't physical tables and can't be seen in Object Explorer.

The ROW_NUMBER() Function

The next ranking function we will learn about is ROW_NUMBER(). As stated at the beginning of this chapter there are some basic character traits that are shared by the RANK(), DENSE_RANK() and ROW_NUMBER() functions. Each of these functions must be followed by an OVER() clause that contains an ORDER BY clause listing the target field and the sort order used by the ranking criteria.

Up until now, we have only seen ranking examples with numeric and date/time data types such as, Amount, RetailPrice, YearlySalary and HireDate. Our next example builds a query that will compare the output of these three ranking functions using values with a character data type.

We know the Employee table contains duplicate values in the FirstName field. Before we start writing a query that includes a ranking function, let's start by taking a quick look at some of the data in the Employee table by narrowing our focus to display only the FirstName and LastName fields in the selection list and sort the result set by the FirstName values in ascending order (Figure 7.21).

```
SELECT FirstName, LastName
FROM Employee
ORDER BY FirstName
```

	FirstName	LastName
1	Alex	Adams
2	Barbara	O'Neil
3	Barry	Brown
4	David	Kennson
5	David	Lonning
6	Eric	Bender

13 rows

Figure 7.21 Begin building a ranking query with a SELECT statement and an ORDER BY clause.

Within the first six records there is a duplicate (tie) value in the FirstName field (David). Do not confuse the fact that these two 'David' values have unique values associated with them in the LastName field by thinking this will not produce a tie when encountered by a ranking function. The ranking function will be performing its evaluation logic on the FirstName field only.

We are now ready to add the RANK() function to the query to test how it responds to this tie in the FirstName field. Make sure this expression field is aliased as AzRank and view the results of running the sample code in Figure 7.22.

```
SELECT FirstName, LastName,
RANK() OVER(ORDER BY FirstName) AS AzRank
FROM Employee
```

	FirstName	LastName	AzRank
1	Alex	Adams	1
2	Barbara	O'Neil	2
3	Barry	Brown	3
4	David	Kennson	4
5	David	Lonning	4
6	Eric	Bender	6

13 rows

Figure 7.22 Add the RANK() function, which will evaluate on the FirstName field (sorted A-Z).

Based on what we have learned so far, the RANK() function should assign the tied FirstName field values of 'David' with the ranked value of 4th place and then it will assign a 6th place ranked value to the next unique value it finds (Eric). When we review the results shown in Figure 7.22, we see this is exactly what happened.

Our next step is to add a column for the DENSE_RANK() function, to test how it responds to the tied value of 'David'. Make sure to distinguish this as a unique field by aliasing it as AzDRank and after running the following code sample, observe that the results resemble those shown in Figure 7.23.

```
SELECT FirstName, LastName,
RANK() OVER(ORDER BY FirstName) AS AzRank,
DENSE_RANK() OVER(ORDER BY FirstName) AS AzDRank
FROM Employee
```

	FirstName	LastName	AzRank	AzDRank
1	Alex	Adams	1	1
2	Barbara	O'Neil	2	2
3	Barry	Brown	3	3
4	David	Kennson	4	4
5	David	Lonning	4	4
6	Eric	Bender	6	5

12 rows

Figure 7.23 Add the DENSE_RANK() function (aliased as AzDRank) to evaluate the same ties.

As expected, the logic for the DENSE_RANK() function assigns a 4th place value to the two FirstName field values of 'David' and then assigns the next sequential value of 5th place (no gap) when it finds the next row with a unique value (Eric).

Finally, we will add a column for the ROW_NUMBER() function, to test how it will respond when it encounters the tied values in the FirstName field. Go ahead and alias this expression with the name AzRRank and after running the sample code, check the results to see if they resemble Figure 7.24.

```
SELECT FirstName, LastName,
RANK() OVER(ORDER BY FirstName) AS AzRank,
DENSE_RANK() OVER(ORDER BY FirstName) AS AzDRank,
ROW_NUMBER() OVER(ORDER BY FirstName) AS AzRRank
FROM Employee
```

	FirstName	LastName	AzRank	AzDRank	AzRRank
1	Alex	Adams	1	1	1
2	Barbara	O'Neil	2	2	2
3	Barry	Brown	3	3	3
4	David	Kennson	4	4	4
5	David	Lonning	4	4	5
6	Eric	Bender	6	5	6

13 rows

Figure 7.24 Add the ROW_NUMBER() function (aliased as AzRRank) to evaluate the same ties.

ROW_NUMBER() Function Logic

We can see by the results shown in Figure 7.24 that when the tied value (David) is encountered by the ROW_NUMBER() function, it ignores the tie and simply assigns unique ranked values in sequential order for every row evaluated.

In other words, the ROW_NUMBER() function always starts with the number 1, followed by 2, 3, 4, 5, 6, etc... until it finishes with the last row. It will never have a row with a ranking value matching any other row (repeating) and there will never be a gap in the ranking values.

Another unique feature of the ROW_NUMBER() function is that it can accept a PARTITION BY clause inside the OVER() clause. This allows for setting the target for evaluation on one field and the sort order on a different field with the ORDER BY clause.

Lab 7.2: ROW_NUMBER

Lab Prep: Each lab has one or more Skill Checks. Start with Skill Check 1 and proceed until reaching the Points to Ponder section.

Before beginning this lab, verify that SQL Server 2012 is properly installed and operating. Before running the lab setup script for resetting the database (SQLQueries2012Vol2Chapter7.2Setup.sql), please make sure to close all query windows within SSMS. An open query window pointing to a database context can lock that database preventing it from updating when the script is executing. A simple way to assure all query windows are closed, is to exit out of SSMS, then open a new instance of SSMS, and lastly run the setup script.

Skill Check 1: In the JProCo database, locate the StateList table to write a query including all fields and records ranked by the smallest to largest value in the LandMass field.

In the SELECT list, add three columns named RankNo, DRankNo and RowNo (representing the RANK(), DENSE_RANK() and ROW_NUMBER() functions) after the four columns already included in the StateList table.

When done, the results of the query should resemble those shown in Figure 7.25.

	StateID	StateName	ProvinceName	RegionName	LandMass	RankNo	DRankNo	RowNo
1	DC	District of Columbia	NULL	USA-Continental	68	1	1	1
2	RI	Rhode Island	NULL	USA-Continental	1545	2	2	2
3	VI	US Virgin Islands	NULL	Other	1545	2	2	3
4	PE	NULL	Prince Edward Island	Canada	2185	4	3	4
5	DE	Delaware	NULL	USA-Continental	2489	5	4	5
6	CO	Connecticut	NULL	USA-Continental	5544	6	5	6

Query executed successfully.   RENO (11.0 RTM)   Reno\Student (51)   JProCo   00:00:00   63 rows

Figure 7.25 Add three columns ranking the LandMass field of the StateList table.

Answer Code: The T-SQL code for this lab is located in the downloadable files as a file named Lab7.2_Row_Number.sql.

Points to Ponder - ROW_NUMBER()

1.   The ROW_NUMBER() function uses the same basic rules as the RANK() and DENSE_RANK() functions.

2.   Use the ROW_NUMBER() function to number rows without ties, repeating ranking values and without introducing a gap in the numbering sequence.

3.   The ROW_NUMBER() function creates ranking values which are unique and sequential without any gaps in the ranking values.

4.   The ROW_NUMBER() function can use the PARTITION BY clause to target a field for the ranking logic in addition to the ORDER BY clause to determine the sort order of the results.

Chapter Glossary

DENSE_RANK(): A SQL Server ranking function that counts ties and uses sequential number sequencing (no gaps). It returns the ranked value of each row within a result set (one plus the previous ranked number).

Derived Table: A temporary object that is only materialized ("made real") while a query is running. The fields and data held in a derived table disappear once the query has completed.

RANK(): A SQL Server ranking function that counts ties and uses non-sequential number sequencing (creates gaps). It returns the ranked value of each row within a result set (one plus the number of rows in a ranked value that comes before the row in question).

Ranking Functions: SQL Server has four ranking functions that return a BIGINT data type:

1) RANK()
2) DENSE_RANK()
3) ROW_NUMBER()
4) NTILE()

ROW_NUMBER(): A SQL Server ranking function that numbers records in a sequential and unique manner, with no ties, skips or repeat values. Unless the following three conditions are true when the query runs, there is no guarantee the order of the results will be the same each time it is executed.

1) Values of partitioned columns are unique.

2) Values of ORDER BY columns are unique.

3) Combinations of values for the partition and ORDER BY columns are unique.

Review Quiz - Chapter Seven

1.) You need to write a query that uses a ranking function that returns a ranked number to each row starting with 1 for the first row. If a tie is encountered, then those rows receive the same ranked number. After the tie, the next number must skip to its exact row position. Which T-SQL ranking function should you use?

O a. `RANK()`

O b. `DENSE_RANK()`

O c. `TOP(n)`

2.) What is the only difference between RANK() and DENSE_RANK()?

O a. `RANK()` does not treat ties with the same number.

O b. `DENSE_RANK()` does not treat ties with the same number.

O c. `RANK()` does not skip numbers after the tie breaker.

O d. `DENSE_RANK()` does not skip numbers after the tie breaker.

3.) Why does the following code fail to find the top 5 grants?

```
SELECT *, RANK() OVER(ORDER BY Amount DESC) as GrantRank
FROM [Grant]
WHERE GrantRank =< 5
```

O a. Because there might be a tie.

O b. We can't use * before the ranked field.

O c. We can't predicate on an expression field until you put it inside an Object like a temp query.

O d. With expression fields you must use `HAVING` instead of `WHERE`.

4.) The following figure shows the scores of 6 contest winners. Tom is the highest and Eric made 6th place. There were 6 people but only 5 distinct scores.

5 Highest Scores	5 Highest Distinct Scores
9.9	9.9
9.8	9.8
9.7	9.7
9.6	9.6
9.6	9.2

You are writing a query to list the 5 highest distinct scores. The Ranked field should be called ScoreRating. You have written the following code:

```
SELECT *
FROM (SELECT   *   More code here.
FROM Contestants)  AS ContestantFinal
WHERE ScoreRating = 5
```

What code will achieve this goal?

O a. `SUM(*) OVER(ORDER BY Score DESC) as ScoreRating`

O b. `RANK() OVER(ORDER BY Score DESC) as ScoreRating`

O c. `COUNT(*) OVER(ORDER BY Score DESC) as ScoreRating`

O d. `DENSE_RANK() OVER(ORDER BY Score DESC) as ScoreRating`

5.) You need to write a query that returns the 5 highest DISTINCT values. Which ranking function would you use?

O a. `RANK`

O b. `NTILE`

O c. `DENSE_RANK`

O d. `ROW_NUMBER`

6.) You are writing a query to list the highest 40 amounts. You have written the following code segment.

```
SELECT *
FROM (SELECT CustomerName, SUM(TotalDue) AS TotalGiven,
--CODE HERE
FROM Customer JOIN SalesOrder
ON Customer.CustomerID = SalesOrder.CustomerID
GROUP BY Customer.CustomerID) AS DonationsToFilter
WHERE FilterCriteria <= 40
```

You need to insert a T-SQL clause in the comment to complete the query. Which T-SQL clause should you insert?

O a. `RANK() OVER (ORDER BY SUM(TotalDue) DESC) AS FilterCriteria`

O b. `DENSE_RANK() OVER (ORDER BY SUM(TotalDue) DESC) AS FilterCriteria`

Answer Key

1.) Because DENSE_RANK() closes the number gap caused by multiple rows having the same ranked number, (b) is incorrect. Since TOP is a row-limiter and is not a function used in expression fields, (c) is also incorrect. Because RANK() is a function that can be used in expression fields and it skips numbers after a tie, (a) will be the correct answer.

2.) Since RANK() and DENSE_RANK() both assign the same number to ties (a) and (b) must both be wrong. Because RANK() does skip numbers after a tie by assigning the next record's row position as the ranked value (c) is wrong too. Because DENSE_RANK() uses sequential numbers to eliminate gaps (d) is the right answer.

3.) Since the query will result in an error because it attempts to predicate on an expression field that is not inside a derived table, (a), (b) and (d) are all incorrect. Since the query will not work unless we use a derived table containing the expression field, (c) is the correct answer.

4.) Because SUM() and COUNT() both expect the PARTITION BY argument in the OVER() clause, the code in (a) and (c) will both return 'Incorrect syntax near the word 'order''. Since RANK() will skip numbers after a tie, the records returned may not be distinct values, making (b) incorrect too. Because DENSE_RANK() assigns the ranked value based on distinct values, (d) is the correct answer.

5.) Since RANK() will skip numbers after a tie, the records returned may not be distinct values, making (a) an incorrect choice. Since NTILE() just divides the result set into equal size groups, (b) is also a wrong choice. Because ROW_NUMBER() will assign a different row number to each record returning the same value, (d) can also return the wrong answer. Because DENSE_RANK() assigns the ranked value based on distinct values, (c) is the correct answer.

6.) Since RANK() will skip numbers after a tie, the records returned may not be distinct values, making (a) incorrect. Because DENSE_RANK() assigns the ranked value based on distinct values, (b) is the correct answer.

Bug Catcher Game

To play the Bug Catcher game, run the SQLQueries2012Vol2BugCatcher07.pps file from the BugCatcher folder of the companion files. We can obtain these files from the www.Joes2Pros.com web site.

[THIS PAGE INTENTIONALLY LEFT BLANK.]

Chapter 8. Predicating and Tiling Ranked Data

A friend of mine recently told me she's very proud of her son, because he is consistently in the upper quarter of every class he takes at school. Although she didn't know it, by making her calculations based on separating each class into four sections and then identifying which section her son belongs to, she had performed a calculation similar to the NTILE() function used by SQL Server.

As with the previous three ranking functions that we have learned about, the NTILE() function requires an OVER() clause that contains an ORDER BY clause to provide it with the target field and sort order for its ranking values. However, instead of assigning a ranked value to each record, the NTILE() function places several rows into one or more groups and then assigns a ranking value to each group (tile) based on its calculations. This chapter covers how to tile and predicate with row functions.

READER NOTE: *Please run the script SQLQueries2012Vol2Chapter8.0Setup.sql in order to follow along with the examples in the first section of Chapter 8. All scripts mentioned in this chapter may be found at www.Joes2Pros.com.*

Tiling Ranked Data

Just like its three fellow ranking functions, NTILE takes data you've sorted and then marches straight down the list in order of row number. Instead of assigning a ranked value to each record, NTILE counts records and assigns them into a group (a.k.a., "tile", or "bucket" in geek speak) based on:
1) the number of tiles/pieces you have specified, and
2) the count of records contained in the query.

We'll start our work by using an example from the Grant table. Like all other ranking functions, we first want to write a SELECT statement and an ORDER BY clause to determine the sort order (Figure 8.1).

```
SELECT *
FROM [Grant]
ORDER BY Amount DESC
```

	GrantID	GrantName	EmpID	Amount
1	007	Ben@MoreTechnology.com	10	41000.00
2	008	www.@-Last-U-Can-Help.com	7	25000.00
3	009	Thank you @.com	11	21500.00
4	004	Norman's Outreach	NULL	21000.00
5	005	BIG 6's Foundation%	4	21000.00
6	006	TALTA_Kishan International	3	18100.00
7	003	Robert@BigStarBank.com	7	18100.00
8	002	K_Land fund trust	2	15750.00
9	010	Call Mom @Com	5	7500.00
10	001	92 Purr_Scents %% team	7	4750.00

10 rows

Figure 8.1 NTILE queries also begin with a SELECT statement and determine the sort order.

For the NTILE() function to be able to make this calculation of how many groups there are and how many rows go into each group, it needs additional information that we must provide as a parameter inside the parentheses. The value we provide will determine how many tiles (groups) there will be.

Of course, calculating the number of tiles derived from or into a percentage is as simple as dividing the number 100 by either the percentage or the number of tiles we want. Let's look at a couple of examples to help understand this concept:

o If we were asked to show the top 25% of sales for a month, then we simply take 100 divided by 25 and the answer is 4. This is the value inside the parentheses as a parameter, so it looks like this… NTILE(4).

o If we were asked by a manager to tell them what percentage of the total each of the five groups in the report represented, then we would simply take 100 divided by 5 and the answer is 20%. That was easy!

Thus, unlike the other three ranking functions, which only have two basic requirements, the NTILE() function has an additional requirement (a parameter). These three requirements are listed in order of appearance:

1) Parameter supplied inside the parentheses of the function
2) OVER() clause
3) ORDER BY clause

In this case, we want four groups, just like my friend's story about her son, so we can identify which grants have an amount in the upper quarter (25%) of the total (Figure 8.2).

```
SELECT *, NTILE(4) OVER (ORDER BY Amount DESC) AS [NTILE(4)]
FROM [Grant]
```

	GrantID	GrantName	EmpID	Amount	NTILE(4)
1	007	Ben@MoreTechnology.com	10	41000.00	1
2	008	www.@-Last-U-Can-Help.com	7	25000.00	1
3	009	Thank you @.com	11	21500.00	1
4	004	Norman's Outreach	NULL	21000.00	2
5	005	BIG 6's Foundation%	4	21000.00	2
6	006	TALTA_Kishan International	3	18100.00	2
7	003	Robert@BigStarBank.com	7	18100.00	3
8	002	K_Land fund trust	2	15750.00	3
9	010	Call Mom @Com	5	7500.00	4
10	001	92 Purr_Scents %% team	7	4750.00	4

10 rows

Figure 8.2 NTILE divides the Grant table into 4 pieces called tiles.

We can see that the upper quarter (ranking value 1) consists of GrantIDs 007, 008 and 009. The lower quarter (ranking value 4) consists of GrantIDs 001 and 010.

What if management decided they wanted a report showing them the top or bottom 50% of grants based on the Amount field? How do we determine the value we need as a parameter? Remember, all we need to do is take 100 and divide it by the number representing the percentage (100 / 50 = 2). Simply modify the parameter value to 2 and we can run the report to see the results (Figure 8.3).

```
SELECT *, NTILE(2) OVER (ORDER BY Amount DESC) AS [NTILE(2)]
FROM [Grant]
```

	GrantID	GrantName	EmpID	Amount	NTILE(2)
1	007	Ben@MoreTechnology.com	10	41000.00	1
2	008	www.@-Last-U-Can-Help.com	7	25000.00	1
3	009	Thank you @.com	11	21500.00	1
4	004	Norman's Outreach	NULL	21000.00	1
5	005	BIG 6's Foundation%	4	21000.00	1
6	006	TALTA_Kishan International	3	18100.00	2
7	003	Robert@BigStarBank.com	7	18100.00	2
8	002	K_Land fund trust	2	15750.00	2
9	010	Call Mom @Com	5	7500.00	2
10	001	92 Purr_Scents %% team	7	4750.00	2

10 rows

Figure 8.3 The NTILE query now divides the grants into an upper half and lower half.

Next, let's apply the NTILE() function to a date/time data type. The Employee table contains data we can use to rank the employees according to their hire date. Begin by writing a basic SELECT query for all fields from the Employee table with the HireDate sorted to show the oldest dates at the top and the most recent dates shown at the bottom (Figure 8.4).

```
SELECT *
FROM Employee
ORDER BY HireDate ASC
```

	EmpID	LastName	FirstName	HireDate	LocationID	ManagerID	Status
1	11	Smith	Sally	1989-04-01...	1	NULL	Active
2	12	O'Neil	Barbara	1995-05-26...	4	4	Has Tenure
3	4	Kennson	David	1996-03-16...	1	11	Has Tenure
4	3	Osako	Lee	1999-09-01...	2	11	Active
5	7	Lonning	David	2000-01-01...	1	11	On Leave
6	1	Adams	Alex	2001-01-01...	1	11	Active

13 rows

Figure 8.4 The Employee table sorted by HireDate (oldest dates to newest).

The next step is to add the NTILE() function as the final column in this query and alias it as [NTILE2]. For this exercise, we want to see the employee records by groups, so pass the number 2 in as a parameter to the function. Run the code sample and compare to the results shown in Figure 8.5

```
SELECT *, NTILE(2) OVER(ORDER BY HireDate ASC) AS [NTILE(2)]
FROM Employee
```

	EmpID	LastName	FirstName	HireDate	LocationID	ManagerID	Status	NTILE(2)
1	11	Smith	Sally	1989-04-01...	1	NULL	Active	1
2	12	O'Neil	Barbara	1995-05-26...	4	4	Has Tenure	1
3	4	Kennson	David	1996-03-16...	1	11	Has Tenure	1
4	3	Osako	Lee	1999-09-01...	2	11	Active	1
5	7	Lonning	David	2000-01-01...	1	11	On Leave	1
6	1	Adams	Alex	2001-01-01...	1	11	Active	1
7	8	Marshbank	John	2001-11-15...	NULL	4	Active	1
8	6	Kendall	Lisa	2001-11-15...	4	4	Active	2
9	2	Brown	Barry	2002-08-12...	1	11	Active	2
10	9	Newton	James	2003-09-30...	2	3	Active	2
11	10	O'Haire	Terry	2004-10-04...	2	3	Active	2
12	5	Bender	Eric	2007-05-17...	1	11	Active	2
13	13	Wilconkinski	Phil	2009-06-11...	1	4	Active	2

Query executed successfully.   RENO (11.0 RTM) Reno\Student (53) JProCo 00:00:00 13 rows

Figure 8.5 There are 7 employees in the first half (piece) and 6 employees in the second half.

Great! We can see from Figure 8.5 that the NTILE() function has assigned the first seven records with a ranking value of 1 and the remaining six records have a ranking value of 2 assigned to them.

NTILE() Function Logic

Hold on a second… it looks like the first group has seven records and the second group has six records in it. Isn't the function supposed to split the table into two equal groups? Yes and No, it actually depends on how many records are in the result set and if the number of tiles can be evenly divided into that number.

For example; In our previous query there are thirteen records in the result set for the Employee table and we are instructing the NTILE(2) function to place these thirteen records into two tiles (groups). However, when we divide 13 by 2 the answer equals an uneven number of 6.5. Since it is impossible to split a row in half, the NTILE() function is designed to place more rows in the first group(s) than in the bottom group(s) to make up for this disparity in records. This way none of the records are missing from the result set.

In other words, the NTILE() function tries to divide the records amongst the groups as equally as possible. If groups don't divide evenly with NTILE(), then the upper group(s) will have more records and the lower group(s) will have fewer.

Let's test this out by modifying the previous query slightly and pass a value of 3 into the NTILE() function. Since 13 / 3 = 4.33, we know the function will be forced to place more records into the first group than the third group, but what about the second group?

Think about how the NTILE() function might resolve this issue and then run the code sample and see if the results are the same as those shown in Figure 8.6.

```sql
SELECT *, NTILE(3) OVER(ORDER BY HireDate ASC) AS WhichTile
FROM Employee
```

	EmpID	LastName	FirstName	HireDate	LocationID	ManagerID	Status	WhichTile
1	11	Smith	Sally	1989-04-01...	1	NULL	Active	1
2	12	O'Neil	Barbara	1995-05-26...	4	4	Has Tenure	1
3	4	Kennson	David	1996-03-16...	1	11	Has Tenure	1
4	3	Osako	Lee	1999-09-01...	2	11	Active	1
5	7	Lonning	David	2000-01-01...	1	11	On Leave	1
6	1	Adams	Alex	2001-01-01...	1	11	Active	2
7	8	Marshbank	John	2001-11-15...	NULL	4	Active	2
8	6	Kendall	Lisa	2001-11-15...	4	4	Active	2
9	2	Brown	Barry	2002-08-12...	1	11	Active	2
10	9	Newton	James	2003-09-30...	2	3	Active	3
11	10	O'Haire	Terry	2004-10-04...	2	3	Active	3
12	5	Bender	Eric	2007-05-17...	1	11	Active	3
13	13	Wilconkin...	Phil	2009-06-11...	1	4	Active	3

Query executed successfully.   RENO (11.0 RTM)   Reno\Student (53)   JProCo   00:00:00   13 rows

Figure 8.6 NTILE adds 1 more record to the first tile when the ratio of tiles to records is uneven.

The NTILE() function tries to divide the records amongst the pieces as equally as possible. When the function was unable to evenly divide the number of records by the number of tiles, it placed five records into the first tile, and the second and third tiles received four records each (Figure 8.6).

Like ROW_NUMBER(), the NTILE() function ignores ties, which means it is always possible for records with the same value to be placed into separate groups. An example of this can be seen in the result set of Figure 8.2, which shows that even though GrantID 006 and 003 are tied on the Amount field with $18,100, they are placed into different tiles (2 and 3).

Lab 8.1: NTILE

Lab Prep: Each lab has one or more Skill Checks. Start with Skill Check 1 and proceed until reaching the Points to Ponder section.

Before beginning this lab, verify that SQL Server 2012 is properly installed and operating. Before running the lab setup script for resetting the database (SQLQueries2012Vol2Chapter8.1Setup.sql), please make sure to close all query windows within SSMS. An open query window pointing to a database context can lock that database preventing it from updating when the script is executing. A simple way to assure all query windows are closed, is to exit out of SSMS, then open a new instance of SSMS, and lastly run the setup script.

Skill Check 1: In the JProCo database, locate the StateList table to write a query including all fields and records ranked by the largest to smallest value in the LandMass field. Group the rankings in 5% increments for all 63 records.

In the selection list, add a column named *StateGroup* (representing the NTILE() function) after the four columns already included in the StateList table.

When done, the query results should resemble those shown in Figure 8.7.

	StateID	StateName	ProvinceName	RegionName	LandMass	StateGroup
1	AK	Alaska	NULL	USA	656425	1
2	QC	NULL	Quebec	Canada	523603	1
3	BC	NULL	British Columbia	Canada	357216	1
4	ON	NULL	Ontario	Canada	354341	1
5	TX	Texas	NULL	USA-Continental	268601	2
6	AB	NULL	Alberta	Canada	247999	2
						63 rows

Figure 8.7 The StateList records grouped in 20 tiles using the NTILE( ) function.

Answer Code: The T-SQL code to this lab can be found in the downloadable files in a file named Lab8.1_NTILE.sql.

Points to Ponder - NTILE

1. Ranking functions always return a value for each row in the result set.

2. All four ranking functions must use the OVER() clause that contains an ORDER BY clause to return a result set.

3. The OVER() clause determines which field is used by the ranking function.

4. Like ROW_NUMBER(), the NTILE() function ignores values and ties. All records are handled in order and assigned to their respective groups, so it is possible that records with the same value can be placed into separate groups.

5. NTILE() distributes rows into a specified number of groups.

6. When using the NTILE() function, the value specified cannot exceed the number of rows produced by the result set. In other words, if the result set contains 100 records, the highest value that can be specified is NTILE(100).

7. If groups don't divide evenly with NTILE(), then the lowest group(s) will have fewer records. For example; Using the NTILE(3) function on a table with 11 records will yield three groups, with the first two groups having four records each and the last group containing three records.

Predicating Row Functions

We have already learned how to locate an exact row or ranked number by using a ranking function with a derived table. What if the job calls for us to locate all the even-numbered rows, like 2, 4, 6, 8, etc. from a data set? In other words, a pattern of displaying every n^{th} row is required for a specific report. What can we do to accomplish this type of task?

Introduction to Modulo

Our ranking and tiling examples have all used integers. For example, we can come in 4th place but we can't come in 4½th place. In this section, we will continue dealing with arithmetic integers.

By definition, an even number is a number evenly divided by 2. While this is a simple concept, let us take a moment to review a couple of examples, as it is essential to understand this as we explore the arithmetic operator, modulo (commonly abbreviated as mod).

- o 30 divided by 2 has a quotient value of 15 with a remainder value of 0, so the number 30 is an even number.

- o 31 divided by 2 has a quotient value of 15 with a remainder value of 1, so the number 31 is an odd number.

In other words, any number divided by two with a remainder of zero is an even number and conversely, any number divided by two with a remainder other than zero is an odd number.

Understanding the quotient and remainder properties of division is important before we move into the basic concept behind the arithmetic operator modulo ("mod" for short).

When you apply modulo to any odd number, you always get the same result: the answer is 1 (one). When you 'mod' any even number by 2, the answer will always be 0. So what do the following numbers have in common?

3, 6, 9, 12, 15…

The answer is they all have a remainder of zero if you mod them by 3. So what do the following numbers have in common?

1, 4, 7, 10, 13…

The answer is they all have a remainder of 1 if you mod them by 3.

Modulo Examples

Let's begin by writing a very simple query to display the numbers 7 and 6.

SELECT 7, 6

	(No column name)	(No column name)
1	7	6

1 rows

Figure 8.8 The result of a simple SELECT statement.

The result in Figure 8.8 is easily predicted. What results should we expect when dividing these two integers by the number 2? We learned at an early age that **7 / 2 = 3.5** (3 with a remainder of 1) and **6 / 2 = 3** (3 with a remainder of 0).

What could we expect if we query six and seven divided by two? They should both be cut in half. **6/2** would be three and **7/2** would be three and a half or three with a remainder of one. Notice in Figure 8.9 the query returned both as three in the result set.

Since we are working with integers there is no half and the remainder is discarded.

SELECT (7 / 2) AS [7 / 2], (6 / 2) AS [6 / 2]

	7 / 2	6 / 2
1	3	3

1 rows

Figure 8.9 The result set demonstrates the remainder is dropped when 7/2 is queried.

So why is 3 shown as the result set for each of these calculations in Figure 8.9? This is because integer data types are whole numbers (no fractions). We need to be careful when dividing integer data types, as the results returned may not always be what we intended.

What results should we see when the dividing operand is replaced with an operand for modulo? The operand sign for modulo used by SQL (and many other languages) is the percent sign '%'. We can expect that 7 mod 2 will have a remainder of 1 and that 6 mod 2 will have a remainder of 0, as seen in Figure 8.10.

SELECT (7 % 2) AS [7 % 2], (6 % 2) AS [6 % 2]

	7 % 2	6 % 2
1	1	0

1 rows

Figure 8.10 This demonstrates how modulo returns the remainder in the result set.

To make sure we fully understand what modulo is doing, run these two separate queries at the same time and confirm the results of our lesson.

```
SELECT (7 / 2) AS Quotient, (7 % 2) AS Remainder
SELECT (6 / 2) AS Quotient, (6 % 2) AS Remainder
```

	Quotient	Remainder
1	3	1
	Quotient	Remainder
1	3	0

2 rows

Figure 8.11 This shows that seven divided by two is three with a remainder of one and six divided by two is three with a remainder of zero.

Predicating Modulo for Row Functions

Modulo is widely used in the world of mathematics and number theory. It also has many uses in the business world from arcane financial calculations, to some fun and creative uses in SQL Server reporting.

One of these common uses is creating reports that will display the result set with every other row highlighted, which makes it much easier to read (Figure 8.12).

	CustomerID	CustomerType	FirstName	LastName	CompanyName
1	1	Consumer	Mark	Williams	NULL
2	2	Consumer	Lee	Young	NULL
3	3	Consumer	Patricia	Martin	NULL
4	4	Consumer	Mary	Lopez	NULL
5	5	Business	NULL	NULL	MoreTechnology.com
6	6	Consumer	Ruth	Clark	NULL

775 rows

Figure 8.12 This shows the Customer table in green board format.

A large company may have their payroll company pay employees with even-numbered ID's on the first and fifteenth of each month and pay employees with odd numbered ID's on the seventh and thirtieth day of each month. This type of payroll arrangement can keep the process manageable by running it in smaller batches.

Without diving into the downstream business process, for simplicity, the JProCo customer table needs to be separated into even and odd numbered records. It may be that the even records need to be fed into one table and odd numbered records into another.

Finding Even-numbered Records

Oftentimes, we are challenged with tasks having more than one solution and it takes a bit more thought to find the most efficient approach. For example; The department heads of JProCo have asked us to create two reports, one with all the even-numbered CustomerID values from the Customer table and the other report should have all the odd numbered CustomerID values.

If we write a simple SELECT query on the Customer table, we find that there are 775 records. By filtering on CustomerID mod two equal to zero, we will limit the records to only those that have a CustomerID with an even number (Figure 8.13).

```
SELECT *
FROM Customer
WHERE CustomerID % 2 = 0
```

	CustomerID	CustomerType	FirstName	LastName	CompanyName
1	2	Consumer	Lee	Young	NULL
2	4	Consumer	Mary	Lopez	NULL
3	6	Consumer	Ruth	Clark	NULL
4	8	Consumer	Jennifer	Garcia	NULL
5	10	Consumer	Robert	Wilson	NULL
6	12	Consumer	Helen	Hernandez	NULL

387 rows

Figure 8.13 Using the mod function in a WHERE clause to return only even-numbered records.

The risk of dividing customers on an identity field is that deletions can cause gaps. With deletions, even-numbered CustomerID values may not be every other row. A much better process to return every other customer would be to use the row numbers. With a simple modification to the WHERE clause, we can produce a report that finds only the records with odd numbered CustomerID values.

```
SELECT *
FROM Customer
WHERE CustomerID % 2 = 1
```

	CustomerID	CustomerType	FirstName	LastName	CompanyName
1	1	Consumer	Mark	Williams	NULL
2	3	Consumer	Patricia	Martin	NULL
3	5	Business	NULL	NULL	MoreTechnology.com
4	7	Consumer	Tessa	Wright	NULL
5	9	Consumer	Linda	Adams	NULL
6	11	Consumer	Kimberly	Taylor	NULL

388 rows

Figure 8.14 Filtering with CustomerID mod 2 = 1 will include only odd numbered records.

We now know that filtering with modulo provides a very simple solution for finding records that have a numeric column that is either odd or even. It is important to take into consideration what effects data modifications (DELETE, INSERT, UPDATE, and MERGE) can have when choosing a numeric column for calculations using modulo in them.

For instance, the example in Figure 8.14 has a business requirement calling for a report with alternating highlighted rows. In this case, it might not be a good idea to perform a calculation using modulo on an identity field, like CustomerID.

What would this report look like if CustomerID 3 were deleted from the table and the criteria for modulo used CustomerID? We are not going to show that but there would be two consecutively highlighted rows (CustomerID 2 and 4), which no longer meets the requirement to display the output with alternating highlighted rows (Figure 8.15).

CustomerID	CustomerType	FirstName	LastName	CompanyName
1	Consumer	Mark	Williams	NULL
2	Consumer	Lee	Young	NULL
4	Consumer	Mary	Lopez	NULL
5	Business	NULL	NULL	MoreTechnology.com
6	Consumer	Ruth	Clark	NULL

Figure 8.15 Effects of deleting a row when using an identity field as criteria with modulo.

In situations like this, we should consider using the ROW_NUMBER() function to create a field that will yield consistent results in our reports, regardless of any data modifications. We will explore this option in our next exercise.

Finding Every Fifth Record

What if we were assigned a more complicated task, such as finding the first record and then every fifth record afterwards in a result set? In other words, we must filter the results from a query to display only the 1st, 5th, 11th, 16th, 21st, etc... records for the required report.

Before we begin working on the solution, let us take a look at all the fields and records in the CurrentProducts table sorted in descending order on RetailPrice. Run the code sample shown here and check the results against those in the CurrentProducts as seen in Figure 8.16.

```
SELECT *
FROM CurrentProducts
ORDER BY RetailPrice DESC
```

	ProductID	ProductName	RetailPrice	Origination...	ToBeDeleted	Category
1	483	Yoga Mtn Getaway 2 Weeks	1695.00	2012-09-26...	1	LongTerm-Stay
2	336	Lakes Tour 2 Weeks West Coast	1161.099	2011-09-29...	1	LongTerm-Stay
3	342	Lakes Tour 2 Weeks East Coast	1147.986	2008-08-31...	1	LongTerm-Stay
4	372	Rain Forest Tour 2 Weeks East Coast	1144.773	2007-04-21...	1	LongTerm-Stay
5	402	River Rapids Tour 2 Weeks East Coast	1116.108	2009-10-23...	1	LongTerm-Stay
6	456	Wine Tasting Tour 2 Weeks West Coast	1101.969	2011-09-09...	1	LongTerm-Stay

Query executed successfully.   RENO (11.0 RTM)   Reno\Student (53)   JProCo   00:00:00   483 rows

Figure 8.16 This shows the CurrentProducts table in descending order by price.

Our next step is to add a ROW_NUMBER() function (aliased as *RowID*) as the first field in the selection list. Recall that this will assign unique sequential values for every row in the table, allowing us to locate every fifth record in the result set. Notice that Figure 8.17 shows *RowID* is now the first column.

```
SELECT
ROW_NUMBER() OVER(ORDER BY RetailPrice DESC) AS RowID, *
FROM CurrentProducts
```

	RowID	ProductID	ProductName	RetailPrice	Origination...	ToBeDeleted	Category
1	1	483	Yoga Mtn Getaway 2 Weeks	1695.00	2012-09-26...	1	LongTerm-Stay
2	2	336	Lakes Tour 2 Weeks West Coast	1161.099	2011-09-29...	1	LongTerm-Stay
3	3	342	Lakes Tour 2 Weeks East Coast	1147.986	2008-08-31...	1	LongTerm-Stay
4	4	372	Rain Forest Tour 2 Weeks East Coast	1144.773	2007-04-21...	1	LongTerm-Stay
5	5	402	River Rapids Tour 2 Weeks East Coast	1116.108	2009-10-23...	1	LongTerm-Stay

Query executed successfully.   RENO (11.0 RTM)   Reno\Student (53)   JProCo   00:00:00   483 rows

Figure 8.17 This is using the OVER clause with ROW_NUMBER() to insert the RowID field into the result.

Notice in Figure 8.17 we created a field called RowID that matches the row numbers to the left. Although it might be tempting to simply add criteria to a WHERE clause filtering for every fifth *RowID*, when we run the following code sample, SQL Server displays an error message stating there is no column named *RowID* (Figure 8.18).

```
SELECT
ROW_NUMBER() OVER(ORDER BY RetailPrice DESC) AS RowID, *
FROM CurrentProducts
WHERE RowID IN (1,6,11)
```

```
Messages
Msg 207, Level 16, State 1, Line 4
Invalid column name 'RowID'.
Msg 207, Level 16, State 1, Line 4
Invalid column name 'RowID'.
Msg 207, Level 16, State 1, Line 4
Invalid column name 'RowID'.
                                                      0 rows
```

Figure 8.18 This shows WHERE does not work as a row limiter with a derived field.

We learned in Chapter 7 that an aliased field cannot be used as a predicate in the WHERE clause, since it is only a label for the ROW_NUMBER() function and the values it produces are not kept in memory by SQL Server.

We must place this entire query (without the WHERE clause) into a temporary object known as a derived table to materialize the RowID field, so that it can be used as filtering criteria while the query is running. For the moment, we will use the hard-coded values of 1, 6 and 11 as the rows to find (Figure 8.19).

```
SELECT * FROM (
  SELECT
  ROW_NUMBER() OVER(ORDER BY RetailPrice DESC) AS RowID, *
  FROM CurrentProducts) AS DrvTbl
WHERE RowID IN (1,6,11)
```

	RowID	ProductID	ProductName	RetailPrice	OriginationDate	ToBeDeleted	Category
1	1	483	Yoga Mtn Getaway 2 Weeks	1695.00	2012-09-26 11...	1	LongTerm-Stay
2	6	456	Wine Tasting Tour 2 Weeks West Coast	1101.969	2011-09-09 11...	1	LongTerm-Stay
3	11	54	History Tour 2 Weeks Canada	1019.583	2004-10-08 21...	1	LongTerm-Stay

Query executed successfully.   RENO (11.0 RTM)   Reno\Student (53)   JProCo   00:00:00   3 rows

Figure 8.19 This uses a derived table for the WHERE to limit the query on the RowID field.

The filtering criteria is now working properly and we are ready to change the hard-coded values to use the modulo operation for locating the first record and then every fifth record afterwards in the result set. Let's do some basic math to help us determine the mod number that will give us the results we are looking for.

o One divided by five is zero with a remainder of one.
o Six divided by five is one with a remainder of one.
o Eleven divided by five is two with a remainder of one.

The pattern emerges, as every fifth number has a mod 5 equal to one. Modify the filtering criteria to replace the hard-coded values with mod 5 equals one and then run the query to display the expected results

```
SELECT * FROM (
  SELECT
  ROW_NUMBER() OVER(ORDER BY RetailPrice DESC) AS RowID, *
  FROM CurrentProducts) AS DrvTbl
WHERE RowID % 5 = 1
```

	RowID	ProductID	ProductName	RetailPrice	OriginationD...	ToBeDeleted	Category	
1	1	483	Yoga Mtn Getaway 2 Weeks	1695.00	2012-09-26...	1	LongTerm-Stay	
2	6	456	Wine Tasting Tour 2 Weeks West Coast	1101.969	2011-09-09...	1	LongTerm-Stay	
3	11	54	History Tour 2 Weeks Canada	1019.583	2004-10-08...	1	LongTerm-Stay	
4	16	414	River Rapids Tour 2 Weeks Canada	978.858	2004-08-06...	1	LongTerm-Stay	
5	21	18	Underwater Tour 2 Weeks Mexico	945.531	2004-12-20...	1	LongTerm-Stay	
6	26	481	Yoga Mtn Getaway 5 Days	875.00	2012-09-26...	0	Medium-Stay	

Query executed successfully.   RENO (11.0 RTM) | Reno\Student (53) | JProCo | 00:00:00 | 97 rows

Figure 8.20 This utilizes modulo to return every fifth record.

Great! Our query has successfully located the first record, and then found every fifth record after that and returned it to our result set as seen in Figure 8.20. With only a slight modification this query can find any row combination we need. By aliasing the ROW_NUMBER() function in a derived table, we are able to use it as criteria for a modulo operation to consistently produce the desired results.

o Find even-numbered rows: WHERE RowID % 2 = 0
o Find odd numbered rows: WHERE RowID % 2 = 1
o Find every 10th row (starting with row 10): WHERE RowID % 10 = 0
o Find every 10th row (starting with row 5): WHERE RowID % 10 = 5

Figure 8.20 pulled out every fifth record. If every other record was needed, replace the mod 5 with % 2 = 1 like a green board format. And if only the even row numbers were wanted, then mod two equal to zero would do the job.

Combining Aggregate Functions with Row Functions

We often wonder how our pay compares to that of the highest paid employee in the company where we work. Is our pay above the average, or below the average of all the other employees? Anyone who is a CEO is very likely to be amongst the highest paid employees. Maybe the majority of employees in the Engineering department make more money than those in the Accounting department. With this in mind, a better question might be, "How might our salary compare to others within our same department?", as this appears to be a better point of comparison.

By making a comparison of results within the same group or department, instead of the entire company, we gain the ability to make decisions based on a partition of the company. In the example of comparing our salary to everyone else in our department, we would want to find the highest paid (MAX) employee and then partition by department to arrive at the results we are looking for.

Partitioning Ranked Records

Many companies contribute to charities every year as part of their desire to give back to the community and to help those in need. Oftentimes a charitable organization assigns labels for different levels of sponsorship to help their cause. These labels, such as Gold, Silver and Bronze help identify the level of financial commitment the company has made to the charity.

As a company, JProCo has made a long-term commitment to make contributions to six charitable organizations that it feels they can help the most. Based on feedback from their employees and customers, the executives for JProCo have decided to make the effort to spread their contributions across the six charities as evenly as possible. This means they need a report to show which charities have received the most contributions. They are also interested to know if there is an imbalance in the level of sponsorship between the different charities.

In other words, to make the best decision for which charities to contribute to this year and at what level to give, the executives at JProCo need a report to show the most recent contribution and level made to each of the six charities they support.

Before we begin please run the SQLQueries2012Vol2Chapter8SpecialSetup.sql script so you have the CharitableEvents table in your JProCo data. To build the queries to provide the requested information to the executives at JProCo, we should simply look at the data contained in the CharitableEvents table, so we know which fields to use for our calculations.

```
SELECT *
FROM CharitableEvents
```

	CharityID	SponsorLevel	OrderDate
1	1	Gold	2008-05-06...
2	1	Silver	2009-05-09...
3	1	Bronze	2009-10-06...
4	2	Gold	2009-09-06...
5	2	Silver	2008-04-09...
6	2	Bronze	2010-02-06...
7	3	Gold	2009-11-06...
8	3	Silver	2009-10-09...
9	3	Bronze	2008-12-06...
10	4	Gold	2010-03-05...
11	4	Silver	2010-08-08...
12	4	Bronze	2011-04-09...
13	5	Gold	2011-02-05...
14	5	Silver	2010-05-08...
15	5	Bronze	2010-09-01...
16	1	Gold	2008-05-06...

18 rows

Figure 8.21 The result set for all records and fields in the CharitableEvents table.

When looking at Figure 8.21, we can see that CharityID 1 received a donation at the Gold level on May 6th, the Silver level on May 9th and the Bronze level on October 6th of 2009. CharityID 2 also received contributions on different dates. The most recent contribution for CharityID 1 is October 6th, 2009 at the Bronze level.

Let's write a query that displays the contributions made to each charity and sort the results by the CharityID and OrderDate in descending order.

```
SELECT * FROM CharitableEvents
ORDER BY CharityID, OrderDate DESC
```

	CharityID	SponsorLevel	OrderDate
1	1	Bronze	2009-10-06…
2	1	Silver	2009-05-09…
3	1	Gold	2008-05-06…
4	2	Bronze	2010-02-06…
5	2	Gold	2009-09-06…
6	2	Silver	2008-04-09…
			18 rows

Figure 8.22 This shows the CharitableEvents table ordered by CharityID and OrderDate.

The result set in Figure 8.22 shows each CharityID grouped together and listed from the most recent to oldest contribution date. To find the most recent date a contribution was made, we can use the MAX() function with the OVER() clause to create a field aliased as *RecentDate* for the most recent OrderDate.

```
SELECT *,
MAX(OrderDate) OVER() AS RecentDate
FROM CharitableEvents
```

	CharityID	SponsorLevel	OrderDate	RecentDate
1	1	Gold	2008-05-06…	2011-08-08…
2	1	Silver	2009-05-09…	2011-08-08…
3	1	Bronze	2009-10-06…	2011-08-08…
4	2	Gold	2009-09-06…	2011-08-08…
5	2	Silver	2008-04-09…	2011-08-08…
6	2	Bronze	2010-02-06…	2011-08-08…
				18 rows

Figure 8.23 Result set shows a comparison of each OrderDate to the most recent OrderDate.

The results shown in Figure 8.23 compare the OrderDate for each contribution to the contribution with the most recent OrderDate made by JProCo. In other words, the value represented by the RecentDate field in this result set is the most recent OrderDate for all contributions contained in the CharitableEvents table.

However, we need to identify the most recent OrderDate for a contribution based on an individual CharityID instead of the most recent OrderDate for the entire CharitableEvents table. To accomplish this, we need to add a PARTITION BY clause inside the OVER() clause to determine the most recent OrderDate based on the CharityID field. Run the code sample shown here and view the results.

```
SELECT *,
MAX(OrderDate) OVER(PARTITION BY CharityID) AS RecentDate
FROM CharitableEvents
```

	CharityID	SponsorLevel	OrderDate	RecentDate
1	1	Gold	2008-05-06...	2009-10-06...
2	1	Silver	2009-05-09...	2009-10-06...
3	1	Bronze	2009-10-06...	2009-10-06...
4	2	Gold	2009-09-06...	2010-02-06...
5	2	Silver	2008-04-09...	2010-02-06...
6	2	Bronze	2010-02-06...	2010-02-06...

18 rows

Figure 8.24 PARTITION BY CharityID displays the most RecentDate for each CharityID.

The result set shown in Figure 8.24 is very close to meeting our requirements. We now have the OrderDate for the most recent contribution (RecentDate) of each CharityID shown alongside the actual OrderDate of each contribution.

Our requirement is to include only the most recent contribution made to each charitable organization (CharityID). How can we modify the current query to display only the requested information? Simply add a WHERE clause to filter the result set with criteria that finds each OrderDate value that is equal to the RecentDate value.

```
SELECT *,
MAX(OrderDate) OVER(PARTITION BY CharityID) AS RecentDate
FROM CharitableEvents
WHERE OrderDate = RecentDate
```

Messages
Msg 207, Level 16, State 1, Line 3
Invalid column name 'RecentDate'

0 rows

Figure 8.25 An aliased expression cannot be used as criteria in a WHERE clause.

By now, we can recognize the error message from SQL Server is the result of our expression field (RecentDate) not being materialized for use elsewhere in the query. So we must implement a derived table (aliased as *SponsorDate*), for the filtering criteria to work in our query.

```
SELECT * FROM (
  SELECT *,
  MAX(OrderDate) OVER(PARTITION BY CharityID) AS RecentDate
  FROM CharitableEvents) AS SponsorDate
WHERE OrderDate = RecentDate
ORDER BY RecentDate DESC
```

	CharityID	SponsorLevel	OrderDate	RecentDate
1	6	Silver	2011-08-08…	2011-08-08…
2	4	Bronze	2011-04-09…	2011-04-09…
3	5	Gold	2011-02-05…	2011-02-05…
4	2	Bronze	2010-02-06…	2010-02-06…
5	3	Gold	2009-11-06…	2009-11-06…
6	1	Bronze	2009-10-06…	2009-10-06…

6 rows

Figure 8.26 The result set shows only the most recent contribution from each CharityID.

We have now met the original requirements set by the executives at JProCo, as this report shows only the most recent contribution for each of the six charities. When looking closer at the results in Figure 8.26, we can see that the values shown in the OrderDate and RecentDate fields are duplicates. In situations like this, it is a good idea to confirm if one or both of these fields need to be in the report. Depending on their needs, they may only want to see one date/time field.

Once this report was distributed, the Accounting department requested a modified report to show only the most recent contribution date for each CharityID at a specific SponsorLevel, such as the Gold level. Run the code sample shown here.

```
SELECT CharityID, SponsorLevel, RecentDate FROM (
    SELECT *,
    MAX(OrderDate) OVER(PARTITION BY CharityID) AS RecentDate
    FROM CharitableEvents) AS SponsorDate
WHERE SponsorLevel = 'Gold'
ORDER BY RecentDate DESC
```

	CharityID	SponsorLevel	RecentDate
1	6	Gold	2011-08-08…
2	4	Gold	2011-04-09…
3	5	Gold	2011-02-05…
4	2	Gold	2010-02-06…
5	3	Gold	2009-11-06…
6	1	Gold	2009-10-06…

6 rows

Figure 8.27 The accounting department report shows the most recent contributions by SponsorLevel.

Reports like this are well suited for conversion to a stored procedure taking a parameter for the SponsorLevel field. This allows the user to run the desired report by simply changing the input value for the sproc, as shown in this example.

```
CREATE PROC RecentContributionByLevel @Level CHAR(10)
AS
SELECT CharityID, SponsorLevel, RecentDate FROM (
  SELECT *,
  MAX(OrderDate) OVER(PARTITION BY CharityID) AS RecentDate
  FROM CharitableEvents) AS SponsorDate
WHERE SponsorLevel = @Level
ORDER BY RecentDate DESC
GO

EXEC RecentContributionByLevel 'Silver'
```

Lab 8.2: Predicating Row Functions

Lab Prep: Before we can begin the lab you must have SQL Server installed and have run the SQLQueries2012Vol2Chapter8.2Setup.sql script. When running a setup script, please first make sure you have closed all your query windows. An open query window pointing to a database context can lock that database preventing it from updating when the script is executing. One great way to do this is to close out of SQL Server, open SQL Server, and then run the script. Each lab has one or more Skill Checks. Start with Skill Check 1 and proceed until reaching the Points to Ponder section.

Skill Check 1: Find even-numbered employees from the Employee table. When done your result should resemble Figure 8.28.

	EmpID	LastName	FirstName	HireDate	LocationID	ManagerID	Status
1	2	Brown	Barry	2002-08-12...	1	11	Active
2	4	Kennson	David	1996-03-16...	1	11	Has Tenure
3	6	Kendall	Lisa	2001-11-15...	4	4	Active
4	8	Marshbank	John	2001-11-15...	NULL	4	Active
5	10	O'Haire	Terry	2004-10-04...	2	3	Active
6	12	O'Neil	Barbara	1995-05-26...	4	4	Has Tenure

6 rows

Figure 8.28 Skill Check 1.

Skill Check 2: From the Employee table of JProCo, show the even-numbered employee rows by HireDate. Alias the ranked row as SeniorRow. When done your result should resemble Figure 8.29.

	SeniorRow	EmpID	LastName	FirstName	HireDate	LocationID	ManagerID	Status
1	2	12	O'Neil	Barbara	1995-05-26 00:00:00.000	4	4	Has Tenure
2	4	3	Osako	Lee	1999-09-01 00:00:00.000	2	11	Active
3	6	1	Adams	Alex	2001-01-01 00:00:00.000	1	11	Active
4	8	6	Kendall	Lisa	2001-11-15 00:00:00.000	4	4	Active
5	10	9	Newton	James	2003-09-30 00:00:00.000	2	3	Active
6	12	5	Bender	Eric	2007-05-17 00:00:00.000	1	11	Active

Query executed successfully.   RENO (11.0 RTM)   Reno\Student (51)   JProCo   00:00:00   6 rows

Figure 8.29 Skill Check 2.

Skill Check 3: From the CurrentProducts table of JProCo find the most recent product in each category. The expression field that finds the most recent origination date by category should be called MaxCatDate. When done your result should resemble Figure 8.30.

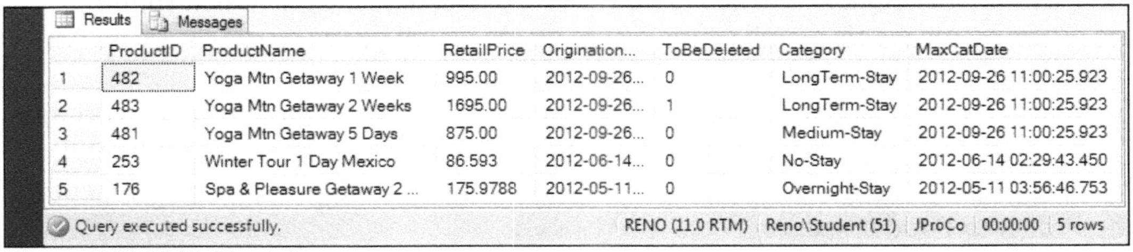

	ProductID	ProductName	RetailPrice	Origination...	ToBeDeleted	Category	MaxCatDate
1	482	Yoga Mtn Getaway 1 Week	995.00	2012-09-26...	0	LongTerm-Stay	2012-09-26 11:00:25.923
2	483	Yoga Mtn Getaway 2 Weeks	1695.00	2012-09-26...	1	LongTerm-Stay	2012-09-26 11:00:25.923
3	481	Yoga Mtn Getaway 5 Days	875.00	2012-09-26...	0	Medium-Stay	2012-09-26 11:00:25.923
4	253	Winter Tour 1 Day Mexico	86.593	2012-06-14...	0	No-Stay	2012-06-14 02:29:43.450
5	176	Spa & Pleasure Getaway 2 ...	175.9788	2012-05-11...	0	Overnight-Stay	2012-05-11 03:56:46.753

Query executed successfully.   RENO (11.0 RTM)   Reno\Student (51)   JProCo   00:00:00   5 rows

Figure 8.30 Skill Check 3.

Answer Code: The T-SQL code to this lab can be found from the downloadable files named Lab8.2_ PredicatingRowFunctions.sql.

Points to Ponder - Predicating Row Functions

1. Modulo is an arithmetic operator that can be used as part of an expression field or predicate in a query.

2. Modulo only works with integer or monetary data, or with the numeric data type.

3. The shorthand term for modulo is "MOD".

4. 50 mod 20 is 10.

5. In the last example (see #4) 50 is the dividend, 20 is the divisor and 10 is the remainder.

6. The syntax to express 50 mod 20 in SQL Server would be 50 % 20.

7. To find all even numbers in the EmpID column, use the following predicate.
   WHERE EmpID % 2 = 0

8. To find all odd numbers in the EmpID column use the following predicate.
   WHERE EmpID % 2 = 1

9. OVER can be used with aggregate functions (like MAX) or analytic functions (like RANK).

10. If you use the OVER clause with an empty set of parentheses, then the aggregate or analytic function is performed over all records in the result set.

11. The OVER clause can allow you to partition the result set into sections. For example, if you partitioned the Employee table for longest serving employee by city, you would find a different aggregate value for each city in your result set.

Chapter Glossary

NTILE(): A SQL Server ranking function that distributes rows into a specified number of tiles (groups), while ignoring values, including ties. First, all records are sorted in their defined order and then assigned to their respective groups.

Tiling: The ranking process used by the NTILE() function to place data into ranked groups (tiles).

Review Quiz - Chapter Eight

1.) You need to write a query that allows you to rank states by total Landmass into four groups, where the top 25 percent of the results are in Group 1, the next 25 percent are in Group 2 and so on. Which NTILE statement should you use?

O a. `NTILE(1) OVER(ORDER BY LandMass DESC)`

O b. `NTILE(4) OVER(ORDER BY LandMass DESC)`

O c. `NTILE(25) OVER(ORDER BY LandMass DESC)`

O d. `NTILE(100) OVER(ORDER BY LandMass DESC)`

2.) You want to find the top 2% of all students' Grade Point Averages (GPA). Which NTILE would you use?

O a. `NTILE(1) OVER(ORDER BY GPA DESC)`

O b. `NTILE(2) OVER(ORDER BY GPA DESC)`

O c. `NTILE(25) OVER(ORDER BY GPA DESC)`

O d. `NTILE(50) OVER(ORDER BY GPA DESC)`

3.) You need to write a query that allows you to rank total sales for each salesperson into four groups, where the top 25 percent of results are in Group 1, the next 25 percent are in Group 2, the next 25 percent are in Group 3, and the lowest 25 percent are in Group 4. Which T-SQL statement should you use?

O a. `NTILE(1)`

O b. `NTILE(4)`

O c. `NTILE(5)`

O d. `NTILE(25)`

4.) You need to write a query that allows you to rank total sales for each salesperson into five groups, where the top 20 percent of results are in Group 1, the next 20 percent are in Group 2, and so on. Which T-SQL statement should you use?

O a. `NTILE(1)`

O b. `NTILE(4)`

O c. `NTILE(5)`

O d. `NTILE(20)`

O e. `NTILE(25)`

5.) You have a table named CurrentProducts that contains 47,000 products. The UnitsSold field shows how many units have been sold for that product. Which query displays the top 5% of products that have been sold most frequently?

O a.
```
WITH Percentages AS (
SELECT *,  NTILE(5) OVER (ORDER BY UnitsSold) AS
GroupingColumn FROM CurrentProducts)
SELECT *
FROM percentages
WHERE GroupingColumn =1;
```

O b.
```
WITH Percentages AS (
SELECT *, NTILE(5) OVER (ORDER BY UnitsSold) AS
GroupingColumn
FROM CurrentProducts)
SELECT *
FROM Percentages
WHERE GroupingColumn = 5;
```

O c.
```
WITH Percentages AS (
SELECT *, NTILE(20) OVER (ORDER BY UnitsSold) AS
GroupingColumn FROM CurrentProducts)
SELECT *
FROM Percentages
WHERE GroupingColumn = 1;
```

O d.
```
WITH Percentages AS (
SELECT *, NTILE(20) OVER (ORDER BY UnitsSold) AS
GroupingColumn FROM CurrentProducts)
SELECT *
FROM Percentages
WHERE GroupingColumn = 20;
```

6.) You have a sales table where you track all customers and when they bought at the Gold, Silver, and Bronze levels. These levels are tracked in a field called BuyerLevel. You want to see each customer's most recent purchase and the BuyerLevel of that most recent purchase. What code will achieve this result?

O a. ```
SELECT *
FROM (SELECT BuyerName, BuyerLevel, OrderDate,
MAX(OrderDate) OVER(PARTITION BY BuyerName) AS
MostRecentBuyerDate
FROM Sales) DrvTbl
WHERE OrderDate = MostRecentBuyerDate
```

O b. ```
SELECT *
FROM (SELECT BuyerName, BuyerLevel, OrderDate,
MAX(BuyerName) OVER(PARTITION BY OrderDate) AS
MostRecentBuyerDate
FROM Sales) DrvTbl
WHERE OrderDate = MostRecentBuyerDate
```

O c. ```
SELECT * FROM (SELECT BuyerName, BuyerLevel, OrderDate,
MAX(OrderDate) OVER( ) AS MostRecentBuyerDate
FROM Sales) DrvTbl
WHERE OrderDate = MostRecentBuyerDate
```

**7.)** You need to find all even-numbered EmployeeID fields. What predicate will achieve this result?

O a. `WHERE EmployeeID / 2 = 0`

O b. `WHERE EmployeeID / 2 = 1`

O c. `WHERE EmployeeID % 2 = 0`

O d. `WHERE EmployeeID % 2 = 1`

**8.)** You need to find all odd numbered EmployeeID fields. What predicate will achieve this result?

O a. `WHERE EmployeeID % 2 = 0`

O b. `WHERE EmployeeID % 2 = 1`

O c. `WHERE EmployeeID % 0 = 2`

O d. `WHERE EmployeeID % 1 = 2`
```

9.) Starting with the first row, you want to pull out every fifth row from the CurrentProducts table (Rows 1, 6, 11…). What code will achieve this result?

O a. `SELECT *`
   `(FROM (SELECT *, (ROW_NUMBER()`
   `OVER ( ORDER BY RetailPrice DESC)) AS ID`
   `FROM CurrentProducts) as DrvTbl`
   `WHERE ID % 5 = 0`

O b. `SELECT *`
   `(FROM (SELECT *, (ROW_NUMBER()`
   `OVER ( ORDER BY RetailPrice DESC)) AS ID`
   `FROM CurrentProducts) as DrvTbl`
   `WHERE ID % 5 = 1`

O c. `SELECT *, (ROW_NUMBER ( )`
   `OVER ( ORDER BY RetailPrice DESC)) AS ID`
   `FROM CurrentProducts`
   `WHERE ID % 5 = 0`

O d. `SELECT * (FROM (SELECT *, (ROW_NUMBER( )`
   `OVER ( ORDER BY RetailPrice DESC)) AS ID`
   `FROM CurrentProducts AS DrvTbl`
   `WHERE ID % 5 = 1`

Answer Key

1.) Because NTILE(x) will return the records divided into x groups and the request is asking for 4 groups, (a), (c) and (d) are wrong for returning 1, 25 and 100 groups respectively. Since NTILE will divide the result set into the number of groups specified in the parentheses, (b) is the correct answer for it will return 4 groups with each group containing 25 percent of the records.

2.) NTILE(1) will return a record set consisting of 1 group that contains 100% of the records, so (a) is not correct. NTILE(2) will split the result set into 2 groups with one group having the upper 50 % of the grades and the other group having the lower 50%, so (b) is also incorrect. Since NTILE(25)'s result set will consist of 25 groups each containing 4% of the grades (c) is also wrong. Because splitting 100% of the grades into 50 equal size groups will create groups that each contain 2% of the grades, NTILE(50) as shown in (d) is the correct answer.

3.)   NTILE(1) will return a record set consisting of 1 group that contains 100% of the records, so (a) is not correct. NTILE(5) will return a record set consisting of 5 groups, each with 20% of the records, so (b) is also not correct. NTILE(25) will return a record set consisting of 25 groups, each with 4% of the records, so (d) is not correct either. NTILE(4) will split the result set into 4 groups with one group having the upper 25 % of the grades, making (b) the correct answer.

4.)   NTILE(4) will return a record set consisting of 1 group that contains 100% of the records, so (a) is not correct. NTILE(4) will return a record set consisting of 4 groups, each with 25% of the records, so (b) is also not correct. NTILE(20) will return a record set consisting of 20 groups, each with 5% of the records, so (d) is incorrect too. NTILE(25) will return a record set consisting of 25 groups, each with 4% of the records, so (e) is also not correct. NTILE(5) will return a record set consisting of 5 groups, each with 20% of the records, making (c) the correct answer.

5.)   NTILE(5) will return a record set consisting of 5 groups, each having 20% of the total, making (a) and (b) incorrect. NTILE(20) will return a record set consisting of 20 groups, each with 5% of the records; since the groups are in ascending order, the last group (Group 20) will have the highest values, making (c) another wrong choice and (d) the right answer.

6.)   You are looking for the most recent date and not the highest buyer, so (b) with MAX(BuyerName) OVER(PARTITION BY OrderDate) is incorrect. Since we want to partition on the BuyerName we can't leave the OVER clause empty, making (c) another wrong choice and (a) the right answer.

7.)   Mod is used to find remainders, so (a) and (b) are incorrect. Since we want even numbers we need a zero remainder. Thus, (c) is the right answer.

8.)   The remainders can never be larger than the divisors, so (c) and (d) are incorrect. Since we want the odd numbers, (b) is the right answer.

9.)   We can't predicate on an expression field, so (c) and (d) are incorrect. Since the numbers 1, 6 and 11 all have a remainder of 1 when divided by 5, (d) is the right answer.

Bug Catcher Game

To play the Bug Catcher game, run the SQLQueries2012Vol2BugCatcher08.pps file from the BugCatcher folder of the companion files. We can obtain these files from the www.Joes2Pros.com web site.

[THIS PAGE INTENTIONALLY LEFT BLANK.]

Chapter 9.   Set Operators

By now, we have regularly been using multi-table joins to find and bring more related data into our record set. Bringing in additional tables and columns in this fashion allows us to create very wide (horizontal) rows of related data. Joins are great when the goal is to have a combined result set of eleven fields made up of one table with seven fields and another table with four fields.

What if the goal is to have a combined result set of 7 fields with 120 records made up of two tables containing seven fields and 60 records each? In other words, we need to stack the data from two tables vertically, instead of having to display the results side-by-side.

Multiple query operators do just what the name implies – they are operators like UNION, UNION ALL, EXCEPT and INTERSECT which allow multiple record sets to be combined together, or compared cleanly and efficiently.

READER NOTE: *Please run the SQLQueries2012Vol2Chapter9.0Setup.sql script in order to follow along with the examples in the first section of Chapter 9. All scripts mentioned in this chapter are available at <u>www.Joes2Pros.com</u>.*

Multiple Queries with Similar Metadata

You'll recognize this graphic from Chapter 4. The table joins we've used thus far have primarily brought data together horizontally. Every join added fields to a record set and extended each row of data to include more information about the row entity. Recall joins can be used to combine as many as 256 tables in one FROM clause (see Chapter 1, "INNER JOINS").

	EmpID	LastName	FirstName	HireDate	LocationID	ManagerID	Status	LocationID	Street	City	State
1	1	Adams	Alex	2001-01-01 ...	1	11	Active	1	111 First ST	Seattle	WA
2	2	Brown	Barry	2002-08-12 ...	1	11	Active	1	111 First ST	Seattle	WA
3	3	Osako	Lee	1999-09-01 ...	2	11	Active	2	222 Second AVE	Boston	MA
4	4	Kennson	David	1996-03-16 ...	1	11	Has Tenure	1	111 First ST	Seattle	WA
5	5	Bender	Eric	2007-05-17 ...	1	11	Active	1	111 First ST	Seattle	WA
6	6	Kendall	Lisa	2001-11-15 ...	4	4	Active	4	444 Ruby ST	Spokane	WA
7	7	Lonning	David	2000-01-01 ...	1	11	On Leave	1	111 First ST	Seattle	WA
8	8	Marshbank	John	2001-11-15 ...	NULL	4	Active	NULL	NULL	NULL	NULL
9	9	Newton	James	2003-09-30 ...	2	3	Active	2	222 Second AVE	Boston	MA
10	10	O'Haire	Terry	2004-10-04 ...	2	3	Active	2	222 Second AVE	Boston	MA
11	11	Smith	Sally	1989-04-01 ...	1	NULL	Active	1	111 First ST	Seattle	WA
12	12	O'Neil	Barbara	1995-05-26 ...	4	4	Has Tenure	4	444 Ruby ST	Spokane	WA
13	13	Wilconkinski	Phil	2009-06-11 ...	1	4	Active	1	111 First ST	Seattle	WA
14	NULL	NULL	NULL	NULL	NULL	NULL	NULL	3	333 Third PL	Chicago	IL

Query executed successfully. RENO (11.0 RTM) Reno\Student (51) JProCo 00:00:00 14 rows

Figure 9.1 The Employee and Location tables joined in an unmatched query.

The only requirement to join two tables is that they share one common field of the same data type. The column names don't need to match. Other than the join field, the data type or number of other fields does not matter (up to SQL Server's maximum of 1024 fields per query).

Stacking queries from multiple tables will require us to follow a few more rules. Each query must have the same structure. In other words, they must each have the same number of fields with compatible data types.

The UNION Operator

The additional rules to stack queries will make more sense after a demonstration. So let's launch into our first example with the Employee table (Figure 9.2).

```
SELECT * FROM Employee
WHERE LocationID = 2

SELECT * FROM Employee
WHERE LocationID = 4
```

	EmpID	LastName	FirstName	HireDate	LocationID	ManagerID	Status
1	3	Osako	Lee	1999-09-01…	2	11	Active
2	9	Newton	James	2003-09-30…	2	3	Active
3	10	O'Haire	Terry	2004-10-04…	2	3	Active
	EmpID	LastName	FirstName	HireDate	LocationID	ManagerID	Status
1	6	Kendall	Lisa	2001-11-15…	4	4	Active
2	12	O'Neil	Barbara	1995-05-26…	4	4	Has T…

5 rows

Figure 9.2 Two separate queries from the Employee table shown in two result sets.

In Figure 9.3, we see the UNION operator combining both queries from Figure 9.2 into one result set.

```
SELECT * FROM Employee
WHERE LocationID = 2

UNION

SELECT * FROM Employee
WHERE LocationID = 4
```

	EmpID	LastName	FirstName	HireDate	LocationID	ManagerID	Status
1	3	Osako	Lee	1999-09-01…	2	11	Active
2	9	Newton	James	2003-09-30…	2	3	Active
3	10	O'Haire	Terry	2004-10-04…	2	3	Active
4	6	Kendall	Lisa	2001-11-15…	4	4	Active
5	12	O'Neil	Barbara	1995-05-26…	4	4	Has T…

5 rows

Figure 9.3 The UNION operator combines both queries into a single result set.

UNION created a single five record stack (the three employees from Location 2 and the two employees from Location 4).

Our next example works with the hire dates for JProCo employees (Figure 9.4).

```
SELECT *
FROM Employee
ORDER BY HireDate ASC
```

Figure 9.4 All JProCo employees listed in order of HireDate (longest serving to newest hired).

Company policy awards three weeks of vacation to employees who have served our company beyond a certain cutoff date. Newer employees receive two weeks of vacation each year.

The cutoff to receive the extra week is 7/1/2001, so we need a query showing all employees hired prior to that date (Figure 9.5).

```
SELECT *
FROM Employee
WHERE HireDate < '7/1/2001'
ORDER BY HireDate ASC
```

	EmpID	LastName	FirstName	HireDate	LocationID	ManagerID	Status
1	11	Smith	Sally	1989-04-01…	1	NULL	Active
2	12	O'Neil	Barbara	1995-05-26…	4	4	Has T…
3	4	Kennson	David	1996-03-16…	1	11	Has T…
4	3	Osako	Lee	1999-09-01…	2	11	Active
5	7	Lonning	David	2000-01-01…	1	11	On Le…
6	1	Adams	Alex	2001-01-01…	1	11	Active
							6 rows

Figure 9.5 The six employees who joined JProCo prior to 7/1/2001.

The policy also allows the first two employees hired after 7/1/2001 to receive the extra week of vacation, so we need the list to include those names.

Write the three week vacation policy criteria as a query (Figure 9.6).

```
SELECT *
FROM Employee
WHERE HireDate < '7/1/2001'
ORDER BY HireDate ASC

SELECT TOP (2) *
FROM Employee
WHERE HireDate > '7/1/2001'
ORDER BY HireDate ASC
```

	EmpID	LastName	FirstName	HireDate	LocationID	ManagerID	Status
1	11	Smith	Sally	1989-04-01 00:00:00.000	1	NULL	Active
2	12	O'Neil	Barbara	1995-05-26 00:00:00.000	4	4	Has Tenure
3	4	Kennson	David	1996-03-16 00:00:00.000	1	11	Has Tenure
4	3	Osako	Lee	1999-09-01 00:00:00.000	2	11	Active
5	7	Lonning	David	2000-01-01 00:00:00.000	1	11	On Leave
6	1	Adams	Alex	2001-01-01 00:00:00.000	1	11	Active

	EmpID	LastName	FirstName	HireDate	LocationID	ManagerID	Status
1	6	Kendall	Lisa	2001-11-15 00:00:00.000	4	4	Active
2	8	Marshbank	John	2001-11-15 00:00:00.000	NULL	4	Active

Query executed successfully.   (local) (11.0 RTM)   Reno\Student (55)   JProCo   00:00:00   8 rows

Figure 9.6 The two criteria statements showing the 8 employees with 3 weeks yearly vacation.

Now let's try combining both queries into one stack with UNION. SQL Server gives us an error, if we try to use both ORDER BY clauses (Figure 9.7).

```
SELECT *
FROM Employee
WHERE HireDate < '7/1/2001'

UNION

SELECT TOP (2) *
FROM Employee
WHERE HireDate > '7/1/2001'
ORDER BY HireDate ASC
```

	EmpID	LastName	FirstName	HireDate	LocationID	ManagerID	Status
1	11	Smith	Sally	1989-04-01 00:00:00.000	1	NULL	Active
2	12	O'Neil	Barbara	1995-05-26 00:00:00.000	4	4	Has Tenure
3	4	Kennson	David	1996-03-16 00:00:00.000	1	11	Has Tenure
4	3	Osako	Lee	1999-09-01 00:00:00.000	2	11	Active
5	7	Lonning	David	2000-01-01 00:00:00.000	1	11	On Leave
6	1	Adams	Alex	2001-01-01 00:00:00.000	1	11	Active
7	2	Brown	Barry	2002-08-12 00:00:00.000	1	11	Active
8	5	Bender	Eric	2007-05-17 00:00:00.000	1	11	Active

Query executed successfully.   (local) (11.0 RTM)   Reno\Student (55)   JProCo   00:00:00   8 rows

Figure 9.7 UNION combines both queries into a single stack. Only one ORDER BY is allowed.

UNION puts the queries into one stack of eight employee records. But closely examine the list in Figure 9.7 and compare it to the names in Figure 9.6. The first six employees appear correctly (the pre July 2001 people), but look at the last two records. We know John Marshbank and Lisa Kendall are the next two individuals hired after July 2001 – not Barry Brown or Eric Bender.

Here SQL Server applied the ORDER BY to the entire result stack, not just on the second query, as we wanted. Since we know TOP can't read dates and relies strictly upon sort order, disrupting the sort order for the post July 2001 people gives us an entirely different result.

Run just the second query without the ORDER BY clause, and you'll get Alex Adams and Lee Osako. A rule consistent for the set operators is that the upper query always dominates. In our Figure 9.7 query, the ORDER BY defers to the upper query and sorts the entire result stack accordingly. We can't put a separate ORDER BY on the bottom query without some extra steps.

For SQL Server to properly apply the ORDER BY, we need to turn the second query into a derived table (Figure 9.8).

READER NOTE: *it is actually not necessary to derive the top query (You will get the same UNION result if you don't nest the upper query) But because we continue using subqueries in future chapters (derived tables and CTE's in Chapter 10 subqueries in Chapter 12, there is a benefit to the method you will use in this section.*

```
SELECT * FROM (
  SELECT *
  FROM Employee
  WHERE HireDate < '7/1/2001') AS PreJulyEmp

UNION

SELECT * FROM (
  SELECT TOP(2) *
  FROM Employee
  WHERE HireDate >= '7/1/2001'
  ORDER BY HireDate ASC) AS NextTwoEmp
```

Figure 9.8 UNION produces the expected result, including Lisa Kendall and John Marshbank.

The legal department informs us that a new local law requires all employees working in Spokane to receive three weeks of vacation no matter when they were hired. Thus, we must add more criteria to our query to include all Spokane employees (LocationID 4) irrespective of hire date.

Let's add the Spokane criteria. Revise, highlight and run just the upper query to see the impact of the legal change before re-running our UNION query (Figure 9.9).

```
SELECT * FROM (
  SELECT *
  FROM Employee
  WHERE HireDate < '7/1/2001'
  OR LocationID = 4 ) AS PreJulyEmpAndSpokane
```

Figure 9.9 Revising the first query to include all Spokane employees now shows Lisa Kendall.

Both Spokane employees, Barbara O'Neil and Lisa Kendall, now appear in the top query result. Barbara was hired in 1995, and Lisa already receives three weeks of vacation as one of the first two individuals hired after July 2001.

So the good news is that JProCo is already compliant with the new law. But how will this impact our UNION query? Lisa Kendall's record now appears in both queries. She won't receive extra vacation because of her dual eligibility, thus we want to see just one instance of her name on our list. UNION removes duplicate records, so her name appears just once (Figure 9.10).

```
SELECT * FROM (
  SELECT *
  FROM Employee
  WHERE HireDate < '7/1/2001'
  OR LocationID = 4 ) AS PreJulyEmpAndSpokane

UNION

SELECT * FROM (
  SELECT TOP(2) *
  FROM Employee
  WHERE HireDate >= '7/1/2001'
  ORDER BY HireDate ASC) AS NextTwoEmp
ORDER BY HireDate
```

	EmpID	LastName	FirstName	HireDate	LocationID	ManagerID	Status
1	11	Smith	Sally	1989-04-01...	1	NULL	Active
2	12	O'Neil	Barbara	1995-05-26...	4	4	Has Tenure
3	4	Kennson	David	1996-03-16...	1	11	Has Tenure
4	3	Osako	Lee	1999-09-01...	2	11	Active
5	7	Lonning	David	2000-01-01...	1	11	On Leave
6	1	Adams	Alex	2001-01-01...	1	11	Active
7	6	Kendall	Lisa	2001-11-15...	4	4	Active
8	8	Marshbank	John	2001-11-15...	NULL	4	Active

Query executed successfully.   RENO (11.0 RTM)   Reno\Student (51)   JProCo   00:00:00   8 rows

Figure 9.10 UNION eliminates duplicate records, so Lisa Kendall appears just once in our list.

The UNION ALL Operator

The UNION ALL operator stacks records from all queries, including any duplicates.

If we had wanted to see Lisa Kendall's record appear twice in the previous example, we could have used a UNION ALL query (Figure 9.11).

```
SELECT * FROM (
  SELECT *FROM Employee
  WHERE HireDate < '7/1/2001'
  OR LocationID = 4 ) AS PreJulyEmpAndSpokane

UNION ALL
```

```
SELECT * FROM (
  SELECT TOP(2) * FROM Employee
  WHERE HireDate >= '7/1/2001'
  ORDER BY HireDate ASC) AS NextTwoEmp
ORDER BY HireDate
```

	EmpID	LastName	FirstName	HireDate	LocationID	ManagerID	Status
1	11	Smith	Sally	1989-04-01...	1	NULL	Active
2	12	O'Neil	Barbara	1995-05-26...	4	4	Has Tenure
3	4	Kennson	David	1996-03-16...	1	11	Has Tenure
4	3	Osako	Lee	1999-09-01...	2	11	Active
5	7	Lonning	David	2000-01-01...	1	11	On Leave
6	1	Adams	Alex	2001-01-01...	1	11	Active
7	6	Kendall	Lisa	2001-11-15...	4	4	Active
8	6	Kendall	Lisa	2001-11-15...	4	4	Active
9	8	Marshbank	John	2001-11-15...	NULL	4	Active

Query executed successfully.   RENO (11.0 RTM)   Reno\Student (51)   JProCo   00:00:00   9 rows

Figure 9.11 UNION ALL *includes duplicate records*, so Lisa Kendall appears twice in our list.

The result now shows Lisa Kendall's record twice, for a total of 9 records in all. Remember that in a UNION query, only distinct records are selected. The UNION ALL query returns all records including duplicates.

UNION Operator Rules

The UNION and UNION ALL operators combine records from multiple sources (two or more queries or tables) into a single stack.

Each query must have the same structure. In other words, they must each have the same number of fields with compatible data types. The columns also need to appear in the same order in all the queries. Our earlier examples combined queries from the Employee table (Figure 9.12).

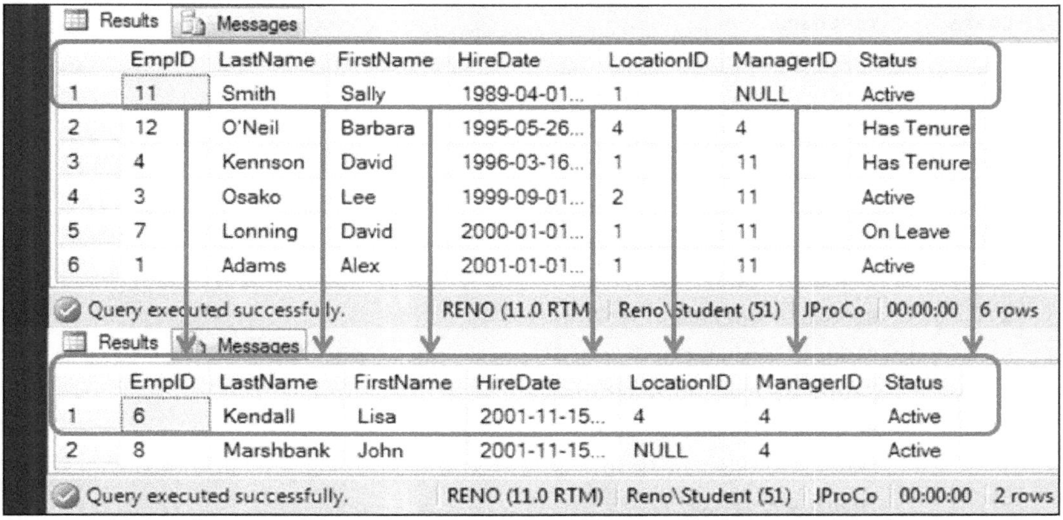

Figure 9.12 Queries must all have the same number of fields with the compatible data types. The columns must appear in the same order in all the queries.

Since all the fields in your UNION queries will have similar metadata, it will not matter if the names match. We can UNION the character data from the Grant and Location tables. The data type for both ID fields is CHAR. GrantName is an NVARCHAR and Street is a VARCHAR (Figure 9.13).

```
SELECT GrantID AS Chars, GrantName AS VarChars
FROM [Grant]

UNION

SELECT LocationID, Street
FROM Location
```

	Chars	VarChars
1	1	111 First ST
2	1	92 Purr_Scents %% team
3	2	222 Second AVE
4	2	K_Land fund trust
5	3	333 Third PL
6	3	Robert@BigStarBank.com
7	4	444 Ruby ST
8	4	Norman's Outreach
9	5	BIG 6's Foundation%
10	6	TALTA_Kishan International
11	7	Ben@MoreTechnology.com
12	8	www.@-Last-U-Can-Help.com
13	9	Thank you @.com
14	10	Call Mom @Com

14 rows

Figure 9.13 The field names don't need to match in UNION queries.

In general, we can combine character data with other character data, and numerical data will combine with other numerals. Let's take a few fields of numerical data. The data type of RetailPrice is money, CustomerID is an integer, and UnitDiscount is SMALLMONEY (Figure 9.14 and Figure 9.15).

```
SELECT TOP 5 RetailPrice
FROM CurrentProducts

SELECT TOP 5 CustomerID
FROM SalesInvoice

SELECT DISTINCT TOP 5 UnitDiscount
FROM SalesInvoiceDetail
```

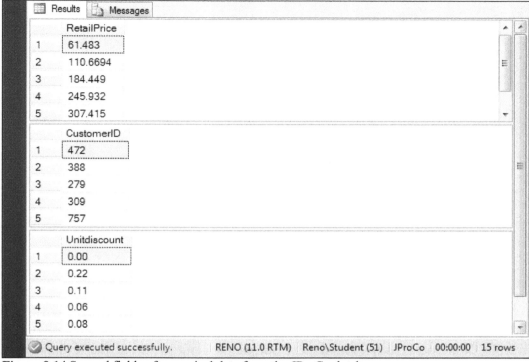

Figure 9.14 Several fields of numerical data from the JProCo database.

Take a moment to recognize that the first query in the union sets the tone for how to display the data. Since RetailPrice is MONEY with decimals, all records (even the CustomerID integer) show as decimals. It also puts the values in order.

```
SELECT TOP 5 RetailPrice
FROM CurrentProducts

UNION

SELECT TOP 5 CustomerID
FROM SalesInvoice

UNION

SELECT DISTINCT TOP 5 UnitDiscount
FROM SalesInvoiceDetail
```

Figure 9.15 A UNION of three TOP 5 queries gets you these 15 records.

In UNION queries, the field names are optional as long as all the queries have the same structure. For example, the two queires in **Figure 9.16** run as one query in Figure 9.17 that works just fine.

```
SELECT * FROM Location

SELECT 5, '99 Union Ave', 'Fargo', 'ND'
```

Figure 9.16 The field names are optional as long as all the queries have the same structure.

```
SELECT *
FROM Location

UNION

SELECT 5, '99 Union Ave', 'Fargo', 'ND'
```

	LocationID	Street	City	State
1	1	111 First ST	Seattle	WA
2	2	222 Second AVE	Boston	MA
3	3	333 Third PL	Chicago	IL
4	4	444 Ruby ST	Spokane	WA
5	5	99 Union Ave	Fargo	ND

5 rows

Figure 9.17 One last example showing UNION.

The examples in this chapter demonstrate the UNION and UNION ALL operators in a two query setting. However, SQL Server's general limitation of 256 tables applies to these operators. UNION and UNION ALL may include up to 256 queries or tables.

Lab 9.1: UNION and UNION ALL

Lab Prep: Each lab has one or more Skill Checks. Start with Skill Check 1 and proceed until reaching the Points to Ponder section.

Before beginning this lab, verify that SQL Server 2012 is properly installed and operating. Before running the lab setup script for resetting the database (SQLQueries2012Vol2Chapter9.1Setup.sql), please make sure to close all query windows within SSMS. An open query window pointing to a database context can lock that database preventing it from updating when the script is executing. A simple way to assure all query windows are closed, is to exit out of SSMS, then open a new instance of SSMS, and lastly run the setup script.

Skill Check 1: The Grant table lists all grants, and vNonEmployeeGrants shows grants that were not found by an employee. Figure 9.18 shows these two result sets run at the same time. We can see they both include Norman's Outreach. This is an example of two different sets of data with similar metadata (in this case the metadata is the same).

	GrantID	GrantName	EmpID	Amount
1	004	Norman's Outreach	NULL	21000.00

	GrantID	GrantName	EmpID	Amount
1	001	92 Purr_Scents %% team	7	4750.00
2	002	K_Land fund trust	2	15750.00
3	003	Robert@BigStarBank.com	7	18100.00
4	004	Norman's Outreach	NULL	21000.00
5	005	BIG 6's Foundation%	4	21000.00
6	006	TALTA_Kishan Internatio...	3	18100.00
7	007	Ben@MoreTechnology.c...	10	41000.00
8	008	www.@-Last-U-Can-Hel...	7	25000.00
9	009	Thank you @.com	11	21500.00
10	010	Call Mom @Com	5	7500.00

Query executed successfully. RENO (11.0 RTM) Reno\Student (53) JProCo 00:00:00 11 rows

Figure 9.18 Two queries with the same fields.

Write a query to combine the records from both tables. Since Norman's Outreach is found in both tables, it should appear in the result set twice. Use the correct set operator to achieve this result. When you're done, your result will look like Figure 9.19.

	GrantID	GrantName	EmpID	Amount
1	004	Norman's Outreach	NULL	21000.00
2	001	92 Purr_Scents %% team	7	4750.00
3	002	K_Land fund trust	2	15750.00
4	003	Robert@BigStarBank.com	7	18100.00
5	004	Norman's Outreach	NULL	21000.00
6	005	BIG 6's Foundation%	4	21000.00

11 rows

Figure 9.19 Combine records from two tables into one result set. Show Norman's Outreach twice.

Skill Check 2: You have two employees whose status shows they have received tenure. You also have two employees who work in Location 4. You have one employee working in Location 4 who has received tenure. Write two separate queries from the Employee table to find each group of employees. Then use the correct operator to put both result sets into one and show the distinct employees.

	EmpID	LastName	FirstName	HireDate	LocationID	ManagerID	Status
1	4	Kennson	David	1996-03-16…	1	11	Has Tenure
2	6	Kendall	Lisa	2001-11-15…	4	4	Active
3	12	O'Neil	Barbara	1995-05-26…	4	4	Has Tenure

3 rows

Figure 9.20 Skill Check 2 shows all employees with tenure OR whose LocationID is 4.

When you are done, your result should resemble Figure 9.20.

Answer Code: The T-SQL code for this lab is located in the downloadable files as a file named Lab9.1_UnionAndUnionAll.sql.

Points to Ponder - UNION and UNION ALL

1. When using the UNION or UNION ALL operators you get record sets that are combined from multiple sources.

2. UNION or UNION ALL operators require that all listed queries have the same number and type of fields in the same order.

3. Since all the fields in the UNION have compatible (if not identical) data types, it does not matter if the column names match. For example, we can union CustomerID and ProductID since both of these fields are the same data type (integer).

4. In a UNION query only distinct records are selected. No duplicates.

5. Using UNION ALL returns all records, including duplicates.

6. Because UNION checks record by record to filter out duplicates, its processing time will be longer than a UNION ALL, which does not check for duplicates.

7. UNION does not guarantee the order of rows. You must use ORDER BY, if you need your result to display in a specific order.

8. In a UNION query, we can only have one ORDER BY clause, at the end. It will apply to the whole result, not to an individual SELECT statement.

9. If the ordering of one or both of the SELECT statement records in the result stack is important to you, then you may need to use a derived table to achieve your needed result. The top table always dominates with UNION (and with all set operators), so any ORDER BY clause will refer to the first query (a.k.a., the left query, the upper query, the top query). It will evaluate your query in that order, and it will stack your result in that same order.

10. Queries with UNION and UNION ALL may include up to 256 queries or tables.

The INTERSECT Operator

INTERSECT is the next set operator we will examine.

Recall the Grant table contains ten grants. Most were registered by JProCo employees. However, Norman's Outreach submitted an unsolicited pledge using the web form, so no employee registered it (Figure 9.21).

```
SELECT *
FROM [Grant]
```

	GrantID	GrantName	EmpID	Amount
1	001	92 Purr_Scents %% team	7	4750.00
2	002	K_Land fund trust	2	15750.00
3	003	Robert@BigStarBank.com	7	18100.00
4	004	Norman's Outreach	NULL	21000.00
5	005	BIG 6's Foundation%	4	21000.00
6	006	TALTA_Kishan International	3	18100.00

10 rows

Figure 9.21 All grants but one (Norman's Outreach) were registered by employees.

```
SELECT *
FROM vNonEmployeeGrants
```

	GrantID	GrantName	EmpID
1	004	Norman's Outreach	NULL

1 rows

Figure 9.22 vNonEmployeeGrants contains only the grants not found by an employee.

In your Object Explorer, you will find the view vNonEmployeeGrants. It serves as a virtual table and will show you all the grants not found by an employee (Figure 9.22).

Notice that Norman's Outreach appears in both results when we run the two queries simultaneously (Figure 9.23).

Results | Messages

	GrantID	GrantName	EmpID	Amount
1	001	92 Purr_Scents %% team	7	4750.00
2	002	K_Land fund trust	2	15750.00
3	003	Robert@BigStarBank.com	7	18100.00
4	004	Norman's Outreach	NULL	21000.00
5	005	BIG 6's Foundation%	4	21000.00
6	006	TALTA_Kishan International	3	18100.00

	GrantID	GrantName	EmpID	Amount
1	004	Norman's Outreach	NULL	21000.00

Query executed successfully. RENO (11.0 RTM) Reno\Student (51) JProCo 00:00:00 11 rows

Figure 9.23 The non-employee grant (Norman's Outreach) appears in both query results.

Just one instance of the non-employee grant (Norman's Outreach) shows in a UNION query (Figure 9.24). And it shows up twice in the UNION ALL query (Figure 9.25).

```
SELECT *
FROM [Grant]

UNION

SELECT *
FROM vNonEmployeeGrants
```

	GrantID	GrantName	EmpID	Amount
1	001	92 Purr_Scents %% team	7	4750.00
2	002	K_Land fund trust	2	15750.00
3	003	Robert@BigStarBank.com	7	18100.00
4	004	Norman's Outreach	NULL	21000.00
5	005	BIG 6's Foundation%	4	21000.00
6	006	TALTA_Kishan International	3	18100.00

10 rows

Figure 9.24 A UNION query shows Norman's Outreach just once.

```
SELECT *
FROM [Grant]

UNION ALL

SELECT *
FROM vNonEmployeeGrants
```

	GrantID	GrantName	EmpID	Amount
3	003	Robert@BigStarBank.com	7	18100.00
4	004	Norman's Outreach	NULL	21000.00
5	005	BIG 6's Foundation%	4	21000.00
6	006	TALTA_Kishan International	3	18100.00
7	007	Ben@MoreTechnology.com	10	41000.00
8	008	www.@-Last-U-Can-Help.com	7	25000.00
9	009	Thank you @.com	11	21500.00
10	010	Call Mom @Com	5	7500.00
11	004	Norman's Outreach	NULL	21000.00

11 rows

Figure 9.25 A UNION ALL query shows Norman's Outreach twice.

It's easy to spot the overlapping record between the queries in these examples. In your database work, however, you will frequently encounter tables or queries containing thousands and or millions of records. Your task will be to find overlapping, duplicate, or missing records in one query versus another query (and/or another list or table).

The operators in this section will help "save the day" in these cases. It's the wise and efficient method to use for any list of 50 or more records. Trying to compare lists manually is a struggle that invariably costs time and/or accuracy.

```
SELECT *
FROM [Grant]

INTERSECT

SELECT *
FROM vNonEmployeeGrants
```

	GrantID	GrantName	EmpID	Amount
1	004	Norman's Outreach	NULL	21000.00

1 rows

Figure 9.26 INTERSECT shows just the record(s) you need. It is a fast and accurate comparison.

The mission for INTERSECT is to compare two queries and search for the distinct records which both queries have in common (Figure 9.26). In this case, we know the one record our two queries have in common is Norman's Outreach.

The EXCEPT Operator

What if we needed a query to display all records from the first query that don't appear in the second query?

```
SELECT *
FROM [Grant]

EXCEPT

SELECT *
FROM vNonEmployeeGrants
```

	GrantID	GrantName	EmpID	Amount
1	001	92 Purr_Scents %% team	7	4750.00
2	002	K_Land fund trust	2	15750.00
3	003	Robert@BigStarBank.com	7	18100.00
4	005	BIG 6's Foundation%	4	21000.00
5	006	TALTA_Kishan International	3	18100.00
6	007	Ben@MoreTechnology.com	10	41000.00

9 rows

Figure 9.27 EXCEPT shows just the record(s) from first query not in the second query.

The EXCEPT operator performs this work by comparing your queries. It subtracts every record in your second query from your first query. So the result output is a list of the distinct records from the first query which are not contained in the second query.

READER NOTE: For every place in this chapter where we mention "the first query" and "the second query", SQL Server considers these as "the left query" and "the right query", respectively. SQL Pros often use these terms, too.

Notice that Norman's Outreach appears in both results when we run the two queries at once (Figure 9.28).

```
SELECT *
FROM [Grant]

SELECT *
FROM vNonEmployeeGrants
```

	GrantID	GrantName	EmpID	Amount		
1	001	92 Purr_Scents %% team	7	4750.00		
2	002	K_Land fund trust	2	15750.00		
3	003	Robert@BigStarBank.com	7	18100.00		
4	004	Norman's Outreach	NULL	21000.00		
5	005	BIG 6's Foundation%	4	21000.00		
6	006	TALTA_Kishan International	3	18100.00		

	GrantID	GrantName	EmpID	Amount	
1	004	Norman's Outreach	NULL	21000.00	

Query executed successfully. RENO (11.0 RTM) Reno\Student (51) JProCo 00:00:00 11 rows

Figure 9.28 The result sets from the original two queries (also shown in Figure 9.23).

In Figure 9.28, the first query contains ten grants and the second query contains one grant. The EXCEPT operator compares both queries, subtracts the common record(s) from the first result (Norman's Outreach in this case), and displays the remaining nine distinct records (Figure 9.27).

INTERSECT and EXCEPT debuted with SQL 2005. UNION and UNION ALL appeared in prior versions of SQL. The same structural rules we mentioned for UNION apply equally to INTERSECT and EXCEPT:

o   All queries must have the same number of expressions (columns).

o   All queries must have compatible data types.

o   The fields in all queries must appear in the same order.

Lab 9.2: INTERSECT and EXCEPT

Lab Prep: Each lab has one or more Skill Checks. Start with Skill Check 1 and proceed until reaching the Points to Ponder section.

Before beginning this lab, verify that SQL Server 2012 is properly installed and operating. Before running the lab setup script for resetting the database (SQLQueries2012Vol2Chapter9.2Setup.sql), please make sure to close all query windows within SSMS. An open query window pointing to a database context can lock that database preventing it from updating when the script is executing. A simple way to assure all query windows are closed, is to exit out of SSMS, then open a new instance of SSMS, and lastly run the setup script.

Skill Check 1: There are 81 records in your CurrentProducts table that are marked for deletion. Those products are to be moved to the RetiredProducts table. When you query the RetiredProducts table, notice there are only 75 records.

Use the correct set operator to find the six ToBeDeleted records from the CurrentProducts table that do not appear in the RetiredProducts table. When you are done, your result should resemble the figure you see here (Figure 9.29).

	ProductID	ProductName	RetailPrice	OriginationD...	ToBeDeleted	Category
1	456	Wine Tasting Tour 2 Weeks We...	1101.969	2011-09-09 ...	1	LongTerm-Stay
2	462	Wine Tasting Tour 2 Weeks Ea...	577.197	2011-01-26 ...	1	LongTerm-Stay
3	468	Wine Tasting Tour 2 Weeks Me...	695.772	2004-11-28 ...	1	LongTerm-Stay
4	474	Wine Tasting Tour 2 Weeks Ca...	398.385	2004-04-18 ...	1	LongTerm-Stay
5	480	Wine Tasting Tour 2 Weeks Sc...	365.076	2005-02-23 ...	1	LongTerm-Stay
6	483	Yoga Mtn Getaway 2 Weeks	1695.00	2012-09-26 ...	1	LongTerm-Stay

Query executed successfully.   RENO (11.0 RTM) Reno\Student (51) JProCo 00:00:00 6 rows

Figure 9.29 Find the six records in the CurrentProducts table not contained in RetiredProducts.

Answer Code: The T-SQL code for this lab is located in the downloadable files as a file named Lab9.2_IntersectAndExcept.sql.

Points to Ponder - INTERSECT and EXCEPT

1. The INTERSECT and EXCEPT operators have the same field and data type requirements as UNION and UNION ALL.

2. As with all set operators, the first query (a.k.a., the left query, the upper query) is dominant in INTERSECT and EXCEPT.

3. The INTERSECT operator finds all records that two tables have in common.

4. The EXCEPT operator finds all records in the first table that are not present in the second table.

5. INTERSECT and EXCEPT are operators that compare two queries or tables.

GROUPING SETS

If you serve on the executive board of a car manufacturer, one decision you must make is how many units of each model to produce. For example, if you were Toyota, should you make more Camry's this year and cut back on the production of the Prius, or vice versa? Running out of stock when a customer has money and wants to buy is a bad situation. If you produce too many, then you will have inventory that you can't sell.

To further complicate the decision, you need to pick the colors. There might be people who really want a Prius but will only buy a yellow or white model. A fleet of blue cars won't help that buyer or your sales. One logical step is to look at sales grouped by year, model and color to see overall car buying trends. One simple GROUP BY query can do the trick.

A big publicly traded company is concerned with more than just good business execution. It needs to keep up a good public image and also be responsible to shareholders. Wall Street does not care what color the cars are but does really care how many you sold. The data you send them would require a different GROUP BY query, one that only shows sales grouped by year.

Finally, suppose you get a press request asking for information on the color trends in recent sales versus previous years. You would need to see the sales units displayed by color for each year.

In SQL Server, each perspective of interest could be solved by performing another GROUP BY query. Notice that our car company story includes seven possible queries to report on:

1) **GROUP BY** [Year], [Model], [Color]
2) **GROUP BY** [Year], [Model]
3) **GROUP BY** [Year], [Color]
4) **GROUP BY** [Model], [Color]
5) **GROUP BY** [Year]
6) **GROUP BY** [Model]
7) **GROUP BY** [Color]

Each query is a grouped query. This combination is a set of seven grouped queries. A feature first introduced in SQL Server 2005 and continuing in SQL Server 2012 is called Grouping Sets. This feature allows you to put all these grouped perspectives into one query. Putting different levels of aggregation into one object until now has been done by SSAS cubes. Cubes are still the king of aggregated analysis, but we can test and sample such data in any SQL Server database using Grouping Sets.

Single Column GROUPING SETS

Let's start off with a recap of a simple grouped query by doing two queries at one time. Once they are both running, we can either combine them with a UNION or put them in one query using grouping sets.

Look at all records from the SalesInvoiceDetail table. Notice that InvoiceID 1 contains five products and a total Quantity of 20 items.

```
SELECT *
FROM SalesInvoiceDetail
```

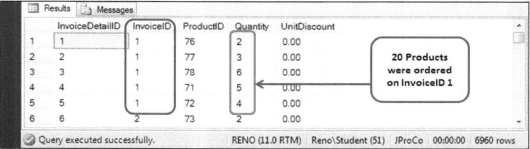

Figure 9.30 The total quantity for InvoiceID 1 is 20, 2 + 3 + 6 + 5 + 4.

We need to do some different groupings in order to see some important facts about our Invoices and Products. In order to see the biggest orders, we have to GROUP BY InvoiceID. To see the most frequently ordered products, we need to GROUP BY ProductID.

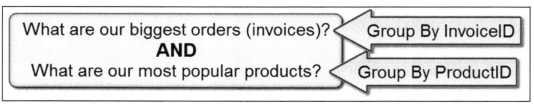

Figure 9.31 To find the invoice totals or the product totals we need a different grouping strategy.

Let's take a look at our orders by grouping the InvoiceIDs. Let's also add a field that totals the Quantity for each InvoiceID and we will alias it as TotalUnits.

```
SELECT InvoiceID, SUM(Quantity) AS TotalUnits
FROM SalesInvoiceDetail
GROUP BY InvoiceID
```

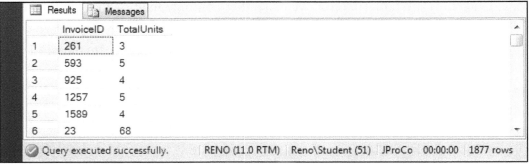

Figure 9.32 This shows the TotalUnits sales for each InvoiceID.

Now let's find TotalUnits sales for each ProductID.

```
SELECT ProductID, SUM(Quantity) AS TotalUnits
FROM SalesInvoiceDetail
GROUP BY ProductID
```

	ProductID	TotalUnits
1	23	4
2	69	207
3	29	377
4	75	473
5	9	460
6	15	671

Query executed successfully.   RENO (11.0 RTM)   Reno\Student (51)   JProCo   00:00:00   60 rows

Figure 9.33 This shows the TotalUnits sales for each ProductID.

In order to get a comprehensive report, we'll need to put these two queries together. However, a simple UNION operation would combine InvoiceID and ProductID values in the same column.

```
SELECT InvoiceID, SUM(Quantity) AS TotalUnits
FROM SalesInvoiceDetail
GROUP BY InvoiceID
UNION
```

```
SELECT ProductID, SUM(Quantity) AS TotalUnits
FROM SalesInvoiceDetail
GROUP BY ProductID
```

	InvoiceID	TotalUnits
1	261	3
2	593	5
3	925	4
4	1257	5
5	1589	4
6	23	68

1937 rows

Figure 9.34 The totals by InvoiceID and ProductID are totaled in the same result set.

We need a report capable of showing InvoiceID and ProductID separately. To accomplish this, we will use NULL to serve as a placeholder. While this may seem unusual, this is a useful way of being able to include both InvoiceID and ProductID records in the same query while at the same time show a correct TotalUnits value in each row (Explained in video 02:15-03:25).

```
SELECT InvoiceID, NULL AS ProductID,
SUM(Quantity) AS TotalUnits
FROM SalesInvoiceDetail
GROUP BY InvoiceID
UNION
SELECT NULL AS InvoiceID, ProductID,
SUM(Quantity) AS TotalUnits
FROM SalesInvoiceDetail
GROUP BY ProductID
```

	InvoiceID	ProductID	TotalUnits
1	261	NULL	3
2	593	NULL	5
3	925	NULL	4
4	1257	NULL	5
5	1589	NULL	4
6	23	NULL	68

1937 rows

Figure 9.35 The two different aggregate queries now have their own marked fields.

While you wouldn't want to see extensive NULL values and placeholders in a typical business report, if you look at cube data (i.e., data contained in a cube built by Analysis Services (SSAS, SQL Server Analysis Services)) you see this is very common.

Now create the equivalent report using GROUPING SETS (Video 03:33-05:15).

```
SELECT InvoiceID, ProductID,
SUM(Quantity) AS TotalUnits
FROM SalesInvoiceDetail
GROUP BY GROUPING SETS(InvoiceID, ProductID)
ORDER BY InvoiceID, ProductID
```

	InvoiceID	ProductID	TotalUnits
1	NULL	7	491
2	NULL	8	505
3	NULL	9	460
4	NULL	10	113
5	NULL	11	504
6	NULL	12	701
			1937 rows

Figure 9.36 The GROUPING SETS query does the same work as the two UNION-ed GROUP BY queries.

Three Single Column GROUPING SETS

In the next example, we will pretend you need one report to show total lifetime sales for a product, total lifetime sales for each customer, and also the total sales for each year the company has been in business. To start let's look at all the records from the vSales table.

```
SELECT *
FROM vSales
```

	CustomerID	OrderDate	RetailPrice	Quantity	ProductID	ProductName	OrderYear
1	597	2009-01-08...	80.859	5	7	Underwater Tour ...	2009
2	736	2009-01-09...	80.859	2	7	Underwater Tour ...	2009
3	47	2009-01-13...	80.859	3	7	Underwater Tour ...	2009
4	251	2009-01-16...	80.859	4	7	Underwater Tour ...	2009
5	529	2009-01-17...	80.859	5	7	Underwater Tour ...	2009
6	151	2009-01-17...	80.859	5	7	Underwater Tour ...	2009

Query executed successfully.　　RENO (11.0 RTM)　Reno\Student (51)　JProCo　00:00:00　6960 rows

Figure 9.37 This shows all the records from the vSales table.

Notice in Figure 9.37 we have a CustomerID, ProductID, OrderYear and Quantity. This is plenty of information to build the report we are looking for. To start we will query from the customer perspective with SUM(Quantity) and GROUP BY CustomerID we will return how much each customer ordered.

```
SELECT CustomerID, SUM(Quantity) AS TotalUnits
FROM vSales
GROUP BY CustomerID
```

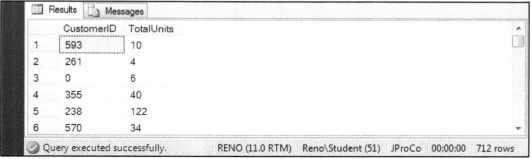

Figure 9.38 This shows TotalUnits sales by CustomerID.

In Figure 9.38 we see the TotalUnits sold for each CustomerID. Using the exact same query format we can see TotalUnits sold from a ProductID perspective.

```
SELECT ProductID, SUM(Quantity) AS TotalUnits
FROM vSales
GROUP BY ProductID
```

Figure 9.39 This shows TotalUnits sales by ProductID.

Using the ProductID perspective Figure 9.39 shows TotalUnits sold of each ProductID. From the OrderYear perspective let's write this query one more time.

```
SELECT OrderYear, SUM(Quantity) AS TotalUnits
FROM vSales
GROUP BY OrderYear
```

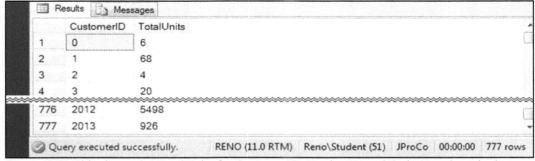

Figure 9.40 This shows the TotalUnits sold in each of the OrderYear values.

The OrderYear perspective is the least granular of the three reports. Figure 9.40 shows how many total products were sold during each OrderYear. What if we want to see all three reports at once? What would happen if we combined all three together in one query with the UNION set operator?

```
SELECT CustomerID, SUM(Quantity) AS TotalUnits
FROM vSales
GROUP BY CustomerID

Union

SELECT ProductID, SUM(Quantity) AS TotalUnits
FROM vSales
GROUP BY ProductID

UNION

SELECT OrderYear, SUM(Quantity) AS TotalUnits
FROM vSales
GROUP BY OrderYear
```

Figure 9.41 This shows the TotalUnits for CustomerID, ProductID and OrderYear in a single column under the field name of CustomerID.

Using union to combine the three queries worked but it is a bit confusing since all three reports are spread down a single column titled CustomerID (Figure 9.41).

This can be fixed however by adding a NULL placeholder in each of the three queries for the missing value.

```
SELECT CustomerID, NULL AS ProductID , NULL AS OrderYear,
SUM(Quantity) AS TotalUnits
FROM vSales
GROUP BY CustomerID

UNION

SELECT NULL, ProductID, NULL, SUM(Quantity) AS TotalUnits
FROM vSales
GROUP BY ProductID

UNION

SELECT NULL, NULL, OrderYear, SUM(Quantity) AS TotalUnits
FROM vSales
GROUP BY OrderYear
```

Figure 9.42 This shows TotalUnits from the CustomerID, ProductID and OrderYear perspective.

In Figure 9.42 we achieved our goal. Building three queries with three perspectives all combined with UNION set operators can be cumbersome.

Let's work to achieve the same goal using GROUPING SETS(). To start we will query FROM vSales and SELECT the three fields from before and create an expression field with SUM(Quantity) to give us TotalUnits. Lastly we will GROUP BY all three fields.

```
SELECT CustomerID, ProductID, OrderYear,
  SUM(Quantity) AS TotalUnits
FROM vSales
GROUP BY CustomerID, ProductID, OrderYear
```

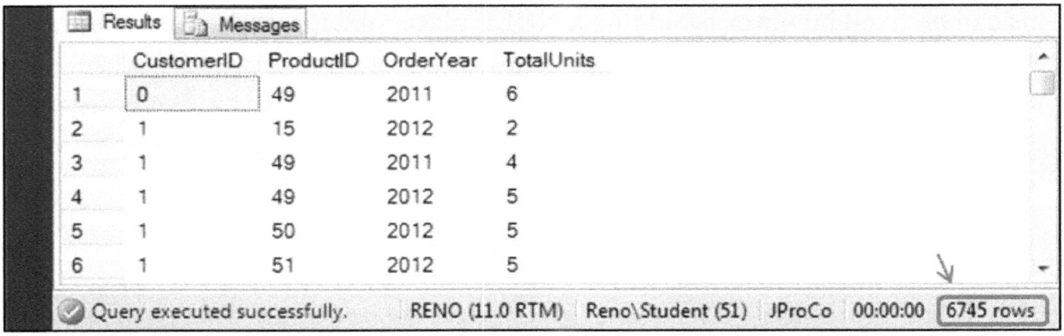

	CustomerID	ProductID	OrderYear	TotalUnits
1	0	49	2011	6
2	1	15	2012	2
3	1	49	2011	4
4	1	49	2012	5
5	1	50	2012	5
6	1	51	2012	5

Query executed successfully. | RENO (11.0 RTM) | Reno\Student (51) | JProCo | 00:00:00 | 6745 rows

Figure 9.43 This shows TotalUnits for each CustomerID by ProductID per OrderYear.

The report in Figure 9.43 is much too granular. Record 1 shows that CustomerID 0 purchased 6 ProductID 49s in the year 2011. To combine the totals to TotalUnits for CustomerID, ProductID and OrderYear we will need to use GROUPING SETS() with the ORDER BY clause.

```
SELECT CustomerID, ProductID, OrderYear, SUM(Quantity) AS
TotalUnits
FROM vSales
GROUP BY GROUPING SETS (CustomerID, ProductID, OrderYear)
```

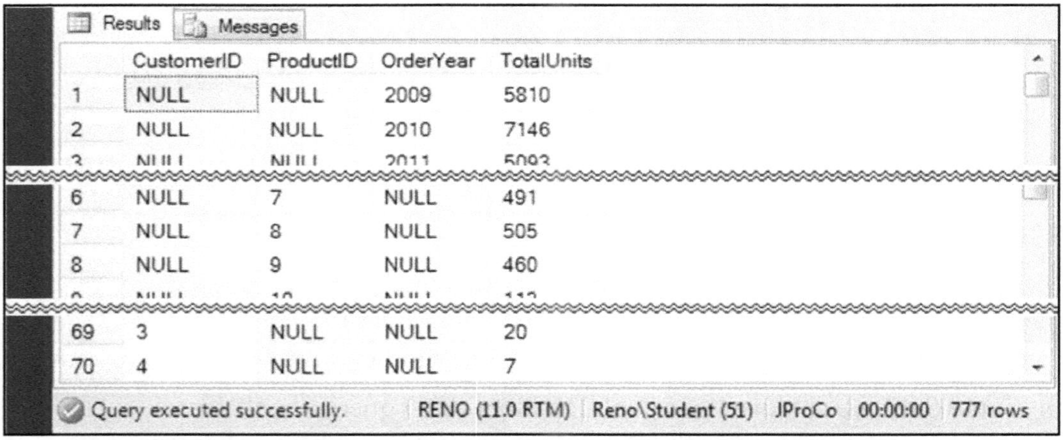

	CustomerID	ProductID	OrderYear	TotalUnits
1	NULL	NULL	2009	5810
2	NULL	NULL	2010	7146
6	NULL	7	NULL	491
7	NULL	8	NULL	505
8	NULL	9	NULL	460
69	3	NULL	NULL	20
70	4	NULL	NULL	7

Query executed successfully. | RENO (11.0 RTM) | Reno\Student (51) | JProCo | 00:00:00 | 777 rows

Figure 9.44 This shows using GROUPING SETS() returned TotalUnits for CustomerID, ProductID, and OrderYear.

We achieved our goal and you can see in Figure 9.44 it was much less code writing to use GROUPING SETS().

Report Granularity

I honestly don't know how many models of cars Toyota makes. Off the top of my head I can name Corolla, Camry, Tercel and Prius. If Toyota only had three car models, then this query would return just three records:

```
SELECT Model, SUM(Quantity)
FROM CarSales
GROUP BY Model
```

Suppose that Toyota creates cars in eight different colors. In that case, this query would return eight records:

```
SELECT Color, SUM(Quantity)
FROM CarSales
GROUP BY Color
```

If you grouped on both Color and Model then you would have 24 records in your result set. The more attributes you combine in a composite, the more records you see.

```
SELECT Model, Color, SUM(Quantity)
FROM CarSales
GROUP BY Model, Color
```

We can also say this last report is more granular and less of a high level summary. Eventually if you included all fields of the table in your group, you would see all records in your summary. With grouping sets, we can use any level of granularity in combination with any other level in the same result set. The following code shows three levels of granularity for the Customer Report:

- **GROUP BY** CustomerID
- **GROUP BY** CustomerID, ProductID
- **GROUP BY** CustomerID, ProductID, OrderYear

By setting subclasses of granularity within your grouping sets, we can have all the levels you want in a single result set.

GROUPING SETS Lists

Let's start this section by looking at the following report.

```
SELECT CustomerID, ProductID, OrderYear,
  SUM(Quantity) AS TotalUnits
FROM vSales
GROUP BY GROUPING SETS (CustomerID, ProductID, OrderYear)
```

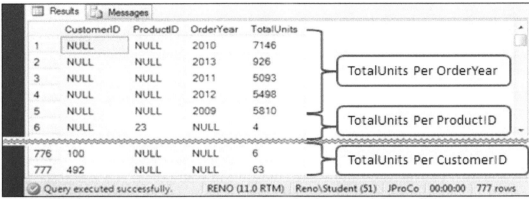

Figure 9.45 This shows the first six and last two records of query and shows all three GROUPING SETS.

Look at Figure 9.45 and notice that records one through five are year totals. Records one through five show the TotalUnits sold by OrderYear. Record six shows the TotalUnits of ProductID 23 that have been sold since the beginning of the company. Records 776 and 777 show the TotalUnits purchased by Customer 100 and 492 respectively.

Currently we have the GROUP BY GROUPING SETS() in the (field1, field2, field3) format which produced 3 sets. If we use the ((field1, field2, field3)) format it should produce one composite set.

```
SELECT CustomerID, ProductID, OrderYear,
SUM(Quantity) AS TotalUnits
FROM vSales
GROUP BY GROUPING SETS((CustomerID, ProductID, OrderYear))
```

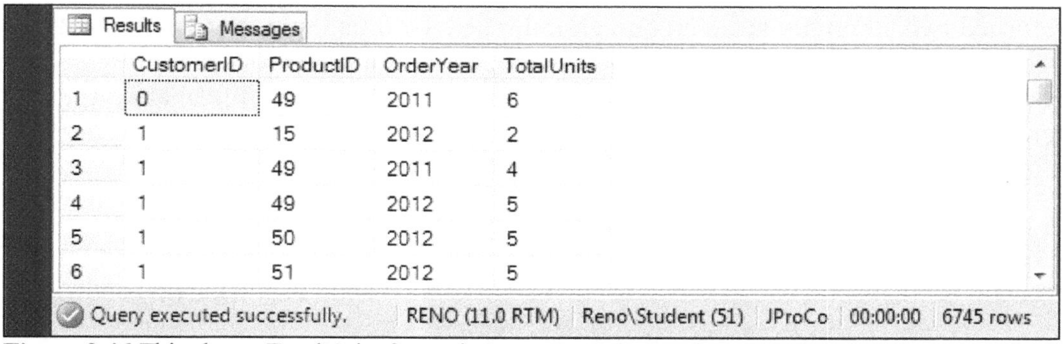

	CustomerID	ProductID	OrderYear	TotalUnits
1	0	49	2011	6
2	1	15	2012	2
3	1	49	2011	4
4	1	49	2012	5
5	1	50	2012	5
6	1	51	2012	5

Figure 9.46 This shows TotalUnits for each CustomerID by ProductID and OrderYear.

The composite set seen in Figure 9.46 is a much more granular report. It shows how many of each ProductID were purchased by every customer in the given OrderYear.

```
SELECT CustomerID, ProductID, OrderYear,
  SUM(Quantity) AS TotalUnits
FROM vSales
GROUP BY GROUPING SETS (CustomerID, ProductID,
  (CustomerID, ProductID, OrderYear))
```

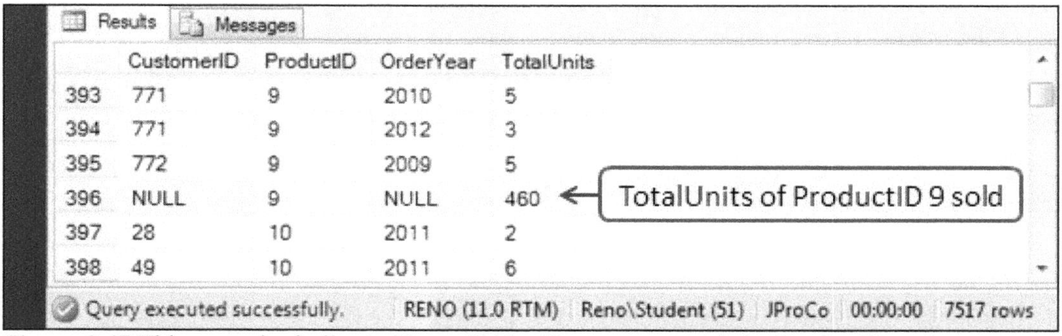

	CustomerID	ProductID	OrderYear	TotalUnits
393	771	9	2010	5
394	771	9	2012	3
395	772	9	2009	5
396	NULL	9	NULL	460
397	28	10	2011	2
398	49	10	2011	6

Figure 9.47 This query is similar to Figure 9.46 with summary totals by ProductID and CustomerID.

Some of our sets are made up of a single field and one set is a composite of a list of fields. Now we have the following three grouped sets:

- CustomerID
- ProductID
- CustomerID, ProductID, OrderYear

The composite set seen in Figure 9.47 is a granular report similar to that in Figure 9.46. The query in Figure 9.47 also includes summary records of TotalUnits by ProductID and TotalUnits by CustomerID. By using the GROUP BY GROUPING SETS in the (Field1, field2, (field1, field2, field3)) format we returned two summary sets and one granular set. To finish this example we will add OrderYear to be included as a summary field before the more granular composite set. The (Field1, field2, field3, (field1, field2, field3)) format will return three summary sets and one composite set.

```
SELECT CustomerID, ProductID, OrderYear,
  SUM(Quantity) AS TotalUnits
FROM vSales
GROUP BY GROUPING SETS (CustomerID, ProductID, OrderYear,
  (CustomerID, ProductID, OrderYear))
```

	CustomerID	ProductID	OrderYear	TotalUnits
1570	772	74	2009	4
1571	772	76	2009	2
1572	773	51	2009	6
1573	NULL	NULL	2009	5810 ← TotalUnits sold per OrderYear
1574	1	61	2010	4
1575	3	25	2010	4

Query executed successfully.   RENO (11.0 RTM)   Reno\Student (51)   JProCo   00:00:00   7522 rows

Figure 9.48 This query is similar to Figure 9.47with summary totals by ProductID, CustomerID and OrderYear.

Now we have four sets in our grouping set. Three are summary sets and one more granular set across multiple fields as listed here:

- o CustomerID
- o ProductID
- o OrderYear
- o CustomerID, ProductID, OrderYear

GROUPING SETS is a Set Operator that enables us to stipulate the precise aggregation we want to return in the result set.

Lab 9.3: GROUPING SETS

Lab Prep: Each lab has one or more Skill Checks. Start with Skill Check 1 and proceed until reaching the Points to Ponder section.

Before beginning this lab, verify that SQL Server 2012 is properly installed and operating. Before running the lab setup script for resetting the database (SQLQueries2012Vol2Chapter9.3Setup.sql), please make sure to close all query windows within SSMS. An open query window pointing to a database context can lock that database preventing it from updating when the script is executing. A simple way to assure all query windows are closed, is to exit out of SSMS, then open a new instance of SSMS, and lastly run the setup script.

Skill Check 1: Turn this complicated UNION query into one that uses GROUPING SETS to achieve the same result.

```
SELECT YEAR([OriginationDate]) AS OriginationYear,
NULL, COUNT(ProductID)
FROM CurrentProducts
GROUP BY YEAR([OriginationDate])

UNION

SELECT NULL AS OriginationYear, Category,
COUNT(ProductID)
FROM CurrentProducts
GROUP BY Category
```

	OriginationYear	(No column name)	(No column name)
1	NULL	LongTerm-Stay	162
2	NULL	Medium-Stay	161
3	NULL	No-Stay	80
4	NULL	Overnight-Stay	80
5	2004	NULL	37
6	2005	NULL	57

13 rows

Figure 9.49 Skill Check 1.

Skill Check 2: From the CurrentProducts table of JProCo, show the count of products by Category and ToBeDeleted.

	Category	ToBeDeleted	(No column name)
1	NULL	0	402
2	NULL	1	81
3	LongTerm-Stay	NULL	162
4	Medium-Stay	NULL	161
5	No-Stay	NULL	80
6	Overnight-Stay	NULL	80

6 rows

Figure 9.50 Skill Check 2.

Skill Check 3: From the CurrentProducts table of JProCo, show the count of products by Category and the count of ToBeDeleted products, as well as a composite of both fields as a grouped list set.

	Category	ToBeDeleted	(No column name)
1	LongTerm-Stay	0	81
2	Medium-Stay	0	161
3	No-Stay	0	80
4	Overnight-Stay	0	80
5	NULL	0	402
6	LongTerm-Stay	1	81

11 rows

Figure 9.51 Skill Check 3.

Answer Code: The T-SQL code for this lab is located in the downloadable files as a file named Lab9.3_GroupingSets.sql.

Points to Ponder - GROUPING SETS

1.   The result set returned by a GROUPING SET can generate what would normally be a combination of GROUP BY queries using a UNION operator.

2.   The GROUPING SETS() clause was a new feature in SQL Server 2008 and continued in SQL 2012.

3.   Using GROUPING SETS() clause allows you to easily specify combinations of fields in your queries to see different perspectives and levels of aggregated data.

4.   The GROUPING SETS() clause is an extension of the GROUP BY clause.

5.   The GROUPING SETS() operator can generate the same result set as that generated by using one or many GROUP BY queries.

6.   When the GROUPING SETS() list contains multiple sets in inner parentheses, separated by commas, the output of the sets are concatenated. The following code is a list of three sets.

   o   GROUPING SETS (Category, ToBeDeleted, (Category, ToBeDeleted))

Chapter Glossary

EXCEPT: This SQL set operator finds all records in the first table that are not present in the second.

INTERSECT: This SQL set operator finds all records that two tables have in common.

Metadata: Data about data.

UNION: This SQL set operator combines *only* distinct records and no duplicates.

UNION ALL: This SQL set operator combines all records, including duplicates.

GROUPING SETS: This clause was a new feature in SQL Server 2005 continued in SQL 2012 which is an extension of the GROUP BY clause. It generates what would normally be a combination of GROUP BY queries using a UNION operator.

Review Quiz - Chapter Nine

1.) What is the only difference between UNION and UNION ALL operators?

O a. UNION does not show duplicates between tables and UNION ALL does.

O b. UNION requires matching field selection order and UNION ALL does not.

O c. UNION cannot use table names and UNION ALL requires table names.

O d. UNION allows the field selection lists of the two queries to be dissimilar.

2.) What does the EXCEPT operator do?

O a. Shows records from the first result set not found in the second result set.

O b. Shows records from the second result set not found in the first result set.

O c. The result set shows all records from both queries.

O d. The result set shows only the records that both queries have in common.

3.) What does the INTERSECT operator do?

O a. Shows records from the first result set not present in the second result set.

O b. Shows records from the second result set not present in the first result set.

O c. The result set shows all records from both queries.

O d. The result set shows only the records that both queries have in common.

4.) What type of UNION operator will always show all records from both queries, even if they are duplicates?

O a. UNION

O b. UNION ALL

O c. INTERSECT

O d. EXCEPT

5.) What T-SQL operator displays rows that exist in both tables?

O a. EXCEPT

O b. INTERSECT

6.) You have two tables named Current Products and Retired Products that have the same field names and data types. The structure of both tables is identical. You write the following two queries:

```
SELECT * FROM CurrentProducts
SELECT * FROM RetiredProducts
```

Between these two queries, you want to use the correct T-SQL operator to display the records that are common between both tables. Which operator would you use?

O a. UNION

O b. EXCEPT

O c. UNION ALL

O d. INTERSECT

7.) You have two tables named LegacyEmployees and SpokaneEmployees that have the same field structure. You run the following query:

```
SELECT * FROM LegacyEmployees
  UNION ALL
SELECT * FROM SpokaneEmployees
```

What list of employees do you expect to return from the query?

O a. Records not listed in both the LegacyEmployees table and the SpokaneEmployees table.

O b. Employees listed in LegacyEmployees who are not from Spokane.

O c. All records from both tables but no duplicate records.

O d. All records from both tables including duplicates found in both tables.

8.) You have two tables, named dbo.CurrentProducts and dbo.ArchiveProducts. You have the following query:

```
SELECT ProductID, Name
FROM dbo.CurrentProducts
   UNION ALL
SELECT ProductID, Name
FROM dbo.ArchiveProducts;
```

Which list of products should the query return?

O a. Only those products listed in the `dbo.CurrentProducts` table.

O b. Only products listed once from both tables.

O c. All products listed in both the `dbo.CurrentProducts` table and the `dbo.ArchiveProducts` table.

O d. Only products listed more than once from both tables.

9.) You have the following query.

```
SELECT Category, ToBeDeleted, COUNT(*)
FROM CurrentProducts
GROUP BY GROUPING SETS (Category, ToBeDeleted,
   (Category, ToBeDeleted))
```

Which GROUPING SETS parameter(s) in the grouping list has the greatest level of granularity?

O a. Category

O b. ToBeDeleted

O c. (Category, ToBeDeleted)

10.) You have the following two queries combined in a UNION query:

```
SELECT YEAR([OriginationDate]) AS OriginationYear, NULL,
COUNT(ProductID)
FROM CurrentProducts
GROUP BY YEAR([OriginationDate])
  UNION
SELECT NULL AS OriginationYear, Category,
COUNT(ProductID)
FROM CurrentProducts
GROUP BY Category
```

You want to write the equivalent query using GROUPING SETS. Which of the following queries achieves this result?

O a.
```
SELECT YEAR([OriginationDate]) AS OriginationYear,
Category, COUNT(ProductID)
FROM CurrentProducts
GROUP BY GROUPING SETS(YEAR([OriginationDate]), Category)
```

O b.
```
SELECT YEAR([OriginationDate]) AS OriginationYear,
Category, COUNT(ProductID)
FROM CurrentProducts
GROUP BY GROUPING SETS((YEAR([OriginationDate]), Category))
```

Answer Key

1.) Since both UNION and UNION ALL require that the field selection list contain the same number of fields with compatible data types both (b) and (d) are incorrect. UNION and UNION ALL both work with SELECT statements that do not query a table, so (c) is wrong too. Since the only difference between UNION and UNION ALL is that UNION ALL will display duplicates while UNION removes them, (a) is the correct answer.

2.) Since UNION ALL shows all records from both result sets, (c) is wrong. INTERSECT will return only those records common to both result sets, making (d) incorrect. Because EXCEPT will display all the records in the first result not found by the second result set, (b) is an incorrect answer, which makes (a) the correct answer.

3.) Since UNION ALL shows all records from both result sets, (c) is wrong. Because EXCEPT will display all the records in the first result set not found by the second result set, (a) is incorrect. INTERSECT will return only those records common to both result sets, making (b) an incorrect answer and (d) the right answer.

4.) Because UNION removes duplicates from the result set, (a) is incorrect. Since INTERSECT will return only those records common to both result sets, (c) is incorrect too. Because EXCEPT will display all records in the first result set not found by the second result set, (d) is also wrong. The UNION ALL operator will display every record returned by both queries including duplicates, making (b) the correct answer.

5.) EXCEPT will display all the records in the first query that are not found in the second query, so (a) is wrong. Because INTERSECT will return those records common to both queries, (b) is the correct answer.

6.) Because UNION and UNION ALL return combined results of both queries, (a) and (c) are incorrect. EXCEPT will display all records in the first query not found by the second query, so (b) is wrong. Because INTERSECT will return only those records common to both result sets, (d) is the right answer.

7.) There is no way to return employees from LegacyEmployees listed in SpokaneEmployees but not both, because if the record exists in LegacyEmployees it also exists in SpokaneEmployees, so (a) is wrong. To get employees listed in LegacyEmployees not from Spokane, the set operator to use would be EXCEPT, so (b) is wrong. The UNION operator would eliminate duplicate records from the result set, making (c) wrong. The UNION ALL operator will display every record returned by both queries including duplicates, so (d) is the correct answer.

8.) Because UNION will display the distinct combined results of the two queries, both (a) and (b) are incorrect. UNION ALL will display all the records from both tables, making (c) the right answer.

9.) The more fields listed in a group, the more granular it becomes, making (c) the right answer.

10.) The goal is to have two high level summaries, each on one field. Since ((YEAR([OriginationDate]), Category)) combines them into one list (b) is incorrect. Doing this as GROUPING SETS (YEAR([OriginationDate]), Category) makes the YEAR([OriginationDate]) as one group and Category as another, so (a) is the right answer.

Bug Catcher Game

To play the Bug Catcher game, run the SQLQueries2012Vol2BugCatcher09.pps file from the BugCatcher folder of the companion files. These files are available from the www.Joes2Pros.com website.

[THIS PAGE INTENTIONALLY LEFT BLANK.]

Chapter 10. Temporary Named Result Sets

When you have access to a table, you can query on any field in the table you want. What about fields not in that table but derived or calculated from that field?

Sometimes you will need to create new objects from existing objects to get queries to run. In previous chapters we used derived tables to materialize queries and expression fields. The code provides more options for your queries, but the code can become complex and make for messy reading.

In this chapter, we will combine different techniques to give you the power of temporary objects and also show how the common table expression (CTE) can make your complex code easy to read.

The CTE was one of the standout debut features in SQL Server 2005 and was widely applauded by SQL Server developers. Readers who are learning SQL Server now can be grateful they don't need to experience the pain and pitfalls of temporary tables (a.k.a., "temp tables", which are different from derived tables) and other messy constructs whose work is now elegantly accomplished by the CTE. Common Table Expressions play an important role when writing recursive queries, so pay close attention to how the CTE works in these exercises.

READER NOTE: *Please run the SQLQueries2012Vol2Chapter10.0Setup.sql script in order to follow along with the examples in the first section of Chapter 10. All scripts mentioned in this chapter are available at www.Joes2Pros.com.*

Derived Tables Recap

We've run many examples with derived tables since we first encountered them back in Chapter 7. While they are a very helpful tool, the next temporary object (Common Table Expression or CTE) we will study has advantages and can do some things that derived tables cannot. For example, we cannot do a self-join with a derived table.

Predicating on Expression Fields

To really see what's cool with Common Table Expressions and other temporary objects let's first see some of the limitations they overcome.

Let's look at a simple query of four fields of the Employee table, which we want to ORDER BY LastName, FirstName. In other words, we want to see all employees alphabetically in order of last name. If there are tie records (i.e., multiple employees with the same last name), then FirstName will be the tie-breaker (Figure 10.1).

```
SELECT FirstName, LastName, EmpID, LocationID
FROM Employee
ORDER BY LastName, FirstName
```

	FirstName	LastName	EmpID	LocationID
1	Alex	Adams	1	1
2	Eric	Bender	5	1
3	Barry	Brown	2	1
4	Lisa	Kendall	6	4
5	David	Kennson	4	1
6	David	Lonning	7	1

13 rows

Figure 10.1 Four fields from the Employee table sorted by LastName, FirstName.

Use one of the ranking functions we learned in Chapter 7 to ROW_NUMBER over the LastName then FirstName, as specified in our ORDER BY clause.

```
SELECT FirstName, LastName, EmpID, LocationID,
ROW_NUMBER() OVER(ORDER BY LastName, FirstName)
FROM Employee
```

	FirstName	LastName	EmpID	LocationID	(No column name)
1	Alex	Adams	1	1	1
2	Eric	Bender	5	1	2
3	Barry	Brown	2	1	3
4	Lisa	Kendall	6	4	4
5	David	Kennson	4	1	5
6	David	Lonning	7	1	6

13 rows

Figure 10.2 ROW_NUMBER adds a new expression field to the Employee query.

Now we see everyone appearing alphabetically, as in the first query and with their row number as a new field. We are going to want to work with this new field, so we will name it Position (Figure 10.3).

```
SELECT FirstName, LastName, EmpID, LocationID,
ROW_NUMBER() OVER(ORDER BY LastName, FirstName) AS Position
FROM Employee
```

	FirstName	LastName	EmpID	LocationID	Position
1	Alex	Adams	1	1	1
2	Eric	Bender	5	1	2
3	Barry	Brown	2	1	3
4	Lisa	Kendall	6	4	4
5	David	Kennson	4	1	5
6	David	Lonning	7	1	6

13 rows

Figure 10.3 Name the new expression field Position, since we want to filter on it.

Our query looks good and appears to have five fields. Suppose our goal was to see who was in 10th position alphabetically. In Figure 10.3 we see the first 6 of the 13 records. The 5th position is David Kennson and if you were to scroll down the 10th position is Barbara O'Neil.

To see just that record, we'll want to filter on the ranking column (Figure 10.4).

```
SELECT FirstName, LastName, EmpID, LocationID,
ROW_NUMBER() OVER(ORDER BY LastName, FirstName) AS Position
FROM Employee
WHERE Position = 10
```

```
Messages
Msg 207, Level 16, State 1, Line 4
Invalid column name 'Position'.
                                                      0 rows
```

Figure 10.4 We can't use an expression field with the WHERE clause of a standard table query.

We get an error because Position isn't actually a column in the table. It is simply a label on top of an expression field. We cannot use an expression field in the WHERE predicate of a standard table query.

To be able to filter on Position, we will need some type of temporary object, and the most common one that's been around for a while is the derived table. We must first materialize this query as a derived table before we can use the expression field as a predicate in the WHERE clause.

Derived Tables

To create the derived table, we'll employ our three steps learned in Chapter 7.

```
SELECT FirstName, LastName, EmpID, LocationID,
ROW_NUMBER() OVER (ORDER BY LastName, FirstName) AS Position
FROM Employee
```

Figure 10.5 Our query before we turn it into a derived table.

Step 1. Alias any expression fields (we have one, which we've already named "Position". Figure 10.3).

Step 2. Name the query (EmpSort). This will become the derived table's name.

Step 3. Nest the query inside another SELECT statement (indent, enclose in parentheses, and add a SELECT * FROM statement at the top as seen in Figure 10.6.).

```
SELECT *
FROM (
  SELECT FirstName, LastName, EmpID, LocationID,
  ROW_NUMBER() OVER(ORDER BY LastName, FirstName) AS
Position
  FROM Employee) AS EmpSort
```

	FirstName	LastName	EmpID	LocationID	Position
1	Alex	Adams	1	1	1
2	Eric	Bender	5	1	2
3	Barry	Brown	2	1	3
4	Lisa	Kendall	6	4	4
5	David	Kennson	4	1	5
6	David	Lonning	7	1	6

13 rows

Figure 10.6 Steps to create the derived table EmpSort

Now run the query to filter WHERE Position = 10 and isolate just the 10th record.

```
SELECT *
FROM (
  SELECT FirstName, LastName, EmpID, LocationID,
  ROW_NUMBER() OVER(ORDER BY LastName, FirstName) AS
Position
  FROM Employee) AS EmpSort
WHERE Position = 10
```

	FirstName	LastName	EmpID	LocationID	Position
1	Barbara	O'Neil	12	4	10

1 rows

Figure 10.7 Position is a field in the derived table EmpSort; it now appears in the WHERE clause.

Common Table Expression (CTE)

As we've just seen, the derived table construct materializes the five fields of the query inside the temporary object EmpSort and allows you to filter on the Position field.

The Common Table Expression (or CTE) shares the advantage that the derived table does but has even more advantages. We won't learn every advantage here, but we will learn some useful ones which will make our code more readable.

First we're going to step back to our query before we made it into the derived table, EmpSort (use the code which appears in Figure 10.5).

Take those same three lines of the query, indent them, and put them inside parentheses. As with the derived table, everything in the parentheses represents what will be contained in the temporary object EmpSort (Figure 10.8).

```
(SELECT FirstName, LastName, EmpID, LocationID,
ROW_NUMBER() OVER(ORDER BY LastName, FirstName) AS Position
FROM Employee)
```

	FirstName	LastName	EmpID	LocationID	Position
1	Alex	Adams	1	1	1
2	Eric	Bender	5	1	2
3	Barry	Brown	2	1	3
4	Lisa	Kendall	6	4	4
5	David	Kennson	4	1	5
6	David	Lonning	7	1	6

13 rows

Figure 10.8 The first step of re-writing our initial query as a Common Table Expression (CTE).

Above it, add the line "WITH EmpSort AS". Unlike derived tables, the CTE declares the name at the beginning of code (Figure 10.9).

```
WITH EmpSort AS
   (SELECT FirstName, LastName, EmpID, LocationID,
   ROW_NUMBER() OVER(ORDER BY LastName, FirstName) AS Position
   FROM Employee)
```

Figure 10.9 Unlike derived tables, the CTE places the name at the beginning of code.

Like derived tables, CTEs also require a SELECT statement to invoke them (the code in Figure 10.9 will not run). However, with the CTE your SELECT statement appears beneath the code. As well, the SELECT statement explicitly names EmpSort, which makes for a more readable code module (Figure 10.10).

```
WITH EmpSort AS (
SELECT FirstName, LastName, EmpID, LocationID,
ROW_NUMBER() OVER(ORDER BY LastName, FirstName) AS Position
FROM Employee)

SELECT * FROM EmpSort
```

	FirstName	LastName	EmpID	LocationID	Position
1	Alex	Adams	1	1	1
2	Eric	Bender	5	1	2
3	Barry	Brown	2	1	3
4	Lisa	Kendall	6	4	4
5	David	Kennson	4	1	5
6	David	Lonning	7	1	6

13 rows

Figure 10.10 The SELECT statement appears below the code and explicitly calls EmpSort.

Add the WHERE clause to filter on the record in 10th position (Figure 10.11).

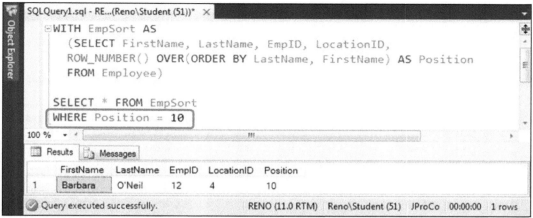

Figure 10.11 Adding the WHERE clause to filter the record with Position of 10.

The Common Table Expression features a clean looking query at the bottom because it handles all the calculations and declarations at the top. This clean, familiar SELECT statement may make you curious as to what else we can try with EmpSort (Figures 10.12, 10.13, and 10.14).

```
WITH EmpSort AS (
SELECT FirstName, LastName, EmpID, LocationID,
ROW_NUMBER() OVER(ORDER BY LastName, FirstName) AS Position
FROM Employee)

SELECT * FROM EmpSort

UNION

SELECT FirstName, LastName, EmpID, LocationID, EmpID
FROM Employee
```

FirstName	LastName	EmpID	LocationID	Position
1 Alex	Adams	1	1	1
2 Barbara	O'Neil	12	4	10
3 Barbara	O'Neil	12	4	12
4 Barry	Brown	2	1	2
5 Barry	Brown	2	1	3
6 David	Kennson	4	1	4

24 rows

Figure 10.12 Our CTE EmpSort shown with the UNION operator.

```
WITH EmpSort AS (
SELECT FirstName, LastName, EmpID, LocationID,
ROW_NUMBER() OVER(ORDER BY LastName, FirstName) AS Position
FROM Employee)
```

```
SELECT * FROM EmpSort AS es
INNER JOIN [Grant] gr
ON es.EmpID = gr.EmpID
ORDER BY Amount DESC
```

	FirstName	LastName	EmpID	LocationID	Position	GrantID	GrantName	EmpID	Amount
1	Terry	O'Haire	10	2	9	007	Ben@MoreTechnology.com	10	41000.00
2	David	Lonning	7	1	6	008	www.@-Last-U-Can-Help.com	7	25000.00
3	Sally	Smith	11	1	12	009	Thank you @.com	11	21500.00
4	David	Kennson	4	1	5	005	BIG 6's Foundation%	4	21000.00
5	Lee	Osako	3	2	11	006	TALTA_Kishan International	3	18100.00
6	David	Lonning	7	1	6	003	Robert@BigStarBank.com	7	18100.00
7	Barry	Brown	2	1	3	002	K_Land fund trust	2	15750.00
8	Eric	Bender	5	1	2	010	Call Mom @Com	5	7500.00
9	David	Lonning	7	1	6	001	92 Purr_Scents %% team	7	4750.00

Query executed successfully. RENO (11.0 RTM) Reno\Student (51) JProCo 00:00:00 9 rows

Figure 10.13 Our CTE EmpSort joined to the Grant table.

```
WITH EmpSort AS (
SELECT FirstName, LastName, EmpID, LocationID,
ROW_NUMBER() OVER(ORDER BY LastName, FirstName) AS Position
FROM Employee)

SELECT *, COUNT(*) OVER() AS EmpSortCount,
COUNT(*) OVER(PARTITION BY LocationID) AS LocationCount
FROM EmpSort
```

	FirstName	LastName	EmpID	LocationID	Position	EmpSortCount	LocationCount
1	John	Marshbank	8	NULL	7	13	1
2	Alex	Adams	1	1	1	13	7
3	Eric	Bender	5	1	2	13	7
4	Barry	Brown	2	1	3	13	7
5	David	Kennson	4	1	5	13	7
6	David	Lonning	7	1	6	13	7

13 rows

Figure 10.14 Our CTE EmpSort combined with aggregation techniques from Chapter 5.

Let's look to the Grant table for our next example. Start with a query showing just the high grants (Figure 10.15).

```
SELECT GrantID, GrantName, Amount
FROM [Grant]
WHERE Amount > 20000
```

	GrantID	GrantName	Amount
1	004	Norman's Outreach	21000.00
2	005	BIG 6's Foundation%	21000.00
3	007	Ben@MoreTechnology.com	41000.00
4	008	www.@-Last-U-Can-Help.com	25000.00
5	009	Thank you @.com	21500.00
			5 rows

Figure 10.15 Our next example features the JProCo grants in excess of $20,000.

Now turn this query into a CTE named HighGrants. Enclose the original query in parentheses and indent it. Then write the declaration statement (WITH HighGrants AS) above and the following SELECT statement (Figure 10.16).

```
WITH HighGrants AS (
SELECT GrantID, GrantName, Amount
FROM [Grant]
WHERE Amount > 20000)

SELECT * FROM HighGrants
```

	GrantID	GrantName	Amount
1	004	Norman's Outreach	21000.00
2	005	BIG 6's Foundation%	21000.00
3	007	Ben@MoreTechnology.com	41000.00
4	008	www.@-Last-U-Can-Help.com	25000.00
5	009	Thank you @.com	21500.00
			5 rows

Figure 10.16 Our Grant table query written as the CTE HighGrants.

These five records represent the high grants. This result looks the same as our query of the Grant table (compare to Figure 10.15).

CTE and Expression Fields

Now here's one more advantage of the CTE. The simple, readable query (SELECT * FROM HighGrants) shows all fields because we built the fields upstairs in the body of the CTE. We can subsequently add items to the CTE code to make the query more complex (Figure 10.17).

```
WITH HighGrants AS (
SELECT GrantID, GrantName, (Amount + 1000) AS DonatedAmount
FROM [Grant]
WHERE Amount > 20000)

SELECT * FROM HighGrants
```

	GrantID	GrantName	DonatedAmount
1	004	Norman's Outreach	22000.00
2	005	BIG 6's Foundation%	22000.00
3	007	Ben@MoreTechnology.com	42000.00
4	008	www.@-Last-U-Can-Help.com	26000.00
5	009	Thank you @.com	22500.00

5 rows

Figure 10.17 An expression field adds to the complexity of our CTE HighGrants.

We've added complexity to the CTE query by re-writing Amount as the expression DonatedAmount. However, the simple SELECT statement is still all that's required to see the result with the new expression DonatedAmount.

```
WITH HighGrants AS (
SELECT GrantID, GrantName, (Amount + 1000) AS DonatedAmount
FROM [Grant]
WHERE Amount > 20000)

SELECT *
FROM HighGrants
WHERE DonatedAmount > 25000
```

	GrantID	GrantName	DonatedAmount
1	007	Ben@MoreTechnology.com	42000.00
2	008	www.@-Last-U-Can-Help.com	26000.00

2 rows

Figure 10.18 We can filter on the new DonatedAmount because it is materialized in the CTE.

For our next example, we'll remove the expression field DonatedAmount and revert back to HighGrants as we first built it (refer to the code in Figure 10.16).

CTE Field Aliasing

Let's start this section with a simple example from the grant table. We will begin by looking at the GrantID, GrantName, and Amount of all the records of the Grant table.

```
SELECT GrantID, GrantName, Amount
FROM [Grant]
```

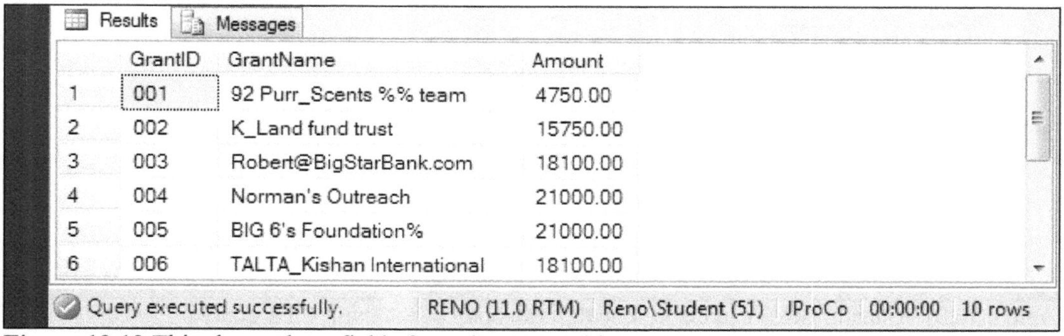

Figure 10.19 This shows three fields from the grant table.

In Figure 10.19 we see there are 10 grants all with varying amounts. Let's narrow our query to just the high grants. We will limit the query to just the grants with amounts greater than 20000 (Figure 10.20).

```
SELECT GrantID, GrantName, Amount
FROM [Grant]
WHERE Amount > 20000
```

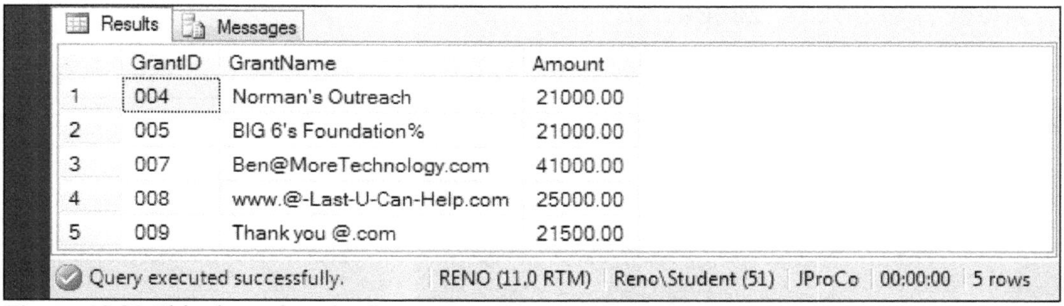

Figure 10.20 This shows just the five grants with amounts greater than 20000.

Figure 10.20 shows the five high grants. Now to create a common table expression we need to take the query from Figure 10.20, wrap it in parenthesis, and precede it with an alias using WITH HighGrants AS. Next we need to call on it with SELECT * FROM HighGrants.

```
WITH HighGrants AS (
SELECT GrantID AS GrantNumber, GrantName AS GName,
Amount AS Pledge
FROM [Grant]
WHERE Amount > 20000)

SELECT * FROM HighGrants
```

Figure 10.21 Aliasing fields can be done within the body of the main CTE query.

The result in Figure 10.21 gives us the same result as Figure 10.20 but has some added advantages. The SELECT * is an easy way to view all the fields from the CTE. What if we make the it a little more complicated using an expression field by making the Amount field Amount + 1000 AS DonatedAmount?

```
WITH HighGrants AS
  (SELECT GrantID, GrantName, Amount + 1000 AS DonatedAmount
  FROM [Grant]
  WHERE Amount > 20000)
SELECT * FROM HighGrants
```

Figure 10.22 This shows the five high grants with Amount + 1000.

In Figure 10.22 we see the expression field DonatedAmount but our general query has not changed in complexity. What if we want to change the name of the fields? (Figure 10.23)

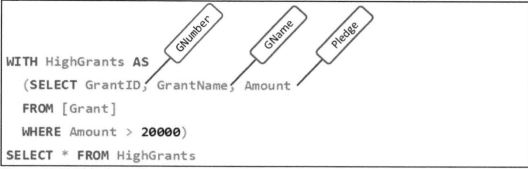

```
WITH HighGrants AS
  (SELECT GrantID, GrantName, Amount
  FROM [Grant]
  WHERE Amount > 20000)
SELECT * FROM HighGrants
```

Figure 10.23 This shows the names we would like the fields to be called.

We could alias all the fields in the query:

```
WITH HighGrants AS
  (SELECT GrantID AS GNumber, GrantName AS GName,
    Amount AS Pledge
  FROM [Grant]
  WHERE Amount > 20000)

SELECT * FROM HighGrants
```

There is another way. The field aliases can be specified before the AS in the WITH statement.

```
WITH HighGrants (GNumber, GName, Pledge) AS
  (SELECT GrantID, GrantName, Amount
  FROM [Grant]
  WHERE Amount > 20000)

SELECT * FROM HighGrants
```

	GNumber	GName	Pledge
1	004	Norman's Outreach	21000.00
2	005	BIG 6's Foundation%	21000.00
3	007	Ben@MoreTechnology.com	41000.00
4	008	www.@-Last-U-Can-Help.com	25000.00
5	009	Thank you @.com	21500.00

Query executed successfully.   RENO (11.0 RTM) Reno\Student (51) JProCo 00:00:00 5 rows

Figure 10.24 Field alias example where names are chosen before the AS in the WITH statement

Aliasing fields can be done inside the body of the main query (Figure 10.22). It gets the job done, but the CTE offers a tidier way to accomplish our goal. We can put the field aliases directly in the declaration statement, which enhances readability (Figure 10.24).

CTE Sorting

Since the CTE resides only in memory (i.e., and isn't an actual table), it doesn't get physically stored in the database. This means their default sort order will be the same as the underlying tables the CTE pulls from. We can sort results the way they are needed but there are a few rules about how we can do that.

Let's start by taking a look at the Grant table in descending ORDER BY Amount.

```
SELECT *
FROM [Grant]
ORDER BY Amount DESC
```

	GrantID	GrantName	EmpID	Amount
1	007	Ben@MoreTechnology.com	10	41000.00
2	008	www.@-Last-U-Can-Help.com	7	25000.00
3	009	Thank you @.com	11	21500.00
4	004	Norman's Outreach	NULL	21000.00
5	005	BIG 6's Foundation%	4	21000.00
6	006	TALTA_Kishan International	3	18100.00

Query executed successfully.   RENO (11.0 RTM)   Reno\Student (51)   JProCo   00:00:00   10 rows

Figure 10.25 This shows the Grant table in descending ORDER BY Amount.

What happens if we create a CTE with the ORDER BY clause inside the CTE?

```
WITH CTE AS
  (SELECT * FROM [Grant]
  ORDER BY Amount DESC)
SELECT * FROM CTE
```

Messages
Msg 1033, Level 15, State 1, Line 4
The ORDER BY clause is invalid in views, inline functions, derived tables, subqueries, and common table expressions, unless TOP, OFFSET or FOR XML is also specified.

0 rows

Figure 10.26 This shows the ORDER BY clause inside the CTE causes an error.

The ORDER BY clause is invalid in a common table expression unless TOP, OFFSET or FOR XML is also specified (Figure 10.26). The ORDER BY clause can be place outside the CTE and it will run without error (Figure 10.27).

```
WITH CTE AS
  (SELECT * FROM [Grant])
```

```
SELECT * FROM CTE
ORDER BY Amount DESC
```

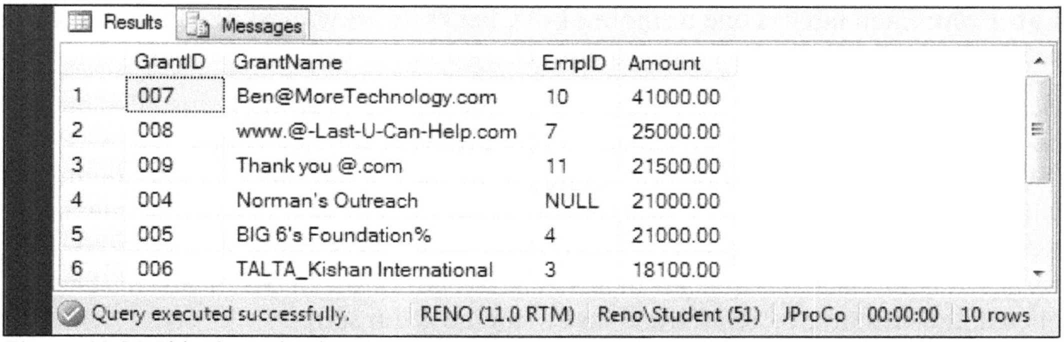

	GrantID	GrantName	EmpID	Amount
1	007	Ben@MoreTechnology.com	10	41000.00
2	008	www.@-Last-U-Can-Help.com	7	25000.00
3	009	Thank you @.com	11	21500.00
4	004	Norman's Outreach	NULL	21000.00
5	005	BIG 6's Foundation%	4	21000.00
6	006	TALTA_Kishan International	3	18100.00

Results
Messages
Query executed successfully.
RENO (11.0 RTM)
Reno\Student (51)
JProCo
00:00:00
10 rows

Figure 10.27 This shows having the ORDER BY clause outside the CTE it runs without error.

Let's run the same query only this time we will specify in the SELECT statement of the CTE TOP(100) PERCENT.

```
WITH CTE AS
  (SELECT TOP (100) PERCENT *
  FROM [Grant]
  ORDER BY Amount DESC)
SELECT * FROM CTE
```

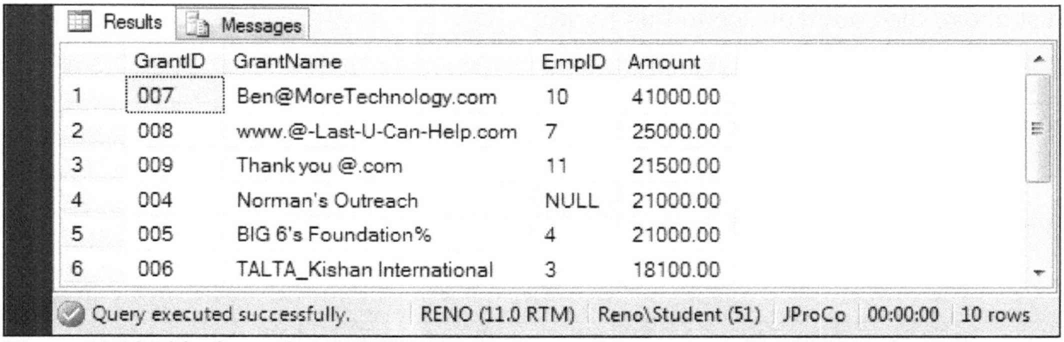

	GrantID	GrantName	EmpID	Amount
1	007	Ben@MoreTechnology.com	10	41000.00
2	008	www.@-Last-U-Can-Help.com	7	25000.00
3	009	Thank you @.com	11	21500.00
4	004	Norman's Outreach	NULL	21000.00
5	005	BIG 6's Foundation%	4	21000.00
6	006	TALTA_Kishan International	3	18100.00

Results
Messages
Query executed successfully.
RENO (11.0 RTM)
Reno\Student (51)
JProCo
00:00:00
10 rows

Figure 10.28 This shows that ORDER BY clause ran without error with TOP() in the CTE.

Using TOP allowed us to put the ORDER BY clause back inside the CTE and have it run without error (Figure 10.28).

Lab 10.1: Common Table Expressions

Lab Prep: Each lab has one or more Skill Checks. Start with Skill Check 1 and proceed until reaching the Points to Ponder section.

Before beginning this lab, verify that SQL Server 2012 is properly installed and operating. Before running the lab setup script for resetting the database (SQLQueries2012Vol2Chapter10.1Setup.sql), please make sure to close all query windows within SSMS. An open query window pointing to a database context can lock that database preventing it from updating when the script is executing. A simple way to assure all query windows are closed, is to exit out of SSMS, then open a new instance of SSMS, and lastly run the setup script.

Skill Check 1: You want to create an external report of your locations with a CTE called LocList. This list should show all fields of the Location table except for LocationID. The fields should also get new names, as shown in the following matrix.

- o Street should be shown as Address
- o City should be shown as Municipality
- o State should be shown as Region

When you're done, your result will resemble Figure 10.29. The CTE code will be just above the code you see in this figure.

```
SELECT * FROM LocList
```

	Address	Municipality	Region
1	111 First ST	Seattle	WA
2	222 Second AVE	Boston	MA
3	333 Third PL	Chicago	IL
4	444 Ruby ST	Spokane	WA

4 rows

Figure 10.29 Skill Check 1 builds a CTE and aliases three fields from the Location table.

Skill Check 2: Create a CTE called EmpGrantRank that joins the Grant and Employee tables. You must be able to see the name of each employee who registered a grant. Include the following four fields in EmpGrantRank:

- o GrantName
- o FirstName
- o LastName
- o Amount

For your fifth field, create an expression field named GrantRank that uses the DENSE_RANK() function based on the amount field in descending order. When you're done, your result should resemble Figure 10.30.

READER NOTE: Amount will be in descending order.

	GrantName	FirstName	LastName	Amount	GrantRank
1	Ben@MoreTechnology.com	Terry	O'Haire	41000.00	1
2	www.@-Last-U-Can-Help.com	David	Lonning	25000.00	2
3	Thank you @.com	Sally	Smith	21500.00	3
4	BIG 6's Foundation%	David	Kennson	21000.00	4
5	TALTA_Kishan International	Lee	Osako	18100.00	5
6	Robert@BigStarBank.com	David	Lonning	18100.00	5

9 rows

Figure 10.30 Write the CTE, GrantRank, with four fields plus a new expression field, GrantRank.

Skill Check 3: Create a CTE called StateRank that queries the StateList table and for all RegionName values that start with the letters USA. Add an expression field called SizeGroup that breaks down the landmass by size into 5 tiles. The top 20% should be in group 1; the next 20% should be in group 2 and the lowest 20% in group 5. When you're done, your result should resemble Figure 10.31.

READER NOTE: LandMass will be in descending order.

```
SELECT * FROM StateRank
```

	StateID	StateName	ProvinceName	RegionName	LandMass	SizeGroup
1	AK	Alaska	NULL	USA	656425	1
2	TX	Texas	NULL	USA-Continental	268601	1
3	CA	California	NULL	USA-Continental	163707	1
4	MT	Montana	NULL	USA-Continental	147046	1
5	NM	New Mexico	NULL	USA-Continental	121593	1
6	AZ	Arizona	NULL	USA-Continental	114006	1

52 rows

Figure 10.31 Skill Check 3.

Skill Check 4: Take the result from Skill Check 3 and change the predicate so that the first group shows the top 20% largest states. You should get 11 records as seen in Figure 10.32.

	StateID	StateName	ProvinceName	RegionName	LandMass	SizeGroup
1	AK	Alaska	NULL	USA	656425	1
2	TX	Texas	NULL	USA-Continental	268601	1
3	CA	California	NULL	USA-Continental	163707	1
4	MT	Montana	NULL	USA-Continental	147046	1
5	NM	New Mexico	NULL	USA-Continental	121593	1
6	AZ	Arizona	NULL	USA-Continental	114006	1
						11 rows

Figure 10.32 Skill Check 4.

Answer Code: The T-SQL code for this lab is located in the downloadable files as a file named Lab10.1_CommonTableExpressions.sql.

Points to Ponder - Common Table Expressions

1. A Common Table Expression (CTE) is a temporary result set we can query like a regular table.

2. A Common Table Expression is similar to a derived table, but the syntax is different. The code for the CTE is generally more readable than that for a derived table.

3. CTEs are created by the "WITH *CTE_Name* AS" syntax. CTEs put the name at the beginning of the code with a declaration statement (WITH *CTE_Name* AS) instead of aliasing within the main body of the code.

4. We can query the CTE with a SELECT clause.

5. The CTE lasts only for the duration of the query. The CTE code must be run each time the CTE is invoked (called upon by a query).

6. CTEs can be used to provide variables for another T-SQL statement, thereby reducing the complexity of queries.

7. CTEs allow users who can't create temp tables to perform more complex queries (e.g., users with read-only permission to the database). Prior to SQL 2005, it was common for users to be given a higher level of permissions (e.g., Admin rights) in order to be able to create temp tables for more complex queries. Therefore, CTEs help secure databases by allowing users with read access to create complex queries.

8. Unlike the old temp table construct, CTEs are not written to disk and do not need to be de-allocated once you are done with them.

PIVOT Operator

In Figure 10.35, you see two result sets which look different but are actually contain the very same data. It breaks down our 483 current products by category and by supplier. The result set on the left organizes each supplier's products in a column. The result set on the right uses a single column for all four SupplierID values listed once with a value grouped for each.

A GROUP BY query would produce the record set you see on the right. In a normalized database you generally would not store or report on data by having field headers contain data values, as you see in the left result set. Every once in a while you will need to create the result set in this way. For example, if you had a reporting application that needed each value expressed as a column, you could PIVOT the result set on the right to achieve the result set on the left.

Aggregate Review

The PIVOT function often has an aggregate function inside of it. If we take a look at the vProductList virtual table (view) we see there are many categories for each SupplierID.

```
SELECT *
FROM vProductList
```

	Category	SupplierID	ProductID
10	Medium-Stay	1	10
11	LongTerm-St...	1	11
12	LongTerm-St...	1	12
13	No-Stay	3	13
14	Overnight-Stay	3	14
15	Medium-Stay	3	15

Query executed successfully.   RENO (11.0 RTM)   Reno\Student (51)   JProCo   00:00:00   485 rows

Figure 10.33 This shows all the different product categories for each supplier.

If we need to know how many categories each SupplierID holds we will need to run an aggregate query. In the field SELECT list let's only look at the Category and SupplierID. We should GROUP BY these same two categories. Let's use the COUNT() function to find out how many products each supplier has.

```
SELECT Category, SupplierID, COUNT(ProductID)
FROM CurrentProducts
GROUP BY Category, SupplierID
```

	Category	SupplierID	(No column name)
1	LongTerm-Stay	0	32
2	Medium-Stay	0	32
3	No-Stay	0	16
4	Overnight-Stay	0	16
5	LongTerm-Stay	1	66
6	Medium-Stay	1	65

Query executed successfully.   RENO (11.0 RTM)   Reno\Student (51)   JProCo   00:00:00   16 rows

Figure 10.34 This shows how many products each SupplierID has for each Category.

In Figure 10.34 we see SupplierID 0 has 32 LongTerm-Stays, 32 Medium-Stays, 16 No-Stays, and 16 Overnight-Stays.

Take a look at Figure 10.35. What is the difference between these two sets of data? In TableA we see a list of Categories with the number of products from each supplier listed in fields. In TableB we see all the categories for each supplier with the number of products listed in the far right field.

	Category	0	1	2	3
1	LongTerm-Stay	32	66	32	32
2	Medium-Stay	34	65	32	32
3	No-Stay	16	32	16	16
4	Overnight-Stay	16	32	16	16

A

	Category	SupplierID	(No column name)
1	LongTerm-Stay	0	32
2	Medium-Stay	0	34
3	No-Stay	0	16
4	Overnight-Stay	0	16
5	LongTerm-Stay	1	66
6	Medium-Stay	1	65
7	No-Stay	1	32
8	Overnight-Stay	1	32
9	LongTerm-Stay	2	32
10	Medium-Stay	2	32
11	No-Stay	2	16
12	Overnight-Stay	2	16
13	LongTerm-Stay	3	32
14	Medium-Stay	3	32
15	No-Stay	3	16
16	Overnight-Stay	3	16

B

Figure 10.35 This shows the vProductList table data two ways.

The data contained in the two record sets of Figure 10.35 are identical. The meta data or design and layout of the two tables is slightly different but tells us the same information. TableB is the result of a GROUP BY Category and SupplierID with a COUNT of Products. TableA shows a grouping of categories and SupplierID values but displays the COUNT values in columns or fields.

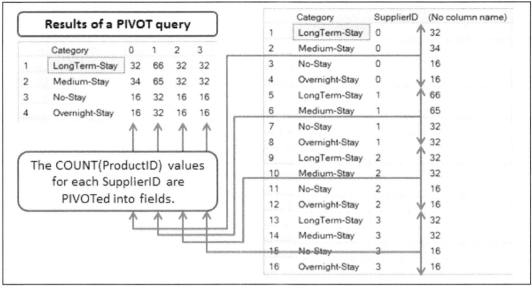

Figure 10.36 This is an explanation of the result of a PIVOT query.

The table on the left shows the COUNT() values as fields rather than repeating sets of rows (Figure 10.36). The table on the left can be accomplished using the PIVOT() command.

Using PIVOT Operator

Let's take the following result set that we have aggregated and PIVOT it across rows by SupplierID as seen in Figure 10.37.

```
SELECT Category, SupplierID, COUNT(ProductID)
FROM vProductList
GROUP BY Category, SupplierID
```

	Category	SupplierID	(No column name)
1	LongTerm-Stay	0	32
2	Medium-Stay	0	34
3	No-Stay	0	16
4	Overnight-Stay	0	16
5	LongTerm-Stay	1	66
6	Medium-Stay	1	65

Query executed successfully.   RENO (11.0 RTM)   Reno\Student (51)   JProCo   00:00:00   16 rows

Figure 10.37 This shows a query of the vProductList table with an aggregated result set.

Let's start with a complete SELECT list and using FROM the vProductList table:

```
SELECT *
FROM vProductList
```

We could group this query like before or PIVOT the query by SupplierID. After the FROM line add the PIVOT() command and create a derived table AS Pvt:

```
SELECT *
FROM vProductList
PIVOT
  () AS Pvt
```

As it stands the code above will not run. We have to tell the query to PIVOT on the COUNT (ProductID) FOR SupplierID. There are several SupplierID values and they should be specified using IN().

```
SELECT *
FROM vProductList
PIVOT
  (COUNT(ProductID)
  FOR SupplierID
  IN ([0],[1],[2],[3])) AS Pvt
```

	Category	0	1	2	3
1	LongTerm-Stay	32	66	32	32
2	Medium-Stay	34	65	32	32
3	No-Stay	16	32	16	16
4	Overnight-Stay	16	32	16	16

Query executed successfully.   RENO (11.0 RTM)   Reno\Student (51)   JProCo   00:00:00   4 rows

Figure 10.38 This shows the ProductID COUNT in fields for each SupplierID using PIVOT().

Figure 10.38 gave us the result we were looking for. The PIVOT() command can layout the result in a more useful format. The PIVOT() command helped us boil the 483 records in the vProductList table down to four rows.

Using PIVOT with Derived Tables

Take a quick look at the CurrentProducts table and see if it has 483 records. It displays the exact same products as the vProductList view.

```
SELECT *
FROM CurrentProducts
```

	ProductID	ProductName	RetailPrice	Origination...	ToBe...	Category	SupplierID
1	1	Underwater Tour...	61.483	2009-05-07...	0	No-Stay	0
2	2	Underwater Tour...	110.6694	2010-06-29...	0	Overnight-Stay	0
3	3	Underwater Tour...	184.449	2012-02-03...	0	Medium-Stay	0
4	4	Underwater Tour...	245.932	2008-11-28...	0	Medium-Stay	0
5	5	Underwater Tour...	307.415	2004-04-13...	0	LongTerm-Stay	0
6	6	Underwater Tour...	553.347	2011-03-27...	1	LongTerm-Stay	0

Query executed successfully.   RENO (11.0 RTM)   Reno\Student (51)   JProCo   00:00:00   483 rows

Figure 10.39 This shows the CurrentProducts table.

The difference is the vProductList table does not have as many fields. Since the CurrentProducts table has all the same information let's use PIVOT() and boil it down to the same result set as Figure 10.38. Let's begin our process the same way we did before:

```
SELECT *
FROM CurrentProducts
PIVOT
  () AS PVT
```

We have to tell the query what to PIVOT on. In the parentheses we need to add COUNT(ProductID) FOR SupplierID. There are several SupplierID values and they should be specified using IN().

```
SELECT *
FROM CurrentProducts
PIVOT
  (COUNT(ProductID)
  FOR SupplierID
  IN ([0],[1],[2],[3])) AS Pvt
```

	ProductName	RetailPrice	Origination...	ToBeD...	Category	0	1	2	3
1	Acting Lessons Tour 1 ...	78.95	2012-05-25...	0	No-Stay	0	0	1	0
2	Acting Lessons Tour 1 ...	52.67	2011-04-16...	0	No-Stay	0	1	0	0
3	Acting Lessons Tour 1 ...	101.068	2005-12-06...	0	No-Stay	0	0	0	1
4	Acting Lessons Tour 1 ...	66.897	2008-06-29...	0	No-Stay	0	1	0	0
5	Acting Lessons Tour 1 ...	111.366	2005-08-21...	0	No-Stay	1	0	0	0
6	Acting Lessons Tour 1 ...	394.75	2010-06-30...	0	LongTerm-Stay	0	0	1	0

Query executed successfully.   RENO (11.0 RTM)   Reno\Student (51)   JProCo   00:00:00   483 rows

Figure 10.40 This shows the CurrentProducts table utilizing PIVOT still returned 483 records.

Why did the CurrentProducts table return all 483 records when the vProductList table boiled down to four records? The reason is when we ran PIVOT on the CurrentProducts table it was sorting by ProductName, RetailPrice, OriginationDate, ToBeDeleted and Category. Our field SELECT list is so vast nothing is getting condensed. There are no two products with the matching values in every field. The result is too granular.

Use the following code to narrow our SELECT list to Category and each SupplierID:

```
SELECT *, [0], [1], [2], [3]
FROM CurrentProducts
    PIVOT
    (COUNT(ProductID)
    FOR SupplierID IN
    ([0], [1], [2], [3])
    ) AS Pvt
```

	ProductName	RetailPrice	OriginationDate	ToBeDeleted	Category	0	1
1	Acting Lessons Tour 1 Day Canada	78.95	2012-05-25 01:45:29.600	0	No-Stay	0	0
2	Acting Lessons Tour 1 Day East Coast	52.67	2011-04-16 20:55:56.943	0	No-Stay	0	1
3	Acting Lessons Tour 1 Day Mexico	101.068	2005-12-06 05:24:17.020	0	No-Stay	0	0
4	Acting Lessons Tour 1 Day Scandinavia	66.897	2008-06-29 00:27:45.787	0	No-Stay	0	1
5	Acting Lessons Tour 1 Day West Coast	111.366	2005-08-21 23:18:38.613	0	No-Stay	1	0

| Query executed successfully. | (local) (11.0 RTM) | Reno\Student (51) | JProCo | 00:00:00 | 483 rows |

Figure 10.41 This shows the same result as Figure 10.40 with a narrowed SELECT list.

The query in Figure 10.41 is still returning 483 records. Narrowing the SELECT list only limits the fields that are displayed. The query is looking at all the fields in the table. What if we created a derived table from the CurrentProducts table that only has the 3 fields we need. Let's SELECT Category, [0], [1], [2], [3] from a derived table that limits the fields to ProductID, Category and SupplierID. We will call the derived table ProductList.

```
SELECT Category, [0],[1],[2],[3]
FROM
   (SELECT ProductID, Category, SupplierID
   FROM CurrentProducts) AS ProductList
PIVOT
   (COUNT(ProductID)
   FOR SupplierID
   IN ([0],[1],[2],[3])) AS Pvt
ORDER BY Category
```

Figure 10.42 This shows the result of PIVOT() on the derived table ProductList.

Using PIVOT() with a derived table that resembled the vProductList table, we were able to get the same result (Figure 10.42).

Changing the PIVOT Fields

For this next example notice we are in the dbBasics database.

Figure 10.43 This shows the Employee table from the dbBasics database.

Notice, in Figure 10.43 there are several departments. Each department has several employees. There are also several locations and each location has several employees. Let's build a grouping query that finds out how many employees are in each department at each location. We will need to limit the field SELECT list to Dept, LocationID and COUNT (EmpNo). We will need to add supporting grouping language to run the aggregate query.

```
SELECT Dept, LocationID, COUNT(EmpNo)
FROM Employee
WHERE LocationID IS NOT NULL
GROUP BY Dept, LocationID
```

	Dept	LocationID	(No column name)
1	Admin	1	3
2	Education	1	3
3	RND	1	1
4	Sales	1	2
5	Admin	2	2
6	Sales	2	3

Query executed successfully.   RENO (11.0 RTM) Reno\Student (51) dbBasics 00:00:00 6 rows

Figure 10.44 This shows how many employees are in each department at each location.

In Figure 10.44 we see there are 3 employees in Admin at location 1, 3 employees in Education at location 1 and so on. Now let's go back to our original query:

```
SELECT *
FROM Employee
WHERE LocationID IS NOT NULL
```

Let's start here and write a query that returns the exact same data but in different design. We will have the departments but the LocationID values will be listed as an individual field for the COUNT(EmpNo) values. Let's start by limiting the field SELECT list to Dept, LocationID and EmpNo. These are the three fields we will be working with.

```
SELECT Dept, LocationID, EmpNo
FROM Employee
WHERE LocationID IS NOT NULL
```

	Dept	LocationID	EmpNo
1	Admin	2	101
2	Sales	2	102
3	Admin	1	103
4	Admin	1	104
5	Sales	2	105
6	Admin	1	106

Query executed successfully.   RENO (11.0 RTM) Reno\Student (51) dbBasics 00:00:00 14 rows

Figure 10.45 This shows the three fields queried from the Employee table.

The reason we narrow the fields is to get a higher report that is less granular. We could create a view but let's go ahead and make this a derived table and name it EmpList:

```
(SELECT Dept, LocationID, EmpNo
FROM Employee
WHERE LocationID IS NOT NULL) AS EmpList
```

We will need to call on the new EmpList table so let's place it in a basic SELECT query:

```
SELECT * FROM
(SELECT Dept, LocationID, EmpNo
FROM Employee
WHERE LocationID IS NOT NULL) AS EmpList
```

	Dept	LocationID	EmpNo
1	Admin	2	101
2	Sales	2	102
3	Admin	1	103
4	Admin	1	104
5	Sales	2	105
6	Admin	1	106

Query executed successfully.   RENO (11.0 RTM)   Reno\Student (51)   dbBasics   00:00:00   14 rows

Figure 10.46 This shows the three fields from the Employee table by querying the derived table EmpList.

Now that we have created a derived table it will be the EmpList table that we will PIVOT the location across two different fields. To start we will add PIVOT() and alias that as pvt:

```
SELECT * FROM
  (SELECT Dept, LocationID, EmpNo
  FROM Employee
  WHERE LocationID IS NOT NULL) AS EmpList
PIVOT
  ()AS pvt
```

In the parentheses we will COUNT the EmpID values going across LocationID values 1 and 2:

```
SELECT * FROM
  (SELECT Dept, LocationID, EmpNo
  FROM Employee
  WHERE LocationID IS NOT NULL) AS EmpList
```

```
PIVOT
  (COUNT(EmpNo)
FOR LocationID IN ([1], [2])) AS pvt
```

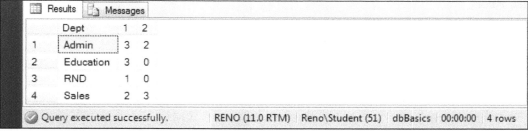

Figure 10.47 This shows the department listed with employee COUNT by LocationID as fields.

We have successfully created a query that listed each department and displayed employee COUNT in fields by LocationID. What if we want to list LocationID values and display employee COUNT in fields by Dept? To do this we need to replace LocationID in the PIVOT with Dept:

```
SELECT * FROM
  (SELECT Dept, LocationID, EmpNo
  FROM Employee
  WHERE LocationID IS NOT NULL) AS EmpList
PIVOT
  (COUNT(EmpNo)
FOR Dept IN ([1], [2])) AS pvt
```

This query will run but it will not return any data because the Depts are not named 1 and 2, they are named Admin, Education etc.

```
SELECT * FROM
  (SELECT Dept, LocationID, EmpNo
  FROM Employee
  WHERE LocationID IS NOT NULL) AS EmpList
PIVOT
  (COUNT(EmpNo)
FOR Dept IN ([Admin], [Education], [RND], [Sales])) AS pvt
```

	LocationID	Admin	Education	RND	Sales
1	1	3	3	1	2
2	2	2	0	0	3

Query executed successfully.   (local) (11.0 RTM)   Reno\Student (51)   dbBasics   00:00:00   2 rows

Figure 10.48 This shows how many employees work in each department at the given locations.

We successfully queried LocationID PIVOT-ed by Dept (Figure 10.48). There is a warning. If you make a spelling error, you will not get an error; it will simply not give you any records in the result. We can test this. Instead of RND we will use R&D.

```
SELECT * FROM
   (SELECT Dept, LocationID, EmpNo
   FROM Employee
   WHERE LocationID IS NOT NULL) AS EmpList
PIVOT
   (COUNT(EmpNo)
FOR Dept IN ([Admin], [Education], [R&D], [Sales])) AS pvt
```

	LocationID	Admin	Education	R&D	Sales
1	1	3	3	0 ←	2
2	2	2	0	0 ←	3

Figure 10.49 Since there are no fields called R&D no records were found.

You need to know what values and what records you are querying for before the PIVOT can be used to pull the data you need. A misspelling will return zero records (Figure 10.49).

Lab 10.2: PIVOT

Lab Prep: Each lab has one or more Skill Checks. Start with Skill Check 1 and proceed until reaching the Points to Ponder section.

Before beginning this lab, verify that SQL Server 2012 is properly installed and operating. Before running the lab setup script for resetting the database (SQLQueries2012Vol2Chapter10.2Setup.sql), please make sure to close all query windows within SSMS. An open query window pointing to a database context can lock that database preventing it from updating when the script is executing. A simple way to assure all query windows are closed, is to exit out of SSMS, then open a new instance of SSMS, and lastly run the setup script.

Skill Check 1: Use PIVOT with the following aggregate query to achieve the result set you see in Figure 10.50.

```
SELECT ProductID, OrderYear, SUM(RetailPrice)
FROM vSales
GROUP BY ProductID, OrderYear
```

	ProductID	2009	2010	2011	2012	2013
1	23	NULL	NULL	427.925	NULL	NULL
2	69	NULL	4268.34	2598.12	3897.18	371.16
3	15	16389.204	17334.735	13237.434	11346.372	2206.239
4	29	18578.88	20320.65	11611.80	9289.44	1741.77
5	75	3423.105	3520.908	3129.696	3423.105	586.818
						60 rows

Figure 10.50 Skill Check 1.

Skill Check 2: Write a query using PIVOT and the dbo.vSales view to achieve the result set you see in Figure 10.51.

	OrderYear	Qty1	Qty2	Qty3	Qty4	Qty5	Qty6
1	2009	136	308	350	326	338	169
2	2010	201	429	400	404	443	176
3	2011	157	282	299	268	285	163
4	2012	169	296	308	322	337	140
5	2013	17	48	55	49	58	27
							5 rows

Figure 10.51 Skill Check 2.

Answer Code: The T-SQL code for this lab is located in the downloadable files as a file named Lab10.2_PIVOT.sql.

Points to Ponder - PIVOT

1. PIVOT is a relational operator.

2. We can use relational operators to change a result set into another result set with the same data but a different layout.

3. PIVOT rotates the result set by turning the unique values from one field into multiple fields in the output.

UNPIVOT Operator

UNPIVOT is the opposite of PIVOT. Take the two result sets from the following figure as an example. If you have repeating columns like you see on the upper left that need to be turned into values within a grouped row, then the UNPIVOT command will help you achieve this goal.

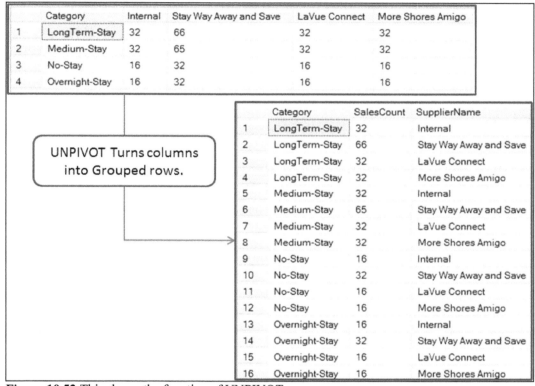

Figure 10.52 This shows the function of UNPIVOT.

Using UNPIVOT Operator

In this section we are going to un-pivot a table called CategoryGrid that is most likely not on your system.

```
SELECT * FROM CategoryGrid
```

Messages
Msg 208, Level 16, State 1, Line 1
Invalid object name 'CategoryGrid'.
0 rows

Figure 10.53 This shows the error message if SQLQueries2012Vol2Chapter10SpecialSetup.sql has not been run on your system.

The CategoryGrid table is not a part of the normal reset scripts. There is a special reset script called SQLQueries2012Vol2Chapter10SpecialSetup.sql that needs to be run before we begin. This file can be found in the C:\Joes2Pros\LabSetupFiles folder.

Now that we have run the reset script take a look at the CategoryGrid table.

```
SELECT * FROM CategoryGrid
```

	Category	Internal	Stay Way Away and Save	LaVue Connect	More Shores Amigo
1	LongTerm-Stay	32	66	32	32
2	Medium-Stay	32	65	32	32
3	No-Stay	16	32	16	16
4	Overnight-Stay	16	32	16	16

Query executed successfully.　　RENO (11.0 RTM)　Reno\Student (51)　JProCo　00:00:00　4 rows

Figure 10.54 This shows the CategoryGrid table.

The CategoryGrid table has four different suppliers and how many sales they have made in each of the four categories (Figure 10.54). Let's use the UNPIVOT command to put all the suppliers back into one field. To start, we need to itemize the fields in the SELECT list:

```
SELECT Category, Internal, [Stay Way Away and Save],
  [LaVue Connect], [More Shores Amigo]
FROM CategoryGrid
```

Notice there are spaces in the supplier names so they need to be placed in square brackets. Next the query needs to be turned into a derived table that we will name Products.

```
SELECT * FROM
  (SELECT Category, [Internal], [Stay Way Away and Save],
  [LaVue Connect], [More Shores Amigo]
  FROM CategoryGrid) AS Products
```

	Category	Internal	Stay Way Away and Save	LaVue Connect	More Shores Amigo
1	LongTerm-Stay	32	66	32	32
2	Medium-Stay	32	65	32	32
3	No-Stay	16	32	16	16
4	Overnight-Stay	16	32	16	16

Query executed successfully.　　RENO (11.0 RTM)　Reno\Student (51)　JProCo　00:00:00　4 rows

Figure 10.55 This shows the CategoryGrid table queried as a derived table named Products.

To UNPIVOT this table we need to add the UNPIVOT command. What are we going to UNPIVOT? We are going to UNPIVOT the SalesCount for

SupplierName. SalesCount and SupplierName will become the field names in the UNPIVOT-ed table. The SalesCount values are found IN the supplier fields which need to be listed. The final step is to name the UNPIVOT drive table AS unpvt.

```
SELECT * FROM
  (SELECT Category, [Internal], [Stay Way Away and Save],
  [LaVue Connect], [More Shores Amigo]
FROM CategoryGrid) AS Products
UNPIVOT
  (SalesCount FOR SupplierName
  IN (Internal,
    [Stay Way Away and Save],
    [LaVue Connect],
    [More Shores Amigo])) AS unpvt
```

	Category	SalesCount	SupplierName
1	LongTerm-Stay	32	Internal
2	LongTerm-Stay	66	Stay Way Away and Save
3	LongTerm-Stay	32	LaVue Connect
4	LongTerm-Stay	32	More Shores Amigo
5	Medium-Stay	32	Internal
6	Medium-Stay	65	Stay Way Away and Save

Query executed successfully.   RENO (11.0 RTM)   Reno\Student (51)   JProCo   00:00:00   16 rows

Figure 10.56 This shows the CategoryGrid table after the UNPIVOT command was applied.

In Figure 10.56 we see the normalized view of the data from the CategoryGrid table. UNPIVOT rotates the result set by turning multiple fields in the output into unique values in a single field.

Lab 10.3: UNPIVOT

Lab Prep: Each lab has one or more Skill Checks. Start with Skill Check 1 and proceed until reaching the Points to Ponder section.

Before beginning this lab, verify that SQL Server 2012 is properly installed and operating. Before running the lab setup script for resetting the database (SQLQueries2012Vol2Chapter10SpecialSetup.sql), please make sure to close all query windows within SSMS. An open query window pointing to a database context can lock that database preventing it from updating when the script is executing. A simple way to assure all query windows are closed, is to exit out of SSMS, then open a new instance of SSMS, and lastly run the setup script.

Skill Check 1: After you run the SQLQueries2012Vol2Chapter10SpecialSetup.sql script then JProCo database will have the SalesGrid table.

```
SELECT *
FROM SalesGrid
```

Write a query using UNPIVOT which will achieve the result set you see in Figure 10.57.

	ProductID	TotalSales	CalYear
1	23	427.925	2011
2	69	4268.34	2010
3	69	2598.12	2011
4	69	3897.18	2012
5	69	371.16	2013
6	15	16389.204	2009

270 rows

Figure 10.57 Skill Check 1.

Answer Code: The T-SQL code for this lab is located in the downloadable files as a file named Lab10.3_UNPIVOT.sql.

Points to Ponder - UNPIVOT

1. UNPIVOT is a relational operator.

2. We can use relational operators to change a result set into another result set with the same data but a different layout.

3. UNPIVOT performs the reverse operation of PIVOT, except there is no aggregation function used while using UNPIVOT.

4. UNPIVOT rotates the result set by turning multiple fields in the output into unique values into a single field.

5. We can only use PIVOT and UNPIVOT in SQL Server 2005 or later.

Chapter Glossary

Clauses: These constitute components of SQL statements and queries. The SQL clauses for SELECT statements are: AS, COMPUTE, COMPUTE BY, FROM, GROUP BY, HAVING, INTO, OPTION, ORDER BY, OVER, SET, TABLESAMPLE, TOP, WHERE and some types of WITH statements.

Common Table Expression (CTE): A CTE is a temporary result set we can query like a regular table; it lasts only for the duration of the query.

PIVOT Operator: Takes a normalized table and transforms it into a new table that has columns based on the values from a single row.

UNPIVOT Operator: Takes a non-normalized table and transforms it into a new table that has unique values in a single row based on field names from the original table.

Review Quiz - Chapter Ten

1.) What is an advantage of a Common Table Expression (CTE) over a derived table?

O a. We can use the SELECT * in a CTE but not in a derived table.

O b. We can predicate on an expression field of the CTE but cannot do so in a derived table.

O c. CTEs can reduce the complexity of a query.

O d. CTEs work faster with the HAVING clause.

2.) Which of the following code segments would implement a CTE?

O a. `WITH LocList ([Address], [Municipality], [Region]) AS`
    `(SELECT [Street], [City], State FROM Location)`
    `SELECT * FROM LocList`

O b. `SELECT *`
    `FROM ([Address], [Municipality], [Region])`
    `(SELECT [Street], [City], State`
    `FROM Location) AS LocList`

O c. `CREATE VIEW LocList AS`
    `SELECT [Street], [City], State`
    `FROM Location`

O d. `SELECT DISTINCT [Street], [City], State`
    `FROM Location`

3.) What operator will turn a normalized result set into multiple fields in the output?

O a. UNION

O b. UNION ALL

O c. PIVOT

O d. UNPIVOT

4.) You have a table with the following design:

```
CREATE TABLE Sales (
SalesID INT PRIMARY KEY,
CustomerID INT NOT NULL,
OrderDate DATETIME,
OrderAmount SMALLMONEY,
ProductID INT,
OrderYear SMALLINT)
```

You have the following aggregate query to find the total order amount for each product in a given year

```
SELECT ProductID, OrderYear, SUM(OrderAmount)
FROM Sales
GROUP BY ProductID, OrderYear
```

You notice you have records from 2009 to 2013. You want each year listed individually in a column. What T-SQL code will achieve this result?

O a.
```
SELECT *
FROM (
   SELECT ProductID, OrderYear, OrderAmount
   FROM Sales) AS drvSales
PIVOT (SUM(OrderAmount)
   FOR OrderYear
   IN ([2009],[2010],[2011],[2012],[2013]) ) AS pvt
```

O b.
```
SELECT *
FROM (
   SELECT ProductID, OrderYear, OrderAmount
   FROM Sales) AS drvSales
UNPIVOT (SUM(OrderAmount)
   FOR OrderYear
   IN ([2009],[2010],[2011],[2012],[2013])) AS pvt
```

O c.
```
SELECT *
FROM (
   SELECT ProductID, OrderYear, OrderAmount
   FROM Sales) AS drvSales
PIVOT (SUM(OrderYear)
   FOR OrderYear
   IN ([2009],[2010],[2011],[2012],[2013])) AS pvt
```

Answer Key

1.) A SELECT statement will work with the all fields wildcard '*' when using either a CTE or a derived table, so (a) is incorrect. Predicating on expression fields is one of the biggest advantages that both CTEs and derived tables have to offer, so (b) is wrong too. While a HAVING clause may make some queries work faster, in other cases it can slow the query down, making (d) an incorrect choice too. Because a CTE is created before the query that is using it, rather than inside, a query using one is generally more readable, making (c) the correct answer.

2.) 'SELECT * FROM (Address, Municipality...' will result in incorrect syntax, so (b) is a wrong answer. 'CREATE VIEW LocList AS...' is the syntax for implementing a view named LocList, so (c) is wrong too. 'SELECT DISTINCT Street, City, State FROM Location' is just a query of the Location table, making (d) another wrong choice. The proper syntax to implement a CTE, WITH *CTE_Name* (*comma separated field list*) AS (SELECT *comma separated field list* FROM *TableName*...) SELECT * FROM *CTE_Name,* is only found in (a), making it the correct answer.

3.) UNION and UNION ALL do not change field orders or field names, so (a) and (b) are wrong. PIVOT turns row values into new columns, making (c) the correct answer.

4.) In order to turn rows into columns you need to use PIVOT, so (b) is wrong. We need to sum the amounts, so (c) is incorrect. Only (a) sums the orders and pivots on the years, making (a) the correct answer.

Bug Catcher Game

To play the Bug Catcher game, run the SQLQueries2012Vol2BugCatcher10.pps file from the BugCatcher folder of the companion files. These files are available from the www.Joes2Pros.com website.

[THIS PAGE INTENTIONALLY LEFT BLANK.]

Chapter 11. Data Recursion

Growing up, my brothers and I had fun competing with each other over all sorts of things. My older brother once compared his height to the rest of us and said, "Except for Dad, I'm the tallest one in the family". Then my younger brother and I exclaimed we were both taller than our mom was.

This chapter includes several examples of hierarchical data, which is all about comparisons between similar items, such as where each item appears in the pecking order. We will run through product pricing data comparing the inexpensiveness of some products versus others. We will also look at the pecking order of JProCo's organizational structure (Management and employee hierarchy).

The concept of recursion is very important in this chapter. Merriam-Webster describes recursion in the following quote:

> *A computer programming technique involving the use*
> *of a procedure, function, or algorithm that calls itself*
> *one or more times until a specific condition is met.*

Advanced students will be familiar with recursive techniques common in many programming languages. For instance, a code loop designed to execute repeatedly until the logic is satisfied. This chapter will give everyone the ability to follow along as we observe a CTE calling on itself through successive iterations in order to establish the JProCo employee hierarchy. Once we understand how recursive queries operate, we will garner the attention of fellow colleagues with advanced coding skills.

The recursive query is an advanced technique, which some developers argue is the most significant and powerful task that CTEs help you accomplish.

READER NOTE: *Please run the SQLQueries2012Vol2Chapter11.0Setup.sql script in order to follow along with the examples in the first section of Chapter 11. All scripts mentioned in this chapter are available at www.Joes2Pros.com.*

Single Table Hierarchies

Before we begin to learn more about how to extract hierarchal data from a single table, it is a good idea to look at what data is contained in the table we are interested in. Write a simple query that shows all the fields and records for the Employee table in the JProCo database.

```
SELECT *
FROM Employee
```

	EmpID	LastName	FirstName	HireDate	LocationID	ManagerID	Status
1	1	Adams	Alex	2001-01-01...	1	11	Active
2	2	Brown	Barry	2002-08-12...	1	11	Active
3	3	Osako	Lee	1999-09-01...	2	11	Active
4	4	Kennson	David	1996-03-16...	1	11	Has T...
5	5	Bender	Eric	2007-05-17...	1	11	Active
6	6	Kendall	Lisa	2001-11-15...	4	4	Active

13 rows

Figure 11.1 The result set for the Employee table has 13 records.

When looking at the result set in Figure 11.1, we can see there are 13 records for each employee working at JProCo. We can also see that each employee record has some additional fields to help identify who they are (EmpID), where they work (LocationID) and whom they work for (ManagerID). In Figure 11.2, we see an illustration of a relationship between the EmpID and ManagerID of Lee Osako.

	EmpID	LastName	FirstName	HireDate	LocationID	ManagerID	Status	
1	1	Adams	Alex	2001-01-01...	1	11	Active	
2	2	Brown	Barry	2002-08-12...	1	11	Active	
3	3	Osako	Lee	1999-09-01...	2	11	Active	
4	4	Kennson	David	1996-03-16...	1	11	Has Tenure	
5	5	Bender	Eric	2007-05-17...	1	11	Active	
6	6	Kendall	Lisa	2001-11-15...	4	4	Active	
7	7	Lonning	David	2000-01-01...	1	11	On Leave	
8	8	Marshbank	John	2001-11-15...	NULL	4	Active	
9	9	Newton	James	2003-09-30...	2	3	Active	
10	10	O'Haire	Terry	2004-10-04...	2	3	Active	
11	11	Smith	Sally	1989-04-01...	1	NULL	Active	
12	12	O'Neil	Barbara	1995-05-26...	4	4	Has Tenure	

Query executed successfully.   RENO (11.0 RTM) Reno\Student (51) JProCo 00:00:00 13 rows

Figure 11.2 James Newton works for Lee Osako and Lee's manager is Sally Smith (CEO).

The illustration makes it possible to piece together this information by looking at the data row by row. Each employee record contains a value in the ManagerID field, which is equal to that manager's EmpID value, so we can indirectly learn the name of the manager for each employee.

While this illustration can be helpful to visualize these relationships, it may not be the best way to look at the employee data from a hierarchy perspective. It is not easy to answer other questions like, "Who's in charge?", "Who works directly below those in charge?", and "Who are the individual contributors at this company?" with a single table query.

For example, James Newton, who is EmpID 9, works at LocationID 2 (Boston) and his boss is ManagerID 3 (Lee Osako). We can then trace a path to Lee Osako (EmpID 3) and learn that he also works at LocationID 2 (Boston) and his boss is ManagerID 11 (Sally Smith). By looking a little closer at all the data, we find that there are no other managers at LocationID 2, so it appears that Lee Osako is the branch manager of the office in Boston.

When we trace a path to Sally Smith, we learn that she works at the JProCo headquarters in Seattle (LocationID 1). Who is Sally's manager? Since Sally has a ManagerID of NULL, we can surmise that she is the CEO of JProCo. This means that she is at the top of the chain of command (reporting hierarchy) and does not report to anyone.

Are there any other employees reporting directly to Sally? We can find this out by adding filtering criteria to our last query for EmpID 11 (her employee number), which will list each employee she manages. The result set is in Figure 11.3.

```
SELECT *
FROM Employee
WHERE ManagerID = 11
```

	EmpID	LastName	FirstName	HireDate	LocationID	ManagerID	Status
1	1	Adams	Alex	2001-01-01...	1	11	Active
2	2	Brown	Barry	2002-08-12...	1	11	Active
3	3	Osako	Lee	1999-09-01...	2	11	Active
4	4	Kennson	David	1996-03-16...	1	11	Has Tenure
5	5	Bender	Eric	2007-05-17...	1	11	Active
6	7	Lonning	David	2000-01-01...	1	11	On Leave

6 rows

Figure 11.3 A list showing the employees Sally Smith manages.

These six are the employees who work directly for ManagerID 11, Sally Smith. They are right below the CEO and thus are the top tier executives. Notice that Sally is not included in this list, since she does not report to anyone.

It is readily apparent that some of the employees at JProCo have the responsibility of managing other employees. It would be useful to create a report showing the manager name alongside the name of each employee. In other words, we want a report that quickly distinguishes Sally Smith as the manager for Alex Adams.

We know there is not a separate table in the JProCo database containing data for each manager, preventing us from joining a Manager table to an Employee table. As we will see later, the realm of temporary objects enables using advanced query techniques to improvise in situations where there is no other table available to meet our specific needs.

In this case, there is an object in the JProCo database, vBossList, allowing us to create a report showing the relationship between managers and employees. Use the Object Explorer to navigate to the Views folder of the JProCo database.

Object Explorer > Databases > JProCo > Views > dbo.vBossList

The vBossList view contains the EmpID, FirstName and LastName fields for the three employees having management responsibilities (Figure 11.4).

```
SELECT *
FROM vBossList
```

	EmpID	FirstName	LastName
1	3	Lee	Osako
2	4	David	Kennson
3	11	Sally	Smith

3 rows

Figure 11.4 The result set for the vBossList object (view) in the JProCo database.

We can write a simple query joining the Employee table and the vBossList view together by finding each ManagerID in the Employee table that is equal to the EmpID value in the vBossList view. In other words, each employee has a manager and that manager is an employee as well. Run the code sample shown here to see the results of using an INNER JOIN between these two objects.

```
SELECT *
FROM Employee AS el
INNER JOIN vBossList AS bl
ON el.ManagerID = bl.EmpID
```

	EmpID	LastName	FirstName	HireDate	LocationID	ManagerID	Status	EmpID	FirstName	LastName	
1	1	Adams	Alex	2001-01-01...	1	11	Active	11	Sally	Smith	
2	2	Brown	Barry	2002-08-12...	1	11	Active	11	Sally	Smith	
3	3	Osako	Lee	1999-09-01...	2	11	Active	11	Sally	Smith	
4	4	Kennson	David	1996-03-16...	1	11	Has Tenure	11	Sally	Smith	
5	5	Bender	Eric	2007-05-17...	1	11	Active	11	Sally	Smith	
6	6	Kendall	Lisa	2001-11-15...	4	4	Active	4	David	Kennson	

Query executed successfully. RENO (11.0 RTM) Reno\j2p (51) JProCo 00:00:00 12 rows

Figure 11.5 An INNER JOIN of Employee and vBossList shows 12 records.

The result set from joining the Employee table to vBossList shows Alex Adams and Barry Brown both work for Sally Smith. Lisa Kendall works for someone else, ManagerID 4, whom we discover is David Kennson (Figure 11.5).

Why are there only 12 records in the result set of Figure 11.5? We know there are thirteen employees working at JProCo, so what happened? The missing record is for EmpID 11, Sally Smith. She does not show up in the result set because of the matching criteria of the INNER JOIN operator (ON el.ManagerID = bl.EmpID).

Since the ManagerID is NULL for Sally in the Employee table, the INNER JOIN is unable to find a match with an EmpID value in the vBossList view. Switching our join type to a LEFT OUTER JOIN will show all records in the Employee table, even if there are no matches in the vBossList view.

```
SELECT *
FROM Employee el
LEFT OUTER JOIN vBossList bl
ON el.ManagerID = bl.EmpID
```

	EmpID	LastName	FirstName	HireDate	LocationID	ManagerID	Status	EmpID	FirstName	LastName	
8	8	Marshbank	John	2001-11-15...	NULL	4	Active	4	David	Kennson	
9	9	Newton	James	2003-09-30...	2	3	Active	3	Lee	Osako	
10	10	O'Haire	Terry	2004-10-04...	2	3	Active	3	Lee	Osako	
11	11	Smith	Sally	1989-04-01...	1	NULL	Active	NULL	NULL	NULL	
12	12	O'Neil	Barbara	1995-05-26...	4	4	Has Tenure	4	David	Kennson	
13	13	Wilconkinski	Phil	2009-06-11...	1	4	Active	4	David	Kennson	

Query executed successfully. RENO (11.0 RTM) Reno\j2p (51) JProCo 00:00:00 13 rows

Figure 11.6 With a LEFT OUTER JOIN, we now see Sally Smith's record in our result.

The result set shown in Figure 11.6 includes the thirteen employee records of the Employee table. The unmatched record, Sally Smith, assigned NULL values for the three fields representing vBossList on the right-hand side of the join (EmpID, FirstName and LastName).

Self-Join Queries

In our last example, the join required two tables. It first needed a table with the list of employees and the manager ID's. The second table then connected to the first table's ManagerID field (el.ManagerID = bl.EmpID) to provide the manager first and last names.

Now we are going to accomplish the same result with a self-join. The key to joining a table to itself is aliasing. Aliasing a table with a different name causes it to behave in memory as two different tables, and therefore we can join them. In fact, "self-join" is just a logical term. We humans see one table being joined to a copy of itself, but all SQL Server sees is two tables being joined. The remainder of examples in this chapter will all include self-joins.

Here we will alias both instances of the Employee table to make our code readable (**Figure 11.6**). As well, we want to make the employee and the manager sides of the table discernible (as in the first example – Figure 11.4).

```
SELECT *
FROM Employee emp

SELECT *
FROM Employee boss
```

Figure 11.7 We can join Employee to a copy of itself and bring in each boss EmpID and name.

Compare the result of Figure 11.7 with that in Figure 11.4. Our SELECT * statement brought in four additional columns on the right side of the table, but otherwise, this result is the same as our join of the Employee table and vBossList.

```
SELECT * FROM Employee emp
INNER JOIN Employee boss
ON emp.ManagerID = boss.EmpID
```

	EmpID	LastName	FirstName	HireDate	LocationID	ManagerID	Status	EmpID	LastName	FirstName	HireDate	LocationID	ManagerID	Status
1	1	Adams	Alex	2001-01-01..	1	11	Active	11	Smith	Sally	1989-04-01..	1	NULL	Active
2	2	Brown	Barry	2002-08-12..	1	11	Active	11	Smith	Sally	1989-04-01..	1	NULL	Active
3	3	Osako	Lee	1999-09-01..	2	11	Active	11	Smith	Sally	1989-04-01..	1	NULL	Active
4	4	Kennson	David	1996-03-16..	1	11	Has Tenure	11	Smith	Sally	1989-04-01..	1	NULL	Active
5	5	Bender	Eric	2007-05-17..	1	11	Active	11	Smith	Sally	1989-04-01..	1	NULL	Active
6	6	Kendall	Lisa	2001-11-15..	4	4	Active	4	Kennson	David	1996-03-16..	1	11	Has Tenure
7	7	Lonning	David	2000-01-01..	1	11	On Leave	11	Smith	Sally	1989-04-01..	1	NULL	Active
8	8	Marshbank	John	2001-11-15..	NULL	4	Active	4	Kennson	David	1996-03-16..	1	11	Has Tenure
9	9	Newton	James	2003-09-30..	2	3	Active	3	Osako	Lee	1999-09-01..	2	11	Active
10	10	O'Haire	Terry	2004-10-04..	2	3	Active	3	Osako	Lee	1999-09-01..	2	11	Active
11	12	O'Neil	Barbara	1995-05-26..	4	4	Has Tenure	4	Kennson	David	1996-03-16..	1	11	Has Tenure
12	13	Wilconkinski	Phil	2009-06-11..	1	4	Active	4	Kennson	David	1996-03-16..	1	11	Has Tenure

Query executed successfully.   RENO (11.0 RTM)   Reno\Student (51)   JProCo   00:00:00   12 rows

Figure 11.8 The self-join brings in our expected result, along with several extra columns to the right.

Figure 11.8 shows all the fields from the Employee table plus all the fields again from the employee table for each employee's boss. To clean up the result let's look at all the fields from Employee (emp) table and just the EmpID, FirstName, and LastName from the Employee boss table. We are keeping the query logic the same but changing the field SELECT list to show all emp fields and just three fields from the boss table alias.

```
SELECT emp.*, boss.EmpID, boss.FirstName, boss.LastName
FROM Employee emp
INNER JOIN Employee boss
ON emp.ManagerID = boss.EmpID
```

	EmpID	LastName	FirstName	HireDate	LocationID	ManagerID	Status	EmpID	FirstName	LastName
1	1	Adams	Alex	2001-01-01...	1	11	Active	11	Sally	Smith
2	2	Brown	Barry	2002-08-12...	1	11	Active	11	Sally	Smith
3	3	Osako	Lee	1999-09-01...	2	11	Active	11	Sally	Smith
4	4	Kennson	David	1996-03-16...	1	11	Has Tenure	11	Sally	Smith
5	5	Bender	Eric	2007-05-17...	1	11	Active	11	Sally	Smith
6	6	Kendall	Lisa	2001-11-15...	4	4	Active	4	David	Kennson

Query executed successfully.   RENO (11.0 RTM)   Reno\Student (51)   JProCo   00:00:00   12 rows

Figure 11.9 With the extra columns removed, our result is identical to our first query (Figure 11.5)

By giving the same table with two different aliases such as emp and boss it allows the table to be joined to itself. Returning hierarchical data is commonly done by joining a table to itself. Joining a table to itself to see a hierarchical relationship is called a self-join.

Lab 11.1: Self-Join Hierarchies

Lab Prep: Each lab has one or more Skill Checks. Start with Skill Check 1 and proceed until reaching the Points to Ponder section.

Before beginning this lab, verify that SQL Server 2012 is properly installed and operating. Before running the lab setup script for resetting the database (SQLQueries2012Vol2Chapter11.1Setup.sql), please make sure to close all query windows within SSMS. An open query window pointing to a database context can lock that database preventing it from updating when the script is executing. A simple way to assure all query windows are closed, is to exit out of SSMS, then open a new instance of SSMS, and lastly run the setup script.

Skill Check 1: In JProCo join the Employee table to itself and just show each employee's EmpID, FirstName and LastName. Show each boss's first and last name as an expression field called *BossFullName*. The expression field should have a space in the middle. Also make sure to use the right type of outer join so that Sally Smith appears, even though she has no boss. When you are done, your result should resemble Figure 11.10.

	EmpID	FirstName	LastName	BossFullName
1	1	Alex	Adams	Sally Smith
2	2	Barry	Brown	Sally Smith
3	3	Lee	Osako	Sally Smith
4	4	David	Kennson	Sally Smith
5	5	Eric	Bender	Sally Smith
6	6	Lisa	Kendall	David Kennson

13 rows

Figure 11.10 Skill Check 1 uses a self-join and adds the new expression field BossFullName.

Answer Code: The T-SQL code for this lab is located in the downloadable files as a file named Lab11.1_SelfJoins.sql.

Points to Ponder - Self-Join Hierarchies

1. Returning hierarchical data is commonly done by joining a table to itself.

2. Joining a table to itself to see a hierarchical relationship is called a self-join.

3. A self-join can be an INNER JOIN or OUTER JOIN and is therefore not really a new type of join, but just a way to use the joins you have already learned.

Range Hierarchies

Our next topic, range hierarchies, is a useful data technique but one that requires some set up before launching into code samples.

Recall me and my brothers comparing the heights in our immediate family. Each of us could easily see where we and the other family members were positioned in the Morelan "height hierarchy".

In our range hierarchy examples, we will be concerned with the "pecking order" of data compared to other surrounding data. A dictionary-style definition for hierarchy is "a graded or ranked series, as in a hierarchy of values". So instead of counting the levels of reporting between the CEO and individual contributors, we will look at how many levels of expensiveness exist between products and how many levels exist between the top grant and other grants. This concept is related to ranking but shows more detail than a simple ranking field.

Begin by simply looking at all the records of the Grant table, which we'll order to find the smallest amount on top and the largest amount on the bottom. We see 10 grants of varying amounts (Figure 11.11).

```
SELECT *
FROM [Grant]
ORDER BY Amount
```

	GrantID	GrantName	EmpID	Amount
1	001	92 Purr_Scents %% team	7	4750.00
2	010	Call Mom @Com	5	7500.00
3	002	K_Land fund trust	2	15750.00
4	003	Robert@BigStarBank.com	7	18100.00
5	006	TALTA_Kishan International	3	18100.00
6	004	Norman's Outreach	NULL	21000.00

10 rows

Figure 11.11 The Grant table sorted by smallest to largest grant amount.

In the Grant table (**Figure 11.11**), the first record we see is the smallest grant amount (the '92 Purr_Scents %% team' grant of $4750). The second smallest grant is from 'Call Mom @Com' in the amount of $7500.

The 'Call Mom @Com' grant is greater than just one grant, '92 Purr_Scents %% team'.

Our third record, the $15,750 grant from 'K_Land fund trust', has actually beaten out two other grants ('92 Purr_Scents %% team' and 'Call Mom @Com').

To see a ranking list for all the grants, we will create a range hierarchy which will reflect the comparisons we've just made verbally (Figure 11.13).

```
SELECT LgGr.GrantID, LgGr.GrantName AS LargerGrantName,
LgGr.EmpID, LgGr.Amount,
SmGr.GrantName AS SmallerGrantName, SmGr.Amount
FROM [Grant] AS LgGr
INNER JOIN [Grant] AS SmGr
ON LgGr.Amount > SmGr.Amount
ORDER BY LgGr.Amount
```

	GrantID	LargerGrantName	EmpID	Amount	SmallerGrantName	Amount	
1	010	Call Mom @Com	5	7500.00	92 Purr_Scents %% team	4750.00	
2	002	K_Land fund trust	2	15750.00	92 Purr_Scents %% team	4750.00	
3	002	K_Land fund trust	2	15750.00	Call Mom @Com	7500.00	
4	003	Robert@BigStarBank.com	7	18100.00	92 Purr_Scents %% team	4750.00	
5	003	Robert@BigStarBank.com	7	18100.00	K_Land fund trust	15750.00	
6	003	Robert@BigStarBank.com	7	18100.00	Call Mom @Com	7500.00	
7	006	TALTA_Kishan International	3	18100.00	92 Purr_Scents %% team	4750.00	
8	006	TALTA_Kishan International	3	18100.00	K_Land fund trust	15750.00	

Query executed successfully.   RENO (11.0 RTM)   Reno\Student (51)   JProCo   00:00:00   43 rows

Figure 11.12 A preview of the range hierarchy comparing all grants from the Grant table.

	GrantID	LargerGrantName	EmpID	Amount	SmallerGrantName	Amount	
1	010	Call Mom @Com	5	7500.00	92 Purr_Scents %% team	4750.00	
2	002	K_Land fund trust	2	15750.00	92 Purr_Scents %% team	4750.00	
3	002	K_Land fund trust	2	15750.00	Call Mom @Com	7500.00	
4	003	Robert@BigStarBank.com		18100.00	92 Purr_Scents %% team	4750.00	
5	003	Robert@BigStarBank.com	7	18100.00	K_Land fund trust	15750.00	
6	003	Robert@BigStarBank.com	7	18100.00	Call Mom @Com	7500.00	
7	006	TALTA_Kishan International	3	18100.00	92 Purr_Scents %% team	4750.00	
8	006	TALTA_Kishan International	3	18100.00	K_Land fund trust	15750.00	

Query executed successfully.   RENO (11.0 RTM)   Reno\Student (51)   JProCo   00:00:00   43 rows

Figure 11.13 The hierarchy displays each grant alongside every grant of a lesser amount.

Each grant in the right hand column (*SmallerGrantName*) has an amount smaller than the corresponding grant listed three columns to the left of it.

For example, 'Robert@BigStarBank.com' is listed in *LargerGrantName* three times because there are three grants smaller than the 'Robert@BigStarBank.com' amount ('92 Purr_Scents %% team', 'K_Land fund trust', and 'Call Mom @Com as seen in **Figure 11.12**, **Figure 11.13**).

Notice the grant with the smallest amount ('92 Purr_Scents %% team') is the only grant which doesn't appear in the left side of the result. It is the smallest value listed in the *SmallerGrantName* field.

As we proceed down the result list, we see each of the larger grants listed more times successively – one instance (one row) for each grant it finds that is smaller than itself.

Now that we have an idea of what the result does, let's write the code for this range comparison hierarchy.

We know we need a self-join and don't want any ambiguities. So we'll alias the tables right from the start. The instance of the Grant table in the upper code will show only the comparatively larger grants (LgGr) (Figure 11.14). Thus, '92 Purr_Scents %% team' ($4750) will not show up because it is the smallest grant. Put another way, it is not larger than any grant, so it won't be shown by the "larger grants" table.

```
SELECT *
FROM [Grant] LgGr --Larger Grants

SELECT *
FROM [Grant] SmGr --Smaller Grants
```

Figure 11.14 The beginning of our range hierarchy query. We alias the tables right from the start.

We will connect to the Grant table using an INNER JOIN, comparing the larger grant amounts (LgGr) to the smaller grant amounts (SmGr). We can accomplish this by using a greater than operator '>' instead of the equals to operator '=' that we typically use in the ON clause when joining tables together. Since LgGr is the left table, each row will list its fields first and when it finds a smaller record in the SmGr table, it places this record on the right-hand side of the same row.

In **Figure 11.15**, we see the join and the ON clause to accomplish these tasks.

```
SELECT LgGr.*, SmGr.GrantName, SmGr.Amount
FROM [Grant] AS LgGr
INNER JOIN [Grant] AS SmGr
ON LgGr.Amount > SmGr.Amount
ORDER BY LgGr.Amount
```

	GrantID	GrantName	EmpID	Amount	GrantName	Amount	
1	010	Call Mom @Com	5	7500.00	92 Purr_Scents %% team	4750.00	
2	002	K_Land fund trust	2	15750.00	92 Purr_Scents %% team	4750.00	
3	002	K_Land fund trust	2	15750.00	Call Mom @Com	7500.00	
4	003	Robert@BigStarBank.com	7	18100.00	92 Purr_Scents %% team	4750.00	
5	003	Robert@BigStarBank.com	7	18100.00	K_Land fund trust	15750.00	
6	003	Robert@BigStarBank.com	7	18100.00	Call Mom @Com	7500.00	

Query executed successfully.   RENO (11.0 RTM)   Reno\Student (51)   JProCo   00:00:00   43 rows

Figure 11.15 The basic code for our range comparison hierarchy.

Finally, we'll modify our code to remove unneeded fields brought in by SmGr. We'll also invest the extra keystrokes to alias the identical GrantName columns and help the readability of our report (**Figure 11.16**).

```
SELECT LgGr.GrantID, LgGr.GrantName AS LargerGrantName,
LgGr.EmpID, LgGr.Amount,
SmGr.GrantName AS SmallerGrantName, SmGr.Amount
FROM [Grant] AS LgGr
INNER JOIN [Grant] AS SmGr
ON LgGr.Amount > SmGr.Amount
ORDER BY LgGr.Amount
```

	GrantID	LargerGrantName	EmpID	Amount	SmallerGrantName	Amount	
1	010	Call Mom @Com	5	7500.00	92 Purr_Scents %% team	4750.00	
2	002	K_Land fund trust	2	15750.00	92 Purr_Scents %% team	4750.00	
3	002	K_Land fund trust	2	15750.00	Call Mom @Com	7500.00	
4	003	Robert@BigStarBank.com	7	18100.00	92 Purr_Scents %% team	4750.00	
5	003	Robert@BigStarBank.com	7	18100.00	K_Land fund trust	15750.00	
6	003	Robert@BigStarBank.com	7	18100.00	Call Mom @Com	7500.00	
7	006	TALTA_Kishan International	3	18100.00	92 Purr_Scents %% team	4750.00	
8	006	TALTA_Kishan International	3	18100.00	K_Land fund trust	15750.00	

Query executed successfully.   RENO (11.0 RTM)   Reno\Student (51)   JProCo   00:00:00   43 rows

Figure 11.16 Remove unneeded fields from SmGr, and alias the main columns for readability.

Let's run another example of a range hierarchy, but this time let's see how it works with criteria. This query is going to show us the most affordable or cheapest item in our CurrentProducts table followed by the second cheapest item, the third cheapest and so on (**Figure 11.17**).

```
SELECT *
FROM CurrentProducts AS scp
WHERE Category = 'No-Stay'
ORDER BY scp.RetailPrice
```

	ProductID	ProductName	RetailPrice	Origination...	ToBeDeleted	Category
1	313	Cherry Festival Tour 1 Day Mexico	31.909	2007-04-11...	0	No-Stay
2	145	Mountain Lodge 1 Day Scandinavia	32.574	2012-01-04...	0	No-Stay
3	73	Ocean Cruise Tour 1 Day Mexico	32.601	2010-01-01...	0	No-Stay
4	265	Winter Tour 1 Day Scandinavia	34.506	2011-03-06...	0	No-Stay
5	319	Cherry Festival Tour 1 Day Canada	34.944	2009-07-02...	0	No-Stay
6	421	Snow Ski Tour 1 Day West Coast	35.308	2008-11-18...	0	No-Stay

Query executed successfully.   RENO (11.0 RTM)   Reno\Student (51)   JProCo   00:00:00   80 rows

Figure 11.17 Our comparison will focus on the small category products (scp) of CurrentProducts.

Not surprisingly, the items in the No-Stay category are generally the cheapest because they are all one day trips. The other categories include medium or long trips and tend to be more expensive (i.e., because of the overnight stays).

So we want to use just the No-Stay trips as our comparison standard. Instead of ranking the comparative expensiveness of all 483 records, we're going to limit that down to compare just the 80 No-Stay products. We've aliased the left table scp for "small category products" and filtered it to include just the No-Stay category (WHERE scp.Category = 'No-Stay') (**Figure 11.17**).

Recall the goal of our result is to show the least expensive trip, followed by the second least expensive item and so forth. In **Figure 11.18**, we see the right hand table acp, which includes "all category products". You might wonder why we don't limit the comparison to No-Stay versus No-Stay prices. Notice that some overnight stay trips are actually cheaper than some No-Stay products. So we want these trips to be included in our result.

```
SELECT *
FROM CurrentProducts AS acp
ORDER BY acp.RetailPrice
```

Figure 11.18 The right hand comparison table will be all category products (acp).

Now let's write the code to build our range hierarchy. Our query will connect the left table (scp) with the right table (acp) using an inner join. The task we want our ON clause to accomplish is to look row by row for any values in acp (right table) that are less expensive than the RetailPrice in scp (left table seen in **Figure 11.19**).

```
SELECT *
FROM CurrentProducts scp
INNER JOIN CurrentProducts acp
ON scp.RetailPrice > acp.RetailPrice
WHERE scp.Category = 'No-Stay'
ORDER BY scp.RetailPrice, acp.RetailPrice
```

Figure 11.19 Our ON clause checks acp.RetailPrice for values less expensive than scp.RetailPrice.

Revise the query to remove extra fields and show just product name and price. We'll also alias our field names to enhance the readability of our report (**Figure 11.20**).

The "Cherry Festival Tour 1 Day Mexico ($31.909)" is the cheapest trip JProCo offers. We can see the second cheapest is the Mountain Lodge trip ($32.574), which is only slightly more expensive than the Cherry Festival at $31.909 (**Figure 11.20**).

```
SELECT scp.productName AS CheapProductName, scp.RetailPrice,
acp.ProductName AS ProductName, acp.RetailPrice
FROM CurrentProducts scp
INNER JOIN CurrentProducts acp
ON scp.RetailPrice > acp.RetailPrice
```

```
WHERE scp.Category = 'No-Stay'
ORDER BY scp.RetailPrice, acp.RetailPrice
```

	CheapProductName	RetailPrice	ProductName	RetailPrice
1	Mountain Lodge 1 Day Scandinavia	32.574 →	Cherry Festival Tour 1 Day Mexico	31.909
2	Ocean Cruise Tour 1 Day Mexico	32.601 →	Cherry Festival Tour 1 Day Mexico	31.909
3	Ocean Cruise Tour 1 Day Mexico	32.601	Mountain Lodge 1 Day Scandinavia	32.574
4	Winter Tour 1 Day Scandinavia	34.506 →	Cherry Festival Tour 1 Day Mexico	31.909
5	Winter Tour 1 Day Scandinavia	34.506	Mountain Lodge 1 Day Scandinavia	32.574
6	Winter Tour 1 Day Scandinavia	34.506	Ocean Cruise Tour 1 Day Mexico	32.601

Query executed successfully.   RENO (11.0 RTM)   Reno\Student (51)   master   00:00:00   4261 rows

Figure 11.20 Our range hierarchy marked to show the activity of each field in scp.RetailPrice.

The Ocean Cruise is more expensive than two items, the Mountain Lodge and the Cherry Festival. The Winter Tour shows three records on the scp (*SmallProductName*) side of the table, so it is more expensive than 3 items (Ocean Cruise, Mountain Lodge, Cherry Festival seen in **Figure 11.20**).

Recall we didn't limit the category to 'No-Stay' for both tables. Scroll through the record set and notice that some of the overnight trips are cheaper than the high end one day trips (**Figure 11.20** and **Figure 11.21**).

For example, of the 25 trips cheaper than Ocean Cruise Tour 1 Day East Coast ($61.86), three of them are 2 day trips (Cherry Festival 2 Days Mexico ($57.43), Mountain Lodge 2 Days Scandinavia ($58.63), and Ocean Cruise Tour 2 Days Mexico ($58.68). In **Figure 11.21**, we limit the query to show just 'No-Stay' products from the first table and all the products that are cheaper than them.

```
SELECT scp.productName AS CheapProductName,
scp.RetailPrice, acp.ProductName AS ProductName,
acp.RetailPrice
FROM CurrentProducts scp
INNER JOIN CurrentProducts acp
ON scp.RetailPrice > acp.RetailPrice
WHERE scp.Category = 'No-Stay'
ORDER BY scp.RetailPrice, acp.RetailPrice
```

Figure 11.21 Some 2 day trips are cheaper than 1 day trips.

In this example, we want to find all 'No-Stay' Products that are more expensive than any of the trips that require at least one night stay. To find the longer trips, we are looking for the cheaper products that are not equal to 'No-Stay'. To see just the unique patterns, use the DISTINCT keyword in your select, as seen in **Figure 11.22**.

```
SELECT DISTINCT acp.ProductName AS CheapProductName,
acp.RetailPrice
FROM CurrentProducts scp
INNER JOIN CurrentProducts acp
ON scp.RetailPrice > acp.RetailPrice
WHERE scp.Category = 'No-Stay'
AND acp.Category != 'No-Stay'
```

Figure 11.22 Our query modified to show the 43 multi-day trips cheaper than No-Stay trips

Lab 11.2: Range Hierarchies

Lab Prep: Each lab has one or more Skill Checks. Start with Skill Check 1 and proceed until reaching the Points to Ponder section.

Before beginning this lab, verify that SQL Server 2012 is properly installed and operating. Before running the lab setup script for resetting the database (SQLQueries2012Vol2Chapter11.2Setup.sql), please make sure to close all query windows within SSMS. An open query window pointing to a database context can lock that database preventing it from updating when the script is executing. A simple way to assure all query windows are closed, is to exit out of SSMS, then open a new instance of SSMS, and lastly run the setup script.

Skill Check 1: From the Employee table in JProCo write a query to see employee # 3 (Lee Osako) and all the people who were hired after him. Show just the FirstName, LastName and HireDate from both tables in the join. Make the fourth field an expression field that says "Was hired before". When you're done, your result will look like the figure you see here (Figure 11.23).

	FirstName	LastName	HireDate	Note	FirstName	LastName	HireDate	
1	Lee	Osako	1999-09-01...	Was hired before	Alex	Adams	2001-01-01 ...	
2	Lee	Osako	1999-09-01...	Was hired before	Barry	Brown	2002-08-12 ...	
3	Lee	Osako	1999-09-01...	Was hired before	Eric	Bender	2007-05-17 ...	
4	Lee	Osako	1999-09-01...	Was hired before	Lisa	Kendall	2001-11-15 ...	
5	Lee	Osako	1999-09-01...	Was hired before	David	Lonning	2000-01-01 ...	
6	Lee	Osako	1999-09-01...	Was hired before	John	Marshbank	2001-11-15 ...	

Query executed successfully. RENO (11.0 RTM) Reno\Student (51) JProCo 00:00:00 9 rows

Figure 11.23 Skill Check 1 uses a self-join of the Employee table.

Skill Check 2: In dbBasics, use the Military table to write a range hierarchy showing the highest Army GradeRank and all the GradeRanks which are below Colonel. When you're done, your result will look like Figure 11.24.

	GradeRank	GradeName	Note	GradeRank	GradeName	
1	8	Colonel	OUTRANKS	1	Private	
2	8	Colonel	OUTRANKS	2	Specialist	
3	8	Colonel	OUTRANKS	2	Corporal	
4	8	Colonel	OUTRANKS	3	Sergeant	
5	8	Colonel	OUTRANKS	4	Master Sergeant	
6	8	Colonel	OUTRANKS	4	First Sergeant	

Query executed successfully. RENO (11.0 RTM) Reno\Student (51) dbBasics 00:00:00 9 rows

Figure 11.24 Skill Check 2 uses a self-join of the Military table in the dbBasics database.

Answer Code: The T-SQL code for this lab is located in the downloadable files as a file named Lab11.2_RangeHierarchies.sql.

Recursive Queries

Now that we've seen some hierarchical examples, we are ready to bring in the power of the CTE. Recursive queries are not a new concept, but thanks to the invention of the CTE they are much easier to use and to write. A recursive CTE repeatedly executes in order to return as many subsets of data you need. The CTE's ability to reference itself makes it a powerhouse for recursive iterations.

Begin with a SELECT statement showing all JProCo employees (**Figure 11.25**).

```
SELECT EmpID, FirstName, LastName, ManagerID
FROM Employee
```

	EmpID	FirstName	LastName	ManagerID
1	1	Alex	Adams	11
2	2	Barry	Brown	11
3	3	Lee	Osako	11
4	4	David	Kennson	11
5	5	Eric	Bender	11
6	6	Lisa	Kendall	4
				13 rows

Figure 11.25 All JProCo employees including EmpID, FirstName, LastName, and ManagerID.

As we did with range hierarchies, it will help us to look ahead to our end goal before beginning to write code (**Figure 11.26**).

	EmpID	FirstName	LastName	ManagerID	EmpLevel
1	11	Sally	Smith	NULL	1
2	1	Alex	Adams	11	2
3	2	Barry	Brown	11	2
4	3	Lee	Osako	11	2
5	4	David	Kennson	11	2
6	5	Eric	Bender	11	2
					13 rows

Figure 11.26 Our end goal is to show the hierarchy level for each person in the Employee table.

Sally Smith is at the top level of our hierarchy, because she doesn't report to anyone. David Kennson, who reports directly to the top person, is at the second level. Lisa Kendall reports to David Kennson, so Lisa is at the third hierarchy level. We need a query which will put each employee's level number right next to the ManagerID (Figure 11.26).

Let's begin by changing our first query so it shows only the top person. The top person has no ManagerID, so we'll add the clause "WHERE ManagerID IS NULL". Alias the Employee table as 'boss' and fully qualify every field. This is our query for everyone at the top level (Figure 11.27).

```
SELECT boss.EmpID, boss.FirstName, boss.LastName, boss.ManagerID
FROM Employee AS boss
WHERE boss.ManagerID IS NULL
```

Figure 11.27 Alias the Employee table as boss and fully qualify every field.

Next we want a query for everyone not at the first level. Paste in another copy of our first query, alias the Employee table as "Emp", and add the clause "WHERE ManagerID IS NOT NULL". Now run both queries (**Figure 11.28**).

```
SELECT boss.EmpID, boss.FirstName, boss.LastName,
boss.ManagerID
FROM Employee AS boss
WHERE boss.ManagerID IS NULL

SELECT emp.EmpID, emp.FirstName, emp.LastName, emp.ManagerID
FROM Employee AS emp
WHERE emp.ManagerID IS NOT NULL
```

	EmpID	FirstName	LastName	ManagerID
1	11	Sally	Smith	NULL

	EmpID	FirstName	LastName	ManagerID
1	1	Alex	Adams	11
2	2	Barry	Brown	11
3	3	Lee	Osako	11
4	4	David	Kennson	11
5	5	Eric	Bender	11
6	6	Lisa	Kendall	4

13 rows

Figure 11.28 Alias the Employee table as emp, and add "WHERE ManagerID IS NOT NULL".

Examine the WHERE clauses. The first query shows just the top boss. The second query shows everyone else (12 people who are not at the top level).

Now let's add UNION ALL to stack both queries together (**Figure 11.29**).

```
SELECT boss.EmpID, boss.FirstName, boss.LastName,
boss.ManagerID
FROM Employee AS boss
WHERE boss.ManagerID IS NULL

UNION ALL

SELECT emp.EmpID, emp.FirstName, emp.LastName, emp.ManagerID
FROM Employee AS emp
WHERE emp.ManagerID IS NOT NULL
```

	EmpID	FirstName	LastName	ManagerID
1	11	Sally	Smith	NULL
2	1	Alex	Adams	11
3	2	Barry	Brown	11
4	3	Lee	Osako	11
5	4	David	Kennson	11
6	5	Eric	Bender	11

13 rows

Figure 11.29 Add UNION ALL to stack both queries together.

Compare this result with Figure 11.26 and notice that we have the same result as our original query. We could have done that with a single SELECT, but there's a benefit associated with stacking these in a UNION ALL. We can now easily transform this UNION-ed query into a CTE. Recursive CTEs require a UNION ALL to connect the final two queries. Here we have just two queries.

Begin transforming this entire query (as shown in **Figure 11.29**) into a CTE by putting parentheses around the entire UNION-ed query, indenting it, moving it down and adding the declaration WITH EmployeeList AS. Then add SELECT * FROM EmployeeList (**Figure 11.30**).

```
WITH EmployeeList AS (
SELECT boss.EmpID, boss.FirstName, boss.LastName,
boss.ManagerID
FROM Employee AS boss
WHERE boss.ManagerID IS NULL

UNION ALL

SELECT emp.EmpID, emp.FirstName, emp.LastName, emp.ManagerID
FROM Employee AS emp
WHERE emp.ManagerID IS NOT NULL)

SELECT * FROM EmployeeList
```

	EmpID	FirstName	LastName	ManagerID	
1	11	Sally	Smith	NULL	
2	1	Alex	Adams	11	
3	2	Barry	Brown	11	
4	3	Lee	Osako	11	
5	4	David	Kennson	11	
6	5	Eric	Bender	11	
					13 rows

Figure 11.30 All the employees are contained in the CTE EmployeeList.

Now we've got all our employees in the CTE. As in Figure 11.30, the first SELECT statement ("boss") inside the CTE represents everyone at Level 1 (i.e., Sally Smith). The second SELECT statement ("emp") represents everyone at Levels 2 and 3.

Add the expression "1 AS EmpLevel" to the top query. Then add "2 AS EmpLevel" in the bottom query (**Figure 11.31**). Before executing the entire query, look closely at the expression field, EmpLevel. The first expression will hard-code the numeral 1 for Sally Smith's level. Everyone else will receive a hard-coded 2 in this step. Now run all the code (**Figure 11.31**).

```
WITH EmployeeList AS (
SELECT boss.EmpID, boss.FirstName, boss.LastName,
boss.ManagerID, 1 AS EmpLevel
FROM Employee AS boss
WHERE boss.ManagerID IS NULL

UNION ALL

SELECT emp.EmpID, emp.FirstName, emp.LastName,
emp.ManagerID, 2 AS EmpLevel
FROM Employee AS emp
WHERE emp.ManagerID IS NOT NULL)

SELECT * FROM EmployeeList
```

	EmpID	FirstName	LastName	ManagerID	EmpLevel
1	11	Sally	Smith	NULL	1
2	1	Alex	Adams	11	2
3	2	Barry	Brown	11	2
4	3	Lee	Osako	11	2
5	4	David	Kennson	11	2
					13 rows

Figure 11.31 We've hardcoded the number 2 as a placeholder to help visualize our next step.

The two new expression fields were a helpful step. In fact, they show the correct EmpLevel information for Sally and for the people at Level 2 (i.e., Adams, Bender, Brown, Kennson, Osako).

However, the 2 is just a hard-coded placeholder to help us visualize our next step. Lisa Kendall and several other employees need to be at Level 3. What we would like to do is drop in "EmpLevel + 1" to replace "2 AS EmpLevel".

Let's take a moment and recognize why this is not going to work quite so simply. The idea to increment EmpLevel in the bottom half of the CTE is on the right track. But "EmpLevel + 1" in the bottom query is unable to reference an expression field which hasn't yet been materialized (i.e., the EmpLevel in the upper query). Thus, the bottom query will try to reference a field called EmpLevel but can't find one. There has been no field materialized as EmpLevel (**Figure 11.32**).

What we need to do is take this second query and join it to a table that has the EmpLevel field materialized. We can use the CTE for this! (**Figure 11.33**)

```
WITH EmployeeList AS (
SELECT boss.EmpID, boss.FirstName, boss.LastName,
boss.ManagerID, 1 AS EmpLevel
FROM Employee AS boss
WHERE boss.ManagerID IS NULL

UNION ALL

SELECT emp.EmpID, emp.FirstName, emp.LastName,
emp.ManagerID, EmpLevel + 1
FROM Employee AS emp
WHERE emp.ManagerID IS NOT NULL)
SELECT * FROM EmployeeList
```

Messages
Msg 207, Level 16, State 1, Line 6
Invalid column name 'EmpLevel'.
0 rows

Figure 11.32 The bottom query tries to reference a field defined as EmpLevel but can't find one.

```
WITH EmployeeList AS (
SELECT boss.EmpID, boss.FirstName, boss.LastName,
boss.ManagerID, 1 AS EmpLevel
FROM Employee AS boss
WHERE boss.ManagerID IS NULL
```

```
UNION ALL
SELECT emp.EmpID, emp.FirstName, emp.LastName,
emp.ManagerID, EmpLevel + 1
FROM Employee AS emp INNER JOIN EmployeeList AS el
ON emp.ManagerID = el.EmpID
WHERE emp.ManagerID IS NOT NULL)

SELECT * FROM EmployeeList
```

	EmpID	FirstName	LastName	ManagerID	EmpLevel
1	11	Sally	Smith	NULL	1
2	1	Alex	Adams	11	2
3	2	Barry	Brown	11	2
4	3	Lee	Osako	11	2
5	4	David	Kennson	11	2
6	5	Eric	Bender	11	2
	7	David	Lonning	11	2
	6	Lisa	Kendall	4	3
	8	John	Marshbank	4	3
	12	Barbara	O'Neil	4	3
	13	Phil	Wilconkinski	4	3
	9	James	Newton	3	3
	10	Terry	O'Haire	3	3

13 rows

Figure 11.33 Our final recursive CTE successfully shows all hierarchy levels.

Success! Sally is at the first level, Alex is at the second level, Lisa appears at the third level. Since a CTE can reference itself, the 'emp' query now can access the EmpLevel field materialized in EmployeeList.

Notice that the code in **Figure 11.33** joins the 'emp' query to the EmployeeList, which was declared by the CTE at the top of our code.

With the EmpLevel field now accessible, the magic of recursion can take place.

Let's quickly recap the recursion process. Recall our step in **Figure 11.31**, where the value 2 was just a hard-coded placeholder to help us visualize our next step. Sally's level, however, remained hard-coded as 1 throughout the entire process.

The expression "1 AS EmpLevel" seeded the first EmpLevel value at 1. In this recursive CTE, the technical term for Sally is the "anchor member". Anchor members are defined in the top query (or queries) of the recursive CTE. They join to the next set of members using UNION, UNION ALL, INTERSECT, or EXCEPT. Recursive members are ones like the 'emp' query, which reference the

CTE in order to increment. Just like in our CTE, a UNION ALL must be used to join an anchor member query to a recursive member query.

"EmpLevel + 1" incremented each EmpLevel value to 2 for all 12 records in the Emp query. Then the INNER JOIN to the CTE (EmployeeList) causes a special recursive step (or iteration) for those employees managed by David Kennson or Lee Osako.

```
INNER JOIN EmployeeList AS el
ON emp.ManagerID = el.EmpID
```

The INNER JOIN finds just six records to join to the 'emp' query (Kendall, Marshbank, Newton, O'Haire, O'Neil and Wilconkinski). The ManagerID for those six employees is ManagerID 3 or ManagerID 4.

The other six individuals (Adams, Brown, Osako, Kennson, Bender and Lonning) each have ManagerID 11, so there is no matching el.EmpID value to join on.

Where the INNER JOIN found an available record, it incremented each EmpLevel value by 1. Those records showed EmpLevel 2 before the INNER JOIN, and after the iteration they receive an EmpLevel of 3.

Points to Ponder - Range Hierarchies

1. The ON clause of your query can use many types of operators, such as:
   - o '=' Exact match
   - o '>' Greater than but not equal to
   - o '<' Less than but not equal to
   - o '!=' Not equal to (every value but…)

2. If there is more than one match in the join, then you will get more records in the result set than the original table.

3. By using a '<' or '>' operator, we can show all results that compare to a particular record.

Lab 11.3: Recursive Queries

Lab Prep: Each lab has one or more Skill Checks. Start with Skill Check 1 and proceed until reaching the Points to Ponder section.

Before beginning this lab, verify that SQL Server 2012 is properly installed and operating. Before running the lab setup script for resetting the database (SQLQueries2012Vol2Chapter11.3Setup.sql), please make sure to close all query windows within SSMS. An open query window pointing to a database context can lock that database preventing it from updating when the script is executing. A simple way to assure all query windows are closed, is to exit out of SSMS, then open a new instance of SSMS, and lastly run the setup script.

Skill Check 1: Change the last query (Figure 11.33) so that you only measure everyone's level of distance from the CEO. For example Alex works directly for Sally, so he is just one level away from the root level of Sally Smith. She is the CEO, so her RootOffset would be zero. Modify the CTE query so that the highest level is 0 and the field is called RootOffset. When you're done, your result will resemble Figure 11.34

	EmpID	FirstName	LastName	ManagerID	RootOffset
1	11	Sally	Smith	NULL	0
2	1	Alex	Adams	11	1
3	2	Barry	Brown	11	1
4	3	Lee	Osako	11	1
5	4	David	Kennson	11	1
6	5	Eric	Bender	11	1
7	7	David	Lonning	11	1
8	6	Lisa	Kendall	4	2
9	8	John	Marshbank	4	2
10	12	Barbara	O'Neil	4	2
11	13	Phil	Wilconkinski	4	2

13 rows

Figure 11.34 You must modify the recursive CTE from our last example to show RootOffset.

Answer Code: The T-SQL code for this lab is located in the downloadable files as a file named Lab11.3_RecursiveQueries.sql.

Points to Ponder - Recursive Queries

1. CTE stands for Common Table Expression.

2. A Common Table Expression is similar to a derived table, but the syntax is different. The code for the CTE is generally more readable than that for a derived table. It puts the name at the beginning of the code with a declaration statement (WITH *CTE_Name* AS) instead of aliasing within the main body of the code.

3. A Common Table Expression is similar to a temp table, but does not require a CREATE TABLE statement.

4. In SQL Server 2005, 2008 and 2012, the CTE is a great way to create recursive queries.

5. Returning hierarchical data is a common use of recursive queries.

6. A recursive CTE repeatedly executes in order to return as many subsets of data you need.

Chapter Glossary

Data Recursion: The use of data in a function or process that calls upon itself to produce a result.

Hierarchical Data: Graded or ranked data.

Range Hierarchies: A data technique that ranks results as compared to other surrounding data.

Recursive Queries: A type of query that runs using the same table twice.

Self-join: A process of joining a table to itself.

Review Quiz - Chapter Eleven

1.)   You have an Employee table with the following data.

EmpID	FirstName	LastName	MgrID
1	David	Kennson	11
2	Eric	Bender	11
3	Lisa	Kendall	4
4	David	Lonning	11
5	John	Marshbank	4
6	James	Newton	3
7	Sally	Smith	NULL

You need to write a recursive CTE that shows the EmpID, FirstName, LastName, MgrID and employee level. The CEO should be listed at Level 1. All people who work for the CEO will be listed at level 2. All of the people who work for those people will be listed at level 3. Which CTE code will achieve this result?

O a.
```
WITH EmpList AS (
SELECT boss.EmpID, boss.FName, boss.LName, boss.MgrID,
1 AS lvl
FROM Employee AS Boss WHERE Boss.MgrID IS NULL
UNION ALL
SELECT e.EmpID, e.FirstName, e.LastName, e.MgrID,
empList.lvl + 1 FROM Employee AS e
INNER JOIN EmpList ON E.MgrID = empList.EmpID)
SELECT * FROM EmpList
```

O b.
```
WITH EmpList AS (
SELECT EmpID, FirstName, LastName, MgrID, 1 AS Lvl
FROM Employee WHERE MgrID IS NULL
UNION ALL
SELECT EmpID,  FirstName, LastName, MgrID, 2 AS Lvl)
SELECT * FROM bossList
```

O c.
```
WITH EmpList AS (
SELECT EmpID,  FirstName, LastName, MgrID, 1 AS Lvl
FROM Employee WHERE MgrID IS NOT NULL
UNION
SELECT EmpID, FirstName, LastName, MgrID, bossList.Lvl + 1
FROM Employee INNER JOIN EmpList BossList
ON Employee.MgrID = bossList.EmpID)
SELECT * FROM EmpList
```

2.) You must create an employee level report. Some employees are directly below the CEO and have a RootOffset of 1. Sally is the CEO, so there is no distance between her and the root level. Her RootOffset is 0 (zero). Some employees are up to 5 levels removed from the root. You must find all employees who are at least 3 levels removed from the CEO. The expression field for the level should be called RootOffset.

O a.
```
WITH EmpList AS (SELECT EmpID,  FirstName, LastName,
ReportsTo, 1 AS RootOffset
FROM Employee WHERE ReportsTo IS NULL
UNION ALL
SELECT EmpID,  FirstName, LastName, ReportsTo,
BossList.RootOffset + 1
FROM Employee INNER JOIN EmpList BossList
ON Employee.ReportsTo = BossList.EmpID)
```

O b.
```
SELECT * FROM EmpList WHERE RootOffset >= 3
WITH EmpList AS (SELECT a.EmpID, a.FirstName, a.LastName,
a.ReportsTo, 0 AS RootOffset
FROM Employee AS a WHERE ReportsTo IS NULL
UNION ALL
SELECT b.EmpID, b.FirstName, b.LastName, b.ReportsTo,
empList.RootOffset + 1
FROM Employee AS b INNER JOIN EmpList
ON b.ReportsTo = EmpList.EmpID)
SELECT * FROM EmpList WHERE RootOffset >= 3
```

O c.
```
WITH EmpList AS (SELECT EmpID,  FirstName, LastName,
ReportsTo, 0 AS RootOffset
FROM Employee WHERE ReportsTo IS NULL
UNION
SELECT EmpID,  FirstName, LastName, ReportsTo,
BossList.RootOffset + 1
FROM Employee INNER JOIN EmpList BossList
ON Employee.ReportsTo = BossList.EmpID)
SELECT * FROM EmpList WHERE RootOffset > 3
```

3.) What is a self-join?

O a. The same table is joined to itself in a query.

O b. Two identical tables from different databases are joined in a query.

O c. Two lookup tables are joined in a query.

4.) Your JProCo database has a table named Employee which has an EmpID for each record. There is also a field called ManagerID which lists the EmpID for the employee's manager. You want to write a self-join query to show the FirstName and LastName of each employee with the FirstName and LastName of the boss next to it. Even the CEO should appear in this query. A co-worker has written part of the query and has gotten stuck.

```
SELECT E.FirstName, E.LastName, B.FirstName, B.LastName
FROM Employee AS e
--PICK ANSWER CODE HERE
```

You need to write the rest of the query. What two lines of code would you add to complete this task?

O a.
```
LEFT JOIN Employee b
ON e.ManagerID = b.ManagerID
```

O b.
```
INNER JOIN Employee b
ON e.ManagerID = b.ManagerID
```

O c.
```
LEFT JOIN Employee b
ON e.ManagerID = b.EmpID
```

O d.
```
INNER JOIN Employee b
ON e.ManagerID = b.EmpID
```

5.) You have a table named Employee. The EmployeeID of each employee's manager is in the ManagerID column. You need to write a recursive query that produces a list of employees and their manager. The query must also include the employee's level in the hierarchy. You write the following code segment:

```
WITH EmployeeList (EmployeeID, FullName, ManagerName, Level)
AS --PICK ANSWER CODE HERE
```

You need to replace the comment "--PICK ANSWER CODE HERE" with what code below?

O a.
```
SELECT EmployeeID, FullName, '' AS [ManagerID],
1 AS [Level]
FROM Employee WHERE ManagerID IS NULL
UNION ALL
SELECT emp.EmployeeID, emp.FullName, mgr.FullName,
1 + 1 AS [Level]
FROM Employee emp JOIN Employee mgr
ON emp.ManagerID = mgr.EmployeeId
```

O b.
```
SELECT EmployeeID, FullName, '' AS [ManagerID],
1 AS [Level]
FROM Employee WHERE ManagerID IS NULL
UNION ALL
SELECT emp.EmployeeID, emp.FullName, mgr.FullName,
mgr.Level + 1
FROM EmployeeList mgr JOIN Employee emp
ON emp.ManagerID = mgr.EmployeeId
```

Answer Key

1.) The code is not even querying the implemented CTE in (b), so it is not correct. 'WHERE MgrID is NOT NULL' will cause 1 to be assigned to every employee's level except the CEO, so (c) is wrong too. To display a hierarchy or chain of command stored with data from one table, implement a CTE that contains a UNION ALL set operator, making sure 'WHERE MgrID IS NULL' is in the first query and the second query properly joins the same table to the CTE being implemented, as in (a), which is the correct answer.

2.) '1 as RootOffset' will be incorrectly assigned to Sally and everyone else's RootOffset will be wrong too, making (a) a wrong answer. Because 'WHERE RootOffset > 3' will not return the records at Level 3, (c) will be incorrect too. Since '0 AS RootOffset' is being assigned to Sally and the query using the CTE has 'WHERE RootOffset >= 3', (b) is the correct answer.

3.) Because neither 'joining tables from two different databases' nor 'joining two lookup tables' is considered a self-join, (b) and (c) are both incorrect. Since a self-join is when a table is joined to itself in a query, (a) is the correct answer.

4.) 'ON e.ManagerID = b.ManagerID' will result in multiple records for each employee with each record consisting of the employee name and either himself again or another employee in the company that has the same manager, making (a) an incorrect answer. Because an INNER JOIN will not return the employee whose ManagerID is NULL, (b) and (d) are also incorrect. Using a LEFT JOIN will ensure that the CEO (employee whose ManagerID is NULL) will be displayed and 'ON e.ManagerID = b.EmployeeID' will ensure that the second employee in each record is the manager and not another employee with the same manager, so (c) is the correct answer.

5.) The anchor query of both answers is right but the second query differs. Since 1+1 always equals 2, every employee below the CEO, no matter how far down the hierarchy, will get a level of 2, making (a) the wrong answer. Because the second query adds 1 to the level in the anchor query, (b) is the correct answer.

Bug Catcher Game

To play the Bug Catcher game, run the SQLQueries2012Vol2BugCatcher11.pps file from the BugCatcher folder of the companion files. These files are available from the www.Joes2Pros.com website.

[THIS PAGE INTENTIONALLY LEFT BLANK.]

Chapter 12. Using Subqueries

We got our first peek at subqueries in Chapter 6 when we worked on the interview question to get only the 5th highest record. In this chapter, we will work in depth with subqueries and see how they can help answer questions about our data.

My younger brother's wedding in 2006 was my first opportunity to go to Hawaii. Having never been there before, I asked my father how I should pack. He didn't tell me what to pack but did say to prepare for the beach, sun and summer like weather. And also to save room in my suitcase for beautiful things I would want to bring home to share with friends. He never specifically told me to pack goggles, snorkel, swim shorts, or sandals but from his list, I could tell what my final list should be. This is exactly what a subquery is. A list from one query determines what the other query should produce. Some subqueries are amazingly simple, and astute observers will discern that our early examples could all be accomplished using a simple join. In other cases, a subquery will be the only way to accomplish the goal.

It won't be an everyday occurrence in your SQL Server work, but there will be situations where a correlated subquery is the only tool that will accomplish a needed task. I encounter those situations about three or four times a year, and I hear similar anecdotes from my former students. You may hear warnings that subqueries are very poor for performance, and those warnings are often accurate for basic subqueries. However, when you work with larger tables, the correlated subquery usually outperforms other available solutions.

In this chapter we will also utilize the comparison operator modifiers ANY, ALL and SOME in our subqueries to see how one value compares to a list of other values.

READER NOTE: *Please run the SQLQueries2012Vol2Chapter12.0Setup.sql script in order to follow along with the examples in the first section of Chapter 12. All scripts mentioned in this chapter are available at www.Joes2Pros.com.*

Basic Subqueries

```
SELECT * FROM CurrentProducts
```

	ProductID	ProductName	RetailPrice	OriginationD...	ToBeDeleted	Category
1	1	Underwater Tour 1 Day W...	61.483	2009-05-07 ...	0	No-Stay
2	2	Underwater Tour 2 Days W...	110.6694	2010-06-29 ...	0	Overnight-Stay
3	3	Underwater Tour 3 Days W...	184.449	2012-02-03 ...	0	Medium-Stay
4	4	Underwater Tour 5 Days W...	245.932	2008-11-28 ...	0	Medium-Stay
5	5	Underwater Tour 1 Week ...	307.415	2004-04-13 ...	0	LongTerm-Stay
6	6	Underwater Tour 2 Weeks ...	553.347	2011-03-27 ...	1	LongTerm-Stay
7	7	Underwater Tour 1 Day Ea...	80.859	2010-01-01 ...	0	No-Stay

Query executed successfully. RENO (11.0 RTM) Reno\Student (51) JProCo 00:00:00 483 rows

Figure 12.1 JProCo currently has 483 products; some are more popular than others.

A simple query from our CurrentProducts table shows we have a total of 483 products (Figure 12.1). Some products are more popular than others. And we may even have some products that have never been sold. In the retail world, these non-selling products are called "no-move SKUs".

How many products in our list have never been sold? Let's look at the activity for all the products by running another query (Figure 12.2).

```
SELECT * FROM SalesInvoiceDetail
```

	InvoiceDetailID	InvoiceID	ProductID	Quantity	UnitDiscount
1	1	1	76	2	0.00
2	2	1	77	3	0.00
3	3	1	78	6	0.00
4	4	1	71	5	0.00
5	5	1	72	4	0.00
6	6	2	73	2	0.00

6960 rows

Figure 12.2 The SalesInvoiceDetail table shows the sales activity for all products.

It looks like there are a total of 6960 transactions – far more sales than we have products (recall the CurrentProducts table contains 483 products). So it looks like we have products which have been sold multiple times. Perhaps some products have moved once, and maybe some products have never moved. Each time a product appears in the SalesInvoiceDetail table, it represents a sale. Wherever a ProductID appears more than once, it means that product has sold again (Figure 12.3).

```
SELECT * FROM SalesInvoiceDetail
```

Figure 12.3 Wherever a ProductID appears more than once, this indicates it has sold again.

Several products have sold more than once. So instead of looking at repeating data, we'll put a DISTINCT in front of ProductID. And let's see how many different products have sold (Figure 12.4).

```
SELECT DISTINCT ProductID
FROM SalesInvoiceDetail
```

	ProductID
1	23
2	69
3	29
4	75
5	9
6	15
	60 rows

Figure 12.4 SELECT DISTINCT shows that just 60 different products have sold many times.

Surprisingly, it appears that we've sold only 60 different products. Since almost all our sales activity is focused within the same products (Figure 12.4), we want to see the list of products that have never sold. One approach might be to take our first query and paste the 60 ProductID values into the WHERE clause criteria (parentheses), which filters out the products which have sold (Figure 12.5).

```
SELECT *
FROM CurrentProducts
WHERE ProductID NOT IN (
23,69,15,72,26,49,29,75,9,52,78,66,32,12,63,
43,55,27,58,38,7,50,30,18,10,61,41,67,64,44,
47,70,65,73,62,42,22,76,33,53,45,25,36,56,59,
39,16,77,11,54,68,57,14,48,71,17,60,74,8,51)
```

	ProductID	ProductName	RetailPrice	Origination...	ToBeDeleted	Category
1	1	Underwater Tour 1 Day W...	61.483	2009-05-0...	0	No-Stay
2	2	Underwater Tour 2 Days ...	110.6694	2010-06-2...	0	Overnight-Stay
3	3	Underwater Tour 3 Days ...	184.449	2012-02-0...	0	Medium-Stay
4	4	Underwater Tour 5 Days ...	245.932	2008-11-2...	0	Medium-Stay
5	5	Underwater Tour 1 Week ...	307.415	2004-04-1...	0	LongTerm-Stay
6	6	Underwater Tour 2 Week...	553.347	2011-03-2...	1	LongTerm-Stay

Query executed successfully.   RENO (11.0 RTM)   Reno\Student (51)   JProCo   00:00:00   423 rows

Figure 12.5 Hard-coding the 60 sold ProductID values is tedious and makes our code inflexible.

The result is correct, but entering the 60 IDs is tedious. As well, our code is inflexible. If we needed to repeat this report next week, we would have to rerun the list of IDs for products which have sold and re-enter those into this query.

A subquery (a SELECT statement nested inside another T-SQL statement) would be far easier and will make our code reusable. We can put this entire list of 60 Product IDs into the WHERE clause criteria of the CurrentProducts query by nesting in the SalesInvoiceDetail query (Figure 12.6).

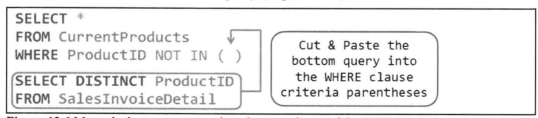

Figure 12.6 Move the bottom query up into the parentheses of the WHERE clause.

In the subquery construct, the CurrentProducts query is termed the outer query. The SELECT statement pulling from SalesInvoiceDetail is the subquery. When used in a WHERE clause, the subquery limits the number of records returned to the outer query (Figure 12.6).

```
SELECT *
FROM CurrentProducts
WHERE ProductID NOT IN (
  SELECT DISTINCT ProductID
  FROM SalesInvoiceDetail)
```

	ProductID	ProductName	RetailPrice	OriginationD...	ToBe...	Category	SupplierID
1	1	Underwater Tour 1 Day ...	61.483	2009-05-07...	0	No-Stay	0
2	2	Underwater Tour 2 Day...	110.6694	2010-06-29...	0	Overnigh...	0
3	3	Underwater Tour 3 Day...	184.449	2012-02-03...	0	Medium...	0
4	4	Underwater Tour 5 Day...	245.932	2008-11-28...	0	Medium...	0
5	5	Underwater Tour 1 We...	307.415	2004-04-13...	0	LongTer...	0
6	6	Underwater Tour 2 We...	553.347	2011-03-27...	1	LongTer...	0

Query executed successfully. | RENO (11.0 RTM) | Reno\Student (51) | JProCo | 00:00:00 | 423 rows

Figure 12.7 The 423 JProCo products which have never been sold.

Both Figure 12.5 and 12.7 achieve the same result. They both show the list of 423 products which have never been sold. And while the code may look different, both subqueries are feeding the same 60 ProductID values into the criteria of the outer queries.

Notice the SupplierIDs appearing in the last result (Figure 12.7). For products which JProCo creates, the SupplierID value shows as 0. JProCo also expands its customer offering with products created by external suppliers. The suppliers have licensed JProCo to resell their products to end customers. Query the Supplier table to see all available supplier information (Figure 12.8).

```
SELECT *
FROM Supplier
```

	SupplierID	SupplierName	ContactFullName
1	1	Stay Way Away and Save	Aaron Jeffries
2	2	LaVue Connect	Lou LaFleur
3	3	More Shores Amigo	Jose Cruz

3 rows

Figure 12.8 JProCo currently sources some products from three external suppliers.

JProCo currently has three external suppliers. Now let's see a list of the products which are supplied by LaVue Connect. We get all of our Canadian trips exclusively from LaVue, which is Supplier #2.

This single table query shows all of Supplier #2's products (Figure 12.9).

```
SELECT *
FROM CurrentProducts
WHERE SupplierID = 2
```

	ProductID	ProductName	RetailPrice	Origination...	To...	Category	SupplierID
1	19	Underwater Tour 1 D...	85.585	2007-01-13...	0	No-Stay	2
2	20	Underwater Tour 2 D...	154.053	2009-07-26...	0	Overnight-Stay	2
3	21	Underwater Tour 3 D...	256.755	2008-07-10...	0	Medium-Stay	2
4	22	Underwater Tour 5 D...	342.34	2004-05-12...	0	Medium-Stay	2
5	23	Underwater Tour 1 W...	427.925	2006-12-05...	0	LongTerm-Stay	2
6	24	Underwater Tour 2 W...	770.265	2010-09-14...	1	LongTerm-Stay	2
7	49	History Tour 1 Day Ca...	113.287	2010-01-04...	0	No-Stay	2

Query executed successfully. RENO (11.0 RTM) Reno\Student (51) JProCo 00:00:00 96 rows

Figure 12.9 A single table query showing products which JProCo has licensed from Supplier #2.

It appears that LaVue Connect currently supplies 96 Canadian trip products to JProCo (Figure 12.9).

With so few external suppliers, JProCo employees always refer to the suppliers by name (i.e., not by SupplierID). So do most reports. Let's modify our prior two queries to reference the Canadian supplier by name only (Figures 12.10-12.12).

```
SELECT SupplierID
FROM Supplier
WHERE SupplierName = 'LaVue Connect'
```

	SupplierID
1	2
	1 rows

Figure 12.10 A lookup query to find the SupplierID for the Canadian supplier, LaVue Connect.

```
SELECT *
FROM CurrentProducts
WHERE supplierID = ( )

SELECT SupplierID
FROM Supplier
WHERE SupplierName = 'LaVue Connect'
```

Cut & Paste the bottom query into the WHERE clause criteria parentheses

Figure 12.11 Move the bottom query up into the parentheses of the WHERE clause.

```
SELECT *
FROM CurrentProducts
WHERE SupplierID = (
  SELECT SupplierID
  FROM Supplier
  WHERE SupplierName = 'LaVue Connect')
```

	ProductID	ProductName	RetailPrice	Origination...	To...	Category	SupplierID
1	19	Underwater Tour 1 Day ...	85.585	2007-01-13...	0	No-Stay	2
2	20	Underwater Tour 2 Days...	154.053	2009-07-26...	0	Overnight-Stay	2
3	21	Underwater Tour 3 Days...	256.755	2008-07-10...	0	Medium-Stay	2
4	22	Underwater Tour 5 Days...	342.34	2004-05-12...	0	Medium-Stay	2
5	23	Underwater Tour 1 Wee...	427.925	2006-12-05...	0	LongTerm-Stay	2
6	24	Underwater Tour 2 Wee...	770.265	2010-09-14...	1	LongTerm-Stay	2

Query executed successfully.   RENO (11.0 RTM)   Reno\Student (51)   JProCo   00:00:00   96 rows

Figure 12.12 A subquery showing products which JProCo has licensed from LaVue Connect.

More than one approach is possible to replicate the result from Figure 12.9. We could have joined the CurrentProducts table to the Supplier table and then filtered on the supplier name LaVue Connect.

But the subquery fits nicely with our supplier example (Figure 12.12). This report would be easy to reuse, even by an employee who didn't know much T-SQL but could open a query, replace a supplier name, and run a query. In our premise, we said JProCo always refers to its suppliers by name. Our final query is an example of the outer query requiring the ID as an input value, but instead we prefer to enter the name. We supply LaVue Connect as criteria to the subquery, which then feeds the SupplierID (2) into the outer query.

Let's add one final variation before leaving this query. More Shores Amigo is the supplier of JProCo's Mexico trip offerings. Suppose an employee wanted to run this report to show all products supplied by both LaVue Connect and MSA (More Shores Amigo). The modified query appears in Figure 12.13.

The subquery feeds the SupplierIDs 2 and 3 into the outer query. Since the equal sign can only handle one value and the subquery might feed many values, we changed the operator in Figure 12.13 to IN. Figure 12.13 shows the 192 products supplied by LaVue Connect and MSA.

```
SELECT *
FROM CurrentProducts
WHERE SupplierID IN (
  SELECT SupplierID
  FROM Supplier
  WHERE SupplierName IN (
    'LaVue Connect', 'More Shores Amigo'))
ORDER BY SupplierID DESC
```

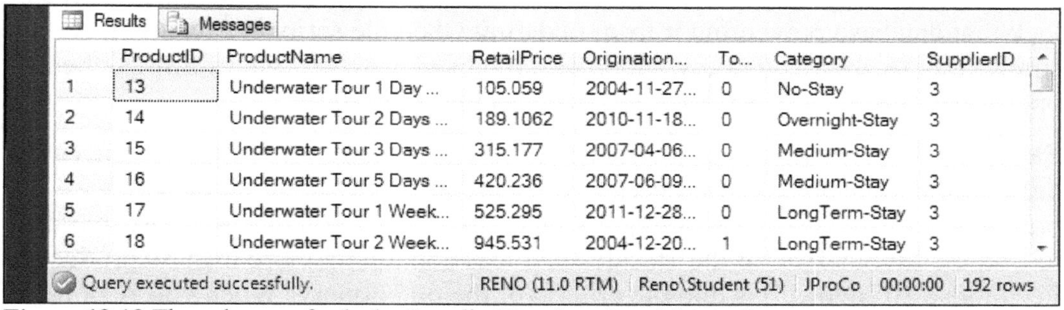

	ProductID	ProductName	RetailPrice	Origination...	To...	Category	SupplierID
1	13	Underwater Tour 1 Day ...	105.059	2004-11-27...	0	No-Stay	3
2	14	Underwater Tour 2 Days ...	189.1062	2010-11-18...	0	Overnight-Stay	3
3	15	Underwater Tour 3 Days ...	315.177	2007-04-06...	0	Medium-Stay	3
4	16	Underwater Tour 5 Days ...	420.236	2007-06-09...	0	Medium-Stay	3
5	17	Underwater Tour 1 Week...	525.295	2011-12-28...	0	LongTerm-Stay	3
6	18	Underwater Tour 2 Week...	945.531	2004-12-20...	1	LongTerm-Stay	3

Query executed successfully.　　RENO (11.0 RTM)　Reno\Student (51)　JProCo　00:00:00　192 rows

Figure 12.13 The subquery feeds the SupplierID values 2 and 3 into the outer query.

Lab 12.1: Basic Subqueries

Lab Prep: Each lab has one or more Skill Checks. Start with Skill Check 1 and proceed until reaching the Points to Ponder section.

Before beginning this lab, verify that SQL Server 2012 is properly installed and operating. Before running the lab setup script for resetting the database (SQLQueries2012Vol2Chapter12.1Setup.sql), please make sure to close all query windows within SSMS. An open query window pointing to a database context can lock that database preventing it from updating when the script is executing. A simple way to assure all query windows are closed, is to exit out of SSMS, then open a new instance of SSMS, and lastly run the setup script.

Skill Check 1: Some invoices are large orders with many products on them. In the SalesInvoice table, 10 of the 1877 sales invoices contain more than 30 products. Run an aggregated subquery using the SalesInvoiceDetail table in order to find the InvoiceIDs for the 10 sales invoices containing more than 30 products. Feed those 10 InvoiceIDs into the criteria of the outer query. When you're done, your result will resemble the figure you see here (Figure 12.14).

	InvoiceID	OrderDate	PaidDate	CustomerID	Comment
1	862	2010-12-08 05:46:37.720	2010-12-22 17:47:43.773	365	NULL
2	9	2009-01-08 21:46:03.093	2009-01-27 04:05:01.967	597	NULL
3	630	2010-06-03 21:26:17.397	2010-07-02 08:55:42.620	621	NULL
4	1091	2011-06-07 09:02:04.440	2011-06-19 14:10:20.427	339	NULL
5	1114	2011-06-23 12:24:39.973	2011-06-23 12:35:11.873	289	NULL
6	880	2010-12-22 01:59:09.067	2011-01-31 21:08:43.377	177	NULL

Query executed successfully.   RENO (11.0 RTM)   Reno\Student (51)   JProCo   00:00:00   10 rows

Figure 12.14 Skill Check 1 finds the 10 sales invoices containing more than 30 products.

Skill Check 2: Write a subquery which will feed EmpIDs into an outer query of the Employee table. Show the records for just those employees who have found grants. When you're done, your result should resemble Figure 12.15.

	EmpID	LastName	FirstName	HireDate	LocationID	ManagerID	Status
1	2	Brown	Barry	2002-08-12 00:00:00.000	1	11	Active
2	3	Osako	Lee	1999-09-01 00:00:00.000	2	11	Active
3	4	Kennson	David	1996-03-16 00:00:00.000	1	11	Has Tenure
4	5	Bender	Eric	2007-05-17 00:00:00.000	1	11	Active
5	7	Lonning	David	2000-01-01 00:00:00.000	1	11	On Leave
6	10	O'Haire	Terry	2004-10-04 00:00:00.000	2	3	Active

Query executed successfully.   RENO (11.0 RTM)   Reno\Student (51)   JProCo   00:00:00   7 rows

Figure 12.15 The employee records of the seven JProCo employees who found grants.

Skill Check 3: Query the Customer table using a subquery, which shows all the customers who have purchased (Hint: everyone appearing in the SalesInvoice table has bought something from JProCo). The query should show all customers who have ordered at least once from JProCo. If a customer has ordered multiple times, make sure they only show once in the result. When you're done, your result will resemble the figure you see here (Figure 12.16).

```
SELECT *
FROM Customer
WHERE CustomerID IN
-- Remaining Code Here
```

Figure 12.16 The customer records of the 711 distinct customers who have bought from JProCo.

Answer Code: The T-SQL code for this lab is located in the downloadable files as a file named Lab12.1_BasicSubqueries.sql.

Points to Ponder - Basic Subqueries

1. A subquery may be nested inside a SELECT, UPDATE, INSERT, or DELETE statement.

2. We can use a subquery as part of an expression in your WHERE clause criteria.

3. The subquery returns results for the outer query to use.

4. Subqueries used after the IN keyword will work if the subquery is returning values from only one field.

5. A subquery which returns a list of values (i.e., a list of values from one field only) may only be used in a WHERE clause.

6. When used in a WHERE clause, the subquery limits the number of records returned to the outer query.

7. A regular subquery can run independently of the outer query.

8. SQL Server allows you to nest up to 32 queries together in a single statement.

Correlated Subqueries

Before we talk about correlated subqueries, let's talk about two tables that we already know relate to each other – or correlate.

We know the location table contains four locations. It has the fields LocationID, Street, City and State. The Employee table also has a LocationID field, which means these two tables do correlate.

```
SELECT *
FROM Location
```

```
SELECT *
FROM Employee
```

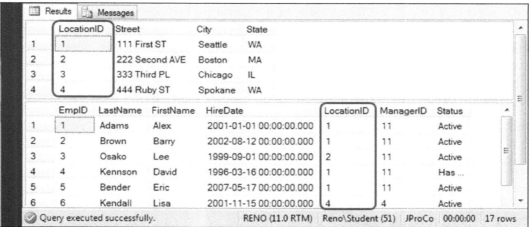

Figure 12.17 The Location and Employee tables correlate on the LocationID field.

Suppose we want to add to the Location table a fifth field called EmpCount. The EmpCount field will specify the number of employees at each location. We would need to join Location to the Employee table in order to find the number of employees working at each location.

Let's first add the aggregation to the query (Figure 12.18). Recall an aggregation (called COUNT) needs some supportive language, so we'll GROUP BY E.LocationID (Figure 12.18).

```
SELECT *
FROM Location AS L
```

```
SELECT E.LocationID, COUNT(*)
FROM Employee AS E
GROUP BY e.LocationID
```

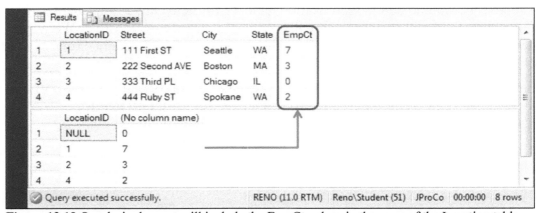

Figure 12.18 Add the COUNT aggregation and the support language GROUP BY.

If we can put these two results together, we will have the report that we're interested in. Look at the four values in the lower part of our result (Figure 12.18). Location 1 is Seattle, so we'd like to see the 7 from the lower result appear at the end of Row 1 in the top result. Next to Location 2, which is Boston, we want to see the 3. We didn't find anybody for Location 3, so we want to see a 0 for Chicago. And for Spokane, we want to see a 2 appear at the end of the fourth row (Figure 12.19).

```
SELECT *, (SELECT COUNT(*) FROM Employee WHERE LocationID =
lo.LocationID) AS EmpCt
FROM Location AS lo
```

```
SELECT LocationID, (SELECT COUNT(*) FROM Employee WHERE
LocationID = em.LocationID)
FROM Employee AS em
GROUP BY em.LocationID
```

Figure 12.19 Our desired report will include the EmpCt values in the rows of the Location table.

One great thing about a correlated subquery is that we can take a summarized aggregate and make it appear as a field. To the upper query, we will add a comma and a set of parentheses to contain the subquery (Figure 12.20).

```
SELECT *, ( )
FROM Location AS L

SELECT E.LocationID, COUNT (*)
FROM Employee AS E
GROUP BY E.LocationID

  WHERE
```

Figure 12.20 Add the COUNT field to the upper query, change the GROUP BY to WHERE.

So let's take the entire lower query and paste it into the new parentheses in the Location query. E.LocationID gets removed from the SELECT statement since L.LocationID is already included in the outer query and thus is already a column in our report (Figure 12.19). As well, just one expression is usually allowed in a subquery's SELECT list. If we try to run the code in Figure 12.20, we will get an error ("Subquery returned more than 1 value").

```
SELECT *, (
  SELECT COUNT(*)
  FROM Employee AS E
  GROUP BY E.LocationID)
FROM Location AS L
```

Even though we can't run this code without an error, we can agree that the subquery portion returns more than one value. From the schematic in Figure 12.19, we know it returns four values. So GROUP BY does not help us here.

What we need is for the subquery to provide the location count to each corresponding row in the outer query. Just like we do when joining tables, we need to equate LocationIDs from the subquery to LocationIDs in the outer query. We do that with this code:

```
SELECT *, (
  SELECT COUNT(*)
  FROM Employee AS E
  WHERE E.LocationID = L.LocationID)
FROM Location AS L
```

The WHERE clause handles the work of the GROUP BY in a correlated subquery. The criteria says, "only include records WHERE the Employee table corresponds to the Location table on E.LocationID=L.LocationID". Each row of the outer query will look through the subquery and pull in the COUNT value wherever E.LocationID finds a matching L.LocationID. If the outer query finds a row in the subquery with no matching LocationID, it ignores it (e.g., the COUNT of 1 for the NULL LocationID value associated with John Marshbank is ignored). Every L.LocationID that doesn't find a corresponding match receives a COUNT of 0 (e.g., L.LocationID 3 (Chicago) shows a 0 in the COUNT). Refer back to Figure 12.19, as needed. Now we see the number of employee counts for each location (Figure 12.21).

```
SELECT *, (
  SELECT COUNT(*)
  FROM Employee AS E
  WHERE E.LocationID = L.LocationID)
FROM Location AS L
```

	LocationID	Street	City	State	(No column name)
1	1	111 First ST	Seattle	WA	7
2	2	222 Second AVE	Boston	MA	3
3	3	333 Third PL	Chicago	IL	0
4	4	444 Ruby ST	Spokane	WA	2

4 rows

Figure 12.21 The number of employee counts is now associated with each location.

```
SELECT *, (
  SELECT COUNT(*)
  FROM Employee AS E
  WHERE E.LocationID = L.LocationID) AS EmpCt
FROM Location AS L
```

	LocationID	Street	City	State	EmpCt
1	1	111 First ST	Seattle	WA	7
2	2	222 Second AVE	Boston	MA	3
3	3	333 Third PL	Chicago	IL	0
4	4	444 Ruby ST	Spokane	WA	2

4 rows

Figure 12.22 Our final report aliases the new expression field as EmpCt.

Now let's try another correlated subquery using a different pair of tables. We'll look at the employee table, which has 13 employees. Some have found grants, some have not. Notice there's an employee ID field, EmpID, in the Employee table. The Grant table also has an EmpID field. Observe that employee ID's may appear multiple times in the Grant table.

READER NOTE: *the Employee query includes all 13 records, even though the Figure 12.23 graphic conserves space by showing just the first six records.*

We would like to have the total number of grants for each employee showing next to his or her name. Next to Barry Brown, we want a 1 to appear. For Lee Osako, we'd also like to see a 1. For David Lonning, we want to see a 3, since he found multiple grants (92 Purr_Scents, BigStarBank, and At-Last-U-Can-Help.com). If no grants were found, then we want to see a 0 in the employee record.

```
SELECT *
FROM Employee AS E
```

```
SELECT *
FROM [Grant] AS G
```

	EmpID	LastName	FirstName	HireDate	LocationID	ManagerID	Status
1	1	Adams	Alex	2001-01-01...	1	11	Active
2	2	Brown	Barry	2002-08-12...	1	11	Active
3	3	Osako	Lee	1999-09-01...	2	11	Active
4	4	Kennson	David	1996-03-16...	1	11	Has Tenure
5	5	Bender	Eric	2007-05-17...	1	11	Active
6	6	Kendall	Lisa	2001-11-15...	4	4	Active

	GrantID	GrantName	EmpID	Amount
1	001	92 Purr_Scents %% team	7	4750.00
2	002	K_Land fund trust	2	15750.00
3	003	Robert@BigStarBank.com	7	18100.00
4	004	Norman's Outreach	NULL	21000.00
5	005	BIG 6's Foundation%	4	21000.00
6	006	TALTA_Kishan Internatio...	3	18100.00

Query executed successfully.   RENO (11.0 RTM)   Reno\Student (51)   JProCo   00:00:00   23 rows

Figure 12.23 The Grant and Employee tables correlate on EmpID.

Modify the Employee query to bring in just the FirstName, LastName, and add the expression field "1 AS GrantCt" as a placeholder (Figure 12.24).

```
SELECT FirstName, LastName, 1 AS GrantCount
FROM Employee AS E
```

	FirstName	LastName	GrantCount
1	Alex	Adams	1
2	Barry	Brown	1
3	Lee	Osako	1
4	David	Kennson	1
5	Eric	Bender	1
6	Lisa	Kendall	1

13 rows

Figure 12.24 The expression "1 AS GrantCt" is a hard-coded placeholder.

Recognize the report in Figure 12.24 is not accurate, because it contains a hard-coded GrantCount value. It shows each employee as having found one grant, but we know one employee has many grants and some employees have none. This 1 is simply a placeholder to get us thinking about what we need the Grant subquery to accomplish. Let's add an aggregation to the Grant query (Figure 12.25).

```
SELECT EmpID, FirstName, LastName, 1 AS GrantCount
FROM Employee AS E

SELECT EmpID, COUNT(*)
FROM [Grant] AS G
GROUP BY EmpID
```

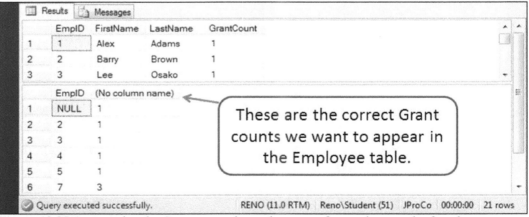

Figure 12.25 Aggregating the Grant query shows the counts for employees who found grants.

The prior figure showed the grant counts for employees who found grants. We need our final result to show a count for each of the 13 employees (Figure 12.26).

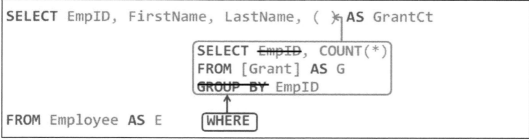

Figure 12.26 The prior result (Fig 12.25) mocked up to show grant counts for every employee.

These last two steps (Figures 12.25 and 12.26) help us see the subquery is going to take the place of the "1" in the placeholder "1 AS GrantCt".

```
1 AS GrantCt --> () AS GrantCt
```

Let's make that change to our code and prepare to move the Grant subquery up into the Employee query (i.e., the outer query). Strike EmpID from the subquery's SELECT statement, since the outer query is already bringing E.EmpID into our report as a column (Figure 12.27).

```
SELECT EmpID, FirstName, LastName, (  *  AS GrantCt

                              SELECT EmpID, COUNT(*)
                              FROM [Grant] AS G
                              GROUP BY EmpID

FROM Employee AS E        WHERE
```

Figure 12.27 We are preparing to move the subquery into the outer (Employee) query.

As we saw in our prior example, the GROUP BY in the subquery will return many values. And we need the outer query and the subquery to correlate on EmpID (WHERE G.EmpID = E.EmpID), so that the outer query will read the subquery row-by-row (Figure 12.28).

```
SELECT EmpID, FirstName, LastName, (
  SELECT COUNT(*)
  FROM [Grant] AS g
  WHERE EmpID = e.EmpID ) AS GrantCt
FROM Employee AS e
```

	EmpID	FirstName	LastName	GrantCt
1	1	Alex	Adams	0
2	2	Barry	Brown	1
3	3	Lee	Osako	1
4	4	David	Kennson	1
5	5	Eric	Bender	1
6	6	Lisa	Kendall	0

13 rows

Figure 12.28 Our final report shows every employee listed with his or her grant count.

Wonderful – we now see every employee listed with the grant count next to his or her name. The outer query has gone through row-by-row and brought in values from the subquery where g.EmpID = e.EmpID. Where it found a match, it brought in the value (i.e., the six 1's and the single 3). Where it found a non-matching record in the subquery, it ignored it (i.e., the NULL EmpID associated with the Norman's Outreach grant; no employee received credit because this was a web pledge – Figure 12.23. Where the outer query contains an employee record but found no corresponding EmpID in the subquery, it arbitrarily assigned the value 0 in our report.

For our last example, we will turn to JProCo's customer list and sales data. Customers purchase trips from JProCo. For each customer, we want to see their total number of trips next to their name in the customer list. The tables we will use are the Customer table and the vSales table view:

```
SELECT * FROM Customer
SELECT * FROM vSales
```

Let's first look at one customer, so we can visualize the data and decide how to aggregate. Customer 11 has taken a total of 12 trips (Figure 12.29 and Figure 12.30).

```
SELECT * FROM Customer
WHERE CustomerID = 11
```

Figure 12.29 This shows the CustomerID 11 from the Customer table.

Notice in Customer 11 has purchased 12 trips (Figure 12.30).

```
SELECT *
FROM vSales
ORDER BY CustomerID
```

	CustomerID	OrderDate	RetailPrice	Quantity		ProductID	ProductName	OrderYear
42	11	2012-01-12 ...	612.205	1	1	65	Ocean Cruise ...	2012
43	11	2011-04-15 ...	339.861	3	3	51	History Tour 3 ...	2011
44	11	2012-03-20 ...	113.287	3	3	49	History Tour 1 ...	2012
45	11	2010-08-19 ...	113.287	4	4	49	History Tour 1 ...	2010
46	11	2010-02-12 ...	339.861	1	+1	51	History Tour 3 ...	2010
47	12	2009-09-21	339.861	4	12	51	History Tour 3	2009

Query executed successfully.   RENO (11.0 RTM)   Reno\Student (51)   JProCo   00:00:00   6960 rows

Figure 12.30 Scroll down to see that Customer 11 has purchased 12 trips so far.

We want an expression field to appear alongside the Customer's record and show the sum of trips taken (i.e., the sum of each customer's Quantity values.)

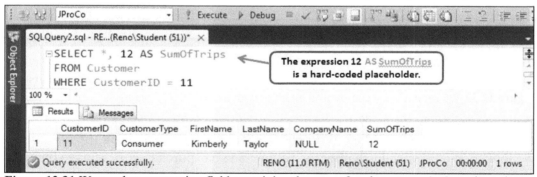

Figure 12.31 We need an expression field containing the sum of each customer's Quantity values.

```
SELECT * FROM Customer

SELECT CustomerID, SUM(Quantity) AS SumOfTrips
FROM vSales
GROUP BY CustomerID
ORDER BY CustomerID
```

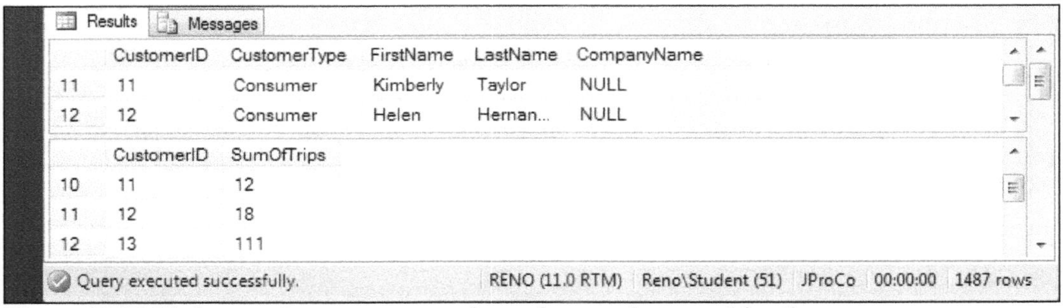

Figure 12.32 We have written our two queries and are ready to combine them.

Now we are ready to combine the two queries into one:

- o add a comma and set of parentheses after the SELECT * clause
- o move the subquery inside the parentheses
- o put the expression field's alias after the subquery, right outside of the parentheses
- o change the GROUP BY to a WHERE (Figure 12.34)
- o equate the common field between the subquery and the outer query

```
SELECT *, (
  SELECT SUM(Quantity)
  FROM vSales V
  GROUP BY c.CustomerID = v.CustomerID) AS SumOfTrips
FROM Customer C
```

```
Messages
Msg 102, Level 15, State 1, Line 2
Incorrect syntax near '='.
                                                    0 rows
```

Figure 12.33 We cannot use a comparison operator with a GROUP BY clause.

Our final result shows each customer's trips alongside their Customer record. We can see that customer 1, Mark Williams, has purchased a total of 68 trips. Earlier we looked at customer 11, Kimberly Taylor. She has purchased 12 trips to date.

```
SELECT *, (
  SELECT SUM(Quantity)
  FROM vSales V
  WHERE c.CustomerID = v.CustomerID ) AS SumOfTrips
FROM Customer C
```

	CustomerID	CustomerType	FirstName	LastName	CompanyName	SumOfTrips
1	1	Consumer	Mark	Williams	NULL	68
2	2	Consumer	Lee	Young	NULL	4
3	3	Consumer	Patricia	Martin	NULL	20
4	4	Consumer	Mary	Lopez	NULL	7
5	5	Business	NULL	NULL	MoreTechnology.com	NULL
6	6	Consumer	Ruth	Clark	NULL	NULL
						775 rows

Figure 12.34 Our final result shows each customer's SumOfTrips.

Lab 12.2: Correlated Subqueries

Lab Prep: Each lab has one or more Skill Checks. Start with Skill Check 1 and proceed until reaching the Points to Ponder section.

Before beginning this lab, verify that SQL Server 2012 is properly installed and operating. Before running the lab setup script for resetting the database (SQLQueries2012Vol2Chapter12.2Setup.sql), please make sure to close all query windows within SSMS. An open query window pointing to a database context can lock that database preventing it from updating when the script is executing. A simple way to assure all query windows are closed, is to exit out of SSMS, then open a new instance of SSMS, and lastly run the setup script.

Skill Check 1: Query the Supplier table and use a subquery from the CurrentProducts table to create a ProductCount expression field. The ProductCount should show the number of products for each supplier. When you are done, your result should resemble the figure you see here (Figure 12.35).

	SupplierID	SupplierName	ContactFullName	ProductCount
1	1	Stay Way Away and Save	Aaron Jeffries	195
2	2	LaVue Connect	Lou LaFleur	96
3	3	More Shores Amigo	Jose Cruz	96

3 rows

Figure 12.35 Skill Check 1 features a subquery, CurrentProducts. The outer query is Supplier.

Skill Check 2: Query the Employee table to find the 7 newest employees by hire date. Create an expression field called GrantCount that shows the number of grants found by each of those newest employees. Only the FirstName, LastName and HireDate columns and the expression field are to be shown. When you are done, your result should resemble the figure you see here (Figure 12.36).

	FirstName	LastName	HireDate	GrantCount
1	Phil	Wilconkinski	2009-06-11 00:00:00.000	0
2	Eric	Bender	2007-05-17 00:00:00.000	1
3	Terry	O'Haire	2004-10-04 00:00:00.000	1
4	James	Newton	2003-09-30 00:00:00.000	0
5	Barry	Brown	2002-08-12 00:00:00.000	1
6	Lisa	Kendall	2001-11-15 00:00:00.000	0

7 rows

Figure 12.36 Skill Check 2 shows grant counts for JProCo's seven newest employees.

Answer Code: The T-SQL code for this lab is located in the downloadable files as a file named Lab12.2_CorrelatedSubqueries.sql.

Points to Ponder - Correlated Subqueries

1. Subqueries can be used as expression fields.

2. A correlated subquery (also known as a repeating subquery) gets the related field IDs from the outer query (WHERE *SubQuery.FieldID = OuterQuery.FieldID*).

3. The correlated subquery executes once for every matching ID found in the outer query (WHERE *SubQuery.FieldID = OuterQuery.FieldID*).

4. Like correlated tables which can be joined because they relate on a common field, correlated subqueries similarly rely upon an overlapping field (e.g., WHERE *SubQuery.FieldID = OuterQuery.FieldID*).

5. A non-correlated subquery can run independently of the outer query. However, a correlated subquery is dependent upon the outer query and will generate an error(s) if run by itself.

Subquery Extensions

T-SQL brings some pretty cool extensions to the power of the subquery. We'll preface our examples with ALL, ANY and SOME by first doing some analysis on the buying patterns of our retail customers.

In this section, JProCo's customer purchases will serve as our sample dataset. We want to know about the activity of our individual customers.

For example, let's look at Customer #2, Lee Young. When Lee buys from us, does he buy one thing at a time? Or does he buy trips by the dozen?

How about Patricia Martin, Customer #3? Or Mary Lopez, Customer #4?

What are their buying patterns? In other words, are they trending up, or trending down? And what might it take to break that pattern?

Let's look at all of Patricia Martin's records from the vSales table. She is Customer #3, and this query shows us her buying pattern (Figure 12.37).

```
SELECT *
FROM Customer

SELECT *
FROM vSales
WHERE CustomerID = 3
```

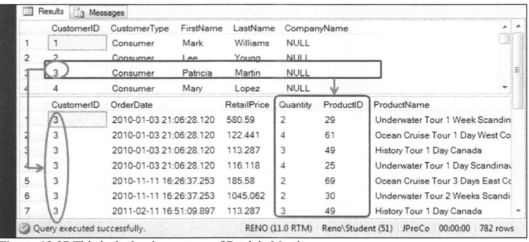

Figure 12.37 This is the buying pattern of Patricia Martin.

It looks like her favorite time to shop for trips is around the winter. The trips encompass Scandinavia and several places in North America. The least she ever buys is two seats per trip. Perhaps she brings along a sister, spouse, or child on every trip. Occasionally she reserves three seats for a trip, but she never buys more than four seats. So if Patricia were to come to us and say she wanted to reserve five places in a European trip, that would be a new personal best.

Let's turn now to Customer #4. Mary Lopez buys infrequently and appears to favor Canadian trips. She may book five seats per trip, or she might book two.

```
SELECT *
FROM Customer
WHERE CustomerID = 4

SELECT *
FROM vSales
WHERE CustomerID = 4
```

Figure 12.38 Customer #4 may book five trips at a time, or she might buy two.

It looks like the most Customer #2 has ever bought at one time is four.

```
SELECT *
FROM Customer
WHERE CustomerID = 2

SELECT *
FROM vSales
WHERE CustomerID = 2
```

Figure 12.39 The most Lee Young has purchased at one time is four trips.

The greatest quantity of trips Lee Young (Customer #2) has ever bought from us is four. The most Patricia Martin (Customer #3) has ever bought is also four. Mary Lopez (Customer #4) previously purchased five of the same product at the same time. So if she returned and bought five, it would not be a personal record for her.

So here's our goal. We want to find customers where, if they were to order five of a product, it would be the single largest purchase they've ever made. In other words, we want to see Lee and Patricia in that query, but not Mary.

ALL Operator

My co-worker and friend, Forest, recently bought a Hybrid car for his daily commute. When I asked how the mileage was, he told me his new car gets better mileage than all the other cars he has ever owned. He proceeded to tell me his old Civic was pretty good (35 MPG) but his Durango from 10 years ago was a guzzler (just 17 MPG). He then reminisced about all the cars he'd owned. Seeing the list he drew on the board, I agreed the 46 MPG he was getting from his new Prius was higher than all the other cars he has ever owned.

We want to see a list of customers where 5 is greater than all the quantities they have purchased to date. In other words, we want a query to look at all of each customer's purchased quantities. And if 5 is greater, we want to see them.

```
--Look for customers WHERE 5 > (the quantity of their best purchase)

SELECT *
FROM Customer
WHERE 5 > ( )

--Look at all of each customer's purchases.

--If 5 is greater than their highest quantity, show that customer.
```

Figure 12.40 The outer query is written and the query logic for the report we want to create is in the comments.

The keyword ALL returns "true" for each set of values in which every record (i.e., "all records") meets the criteria. So place ALL before the set of parentheses.

```
SELECT *
FROM Customer
WHERE 5 > ALL ( )

    SELECT * Quantity
    FROM vSales
    WHERE CustomerID = 2
```

Figure 12.41 Add the keyword ALL and prepare the vSales query to become the subquery.

In preparing vSales to become the subquery, we need to remove the * from the SELECT statement (we are evaluating just Quantity, not all fields). We also need to remove the hardcoded 2 in the subquery's criteria (i.e., WHERE clause) (see the strikethrough notations for these shown in Figure 12.41).

The subquery captures the history of all customer sales. We nest it inside the query from the Customer table. The subquery correlates to the outer query on the CustomerID field (WHERE Customer.CustomerID=vSales.CustomerID).

The "WHERE 5 > ALL" criteria evaluates each row that contains a matching CustomerID. For every customer in the subquery which meets the criteria (5 > Quantity), the WHERE clause returns a "true" to the outer query (Figure 12.42).

```
SELECT *
FROM Customer
WHERE 5 > ALL (
  SELECT Quantity
  FROM vSales
  WHERE Customer.CustomerID = vSales.CustomerID)
```

	CustomerID	CustomerType	FirstName	LastName	CompanyName
1	2	Consumer	Lee	Young	NULL
2	3	Consumer	Patricia	Martin	NULL
3	5	Business	NULL	NULL	MoreTechnology.com
4	6	Consumer	Ruth	Clark	NULL
5	7	Consumer	Tessa	Wright	NULL
6	8	Consumer	Jennifer	Garcia	NULL

Query executed successfully.   RENO (11.0 RTM)   Reno\Student (51)   JProCo   00:00:00   258 rows

Figure 12.42 Our final result shows the 258 customers who have not yet purchased a quantity >4.

Our final result shows the list of 258 customers whose sales histories do not yet contain a product purchase with a quantity higher than 4.

We expected to see Lee Young and Patricia Martin in this list, and they both are there. If Lee were to buy five of a product, it would be a personal best. The same would be true for Patricia.

We expected to not see Mary Lopez, and she does not appear. She already bought five from us and thus does not appear in the result. Put another way, "5 is not greater than the individual comparison of all the Quantities we found for Customer #4".

In case you are curious and would like to see the detail and quantity for each of the 258 customers in our final result, the next figure joins the outer query to vSales to show each customer's individual sales records. Try copying this query into a new query window and scrolling through, to see for yourself that all the quantities are less than 5 (Figure 12.43). Since customers can place orders for more than one of each item, we see 396 records for the 258 customers that have never ordered 5 or more of an item at a time.

```
SELECT c.CustomerID, c.FirstName, c.LastName, c.CompanyName,
s.OrderDate, s.RetailPrice, s.Quantity, s.ProductID,
s.ProductName
FROM Customer AS c
INNER JOIN vSales AS s
ON c.CustomerID = s.CustomerID
WHERE 5 > ALL (
  SELECT Quantity
  FROM vSales AS s
  WHERE c.CustomerID = s.CustomerID)
ORDER BY c.CustomerID
```

	CustomerID	FirstName	LastName	Company...	OrderDate	RetailPrice	Quantity	ProductID	ProductName
1	2	Lee	Young	NULL	2011-02-07...	556.74	4	72	Ocean Cruise Tour 2 Weeks East Coast
2	3	Patricia	Martin	NULL	2010-01-03...	122.441	4	61	Ocean Cruise Tour 1 Day West Coast
3	3	Patricia	Martin	NULL	2010-11-11...	185.58	2	69	Ocean Cruise Tour 3 Days East Coast
4	3	Patricia	Martin	NULL	2010-01-03...	116.118	4	25	Underwater Tour 1 Day Scandinavia
5	3	Patricia	Martin	NULL	2010-01-03...	580.59	2	29	Underwater Tour 1 Week Scandinavia
6	3	Patricia	Martin	NULL	2010-11-11...	1045.062	2	30	Underwater Tour 2 Weeks Scandinavia

Query executed successfully.   RENO (11.0 RTM) Reno\Student (51) JProCo 00:00:00 396 rows

Figure 12.43 A bonus perspective showing the 396 detailed sales records for the same 258 customers.

ANY and SOME Operators

Recall my friend Forest loves his Prius because it gets better mileage than all the other cars he has ever owned. Two years after my friend bought his Hybrid car, I was thinking about getting a Ford Escape Hybrid. An SUV hybrid meant the freedom to carry many things and still get great mileage. In fact, I average about 32 MPG. When people ask, I give the Ford Escape Hybrid a glowing review, although I phrase it a little differently than Forest. I say this is one of the best mileage vehicles I have ever owned. It's far better than my RX8 (18 MPG). In fact it gets better mileage than most of the cars I've owned, except for my Geo back in 1994. My new Ford Escape does beat most of the cars' mileage I have owned but not all of them. If I were to use the ALL keyword, then my Ford Escape would not show up in my list of cars. We are going to explore other clauses that can help to stack rank the comparison when a quantity beats only some – but not all – of the other compared values.

We'll now turn to another subquery example using the same Customer and vSales record sets. Here we will use the keywords ANY and SOME to modify our comparison operators. Look at the Customer table. We will compare some customers' purchases versus those of other customers (Figure 12.44).

```
SELECT * FROM Customer
```

Figure 12.44 We will compare Mark Williams's purchases with other customers.

So let's look at the purchases made by customer #1, Mark Williams. Mark has purchased many times with product quantities ranging between 1 and 5.

```
SELECT * FROM vSales
WHERE CustomerID = 1
```

Figure 12.45 Mark has purchased many times with product quantities ranging between 1 and 5.

Now let's look at the purchases of the next two customers, Lee Young and Patricia Martin . Lee has purchased a quantity of 4. Patricia has purchased quantities ranging from 2 to 4 seats per trip in any one order (Figure 12.46).

```
SELECT * FROM Customer
WHERE CustomerID IN (2, 3)
```

```
SELECT * FROM vSales
WHERE CustomerID = 2 OR CustomerID = 3
ORDER BY CustomerID
```

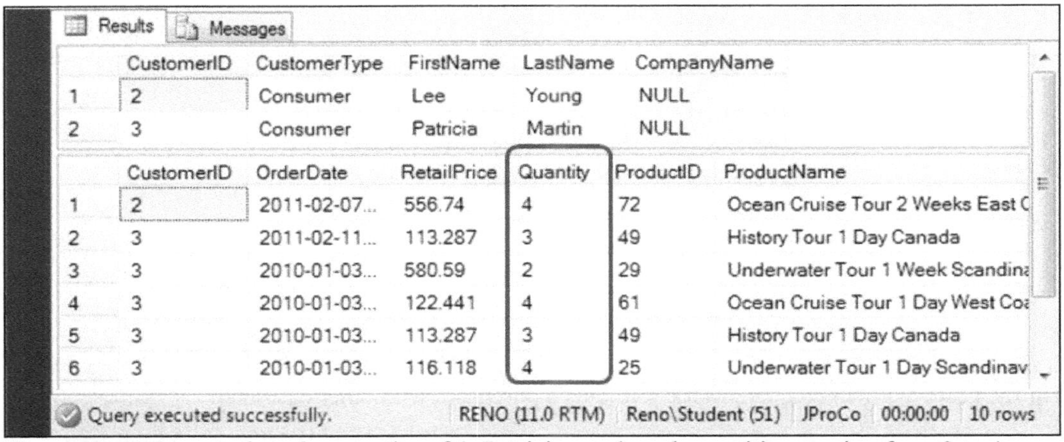

	CustomerID	CustomerType	FirstName	LastName	CompanyName
1	2	Consumer	Lee	Young	NULL
2	3	Consumer	Patricia	Martin	NULL

	CustomerID	OrderDate	RetailPrice	Quantity	ProductID	ProductName
1	2	2011-02-07...	556.74	4	72	Ocean Cruise Tour 2 Weeks East C
2	3	2011-02-11...	113.287	3	49	History Tour 1 Day Canada
3	3	2010-01-03...	580.59	2	29	Underwater Tour 1 Week Scandin
4	3	2010-01-03...	122.441	4	61	Ocean Cruise Tour 1 Day West Co
5	3	2010-01-03...	113.287	3	49	History Tour 1 Day Canada
6	3	2010-01-03...	116.118	4	25	Underwater Tour 1 Day Scandinav

Figure 12.46 Lee purchased a quantity of 4; Patricia purchased quantities ranging from 2 to 4.

For which of these customers could you say that the quantity 2 is greater than the quantity of any of their purchases? It's not true for Patricia, because all of her purchases are for 2 or more (Refer back to Figure 12.46). Patricia always buys 2.

How about Lee? Is the value of 2 greater than any of the purchases Lee has made? No, Lee's single purchase contained a quantity of 4.

However, if we go to Customer #1, the quantity 2 is greater than one of his purchases (See row 3 in Figure 12.45). So, is the quantity 2 higher than any one of the purchases? Yes.

In our report we want to know if the value of 2 is greater than the quantity of any one of a customer's purchases. The keyword ANY is a comparison operator modifier. For each set of values in the subquery, ANY returns a "true" where at least one record (any record) meets the criteria.

The subquery and the outer query correlate on the CustomerID field. For every set of records in the subquery with a matching CustomerID, we want to evaluate every Quantity in that set of records to evaluate whether 2 is greater than any of the quantities (Figure 12.47).

```
SELECT *
FROM Customer
WHERE 2 > ANY (
  SELECT Quantity
  FROM vSales
  WHERE vSales.CustomerID = Customer.CustomerID)
```

	CustomerID	CustomerType	FirstName	LastName	CompanyName
1	1	Consumer	Mark	Williams	NULL
2	8	Consumer	Jennifer	Garcia	NULL
3	11	Consumer	Kimberly	Taylor	NULL
4	13	Consumer	Linda	Hernandez	NULL
5	15	Consumer	Anthony	Scott	NULL
6	16	Consumer	Paul	Perez	NULL

333 rows

Figure 12.47 There are 333 customers who have purchased a quantity of 1.

So what happens if we change ANY to ALL? We would get a different record set because the quantity 2 is greater than all of these (Figure 12.48). In other words, when using ANY, Mark Williams is shown because the quantity 2 is greater than the quantity of -ANY- of his purchases. This is true since he has an order with an item with a quantity of 1. He also has an order where he bought 5 items. Using ALL, Mark is not shown because the quantity 2 is not greater than the quantity of -ALL- of his purchases (5), so this is not true.

```
SELECT *
FROM Customer
WHERE 2 > ALL (
  SELECT Quantity
  FROM vSales
  WHERE vSales.CustomerID = Customer.CustomerID)
```

	CustomerID	CustomerType	FirstName	LastName	CompanyName
1	5	Business	NULL	NULL	MoreTechnology.com
2	6	Consumer	Ruth	Clark	NULL
3	16	Consumer	Paul	Perez	NULL
4	18	Consumer	Donald	Walker	NULL
5	23	Consumer	Daniel	Gonzalez	NULL
6	39	Consumer	John	Jackson	NULL

81 rows

Figure 12.48 ALL will show an entirely different result set.

In other words, Customer #5 has never ordered 2 at once. The same is true for Customer #6, who has never ordered >1 at once.

ANY will show more records because it's comparing against and beating out just one of them.

Let's return to our main result with ANY. Notice we have 333 records in that result set (Figure 12.47). What happens if we change this ANY to SOME?

```
SELECT *
FROM Customer
WHERE 2 > SOME (
  SELECT Quantity
  FROM vSales
  WHERE vSales.CustomerID = Customer.CustomerID)
```

	CustomerID	CustomerType	FirstName	LastName	CompanyName
1	5	Business	NULL	NULL	MoreTechnology.com
2	6	Consumer	Ruth	Clark	NULL
3	16	Consumer	Paul	Perez	NULL
4	18	Consumer	Donald	Walker	NULL
5	23	Consumer	Daniel	Gonzalez	NULL

333 rows

Figure 12.49 The keywords SOME and ANY are equivalent and achieve the same result.

We get the same 333 records as we did with ANY. The keyword SOME is not a T-SQL extension. It is the ISO standard equivalent of the ANY extension, so we can use ANY and SOME interchangeably in SQL Server.

Lab 12.3: Subquery Extensions

Lab Prep: Each lab has one or more Skill Checks. Start with Skill Check 1 and proceed until reaching the Points to Ponder section.

Before beginning this lab, verify that SQL Server 2012 is properly installed and operating. Before running the lab setup script for resetting the database (SQLQueries2012Vol2Chapter12.3Setup.sql), please make sure to close all query windows within SSMS. An open query window pointing to a database context can lock that database preventing it from updating when the script is executing. A simple way to assure all query windows are closed, is to exit out of SSMS, then open a new instance of SSMS, and lastly run the setup script.

Skill Check 1: We want to compare the RetailPrice values of products supplied by JProCo's three external suppliers. Show the supplier who, if it were to introduce a $1000 product, that would represent the highest RetailPrice they offer. Find all suppliers (from the Supplier table) whose current products are less than $1000 (from the CurrentProducts table). Run the comparison using a correlated subquery (as we did in the last section examples) and use ANY, ALL, or SOME to modify your comparison operator. Use the CurrentProducts and Supplier tables in JProCo for your correlated subquery.

	SupplierID	SupplierName	ContactFullName
1	3	More Shores Amigo	Jose Cruz

1 rows

Figure 12.50 Skill Check 1 uses a correlated subquery comparison with ANY, ALL, or SOME.

Skill Check 2: Show all employees who, if they were to find a $5000 grant, it would represent the highest grant they have ever found. Use the ALL operator with your correlated subquery. When you're done, your result will resemble the figure you see here (Figure 12.51).

	EmpID	LastName	FirstName	HireDate	LocationID	ManagerID	Status
1	1	Adams	Alex	2001-01-01	1	11	Active
2	6	Kendall	Lisa	2001-11-15	4	4	Active
3	8	Marshbank	John	2001-11-15	NULL	4	Active
4	9	Newton	James	2003-09-30	2	3	Active
5	12	O'Neil	Barbara	1995-05-26	4	4	Has Tenure
6	13	Wilconkins…	Phil	2009-06-11	1	4	Active

6 rows

Figure 12.51 Skill Check 2 uses a correlated subquery between the Employee and Grant tables.

Answer Code: The T-SQL code for this lab is located in the downloadable files as a file named Lab12.3_SubqueryExtensions.sql.

Points to Ponder - Subquery Extensions

1.   ANY, ALL and SOME are keywords which modify comparison operators.

2.   The keyword ALL returns a "true" for each set of values in which every record (i.e., "all records") meets the criteria.

3.   ANY returns a "true" for each set of values in which at least one record (i.e., "any record") meets the criteria.

4.   SOME is the ISO standard equivalent of ANY.

Chapter Glossary

ALL: A keyword which returns a "true" for each set of values in which every record meets the criteria.

ANY: A keyword which returns a "true" for each set of values in which at least one record meets the criteria.

Correlated Subqueries: This type of query, also called a repeating subquery, uses two tables that relate to one another and executes once for every matching ID found in the outer query.

SOME: A keyword that is the ISO standard equivalent of ANY.

Subquery: A SELECT statement nested inside another T-SQL statement.

Review Quiz - Chapter Twelve

1.) Your Customer table has 775 records. The SalesInvoice table has 1877 records from 712 different customers. There are 64 customers that have never ordered from JProCo and are not listed in the SalesInvoice table. All of the CustomerIDs listed in the SalesInvoice table have a valid CustomerID. How many records will result from the following query?

```
SELECT * FROM Customer
WHERE CustomerID IN (
  SELECT DISTINCT CustomerID
  FROM  SalesInvoice)
```

O a. 1877

O b. 775

O c. 712

O d. 64

2.) You need to query the 6 newest employees by HireDate. The Grant table links to the Employee table by EmpID. You want to show these employees and the number of Grants they have found. Which query should you use?

O a. `SELECT TOP(6) FirstName, LastName, HireDate, (`
      `SELECT COUNT(*)`
      `FROM [Grant] G`
      `WHERE G.EmpID = E.EmpID) AS GrantCount`
    `FROM Employee E`
    `ORDER BY HireDate DESC`

O b. `SELECT TOP(6) FirstName, LastName, HireDate, (`
      `SELECT COUNT(*)`
      `FROM [Grant]) AS GrantCount`
    `FROM Employee E`
    `ORDER BY HireDate DESC`

O c. `SELECT TOP(6) FirstName, LastName, HireDate (`
      `SELECT COUNT(`
        `FROM [Grant] G`
      `WHERE G.EmpID = E.EmpID)) AS GrantCount`
    `FROM Employee E`
    `ORDER BY HireDate DESC`

3.) All CurrentProducts from "LaVue Connect" are going up in price 10% across the board. Create an update statement using a basic subquery that sets all CurrentProducts from "LaVue Connect" to increase by 10%. Which query should you use?

O a.
```
UPDATE CurrentProducts
SET RetailPrice = RetailPrice + 10
WHERE SupplierID IN (
    SELECT SupplierID
    FROM Supplier
    WHERE SupplierName = 'LaVue Connect')
```

O b.
```
UPDATE CurrentProducts
SET RetailPrice = RetailPrice * 1.1
WHERE SupplierID IN (
    SELECT SupplierID
    FROM Supplier
    WHERE SupplierName = 'LaVue Connect')
```

O c.
```
UPDATE CurrentProducts
SET RetailPrice = RetailPrice * 1.1
WHERE SupplierID EXISTS (
    SELECT SupplierID
    FROM Supplier
    WHERE SupplierName = 'LaVue Connect')
```

4.) Complete the following query to find all the employee counts for each location.
```
SELECT *, (
    SELECT COUNT(*)
    FROM Employee E
    --Remaining Code Here)
FROM Location L
```

O a. `ON E.LocationID = L.LocationID`

O b. `IF E.LocationID = L.LocationID`

O c. `WHERE E.LocationID = L.LocationID`

O d. `ON E.LocationID != L.LocationID`

5.)   Your SalesInvoice table has one record for each time a customer placed an order. In each order, a customer may order many different products as listed in the SalesInvoiceDetail table. You want to write a query to show all the Invoices that have more than 20 products on them. Which query should you use?

O a. `SELECT *`
`FROM SalesInvoice`
`WHERE SalesInvoiceID IN (`
`SELECT SalesInvoiceID, COUNT(*)`
`FROM SalesInvoiceDetail`
`GROUP BY SalesInvoiceID`
`HAVING COUNT(*) > 20 )`

O b. `SELECT *`
`FROM SalesInvoice`
`WHERE SalesInvoiceID EXISTS (`
`SELECT SalesInvoiceID`
`FROM SalesInvoiceDetail`
`GROUP BY SalesInvoiceID`
`HAVING COUNT(*) > 20 )`

O c. `SELECT *`
`FROM SalesInvoice`
`WHERE SalesInvoiceID IN (`
`SELECT SalesInvoiceID`
`FROM SalesInvoiceDetail`
`GROUP BY SalesInvoiceID`
`HAVING COUNT(*) > 20 )`

6.)　You have two tables named Drivers and Violations. You need to identify all Drivers that have not yet made any moving violations and those that have only made violations with an Amount less than 50. Which query should you use?

O a. `SELECT *`
　　`FROM Drivers`
　　`WHERE 50 > ANY (`
　　　`SELECT Amount`
　　　`FROM Violations`
　　　`WHERE Drivers.DriversID = Violations.DriversID)`

O b. `SELECT *`
　　`FROM Drivers`
　　`WHERE 50 > ALL (`
　　　`SELECT Amount`
　　　`FROM Violations`
　　　`WHERE Drivers.DriversID = Violations.DriversID)`

7.)　All items in your database are used to monitor activity for products supplied by approved vendors. Each product has a list price. You need to increase the list price for all products of only the vendor named CoolGear by 5.00. Which query should you use?

O a. `UPDATE Production. Product`
　　`SET ListPrice = ListPrice + 5.00`
　　`WHERE VendorID NOT IN (`
　　　`SELECT VendorID`
　　　`FROM Purchasing.Vendor`
　　　`WHERE VendorName = 'CoolGear');`

O b. `UPDATE Production. Product`
　　`SET ListPrice = ListPrice + 5.00`
　　`WHERE EXISTS (`
　　　`SELECT VendorID`
　　　`FROM Purchasing.Vendor`
　　　`WHERE VendorName = 'CoolGear');`

O c. `UPDATE Production. Product`
　　`SET ListPrice = ListPrice + 5.00`
　　`WHERE VendorID IN (`
　　　`SELECT VendorID`
　　　`FROM Purchasing.Vendor`
　　　`WHERE VendorName = 'CoolGear');`

8.) You have two tables, named Customer and SalesOrder. You need to identify all customers that have not made any purchases or those who have never ordered more than 40 at any given time. Which query should you use?

O a.
```
SELECT *
FROM Customer
WHERE 40 > ALL (
   SELECT OrderTotal
   FROM SalesOrder
   WHERE Customer.CustomerID = SalesOrder.CustomerID)
```

O b.
```
SELECT *
FROM Customer
WHERE 40 > ANY (
   SELECT OrderTotal
   FROM SalesOrder
   WHERE Customer.CustomerID = SalesOrder.CustomerID)
```

O c.
```
SELECT *
FROM Customer
WHERE 40 > (
   SELECT MAX(OrderTotal)
   FROM SalesOrder
   WHERE Customer.CustomerID = SalesOrder.CustomerID)
```

Answer Key

1.) 1877 is more records than exist in the Customer table, so (a) is wrong. Since there are 64 customers who have not ordered, the query will not return all 775 records in the Customer table, so (b) is wrong too. Because the WHERE clause is predicating on all the customers who have ordered products, the result set will not return the 64 customers who have not ordered products, making (d) another wrong answer. Because the WHERE clause is predicating on CustomerIDs in a list that contains only the 712 distinct customers who have ordered products, (c) is the correct answer.

2.) '(SELECT Count (*) FROM [Grant]) As GrantCount' will return the total number of grants found by all the employees appended to each record of the 6 newest employees, so (b) is incorrect. '(SELECT Count (FROM Grant G WHERE G.EmpID = E.EmpID))' will return an error because the COUNT function is not used correctly, so (c) is also incorrect. Since '(SELECT Count (*) FROM Grant G WHERE G.EmpID = E.EmpID)' will correctly count the number of grants for each individual employee, (a) is the correct answer.

3.) Since 'SET RetailPrice = RetailPrice + 10' will only add 10 to each RetailPrice and 10 may not be 10 percent of the RetailPrice in each case, (a) is not correct. As long as there is a Supplier named 'La Vue Connect' EXISTING in the Supplier table, every record in the Supplier table will have its RetailPrice increased by 10 percent, otherwise none of them will, if using the code from (c), making it incorrect. Since the RetailPrice is multiplied by 1.1 and the WHERE clause is predicating on 'SupplierID IN ...', (b) will be the correct answer.

4.) Because ON and IF will result in syntax errors, (a), (b) and (d) are all incorrect. Because the code in (c) is correlating on the LocationID field properly with 'WHERE E.LocationID = L.LocationID', it is the correct answer.

5.) A subquery must return only one field to be used in a WHERE clause, so (a) will not work. Because the query will return every SalesInvoice or none of them based on the use of EXISTS in the WHERE clause, (b) will be wrong too. The code in (c) is the only one to correctly use 'WHERE SalesInvoice IN' with the proper Subquery, making it the correct answer.

6.) Because (a) will return a driver if any one of his violations is less than 50, even if some of them are over 50, it cannot be correct. Only (b) will find drivers who have never had a violation over 50.

7.) Because the code in (a) uses NOT IN, it affects only gear that is not CoolGear, making it incorrect. Using EXISTS updates every product, even non-CoolGear products, as long as there is a Vendor named CoolGear, so (b) is incorrect too. Since IN finds the subquery records you want to see, (c) is the correct answer.

8.) Because ANY finds records where a customer has at least one order below 40, even if other orders are over 40, (b) will show too many records, making it incorrect. There is no subquery keyword in (c), so that won't even compile. Using the ALL keyword means that 40 is greater than every order placed by that customer, making (a) the correct answer.

Bug Catcher Game

To play the Bug Catcher game, run the SQLQueries2012Vol2BugCatcher12.pps file from the BugCatcher folder of the companion files. These files are available from the www.Joes2Pros.com website.

[THIS PAGE INTENTIONALLY LEFT BLANK.]

Chapter 13. Advanced Subqueries

When you have just a few records which need to be handled by SQL Server, the best practice is to process just the needed records. Suppose your database contains 1 million records, and you need to run an update that should impact only 15 records. There is no point processing all of the records. Besides wasting time and system resources, you run the risk of an unintended change to all 1 million records.

READER NOTE: *Please run the SQLQueries2012Vol2Chapter13.0Setup.sql script in order to follow along with the examples in the first section of Chapter 13. All scripts mentioned in this chapter are available at www.Joes2Pros.com.*

Correlated Subquery Recap

Subqueries run once for every row in the outer query. If the outer query has millions of records and the subquery has just a few, then you have created certain risks and/or waste. This section will analyze times when the subquery may be doing more than you want it to and what to do about those situations.

There are going to be times when we want to use a correlated subquery as part of an update statement. There will be other times when combining a basic subquery with a correlated subquery will be more desirable.

Updates with Subqueries

To start, let's take a look and become familiar with the following two tables and come up with an objective.

```
SELECT *
FROM [Grant] AS gr
```

	GrantID	GrantName	EmpID	Amount
1	001	92 Purr_Scents %% team	7	4750.00
2	002	K_Land fund trust	2	15750.00
3	003	Robert@BigStarBank.com	7	18100.00
4	004	Norman's Outreach	NULL	21000.00
5	005	BIG 6's Foundation%	4	21000.00
6	006	TALTA_Kishan International	3	18100.00

Query executed successfully.   RENO (11.0 RTM)   Reno\Student (51)   JProCo   00:00:00   10 rows

Figure 13.1 This shows the records of the Grant table.

In Figure 13.1 we see the first six records of the 10 grants in the Grant table. Sometimes more money is received for the same grant. That information is stored in the GrantAdder table (Figure 13.2).

```
SELECT *
FROM GrantAdder AS ga
```

	GrantID	Amount
1	001	2000.00
2	005	500.00
3	005	1000.00

Query executed successfully.   RENO (11.0 RTM)   Reno\Student (51)   JProCo   00:00:00   3 rows

Figure 13.2 This shows the records from the GrantAdder table.

When we look at the GrantAdder table in Figure 13.2 we see that $2000 will need to be added to GrantID 001. $500 and $1000 for a total of $1500 will need to be added to GrantID 005.

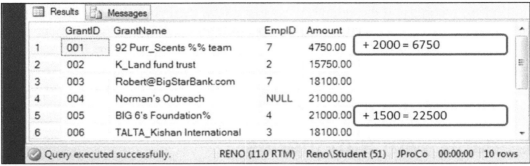

Figure 13.3 This shows the total after the new money is added to the old grant Amount.

It looks like we are going to need a SUM of the Amounts in the GrantAdder table.

```
SELECT SUM(Amount)
FROM GrantAdder AS ga
WHERE GrantID = '001'
```

Figure 13.4 This shows $2000 is the SUM() total that needs to be added to GrantID 001.

```
SELECT SUM(Amount)
FROM GrantAdder AS ga
WHERE GrantID = '005'
```

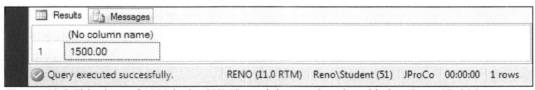

Figure 13.5 This shows $1500 is the SUM() total that needs to be added to Grant ID 005.

If we want to add these values to our query of the Grant table as a field we can put the entire query in parentheses in the SELECT list:

```
SELECT *, (SELECT SUM(Amount)
FROM GrantAdder
WHERE GrantID = '001')
FROM [Grant] AS gr
```

We don't want the subquery to be hardcoded for GrantID 001 in the WHERE clause. We want the SELECT statement to pull out the GrantID that is coming up at the time. To do this we will have the GrantID values from both tables equal each other in the WHERE clause.

```
SELECT *, (SELECT SUM(Amount)
          FROM GrantAdder AS ga
          WHERE ga.GrantID = gr.GrantID)
FROM [Grant] AS gr
```

	GrantID	GrantName	EmpID	Amount	(No column name)
1	001	92 Purr_Scents %% team	7	4750.00	2000.00
2	002	K_Land fund trust	2	15750.00	NULL
3	003	Robert@BigStarBank.com	7	18100.00	NULL
4	004	Norman's Outreach	NULL	21000.00	NULL
5	005	BIG 6's Foundation%	4	21000.00	1500.00
6	006	TALTA_Kishan International	3	18100.00	NULL

Query executed successfully.   RENO (11.0 RTM)   Reno\Student (51)   JProCo   00:00:00   10 rows

Figure 13.6 This shows the sums from the GrantAdder table were returned in the result using a subquery.

Using a subquery, we were able to list the amounts from the GrantAdder table into our result (Figure 13.6). Notice there were no amounts in the GrantAdder table for records other than 001 and 005, NULLs were returned.

What would happen if we changed this from a SELECT statement to an UPDATE statement? For fun and learning, let's replace SELECT with UPDATE and we want to update the Grant (gr) table. Next let's set the Amount equal to the Amount plus the result of the subquery.

```
UPDATE [Grant] SET Amount =
  Amount + (SELECT SUM(Amount)
            FROM GrantAdder  AS ga
            WHERE ga.GrantID = gr.GrantID)
FROM [Grant] AS gr
```

```
Messages
(10 row(s) affected)
                                                           0 rows
```

Figure 13.7 This shows the UPDATE statement affected 10 rows.

Figure 13.7 shows 10 rows were affected by the UPDATE statement. Let's check the Grant table.

```
SELECT *
FROM [Grant]
```

	GrantID	GrantName	EmpID	Amount
1	001	92 Purr_Scents %% team	7	6750.00
2	002	K_Land fund trust	2	NULL
3	003	Robert@BigStarBank.com	7	NULL
4	004	Norman's Outreach	NULL	NULL
5	005	BIG 6's Foundation%	4	22500.00
6	006	TALTA_Kishan International	3	NULL

Query executed successfully.   (local) (11.0 RTM)   Reno\Student (51)   JProCo   00:00:00   10 rows

Figure 13.8 This shows GrantID 001 and 005 were updated but cleared the amounts for grants without changes.

The good news is we successfully updated the Amount for GrantID 001 and 005 but the bad news is we cleared the values that were not supposed to change. We should have only updated the two records that changed.

Before we figure out how to fix this problem we will need to restore the Grant table by running the SQLQueries2012Vol2Chapter13SpecialSetup.sql script found in the C:\Joes2Pros\LabSetupFiles folder.

Let's verify that our Grant table is back to normal.

```
SELECT *
FROM [Grant] AS gr
```

	GrantID	GrantName	EmpID	Amount
1	001	92 Purr_Scents %% team	7	4750.00
2	002	K_Land fund trust	2	15750.00
3	003	Robert@BigStarBank.com	7	18100.00
4	004	Norman's Outreach	NULL	21000.00
5	005	BIG 6's Foundation%	4	21000.00
6	006	TALTA_Kishan International	3	18100.00

Query executed successfully.   RENO (11.0 RTM)   Reno\Student (51)   JProCo   00:00:00   10 rows

Figure 13.9 This shows the Grant table restored with its original values.

Combining Basic and Correlated Subqueries

To begin this section, take a look at the following five queries:

```
SELECT 5
SELECT 5 + 1
SELECT 5 + 0
SELECT 5 + NULL
SELECT 15750 + NULL
```

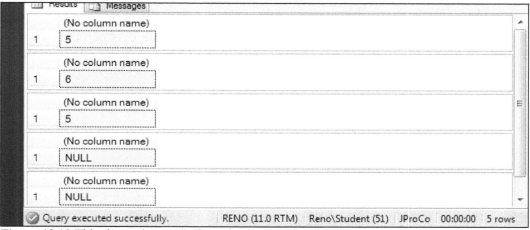

Figure 13.10 This shows the results from the five queries above.

Everyone knows 5+1=6 and 5+0=5. What does 5+NULL= ? No matter what number is added to a NULL the answer will always be NULL (Figure 13.10). Let's go back to the query we started with.

```
SELECT *
FROM [Grant] AS gr
```

	GrantID	GrantName	EmpID	Amount
1	001	92 Purr_Scents %% team	7	4750.00
2	002	K_Land fund trust	2	15750.00
3	003	Robert@BigStarBank.com	7	18100.00
4	004	Norman's Outreach	NULL	21000.00
5	005	BIG 6's Foundation%	4	21000.00
6	006	TALTA_Kishan International	3	18100.00

Query executed successfully.　　RENO (11.0 RTM)　Reno\Student (51)　JProCo　00:00:00　10 rows

Figure 13.11 This shows the records of the Grant table.

Look at the following figure to see exactly what happened when the Grant table was updated in Figure 13.7.

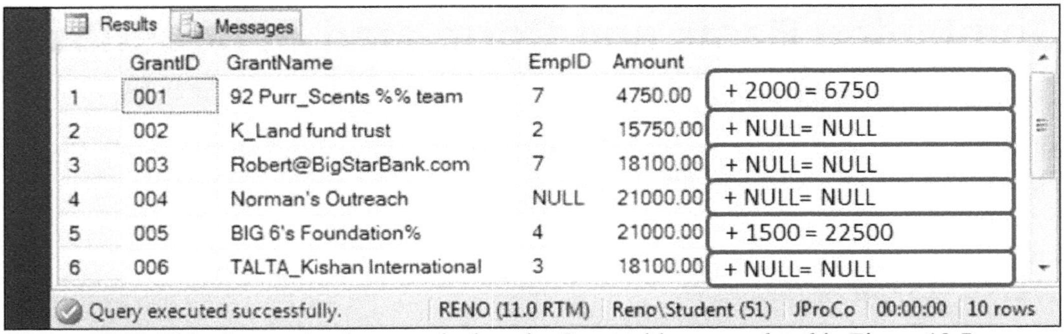

Figure 13.12 This shows what happened when the Grant table was updated in Figure 13.7.

We did not want to UPDATE every record that was relatable between the two tables; we wanted to add the records that actually had a value. Take a look at the results from the SELECT query.

```
SELECT *, (SELECT SUM(Amount)
          FROM GrantAdder AS ga
          WHERE ga.GrantID = gr.GrantID)
FROM [Grant] AS gr
```

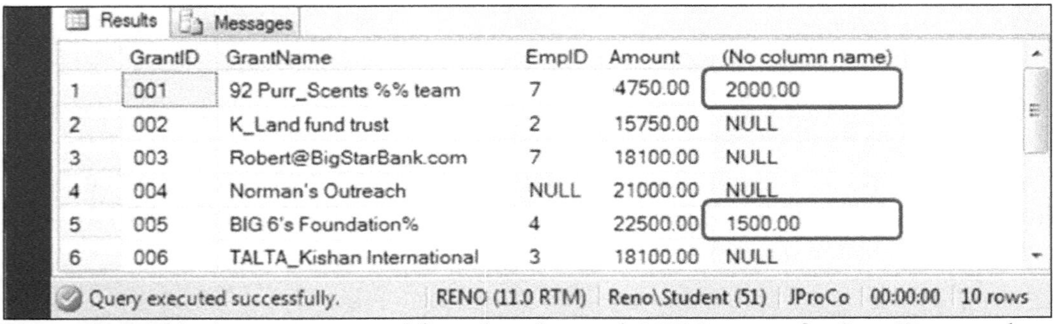

Figure 13.13 This shows every record from the subquery is NULL except for GrantID one and five.

In the results from Figure 13.13 we see that every record that does not have a value was returned as NULL. We want record 001 and record 005 to show up in the subquery but that is all. How do we write a query that says if the record is in the GrantAdder table, then update the matching record in the Grant table, but if it is not, then don't update the record?

Let's take a look at the GrantAdder table.

```
SELECT *
FROM GrantAdder AS ga
```

Figure 13.14 This shows the records from the GrantAdder table.

Record 001 and 005 are the only two that need to be updated in the Grant table. We don't need GrantID 005 listed twice, so instead of SELECT *, let's use SELECT DISTINCT.

```
SELECT DISTINCT GrantID
FROM GrantAdder AS ga
```

Figure 13.15 This shows there are two DISTINCT GrantID values.

Even though the GrantAdder table has three records, there are only two DISTINCT GrantID values (Figure 13.15). If the Grant table has a GrantID that is actually IN the GrantAdder table then it is eligible for UPDATE. Let's pass the SELECT DISTINCT basic subquery into a WHERE clause for our criteria.

```
SELECT *, (SELECT SUM(Amount)
           FROM GrantAdder AS ga
           WHERE ga.GrantID = gr.GrantID)
FROM [Grant] AS gr
WHERE GrantID IN (SELECT DISTINCT GrantID FROM GrantAdder)
```

	GrantID	GrantName	EmpID	Amount	(No column name)	
1	001	92 Purr_Scents %% team	7	4750.00	2000.00	
2	005	BIG 6's Foundation%	4	21000.00	1500.00	

Query executed successfully.   RENO (11.0 RTM)   Reno\Student (51)   JProCo   00:00:00   2 rows

Figure 13.16 This shows the WHERE clause containing the basic subquery limited the query to just the records needing to be updated from the GrantAdder table.

Updating with Basic and Correlated Subqueries

Let's add the same WHERE clause to the UPDATE statement.

```
UPDATE [Grant]
SET Amount = Amount + (SELECT SUM(Amount)
                       FROM GrantAdder AS ga
                       WHERE ga.GrantID = gr.GrantID)
FROM [Grant] AS gr
WHERE GrantID IN (SELECT DISTINCT  GrantID FROM GrantAdder)
```

Messages
(2 row(s) affected)
0 rows

Figure 13.17 This shows the UPDATE statement updated two records.

This time the UPDATE statement only updated two records. Let's take a look at the Grant table and check our results.

```
SELECT *
FROM [Grant] AS gr
```

	GrantID	GrantName	EmpID	Amount
1	001	92 Purr_Scents %% team	7	6750.00
2	002	K_Land fund trust	2	15750.00
3	003	Robert@BigStarBank.c...	7	18100.00
4	004	Norman's Outreach	NULL	21000.00
5	005	BIG 6's Foundation%	4	22500.00
6	006	TALTA_Kishan Internati...	3	18100.00

Query executed successfully.   RENO (11.0 RTM) Reno\Student (51) JProCo 00:00:00 10 rows

Figure 13.18 This shows the two updated values of the Grant table.

When you use a correlated subquery in an UPDATE statement, the correlation alias refers to the table you wish to update.

Lab 13.1: Updates with Subqueries

Lab Prep: Each lab has one or more Skill Checks. Start with Skill Check 1 and proceed until reaching the Points to Ponder section.

Before beginning this lab, verify that SQL Server 2012 is properly installed and operating. Before running the lab setup script for resetting the database (SQLQueries2012Vol2Chapter13SpecialSetup.sql), please make sure to close all query windows within SSMS. An open query window pointing to a database context can lock that database preventing it from updating when the script is executing. A simple way to assure all query windows are closed, is to exit out of SSMS, then open a new instance of SSMS, and lastly run the setup script.

Skill Check 1: Review the data shown here in the PriceIncrease table. Turn the records of this table into a subquery which will increment prices in the CurrentProducts table.

READER NOTE: *You should update only three records in the CurrentProducts table.*

```
SELECT * FROM PriceIncrease

SELECT * FROM CurrentProducts
```

	ProductID	Change
1	1	5.75
2	1	1.00
3	2	9.50
4	3	1.50
5	3	2.50

	ProductID	ProductName	RetailPrice	OriginationD...	To...	Category	Supp
1	1	Underwater Tour 1 Day West...	61.483	2009-05-07...	0	No-Stay	0
2	2	Underwater Tour 2 Days We...	110.6694	2010-06-29...	0	Overni...	0
3	3	Underwater Tour 3 Days We...	184.449	2012-02-03...	0	Mediu...	0
4	4	Underwater Tour 5 Days We...	245.932	2008-11-28...	0	Mediu...	0
5	5	Underwater Tour 1 Week W...	307.415	2004-04-13...	0	LongT...	0
6	6	Underwater Tour 2 Weeks W...	553.347	2011-03-27...	1	LongT...	0

Query executed successfully. RENO (11.0 RTM) Reno\Student (51) JProCo 00:00:00 488 rows

Figure 13.19 Your records before you start Skill Check 1.

When you are done with Skill Check 1, notice that ProductID 1 has a price of $68.233 and ProductID 4 is unchanged at $245.932.

```
SELECT * FROM CurrentProducts
```

	ProductID	ProductName	RetailPrice	OriginationDate	ToBeDeleted	Category	Sup
1	1	Underwater Tour 1 Day ...	68.233	2009-05-07 1...	0	No-Stay	0
2	2	Underwater Tour 2 Day...	120.1694	2010-06-29 2...	0	Overnight-Stay	0
3	3	Underwater Tour 3 Day...	188.449	2012-02-03 1...	0	Medium-Stay	0
4	4	Underwater Tour 5 Day...	245.932	2008-11-28 0...	0	Medium-Stay	0
5	5	Underwater Tour 1 We...	307.415	2004-04-13 1...	0	LongTerm-Stay	0
6	6	Underwater Tour 2 We...	553.347	2011-03-27 2...	1	LongTerm-Stay	0
7	7	Underwater Tour 1 Day ...	80.859	2010-01-01 0...	0	No-Stay	1

Query executed successfully.   (local) (11.0 RTM) Reno\Student (54) JProCo 00:00:00 483 rows

Figure 13.20 Skill Check 1 result should reflect these RetailPrice values.

Answer Code: The T-SQL code for this lab is located in the downloadable files as a file named Lab13.1_UpdatesWithSubqueries.sql.

Points to Ponder - Updates with Subqueries

1. An UPDATE, DELETE, or INSERT statement with another query nested inside of it is known as a subquery.

2. The UPDATE command can update records for one table only.

3. When using a correlated subquery in an UPDATE statement, the correlation alias refers to the updated table.

Existence Subqueries

Of all types of subqueries, existence subqueries are the most performant. This is true for two reasons. The outer query only needs to find one or more matches from the inner query to be considered matched. In other words, not all the records need to be processed. The next reason is that the subquery returns only a true or false indicator to the query, not actual data values.

A drawback to the existence subquery is that you won't be able to display any data from the inner query in your result set. If it finds one or more values in the inner query, then it will show those records in the result set.

Using EXISTS Operator

There is one big advantage to an EXISTS subquery over an INNER JOIN. If you join to a table with duplicates, then you get duplicates in your final result set. We can filter those results with the DISTINCT keyword, but then you will have taken two performance hits. First you processed more records than you needed to and then you ran a costly DISTINCT query.

The EXISTS keyword is much faster than an inner join since it does not return any data from the other table. It just returns a "true" if one or more matches is found. This also saves time since it does not need to perform multiple searches.

We're going to look at employees who have found grants. Begin by looking at all records in the Employee and Grant tables.

```
SELECT *
FROM Employee AS em
```

	EmpID	LastName	FirstName	HireDate	LocationID	ManagerID	Status
1	1	Adams	Alex	2001-01-01 ...	1	11	Active
2	2	Brown	Barry	2002-08-12 ...	1	11	Active
3	3	Osako	Lee	1999-09-01 ...	2	11	Active
4	4	Kennson	David	1996-03-16 ...	1	11	Has Tenure
5	5	Bender	Eric	2007-05-17 ...	1	11	Active
6	6	Kendall	Lisa	2001-11-15 ...	4	4	Active

Query executed successfully.   RENO (11.0 RTM) Reno\Student (51) JProCo 00:00:00 13 rows

Figure 13.21 This shows the first six records from the Employee table.

Which of the employees in the Employee table have found grants? To see that information we will need to look at the Grant table.

```
SELECT *
FROM [Grant] AS gr
```

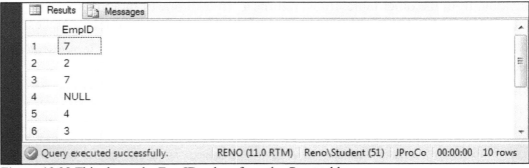

Figure 13.22 This shows the first six records of the Grant table.

Here we see a list of grants and the EmpID of the employees that found them (Figure 13.22).

Let's look at the Grant table but this time lets limit the fields to just the EmpID field.

```
SELECT EmpID
FROM [Grant] AS gr
```

Figure 13.23 This shows the EmpID values from the Grant table.

If this was ultimately going to be a basic subquery then it would be good to use DISTINCT to eliminate repeat values. What we are working toward is demonstrating a relationship with a correlated subquery using the EXISTS keyword. To begin, let's take the query of the Employee table and in a WHERE clause let's use EXISTS with our query of the Grant table EmpID values.

```
SELECT *
FROM Employee AS em
WHERE EXISTS (SELECT EmpID
              FROM [Grant] AS gr)
```

Figure 13.24 The query returned all 13 records of the Employee table.

This query returned all the records of the Grant table because we have not defined the relationship it EXISTS on. To establish the relationship between the inner and outer queries of this subquery let's add a WHERE clause to the subquery that says we want all the EmpID values WHERE em.EmpID is equal to gr.EmpID.

```
SELECT *
FROM Employee AS em
WHERE EXISTS (SELECT EmpID
              FROM [Grant] AS gr
              WHERE em.EmpID = gr.EmpID)
```

Figure 13.25 This shows a list of just the employees from the Employee table that have found grants.

When a subquery uses the EXISTS keyword it acts like an existence test of records from the inner query. With the EXISTS subquery it does not matter which field is selected. We could run the same query with SELECT * in the subquery and it would work the same because the correlation is made in the WHERE clause.

If we want to pull out just the employees that have found large grants over $20000 we will need to add to the correlated subquery. At the end of the WHERE clause add AND gr.Amount > 20000.

```
SELECT *
FROM Employee AS em
WHERE EXISTS (SELECT EmpID
              FROM [Grant] AS gr
              WHERE em.EmpID = gr.EmpID
              AND gr.Amount > 20000)
```

	EmpID	LastName	FirstName	HireDate	LocationID	ManagerID	Status
1	4	Kennson	David	1996-03-16 00:00:00.000	1	11	Has Te
2	7	Lonning	David	2000-01-01 00:00:00.000	1	11	On Lea
3	10	O'Haire	Terry	2004-10-04 00:00:00.000	2	3	Active
4	11	Smith	Sally	1989-04-01 00:00:00.000	1	NULL	Active

Query executed successfully.   RENO (11.0 RTM) Reno\Student (51) JProCo 00:00:00 4 rows

Figure 13.26 This shows the four employees of the Employee table that found grants over $20000.

Comparing EXISTS Subquery with Basic Subquery

You may remember from the last chapter that basic subqueries find only records that exist. We just learned that EXISTS subqueries also find only records that exist. Therefore, the output between the two will be the same. Let's see this by comparing the result of a basic subquery and an EXISTS subquery run against the same table and using the same criteria.

Let's take a look at the following four locations.

```
SELECT *
FROM Location AS lo
```

	LocationID	Street	City	State
1	1	111 First ST	Seattle	WA
2	2	222 Second AVE	Boston	MA
3	3	333 Third PL	Chicago	IL
4	4	444 Ruby ST	Spokane	WA

Query executed successfully.   RENO (11.0 RTM) Reno\Student (51) JProCo 00:00:00 4 rows

Figure 13.27 This shows the four location records found in the Location table.

If we need to find out how many locations have more than two employees we will need to also look at the Employee table.

```
SELECT *
FROM Employee AS em
```

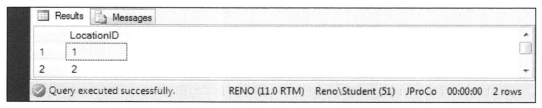

	EmpID	LastName	FirstName	HireDate	LocationID	ManagerID	Status
1	1	Adams	Alex	2001-01-01 00:00:00.000	1 ←	11	Active
2	2	Brown	Barry	2002-08-12 00:00:00.000	1 ←	11	Active
3	3	Osako	Lee	1999-09-01 00:00:00.000	2 ←	11	Active
4	4	Kennson	David	1996-03-16 00:00:00.000	1 ←	11	Has Ter
5	5	Bender	Eric	2007-05-17 00:00:00.000	1	11	Active
6	6	Kendall	Lisa	2001-11-15 00:00:00.000	4	4	Active
7	7	Lonning	David	2000-01-01 00:00:00.000	1	11	On Lea
8	8	Marshb...	John	2001-11-15 00:00:00.000	NULL	4	Active
9	9	Newton	James	2003-09-30 00:00:00.000	2 ←	3	Active
10	10	O'Haire	Terry	2004-10-04 00:00:00.000	2 ←	3	Active
11	11	Smith	Sally	1989-04-01 00:00:00.000	1	NULL	Active
12	12	O'Neil	Barbara	1995-05-26 00:00:00.000	4	4	Has Ter
13	13	Wilconki...	Phil	2009-06-11 00:00:00.000	1	4	Active

Query executed successfully.　　RENO (11.0 RTM)　Reno\Student (51)　JProCo　00:00:00　13 rows

Figure 13.28 This shows locations 1 and 2 are the only ones with more than two employees.

When we look at Figure 13.28 we notice only locations 1 and 2 have more than two employees. Locations 1 and 2 are the ones we're going to want to see in our final result. Instead of having to scan the entire document let's have the query pull them out for us. We will limit the fields to just the LocationID and GROUP BY LocationID as well. We are looking for total number of employees at each location. We cannot use a WHERE clause with GROUP BY so we will use HAVING COUNT(*) > 2.

```
SELECT LocationID
FROM Employee AS em
GROUP BY LocationID
HAVING COUNT(*) > 2
```

	LocationID
1	1
2	2

Query executed successfully.　　RENO (11.0 RTM)　Reno\Student (51)　JProCo　00:00:00　2 rows

Figure 13.29 This shows the two locations that have more than two employees.

Take a look at the following two queries. The first query is selecting the two records that have a LocationID of 1 or 2. The second query returns LocationID 1 and 2. The second query could easily replace the hard-coded 1 and 2 in the first query.

```
SELECT *
FROM Location AS lo
WHERE LocationID IN (1,2)

SELECT LocationID
FROM Employee AS em
GROUP BY LocationID
HAVING COUNT(*) > 2
```

Figure 13.30 This shows the second query could replace the hard-coded 1 and 2.

```
SELECT *
FROM Location AS lo
WHERE LocationID IN (SELECT LocationID
                     FROM Employee AS em
                     GROUP BY LocationID
                     HAVING COUNT(*) > 2)
```

	LocationID	Street	City	State
1	1	111 First ST	Seattle	WA
2	2	222 Second AVE	Boston	MA

Query executed successfully.   RENO (11.0 RTM) Reno\Student (51) JProCo 00:00:00 2 rows

Figure 13.31 This shows the basic subquery limited the fields from the location table to the ones with more than 2 employees.

Let's convert the query in Figure 13.31 to an EXISTS subquery. Replace the LocationID IN with EXISTS in the outer query and add a correlating WHERE clause to the inner query that relates the two tables on the LocationID.

```
SELECT *
FROM Location AS lo
WHERE EXISTS (SELECT LocationID
             FROM Employee AS em
             WHERE em.LocationID = lo.LocationID
             GROUP BY LocationID
             HAVING COUNT(*) > 2)
```

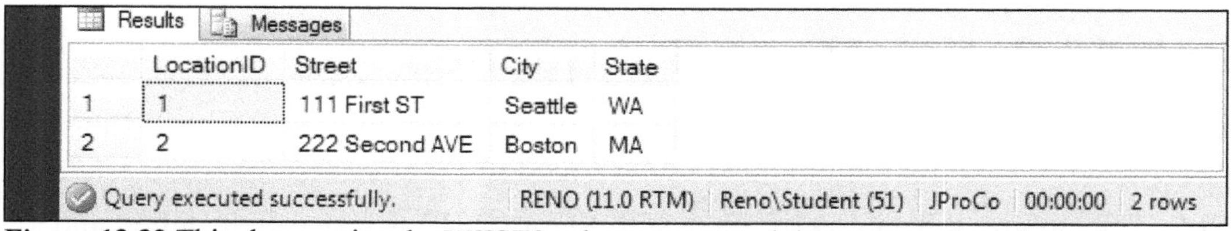

Figure 13.32 This shows using the EXISTS subquery returned the same result as the basic subquery.

Both the basic subquery and EXISTS query appear to work exactly the same (Figure 13.31 and Figure 13.32). Why would you use one over the other? There is a lot of evidence and many examples showing the EXISTS subquery performs much faster than the basic subquery that uses an IN.

Lab 13.2: Existence Subqueries

Lab Prep: Each lab has one or more Skill Checks. Start with Skill Check 1 and proceed until reaching the Points to Ponder section.

Before beginning this lab, verify that SQL Server 2012 is properly installed and operating. Before running the lab setup script for resetting the database (SQLQueries2012Vol2Chapter13.2Setup.sql), please make sure to close all query windows within SSMS. An open query window pointing to a database context can lock that database preventing it from updating when the script is executing. A simple way to assure all query windows are closed, is to exit out of SSMS, then open a new instance of SSMS, and lastly run the setup script.

Skill Check 1: Use an EXISTS subquery to find all products that have been sold according to the SalesInvoiceDetail table.

```
SELECT *
FROM CurrentProducts AS cp
WHERE EXISTS (--Remaining Code Here)
```

	ProductID	ProductName	RetailPrice	OriginationD...	To...	Category	SupplierID
1	23	Underwater Tour 1 Week C...	427.925	2006-12-05...	0	LongTerm-Stay	2
2	69	Ocean Cruise Tour 3 Days E...	185.58	2011-11-15...	0	Medium-Stay	1
3	29	Underwater Tour 1 Week Sc...	580.59	2006-12-03...	0	LongTerm-Stay	1
4	75	Ocean Cruise Tour 3 Days ...	97.803	2011-12-03...	0	Medium-Stay	3
5	9	Underwater Tour 3 Days Ea...	242.577	2005-12-26...	0	Medium-Stay	1
6	15	Underwater Tour 3 Days Me...	315.177	2007-04-06...	0	Medium-Stay	3

Query executed successfully. RENO (11.0 RTM) Reno\Student (51) JProCo 00:00:00 60 rows

Figure 13.33 Skill Check 1 finds all products that have been sold.

Skill Check 2: Use an EXISTS subquery to find all customers who have made a purchase according to the SalesInvoice table.

```
SELECT *
FROM Customer AS cu
WHERE EXISTS (--Remaining Code Here)
```

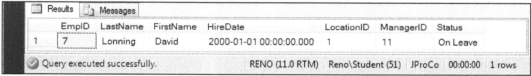

Figure 13.34 Skill Check 2 finds all customers who have made a purchase.

Skill Check 3: Use an EXISTS subquery to find all employees who have found more than two grants.

```
SELECT *
FROM Employee AS em
WHERE EXISTS (--Remaining Code Here)
```

	EmpID	LastName	FirstName	HireDate	LocationID	ManagerID	Status
1	7	Lonning	David	2000-01-01 00:00:00.000	1	11	On Leave

Query executed successfully.   RENO (11.0 RTM) Reno\Student (51) JProCo 00:00:00 1 rows

Figure 13.35 Skill Check 3 finds employees that have procured at least three grants.

Answer Code: The T-SQL code for this lab is located in the downloadable files as a file named Lab13.2_ExistenceSubqueries.sql.

Points to Ponder - Existence Subqueries

1. When a subquery uses the EXISTS operator it acts like an existence test of records from the inner query.

2. The WHERE clause of the outer query checks for records that are in the inner query.

3. With an EXISTS subquery it does not matter which field you select. In fact often times SELECT * is used in the inner query.

Chapter Glossary

EXISTS Condition: Considered to be met if the inner query returns at least one row.

Inner Query: The subquery runs once for each row in the outer query.

Review Quiz - Chapter Thirteen

1.) You have a Credit Union database with an Accounts table containing 3 million records. The amount of activity during the day is too much for the Accounts table. The company wants to load all the daily activity for account deposits during the day into a Deposits table and at night load the records from the Deposits table to the Accounts table. The bank should load into the accounts table the AccountID values. The design of the Deposits and Accounts table is seen here:

```
CREATE TABLE Accounts (
AccountID INT PRIMARY KEY,
CustomerID INT,
Balance SMALLMONEY)
GO

CREATE TABLE Deposits (
ReferenceNo INT PRIMARY KEY,
AccountID INT,
Amount SMALLMONEY,
DepositDate DATETIME)
GO
```

If a customer makes multiple deposits on one day, then we want the sum of the amounts recorded in the Accounts table to run as one update. Which T-SQL code will perform this result?

O a.
```
UPDATE Accounts ac
  SET ac.Balance = ac.Balance + (
    SELECT SUM(Amount) FROM Deposits dep
    WHERE ac.AccountID = dep.AccountID)
  WHERE ac.AccountID IN (
    SELECT AccountID FROM Deposits)
```

O b.
```
UPDATE Accounts
  SET Balance = Balance + (
    SELECT SUM(Amount) FROM Deposits dep
    WHERE Accounts.AccountID = dep.AccountID)
```

O c.
```
UPDATE ac
  SET Balance = Balance + (
    SELECT SUM(Amount) FROM Deposits dep
    WHERE ac.AccountID = dep.AccountID)
  FROM Accounts ac
  WHERE ac.AccountID IN (
    SELECT AccountID FROM Deposits)
```

2.) Which subquery keyword acts like a simple existence test for a correlated subquery?

  O a. ANY

  O b. ALL

  O c. IN

  O d. EXISTS

3.) You have a database that contains two tables named MovieCategory and MovieSubCategory. You need to write a query that returns a list of movie categories containing more than 5 subcategories. Which query should you use?

O a.
```
SELECT [Name]
FROM MovieSubCategory
WHERE MovieCategoryID IN (
    SELECT MovieCategoryID
    FROM MovieCategory
    GROUP BY [Name]
    HAVING COUNT(*) > 5)
```

O b.
```
SELECT [Name]
FROM MovieSubCategory
WHERE MovieCategoryID NOT IN (
    SELECT MovieCategoryID
    FROM MovieCategory
    GROUP BY [Name]
    HAVING COUNT(*) > 5)
```

O c.
```
SELECT [Name]
FROM Movie Category c
WHERE EXISTS (
    SELECT MovieCategoryID
    FROM MovieSubCategory
    WHERE MovieCategoryID = c.MovieCategoryID
    GROUP BY MovieCategoryID
    HAVING COUNT(*) > 5)
```

O d.
```
SELECT [Name]
FROM Movie Category c
WHERE NOT EXISTS (
    SELECT MovieCategoryID
    FROM MovieSubCategory
    WHERE MovieCategoryID = c.MovieCategoryID
    GROUP BY MovieCategoryID
    HAVING COUNT(*) > 5)
```

4.) You have a CurrentProducts table and a Supplier table. Each product has a RetailPrice. One of your suppliers increased the price of the goods they supply to you. You need to increase the RetailPrice for all CurrentProducts by 2.75 for products supplied by "LaVue Connect". All of the following queries will work except for one. Which query will <u>not</u> update only the "LaVue Connect" records?

O a.
```
UPDATE CurrentProducts
SET RetailPrice = RetailPrice + 2.75
WHERE EXISTS (
   SELECT SupplierID
   FROM Supplier
   WHERE SupplierName = 'LaVue Connect')
```

O b.
```
UPDATE CurrentProducts
SET RetailPrice = RetailPrice + 2.75
WHERE EXISTS (
   SELECT SupplierID
   FROM Supplier
   WHERE Supplier.SupplierID = CurrentProducts.SupplierID
   AND SupplierName = 'LaVue Connect')
```

O c.
```
UPDATE CurrentProducts
SET RetailPrice = RetailPrice + 2.75
WHERE SupplierID IN (
   SELECT SupplierID
   FROM Supplier
   WHERE SupplierName = 'LaVue Connect')
```

Answer Key

1.) If you have a join or subquery and want to do an update you must use the table alias (not the table name) right after the UPDATE keyword, making (a) wrong. If you make the update as a subquery to the account table it will do all records and you only want to update the records with deposits, this makes (b) incorrect. By using a basic subquery to filter out only records from the Deposits table, (c) is the right answer.

2.) ANY and ALL compare values from one query to another, so (a) and (b) are incorrect. The IN keyword is used for basic subqueries and not correlated subqueries, so (c) is also incorrect. EXISTS checks for records present at least once in the inner query, so (d) is the right answer.

3.)   When you do a GROUP BY you can only list fields in your SELECT statement if they use an aggregated function or they are explicitly listed in the GROUP BY. This makes answers (a) and (b) incorrect. Since we are looking for more than 5 to exist, (d) is wrong, since it says NOT EXISTS. Therefore (c) is the right answer.

4.)   The only query that does not work as planned is (a) because when you use an EXISTS with no correlation it handles every record. Answer (b) correlates and (c) is a basic subquery impacting the correct number of records. Since the question is looking for the only query that handles every record, (a) is the correct answer to this question.

Bug Catcher Game

To play the Bug Catcher game, run the SQLQueries2012Vol2BugCatcher13.pps file from the BugCatcher folder of the companion files. These files are available from the www.Joes2Pros.com website.

[THIS PAGE INTENTIONALLY LEFT BLANK.]

Chapter 14. The MERGE Statement

The MERGE statement was new to SQL Server 2008 and continues in SQL 2012. It is an excellent tool for handling table data. For years, database professionals have used the informal term "upsert" with respect to bringing new data into an existing table. If the record is brand new, you want your query logic to insert that entire record into the table. However, if the record already exists, you want your query to compare the old record with the new and update only the incremental changes. That logical process has been formalized as the MERGE statement.

READER NOTE: *Please run the SQLQueries2012Vol2Chapter14.0Setup.sql script in order to follow along with the examples in the first section of Chapter 14. All scripts mentioned in this chapter are available at <u>www.Joes2Pros.com</u>.*

Introducing MERGE

The underlying logic for the MERGE statement has been around for quite a while, even though MERGE is a new feature since SQL Server 2008. That logic was informally termed "upsert" – shorthand for "update or insert". If a record is brand new, your query logic should insert that entire record into the table. If the record already exists, your query compares the old record with the new to update just the incremental changes.

To add variety, this lesson will primarily include MERGE statements as part of a stored procedure, so we can re-use our code. This serves as excellent practice for your real world database work, where you will find it extremely rare to ever update tables directly. It's more likely you will build a stored procedure (sproc) to update these records and have that sproc pull in the new records from a data feed or some sort of user interface (UI).

Let's begin by reviewing the Grant table and some changes which must be reflected in the Grant table. We will begin by updating existing grants.

```
SELECT * FROM [Grant]
```

	GrantID	GrantName	EmpID	Amount	
1	001	92 Purr_Scents %% team	7	4750.00	
2	002	K_Land fund trust	2	15750.00	
3	003	Robert@BigStarBank.com	7	18100.00	
4	004	Norman's Outreach	NULL	21000.00	
5	005	BIG 6's Foundation%	4	21000.00	
6	006	TALTA_Kishan International	3	18100.00	
7	007	Ben@MoreTechnology.com	10	41000.00	
8	008	www.@-Last-U-Can-Help.com	7	25000.00	
9	009	Thank you @.com	11	21500.00	
10	010	Call Mom @Com	5	7500.00	
	010	Call Mom @Com	5	9900.00 ←	Update Grant 010 values
	011	Big Giver Tom	7	95900.00 ←	Insert new Grant 011 record

Query executed successfully.   RENO (11.0 RTM)   Reno\Student (51)   JProCo   00:00:00   10 rows

Figure 14.1 Some data changes must be made to the Grant table.

Look at the last record. Grant 010 is from Call Mom @Com and was found by Employee 5 for $7500. Two things must be updated here. Call Mom @Com has been renamed "Call Mom". The amount of the donation was incorrectly keyed in as $7500, but it was actually a $9900 grant.

The changes to Grant 010 can be accomplished with a simple update statement. So let's build our stored procedure step by step.

We're first going to type CREATE PROC and call it UpdateGrant. Now UpdateGrant will need to know the ID (GrID), name (GrName), which employee (EmpID), and what the new amount (Amt) will be. We must specify a variable to correlate with each field. Define the data types of the variables by opening Object Explorer and referencing the fields of the Grant table.

```
CREATE PROC UpdateGrant
@GrID CHAR (3), @GrName VARCHAR (50)
, @EmID int, @Amt SMALLMONEY
```

Figure 14.2 Step one. Write the CREATE PROC statement and define the four variables.

Next, we'll add the keywords AS, BEGIN, and END.

```
CREATE PROC UpdateGrant
@GrID CHAR (3), @GrName VARCHAR (50)
, @EmID int, @Amt SMALLMONEY
AS
BEGIN
END
```

Figure 14.3 Step two. Add keywords AS, BEGIN, and END.

We know the heart of the sproc appears between the BEGIN and END statements, so this is where we will add our UPDATE statement. This is also where we must SET each Grant table field equal to its respective parameter. We'll SET GrantName = @GrName, EmpID = @EmpID, and so forth. Since we don't want every record in the table to contain the same values, we need to correlate each GrantID. WHERE GrantID = @GrID.

Now run this code in order to create the UpdateGrant sproc.

```
CREATE PROC UpdateGrant
  @GrID CHAR (3), @GrName VARCHAR (50),
  @EmpID INT, @Amt SMALLMONEY
AS
BEGIN
  UPDATE [Grant]
  SET GrantName = @GrName, EmpID = @EmpID, Amount = @Amt
```

```
    WHERE GrantID = @GrID
END
```

Messages
Command(s) completed successfully.
0 rows

Figure 14.4 This stored procedure will update an existing grant record.

Now we're going to change Grant 010 by executing the sproc. Figure 14.1 contains the specified values we've been asked to change in the Grant table.

```
EXEC UpdateGrant '010','Call Mom', 5, 9900
```

Messages
(1 row(s) affected)
0 rows

Figure 14.5 Update Grant 010 by passing in the values to the sproc and executing.

After executing UpdateGrant, rerun the SELECT statement to see the changes. Confirm that Grant 010's name is reflected as "Call Mom" and the amount shows as $9900 (Figure 14.6).

```
SELECT * FROM [Grant]
```

	GrantID	GrantName	EmpID	Amount
5	005	BIG 6's Foundation%	4	21000.00
6	006	TALTA_Kishan International	3	18100.00
7	007	Ben@MoreTechnology.com	10	41000.00
8	008	www.@-Last-U-Can-Help.com	7	25000.00
9	009	Thank you @.com	11	21500.00
10	010	Call Mom	5	9900.00
				10 rows

Figure 14.6 After executing UpdateGrant, look at the Grant table to confirm the changes.

This works great for updates, but what if we try using it to enter the brand new record for GrantID 011? Look back to the code we used to build the sproc and recognize why this won't work (Figure 14.3).

```
EXEC UpdateGrant '011','Big Giver Tom', 7, 95900
```

Messages
(0 row(s) affected)
0 rows

Figure 14.7 UpdateGrant will not add a new record to the Grant table.

This will not work because we wrote our UPDATE statement to correlate each incoming ID value to an existing GrantID (WHERE GrantID=@GrID). Since there's no existing ID value "011", the sproc UpdateGrant does not provide a path for new records to connect to the Grant table.

We could add complexity to our sproc code (e.g., add IF conditions checking for the existence of a record:

1) if it finds the record, it can then update the record with the incremental changes;

2) if it doesn't, it can insert the entire record. This would make for a very complicated stored procedure with multiple code paths robust enough to handle both inserts and updates.

Fortunately, the MERGE statement makes update-or-insert (a.k.a., "upsert") logic very easy. MERGE will allow us to write a stored procedure so smart that it will UPDATE an existing record wherever it finds a match between the parameters fed and a record in the target table. And where it finds that the input parameter constitutes a brand new record, it will INSERT that record into the target table.

UPDATE if existing records are found

INSERT if new records are found

Figure 14.8 The "upsert" (upsert = Update or Insert) logic for the MERGE command.

In the MERGE context, there are two types of tables: the source table and the target table. When you need to update or insert records, it's usually because you have been provided a revised input list or table which is the source table. In this chapter we will use GrantFeed and GrantCheckMaster as source tables. The Grant table is an example of a target table. It is the existing table, and new data from the source table will be evaluated and then updated or inserted into the target table.

So the sproc we need in order to add Grant 011 to the Grant table should be smart enough to update or insert based on what it finds in the target table.

We will use the MERGE command, and we're going to use a stored procedure similar to our last example (Figure 14.9 and Figure 14.10).

Before writing the UpsertGrant code, rerun the last setup script (SQLQueries2012Vol2Chapter14.0Setup.sql) to replace all the original values in the Grant table records. The UpsertGrant will do the work of our first sproc, so we'll want to rerun the earlier change (Figure 14.7) using the new sproc.

First look at all the records from the Grant table. Since we just reran the reset script, we expect to find all records in their original condition. Look for Grant 010 to be restored back to its original GrantName (Call Mom @Com) and its amount restored back to $7500.

```
SELECT * FROM [Grant]
```

	GrantID	GrantName	EmpID	Amount
5	005	BIG 6's Foundation%	4	21000.00
6	006	TALTA_Kishan International	3	18100.00
7	007	Ben@MoreTechnology.com	10	41000.00
8	008	www.@-Last-U-Can-Help.com	7	25000.00
9	009	Thank you @.com	11	21500.00
10	010	Call Mom @Com	5	7500.00

10 rows

Figure 14.9 The Grant table has been reset back to its original condition.

```
CREATE PROC UpsertGrant
@GrID CHAR(3), @GrName VARCHAR(50),
@EmID INT, @Amt SMALLMONEY

AS
BEGIN
      MERGE [Grant] AS gr

      USING (SELECT @GrID, @GrName, @EmID, @Amt )
      AS src (GrantID, GrantName, EmpID, Amount)
      ON gr.GrantID = src.GrantID

      WHEN MATCHED THEN

      WHEN NOT MATCHED THEN
END
```

Figure 14.10 Early steps to create UpsertGrant. Replace UPDATE code with MERGE.

Notice the sproc name has been changed to UpsertGrant. The four parameters match the four fields of the destination or target table (i.e., the Grant table).

We've replaced the UPDATE code with the MERGE code between the BEGIN and END command of this sproc. We're going to MERGE the Grant table using the four parameters. We need to treat those parameters as values inside of a record we're going to compare to the target table, which is what the USING code accomplishes (USING (SELECT @GrID, @GrName, @EmID, @Amt)). Notice those names don't quite match the names of the target table, which is ok because we can alias those to match the actual field names (AS src (GrantID, GrantName, EmpID, Amount)).

The src alias stands for "source" table, or in this case source record(s). Later we will use an actual source table, but for now we are still trying to enter an individual record (e.g., Grant 011) into the Grant table.

For each source record, UpsertGrant will attempt to answer the question, "Does the source GrantID record match an existing Grant.GrantID?" It "asks" this question by correlating each src.GrantID with an existing GrantID:
ON gr.GrantID = src.GrantID

If UpsertGrant finds a matching ID, then it updates the existing record (in the Grant table, which is the target table) with any new values showing in the source record ("WHEN MATCHED THEN…"). Notice the code for the UPDATE is similar to that in our first sproc.

If it doesn't find a match, then it inserts the entire record into the Grant table ("WHEN NOT MATCHED THEN…"). The INSERT code directs the four source VALUES into their respective fields in the Grant table.

The final step before running the CREATE PROC code is to place a semicolon after the VALUES clause, which is the final part of the MERGE statement (END completes the stored procedure creation, not the MERGE). Now run all the code and make sure you see the message "Command(s) completed successfully.".

```
CREATE PROC UpsertGrant
  @GrID CHAR(3), @GrName VARCHAR(50),
  @EmpID INT, @Amt SMALLMONEY
AS
BEGIN
  MERGE [Grant] AS gr
  USING (SELECT @GrID, @GrName, @EmpID, @Amt) AS src
  (GrantID, GrantName, EmpID, Amount)
  ON gr.GrantID = src.GrantID

  WHEN MATCHED THEN UPDATE
  SET gr.GrantName = src.GrantName,
  gr.EmpID = src.EmpID, gr.Amount = src.Amount

  WHEN NOT MATCHED THEN INSERT
  (GrantID, GrantName, EmpID, Amount) VALUES
  (src.GrantID, src.GrantName, src.EmpID, src.Amount);
END
```

Messages
Command(s) completed successfully.
0 rows

Figure 14.11 A MERGE statement must be terminated by a semicolon.

Look once more at the UPDATE and INSERT statements in Figure 14.11 and notice that there is no FROM clause. Since these statements are within a MERGE statement, the information normally supplied by the FROM clause is specified implicitly by the target table (i.e., the Grant table).

Now we will run the two changes from the last example (Figures 14.5, 14.7).

```
EXEC UpsertGrant '010','Call Mom',5,9900
```

```
EXEC UpsertGrant '011','Big Giver Tom',7,95900
```

Messages
(1 row(s) affected)
(1 row(s) affected)
0 rows

Figure 14.12 The new sproc UpsertGrant has successfully upserted both of the change records.

We expect to see that the first statement updates Grant 010 to Call Mom and $9900. We expect the second statement to run an insert of brand new data.

```
SELECT * FROM [Grant]
```

Figure 14.13 The new sproc UpsertGrant updated Grant 010 and inserted Grant 011.

Just as we expected – Grant 010 has been updated and Grant 011 now shows. That's how you UPSERT using a MERGE inside of a stored procedure.

Upserting Multiple Records at Once

Our last example here will use MERGE with one of the source tables we mentioned earlier, GrantFeed. Rather than using a stored procedure, this example will demonstrate using MERGE ad hoc when you're trying to update a table from another table (e.g., a staging table or a feed table).

First we will look at all the records in our target table (Grant) and our source table (GrantFeed). If GrantFeed doesn't appear in your instance of the JProCo database, then please run SQLQueries2012Vol2Chapter14.1Setup.sql before proceeding.

```
SELECT * FROM [Grant]
```

```
SELECT * FROM GrantFeed
```

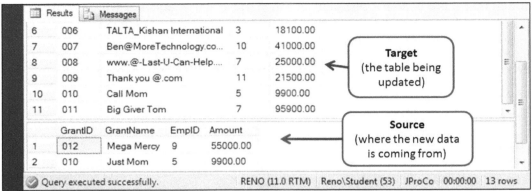

Figure 14.14 The target table, [Grant], and the source table, GrantFeed.

In the Grant table, we see all grants (Grant 001 through Grant 011). The two records from GrantFeed are additional new data that we need to have reflected in our database. It looks like Grant 010 is again going to change its name from Call Mom to Just Mom. So we have one update to make from this GrantFeed table. Grant 012, Mega Mercy, was found by Employee 9 in the amount of $55000 and is a brand new grant.

The action needed here is to take GrantFeed (the source table), MERGE it into the Grant table (the target table), and perform an upsert (UPDATE where records are found, INSERT where records aren't found).

So what we're going to do is open a new query window and begin with the basic parts of the MERGE statement we saw in our last example:

- o MERGE into the target table (MERGE Grant AS gr)
- o USING the source table (USING GrantFeed AS gf)
- o ON the correlating field (ON gr.GrantID = gf.GrantID)
- o WHEN MATCHED THEN…we want to update
- o WHEN NOT MATCHED THEN…we want to insert

```
MERGE [Grant] AS gr
USING GrantFeed AS gf
ON gr.GrantID = gf.GrantID

WHEN MATCHED THEN  --Update

WHEN NOT MATCHED THEN -- insert
```

Figure 14.15 Begin with the basic parts of the MERGE statement we saw in our last example.

Now fill in the two missing pieces – the UPDATE statement and the INSERT statement. Then remember to end the MERGE statement with a semicolon.

When the GrantIDs are matched, it means the source record already contains the GrantID. So we just need to line up (i.e., correlate) the other fields (GrantName, EmpID and Amount) between target and source (i.e., between gr and gf) in order to allow the updates. Wherever there is a match on GrantID, we want every field in the source record to UPDATE its value into the target record.

When the source record's GrantID is not matched, then we INSERT. Like other INSERT statements we've written in this book, we list each target column name in order. The only difference here is we list the target field names in place of the literal values we are used to seeing. But the idea is the same. We want each target field to bring in the value it finds in the source field.

Remember your delimiting semicolon and then run all of this code (Figure 14.16).

```
MERGE [Grant] AS gr
USING GrantFeed AS gf
ON gr.GrantID = gf.GrantID

WHEN MATCHED THEN UPDATE
SET gr.GrantName = gf.GrantName,
gr.Amount = gf.Amount, gr.EmpID = gf.EmpID

WHEN NOT MATCHED THEN INSERT
(GrantID, GrantName, EmpID, Amount) VALUES
(gf.GrantID, gf.GrantName, gf.EmpID, gf.Amount);
```

Messages
(2 row(s) affected)
0 rows

Figure 14.16 Remember to end the MERGE statement with a semicolon, and then run this code.

Two rows have been affected, and there were two records in the source table (Look back to Figure 14.14). Now look at the Grant table to confirm the result.

```
SELECT * FROM [Grant]
```

	GrantID	GrantName	EmpID	Amount	GrantID
1	007	Ben@MoreTechnology.com	10	41000.00	007
2	008	www.@-Last-U-Can-Help.com	7	25000.00	008
3	009	Thank you @.com	11	21500.00	009
4	010	Just Mom	5	9900.00	010
5	011	Big Giver Tom	7	95900.00	011
6	012	Mega Mercy	9	55000.00	012

12 rows

Figure 14.17 Our MERGE statement worked perfectly. One record updated, one record inserted.

Our MERGE statement worked perfectly! Grant 010 has been updated to "Just Mom" and the new grant Mega Mercy has been inserted.

After the next section, we will see some permanent changes to the Grant table. However, the tables in this section will all be reset with the next setup script (SQLQueries2012Vol2Chapter14.1Setup.sql script), so that we can keep working with MERGE and merging deletes in the next section.

Lab 14.1: Using Merge

Lab Prep: Each lab has one or more Skill Checks. Start with Skill Check 1 and proceed until reaching the Points to Ponder section.

Before beginning this lab, verify that SQL Server 2012 is properly installed and operating. Before running the lab setup script for resetting the database (SQLQueries2012Vol2Chapter14.1Setup.sql), please make sure to close all query windows within SSMS. An open query window pointing to a database context can lock that database preventing it from updating when the script is executing. A simple way to assure all query windows are closed, is to exit out of SSMS, then open a new instance of SSMS, and lastly run the setup script.

Skill Check 1: Create a stored procedure called UpsertLocation that accepts four parameters – one for each field in the Location table. This stored procedure should make updates to existing records and insert any new records. After creating the stored procedure, call on it with the following code.

```
EXEC UpsertLocation 1,'545 Pike', 'Seattle', 'WA'

EXEC UpsertLocation 5,'1595 Main', 'Philadelphia', 'PA'
```

Check to see that the update was made to Location 1 and a new record (Location 5) was inserted by running a query on the Location table. When you are done, your result should resemble Figure 14.18.

```
SELECT * FROM Location
```

	LocationID	Street	City	State
1	1	545 Pike	Seattle	WA
2	2	222 Second AVE	Boston	MA
3	3	333 Third PL	Chicago	IL
4	4	444 Ruby ST	Spokane	WA
5	5	1595 Main	Philadelphia	PA

5 rows

Figure 14.18 Skill Check 1 updates one record and inserts one record.

Skill Check 2: You have a table named PayRatesFeed with the updated pay information that needs to be fed into the PayRates table (Figure 14.19).

SELECT * FROM PayRatesFeed

	EmpID	YearlySalary	MonthlySalary	HourlyRate	Selector	Estimate
1	1	97500.00	NULL	NULL	1	1
2	2	85500.00	NULL	NULL	1	1
3	14	52000.00	NULL	NULL	1	1

3 rows

Figure 14.19 Skill Check 2 uses PayRatesFeed as a source table for the target table, PayRates.

Write a MERGE statement that will update employee 1 to a YearlySalary of $97500 and insert a new pay record for EmpID 14 with year salary of $52000. When you are done, your result should resemble Figure 14.20.

SELECT * FROM PayRates

	EmpID	YearlySalary	MonthlySalary	HourlyRate	Selector	Estimate
2	2	85500.00	NULL	NULL	1	1
3	3	NULL	NULL	45.00	3	2080
4	4	NULL	6500.00	NULL	2	12
5	5	NULL	5800.00	NULL	2	12
6	6	52000.00	NULL	NULL	1	1
7	7	NULL	6100.00	NULL	2	12
8	8	NULL	NULL	32.00	3	2080
9	9	NULL	NULL	18.00	3	2080
10	10	NULL	NULL	17.00	3	2080
11	11	115000.00	NULL	NULL	1	1
12	12	NULL	NULL	21.00	3	2080
13	13	72000.00	NULL	NULL	1	1
14	14	52000.00	NULL	NULL	NULL	NULL

Query executed successfully.   RENO (11.0 RTM) Reno\Student (53) JProCo 00:00:00 14 rows

Figure 14.20 Your MERGE statement will update the target table with data from the source table.

Skill Check 3: Create a stored procedure called UpsertMgmtTraining that accepts four parameters for each field in the MgmtTraining table. This stored procedure should make updates to existing records and insert any new records. Create the stored procedure and call on it with the following code.

Check to see that the updates were made to Class 3 and a new class was inserted by running a query on the MgmtTraining table. When you are done, your result should resemble Figure 14.21.

```
EXEC UpsertMgmtTraining 3, 'Challenging Negotiations', 40,
'12/1/2009'

EXEC UpsertMgmtTraining 0, 'Corporate Privacy', 8,
'12/1/2009'

SELECT * FROM MgmtTraining
```

	ClassID	ClassName	ClassDurationHours	ApprovedDate
1	1	Embracing Diversity	12	2007-01-01 00:00:00.000
2	2	Interviewing	6	2007-01-15 00:00:00.000
3	3	Challenging Negotiations	40	2009-12-01 00:00:00.000
4	4	Empowering Others	18	2012-11-14 13:01:18.570
5	8	Corporate Privacy	8	2009-12-01 00:00:00.000

Query executed successfully.   RENO (11.0 RTM) Reno\Student (51) JProCo 00:00:00 5 rows

Figure 14.21 After creating and executing your sproc UpsertMgmtTraining, check your results.

Answer Code: The T-SQL code for this lab is located in the downloadable files as a file named Lab14.1_UsingMerge.sql

Points to Ponder - Using Merge

1. MERGE is a DML statement.

2. The MERGE clause was first introduced in SQL Server version 2008.

3. MERGE compares data between two identically structured tables (a source table and a target table).

4. The source table contains the new comparison data.

5. The target table is the one being updated.

6. UPSERT is shorthand for the query logic updating field values if a record is already present and inserting a new record when the source record is not found in the target.

7. MERGE requires a semicolon to delimit the end of the statement.

Merging Deletes

Our next example will include a different source table, GrantCheckMaster, which we will use with a MERGE statement. However, instead of containing a few change examples, GrantCheckMaster will be treated as the master file which will dictate inserts, updates and deletes in the Grant table. We will step up the code in our MERGE statement to handle all of these changes for us, including deleting records from the target which are not matched by the source.

```
SELECT *
FROM [Grant]
ORDER BY GrantID

SELECT *
FROM GrantCheckMaster
ORDER BY GrantID
```

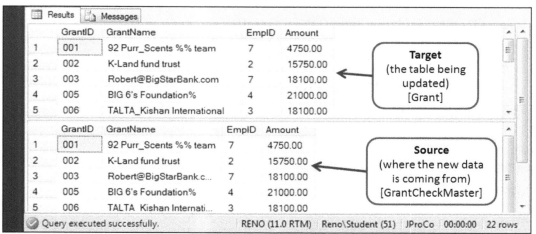

Figure 14.22 The target table, Grant, and the source table, GrantCheckMaster.

These two tables have the same number of records. There are 11 records in the Grant table and 11 records in the GrantCheckMaster table, but notice a few differences. 'K_Land fund trust' has been changed to 'K-Land fund trust' with a hyphen, so the record for Grant 002 should be updated from GrantCheckMaster, which is the source table. Grant 010 has also had a name change to "Just Mom".

One significant change is that Grant 004 does not appear in the source table, GrantCheckMaster. Our guidelines from the prior section would have ignored this record. However, this section is about MERGE with DELETE. So in this case we'll say, "if a record's missing in the source, we want it deleted from the target".

We have one other change. There is a Grant 012 Mega Mercy in the source, but there is no Grant 012 in the target table. In other words, we will want one insert, two updates, and one delete. We want to insert Mega Mercy, we want to update GrantName values of K_Land fund trust and Call Mom. We also want to delete grant 004.

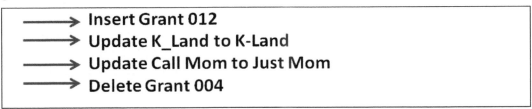

Figure 14.23 We need MERGE to perform one INSERT, two UPDATEs, and one DELETE.

Let's begin building the code to accomplish these four actions. We will build it in steps and add in the new components to handle the DELETE. Begin with the basic parts of the MERGE statement we know:

- o MERGE into the target table (MERGE Grant AS gr)
- o USING the source table (USING GrantCheckMaster AS gcm)
- o ON the correlating field (ON gr.GrantID = gcm.GrantID)
- o WHEN MATCHED THEN...update
- o WHEN NOT MATCHED BY TARGET THEN...insert
- o WHEN NOT MATCHED BY SOURCE THEN...delete

```
MERGE [Grant] AS gr
USING GrantCheckMaster AS gcm
ON gr.GrantID = gcm.GrantID
WHEN MATCHED THEN --Update

WHEN NOT MATCHED BY TARGET THEN --Insert

WHEN NOT MATCHED BY SOURCE THEN --Delete
```

Figure 14.24 Begin with the basics of the MERGE statement.

Note that there are two types of NOT MATCHED – "NOT MATCHED BY TARGET" and "NOT MATCHED BY SOURCE". If it's not matched by the target (i.e., the Grant table) – meaning that the Grant table doesn't have it, but the GrantCheckMaster table does – then it should do an insert. Now how about when it's "NOT MATCHED BY SOURCE"? In other words, if the source doesn't have Grant 004, and the target (the Grant table) does have Grant 004, then we want to delete it.

Now fill in any missing pieces. Write the UPDATE, INSERT, and DELETE statements before ending the MERGE statement with a semicolon.

```
MERGE [Grant] AS gr
USING GrantCheckMaster AS gcm
ON gr.GrantID = gcm.GrantID

WHEN MATCHED THEN UPDATE
SET gr.EmpID = gcm.EmpID,
gr.GrantName = gcm.GrantName, gr.Amount = gcm.Amount

WHEN NOT MATCHED BY TARGET THEN INSERT
(GrantID, GrantName, EmpID, Amount) VALUES
(gcm.GrantID, gcm.GrantName, gcm.EmpID, gcm.Amount)

WHEN NOT MATCHED BY SOURCE THEN DELETE;
```

Messages
(12 row(s) affected)
0 rows

Figure 14.25 Fill in the UPDATE, INSERT, and DELETE statements, then add the semicolon.

It confirms 12 rows have been affected. Let's take a look at the result. We're expecting to see four things: 1) K-Land with a hyphen, 2) Grant 004 should be gone, 3) the new name Just Mom, and 4) Mega Mercy should have been added.

```
SELECT * FROM [Grant]
ORDER BY GrantID
```

	GrantID	GrantName	EmpID	Amount
1	001	92 Purr_Scents %% team	7	4750.00
2	002	K-Land fund trust	2	15750.00 ←
3	003	Robert@BigStarBank.com	7	18100.00 ←
4	005	BIG 6's Foundation%	4	21000.00
5	006	TALTA_Kishan International	3	18100.00
6	007	Ben@MoreTechnology.com	10	41000.00
7	008	www.@-Last-U-Can-Help.com	7	25000.00
8	009	Thank you @.com	11	21500.00
9	010	Just Mom	5	9900.00 ←
10	011	Big Giver Tom	7	95900.00
11	012	Mega Mercy	9	55000.00 ←

Query executed successfully.   RENO (11.0 RTM)   Reno\Student (51)   JProCo   00:00:00   11 rows

Figure 14.26 The MERGE successfully handled the INSERT, UPDATE, and DELETE actions.

And we do find all four items in our result. In fact, an EXCEPT query between the source and target tables indicates the tables are identical following the MERGE. Both tables contain all the same fields and the same records (For more on EXCEPT, see Chapter 9 Set Operators).

```
SELECT * FROM [Grant]
EXCEPT
SELECT * FROM GrantCheckMaster
```

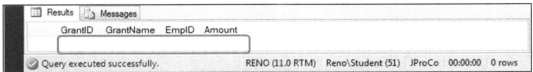

Figure 14.27 After the MERGE, the source and target tables are identical.

We can also confirm visually that identical records now appear in both tables.

```
SELECT *
FROM [Grant]
ORDER BY GrantID
```

```
SELECT *
FROM GrantCheckMaster
ORDER BY GrantID
```

	GrantID	GrantName	EmpID	Amount
1	001	92 Purr_Scents %% team	7	4750.00
2	002	K-Land fund trust	2	15750...
3	003	Robert@BigStarBank.c...	7	18100...
4	005	BIG 6's Foundation%	4	21000...
5	006	TALTA_Kishan Internati...	3	18100...
6	007	Ben@MoreTechnology....	10	41000...

	GrantID	GrantName	EmpID	Amount
1	001	92 Purr_Scents %% team	7	4750.00
2	002	K-Land fund trust	2	15750.00
3	003	Robert@BigStarBank.c...	7	18100.00
4	005	BIG 6's Foundation%	4	21000.00
5	006	TALTA_Kishan Internati...	3	18100.00
6	007	Ben@MoreTechnology....	10	41000.00

Query executed successfully.   RENO (11.0 RTM)   Reno\Student (51)   JProCo   00:00:00   22 rows

Figure 14.28 After the MERGE, all fields and records in the source and target tables are identical.

Merging Only Changes

When running MERGE operations, you frequently will encounter records that don't actually need to be processed. Consider the GrantCheckMaster example we just completed. Only four records were changed (one INSERT, two UPDATEs, and one DELETE), but SQL Server confirmed that our MERGE query affected 12 records (Figure 14.25).

In that case, we didn't experience a downside to having MERGE process all the records, even though it only needed to touch four. Our result was perfect and the tables were small enough that we didn't detect any performance delay that may have been incurred by MERGE needlessly processing those extra records. But what if you had source and target tables each with 1 million or more records? Then you would definitely be concerned about ensuring MERGE handled only the needed records.

One way to do this is to have MERGE check the matched records to see whether or not they have any changes before running the update. Our next example shows us how to build this into our MERGE statement.

Take a moment to notice two things about the Employee table. There are currently 13 records, and shows Phil works for Manager 4.

```
SELECT *
FROM Employee
```

	EmpID	LastName	FirstName	HireDate	LocationID	ManagerID	Status
8	8	Marshbank	John	2001-11-15…	NULL	4	Active
9	9	Newton	James	2003-09-30…	2	3	Active
10	10	O'Haire	Terry	2004-10-04…	2	3	Active
11	11	Smith	Sally	1989-04-01…	1	NULL	Active
12	12	O'Neil	Barbara	1995-05-26…	4	4	Has Tenure
13	13	Wilconkinski	Phil	2009-06-11…	1	4	Active
							13 rows

Figure 14.29 This shows records of Employee table.

PromotionList is a staging table for the Employee table, and it's designed to insert or update changes to an employee's ManagerID due to a promotion.

```
SELECT * FROM PromotionList
```

	EmpID	LastName	FirstName	HireDate	LocationID	ManagerID	Status
1	14	Smith	Janis	2009-10-18…	1	4	Active
2	10	O'Haire	Terry	2004-10-04…	2	3	Active
3	11	Smith	Sally	1989-04-01…	1	NULL	Active
4	12	O'Neil	Barbara	1995-05-26…	4	4	Has Tenu…
5	13	Wilconkinski	Phil	2009-06-11…	1	11	Active
							5 rows

Figure 14.30 This table should insert or update manager changes to the Employee table.

This staging table contains brand new employees who are getting a new boss, in addition to existing employees who are getting a new boss. Let's look at the five records from the source table and see if we should update or insert them into the target table (Figure 14.31).

```
--Target Table
SELECT *
FROM Employee

--Source Table
SELECT *
FROM PromotionList
```

	EmpID	LastName	FirstName	HireDate	LocationID	ManagerID	Status
7	7	Lonning	David	2000-01-01 00:00:00.000	1	11	On Leave
8	8	Marshb...	John	2001-11-15 00:00:00.000	NULL	4	Active
9	9	Newton	James	2003-09-30 00:00:00.000	2	3	Active
10	10	O'Haire	Terry	2004-10-04 00:00:00.000	2	3	Active
11	11	Smith	Sally	1989-04-01 00:00:00.000	1	NULL	Active
12	12	O'Neil	Barbara	1995-05-26 00:00:00.000	4	4	Has Tenure
13	13	Wilconki...	Phil	2009-06-11 00:00:00.000	1	4	Active

	EmpID	LastName	FirstName	HireDate	LocationID	ManagerID	Status
1	14	Smith	Janis	2009-10-18 00:00:00.000	1	4	Active
2	10	O'Haire	Terry	2004-10-04 00:00:00.000	2	3	Active
3	11	Smith	Sally	1989-04-01 00:00:00.000	1	NULL	Active
4	12	O'Neil	Barbara	1995-05-26 00:00:00.000	4	4	Has ...
5	13	Wilconki...	Phil	2009-06-11 00:00:00.000	1	11	Active

Query executed successfully.   RENO (11.0 RTM)   Reno\Student (53)   JProCo   00:00:00   18 rows

Figure 14.31 Review the five PromotionList records. Which should MERGE into the target table?

Janis Smith (Employee 14) doesn't exist in the target table, so that record should be inserted. Terry O'Haire (Employee 10) works for ManagerID 3 in the Employee table, and he still works for ManagerID 3 in the PromotionList table. Sally Smith and Barbara O'Neil each show the same ManagerID in both tables and will not need to be updated.

We do see one manager change in PromotionList, which is that Phil Wilconkinski is going to report to ManagerID 11. He is being promoted and will report to the CEO, Sally Smith.

It appears that only two of the five PromotionList records will actually need to be updated or inserted into the target (Employee) table. Three of the five records have no change between the source and target tables. So should we have MERGE run an update statement against those three records, or would that be a waste of processing power?

We would like our MERGE statement to only merge changed records. Whether it inserts or updates them, we only want MERGE to update records where there is a difference between the source record and the target record.

Thus, we want to see MERGE affect just two of the five records. Our goal is to insert the one new record (Janis), update the one changed record (Phil), and leave alone the three identical records.

This MERGE statement will be similar to the previous MERGE statements we've run. We want to take any existing records from PromotionList that have a new Manager ID and update them. The one new element we will introduce is the "WHEN MATCHED AND...THEN" clause. After the ON clause locates the matches, the AND clause adds a condition where not only does a record need to match to get updated, but the record must also contain a change in ManagerID. Otherwise, MERGE will simply leave that record alone.

- o MERGE into the target table (MERGE Employee AS em)
- o USING the source table (USING PromotionList AS pl)
- o ON the correlating field (ON em.EmpID = pl.EmpID)
- o WHEN MATCHED AND
  - • [condition: NOT (em.ManagerID = pl.ManagerID)] THEN...update
- o WHEN NOT MATCHED THEN...insert

```
MERGE Employee AS em
USING PromotionList as pl
ON em.EmpID = pl.EmpID

WHEN MATCHED AND NOT (em.ManagerID = pl.ManagerID) THEN --Update

WHEN NOT MATCHED THEN --Insert
```

Figure 14.32 The MERGE statement is marked but not yet completed.

If it does not match, what do we do? We're going to INSERT the values from the source table. There are seven fields in the Employee table, and we want every single field to be coming from the source, which is PromotionList. And finally we've got to make sure we terminate our MERGE statement with a semicolon.

Before we run our query, notice we have five records in the PromotionList table. One record is completely new. The other four records exist, but only one of those records will be updated. So we expect to see two records updated.

```
MERGE Employee AS em
USING PromotionList as pl
ON em.EmpID = pl.EmpID

WHEN MATCHED
AND NOT (em.ManagerID = pl.ManagerID) THEN UPDATE
SET em.ManagerID = pl.ManagerID
```

```
WHEN NOT MATCHED THEN INSERT
(EmpID, LastName, FirstName, HireDate,
LocationID, ManagerID, Status) VALUES
(pl.EmpID, pl.LastName, pl.FirstName, pl.HireDate,
pl.LocationID, pl.ManagerID, pl.[Status]);
```

Messages
(2 row(s) affected)

0 rows

Figure 14.33 This MERGE statement is completed and will upsert the new records.

Perfect – just two rows were affected. Now let's check our PromotionList and our Employee table.

	EmpID	LastName	FirstName	HireDate	LocationID	ManagerID	Status
11	11	Smith	Sally	1989-04-01 00:00:00.000	1	NULL	Active
12	12	O'Neil	Barbara	1995-05-26 00:00:00.000	4	4	Has Tenure
13	13	Wilconkinski	Phil	2009-06-11 00:00:00.000	1	11	Active
14	14	Smith	Janis	2009-10-18 00:00:00.000	1	4	Active

	EmpID	LastName	FirstName	HireDate	LocationID	ManagerID	Status
1	14	Smith	Janis	2009-10-18 00:00:00.000	1	4	Active
2	10	O'Haire	Terry	2004-10-04 00:00:00.000	2	3	Active
3	11	Smith	Sally	1989-04-01 00:00:00.000	1	NULL	Active
4	12	O'Neil	Barbara	1995-05-26 00:00:00.000	4	4	Has ...
5	13	Wilconki...	Phil	2009-06-11 00:00:00.000	1	11	Active

Query executed successfully.   RENO (11.0 RTM)   Reno\Student (53)   JProCo   00:00:00   19 rows

Figure 14.34 This shows the updated Employee table.

And the change has been made. We have a newly inserted Employee 14 record, and Phil now reports to ManagerID 11 instead of ManagerID 4

Lab 14.2: MERGE Updating Options

Lab Prep: Each lab has one or more Skill Checks. Start with Skill Check 1 and proceed until reaching the Points to Ponder section.

Before beginning this lab, verify that SQL Server 2012 is properly installed and operating. Before running the lab setup script for resetting the database (SQLQueries2012Vol2Chapter14.2Setup.sql), please make sure to close all query windows within SSMS. An open query window pointing to a database context can lock that database preventing it from updating when the script is executing. A simple way to assure all query windows are closed, is to exit out of SSMS, then open a new instance of SSMS, and lastly run the setup script.

Skill Check 1: The PayRatesFeed table has three records. The first record shows a yearly salary of 97500 per year which is identical to employee 1's pay in the PayRates table. This record should not be updated. The PayRatesFeed table shows the new pay for employee 2 will be 85500 per year, which is higher than the current 79000 in the PayRates table. This record will need to be updated. The last record from the PayRatesFeed table shows a pay of 52000 per year for employee 14. Since there is no employee 14 in the PayRates table, you must insert this record. Write a MERGE statement that will insert new records and update existing records only if their YearlySalary has changed. When done, your result will look like Figure 14.35.

```
SELECT * FROM PayRatesFeed
SELECT * FROM PayRates
```

	EmpID	YearlySalary	MonthlySalary	HourlyRate	Selector	Estimate
1	1	97500.00	NULL	NULL	1	1
2	2	85500.00	NULL	NULL	1	1
3	14	52000.00	NULL	NULL	1	1

	EmpID	YearlySalary	MonthlySalary	HourlyRate	Selector	Estimate
1	1	97500.00	NULL	NULL	1	1
2	2	85500.00	NULL	NULL	1	1
3	3	NULL	NULL	45.00	3	2080
4	4	NULL	6500.00	NULL	2	12
5	5	NULL	5800.00	NULL	2	12
6	6	52000.00	NULL	NULL	1	1
7	7	NULL	6100.00	NULL	2	12
8	8	NULL	NULL	32.00	3	2080
9	9	NULL	NULL	18.00	3	2080
10	10	NULL	NULL	17.00	3	2080
11	11	115000.00	NULL	NULL	1	1
12	12	NULL	NULL	21.00	3	2080
13	13	72000.00	NULL	NULL	1	1
14	14	52000.00	NULL	NULL	NULL	NULL

Query executed successfully. RENO (11.0 RTM) Reno\Student (51) JProCo 00:00:00 17 rows

Figure 14.35 Write code to update one record and insert one record into the PayRates table.

Answer Code: The T-SQL code for this lab is located in the downloadable files as a file named Lab14.2_MergeUpdateOptions.sql

Points to Ponder - MERGE Updating Options

1. A WHEN MATCHED clause will UPDATE or DELETE rows in the target table.

2. A WHEN NOT MATCHED BY TARGET will INSERT rows into the target table which are found only in the source table.

3. Use WHEN NOT MATCHED BY SOURCE to UPDATE or DELETE rows in the target table. We can specify DELETE to remove rows from the target table which are not present in the source table.

4. We can have MERGE check the matched records to detect changes before running an update. A "WHEN MATCHED AND" clause with a condition can instruct MERGE to update only change records. Particularly with larger tables, this can make your code more efficient and save processing time wasted by applying UPDATE logic to records which have not changed.

Chapter Glossary

MERGE: A DML statement that compares data between two identically structured tables.

Source Table: In a MERGE statement, a table or list that is providing new records to input.

Target Table: The existing table in a MERGE statement which will receive new records.

Upsert: The term for the query logic updating field values if a record is already present and inserting a new record when the source record is not found in the target.

Using Code: The part of the code in a MERGE statement that compares values to the target table.

WHEN MATCHED: A clause that will UPDATE or DELETE rows in the table.

WHEN NOT MATCHED: A clause that will INSERT rows into a target table which are only found in the source table.

Review Quiz - Chapter Fourteen

1.) You have a stored procedure name UpsertLocation with the following structure.

```
CREATE PROC UpsertLocation @LocID INT, @Street VARCHAR(50),
@City VARCHAR(25), @State VARCHAR(25)
AS
BEGIN
  --Remaining Code Here
END
```

You need to complete the code which will update or insert new records into the variables based on the values found in the Location table. What code will achieve this result?

O a. MERGE Statement

O b. INSERT Statement

O c. UPDATE Statement

O d. OUTPUT Clause

2.) Which table do you put right after the MERGE statement?

O a. All tables

O b. The source table

O c. The target table

O d. Any virtual table

3.) You have a stored procedure name UpsertLocation with the following structure.

```
CREATE PROC UpsertLocation @LocID INT, @Street VARCHAR(50),
@City VARCHAR(25), @State VARCHAR(25)
AS
BEGIN
  --Remaining Code Here
END
```

You need to complete the code which will update or insert new records into the Location table based on the values found in the variables. What code will achieve this result?

O a.
```
MERGE Location AS loc
  USING (SELECT @LocID, @Street, @City, @State) AS LocScr
  (LocationID, street, city, state)
  ON loc.LocationID = LocScr.LocationID
  WHEN NOT MATCHED THEN UPDATE
  SET loc.street = @Street, loc.City = @City,
  loc.State = @State
  WHEN NOT MATCHED THEN INSERT (LocationID, street,
  city, state) VALUES
  (@LocID, @Street, @City, @State);
```

O b.
```
USING Location AS loc
  MERGE (SELECT @LocID, @Street, @City, @State) AS LocScr
  (LocationID, street, city, state)
  ON loc.LocationID = LocScr.LocationID
  WHEN NOT MATCHED THEN UPDATE
  SET loc.street = @Street, loc.City = @City,
  loc.State = @State
  WHEN NOT MATCHED THEN INSERT
  (LocationID, street, city, state) VALUES
  (@LocID, @Street, @City, @State);
```

O c.
```
MERGE Location AS loc
  USING (SELECT @LocID, @Street, @City, @State) AS LocScr
  (LocationID, street, city, state)
  ON loc.LocationID = LocScr.LocationID
  WHEN MATCHED THEN UPDATE
  SET loc.street = @Street, loc.City = @City,
  loc.State = @State
  WHEN NOT MATCHED THEN INSERT
  (LocationID, street, city, state) VALUES
  (@LocID, @Street, @City, @State);
```

4.)   You have a table named LocationFeed which contains the latest changes that need to be made to the Location table. Sometimes the records in the LocationFeed table are new records and sometimes they are updates to existing records. You want to ensure that all changes from LocationFeed are made to the Location table. What code will achieve this result?

O a.
```
MERGE dbo.Location AS Loc
USING dbo.LocationFeed AS LFeed
ON Loc.LocationID = LFeed.LocationID
WHEN MATCHED THEN UPDATE
SET Loc.Street = LFeed.Street, Loc.City = LFeed.City,
Loc.State = LFeed.State
WHEN NOT MATCHED THEN INSERT
(LocationID, Street, City, State) VALUES
(LFeed.LocationID, LFeed.Street, LFeed.City,LFeed.[State]);
```

O b.
```
MERGE dbo.Location AS Loc
USING dbo.LocationFeed AS LFeed
ON Loc.LocationID = LFeed.LocationID
WHEN MATCHED THEN DELETE UPDATE
SET Loc.Street = LFeed.Street, Loc.City = LFeed.City,
Loc.State = LFeed.State
WHEN NOT MATCHED THEN INSERT
(LocationID, Street, City, State) VALUES
(LFeed.LocationID, LFeed.Street, LFeed.City,LFeed.[State]);
```

O c.
```
MERGE dbo.Location AS Loc
USING dbo.LocationFeed AS LFeed
ON Loc.LocationID = LFeed.LocationID
WHEN MATCHED THEN SELECT * FROM LFeed
UPDATE SET Loc.Street = LFeed.Street,
Loc.City = LFeed.City, Loc.State = LFeed.State
WHEN NOT MATCHED THEN INSERT
(LocationID, Street, City, State) VALUES
(LFeed.LocationID,LFeed.Street,LFeed.City,LFeed.[State]);
```

5.) You have a table named LocationFinal which contains the final approved list for the Location table. You need to create a MERGE statement that does the following.

> o Records in LocationFinal that are new should be inserted in the Location table.
> o Records that exist in both tables should be updated to the values in the LocationFinal table.
> o Records that exist in Location but not in LocationFinal should be deleted from the Location Table

What code will achieve this result?

O a.
```
MERGE dbo.Location AS Loc
USING dbo.LocationFinal AS LFeed
ON Loc.LocationID = LFeed.LocationID
WHEN MATCHED THEN UPDATE
SET Loc.Street = LFeed.Street, Loc.City = LFeed.City,
Loc.State = LFeed.State
WHEN NOT MATCHED BY TARGET THEN INSERT
(LocationID, Street, City, State) VALUES
(LFeed.LocationID, LFeed.Street, LFeed.City, LFeed.[State])
WHEN NOT MATCHED BY SOURCE THEN DELETE;
```

O b.
```
MERGE dbo.Location AS Loc
USING dbo.LocationFinal AS LFeed
ON Loc.LocationID = LFeed.LocationID
WHEN MATCHED THEN UPDATE
SET Loc.Street = LFeed.Street, Loc.City = LFeed.City,
Loc.State = LFeed.State
WHEN NOT MATCHED BY TARGET THEN DELETE
WHEN NOT MATCHED BY SOURCE THEN INSERT
(LocationID, Street, City, State) VALUES
(LFeed.LocationID,LFeed.Street,LFeed.City,LFeed.State);
```

O c.
```
MERGE dbo.Location AS Loc
USING dbo.LocationFinal AS LFeed
ON Loc.LocationID = LFeed.LocationID
WHEN MATCHED THEN UPDATE
SET Loc.Street = LFeed.Street, Loc.City = LFeed.City,
Loc.State = LFeed.State
WHEN NOT MATCHED THEN DELETE OR INSERT
LocationID, Street, City, State) VALUES
(LFeed.LocationID,LFeed.Street,LFeed.City,LFeed.State);
```

6.) You have a Contestant and a CFeed table. The Contestant table holds all current contestants and their highest score. The CFeed table holds information waiting to be verified and then later merged with the Contestant table. Both tables have identical structure as seen in Figure 14.36. Use the following code to update the Contestant table from the source table, CFeed:

```
SELECT * FROM Contestant
SELECT * FROM CFeed
```

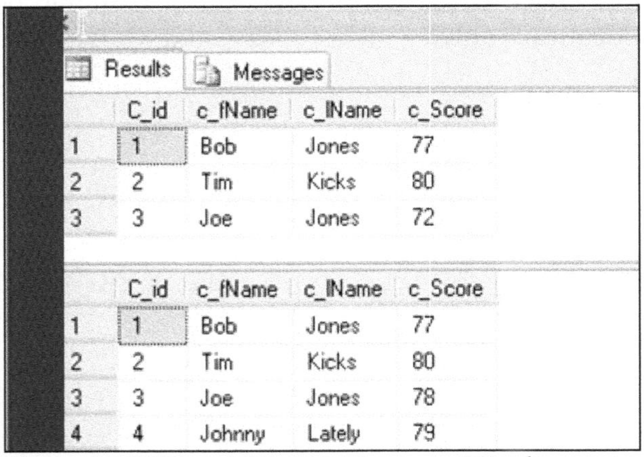

Results | Messages

	C_id	c_fName	c_lName	c_Score
1	1	Bob	Jones	77
2	2	Tim	Kicks	80
3	3	Joe	Jones	72

	C_id	c_fName	c_lName	c_Score
1	1	Bob	Jones	77
2	2	Tim	Kicks	80
3	3	Joe	Jones	78
4	4	Johnny	Lately	79

Figure 14.36 Target Contestant, source CFeed.

```
MERGE Contestant AS ct
USING CFeed AS fd
ON ct.C_id = fd.C_id
WHEN MATCHED THEN UPDATE
SET ct.c_Score = fd.c_Score
WHEN NOT MATCHED THEN INSERT
(c_id, c_fName, c_lName, c_Score) VALUES
(fd.c_id, fd.c_fName, fd.c_lName, fd.c_Score);
```

How many records will be inserted and how many will be updated?

O a. 1 record is inserted and 3 records are updated.

O b. 3 records are inserted and 1 record is updated.

O c. 3 records are inserted and 3 records are updated.

O d. 1 record is inserted and 1 record is updated.

7.) You have a Contestant and a CFeed table. The Contestant table holds all current contestants and their highest score. The CFeed table holds information waiting to be verified and then later merged with the Contestant table. Both tables have identical structure as seen in Figure 14.37

Use the following code to update the Contestant table from the source table, CFeed:

```
SELECT * FROM Contestant
SELECT * FROM CFeed
```

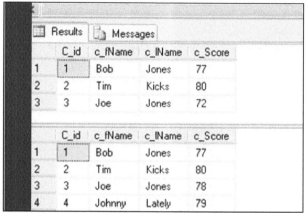

Figure 14.37 Target Contestant, source CFeed.

```
MERGE Contestant AS ct
USING CFeed as fd
ON ct.C_id = fd.C_id
WHEN MATCHED
AND NOT (ct.C_Score = fd.C_Score) THEN UPDATE
SET ct.c_Score = fd.c_Score
WHEN NOT MATCHED THEN INSERT
(c_id, c_fName, c_lName, c_Score) VALUES
(fd.c_id, fd.c_fName, fd.c_lName, fd.c_Score);
```

How many records will be inserted and how many will be updated?

O a. 1 record is inserted and 3 records are updated.

O b. 3 records are inserted and 1 record is updated.

O c. 3 records are inserted and 3 records are updated.

O d. 1 record is inserted and 1 record is updated.

8.) You have two tables. The Student.Students table contains the names of all students enrolled for the current year. The Student.Applicants table contains the names of students who have enrolled for the upcoming year. You have been hired to write a MERGE statement, to insert all the names of students who are enrolled for the upcoming year, but not for the current year, into the Student.Students table. For students who are enrolled in both the current year and the upcoming year, update their address and age. Delete all students who are not re-enrolling for the upcoming year. Which T-SQL MERGE statement should you use?

O a.
```
MERGE Student.Students AS T
USING Student.Applicants AS S
ON S.LastName = T.LastName AND S.FirstName = T.FirstName
WHEN MATCHED THEN UPDATE
SET Address = S.Address, Age = S.Age
WHEN NOT MATCHED BY TARGET THEN INSERT
(LastName, FirstName, Address, Age) VALUES
(S.LastName, S.FirstName, S.Address, S.Age)
WHEN NOT MATCHED BY SOURCE THEN DELETE;
```

O b.
```
MERGE Student.Students AS T
USING Student.Applicants  AS S
ON S.LastName = T.LastName AND S.FirstName = T.FirstName
WHEN MATCHED THEN DELETE
WHEN NOT MATCHED THEN INSERT
(LastName, FirstName, Address, Age) VALUES
(S.LastName, S.FirstName, S.Address, S.Age)
WHEN NOT MATCHED BY SOURCE THEN UPDATE
SET Address = T.Address, Age = T.Age;
```

Answer Key

1.) Because INSERT or UPDATE alone will only do half of what is required, (b) and (c) are both incorrect. OUTPUT will neither UPDATE nor INSERT any records, so (d) is wrong too. Since MERGE will perform either an UPDATE or an INSERT depending on the values in the records, (a) is the correct answer.

2.) The only thing that comes immediately after the MERGE statement is the target table, making (a), (b) and (d) all incorrect. Since the target table is the first thing to follow the MERGE statement, (c) is the correct answer.

3.) The two WHEN NOT MATCHED clauses make (a) an incorrect choice. USING is a directive telling the MERGE statement what object to use as the data source and must come within the body of the code implementing it, so (b) is incorrect too. Because the proper syntax of a MERGE statement is displayed in (c) it is the correct answer.

4.) DELETE must be followed by a semi-colon to end the MERGE statement or another WHEN clause to contain UPDATE or INSERT code, making (b) an incorrect answer. WHEN MATCHED THEN must be followed by UPDATE, INSERT or DELETE to work correctly, so (c) is wrong too. The right answer is (a) because it is the only code that performs an UPDATE on matching records and an INSERT on new (NOT MATCHED) records.

5.) WHEN NOT MATCHED BY TARGET THEN DELETE will attempt to delete a record that does not exist from the Location table, making (b) one of the wrong answers. Since WHEN NOT MATCHED must include a BY TARGET or BY SOURCE clause to determine WHEN to DELETE rather than INSERT, (c) is the other incorrect answer. Since the only code that properly updates MATCHED records, inserts records WHEN NOT MATCHED BY TARGET and DELETE a record WHEN NOT MATCHED BY SOURCE is (a), that makes it the correct answer.

6.) 3 records in both tables match and will be updated, while only 1 record in the source table does not exist in the target table and will be inserted, so (b), (c) and (d) are all wrong. Since the source table has 1 record that does not have a match in the target table and the other 3 records do have a match, (a) is the correct answer.

7.) 3 records in both tables match on the ID field but only 1 of those has a different score (AND NOT (ct.C_Score = fd.C_Score)) and will be updated, while only 1 record in the source table does not exist in the target table and will be inserted, so (a), (b) and (c) are all wrong. Since the source table has 1 record that does not have a match in the target table and only 1 of the remaining 3 records that match on ID have a differing score, (d) is the correct answer.

8.) WHEN NOT MATCHED will run when an applicant exists and a student does not. In this case we want to insert and since (b) is attempting to delete new students, this answer is wrong. Answer (a) inserts new records and deletes old records which are not in the source (applicants), making this the correct answer.

Bug Catcher Game

To play the Bug Catcher game, run the SQLQueries2012Vol2BugCatcher14.pps file from the BugCatcher folder of the companion files. These files are available from the www.Joes2Pros.com website.

[THIS PAGE INTENTIONALLY LEFT BLANK.]

Chapter 15. The OUTPUT Clause

The OUTPUT feature made its debut in SQL Server 2005 and is a pretty exciting tool. The OUTPUT statement generates a temporary copy of table records you insert, update, delete, or merge. Much like a confirmation page that shows when you make an online payment or a purchase, we can choose to view and discard the confirmation detail, or we can store it.

The OUTPUT statement provides a confirmation copy of the records you just inserted, updated, deleted, or "upserted" using MERGE. Our chapter examples will demonstrate both simply viewing the confirmation as it flashes on screen, as well as storing the record(s).

READER NOTE: *Please run the SQLQueries2012Vol2Chapter15.0Setup.sql script in order to follow along with the examples in the first section of Chapter 15. All scripts mentioned in this chapter are available at www.Joes2Pros.com.*

The JProCo database will need to be reset after most data deletions (You will be prompted each time you need to reset the database). Because of the many resets needed in this chapter, you will be provided several stored procedure "shortcuts" to help make the reset process quicker and easier.

In the first half of the chapter we can elect to either rerun the setup script (SQLQueries2012Vol2Chapter15.0Setup.sql) or the sproc. However, examples in the latter half of the chapter will require you to use stored procedures in order to reset the JProCo database.

OUTPUT

We will first begin our work with the OUTPUT clause, by diving into hands-on examples of deleting, inserting and updating table data. Later, we will demonstrate logging these types of changes in a separate storage table.

READER NOTE: *The OUTPUT statement uses temporary INSERTED and/or DELETED tables. These memory-resident tables are used to determine the changes being caused by the INSERT, DELETE or UPDATE statements.*

Delete Actions with OUTPUT

JProCo has five locations, two of them in Washington State. The DELETE query will remove both the Seattle headquarters and the Spokane office.

```
SELECT * FROM Location
```

	LocationID	Street	City	State
1	1	545 Pike	Seattle	WA
2	2	222 Second AVE	Boston	MA
3	3	333 Third PL	Chicago	IL
4	4	444 Ruby ST	Spokane	WA
5	5	1595 Main	Philadelphia	PA

Query executed successfully.   RENO (11.0 RTM)   Reno\Student (51)   JProCo   00:00:00   5 rows

```
DELETE FROM Location WHERE [State] = 'WA'
```

Messages

```
(2 row(s) affected)
```

100 %

Query executed successfully.   RENO (11.0 RTM)   Reno\Student (51)   JProCo   00:00:00   0 rows

Figure 15.1 By default, SQL Server does not show details of deleted records.

SQL Server confirms that 2 rows were affected, but which 2 rows? It doesn't say, and oftentimes you're not interested in that detail. The OUTPUT clause displays the exact affected rows, even though they're no longer present in your table.

Now reset the Location table to show all the original records. To do this, you may either 1) rerun the current setup script (SQLQueries2012Vol2Chapter15.0Setup.sql) to reset your database; or 2) execute a sproc which resets the Location table (EXEC ResetLocationTables).

Our DELETE query will again remove those same two records from the Location table. But first we will place an OUTPUT statement between the FROM and WHERE clauses. OUTPUT Deleted.* states that we want to see all deleted records and all of their fields in order. When we run this code, instead of saying "2 row(s) affected," it will show us the actual deleted data (Figure 15.2).

```
DELETE
FROM Location
OUTPUT deleted.*
WHERE State = 'WA'
```

	LocationID	Street	City	State
1	1	545 Pike	Seattle	WA
2	4	444 Ruby ST	Spokane	WA

2 rows

Figure 15.2 OUTPUT Deleted.* shows us the two records which we just deleted.

The Deleted.* worked because the OUTPUT clause accessed the deleted memory-resident table. Let's check to confirm that all WA locations have been removed (Figure 15.3).

```
SELECT * FROM Location
```

	LocationID	Street	City	State
1	2	222 Second AVE	Boston	MA
2	3	333 Third PL	Chicago	IL
3	5	1595 Main	Philadelphia	PA

3 rows

Figure 15.3 All WA locations have been removed from the Location table.

Now please reset the Location table once more before moving ahead to the next section. It's your choice whether to rerun the script or EXEC ResetLocationTables as seen in the following code:

```
EXEC ResetLocationTables
```

Insert Actions with OUTPUT

The OUTPUT keyword exposes a special type of temporary table, or tables, based on the type of action you take. In our example, it created a table called Deleted to show us the records it removed. However, if we INSERT records, OUTPUT will not be able to create a Deleted table (Figure 15.4).

```
INSERT INTO Location
OUTPUT Deleted.*
VALUES (6,'555 CanDo St', 'Portland', 'OR')
```

```
Messages
Msg 107, Level 15, State 1, Line 2
The column prefix 'Deleted' does not match with a table name or alias name
used in the query.
```
0 rows

Figure 15.4 If you INSERT records, OUTPUT cannot create a Deleted table.

Now let's reattempt this query with an OUTPUT table called Inserted. This should display what is now the sixth record in the Location table.

```
INSERT INTO Location
OUTPUT inserted.*
VALUES (6,'555 CanDo St', 'Portland', 'OR')
```

	LocationID
1	6

1 rows

Figure 15.5 OUTPUT creates and populates an Inserted table when you INSERT records.

As expected, we successfully ran the insert and saw confirmation in the form of the inserted record's detail. Now let's double check and see the new record showing in the Location table (Figure 15.6).

```
SELECT * FROM Location
```

	LocationID	Street	City	State
1	1	545 Pike	Seattle	WA
2	2	222 Second AVE	Boston	MA
3	3	333 Third PL	Chicago	IL
4	4	444 Ruby ST	Spokane	WA
5	5	1595 Main	Philadelphia	PA
6	6	555 CanDo St	Portland	OR

6 rows

Figure 15.6 Confirm the INSERT was successful by looking at all records in the Location table.

Update Actions with Output

We now know that the OUTPUT keyword will create an Inserted or a Deleted memory-resident table based on the query action you are running. The OUTPUT clause creates an Inserted table when you run an INSERT statement, and it creates the Deleted table when you run a DELETE operation. When you run an UPDATE statement, it creates both tables.

DELETE action + OUTPUT ⟹ Deleted table
INSERT action + OUTPUT ⟹ Inserted table
UPDATE action + OUTPUT ⟹ Deleted AND Inserted tables

Figure 15.7 The OUTPUT keyword creates a table(s) based on the type of query action you run.

Let's think about the UPDATE statement for a moment. DELETE and INSERT each perform a single action – namely, they either add or remove records.

However, an UPDATE statement is a little different. While it also performs a single action (replaces an existing value with a new value), reflecting that change with an OUTPUT statement is a little more complex. If your manager asked you to track the changes made with an UPDATE statement, you really would want to capture two things: 1) the existing record and 2) the updated record.

The OUTPUT clause handles this situation for you. When you run an UPDATE statement, the OUTPUT clause can create and populate both an Inserted and a Deleted table. This is a great way to see each old record next to the new record. Later we will see examples where the old and new records are entered side by side into the same storage table.

Let's see the UPDATE statement in action. First we'll look just at Location 1, which is JProCo's Seattle location (Figure 15.8).

```
SELECT * FROM Location
WHERE LocationID = 1
```

LocationID			
1 1	545 Pike	Seattle	WA
			1 rows

Figure 15.8 Location 1 is JProCo's Seattle headquarters.

Now let's run an UPDATE to change the city to Kirkland.

```
UPDATE Location
SET City = 'Kirkland'
WHERE LocationID = 1
```

Messages
(1 row(s) affected)

Figure 15.9 Run an UPDATE statement to change the city to Kirkland for Location 1.

Kirkland is now the city for Location 1. So if we were to use OUTPUT to generate the confirmation, would we want to see Seattle, or would we want to see Kirkland? As stated earlier, we can look at either one or both. We can see the record we just got rid of (i.e., the Seattle record), the record we just gained (i.e., the Kirkland record), or we can see both together.

Let's change the city once more to Tacoma and then observe OUTPUT generating both Deleted and Inserted tables (Figure 15.10).

```
UPDATE Location
SET City = 'Tacoma'
OUTPUT Deleted.*, Inserted.*
WHERE LocationID = 1
```

Figure 15.10 Run an UPDATE statement to change the city to Tacoma for Location 1.

The OUTPUT statement shows just what we asked for. First we see the old record, and the new record appears right next to it. OUTPUT Deleted.*, Inserted.* is how we were able to specify that the old record should show on the left side and the new record on the right. If we reversed the order, SQL Server would put the new record first and the old record second.

To demonstrate this, let's change the city one last time to Anacortes.

```
UPDATE Location
SET City = 'Anacortes'
OUTPUT Inserted.*, Deleted.*
WHERE LocationID = 1
```

Figure 15.11 OUTPUT orders the Deleted and Inserted tables according to your specification.

Before proceeding to the next section, please reset the Location table back to its original condition by running the sproc (EXEC ResetLocationTables) or the setup script. If you rerun the script, either close all query windows before running it OR make sure that no open windows have JProCo selected in the context dropdown.

Any window pointing to JProCo will lock the JProCo database and cause the script to run improperly.

Using OUTPUT to Log Changes to a Table

The final action to review for the OUTPUT statement is storing information from the Deleted.* and/or Inserted.* tables into a table you create for this purpose. Essentially, we just need to add an "INTO *TableLog*" statement to our prior code (OUTPUT Deleted.* INTO *StorageTable*, OUTPUT Inserted.* INTO *StorageTable*). "*StorageTable*" represents a copy of the table you are changing (i.e., the table in which you are deleting, inserting, or updating records).

Since the Deleted and Inserted tables created by OUTPUT are temporary, they have only a short lifespan. Similar to other temporary objects we covered in Chapters 9 and 10, these tables are available only as long as the query is running. If you want to keep a record of changes you make to a table, you must send the OUTPUT table information into a storage table.

LocationChanges is just such a table. Run SELECT * FROM LocationChanges and confirm you find the empty table LocationChanges in your JProCo database.

This table is identical in structure to the Location table, as shown in the Design interface (Figure 15.12) If you wish to find this in your instance of SQL Server, just right-click the LocationChanges table in Object Explorer and select **Design > Object Explorer > Databases > JProCo > Tables > LocationChanges > Design**

Figure 15.12 LocationChanges is identical in structure to the Location table and is empty.

In the next section, we will see examples where storage tables contain more fields than just columns from the Deleted.* and/or Inserted.* tables. But while we are familiarizing ourselves with the OUTPUT clause and its tables, we want straightforward examples to build upon.

We would like this second table to contain the data for every deleted record from the Location table. Whenever a change takes place, we expect to see that change reflected in our storage table, LocationChanges.

Before we run our OUTPUT statement, run the following queries to see the Location and LocationChanges tables together. Make sure your Location table has been reset (i.e., our practice changes have been erased – Location 1 is reset to Seattle, there is no Portland location, and the LocationChanges table is empty).

```
SELECT *
FROM Location

SELECT *
FROM LocationChanges
```

	LocationID	Street	City	State
1	1	545 Pike	Seattle	WA
2	2	222 Second AVE	Boston	MA
3	3	333 Third PL	Chicago	IL
4	4	444 Ruby ST	Spokane	WA
5	5	1595 Main	Philadelphia	PA
6	6	555 CanDo St	Portland	OR
	LocationID	Street	City	State

6 rows

Figure 15.13 The Location and LocationChanges tables before we run an OUTPUT statement.

Now add an "INTO LocationChanges" statement to our prior code. Instead of displaying the changes on screen, the OUTPUT statement will send the changes into the LocationChanges table (Figure 15.14).

```
DELETE
FROM Location
OUTPUT deleted.* INTO LocationChanges
WHERE State = 'WA'
```

Messages
(2 row(s) affected)

0 rows

Figure 15.14 Instead of displaying changes, OUTPUT sends them into the LocationChanges table.

```
SELECT *              --Location contains 3 records
FROM Location         --following the DELETE

SELECT *              --LocationChanges Stores the
FROM LocationChanges --changes we wish to track
```

	LocationID	Street	City	State
1	2	222 Second AVE	Boston	MA
2	3	333 Third PL	Chicago	IL
3	5	1595 Main	Philadelphia	PA
4	5	**555 CanDo St**	**Portland**	**OR**
	LocationID	street	city	state
1	1	545 Pike	Seattle	WA
2	4	444 Ruby ST	Spokane	WA

6 rows

Figure 15.15 Location and LocationChanges following the DELETE + OUTPUT statement.

Ok, hold onto your seats because next we're going to combine the OUTPUT clause with another advanced technique from a previous chapter. But first we need to reset the Location tables back to their original condition. Either run the script or sproc and see JProCo's current locations in the Location table. It's your choice whether to rerun the script or EXEC ResetLocationTables as seen in the following code:

```
EXEC ResetLocationTables
```

Confirm the five original locations are present and LocationChanges is empty.

```
SELECT *
FROM Location

SELECT *
FROM LocationChanges
```

	LocationID	Street	City	State
1	1	545 Pike	Seattle	WA
2	2	222 Second AVE	Boston	MA
3	3	333 Third PL	Chicago	IL
4	4	444 Ruby ST	Spokane	WA
5	5	1595 Main	Philadelphia	PA
	LocationID	Street	City	State
				5 rows

Figure 15.16 Run the setup script or EXEC ResetLocationTables one last time; confirm 5 locations.

This final example is based upon a hypothetical scenario. Suppose the abbreviation for Washington State changed from WA to WS. We would need to write an UPDATE statement to change the Location table accordingly. Don't run the code yet – we first need to add a few more steps to our query.

```
UPDATE Location
SET [state] = 'WS'
WHERE [State] = 'WA'
```

Figure 15.17 Our hypothetical example updates the official abbreviation for Washington to WS.

The UPDATE code above is correct, but we don't want to lose visibility to the changes being made. Thus, we're going to add the OUTPUT keyword with Inserted.* to our code. Don't run the code yet – we will do that in Figure 15.20.

```
UPDATE Location
SET [state] = 'WS'
OUTPUT Inserted.*
WHERE [State] = 'WA'
```

Figure 15.18 Add OUTPUT Inserted.* to the code, but don't run the query yet.

This UPDATE statement should show two records in the Inserted.* table. If you are uncertain of this, we can run the code to confirm this yourself. If you do, remember to again rerun the sproc ResetLocationTables or the setup script before proceeding. As before, we want to send pre-UPDATE and UPDATE data into the LocationChanges table. But there's more than one way to accomplish this.

Indent the above query; enclose it inside parentheses; and alias it as LocIns (short for "location insert"). Be sure to add SELECT * FROM at the top of your code. Again, we aren't ready to execute this code yet. The code here (Figure 15.19) would generate a SQL Server error, because a nested UPDATE is not allowed in a SELECT statement unless the SELECT feeds rows into an INSERT statement. That is precisely the code we will add in our next and final step.

```
SELECT * FROM   ←—
  (UPDATE Location
  SET [state] = 'WS'
  OUTPUT Inserted.*
  WHERE [State] = 'WA') AS LocIns   ←—
```

Figure 15.19 We have re-written our UPDATE + OUTPUT statement as a derived table.

What we now have is a query which will create LocIns, a derived table. LocIns will contain the two newly updated records from the Inserted table. Recall we intended to populate LocationChanges with the updated records we have to store for tracking purposes. We will do this by writing INSERT INTO LocationChanges above the SELECT statement. We are instructing the derived table to insert its contents into the LocationChanges table. Now run all of this code (Figure 15.20).

```
INSERT INTO LocationChanges
SELECT *
FROM (
  UPDATE Location
  SET State = 'WS'
  OUTPUT Inserted.*
  WHERE State = 'WA') AS LocIns
```

```
Messages
(2 row(s) affected)
                                                    0 rows
```

Figure 15.20 We are instructing the derived table to insert its contents into LocationChanges.

The confirmation message indicates "2 row(s) affected," meaning that the two records in the Location table have been successfully updated. But let's look closer at how many records were impacted overall.

The code actually updated two records in the Location table and then inserted the records affected by the UPDATE + OUTPUT statement into the LocationChanges table. The records formerly containing WA now show WS as the state.

```
SELECT * FROM Location

SELECT * FROM LocationChanges
```

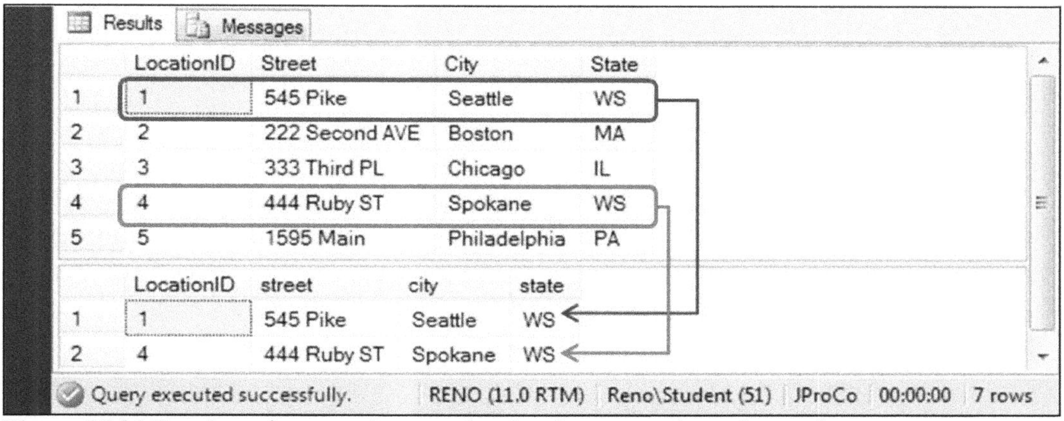

Figure 15.21 Two Location records are updated and two records are inserted.

Notice that, if you take your output and turn it into a derived table, the effects still take place inside of the derived table AND the insert also gets logged in your storage table. You get two inserts and two deletes from using this technique. Run the following code you see in Figure 15.23.

```
INSERT INTO LocationChanges2
SELECT *
FROM (
  UPDATE Location
  SET State = 'WS'
  OUTPUT Inserted.*, Deleted.LocationID AS delLocID,
  Deleted.Street AS delStreet, Deleted.City AS delCity,
  Deleted.State AS delState
  WHERE State = 'WA') AS LocIns
```

Messages
(2 row(s) affected)
0 rows

Figure 15.22 In the next section, we'll see how old and new records can be archived side by side.

Results | Messages

	LocationID	street	city	state	delLocID	delStreet	delCity	delState
1	1	545 Pike	Seattle	WS	1	545 Pike	Seattle	WA
2	4	444 Ruby ST	Spokane	WS	4	444 Ruby ST	Spokane	WA

Query executed successfully. | RENO (11.0 RTM) | Reno\Student (51) | JProCo | 00:00:00 | 2 rows

Figure 15.23 The two inserted records sit next to the deleted records produced during the UPDATE.

Lab 15.1: Using Output

Lab Prep: Each lab has one or more Skill Checks. Start with Skill Check 1 and proceed until reaching the Points to Ponder section.

Before beginning this lab, verify that SQL Server 2012 is properly installed and operating. Before running the lab setup script for resetting the database (SQLQueries2012Vol2Chapter15.1Setup.sql), please make sure to close all query windows within SSMS. An open query window pointing to a database context can lock that database preventing it from updating when the script is executing. A simple way to assure all query windows are closed, is to exit out of SSMS, then open a new instance of SSMS, and lastly run the setup script.

Skill Check 1: The Contractor table has four records: three records from Location 1 and one from Location 2. JProCo is closing down Location 2 next year and thus must delete one record from the Contractor table. As this record is being deleted, we want to see the affected record displayed in our result pane. Write this query and execute the deletion with the appropriate output statement. When you're done, the output will show on your screen (Figure 15.24).

```
DELETE FROM Contractor
--Remaining Code Here
```

	ctrID	LastName	FirstName	HireDate	LocationID
1	3	Fortner	Linda	2009-11-22…	2

1 rows

Figure 15.24 Delete Location 2 from the Contractor table. Use OUTPUT to display the change.

Skill Check 2: A new contractor named Vern Anderson is coming onboard to work in Location 1. Write the code to execute this insert, and use the GETDATE() function to populate the current date and time in the HireDate field of the Contractor table. Use the OUTPUT clause to show the results of your insertion as you run it. When you're done, your result should resemble Figure 15.25.

```
INSERT INTO Contractor
--Remaining Code Here
VALUES ('Anderson', 'Vern', GETDATE(), 1)
```

	ctrID	LastName	FirstName	HireDate	LocationID
1	5	Anderson	Vern	2012-09-27…	1

1 rows

Figure 15.25 Insert Vern Anderson into the Contractor table. Use OUTPUT to display the insertion.

Skill Check 3: All six yearly salaried employees are getting a raise of $1500 per year. Run the appropriate UPDATE statement on the PayRates table and show the results on screen. When you are done, your result should resemble Figure 15.26.

	EmpID	YearlySalary	MonthlySalary	HourlyRate	Selector	Estimate	EmpID	YearlySalary	MonthlySalary	HourlyRate	Selector	Estimate
1	1	99000.00	NULL	NULL	1	1	1	97500.00	NULL	NULL	1	1
2	2	87000.00	NULL	NULL	1	1	2	85500.00	NULL	NULL	1	1
3	6	53500.00	NULL	NULL	1	1	6	52000.00	NULL	NULL	1	1
4	11	116500.00	NULL	NULL	1	1	11	115000.00	NULL	NULL	1	1
5	13	73500.00	NULL	NULL	1	1	13	72000.00	NULL	NULL	1	1
6	14	53500.00	NULL	NULL	NULL	NULL	14	52000.00	NULL	NULL	NULL	NULL

Query executed successfully.　　　RENO (11.0 RTM)　Reno\Student (54)　JProCo　00:00:00　6 rows

Figure 15.26 UPDATE the PayRates table and use OUTPUT to show the changed records.

Skill Check 4: Due to cutbacks, you need to reduce your contractor workforce. You have decided to keep the two contractors who were hired before January 1, 2007. You will delete any contractor hired after January 1, 2007. You want to send the records affected by this delete operation into a separate table named ContractorLog. Run the code to achieve this and check your Contractor table and your ContractorLog table. Each should have two records, as shown in Figure 15.27.

```
SELECT * FROM Contractor
SELECT * FROM ContractorLog
```

	ctrID	lastname	firstname	hiredate	LocationID
1	1	Barker	Bill	2006-01-07 00:00:00.000	1
2	2	Ogburn	Maurice	2006-10-27 00:00:00.000	1

	ctrID	lastname	firstname	hiredate	LocationID
1	4	Johnson	Davey	2009-03-07 00:00:00.000	1
2	5	Anderson	Vern	2012-09-27 22:56:25.170	1

Query executed successfully.　　|　RENO (11.0 RTM)　Reno\Student (54)　JProCo　00:00:00　4 rows

Figure 15.27 DELETE two records from Contractor. Send the changes to the ContractorLog table.

Skill Check 5: You want to insert two new trips in the CurrentProducts table that have the following insert statement.

```
INSERT INTO CurrentProducts VALUES
('Baja 3 Day', 595, GETDATE(), 0, 'Medium-Stay', 0),
('Baja 5 Day', 795, GETDATE(), 0, 'Medium-Stay', 0)
```

You will not need to insert the ID values 484 or 485, because the ProductID in the CurrentProducts table is auto generated by the identity property. You want to use the OUTPUT clause with the INSERT statement to show the two inserted ID's and the OriginationDate in the result. When you are done, your result should resemble Figure 15.28.

	ProductID	OriginationDate
1	484	2012-09-27 23:03:20.180
2	485	2012-09-27 23:03:20.180

2 rows

Figure 15.28 Insert two new products and then show the changed records.

Answer Code: The T-SQL code for this lab is located in the downloadable files as a file named Lab15.1_UsingOutput.sql

Points to Ponder - Using OUTPUT

1. The OUTPUT statement exposes a temporary copy of table records affected by INSERT, UPDATE, DELETE, or MERGE.

2. The OUTPUT keyword exposes a special type of memory-resident temporary table, or tables, based on the type of action you take.

3. There are 2 memory-resident tables exposed by the OUPTUT keyword in SQL Server, Inserted and Deleted.

4. These memory-resident tables are maintained by SQL Server for internal processing whenever an update is made.

5. Every DML statement (except SELECT) generates one or more of these memory-resident tables. The OUTPUT statement just exposes a temporary table for your use.

6. The Inserted and Deleted tables are temporary objects only available while the SQL statement is running.

7. Records which have been deleted, inserted, or upserted (updated or inserted) may be saved into an output table for storage or archival purposes.

8. OUTPUT cannot guarantee the order of rows.

9. An UPDATE, INSERT, or DELETE statement containing an OUTPUT clause will return rows even if the statement later encounters an error or is rolled back. So if any error occurs when you run the statement, the OUTPUT result should not be used.

OUTPUT Code Combinations

OUTPUT returns a result set very much like the SELECT statement. We can use this result set in a derived table, which in turn can be used to insert or update other tables. As we saw toward the end of our last example, this capability is very useful for populating tables which track record changes. In this section we also use OUTPUT in combination with MERGE.

OUTPUT with Derived Tables

```
CREATE TABLE TrainingChangeLog
(classID INT NOT NULL,
CClassName VARCHAR (50) NULL,
ClassDurationHours INT NULL,
ApprovedDate DATETIME NULL)
GO
```

Figure 15.29 TrainingChangeLog will store changed records removed from MgmtTraining.

We have created the TrainingChangeLog table to track all changed and deleted records from the MgmtTraining table. TrainingChangeLog is used as a storage table to contain these records for archival purposes. Since changes to MgmtTraining are a frequent occurrence, we want to keep a record of each deletion made from MgmtTraining.

Let's look at the five records in the MgmtTraining table. We recently added the last record, which is the Corporate Privacy curriculum (Figure 15.30).

```
SELECT * FROM MgmtTraining
```

	ClassID	ClassName	ClassDurationHours	ApprovedDate
1	1	Embracing Diversity	12	2007-01-01...
2	2	Interviewing	6	2007-01-15...
3	3	Challenging Negotiations	40	2009-12-01...
4	4	Empowering Others	18	2012-09-27...
5	8	Corporate Privacy	8	2009-12-01...

5 rows

Figure 15.30 MgmtTraining is the main table for training data and contains all current classes.

If we decided to cancel this class, we could run the following statement and delete Class 8. Don't run the DELETE yet (otherwise you'll need to rerun the setup script). First observe the demonstration in Figure 15.31where we see the DELETE statement run alone. OUTPUT shows us the record as it is removed.

```
DELETE FROM MgmtTraining
OUTPUT Deleted.*, GETDATE() AS ClassChangeDate
WHERE ClassID = 8
```

	ClassID	ClassName	ClassDurationHours	ApprovedDate	ClassChangeDate
1	8	Corporate Privacy	8	2009-12-01 00:00:00.000	2012-09-27 23:26:43.890

Query executed successfully.　　RENO (11.0 RTM)　Reno\Student (51)　JProCo　00:00:00　1 rows

Figure 15.31 The OUTPUT clause confirms which record(s) has been deleted.

Notice this result set can be treated like many other SELECT statement results we've seen. For example, if we put parentheses around this statement, add a SELECT * FROM, and then alias the table as TrainChange, we can actually materialize (To make real) this query result as the derived table TrainChange. We can then insert the contents of TrainChange into the TrainingChangeLog table.

```
INSERT INTO TrainingChangeLog
SELECT * FROM
(DELETE FROM MgmtTraining
OUTPUT Deleted.*, GETDATE() AS ClassChangeDate
WHERE ClassID = 8) AS TrainChange
```

Messages
(1 row(s) affected)
0 rows

Figure 15.32 INSERT the contents of the derived table TrainChange INTO TrainingChangeLog.

Let's look at MgmtTraining and TrainingChangeLog. The deletion of the Corporate Privacy class record is now reflected in the storage table.

```
SELECT * FROM MgmtTraining
SELECT * FROM TrainingChangeLog
```

	ClassID	ClassName	ClassDurationHours	ApprovedDate	
1	1	Embracing Diversity	12	2007-01-01 00:00:00.000	
2	2	Interviewing	6	2007-01-15 00:00:00.000	
3	3	Challenging Negotiations	40	2009-12-01 00:00:00.000	
4	4	Empowering Others	18	2012-11-04 01:56:12.800	

	ClassID	ClassName	ClassDurationHours	ApprovedDate	ClassChangeDate
1	8	Corporate Privacy	8	2009-12-01 00:00:00.000	2012-11-04 01:07:45.407

Query executed successfully.　　RENO (11.0 RTM)　Reno\Student (51)　JProCo　00:00:00　5 rows

Figure 15.33 The deleted class record has been sent into the storage table TrainingChangeLog.

Another class needs a change. Challenging Negotiations is being changed to a 32 hour class. Rather than just a quick flash of the confirmation on our screen, we want the old 40 hour record for Challenging Negotiations to be sent into the storage table (Figure 15.34).

```
INSERT INTO TrainingChangeLog
SELECT * FROM
(UPDATE MgmtTraining
SET ClassDurationHours = 32
Output Deleted.*, GETDATE() AS ClassChangeDate
WHERE ClassID = 3) AS TrainChange
```

Messages
(1 row(s) affected)
0 rows

Figure 15.34 Class 3 has been updated, and the old record will be stored in TrainingChangeLog.

When we run this statement, it says "1 row(s) affected". Thus, we should be able to see the updated record in MgmtTraining and the old record archived in the storage table, TrainingChangeLog.

```
SELECT * FROM MgmtTraining
SELECT * FROM TrainingChangeLog
```

	ClassID	ClassName	ClassDurationHours	ApprovedDate	
1	1	Embracing Diversity	12	2007-01-01 00:00:00.000	
2	2	Interviewing	6	2007-01-15 00:00:00.000	
3	3	Challenging Negotiations	32	2009-12-01 00:00:00.000	
4	4	Empowering Others	18	2012-11-04 01:56:12.800	

	ClassID	ClassName	ClassDurationHours	ApprovedDate	ClassChangeDate
1	8	Corporate Privacy	8	2009-12-01 00:00:00.000	2012-11-04 01:07:45.407
2	3	Challenging Negotiations	32	2009-12-01 00:00:00.000	2012-11-04 01:15:12.890

Query executed successfully.　　　　RENO (11.0 RTM)　Reno\Student (51)　JProCo　00:00:00　6 rows

Figure 15.35 We see the updated record in MgmtTraining; the old record was sent to storage.

OUTPUT with MERGE Statements

Our final examples will combine OUTPUT with MERGE, the spiffy new tool we picked up. We will leverage three final results from earlier, in order to keep the focus on the OUTPUT aspect of the examples.

Each of the three examples we'll revisit involves a MERGE operation. Therefore, a source table is updating a target table. We have created the GrantFeedAudit table to track all affected or deleted records flowing from the source table (GrantFeed) into the target table (Grant).

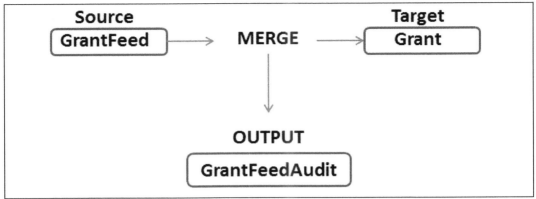

Figure 15.36 The Grant MERGE using GrantFeed sends an output to the GrantFeedAudit table.

Just like we saw with our earlier OUTPUT examples (e.g., Location-LocationChanges and Contractor-ContractorLog), our MERGE examples also require a separate table to track changes if we want to do anything with the OUTPUT besides see it appear briefly on screen. GrantFeedAudit is the table which contains the changes made during the MERGE operation between Grant and GrantFeed (As illustrated in Figure 15.36). GrantChangesAudit and PromotionListArchive are two other tables we will utilize to track changes from our MERGE examples. After we run the example, we'll take a closer look at setup and design consideration for tables which store your OUTPUT data.

Since we will speed our learning by building upon the MERGE results we saw in the last chapter, two stored procedures will serve as shortcuts to help us temporarily reset the Grant and Employee tables to their pre-MERGE condition.

```
EXEC ResetGrantTables
EXEC ResetEmployeeTables
```

Use these stored procedures each time you need to reset the tables in this section. The sproc ResetGrantTables will reset the Grant table, as well as the tables we've created to store the OUTPUT data (GrantFeedAudit, GrantChangesAudit), back to their pre-MERGE states. The sproc ResetEmployeeTables will similarly reset the Employee table to its pre-MERGE state and truncate the PromotionListArchive.

In our first example (Figure 15.37), the GrantFeed table contained two records destined for the Grant table, and thus the MERGE query affected two rows. The addition of the OUTPUT code now sends a copy of those changes into the GrantFeedAudit table (When running this example yourself, remember to first run the reset code EXEC ResetGrantTables).

```
MERGE [Grant] AS gr
USING GrantFeed AS gf
ON gr.GrantID = gf.GrantID
WHEN MATCHED THEN --Update
  UPDATE SET gr.GrantName = gf.GrantName,
             gr.EmpID = gf.EmpID, gr.Amount = gf.Amount
WHEN NOT MATCHED THEN --Insert
  INSERT (GrantID, GrantName, EmpID, Amount)
  VALUES (gf.GrantID, gf.GrantName, gf.EmpID, gf.Amount)
OUTPUT GETDATE(), $Action, Inserted.*, Deleted.* INTO
                GrantFeedAudit;
```

Messages
(2 row(s) affected)
0 rows

Figure 15.37 This code will merge records from the GrantFeed table to the Grant table.

```
SELECT * FROM GrantFeedAudit
```

	GrChangeD...	HowUpdated	insGrantID	insGrantName	insEmpID	insAmount	delGrantID	delGrantName	delEmpID	delAmount
1	2012-11-23...	INSERT	012	Mega Mercy	9	55000.00	NULL	NULL	NULL	NULL
2	2012-11-23...	UPDATE	010	Just Mom	5	9900.00	010	Call Mom	5	9900.00

Query executed successfully.   RENO (11.0 RTM)   Reno\Student (51)   JProCo   00:00:00   2 rows

Figure 15.38 The Grant MERGE using GrantFeed sends an output to the GrantFeedAudit table.

Where UPDATE performs an INSERT and DELETE as part of one action, we want the inserted ("new") and the deleted ("old") records to sit side by side, as seen in Record 2 of Figure 15.38 (Grant 010, Just Mom). For other actions, like a simple INSERT or DELETE, each OUTPUT record will occupy its own row (as seen in Record 1, Grant 012). Because it's possible that each GrantFeedAudit record may include four empty fields, we want each field in the Inserted.* ("ins") and the Deleted.* ("del") table to accept NULL values. See the NULLs shown in Figure 15.38.

The nullable fields here are a departure from most constructs where we use a copy of a table. Normally we use an identically structured copy of the table. We couldn't do that here because we're combining records from the Inserted and Deleted tables within the same row. Without nullable fields, our storage tables (GrantFeedAudit, GrantChangesAudit) could accept only records produced by an UPDATE statement, and our code in Figure 15.37and Figure 15.39 would generate an error. Our code would fail wherever a record was simply inserted or deleted.

OUTPUT allows you to include fields in your output record besides fields from the Inserted or Deleted tables. The GrantFeedAudit table includes two metadata fields in each record. The first field, GrChangeDate, simply documents the date a record is inserted into GrantFeedAudit. The second field, HowUpdated, contains the initials of the person who entered the record(s) into the storage table.

```
CREATE TABLE GrantFeedAudit
(GrChangeDate DATETIME NULL,
HowUpdated CHAR (5) NOT NULL,
InsGrantID CHAR (3) NULL, --Inserted.*
InsEmpID INT NULL,
InsAmount SMALLMONEY NULL,
DelGrantID CHAR (3) NULL, --Deleted.*
DelGrantName NVARCHAR (50) NULL,
DelEmpID INT NULL,
DelAmount SmallMoney NULL)
```

Figure 15.39 The design of the GrantFeedAudit table.

As in all our previous OUTPUT examples, the OUTPUT statement with MERGE is included in the main query just after the final WHEN statement. The semicolon delimiting the MERGE appears immediately after the OUTPUT statement.

We have arranged the records in our next storage table in a similar fashion. GrantChangesAudit tracks records sent to the Grant table by the source table, GrantCheckMaster. Recall that MERGE processed all 12 records between the source and target tables, even though just four records were actually impacted by the MERGE. Since this is the same query, our result here is the same ("12 row(s) affected"). Unfortunately this makes visibility to our audit report less tidy, because GrantChangesAudit contains so many extra records (Figure 15.41). The four outlined records are the four grants which were inserted, updated, or deleted by the MERGE query.

READER NOTE: Before you run the Grant-GrantCheckMaster MERGE, remember to reset the Grant tables again using the reset sproc (EXEC ResetGrantTables).

```
EXEC ResetGrantTables
MERGE [Grant] AS gr
USING GrantCheckMaster AS gcm
ON gr.GrantID = gcm.GrantID
WHEN MATCHED THEN
  UPDATE SET gr.GrantName = gcm.GrantName,
    gr.EmpID = gcm.EmpID, gr.Amount = gcm.Amount
WHEN NOT MATCHED BY TARGET THEN
  INSERT (GrantID, GrantName, EmpID, Amount)
  VALUES (gcm.GrantID, gcm.GrantName, gcm.EmpID, gcm.Amount)
WHEN NOT MATCHED BY SOURCE THEN
  DELETE
OUTPUT GETDATE(), $Action, Inserted.*, Deleted.* INTO
  GrantChangesAudit;
```

Messages
(12 row(s) affected)
0 rows

Figure 15.40 The MERGE into GrantCheckMaster also outputs to GrantChangesAudit.

Next run the following query to check our results:

```
SELECT * FROM GrantChangesAudit
```

GrantChangesAudit contains a timestamp field (GrChangeDt). The other eight possible fields are the four fields from Inserted.* and the four fields from Deleted.*. Since each record may contain up to four empty fields, we have also designed the "INS" and "DEL" fields to accept NULLs.

	GrChangeDt	MergeAction	INSGrID	INSGrName	INSEmID	INSAmt	DELGrID	DELGrName	DELEmID	DELAmt
1	2012-11-04...	UPDATE	001	92 Purr_Scents %...	7	4750.00	001	92 Purr_Scents %%...	7	4750.00
2	2012-11-04...	UPDATE	002	K-Land fund trust	2	15750.00	002	K_Land fund trust	2	15750.00
3	2012-11-04...	UPDATE	003	Robert@BigStarBa...	7	18100.00	003	Robert@BigStarBa...	7	18100.00
4	2012-11-04...	UPDATE	005	BIG 6's Foundation%	4	21000.00	005	BIG 6's Foundation%	4	21000.00
5	2012-11-04...	UPDATE	006	TALTA_Kishan Inter...	3	18100.00	006	TALTA_Kishan Inter...	3	18100.00
6	2012-11-04...	UPDATE	007	Ben@MoreTechnol...	10	41000.00	007	Ben@MoreTechnol...	10	41000.00
7	2012-11-04...	UPDATE	008	www.@-Last-U-Ca...	7	25000.00	008	www.@-Last-U-Can...	7	25000.00
8	2012-11-04...	UPDATE	009	Thank you @.com	11	21500.00	009	Thank you @.com	11	21500.00
9	2012-11-04...	UPDATE	010	Just Mom	5	9900.00	010	Call Mom	5	9900.00
10	2012-11-04...	UPDATE	011	Big Giver Tom	7	95900.00	011	Big Giver Tom	7	95900.00
11	2012-11-04...	INSERT	012	Mega Mercy	9	55000.00	NULL	NULL	NULL	NULL
12	2012-11-04...	DELETE	NULL	NULL	NULL	NULL	004	Norman's Outreach	NULL	21000.00

Query executed successfully.   RENO (11.0 RTM)   Reno\Student (51)   JProCo   00:00:00   12 rows

Figure 15.41 Outlined are the 4 Grant records affected by the MERGE using GrantCheckMaster.

Open Object Explorer (**Object Explorer** > **Databases** > **JProCo** > **Tables**) to view the structure of GrantChangesAudit or any storage table shown in this section.

Our next example is based on the most robust of the MERGE queries we wrote in Chapter 14. Before the upsert code in the Employee-PromotionList, we added secondary criteria to instruct MERGE to not process any unnecessary records. Matched records could only be processed if they had a ManagerID change. So MERGE processed one insert (new employee Janis Smith) and one update (Phil Wilconkinski was promoted to report to the CEO) for a total of just two affected records. Accordingly, those are the only two employee records which were moved into the PromotionListArchive table (Figure 15.41).

Since PromotionListArchive mirrors the target (Employee) and source (PromotionList) tables, it already includes seven main fields. Thus, we defined just one new field in the storage table to document the PromotedDate.

Before running the Employee-PromotionList MERGE, remember to reset the Employee tables using the reset sproc:

```
EXEC ResetEmployeeTables
```

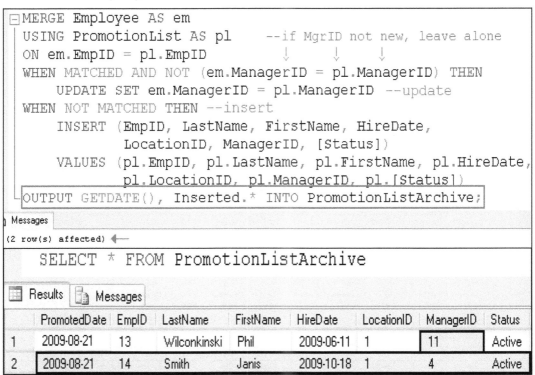

Figure 15.42 The Employee MERGE using PromotionList now outputs to PromotionListArchive, which shows the two records merged into the Employee table on 8/21/09.

Before running the next example, you will want to reset the Grant tables using the reset sproc, EXEC ResetGrantTables.

Be aware that it's possible to choose just certain fields you may want from the Inserted and Deleted tables generated by OUTPUT. The examples we've shown used all the fields in order (i.e., Inserted.* and/or Deleted.*), but we easily could have included just a subset of fields. Our OUTPUT could have specified a single field, multiple fields, or even all the fields from the Inserted/Deleted table arranged in a different order. Example:

OUTPUT GETDATE(), Inserted.TargetField **INTO** StorageTable;

OUTPUT is quite specific about the order of fields in the output record. Decide which fields you need and in what order, then design a storage table accordingly. If the following output were an actual report, we would redesign GrantChangesAudit as a two-field storage table containing just GrChangeDt and INSGrName.

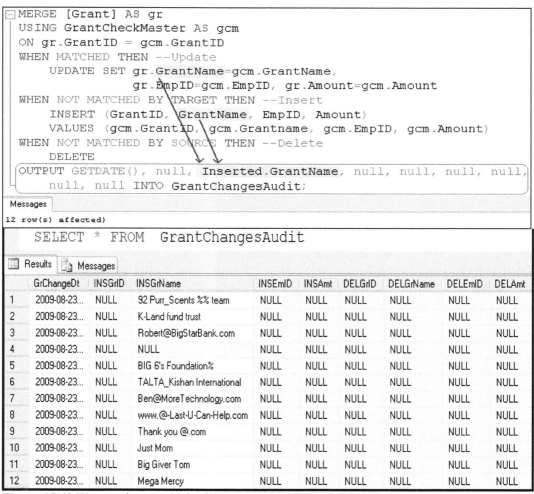

```
MERGE [Grant] AS gr
USING GrantCheckMaster AS gcm
ON gr.GrantID = gcm.GrantID
WHEN MATCHED THEN --Update
    UPDATE SET gr.GrantName=gcm.GrantName,
            gr.EmpID=gcm.EmpID, gr.Amount=gcm.Amount
WHEN NOT MATCHED BY TARGET THEN --Insert
    INSERT (GrantID, GrantName, EmpID, Amount)
    VALUES (gcm.GrantID, gcm.Grantname, gcm.EmpID, gcm.Amount)
WHEN NOT MATCHED BY SOURCE THEN --Delete
    DELETE
OUTPUT GETDATE(), null, Inserted.GrantName, null, null, null, null,
    null, null INTO GrantChangesAudit;
```

Messages

12 row(s) affected)

SELECT * FROM GrantChangesAudit

Results | Messages

	GrChangeDt	INSGrID	INSGrName	INSEmID	INSAmt	DELGrID	DELGrName	DELEmID	DELAmt
1	2009-08-23...	NULL	92 Purr_Scents %% team	NULL	NULL	NULL	NULL	NULL	NULL
2	2009-08-23...	NULL	K-Land fund trust	NULL	NULL	NULL	NULL	NULL	NULL
3	2009-08-23...	NULL	Robert@BigStarBank.com	NULL	NULL	NULL	NULL	NULL	NULL
4	2009-08-23...	NULL	NULL	NULL	NULL	NULL	NULL	NULL	NULL
5	2009-08-23...	NULL	BIG 6's Foundation%	NULL	NULL	NULL	NULL	NULL	NULL
6	2009-08-23...	NULL	TALTA_Kishan International	NULL	NULL	NULL	NULL	NULL	NULL
7	2009-08-23...	NULL	Ben@MoreTechnology.com	NULL	NULL	NULL	NULL	NULL	NULL
8	2009-08-23...	NULL	www.@-Last-U-Can-Help.com	NULL	NULL	NULL	NULL	NULL	NULL
9	2009-08-23...	NULL	Thank you @.com	NULL	NULL	NULL	NULL	NULL	NULL
10	2009-08-23...	NULL	Just Mom	NULL	NULL	NULL	NULL	NULL	NULL
11	2009-08-23...	NULL	Big Giver Tom	NULL	NULL	NULL	NULL	NULL	NULL
12	2009-08-23...	NULL	Mega Mercy	NULL	NULL	NULL	NULL	NULL	NULL

Figure 15.43 We can choose which of the Inserted or Deleted field(s) you want to use.

Lab 15.2: OUTPUT Code Combinations

Lab Prep: Each lab has one or more Skill Checks. Start with Skill Check 1 and proceed until reaching the Points to Ponder section.

Before beginning this lab, verify that SQL Server 2012 is properly installed and operating. Before running the lab setup script for resetting the database (SQLQueries2012Vol2Chapter15.2Setup.sql), please make sure to close all query windows within SSMS (An open query window pointing to a database context can lock that database preventing it from updating when the script is executing). A simple way to assure all query windows are closed, is to exit out of SSMS, then open a new instance of SSMS, and lastly run the setup script.

Skill Check 1: Using the MERGE query shown in Figure 15.43, modify the OUTPUT statement to populate into the MyGrantChanges table. Create an archive table called MyGrantChanges to contain your output using the following code:

```
CREATE TABLE MyGrantChanges
(GrChangeDt DATETIME,
INSGrName NVARCHAR(40),
INSGrAmt MONEY)
GO
```

Hard-code the GrChangeDt value to make your result match Figure 15.45. In order to get all 12 records to appear in your output, you will need to reset the Grant table using the sproc (EXEC ResetGrantTables). If you do not reset the Grant table, you will see just 11 records in your result.

If you would like to view the code contained in this sproc, go to
Object Explorer > **Databases** > **JProCo** > **Programmability** > **Stored Procedures** > right-click **ResetGrantTables** > **Script Stored Procedure as** > **CREATE To** > **New Query Editor Window**.

```
SELECT * FROM MyGrantChanges
```

	GrChangeDt	INSGrName	INSGrAmt
1	2009-08-15 00:00:00.000	92 Purr_Scents %% team	4750.00
2	2009-08-15 00:00:00.000	K-Land fund trust	15750.00
3	2009-08-15 00:00:00.000	Robert@BigStarBank.com	18100.00
4	2009-08-15 00:00:00.000	BIG 6's Foundation%	21000.00
5	2009-08-15 00:00:00.000	TALTA_Kishan International	18100.00
6	2009-08-15 00:00:00.000	Ben@MoreTechnology.com	41000.00
7	2009-08-15 00:00:00.000	www.@-Last-U-Can-Help.com	25000.00
8	2009-08-15 00:00:00.000	Thank you @.com	21500.00
9	2009-08-15 00:00:00.000	Just Mom	9900.00
10	2009-08-15 00:00:00.000	Big Giver Tom	95900.00
11	2009-08-15 00:00:00.000	Mega Mercy	55000.00

Query executed successfully.   RENO (11.0 RTM)   Reno\Student (51)   JProCo   00:00:00   11 rows

Figure 15.44 Modify the output from 15.43 and send it to the storage table MyGrantChanges.

Skill Check 2: You have seven products that each cost less than $40.

	ProductID	ProductName	RetailPrice	OriginationD...	To...	Category
1	73	Ocean Cruise Tour 1 Day Mexico	35.601	2010-01-01...	0	No-Stay
2	145	Mountain Lodge 1 Day Scandinavia	35.574	2012-01-04...	0	No-Stay
3	265	Winter Tour 1 Day Scandinavia	37.506	2011-03-06...	0	No-Stay
4	313	Cherry Festival Tour 1 Day Mexico	34.909	2007-04-11...	0	No-Stay
5	319	Cherry Festival Tour 1 Day Canada	37.944	2009-07-02...	0	No-Stay
6	415	River Rapids Tour 1 Day Scandinavia	39.042	2004-09-15...	0	No-Stay
7	421	Snow Ski Tour 1 Day West Coast	38.308	2008-11-18...	0	No-Stay

Query executed successfully.   RENO (11.0 RTM)   Reno\Student (51)   JProCo   00:00:00   7 rows

Figure 15.45 Seven products in CurrentProducts currently cost less than $40.

You plan to write the following update statement to raise the price of each of these products by $3.00:

```
UPDATE CurrentProducts
SET RetailPrice = RetailPrice + 3.00
WHERE RetailPrice < 40
```

You want to capture the results of the update into a table called ProductPriceChange. Capture the ProductID and OldPrice from the Deleted table and NewPrice from the Inserted table. When you are done, you should query the ProductPriceChange table and see the results as seen in Figure 15.45. Hint: We can accomplish a correct solution without a derived table and an INSERT INTO statement, but it is highly recommended that you also attempt it using the method demonstrated in this chapter.

```
SELECT * FROM ProductPriceChange
```

Figure 15.46 This shows OldPrice and NewPrice.

Skill Check 3: When you need to test some code but don't want to experiment on a live table, this code quickly creates a copy of a table. Be sure to run this code before completing the Skill Check:

```
SELECT * INTO ImportantTableCopy
FROM ImportantTable
```

Use a similar query to create a test copy of the Employee table:

```
SELECT * INTO EmployeeLMO
FROM Employee
```

Use MERGE to update EmployeeLMO (alias as ELMO) with the changes contained in EmpCheckMaster (alias as ECM). ECM is a reconciliation table prepared at the start of each fiscal year to update the master employee list once performance reviews and promotions have been processed. Your MERGE query should ensure that all changes contained in ECM are carried over to ELMO. In fact, when the MERGE is complete, ELMO and ECM should be identical.

Insert any records in the source table (EmpCheckMaster) not found in the target (ELMO). Update any common records between the two tables, so that matched records in ELMO will become identical to those in ECM. If there are any records in the target not contained in the source, delete them. Before it processes any changes to matched records, your code must first confirm there has been a change in ManagerID. Any matched records not containing a manager change should be ignored and not affected by the MERGE.

Use OUTPUT to contain the records inserted during the MERGE. Make sure your OUTPUT result populates the archive table EmpMergeArchive and the fields appear in the order shown in Figure 15.47. Be sure to run the queries at the beginning of this Skill Check or you will get the following error message.

```
Messages
Msg 208, Level 16, State 1, Line 1
Invalid object name 'EmpCheckMaster'

                                                    0 rows
```

Figure 15.47 If you see this error message run the query at the beginning of Skill Check 3.

SELECT * **FROM** EmpCheckMaster

	EmpID	LastName	FirstName	HireDate	LocationID	ManagerID	Status
1	1	Adams	Alex	2001-01-01...	1	11	Active
2	2	Brown	Barry	2002-08-12...	1	11	Active
3	3	Osako	Lee	1999-09-01...	2	11	Active
4	4	Kennson	David	1996-03-16...	1	11	Has Tenure
5	6	Kendall	Lisa	2001-11-15...	4	4	Active
6	7	Lonning	David	2000-01-01...	1	11	On Leave
7	8	Marshbank	John	2001-11-15...	NULL	4	Active
8	9	Newton	James	2003-09-30...	2	3	Active
9	10	O'Haire	Terry	2004-10-04...	2	9	Active
10	11	Smith	Sally	1989-04-01...	1	NULL	Active
11	12	O'Neil	Barbara	1995-05-26...	4	9	Has Tenure
12	13	Wilconkinski	Phil	2009-06-11...	1	11	Active
13	14	Smith	Janis	2009-10-18...	1	4	Active
14	15	Jones	Mary	2008-03-03...	3	4	Active
15	16	Mehta	Vijya	2009-05-01...	2	3	Has Tenure
16	17	Asterov	Sergei	2009-06-15...	2	3	Active

Query executed successfully.   (local) (11.0 RTM)   Reno\Student (51)   JProCo   00:00:00   16 rows

Figure 15.48 EmpCheckMaster is a table in JProCo.

SELECT * **FROM** EmpMergeArchive

	FirstName	LastName	ManagerID	LocationID	HireDate	Status	EmpID
1	Mary	Jones	4	3	2008-03-03 00:00:00.000	Active	15
2	Vijya	Mehta	3	2	2009-05-01 00:00:00.000	Has Tenure	16
3	Sergei	Asterov	3	2	2009-06-15 00:00:00.000	Active	17
4	NULL	NULL	NULL	NULL	NULL	NULL	NULL
5	Terry	O'Haire	9	2	2004-10-04 00:00:00.000	Active	10
6	Barbara	O'Neil	9	4	1995-05-26 00:00:00.000	Has Tenure	12

Query executed successfully.   (local) (11.0 RTM)   Reno\Student (51)   JProCo   00:00:00   6 rows

Figure 15.49 Use OUTPUT to send the results of your MERGE into EmpMergeArchive.

Answer Code: The T-SQL code for this lab is located in the downloadable files as a file named Lab15.2_OutputCodeCombinations.sql

Points to Ponder - OUTPUT Code Combinations

1. A derived query may use the result set of an OUTPUT statement.

2. The result set from a derived query can insert records into other tables.

3. The OUTPUT clause used in conjunction with an INTO clause will specify the table where the OUTPUT fields will be inserted. This is sometimes easier than using a derived query with an INSERT statement.

4. When the OUTPUT clause is used as part of a MERGE statement, it must appear between the last WHEN clause and the semicolon.

5. A WHEN MATCHED clause will UPDATE rows in the target table.

6. A WHEN NOT MATCHED BY TARGET will INSERT rows into the target table, which are only in the source table.

7. Use WHEN NOT MATCHED BY SOURCE to UPDATE or DELETE rows in the target table. For example, specify DELETE with this clause to remove rows from the target table, which are not present in the source table.

8. An AND condition can be used with a WHEN MATCHED clause to instruct MERGE to update only the changed records. Particularly with larger tables, this can make code more efficient and save processing time used to unnecessarily iterate through and apply logic to unchanged records.

Chapter Glossary

Memory-Resident Table: A special type of temporary table that is created automatically by SQL.

OUTPUT: This statement generates a copy of table records affected by INSERT, UPDATE, DELETE or MERGE.

OUTPUT Code Combination: An OUTPUT statement combined with code allows you to create a derived query to insert records into other tables.

UPDATE: A statement that changes – or *manipulates* – existing data without adding any new records.

Review Quiz - Chapter Fifteen

1.) The OUTPUT clause can create two different tables based on the statement using it. Which two tables can the OUTPUT clause create? (choose two)

☐ a. Inserted

☐ b. Updated

☐ c. Deleted

☐ d. Changed

☐ e. Logged

2.) Which two DML statements will create an Inserted table? (choose two)

☐ a. SELECT

☐ b. INSERT

☐ c. UPDATE

☐ d. DELETE

3.) Which two DML statements will create a Deleted table? (choose two)

☐ a. SELECT

☐ b. INSERT

☐ c. UPDATE

☐ d. DELETE

4.) The magic tables created by the OUTPUT keyword are (choose one):

O a. Permanent and can be seen in the Object Explorer.

O b. Temporary can be viewed for about 5 minutes

O c. Temporary and can only be accessed while the SQL statement runs.

5.) What type of SQL statement works with the OUTPUT clause?

O a. DML

O b. DDL

O c. DCL

O d. TCL

6.) You want to delete all records from the Location table with the state abbreviation of WA. You know that will affect two records. You want to see the affected records at the time the query is running. What code will achieve this result?

O a. `DELETE FROM dbo.Location`
`OUTPUT Deleted.*`
`WHERE State = 'WA'`

O b. `DELETE FROM dbo.Location`
`OUTPUT Inserted.*`
`WHERE State = 'WA'`

O c. `DELETE FROM dbo.Location`
`WHERE State = 'WA'`
`OUTPUT Deleted.*`

O d. `DELETE FROM dbo.Location`
`WHERE State = 'WA'`
`OUTPUT Inserted.*`

7.) The HourlyPay table allows you to give all hourly employees a $1 raise. When running the UPDATE statement you want to see the EmpID, the old hourly pay and the new hourly pay. What code will achieve this result?

O a. `UPDATE HourlyPay SET Hourly = Hourly + 1`
`OUTPUT Deleted.EmpID , Deleted.Hourly AS OldPay,`
`Updated.Hourly AS NewPay`
`WHERE Hourly IS NOT NULL`

O b. `UPDATE HourlyPay SET Hourly = Hourly + 1`
`OUTPUT Deleted.EmpID , Updated.Hourly AS OldPay,`
`Deleted.Hourly AS NewPay`
`WHERE Hourly IS NOT NULL`

O c. `UPDATE HourlyPay SET Hourly = Hourly + 1`
`OUTPUT Deleted.EmpID , Inserted.Hourly AS OldPay,`
`Deleted.Hourly AS NewPay`
`WHERE Hourly IS NOT NULL`

O d. `UPDATE HourlyPay SET Hourly = Hourly + 1`
`OUTPUT Deleted.EmpID , Deleted.Hourly AS OldPay,`
`Inserted.Hourly AS NewPay`
`WHERE Hourly IS NOT NULL`

8.) You want to increase the RetailPrice of all No-Stay products by 15% in a table named CurrentProducts. You want the query results to list the ProductName and the new price. What code will achieve this result?

O a. ```
UPDATE CurrentProducts
SET RetailPrice = RetailPrice * 1.15
OUTPUT Updated.ProductName, Updated.RetailPrice
WHERE Category = 'No-Stay'
```

O b.  ```
UPDATE CurrentProducts
SET RetailPrice = RetailPrice * 1.15
OUTPUT Deleted.ProductName, Deleted.RetailPrice
WHERE Category = 'No-Stay'
```

O c. ```
UPDATE CurrentProducts
SET RetailPrice = RetailPrice * 1.15
OUTPUT Inserted.ProductName, Inserted.RetailPrice
WHERE Category = 'No-Stay'
```

**9.)** You have a table named Employees and EmployeeArchive. These two tables have the same fields and data types. You want to delete all employees from LocationID 3 and record these changes in the EmployeeArchive table. What code will achieve this result?

O a.  ```
DELETE Employee
OUTPUT Deleted.* INTO EmployeeArchive
WHERE LocationID = 3
```

O b. ```
DELETE EmployeeArchive
OUTPUT Deleted.* INTO Employee
WHERE LocationID = 3
```

O c.  ```
DELETE Employee
OUTPUT Updated.* INTO EmployeeArchive
WHERE LocationID = 3
```

10.) What type of DML statement used in conjunction with the OUTPUT statement will create both an Inserted and a Deleted table?

O a. SELECT

O b. INSERT

O c. UPDATE

O d. DELETE

11.) You want to insert two new products named 'Baja Trip 3 days' for $595 and 'Baja Trip 5 days' for $795 into a table named CurrentProducts with a ProductID field that is auto generated. You want to capture the ProductID field and the current time into a table called dbo.CuLog. The following code created the dbo.CuLog table.

```
CREATE TABLE dbo.CuLog (
ProductID INT NOT NULL,
ChangeTime DATETIME)
```

What code will achieve this result?

O a.
```
INSERT INTO CurrentProducts
OUTPUT Inserted.ProductID, CURRENT_TIMESTAMP INTO CuLog
VALUES ('Baja 3 Day', 595), ('Baja 5 Day', 795)
```

O b.
```
INSERT INTO CurrentProducts
OUTPUT Inserted.ProductID, Inserted.RetailPrice INTO CuLog
VALUES ('Baja 3 Day', 595), ('Baja 5 Day', 795)
```

O c.
```
INSERT INTO CurrentProducts
OUTPUT Inserted.ProductID, CURRENT_TIMESTAMP INTO CuLog
VALUES (DEFAULT, 'Baja 3 Day', 595),
(DEFAULT, 'Baja 5 Day', 795)
```

12.) You have five records in the Location table. A statement using a derived table to delete both Washington locations from the Location table uses an OUTPUT statement as seen below.

```
INSERT INTO LocationLog
SELECT * FROM (
  DELETE FROM Location OUTPUT Deleted.*
  WHERE State = 'WA') AS DelLoc
```

What result will this code achieve?

O a. 3 records will be inserted into the LocationLog table and 3 records will be deleted from the Location table.

O b. 3 records will be inserted into the LocationLog table and 2 records will be deleted from the Location table.

O c. 2 records will be inserted into the LocationLog table and 3 records will be deleted from the Location table.

O d. 2 records will be inserted into the LocationLog table and 2 records will be deleted from the Location table.

13.) Using the same scenario and query from the previous question (#12), what result will the following statement achieve?

```
SELECT * FROM LocationLog
```

O a. The SELECT statement shows the 2 records generated from the derived table (DelLoc), since 2 records were deleted from the Location table.

O b. The SELECT statement will not show any records in this case.

O c. The SELECT statement will show 4 records.

O d. The SELECT statement will show the 4 records (2 generated from the DelLoc derived table and 2 more from the Location table).

14.) You have a table named CurrentProducts that has 485 records. Only seven of those records cost less than $40. These low cost trips will all be going up in price by $3.50 in the next day. You have the following query.

```
CREATE TABLE ProductPriceChange (
ProductID INT,
OldPrice MONEY,
NewPrice MONEY)
GO

INSERT INTO ProductPriceChange
SELECT *
FROM (
  UPDATE CurrentProducts
  SET RetailPrice = RetailPrice + 3.50
  OUTPUT Inserted.ProductID, Deleted.RetailPrice,
  Inserted.RetailPrice
  WHERE RetailPrice < 40) AS updCurProd
  (ProductID, OldPrice, NewPrice)
```

How many rows are affected?

O a. 7

O b. 478

15.) You have a table, named Product, which has products from many different vendors. You need to increase product prices, only for the vendor named "Yakima Winery", by 10 percent. When this update statement runs, you want to return a list of the products and the new updated prices. Which code segment should you use?

O a.
```
UPDATE Product
SET Price = Price * 1.10, ProductName = ProductName
WHERE Product.VendorName = 'Yakima Winery'
```

O b.
```
UPDATE Product
SET Price = Price * 1.10
OUTPUT Inserted.ProductName, Deleted.Price
WHERE Product.VendorName = 'Yakima Winery'
```

O c.
```
UPDATE Product
SET Price = Price * 1.10
OUTPUT Inserted.ProductName, Inserted.Price
WHERE Product.VendorName = 'Yakima Winery'
```

O d.
```
UPDATE Product
SET Price = Price * 1.10, VendorName = 'Yakima Winery'
OUTPUT Inserted.ProductName, Inserted.Price
```

Answer Key

1.) Since the OUTPUT clause can create the Inserted and Deleted tables, (b), (d) and (e) are all incorrect, which makes (a) and (c) the correct answers.

2.) Since the INSERT and UPDATE statements create an Inserted table, (a) and (d) are not correct, which makes (b) and (c) the right answers.

3.) Both the UPDATE and the DELETE statement create a Deleted table, which make (a) and (b) the wrong choices, thus (c) and (d) are the right choices.

4.) Because the magic tables are temporary (not permanent) and can be viewed only while the statement is running (no matter how long it runs), both (a) and (b) are wrong answers, which makes (c) the correct answer.

5.) Since the OUTPUT clause works with statements from the DML family and not the DDL, DCL or TCL families (b), (c) and (d) are all incorrect. The OUTPUT clause will work with the INSERT, UPDATE and DELETE statements, which belong to the DML family, so (a) is the correct answer.

6.) Since the DELETE statement creates the Deleted temporary table (b) is incorrect for attempting to OUTPUT Inserted.*. Because the OUTPUT clause must be located within the DML statement and not after it, (c) and (d) are both wrong. Since the Deleted table is being OUTPUT and is within the DELETE statement, (a) is the correct answer.

7.) Since the UPDATE statement does not create an Updated table, (a) and (b) are both incorrect. Because Inserted.Hourly will contain the new value inserted by the UPDATE statement and Deleted.Hourly will contain the old value deleted, (c) will not be correct either. Since the code in (d) is referring to the Deleted.Hourly field as the OldPay and the Inserted.Hourly field as the NewPay it is the correct answer.

8.) Since there is no Updated temporary table, (a) will be wrong and result in an error. The Deleted temporary table contains the record, as it existed prior to updating, so (b) will be wrong too. The Inserted temporary table will contain the record as it exists after it has been updated, making (c) the right answer.

9.) Since 'DELETE EmployeeArchive' deletes a record from EmployeeArchive rather than the Employee table, (b) is incorrect. Because an Updated temporary table does not exist, (c) is wrong also. 'DELETE Employee' will delete records from the Employee table and 'OUTPUT Deleted.* INTO EmployeeArchive' will insert a copy of the deleted records into the EmployeeArchive table, making (a) the correct answer.

10.) SELECT does not create any temporary tables with the OUTPUT statement, so (a) is incorrect. OUTPUT used with the INSERT statement will only create an Inserted temporary table, so (b) is incorrect. Since OUTPUT used with the DELETE statement will only create a Deleted temporary table, (d) is also incorrect. The UPDATE statement will create both the Deleted and Inserted temporary tables with the OUTPUT statement, so (c) is correct.

11.) 'OUTPUT Inserted.ProductID, Inserted.RetailPrice' will attempt to insert the new RetailPrice into the ChangeTime field of the CuLog table, so (b) is wrong. When inserting a row into a table that has an identity field there is no need to supply a value for that field, so (c) is wrong also. The line 'OUTPUT Inserted.ProductID, CURRENT_TIMESTAMP' will insert the right data into CuLog and 'VALUES ('Baja 3 Day', 595), ('Baja 5 Day', 795)' does not refer to the ProductID field, making (a) the right answer.

12.) The derived table DelLoc results in two records deleted from Location, so (a) and (c) are both incorrect. The INSERT statement inserts two records of data deleted by DelLoc into the LocationLog table, making (b) incorrect. Since the INSERT statement inserts two records into the LocationLog table and those are the same two records deleted from Location within the DelLoc derived table, (d) is the correct answer.

13.) Since there are only two records in LocationLog after running the query in question #12, (b), (c) and (d) are all wrong choices. Because the scenario resulted in two rows being inserted into the LocationLog table 'SELECT * FROM LocationLog' will also show those two records, making (a) correct.

14.) Since there are 485 records and seven of those records will be updated, 478 of the records will be unaffected, making (b) the wrong answer. Because there are only seven records that cost less than $40 and the code is only updating the CurrentProducts table 'WHERE RetailPrice < 40' only those seven records will be affected, making (a) the correct answer.

15.) Since the OUTPUT clause to display the new price is missing, (a) is wrong. The new records are in the Inserted table, so (b) is incorrect, because it returns the old price. Since the WHERE clause is missing, (d) updates all records to have 'Yakima Winery' as a VendorName value. We want to increase the price of products from 'Yakima Winery' and display the product's name and new price, so (c) is the correct answer.

Bug Catcher Game

To play the Bug Catcher game, run the SQLQueries2012Vol2BugCatcher15.pps file from the BugCatcher folder of the companion files. These files are available from the www.Joes2Pros.com website.

[THIS PAGE INTENTIONALLY LEFT BLANK]

Chapter 16. Next Steps for Aspiring SQL Pros

Congratulations to those who have successfully made it all the way through this book, which is an important leg on your journey to becoming a SQL Pro!

I have tried to write each book in this series to be of help to anyone seeking knowledge about SQL Server – whether an intermediate looking to fill in gaps in their knowledge, an expert looking for new features of SQL Server, or even a developer picking up SQL Server as their second or third programming language. But the heart of my mission as an educator remains dedicated to the brand new beginner who learns about the power of SQL Server and becomes committed to mastering this awesome technology and 'making it their own'.

Those earnest seekers who have successfully studied these first two books in "cover-to-cover" fashion are well prepared for the next step in your journey to becoming a SQL Pro. As all my students and readers know, I am a big believer in the certification method of demonstrating your seriousness and expertise in SQL Server. I have designed the Joes 2 Pros curriculum to help prepare you on the journey toward becoming a Microsoft Certified Technology Specialist, and I recommend you consider this important step in building your SQL Server knowledge and career.

The next step in the Joes 2 Pros curriculum will build your knowledge of SQL Server design and programming. This area of focus primarily utilizes DDL (Data Definition Language), which you've used in the first two books (Figure 16.1).

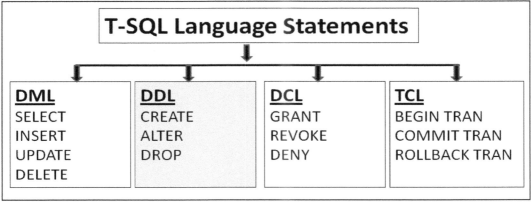

Figure 16.1 SQL Server design and programming largely uses DDL (Data Definition Language).

The interesting thing about DDL is that you need it to create and work with objects like tables, views, functions and stored procedures (just to name a few). Those are the key objects you will use to work with data – in fact, lots of data! So most often, enclosed within DDL statements will be DML statements handling the data work for the object. So far we've seen this when we altered existing tables or built stored procedures. We will see more of that in the next book when we work with views and functions. This is one reason why I've always had my students first become expert at data queries before proceeding to the design and programming topics. In reality, DML is the greatest tool to help you succeed at programming inside of SQL Server objects (DDL).

In the familiar Joes 2 Pros roadmap, you will recognize the first two books, representing the first two classes in my yearlong SQL preparatory track.

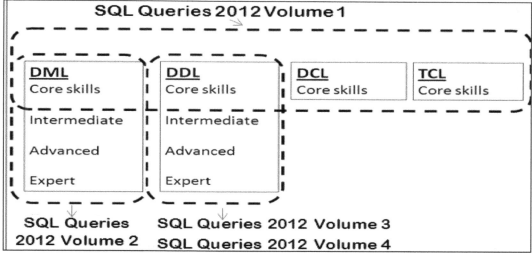

Figure 16.2 You have now mastered the knowledge in Books 1 and 2 and utilized expert level DML and DDL concepts.

You have now successfully mastered the knowledge contained in Book 1 and Book 2 and are ready to proceed to the next class, which is contained in Book 3 and covers SQL Server design and programming. Book 2 covered an advanced level of DML bringing our overall SQL skill set up to the intermediate level. Therefore, this is considered an intermediate book that gives you some expert level specialization. To become a true SQL Expert, you must attain the Expert level for all family statement types within SQL.

In the first two books, we used the default settings provided by SQL Server whenever we created databases and database objects.

In Book 3, we begin by learning database file structures and how we can customize those available structures and settings to best fit our data traffic and system performance needs. We also cover indexes, and partitions.

In Book 4, we go straight into programming objects like functions, stored procedures, views and triggers just to name a few. All of these SQL objects either contain data or work with data. We also cover the creation, usage and maintenance of advanced objects, such as views, triggers and functions.

A true expert would even know about how SQL interacts with XML. This includes shredding, binding and using XML indexes.

Best wishes for your continued progress in the realm of SQL Server databases!!

*　　　　*　　　　*　　　　*　　　　*　　　　*

Find more detail on forthcoming titles and keep in touch with the *Joes 2 Pros* community at *www.Joes2Pros.com*.

SQL Queries 2012 Joes 2 Pros Volume 1/Beginning SQL 2012 Joes 2 Pros *Volume 1*

SQL Queries 2012 Joes 2 Pros Volume 2

SQL Queries 2012 Joes 2 Pros Volume 3

SQL Queries 2012 Joes 2 Pros Volume 4

SQL Queries 2012 Joes 2 Pros Volume 5

SQL Wait Stats Joes 2 Pros: SQL Performance Tuning Techniques Using Wait Statistics, Types & Queues

INDEX

CPSIA information can be obtained
at www.ICGtesting.com
Printed in the USA
LVHW011555021221
705096LV00006B/259